53 rd Locarno International Film Festival

August, 2-12 2000

"Showing my films in Piazza Grande in Locarno was amongst the most exciting evenings of my life.

Atom Egoyan

"Faced with the idea of being actually present at the festival, the excitement could kill me. The Locarno Festival is just too exciting."

Roberto Benigni

Locarno International Film Festival

The International Competition, the Piazza Grande, the Filmakers of the Present, the Leopards of Tomorrow, the Special Sidebar: a wide selection of films discovered every year by more than 170,000 visitors, over 1,000 journalists from 32 countries and 4,000 European film professionals. New and established talents come to Locarno from all over the world to screen their films in a unique environment.

Via Luini 3a - CH-6601 Locarno
Phone: (41 91) 756 2121 Fax: (41 91) 756 2149 · E-mail: info@pardo.ch - http://www.pardo.ch

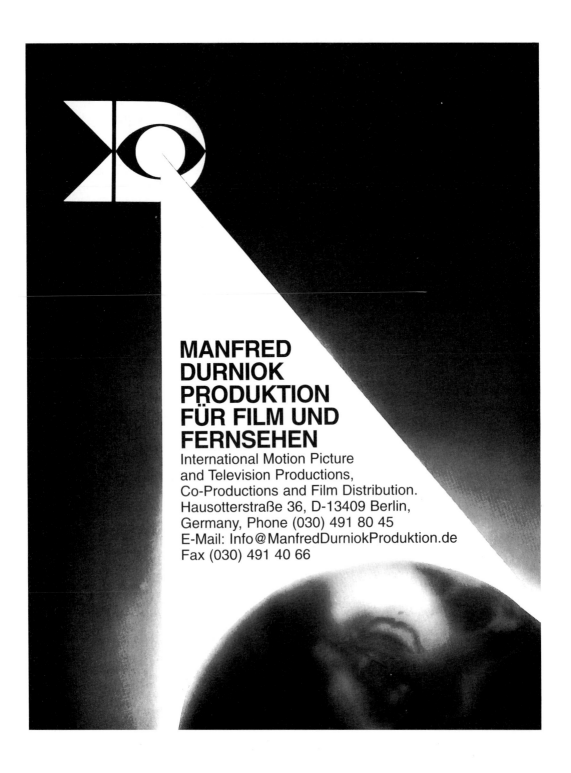

MANFRED DURNIOK PRODUKTION FÜR FILM UND FERNSEHEN
International Motion Picture
and Television Productions,
Co-Productions and Film Distribution.
Hausotterstraße 36, D-13409 Berlin,
Germany, Phone (030) 491 80 45
E-Mail: Info@ManfredDurniokProduktion.de
Fax (030) 491 40 66

EDITED BY PETER COWIE

Managing Editor: Daniel Rosenthal

faber and faber
LONDON

SILMAN-JAMES PRESS
LOS ANGELES

THE *VARIETY* ALMANAC

1999

THE ONLY COMPREHENSIVE REFERENCE GUIDE TO ENCOMPASS ALL ENTERTAINMENT CATEGORIES, FROM FILM AND TELEVISION (INCLUDING VIDEO RELEASES), TO MUSIC AND THEATRE.

BOXTREE

CONTENTS

Editor: Peter Cowie

Managing Editor: Daniel Rosenthal

Consulting Editor: Derek Elley

Editorial Assistants: Sue Harper, Damjana Finci, Elizabeth Prestwood, David Murray

Advertising Co-ordination: Sandrine Bentata, Frederic Fenucci

Cover Design: Stefan Dreja

Photo Consultants: The Kobal Collection

Editorial and Business Offices:
Variety
6 Bell Yard
London WC2A 2JR
Tel: (0171) 520 5222
Fax: (0171) 520 5219

ISBN 0-571-20251-9 (United Kingdom)
ISBN 1-879505-52-5 (United States)
British Library Cataloging in Publication
Data
Variety International Film Guide 1999
1. Cowie, Peter
011.37

Published in the US by
Silman-James Press
Tel: (323) 661 9922
Fax: (323) 661 9933

Copyright © 1999 by
Variety Media Publications Ltd.

Photoset/Origination by Columns
Design Limited, Reading
Printed and bound in Great Britain by
Cromwell Press Ltd.

CONTENTS

INTERNATIONAL LIAISON

Africa: Roy Armes (Algeria, Morocco, Tunisia); Judy Kendall (Burkina Faso, Mali, Zimbabwe)
Australia: David Stratton, Peter Thompson
Austria: Beat Glur
Belgium: Patrick Duynslaegher
Bosnia & Hezegovina: Rada Šesić
Brazil: Nelson Hoineff
Bulgaria: Pavlina Jeleva
Canada: Gerald Pratley
Chile: Hans Ehrmann†
Croatia: Tomislav Kurelec
Cuba: Andrew Paxman
Czech Republic: Eva Zaoralová
Denmark: Ebbe Iversen
Egypt: Fawzi Soliman
Estonia: Jaan Ruus
Far East: Derek Elley (China, Hong Kong, Taiwan)
Finland: Antti Selkokari
France: Michel Ciment
Germany: Jack Kindred
Greece: Yannis Bacoyannopoulos
Hungary: Derek Elley

Iceland: Ásgrímur Sverrisson
India: Uma da Cunha
Indonesia: Marselli Sumarno
Iran: Jamal Omid
Ireland: Michael Dwyer
Israel: Dan Fainaru
Italy: Lorenzo Codelli
Japan: Frank Segers
Kazakhstan: Eugene Zykov
Latvia: Andris Rozenbergs
Lithuania: Gražina Arlickaite
Malaysia: Baharudin A. Latif
Mexico: Tomás Pérez Turrent
Nepal: Uzzwal Bhandary
Netherlands: Pieter van Lierop
New Zealand: Peter Calder
Norway: Trond Olav Svendsen
Pakistan: Aijaz Gul
Peru: Isaac León Frías
Philippines: Agustin Sotto
Poland: Rick Richardson
Portugal: Martin Dale
Puerto Rico: José Artemio Torres
Romania: Cristina Corciovescu
Russia: Michael Brashinsky
Serbia & Montenegro: Goran Gocić
Singapore: Yvonne Ng
Slovakia: Hana Cielová
South Africa: Martin Botha
South Korea: Frank Segers
Spain: Peter Besas
Sri Lanka: Amarnath Jayatilaka
Sweden: Bengt Forslund
Switzerland: Pierre Lachat
Syria: Rafik Atassi
Thailand: Anchalee Chaiworaporn
Turkey: Atilla Dorsay
United Kingdom: Philip Kemp
United States: Harlan Jacobson
Venezuela: Irene Herrera

At the top of Scandinavia

From now on you can reach the entire Scandinavian market, with more than 20 million people, through one new powerful film company.

In key cities of Denmark, Finland, Norway and Sweden 140 screens are waiting for you. And more well-equipped multi-movie theatres are under way.

So, whenever you are ready to launch a new film, welcome to the number one film company of Scandinavia.

Cate Blanchett won a BAFTA for ELIZABETH
photo: Alex Bailey/Gramercy Pictures

Gwyneth Paltrow, Oscar-winner for SHAKESPEARE IN LOVE

US Academy Awards: 1999

Best Film: *Shakespeare in Love.*
Best Direction: Steven Spielberg for *Saving Private Ryan.*
Best Actor: Roberto Benigni for *Life is Beautiful.*
Best Actress: Gwyneth Paltrow for *Shakespeare in Love.*
Best Supporting Actor: James Coburn for *Affliction.*
Best Supporting Actress: Judi Dench for *Shakespeare in Love.*
Best Original Screenplay: Marc Norman & Tom Stoppard for *Shakespeare in Love.*
Best Adapted Screenplay: Bill Condon for *Gods and Monsters.*
Best Cinematography: Janusz Kaminski for *Saving Private Ryan.*
Best Costume Design: Sandy Powell for *Shakespeare in Love.*
Best Art Direction: Martin Childs, Jill Quertier for *Shakespeare in Love.*
Best Editing: Michael Kahn for *Saving Private Ryan.*
Best Original Musical or Comedy Score: Stephen Warbeck for *Shakespeare in Love.*
Best Dramatic Score: Nicola Piovani for *Life is Beautiful.*
Best Original Song: "When You Believe" from *The Prince of Egypt.* Music and lyrics by Stephen Schwartz.
Best Sound: Gary Rydstrom, Gary Summers, Andy Nelson, Ronald Judkins for *Saving Private Ryan.*
Best Make-up: Jenny Shircore for *Elizabeth.*
Best Visual Effects: Joel Hynek, Nicholas Brooks, Stuart Robertson, Kevin Mack for *What Dreams May Come.*
Best Sound-Effects Editing: Gary Rydstrom, Richard Hymns for *Saving Private Ryan.*
Best Foreign-Language Film: *Life is Beautiful* (Italy).

British Academy of Film and Television Awards: 1999

Best Film: *Shakespeare in Love.*
Best British Film: *Elizabeth.*
Best Direction: Peter Weir for *The Truman Show.*
Best Actor: Roberto Benigni for *Life is Beautiful.*
Best Actress: Cate Blanchett for *Elizabeth.*
Best Supporting Actor: Geoffrey Rush for *Shakespeare in Love.*
Best Supporting Actress: Judi Dench for *Shakespeare in Love.*
Best Original Screenplay: Andrew Niccol for *The Truman Show.*
Best Adapted Screenplay: Elaine May for *Primary Colors.*
Best Foreign-Language Film: *Central Station* (Brazil).
Audience Award: *Lock, Stock and Two Smoking Barrels.*
Fellowship Award: Elizabeth Taylor.

European Film Awards: 1998

Best Film: *La vita é bella* (*Life is Beautiful*) (Italy).
Best Actor: Roberto Benigni for *Life is Beautiful* (Italy).
Best Actress: Elodie Bouchez & Natacha Régnier, *La vie rêvée des anges* (*The Dreamlife of Angels*) (France).
Best Screenwriter: Peter Howitt for *Sliding Doors.*

DOLBY LABORATORIES

SOUND INNOVATIONS

When it comes to sound innovation, Dolby Laboratories leads the way, revolutionizing the audio and film industry with technological breakthroughs ranging from analog sound systems to Digital Video Broadcasting. Film and cinema sound in particular have benefited the most from Dolby's research and development programs:

- 1974, *Callan*, first film with optical soundtrack (mono) encoded with A-type noise reduction, shown at Cannes film festival. Dolby model number 364 used in the cinema to standardize the reproduction characteristics.

- 1974, *Lisztomania*, first feature film for general release with DOLBY STEREO optical soundtrack.

- 1975, *A Star Is Born*, first 35 mm DOLBY STEREO optical film with encoded surround effects.

- 1977, *Star Wars*, first standard commercial release of four channel DOLBY STEREO with *Close Encounters of the Third Kind* released later in year.

- 1979, *Apocalypse Now* and *Superman*, first 70 mm releases to high-quality six-track sound with stereo surround channels.

- 1987, An improved noise reduction system called Spectral Recording—DOLBY SR— used on the stereo optical soundtrack for *Innerspace* and *Robocop*.

- 1989, Ray Dolby and Vice President Ioan Allen awarded Oscars for "continuing contributions to motion picture sound through the research and development programs of Dolby Laboratories" by Academy of Motion Picture Arts and Sciences.

- 1992, *Batman Returns*, first film released in DOLBY DIGITAL providing six channels of digital sound recorded alongside the standard analog soundtrack, on the print.

- 1999, DOLBY DIGITAL SURROUND EX adds a third channel of surround on the back wall, developed with Lucasfilm's THX division for the release of *Star Wars*: Episode 1— The Phantom Menace.

- 21 of 22 Academy Award[TM] Winners for Best Sound and Best Picture have included Dolby sound technology.

- Dolby cinema processors have evolved from the CP100 through the CP50, CP200, CP55, CP65, DA10, and DA20 to today's industry standard CP500.

- Over 30 sound consultants worldwide support the film program providing technical services at film mixes, premieres and film festivals.

As the only cinema sound company dedicated to research and development, you can be sure that Dolby films will continue to thrill audiences the world over, for many years to come. To review the next episode in sound innovation, visit Dolby's web site at *www.dolby.com.*   S99/12658

European Cinematographer: Adrian Biddle for *The Butcher Boy* (Ireland).

European Achievement in World Cinema: Stellan Skarsgård, Sweden, *Amistad/Good Will Hunting*

Screen International award for a non-European film: *The Truman Show*, Peter Weir, (US).

The People's Choice Award: (voted for by movie fans across Europe):

Best European Director: Roland Emmerich (Germany) for *Godzilla*.

Best European Actor: Antonio Banderas (Spain) for *The Mask of Zorro*.

Best European Actress: Kate Winslet (UK), *Titanic*.

European Discovery – Fassbinder award: Joint winners: *Festen* (*The Celebration*) Thomas Vinterberg, Denmark and *La vie rêvée des anges* (*The Dreamlife of Angels*) Erick Zonca, France

Documentary Award – Prix Arte: Claudio Pazienza (Belgium).

European Short Film: *Un Jour*, Marie Paccou, France

FIPRESCI Award: Goran Paskaljević for *The Powder Keg* (Yugoslavia).

European Film Academy Special Achievement Award: Jeremy Irons (UK.)

Thomas Vinterberg's FESTEN, joint winner of the European Discovery award

French César Academy Awards: 1998

Best Director: Patrice Chéreau for *Ceux qui m'aiment prendront le train*.

Best Film: *La vie rêvée des anges*.

Best Actor: Jaques Villeret for *Le dîner de cons*.

Best Actress: Elodie Bouchez for *La vie rêvée des anges*.

Best Supporting Actor: Daniel Prévost for *Le dîner de cons*.

Best Supporting Actress: Dominique Blanc for *Ceux qui m'aiment prendront le train*.

AFI Australian Film Awards: 1998

Best Film: *The Interview*.

Best Direction: Rowan Woods for *The Boys*.

Best Original Screenplay: Craig Monahan, Gordon Davie for *The Interview*.

Best Adapted Screenplay: Stephen Sewell for *The Boys*.

Best Actress: Deborah Mailman for *Radiance*.

Best Actor: Hugo Weaving for *The Interview*.

Best Supporting Actress: Toni Collette for *The Boys*.

Best Supporting Actor: John Polson for *The Boys*.

Best Cinematography: Geoffrey Simpson for *Oscar and Lucinda*.

Best Editing: Jill Bilcock for *Head On*.

Best Original Music Score: Thomas Newman for *Oscar and Lucinda*.

Best Production Design: Luciana Arrighi for *Oscar and Lucinda*.

Best Costume Design: Janet Patterson for *Oscar and Lucinda*.

Best Foreign Film: *L.A. Confidential* (US).

Byron Kennedy Award for Excellence: Alison Barrett, Arthur Cambridge.

Best Documentary: *The Dragon of Galapogas*.

Best Sound: Andrew Plain, Ben Osmo, Gethin Creagh, *Oscar and Lucinda*.

Bill Condon won the Best Adapted Screenplay Oscar for GODS AND MONSTERS

Flanders International

Film
Festival
Ghent

Cultural Ambassador of Flanders
City Ambassador of Ghent

Every year in October

Over 120,000 US$ money prizes for distributors, filmmakers & composers

FOR INFORMATION, CONTACT OUR AGENTS:

L.A.	Ronni Chasen	+1/310/274 4400
N.Y.	Lucius Barre	+1/212/595 1773
London	Corbett & Keene	+44/171/494 3478
Paris	Denise Breton	+33/1/42 66 20 02

Flanders International Film Festival • Ghent
Kortrijksesteenweg 1104 • B-9051 Ghent • Belgium
tel.: +32/9/242 80 60 • fax: +32/9/221 90 74
e-mail: info@filmfestival.be • website: http://www.filmfestival.be

15020

Photo: Tony Stone images

Realisation: ● CLAERHOUT nv · (09) 242 82 00

For more information: http://www.filmfestival.be

Best Young Actor: Bruno Putzulu for *Petits désordres amoureux*.
Best Young Actress: Natacha Régnier for *La vie rêvée des anges*.
Best First Film: *Dieu seul me voit*.
Best Foreign Film: *Life is Beautiful* (Italy).
Best Original or Adapted Screenplay: Francis Veber for *Le dîner de cons*.
Best Music: Tony Gatlif for *Gadjo Dilo*.
Best Photography: Eric Gauthier for *Ceux qui m'aiment prendront le train*.
Best Editing: Véronique Lange for *Taxi*.
Best Sets: Jacques Rouxel for *Lautrec*.
Best Costumes: Pierre-Jean Larroque for *Lautrec*.
Best Short Film: Xavier Giannoli for *L'Interview*.

German Film Awards: 1999

Best Film: *Run Lola, Run*.
Best Director: Tom Tykwer for *Run Lola, Run*.
Best Actor: August Diehl for *23*.
Best Actress (shared): Juliane Koehler for *Aimee & Jaguar* and Maria Schrader for *Aimee & Jaguar* and *Meschugge*.
Best Supporting Actor: Herbert Knaup for *Run Lola, Run*.
Best Supporting Actress: Nina Petri for *Bin ich Schön* and *Run Lola, Run*.
Best Cinematography: Frank Griebe for *Run Lola, Run*.
Best Editing: Mathilde Bonnefoy for *Run Lola, Run*.

Best Foreign Film: *Life is Beautiful* (Italy).
Best Film Music: Niki Reiser for *Meschugge* and *Pünktchen und Anton*.
Lifetime Achievement Award: Egon Günther.

Italian Donatello Awards: 1999

Best Film: *Not of This World*.
Best Director: Giuseppe Tornatore for *The Legend of the Pianist on the Ocean*.
Best Producer: Lionello Cerri for *Not of This World*.
Best Debuting Director: Luciano Ligabue for *Radio Freccia*.
Best Actor: Stafano Accorsi for *Radio Freccia*.
Best Actress: Margherita Buy for *Not of This World*.
Best Supporting Actor: Fabrizio Bentivoglio for *Of Lost Love*.
Best Supporting Actress: Cecilia Dazzi for *Marriages*.
Best Screenplay: Giuseppe Piccioni, Gualtiero Rosell, Lucia Zei for *Not of This World*.
Best Cinematography: Lajos Koltai for *The Legend of the Pianist on the Ocean*.
Best Art Direction: Francesco Frigeri for *The Legend of The Pianist on the Ocean*.
Best Costumes: Maurizion Millenotti for *The Legend of the Pianist on the Ocean*.
Best Editing: Esmerelda Calabria for *Not of This World*.
Best Sound: Gaetano Carito for *Radio Freccia*.
Best Foreign Film: *Train of Life* (French/Belgian/Romanian/Dutch).

Spielberg's SAVING PRIVATE RYAN claimed five Oscars   *photo: David James*

DIRECTORS
of the year

Danny Boyle

by Philip Kemp

According to Danny Boyle, "the really great work comes from partnerships". It is a belief that, to date, he has adhered to faithfully. So inextricably is he bound up in the film-making triumvirate that also includes producer Andrew MacDonald and screenwriter John Hodge, that it is often difficult to disentangle their respective contributions. "You've got to take us as a job lot," MacDonald told the Hollywood studios that tried to pick them off one by one after the sensation of *Trainspotting*, and so far it is together that they have stood or fallen.

If and when Boyle splits off – even temporarily – from his partners to make a film independently, it may become easier to define his directorial personality. On the evidence to date he seems to be a director who is at the mercy of his script. Armed with good writing, Boyle's style is taut, energetic and to the point. Given a bad script, his stylistic quirks come to seem meretricious and tacked on: flash without substance.

It could also be that, like many directors who moved over from theatre and television, he thrives on restrictions. His first two cinematic hits, *Shallow Grave* and *Trainspotting*, were made on tight budgets and few sets, with a minimum of location work. *A Life Less Ordinary* had a longer shooting schedule, a far larger budget and all the wide open spaces of Utah to shoot in. The result was a disaster, both critically and financially; but again, should the accusing finger be pointed primarily at Boyle, or at Hodge's script? Or indeed at MacDonald, for enabling the whole project in the first place?

DANNY BOYLE was born in Bury, Manchester, of working-class Irish stock, in 1956, making him the oldest member of the trio heading Figment Films (Hodge was born in 1964 and MacDonald in 1966, both in Glasgow). Boyle grew up an avid cinemagoer: he recalls his father taking him to see *The Battle of the Bulge*, and he later sneaked in, under-age, to see *A Clockwork Orange*. From there he graduated to the local, scruffy arthouse to catch European movies: "I used to go there to see sex. But I came home having seen these incredible films – Bertolucci, Chabrol – and that was what I fed on."

Early stages

Theatre scarcely figured in Boyle's upbringing; he was 18, he claims, before he so much as set foot in a playhouse. Even so, having chosen a career in the performing arts, it was in the theatre that he started out. "Theatre seemed a much easier and more accessible way of getting into the arts," he explains. He began with the Joint Stock Company, then joined the Royal Court, liveliest and most adventurous of London's producing theatres.

From 1982 to 1987 Boyle was artistic director of the Court's Theatre Upstairs, the smaller and more experimental of its two stages; from 1985 to 1987 he was deputy artistic director of the whole theatre. Among the productions he mounted were Howard Brenton's *Victory* and *The Genius*, and Edward Bond's *Saved* – all socially and politically challenging pieces. During this period he also directed five productions – mainly new writing rather than classics – for the Royal Shakespeare Company.

Boyle values his time in the theatre. "You get a background working with actors, which is incredibly beneficial later on." Nonetheless, he feels the stage is mainly "an actor's tool", control of which must ultimately be relinquished by directors: "It's a salutary process. You spend six weeks dominating rehearsals, and then as soon as they get an audience the actors push you away, very gently, and you just float off … They're very respectful when you bring them your notes but what they're really thinking is, 'Fuck me, I'm out there, pal! You've no idea what it's like.' But with film, you take the material and you shape it and the actors float away from you."

Taking the next logical step towards film directing, Boyle moved into television in 1987 and joined the BBC in Belfast, where he directed – and in some cases produced – a series of hard-hitting plays about the Troubles. Moonlighting for independent television, he also directed two films for the prestigious, high-profile detective series *Inspector Morse*. One of these,

"Cherubim and Seraphim", offered a foretaste of *Trainspotting* when Morse and his sidekick, Sergeant Lewis, infiltrated an unofficial rave and watched teenagers taking Ecstasy. Morse took an uncensorious view of the drug scene, reflecting Boyle's own attitude.

The series that made Boyle's name was *Mr Wroe's Virgins*, a four-part BBC period drama adapted from a fact-based novel by Jane Rogers. Set in 1820s Lancashire, it told of a charismatic preacher who sets up his own church, the Christian Israelites, and asks his congregation to provide seven young women to serve in his household. A prime cast (Jonathan Pryce, Kerry Fox, Minnie Driver, Kathy Burke, Lia Williams) and the potent mix of sex, scandal and religion made for compelling drama, and confirmed Boyle's skill at directing actors and creating atmosphere. Some vivid near-fantasy sequences also hinted at his impatience with the prevailing realist mode that dominates most British television drama.

New talents unearthed

Impressed by *Mr Wroe's Virgins*, MacDonald and Hodge sent Boyle the script of *Shallow Grave*. The project had originated with Hodge, a doctor attempting to establish himself as a screenwriter. In 1991, he had brought the script to MacDonald, then looking to launch himself as a producer. Having sold the idea to the Scottish and Glasgow Film Funds, and secured backing from Channel Four, the pair started auditioning directors. Boyle's enthusiasm, and his cinematic reference points, convinced them he was the ideal choice. Boyle has said: "I thought the script was wonderful – lean and mean, and a very clean read – so I went in and pitched my ideas. The first words out of my mouth were '*Blood Simple*', which was crucial, I think: that dedication to the narrative, to the drive of the story."

The analogy was apt: *Shallow Grave* shares much of the Coen brothers' stylistic sharpness and their gleeful delight in pitch-black humour, in setting up a

The three greedy flat-mates in SHALLOW GRAVE
photo: Nigel Robertson/Gramercy Pictures

situation tight as a coiled watch-spring and letting it unwind into mayhem and disaster. We watch three young professionals sharing an Edinburgh flat take in a fourth, who promptly dies of an overdose, a suitcase full of loot left at his side. They decide to bury him, keep his ill-gotten cash and say nothing – a fatal decision that leads to dismemberment, madness and violent death.

Right from the start, as Boyle unleashes his camera in a headlong rush through the elegant Georgian streets of Edinburgh New Town, the film fizzes with bite and energy. The unsentimental, even cruel take on the characters is refreshing. *Shallow Grave*, Boyle has suggested, "is not about class or society, or people being crushed by forces they can't control. Everybody takes responsibility for their decisions. We didn't want this film soaked in British social realism."

Most of the film was shot on a single set – a desirable flat, built (in a Glasgow warehouse) slightly larger than life-size and complete with all services – enhancing the sense of a close-textured chamber piece. Boyle's three leads (Kerry Fox, Christopher Eccleston and Ewan McGregor) play off each other like musicians, weaving and manoeuvring as the lines of attraction, greed and power shift between them. Boyle's collaborative rapport with actors paid dividends.

"There's this impression that to get what they want, directors have to have these monstrous egos that just gobble everyone and everything up," he says. "What I've found is that if you want to get the best out of the actors, you have to trust and respect them. If you do that, then they'll come up with a lot of amazing ideas which you can nick – and take all the credit."

Witty, stylish and hard-edged, *Shallow Grave* was widely hailed as an exhilarating breakthrough for British – and indeed Scottish – cinema. It took $8m at the UK box-office (more than three times as much as any other home-grown feature released in 1995) and went on to win the BAFTA award for Best British Film. Along with its vigour, many critics were struck by the disquieting beauty of Boyle's images (his cinematographer, Brian Tufano, had worked on *Mr Wroe's Virgins*, as had his editor, Masahiro Hirakubo; both stayed with him on his subsequent films). When the new flatmate, Hugo, is found dead, he lies naked, face up, limbs sprawling, on a blood-red blanket against a royal-blue background – an image with all the cool lushness of a Caravaggio.

An exhilarating injection

After briefly toying with a curious, abortive assignment – an English-language remake of Julio Medem's quirky romance *The Red Squirrel* – Boyle rejoined his Figment partners for a film version of Irvine Welsh's cult novel *Trainspotting*. Set among the young heroin addicts of Edinburgh's less salubrious quarter, Welsh's novel – recounted in multiple voices and caustically demotic Scots patois – captures the rhythm and energy of the fractured, street-level junk culture it portrays. Hodge's script skilfully narrowed down the viewpoint to one character, Renton – played by Ewan McGregor with crop-haired, weasel charm – and marshalled the novel's rambling structure into a coherent narrative.

If *Shallow Grave* was a smash hit, *Trainspotting* was a phenomenon, taking almost $20m at home and $40m abroad. Sharing the earlier film's headlong trajectory and its passion for colour and light, it replaced *Shallow Grave*'s visual elegance and poised, cruel humour with a mass of relentlessly shitty detail and a manic cackle of wrecked mirth. At once exhilarating and despairing, lurching from exuberance to inertia, from frenetic humour to gut-wrenching squalor, it enters into the lives of its deadbeat junkies on their own terms, without patronising or pitying. Boyle's signature visual tropes – frenetic camera, skewed framing, overheated colours – are even more in evidence. Again he draws superb ensemble acting from his cast – especially from Robert Carlyle as Begbie, a scarifying psychotic so high on mindless violence he doesn't even need drugs.

The film's pace and scabrous humour, set to a pulsing Britpop and dance music score (the album went multi-platinum), appealed strongly to younger audiences, as did its unpreachy attitude to drugs. Though never discounting the ravages of heroin addiction, Boyle and his colleagues rejected any simplistic 'Just Say No' attitude. "The whole reason we wanted to do this film," he remarked at the time, "is to say people do drugs because you actually have a good time. That's the bit that's always left out …

In the end the film conforms like every other film about heroin; it shows you how in fact it will destroy you. But there are people, like Irvine Welsh, who go through it and come out the other side. You have to tell the truth about that, even though you're accused of encouraging drug use."

As of course they were. The ensuing controversy did the film nothing but good at the box-office, and *Trainspotting* – along with its distinctive orange-toned publicity material – became one of the most influential films of the decade, headbutting audiences the world over into a lastingly new perception of what British films could look like. Boyle found himself compared to Scorsese, Kubrick, Tarantino and other masters of guerrilla cinema – influences he readily acknowledges, along with those of Dick Lester and Kathryn Bigelow. "I feed off other stuff deliberately. That's not un-healthy… I love looting people and ideas."

Third-time unlucky

Now ultra-hot property, the trio found themselves wooed by Hollywood, and for

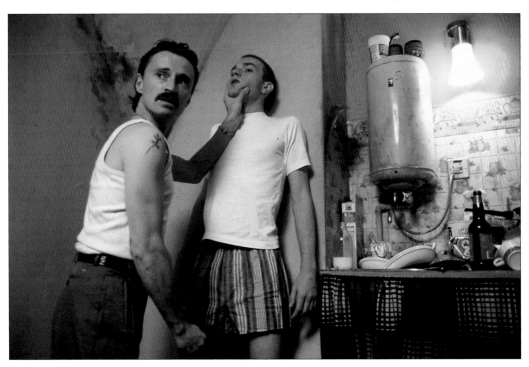

Begbie (Robert Carlyle) gets to grips with Renton (Ewan McGregor) in TRAINSPOTTING

photo: Liam Longman/PolyGram

a while toyed with the idea of making the fourth *Alien* film. But the prospect of dealing with the studio interference inseparable from mega-budget movie-making put them off. Instead they opted for a rather less ambitious, US-based project that they could control: *A Life Less Ordinary*, from another original script by Hodge.

The remarkable thing about *A Life Less Ordinary* is that, by all accounts, Boyle and Co. did retain complete creative control, since the film looks like nothing so much as the kind of sprawling, soggy mess that often results when Hollywood gets hold of, and tries to remould, spiky European talents. An attempt at a screwball romance after the model of *It Happened One Night*, the film contrives to misfire in virtually every department. The main, road-movieish plotline of inept would-be kidnapper Ewan McGregor and spoilt rich girl Cameron Diaz on the run together, is cluttered with a footling and superfluous

Delroy Lindo and Holly Hunter as angels in A LIFE LESS ORDINARY

photo: Darren Michaels/Fox

subplot about two angels sent from heaven to bring the young couple together in true love. Most of the cast, as if uneasy with their material, shout too much.

At one point both Diaz and the female angel (Holly Hunter) are shown reading a Mills & Boon-ish romance (*Perfect Love* by Jennifer Hodge) which Diaz sums up as follows: "There's this girl, she meets this guy, they fall in love. It's bullshit." This self-conscious attempt to deflect criticism backfires badly, since the film itself features emetic lines like "Love comes from a strange and wonderful place that we don't know about." Boyle attempts to jazz things up with high-octane stylistic tricks – overhead shots, saturated colours, jump-cuts, flash forwards, fantasy sequences and so forth – but they skid about on the surface, never getting a hold on the trite material. The film ends in what seems sheer desperation – a sequence with the characters transformed into animated plasticine figures.

Even before *A Life Less Ordinary* was released, the film-makers evidently feared they were serving up a turkey. "It's about time we got some flak," Boyle commented uneasily, and they did – both from the critics, universally dismissive, and the public, who stayed away in droves, leaving the film with a domestic gross half the size of *Shallow Grave*'s.

It says a lot for the strength of their partnership – which is not bound by any formal contract – that the trio stayed together without recrimination and embarked on their fourth film: an adaptation of another cult novel, Alex Garland's bestseller *The Beach*, in which a back-packer in Thailand stumbles upon a seemingly idyllic hippie colony. However, to up the chances of commercial success, Ewan McGregor was dropped from the lead – a decision that still rankles with the actor – in favour of Leonardo DiCaprio, whose post-*Titanic* fee boosted the budget by $20m.

The Beach will certainly not want for publicity on its release. Already the shoot has attracted copious coverage, with

DiCaprio reportedly suffering from loneliness and jelly-fish stings, and environmentalists irate over despoiled Thai beaches. At the end of the 1990s, it remains to be seen whether Boyle and his colleagues can recapture the bite, inventiveness and brio of their first two films. It's certain, however, that *Shallow Grave* and, even more so, *Trainspotting*, will be acknowledged as two of the most influential films of the decade, for their role in sparking the current revitalisation of British cinema.

Boyle (right) with Ewan McGregor on the set of A LIFE LESS ORDINARY   *photo: 20th Century Fox*

PHILIP KEMP is a freelance writer on film, contributing regularly to *Film Comment* and *Sight and Sound*. He is currently working on a biography of Michael Balcon.

Boyle Filmography

TELEVISION

1987: *Next: Scout* (also Prod); *The Rockingham Shoot* (Prod only). 1989: *Elephant* (Prod only); *Monkeys* (also Prod); *Nightwatch* (also Prod); *Screenplay: Hen House*. 1990: *Inspector Morse*: "Masonic Mysteries". 1991: *For the Greater Good* (3-part drama); *Screenplay: Arise and Go Now*. 1992: *Inspector Morse*: "Cherubim and Seraphim". 1993: *Mr Wroe's Virgins* (4-part drama); *Screenplay: Not Even God Is Wise Enough*.

1994
SHALLOW GRAVE

Script: John Hodge. Direction: DB. Photography: Brian Tufano. Editing: Masahiro Hirakubo. Production Design: Kave Quinn. Music: Simon Boswell. Players: Kerry Fox (*Juliet Miller*), Christopher Eccleston (*David Stephens*), Ewan McGregor (*Alex Law*), Ken Stott (*DI McCall*), Keith Allen (*Hugo*). Produced by Andrew Macdonald for Figment Films and Channel Four. 92 mins.

1995
TRAINSPOTTING

Script: John Hodge, from the novel by Irvine Welsh. Direction: DB. Photography: Brian Tufano. Editing: Masahiro Hirakubo. Production Design: Kave Quinn. Music: Iggy Pop, Lou Reed, Brian Eno, Blur et al. Players: Ewan McGregor (*Renton*), Ewen Bremner (*Spud*), Jonny Lee Miller (*Sick Boy*), Robert Carlyle (*Begbie*), Kevin McKidd (*Tommy*), Kelly Macdonald (*Diane*), Peter Mullan (*Swanney*). Produced by Andrew Macdonald for Figment Films, Noel Gay Motion Picture Co and Channel Four. 93 mins.

1997
A LIFE LESS ORDINARY

Script: John Hodge. Direction: DB. Photography: Brian Tufano. Editing: Masahiro Hirakubo. Production Design: Kave Quinn. Music: David Arnold. Players: Ewan McGregor (*Robert*), Cameron Diaz (*Celine*), Holly Hunter (*O'Reilly*), Delroy Lindo (*Jackson*), Ian Holm (*Naville*), Dan Hedaya (*Gabriel*), Ian McNeice (*Mayhew*), Stanley Tucci (*Elliot*), Maury Chaykin (*Tod Johnson*). Produced by Andrew Macdonald for Figment Films, Channel Four and Polygram Filmed Entertainment. 102 mins.

1999
THE BEACH

Script: John Hodge, Alex Garland, from Garland's novel. Direction: DB. Players: Leonardo DiCaprio, Virginie Ledoyen, Guillaume Canet, Tilda Swinton. Produced by Andrew Macdonald.

Takeshi Kitano

by Tad Osaki

His works are "imbued with a charm that incorporates both brutality and kindness". So said Maurice Gourdault-Montagne, France's Ambassador to Japan, as the French government bestowed Takeshi Kitano with the honorary title of Chevalier at the French Film Festival in Yokohama on June 12, 1999. The French medal, created in 1957 by the late André Malraux when he was Minister of Education, to decorate those who excel in creative arts, was given to Kitano two weeks after his latest film, *Kikujiro*, had been in competition at Cannes.

Kikujiro, named after Kitano's father, is the eighth film he has directed since 1989, and the follow-up to the 1997 Golden Lion-winning *Hana-Bi*, which had brought Kitano the greatest acclaim and exposure of his directorial career. Entitled *Kikujiro-no-Natsu* ("Kikujiro's Summer") in Japanese, the film follows the journey of a middle-aged bum (Kitano) and a boy whose mother has walked out on him. It was a dramatic departure from the mob violence which featured in his earlier works.

The juxtaposition of violence and mute, reflective passages had confused spectators and resulted in polarised reviews of his movies in Japan. Some labelled Kitano as being too fond of cheap violence, while others praised him for employing the heightened language of pure cinematic art, next to or even surpassing the legendary Kurosawa.

At Cannes, Kitano said: "After *Hana-Bi*, I couldn't help feeling my films were being stereotyped: 'gangster violence, life and death', and I found it difficult to identify myself with them. So I decided to make a film no one would have predicted. In truth, the story belongs to a genre outside my speciality, because it would be a challenge for me to cope with this ordinary story. I tried a lot of experiments in the imagery, and think it has become a rather strange film, with my trademark all over it. I hope to continue betraying people's expectations in a positive way."

For Kitano, however, "betraying people's expectations" has been a paramount goal throughout his life as a comedian, TV personality, radio talk show host, actor, writer, director and all-round entertainer. From the very first day he appeared on stage at the France-za striptease theatre in Asakusa, Tokyo, in 1974, Takeshi "Beat" Kitano ignored traditional rules – and common sense.

It is anybody's guess if he knew then that his stage name "Beat" would contradict what became his trademark: bombarding audiences on stage and television with off-beat gags full of swear words. He was and still is known for raw jokes which strain or even break Japan's broadcasting code of ethics on discrimination against the elderly, women, ethnic minorities, the ugly and the poor. In fact, "Beat"'s off-beat characteristics have been with him since childhood.

The Beat generation

TAKESHI KITANO was born in Tokyo on January 18, 1947, the fourth son of a house painter. He was doted on by his parents and grandmother, who called him Prince Takeshi. At junior school, he was adept at swimming, softball and baseball and a gifted mimic, always making his classmates laugh. Despite spending more time on baseball and in the boxing gym than on his high school studies, he made it to the

Detective Nishi (Kitano) with his wife Miyuki (Kayoko Kishimoto) in HANA-BI   *photo: Office Kitano*

mechanical engineering department of Meiji University in 1965.

Once there, however, he spent most of his time working as a coffee shop waiter in Shinjuku, Tokyo, for 60 cents an hour. Later, he worked as a department store sales agent, Ginza hostess bar waiter, cab driver and construction worker. He did not last long in any of these jobs because he simply ignored the rules; for example, he drank while on duty as a cab driver.

His life reached a turning point when in 1972 he got an elevator operator job at the old striptease theatre, France-za, where he became fascinated by the comedians who acted as warm-up. He volunteered to become a disciple of the France-za's chief comedian, Senzaburo Fukami, and underwent basic comedic training. He formed a duo with his buddy Jiro Kaneko and worked out a few numbers on the road, with minimal success, splitting with Kaneko once, before teaming up as a duo again under the name Two Beat, in 1974, back at France-za, when Kitano was 27.

As their unconventional, stinging jokes developed a following, the duo were offered occasional spots on Tokyo radio and television stations, the first being *Rivals Guffaw* in 1975, the TV Tokyo show which triggered a boom in stand-up, dialogue comedy on television that was to last for several years. In their first magazine interview, in a November 1978 issue of *Heibon Punch*, then the widest-circulation pop magazine for young men, Two Beat were described as "a young, fast rising dialogue comedy duo that takes full advantage of all the criticisms hurled at them: rude, incoherent, preposterous and cheeky".

The rest is now history. Two Beat became the most sought-after act of the early 1980s, at one point appearing in 45 programmes a week. Kitano was in huge demand in his own right on radio and TV and his childhood was dramatised in a serial based on his best-selling (almost a million copies) memoir, *Master Takeshi, Yes*, on the national NHK network in 1985. As the demand for Takeshi's solo performance soared and the dialogue comedian boom peaked around that time, Takeshi's Two Beat partner, Kiyoshi (as Kaneko is now known), also began working solo. However, the duo still play the occasional gig together.

From small to big screen

After starring in three Japanese movies in 1981 and 1982, Kitano made his international movie debut as an actor in 1983 with the British-funded *Merry Christmas, Mr. Lawrence*, directed by Nagisa Oshima, as a Japanese sergeant in a prisoner-of-war camp in Batavia. The movie lost to Shohei Imamura's *The Ballad of Narayama* at Cannes that year, much to Kitano's chagrin, and was only a minor box-office hit in Japan. However, *Merry Christmas, Mr. Lawrence* hooked him into the film world.

Kitano made his debut as a director in 1989, with the hard-boiled police thriller *Beware, That Man Is Violent* (*Sono Otoko Kyobo ni tsuki*), or *Violent Cop*, as it was released and known in the US. The film sees maverick detective Azuma, who has a mentally handicapped sister, become locked in a life-and-death battle with a drug dealer. Since then, Kitano has directed a new movie virtually every year, going against the original scheduling

suggested by his manager, Masayuki Mori, who wanted him to work at the rate of at most two movies every three years.

He wrote, directed and also played the leading role in his second film, *Boiling Point* (aka *3-4 October*), in 1990, a fantasy set on Okinawa one October, in which an amateur baseball team fights gangsters. *A Scene at the Sea* (aka *The Quietest See That Summer*), in 1991, centred on a deaf couple (Kurodo Maki and Hiroko Oshima) who join a surfing competition, never speaking to each other or anyone else. The fourth feature, *Sonatine*, in 1993, charted the last week in the life of a brutal, disillusioned and ultimately suicidal gangster, played by Kitano.

After four features in which the leading characters are relatively expressionless and impassive, destined for self-destruction or death, Kitano changed tack with the comedy of *Getting Any?* in 1994, in which Asao (Minoru Iizuka), a self-styled play-boy, keeps failing to pick up girlfriends via abortive efforts at bank robbery, drug trafficking and other crimes.

Kitano as the eponymous VIOLENT COP, his debut feature as director   photo: The Kobal Collection

A deaf couple enter a surfing competition in A SCENE AT THE SEA   *photo: Office Kitano*

A pair of high school dropouts in KIDS RETURN   *photo: Office Kitano*

Enforced retreats

It was after *Getting Any?* that Kitano went temporarily quiet for the second time in his career. The first hiatus had come in December 1986, when Kitano and 11 members of "Takeshi's Army" physically assaulted the editorial department of the photo weekly *Friday*, after the magazine carried an exposé of his extramarital affair.

He had gathered his disciples as "Takeshi's Army" in 1983. These young men, fiercely loyal, are given the chance to appear as bit part players in his television shows or on stage, mostly as Kitano's guests' servants. They also play baseball as a team managed by Kitano, and work as his bodyguards and servants, in the tradition of Japanese entertainers who are trained by their grand masters.

After the incident at the *Friday* offices, Kitano was found guilty of assault and given a suspended sentence in April 1994, after which he went quiet for about three months. Shortly after returning to the spotlight, however, in the early hours of August 2, 1994, Kitano had a serious motorbike accident while riding under the influence of alcohol, and suffered near-fatal injuries. He was immobilised in hospital for several months, before reappearing on a talk show in March 1995.

He has said that *Kids Return*, in 1996, was "my rehabilitation as a director", and he came back from the accident with another departure from the gangster genre: a social realist drama focusing on high-school dropouts who try to do the best they can by pursuing various avenues, such as prize-fighting or motorbike riding.

Hana-Bi, in 1997, saw him return to *Violent Cop* and *Sonatine* territory, with detective Nishi (Kitano) taking on the mobsters who killed his fellow cops and confined his best friend to a wheelchair. He robs a bank to fund the widow of one of the dead cops and to take his wife, bed-ridden with cancer, on a final, honeymoon-like journey before her death. Here, Kitano's gifts as an editor (he has edited all his films since *A Scene at the Sea*) are seen to great effect, with the main narrative progression alternating with flashbacks and occasional flash forwards.

None of his movies has relied heavily on dialogue, with Kitano preferring silent acting and imagery to convey his ideas. Many spectators and some critics are fascinated by his sense of colour. The term "Kitano Blue" was coined during the Venice Film Festival in 1998 to describe his persistent use of blue in various shades: tropical fish, suits worn by leading characters, the sky, cars, or night lights.

His modus operandi as a director is quite flamboyant and unpredictable; he will change the script on a whim while out on location, often confusing his cast and crew. He does, however, have a set style of directing a film: in four 'chapters', each comprising 20 to 30 scenes.

Kitano set up Office Kitano as his own management office in 1989, with Masayuki

Kitano assaults a fellow gangster in SONATINE   *photo: The Kobal Collection*

Mori, a long-time director of his television programmes, as president. Office Kitano, now fully incorporated, is located in Akasaka, not far from Tokyo Broadcasting System (TBS) and TV Tokyo, with about 20 employees working on promotion, scheduling, video production and movie distribution. Some of Kitano's two-dozen 'soldiers' have gradually been given better roles, with a few now working as comedians and actors in their own right, but still pledging absolute loyalty to Kitano.

Kitano has occasionally taken on other commercial ventures unrelated to his art. He appeared in a health food commercial with his mother, Saki, in 1982. In 1987 and 1988, he opened a chain of Indian curry restaurants, Kitano Indian Co., in Karuisawa and Lake Yamanaka resorts, a fashion boutique, Kitano Club, in Harajuku, Tokyo, and an ice cream and pancake shop in Maebashi, Gunma. However, he quickly lost interest in these businesses and wound them up.

In the summer of 1999, Kitano was shooting another Nagisa Oshima movie,

Gohatto (*Forbidden*), scheduled to be released in December, in which he plays a samurai. As most of the location work was taking place in Kyoto, Kitano was running back and forth between the old capital of Japan and Tokyo, where most of his television shows are produced.

Kitano today appears in eight regular network TV programmes, five in prime-time slots – Mori has noted that "the more tension rises on his movie work schedule, the more hyperactive he gets in his television work". Kitano has won more than two dozen best programme awards in 23 years, written more than 70 books, selling more than 100,000 copies each, as well as regular columns for magazines, many of them illustrated with his own paintings and drawings. He sings and plays keyboards, and has released 24 CD singles and albums.

Mori began adjusting Kitano's television work schedule in February in preparation for his next feature, tentatively entitled *Brothers*, to be jointly produced by Jeremy Thomas of RPC and Office Kitano. The Japanese location work will start in

Kitano with Yusukae Sekiguchi in KIKUJIRO — — — *photo: Office Kitano*

November, 1999, with shooting in the US in January and February, 2000, for completion in May.

Before shooting begins, he will have received the 1999 Japanese Cultural Design Grand Prix from the Japan Cultural Design Forum (JCDF). This is due recognition, says JCDF president Kisho Kurokawa, for the man who has revolutionised Japanese television humour and rejuvenated Japanese movies in the eyes of the world.

N. TAD OSAKI writes for *Variety, Television Asia* and *Asia Image* from Tokyo, where he has been a journalist for more than 30 years.

Takeshi Kitano Filmography

1989
SONO OTOKO KYOBO NI TSUKI
(Violent Cop)

Script: Hisashi Nozawa. Dir: TK. Editing: Nobutake Kamiya. Photography: Yasushi Sasakibara. Music: Daisaku Kume. Players: TK (*Detective Azuma*), Maiko Kawakami (*Akari, Azuma's sister*), Shiro Sano (*Yoshinari*). Produced by Kazuhisa Okuyama for Shochiku-Fuji.103 mins.

1990
BOILING POINT
(aka 3-4 October)

Script and Direction: TK. Photography: Katsumi Yanagijima. Editing: Toshio Taniguchi. Players: TK (*Uehara*), Masahiko Ono (*Masaki*), Yuriko Ishida (*Sayaka*), Hisashi Iguchi (*Takashi*), Minoru Iizuka (*Kazuo*). Produced by Kazuhisa Okuyama for Shochiku-Fuji. 96 mins.

1991
ANO NATSU ICHIBAN
SHIZUKANA UMI
(A Scene at the Sea)

Script, Direction and Editing: TK. Photography: Katsumi Yana-gijima. Music: Jo Hisaishi. Players: Hiroko Oshima (*Takako*), Kurodo Maki (*Shigeru*), Susumu Terashima (*Truck driver*). Produced by Yukio Tachi for Office Kitano, Totsu. 101 mins.

1993
SONATINE

Script, Direction and Editing: TK. Photography: Katsumi Yana-gijima. Music: Jo Hisaishi. Players: TK (*Murakawa*), Aya Kokumai (*Miyuki*). Produced by Kazuyoshi Okuyama for Bandai Visual, Shochiku. 94 mins.

1994
MINNA YATTERUKAI!
(Getting Any?)

Script, Direction and Editing: TK. Photography: Katsumi Yanagijima. Music: Hidehiko Koike. Players: TK (*Doctor to promote Invisible Man*), Susumu Terashima (*Hoodlum*), Ken Osugi (*Hitman*), Minoru Iizuka (*Asao*), Tokie Hidari (*Asao's mother*). Produced by Masyuki Mori and Hisao Nabeshima for Office Kitano, Bandai Visual. 110 mins.

1996
KIDS RETURN

Script and Direction: TK. Editing: TK, with Yoshinori Ota. Photography: Katsumi Yanagijima. Music: Jo Hisaishi. Players: Ken Kaneko (*Masaru*), Masanobu Ando (*Shinji*), Yuko Daike, Susumu Terashima (*Young mob leaders*). Produced by Masayuki Mori, Yasuji Tsuge and Takio Yoshida for Office Kitano, Bandai Visual. 108 mins.

1997
HANA-BI

Script, Direction and Editing: TK. Photography: Hideo Yamamoto. Music: Jo Hisaishi. Players: TK (*Detective Nishi*), Kayoko Kishimoto (*Miyuki, Nishi's wife*), Ren Osugi (*Horibe*), Susumu Terashima (*Nakamura*). Produced by Masayuki Mori, Takio Yoshida and Yasuji Tsuge for Office Kitano, Nippon Herald. 103 mins.

1998
KIKUJIRO NO NATSU
(Kikujiro)

Script and Direction: TK. Editing: TK, with Yoshinori Ota. Photography: Katsumi Yanagijima. Music: Jo Hisaishi. Players: TK (*Kikujiro*), Kayoko Kishimoto (*Neighbour*), Yusuke Sekiguchi (*Masao*), Kazuko Yoshiyuki (*Auntie*). Produced by Masayuki Mori and Takio Yoshida for Bandai Visual, Nippon Herald and Office Kitano. 121 mins.

Søren Kragh-Jacobsen

by Ebbe Iversen

Everybody is good at something - it's just a matter of finding out what. This line from Søren Kragh-Jacobsen's *Rubber Tarzan* could almost serve as a motto for his entire œuvre. The Danish director likes to tell us stories about underdogs, who at first seem to be born losers, but have hidden resources which emerge in the face of adversity. Their final triumph comes not in defeating the bad guys, but in proving themselves as valuable human beings, good at something.

Kragh-Jacobsen's protagonists – from Claus in his first film, *Wanna See My Beautiful Navel*, to Kresten in his most recent, *Mifune*, discover their hitherto hidden qualities when transformed by friendship or love. Personal improvement and growth are the themes of Kragh-Jacobsen's optimistic films, yet he is no naive escapist, blind to the problems of life. It is through conflict, and often humiliation, that his main characters find maturity and self-esteem.

At the 1999 Berlin Film Festival, *Mifune* was not only awarded a Silver Bear, but had distributors literally fighting to secure the rights, which were sold to almost every territory in the world. Although Kragh-Jacobsen's contribution to the much-debated Dogma movement – following Thomas Vinterberg (*The Celebration*) and Lars von Trier (*Idiots*) – looks like becoming his international breakthrough, it is worth stressing that *Mifune* is not so much typical Dogma as typical Kragh-Jacobsen. He has loyally obeyed the ten strict Dogma commandments, but within these technical limitations he has chosen the same kind of story and themes as in his previous films.

SØREN KRAGH-JACOBSEN was born in Copenhagen in 1947, the second-oldest of four brothers, one of whom, Ole, is now an eminent photographer. Their father was in charge of part of the production process at an ice cream factory, his mother had worked in an office, and Søren grew up in a safe, solid middle-class family.

He had two uncles with artistic interests. Bamse Kragh-Jacobsen was a painter and jazz musician, and Svend Kragh-Jacobsen was for decades the best-known theatre, ballet and film critic in Denmark. He wrote for the *Berlingske Tidende* newspaper and was a living legend within his profession. He took his nephew Søren to theatre first nights and film press screenings. As a boy, Søren fell in love with films, but dutifully followed his father's advice and trained as an electrical engineer from the age of 16.

After completing his education he held a number of blue-collar jobs, including spells at a shipyard and with the postal service, and today he claims these experiences taught him a great deal about co-operation and professional discipline. He also cites these jobs as the reason for *Rubber Tarzan* being, among other things, a "ballet for heavy industrial equipment".

First films are kids' stuff

He still wanted to make films, and, spurred on by his admiration for directors like Robert Flaherty and Joris Ivens, his early ambition was to become a documentarist. In 1969-70 he attended the FAMU film school in Prague (a period which he now calls the most important in his life), after which he landed a job at Danmarks Radio, the national public broadcaster, where from 1971 to 1983 he made numerous radio and television programmes, especially for children and young people. Simultaneously he carved out a career as a singer and songwriter, releasing a couple of domestically very successful pop albums. In 1986, he married copyright lawyer Cæcilie, and they have two sons.

He belongs to the same generation of Danish film-makers as Nils Malmros, Anders Refn, Morten Arnfred and Bille August, and 1978 saw his feature debut, *Wanna See My Beautiful Navel*, based on a novel by Hans Hansen. It tells of first love,

Ole (Otto Brandenburg), with Alex Svanbjerg as RUBBER TARZAN

Peter Hesse Overgaard and Michael Falch in THUNDERBIRDS

as teenagers Claus and Lene are shyly attracted to each other during a week-long school excursion to a remote cabin in a Swedish forest.

The film was well-received by audiences and critics, who appreciated its natural freshness, romantic gentleness and humour. Claus is convincingly played by Birger Larsen, who, aided by Kragh-Jacobsen, has since become a director himself (*Let the Polar Bears Dance, The Big Dipper*).

Although very loosely structured, with a visually raw, almost improvised look, *Wanna See My Beautiful Navel* is still enjoyable thanks to its relaxed realism and witty description of girls being more mature and sensible than boys, who try to hide their insecurity behind silly practical jokes. It also holds a rare distinction, as a film whose catchy theme song is sung by its director.

Kragh-Jacobsen's second film, *Rubber Tarzan*, has been described as the best

children's film ever made – an accolade impossible to prove or disprove. Based on a novel by the late Ole Lund Kirkegaard it recounts the story of eight-year-old Ivan Olsen, played with wonderful sensitivity by Alex Svanberg, who is constantly mobbed at school and scolded by his father for seemingly being hopeless at absolutely everything, including gymnastics and reading (the latter perhaps an autobiographical reflection of the fact that Kragh-Jacobsen was suspected of suffering from dyslexia at school).

However, Ivan (nicknamed Rubber Tarzan by his father, who reads Tarzan comics and mocks the physical weakness which prevents his son from climbing trees) finds a friend in harbour worker Ole – a politically incorrect hero, who swears and smokes. He teaches the boy to manoeuvre a gigantic crane, and utters the now classic line about everybody being good at something, the trick being to find out what. Whereas the novel ends on a very dark note, Kragh-Jacobsen provides an uplifting, gently satirical, but not sugar-coated ending to this charming story, which combines realism with a magical dream world.

Rubber Tarzan was awarded three Danish Bodil prizes and the UNICEF prize at the Berlin Film Festival. Its vivid images marked the first collaboration between Kragh-Jacobsen and cinematographer Dan Laustsen, who has shot five of the director's eight features, and now works in the United States.

Something to prove?

With his following film, *Thunderbirds*, in 1983, Kragh-Jacobsen probably wanted to demonstrate (especially to himself) that he was capable of making a serious film about adults. He wrote the script with Hans Hansen and the male protagonist John, a power plant worker still living with his mother, is a sort of grown-up Rubber Tarzan, with little going for him.

John's life changes when he meets tough desperado René, who insists on befriending him. René terrorises his wealthy father, whom he blames for his mother's suicide. Ultimately this costs René his life, but the introvert John matures through their stormy friendship and probably faces a brighter future with his new girlfriend, single mother Vivi.

Thunderbirds is a personal, ambitious and partly tragic film, worthy of respect, although its dramatic potential is not fully explored: the initially promising story gradually loses momentum and ends with a whimper. Despite strong images and an occasionally icy atmosphere, it seems to prove that Kragh-Jacobsen deals with serious subjects most convincingly when employing his generous, unique sense of humour.

His subsequent film, *Shower of Gold*, has no serious ambitions at all. This light, attractive entertainment for very young people is actually an edited version of a six-part television series from 1986. Based on a script by popular suspense writer Anders Bodelsen its heroes are four bright children who find a large sum of stolen money buried in a wood north of Copenhagen. The thieves set out to recover the loot and a number of dramatic chases follow. The most interesting point of the story is that the girls are more sensible and morally aware than the boys. Women are almost always stronger and wiser than men in Kragh-Jacobsen's films.

Poor little rich girl

After *Shower of Gold*, he decided not to make any more films about kids. He recently said, with excessive modesty, that directing young children is very unpredictable and risky – a bit like "pulling the pin on a hand grenade and then waiting and watching". Nevertheless, part of the financing for his next project, *Emma's Shadow*, was allocated from the Danish Film Institute's fund for children's films, and without much enthusiasm Kragh-Jacobsen felt obliged to direct yet another story about a child: 12-year-old Emma, who feels ignored by her wealthy, busy parents, and, inspired by the recent, tragic abduction of Charles Lindbergh's son (the story takes place in 1932), fakes her own "kidnapping".

Line Kruse and Börje Ahlstedt in EMMA'S SHADOW

The decisive point here is that Emma is not cute: she is a spoiled, snobbish and quite obnoxious little pain in the neck. Like a fish out of water when hiding in a working-class district of Copenhagen, she needs help, and befriends a gentle giant, the humble, insecure Swedish-born worker Malthe, who makes his malodorous living in the city sewers.

Emma's Shadow movingly describes the girl's transformation from selfish brat to caring, generous person, as her friendship with Malthe grows stronger. It is, however, also a suspense story, as the police investigating the presumed kidnapping pick Malthe, who has done time for violence, as their prime suspect. The drama culminates in a spectacular chase through the sewers, an arrest and a wordless, touching reunion.

With Copenhagen of the 1930s carefully recreated, and strong performances from talented newcomer Line Kruse (who has since made a career in Danish cinema) as Emma and the great Swedish actor Börje Ahlstedt as Malthe, *Emma's Shadow* is one of Kragh-Jacobsen's finest films. It is romantically naive and occasionally didactic in its colourful depiction of proletarian life, but also visually splendid and extremely satisfying emotionally – a beautiful tribute to the redemption found in friendship based on loyalty and self-sacrifice.

The Boys from St. Petri (1991), written by Kragh-Jacobsen with prolific novelist Bjarne Reuter, recounts a fictional story based on fact. During the German occupation of Denmark one of the very first resistance groups – known as the Churchill Club – was formed by a handful of grammar school students in the northern town of Aalborg in 1942. Although their success as urban guerrillas was limited, they were an inspiration for the Danish resistance movement over the next three years.

Kragh-Jacobsen's handsome film, partly shot in Poland, is less a story of heroic deeds (the young freedom fighters fumble when trying to blow up a German train),

Kragh-Jacobsen with Line Kruse, filming EMMA'S SHADOW

than an intimate study of the psychological hierarchy within the group – a coming-of-age tale about maturity achieved too quickly under dramatic circumstances.

Unfortunately, the film fails to provide the seven fighters with sufficiently clear profiles, depriving the narrative of a strong focus. One interesting character does emerge, in the shape of the dark, gloomy Otto, whose working-class background makes him a misfit in the bourgeois group, only accepted because he knows how to acquire guns. Otto was the screen debut of Nikolaj Lie Kaas, who won a Bodil prize as Best Supporting Actor (an award he recently received again for *Idiots*). *The Boys from St. Petri* is technically very accomplished, containing strong, dramatic images by the meticulous Laustsen, and was a fair success in domestic cinemas, selling about 270,000 tickets.

Kragh-Jacobsen's next assignment was the four-part series *The Bishop from Corsica*, written with Bjarne Reuter and made for Swedish television. It was a suspense story for kids about two boys caught up in a mysterious case involving a crashed aeroplane and a stolen Nubian water wheel.

Same themes, different language

Kragh-Jacobsen now seemed ready for an international co-production, the result being the English-language *The Island on Bird Street*, shot in the Polish town of Wroclaw and on sets in Cologne. It is based on Uri Olev's autobiographical novel about Alex, a Jewish boy left alone in the remains of a Polish ghetto during the Second World War after his father has been taken away by the Nazis.

For Kragh-Jacobsen, the film was not an entirely smooth experience, as, in his own words, the producers wanted something like "*Home Alone in the Ghetto*" He finds the film a bit stiff, and would have liked it to contain more humour. Nevertheless, it is easy to see Alex as a relative of both Ivan in *Rubber Tarzan* and Emma in *Emma's Shadow*, as this gentle boy uses his imagination (nourished by Defoe's *Robinson Crusoe*) to survive against all odds. The portrait of Alex – beautifully played by British boy Jordan Kiziuk – is illuminated by warm and loving tenderness.

On the other hand, the anti-Semitic Nazi terror is too gigantic an evil to be contained in a film by Kragh-Jacobsen, who has never divided the human race into heroes and villains; the ruins of the ghetto, whose inhabitants have been forced into the death camps, have a picturesque, rather than tragic quality.

In May 1999, *The Island on Bird Street*, having been shown on television in the United States, was awarded three Emmys: Best Film for Children, Best Direction and Best Male Lead (Kiziuk). In Denmark, however, the film fared poorly, selling only 15,000 tickets.

Obeying the commandments

Although the optimistic humanity of *The Island on Bird Street* should not be underestimated, it is obvious that shooting *Mifune* according to Dogma principles was a relief, even a liberation, for Kragh-Jacobsen. He has said: "With *Mifune* I rediscovered a lost spontaneity and joy in my work, the pleasure of indulging in the dynamic and elusive without depending

The Second World War resistance group honoured in THE BOYS FROM ST. PETRI

on technical equipment. Making a Dogma film is like playing music unplugged; it gives great freedom to the actors, and it gives you final cut from the day you start writing the script.

"It is an extremely useful exercise to direct a Dogma film and find out what you can accomplish with three nails and not much more. I didn't want to make shaky images, I wanted summer and sensuous women, and shooting the film was a very happy experience because I have always made films more with my heart than with my head. Now I could finally freely show how banal I am."

Not quite true. *Mifune* is far from banal, with its joyfully unpredictable story about the newly-married yuppie, Kresten, who lives a lie until his estranged father's death forces him to return to the derelict family farm on his native island, Lolland, where he is reunited with his slightly retarded, sweet and innocent brother Rud.

The attractive Liva, whom Kresten hires as a housekeeper, is less innocent. She is a call-girl on the run, also hiding behind a false identity, and as Kresten and Liva fall in love, they both have to learn to stop lying. Of the film's happy ending, Kragh-Jacobsen has said: "In *The Celebration*, Thomas Vinterberg blew up the family, and in *Mifune* I put it back together."

Mifune takes its title from the moment when, to entertain Rud, Kresten impersonates a fierce samurai, inspired by the great Toshiro Mifune in Kurosawa's films – one of the film's many funny and surprising moments. As a Dogma movie, it is less weird and provocative than *Idiots*, less tense and tight than *The Celebration*. It was a major commercial hit domestically.

Anders W. Berthelsen plays Kresten, a basically decent guy in search of an identity, Jesper Asholt is a small poetic miracle as Rud, and the expressive Iben Hjejle, who plays Liva, seems headed for

Jack Warden, Jordan Kiziuk, and Patrick Bergin in THE ISLAND ON BIRD STREET

an international career, with a part in a new film by Stephen Frears.

As for Kragh-Jacobsen, he would like at some point to make a historical film about events in the eighteenth century, "but not about kings and noblemen". That proviso sounds perfectly convincing from an artist who has always made films about seemingly born losers, who turn out to be likeable, valuable human beings. For directors, too, it is just a matter of discovering what it is you are good at.

EBBE IVERSEN has been film critic of *Berlingske Tidende* since 1973. He is a former co-editor of the magazine *Kosmorama*.

Kragh-Jacobsen Filmography

1978
VIL DU SE MIN SMUKKE NAVLE
(Wanna See My Beautiful Navel)

Script: Hans Hansen, based on his novel. Direction: SKJ. Photography: Peter Roos. Editing: Janus Billeskov Jansen. Music: SKJ, Leif Lindskov, Jacob Groth. Production Design: Søren Skjaer. Players: Birger Larsen (*Claus*), Lise-Lotte Rau (*Lene*), Henning Palner (*Svendsen*), Gertrud Mollerup (*Kirsten*).

Produced by Ib Tardini for Steen Herdel Filmproduktion. 92 mins.

1981
GUMMI TARZAN
(Rubber Tarzan)

Script: SKJ, Hans Hansen, based on a novel by Ole Lund Kirkegaard. Direction: SKJ. Photography: Dan Laustsen. Editing: Anders Refn. Music: Kenneth Knudsen. Production Design: Søren Skjaer. Players: Alex Svanbjerg (*Ivan*

Olsen), Otto Brandenburg (*Ole*), Peter Schrøder (*Ivan's father*), Susanne Heinrich (*Ivan's mother*), Jens Okking (*Teacher*). Produced by Ib Tardini for Metronome Productions. 86 mins.

1983
ISFUGLE
(Thunderbirds)

Script: SKJ, Hans Hansen. Direction: SKJ. Photography: Dan Laustsen. Editing: Janus

Kresten (Anders W. Berthelsen) falls for Liva in MIFUNE   *photo: Lars Høgsted/Nimbus Film*

Billeskov Jansen. Music: Kenneth Knudsen. Production Design: Palle Arrestrup. Players: Peter Hesse Overgaard (*John*), Michael Falch (*René*), Mette Munk Plum (*Vivi*), Dick Kaysø (*René's father*), Holger Boland (*Karl Sand*), Rita Angela (*John's mother*). Produced by Michael Christensen for Metronome Productions. 96 mins.

1988
GULDREGN
(Shower of Gold)

Script: Anders Bodelsen. Direction: SKJ. Photography: Dan Laustsen. Editing: Leif Axel Kjeldsen. Music: Jacob Groth. Production Design: Gunilla Allard. Players: Ricki Rasmussen (*Jørn*), Ken Vedsegaard (*Lasse*), Tania Frydensberg (*Karen*), Nanna Bøndergaard (*Nanna*), Torben Jensen (*Solskaermen*), Søren Østergaard (*Mannicke*). Produced by Metronome Productions. 96 mins.

1988
SKYGGEN AF EMMA
(Emma's Shadow)

Script: SKJ, Jørn O. Jensen. Direction: SKJ. Photography: Dan Laustsen. Editing: Leif Axel Kjeldsen. Music: Thomas Lindahl. Production Design: Lars Nielsen. Players: Line Kruse (*Emma*), Börje Ahlstedt (*Malthe*), Henrik Larsen (*Emma's father*), Inge Sofie Skovbo (*Emma's mother*), Ulla Henningsen (*Ruth*), Erik Wedersøe (*Chief detective*). Produced by Tivi Magnusson for Metronome Productions. 95 mins.

1991
DRENGENE FRA SANKT PETRI
(The Boys from St. Petri)

Script: SKJ, Bjarne Reuter. Direction: SKJ. Photography: Dan Laustsen. Editing: Leif Axel

Kragh-Jacobsen directing Jesper Asholt as Rud in MIFUNE
photo: Lars Høgsted/Nimbus Film

Kjeldsen. Music: Jacob Groth. Production Design: Lars Nielsen. Players: Tomas Villum Jensen (*Lars Balstrup*), Morten Buch Jørgensen (*Gunnar Balstrup*), Nikolaj Lie Kaas (*Otto Hvidmann*), Christian Grønvall (*Søren Brinck*), Karl Bille (*Oluf 'Luffe' Juhl*), Søren Hytholm Jensen (*Anders Møller*), Joachim Knop (*Aage Terkilsen*). Produced by Mads Egmont Christensen for Metronome Productions. 106 mins.

1997
THE ISLAND ON BIRD STREET

Script: John Goldsmith, Toni Grisoni, based on the novel by Uri Orlev. Direction: SKJ. Photography: Ian Wilson. Editing: David Martin. Music: Zbigniew Preisner. Production Design: Norbert Scherer. Players: Patrick Bergin (*Stefan*), Jordan Kiziuk (*Alex*), Jack Warden (*Boruch*), James Bolam (*Doctor Studjinsky*),

Stefan Sauk (*Goehler*), Simon Gregor (*Henryk*), Sian Nicola Liquorish (*Stasya*), Suzanna Hamilton (*Stasya's mother*). Produced by Rudy Cohen, Tivi Magnusson for April Productions, M&M Productions, Connexion Film. 106 mins.

1999
MIFUNES SIDSTE SANG
(Mifune)

Script: SKJ, Anders Thomas Jensen. Direction: SKJ. Photography: Anthony Dod Mantle. Editing: Valdir Oskarsdóttir. Players: Anders W. Berthelsen (*Kresten*), Iben Hjejle (*Liva*), Jesper Asholt (*Rud*), Sofie Graabøl (*Claire*) Emil Tarding (*Bjarke*), Anders Hove (*Gerner*), Paprika Steen (*Pernille*), Ellen Hillingsø (*Lykke*), Sidse Babett Knudsen (*Bibbi*). Produced by Birgitte Hald, Morten Kaufmann for Nimbus Film. 98 mins.

Spike Lee

by Carrie Rickey

Remarkably, Spike Lee made the leaps from film school maverick to independent phenomenon to Hollywood auteur in the space of five years and three films. That he is African-American makes this achievement all the more remarkable – given that America is notoriously snow-blind: it sees pre-dominantly white. Though Lee is as uneven a film-maker as his artistic hero and fellow New York University film school graduate, Martin Scorsese, he has demonstrated great virtuosity and versatility, working with minuscule and large budgets, as an independent and for studios, in drama, comedy and documentary.

SHELTON JACKSON LEE was born in Atlanta, Georgia, on March 20, 1957, the first of five children raised by jazz bassist and composer Bill Lee and his wife, art teacher Jacquelyn Shelton Lee. After a brief stay in Chicago, in 1959 the Lees relocated to New York, specifically the Brooklyn neighbourhood of Fort Greene, where the tenacity of their toddler earned him the nickname Spike. Before the term existed, Lee's parents were Afrocentric, instilling in their children knowledge of and pride in black achievement. Whether it was the poetry of Langston Hughes, the novels of Zora Neale Hurston, the music of Miles

Davis or the art of Romare Bearden, Spike and his siblings were shaped by the titans of black culture who were redirecting the American mainstream.

That his father was a musician and his mother an artist clearly fuelled the jazzy rhythms and edgy montages that would later distinguish Lee's films. Though during the school year he lived in the urban North, Lee spent his summers in the South, dividing his vacations between his two sets of grandparents, the Sheltons of Snow Hill, Alabama, and the Lees of Atlanta, broadening his vistas beyond the Brooklyn skyline.

Lee remembers reading that formative work of black evolution, *The Autobiography of Malcolm X*, when he was about 13, and would 20 years later make his masterpiece on the life of the slain leader. Yet while he was growing up, Lee has recalled: "I never saw black people kissing on screen." Prior to Lee, one of the few black Americans to build an enduring film career was Oscar Micheaux, who made 50 movies between 1918 and 1948. Yet, although Lee came of age during the Civil Rights era, a period of momentous social and political trans-formation, there were precious few images of blacks in contemporary American cinema, except for the solitary figure of Sidney Poitier in Hollywood films, playing characters who traversed an arc from discrimination to acceptance.

Furthermore, apart from a milestone such as Melvin van Peebles' *Sweet*

Lee (centre) with his two rivals in love in SHE'S GOTTA HAVE IT   *photo: The Kobal Collection*

Sweetback's Baad Asss Song, in 1971, or Michael Schultz's *Cooley High*, in 1975, the only blacks on screen were defined by whites. Inevitably, therefore, any African-American film-maker who could create a body of work would be judged not only on his artistry but also on his socio-cultural impact. Whatever one says about Lee's energetic if inconsistent aesthetic, which runs the gamut from experimental to classical to agit-prop, he consistently, in the words of the African-American sociologist and intellectual W.E.B. DuBois, depicts "life behind the veil" – i.e. what black people do when white people aren't watching.

Film school daze

Given his culturally rich family background, Lee was probably destined for a career in the arts. But movies and movie-making were not a particular passion, as they were for other prodigies such as Scorsese and Stanley Kubrick. It was not until 1977, during his sophomore year at Atlanta's historically black Morehouse College, alma mater of his father and grandfather, that Lee first

picked up a borrowed Super-8 camera. In a momentous summer, during which his beloved mother died of cancer and the New York blackout ominously shut down the city, Lee bought a movie camera of his own. One of his early efforts, *Last Hustle in Brooklyn*, inter-cut footage of the blackout with shots of disco dancers, a blend which presaged his 1999 film, *Summer of Sam*.

After receiving his bachelor's degree from Morehouse in 1979, Lee was awarded a summer internship at Columbia Pictures in Hollywood. That fall he enrolled in the master's program at New York University film school, breeding ground for off-Hollywood film-makers such as Scorsese, Oliver Stone, Susan Seidelman and Jim Jarmusch. Almost immediately, he was at the centre of a storm triggered by his first-year project, a 10-minute 'epic' called *The Answer*, in which an African-American film-maker reimagines D.W. Griffith's infamously racist (and cinematically influential) *Birth of a Nation*. Lee's instructors were not amused by the student's lampooning of a masterwork. Establishing what was to become a characteristic of most Lee feature releases, the controversy created plenty of publicity and mystique.

Samuel L. Jackson as the neighbourhood DJ in DO THE RIGHT THING   *photo: The Kobal Collection*

His thesis film, *Joe's Bed-Stuy Barbershop: We Cut Heads* (1983), an affectionate portrait of an ad hoc neighbourhood community centre and numbers-running joint, boasted a slice-of-life flavour that earned Lee a Student Academy Award (future director Ang Lee was his assistant cameraman). The laurels helped Lee get federal and state arts grants for his next project, *The Messenger*, a coming-of-age story about a bike messenger in Manhattan. Meanwhile, he worked in a film distribution centre, cleaning and shipping movies.

Just as production on *The Messenger* was about to commence, Lee scuttled the project when the Screen Actors Guild refused to grant him a waiver because his script was "too commercial" – meaning that his actors would have to be paid at full rate. In a portent of the budgetary crises he would face on many of his future films, Lee had to return a $20,000 grant to the American Film Institute. However, the New York State Council on the Arts allowed him to transfer its $18,000 award to *She's Gotta Have It*, a black-and-white comedy about a young woman juggling three very different boyfriends.

Written on the fly and shot on a shoestring ($175,000), *She's Gotta Have It* (released in 1986) rewrote the rules for American independent film. At a time when "independent" was synonymous with "inaccessible and experimental" Lee created a comedy with universal appeal and earned himself the Prix de Jeunesse at Cannes. His episodic treatment of the life and loves of Nola Darling (Tracy Camila Johns) was revolutionary because it marked one of the first times in modern film that blacks were portrayed as ordinary human beings, instead of what Lee called "the stereotypical singer-dancer-comedian-drug addict-prostitute-policeman."

Lee himself had a significant role in the film as Mars Blackmon (characters in his

Lee in MO' BETTER BLUES
photo: The Kobal Collection

Wesley Snipes in JUNGLE FEVER
photo: The Kobal Collection

scripts typically have such symbolic, Dickensian handles), a scene-stealing motor-mouth and amusing loser who tickles Nola's funnybone, if not her G-spot. Perhaps because he had starred in, written and directed his own sex comedy, he was immediately dubbed "the black Woody Allen". *She's Gotta Have It* grossed more than $7m in the US, tapping a previously unexploited audience of middle-class blacks, and proving to exhibitors that, contrary to superstition, some whites would flock to strong movies with black characters.

Summer in the city

This success convinced the film's distributors, Island Pictures, to budget Lee's next project, *School Daze*, at $4m, but when it looked as though Lee's campus musical, set at Mission, a fictional all-black college in Atlanta, would go over budget, they decamped, leaving Lee scrambling for a backer. Columbia Pictures agreed to provide $6m and the resulting 1988 film, which introduced Laurence Fishburne and Samuel L. Jackson to wide audiences, was a pastiche of Vincente Minnelli and Luis Buñuel, freely mixing surrealism, music and intra-racial politics in a cocktail that is initially potent, but loses its fizz.

The campus conflict between the jocks, called Wannabes, as in Wannabe Whites, and the politicos, called Jigs, an abbreviation of the epithet for blacks, comes to a head over hair. The Wannabes favour chemically-treated, straightened hair, and the Jigs the natural African, nappy hair. Both as social criticism and as a musical, the film had mixed results.

It was in *School Daze* that Lee first quilted a patchwork of different film styles – comic, melodramatic and musical – within one movie, something he would do more effectively in *Malcolm X*, *Girl 6* and his third movie, *Do the Right Thing*. One of the most important films of the 1980s – and one of the three best features of Lee's career – *Do the Right Thing* vividly illustrates how the round robin of escalating suspicion distorts human relations in America. Set in Bedford-Stuyvesant, a multi-racial Brooklyn

Lee directing CROOKLYN

photo: *The Kobal Collection*

neighbourhood, on a summer day so hot that the sun blisters the soul, Lee shows how heat can magnify tensions and sear the heart.

Shot in a documentary-like style, and punctuated by the rhythms of Public Enemy's rap anthem "Fight the Power", the film transcends realism with its palette of brick reds and blood reds. It is like a Jean Renoir film as painted by that Raphael of film-makers, Vincente Minnelli, whose super-charged compositions and emotions are surpassed here in Lee's story of a neighbourhood in which whites are the landlords and shopkeepers, and blacks the tenants and customers.

As in the best of Renoir, there are no heroes and villains, just people with a complement of admirable and deplorable traits: Danny Aiello as the Italian-American owner of a pizzeria (he earned an Oscar nomination for Best Supporting Actor; Lee was nominated for Best Original Screenplay), Ossie Davis as a black elder, and Bill Nunn as the doomed homeboy, Radio Raheem, as proud of his boom box as Sal is of his pizzeria. By the violent conclusion, Lee has left viewers with indelible images of a scorched community.

Modestly budgeted, *DTRT* earned $27.1m, fulfilling both the artistic and box-office promise of *She's Gotta Have It*. As with Lee's best work – which includes *Malcolm X*, *Get on the Bus* and the documentary *4 Little Girls* – *DTRT* was inspired by real-life figures and events, in this case an incident in Howard Beach, New York, in which a black man was knocked down and killed by a car while trying to flee a pack of bat-wielding whites.

Two misses, and a masterpiece

Another hallmark of *DTRT* is that, with the exception of *Malcolm X*, Lee is more successful in characterising a community than he is in evoking the inner life of an individual, a trait which may account for the still-born quality of his next two films, *Mo' Better Blues* and *Jungle Fever*, in which he failed to juggle multiple storylines and characters as skilfully as he did in *DTRT*.

Mo' Better Blues, starring Denzel Washington as a jazz trumpeter too obsessed with his music to have a life, plays like a riff that loses the original theme. Not only is the trumpeter torn between career and personal life, his personal life is torn between two women. A story about fragmentation is too fragmented to be coherent.

Similarly, *Jungle Fever* (1991) is on the one hand about a black architect (Wesley Snipes) who has an extramarital affair with his white temp (Annabella Sciorra), and on the other about the architect's crack-addicted brother, whose habit destroys the family and divides their neighbourhood as forcefully as the inter-racial romance. The film loses its identity to narrative schizophrenia.

In *Malcolm X* (1992), starring a majestic Denzel Washington as the black leader, Lee found a subject with themes enough for a symphony. Composed in four movements, the gripping biopic is about the search for father and self, a remarkable account of transition and transformation that represents not just one man or one African-American, but all men.

The first movement, with the saturated colour and jazzy rhythms of a Vincente Minnelli musical, depicts a young

Denzel Washington addresses a crowd as MALCOLM X

photo: The Kobal Collection

Lee's childhood recalled in CROOKLYN
photo: David Lee/Kobal Collection

Theresa Randall as GIRL 6
photo: David Lee/Fox

hoodlum, haunted by his father's death and finding a father figure in a racketeer. The second movement, monochromatic grey, and quiet, depicts Malcolm's conversion in prison to the teachings of Black Islam. Next comes his release from prison, after which he embraces surrogate father Elijah Muhammad (Al Freeman Jr.) and becomes his acolyte. The fourth movement, sundrenched and bright like a David Lean epic, shows Malcolm's conversion in Mecca, where he finds his true father in Allah. The coda, involving Malcolm's martyrdom and political resurrection, reprises the themes of Lee's most fully realised work.

New York stories

After the career peak of *Malcolm X*, *Crooklyn* (1994), Lee's semi-auto-biographical story about how his family dealt with his mother's cancer, and *Clockers* (1995), about lowly drug dealers in Brooklyn, were disappointments. Both are marked by excellent performances and expressionistic camerawork that sabotages the narratives – though they testify to a film-maker committed to finding visual equivalents for emotional states. The innovative cinematography which makes Lee such a sought-after director of commercials, was more integrated into the

Detectives Harvey Keitel (left) and John Turturro (right) arrest street dealer Strike (Mekhi Phifer) in CLOCKERS
photo: David Lee/The Kobal Collection

plot of *Girl 6* (1996), starring Theresa Randle as an aspiring actress who hones her acting skills as a phone-sex operator and whose diverse fantasies demand different film-making styles.

After *Girl 6*, a real-life event once again sparked Lee into making one of his best films. *Get On the Bus* (1996) is a powerful melodrama about black manhood, focusing on a group of men attempting to join the historic 1995 Million Man March. Working from a screenplay by Reggie Rock Bythewood, Lee had a solid base from which to improvise his narrative riffs and produced a critical hit which flopped at the box-office.

4 Little Girls, his Oscar-nominated documentary about the 1963 bombing of a black church in Birmingham, Alabama, is his most straightforward work. Lee's sensitive interviews with survivors show how the tragedy was a transforming moment in the nation's history. More powerfully than his militant films, *4 Little Girls* educates and politicises an audience.

Lee merged his love of movies and of basketball in *He Got Game* (1998), a family melodrama starring Denzel Washington as an inmate granted furlough by a prison governor so that he can persuade his estranged son, a hoops star, to attend the state university. As in *Jungle Fever*, the film is beautifully shot, but fails to integrate the competing storylines about father and son.

Summer of Sam, his thirteenth and most recent film, is a kaleidoscopic look at the mean season of 1977, when New York was on the brink of insolvency, stalked by serial killers, and when punk and disco reverberated through humid, stagnant air. As a mood piece it is powerful. But, as ever with Lee's lesser works, the lack of narrative coherence is frustrating. One senses though, that as with the career lows preceding *Malcolm X* and *Get on the Bus*, Lee is gathering steam for his next breakout project.

CARRIE RICKEY has been a film critic for *The Philadelphia Inquirer* since 1986. She has contributed to many books and anthologies, including *The American Century*, which is published this autumn.

John Leguizamo reads the latest news during the SUMMER OF SAM

photo: Downtown Pictures

Spike Lee Filmography

1986
SHE'S GOTTA HAVE IT

Script and Direction: SL. Photography: Ernest Dickerson. Editing: SL. Production Design: Wynn Thomas. Music: Bill Lee. Players: Tracy Camila Johns (*Nola Darling*), Tommy Redmond Hicks (*Jamie Overstreet*), John Canada Terrell (*Greer Childs*), SL (*Mars Blackmon*). Produced by SL. 84 mins.

1988
SCHOOL DAZE

Script and Direction: SL. Photography: Ernest Dickerson. Editing: Barry Alexander Brown. Production Design: Wynn Thomas. Music: Bill Lee. Players: Larry Fishburne (*Slap Dunlap*), Giancarlo Esposito (*Julian Eaves*), Tisha Campbell (*Jane Toussaint*), SL (*Half Pint*). Produced by SL. 120 mins.

1989
DO THE RIGHT THING

Script and Direction: SL. Photography: Ernest Dickerson. Editing: Barry Alexander Brown. Production Design: Wynn Thomas. Music: Bill Lee. Players: Danny Aiello (*Sal*), Ossie Davis (*Da Mayor*), Ruby Dee (*Mother Sister*), SL (*Mookie*), Bill Nunn (*Radio Raheem*). Produced by SL and Monty Ross. 120 mins.

1990
MO' BETTER BLUES

Script and Direction: SL. Photography: Ernest Dickerson. Editing: Samuel D. Pollard. Production Design: Wynn Thomas. Music: Bill Lee and various artists. Players: Denzel Washington (*Bleek Gilliam*), Spike Lee (*Giant*), Wesley Snipes (*Shadow Henderson*), Joie Lee (*Indigo Downes*), Cynda Williams (*Clarke Bentancourt*). Produced by SL. 129 mins.

Lee directing a fine ensemble cast in GET ON THE BUS

photo: The Kobal Collection

1991
JUNGLE FEVER

Script and Direction: SL. Photography: Ernest Dickerson. Editing: Samuel D. Pollard, Brunilda Torres. Production Design: Wynn Thomas. Music: Terence Blanchard. Players: Wesley Snipes (*Flipper Purify*), Anabella Sciorra (*Angie Tucci*), Spike Lee (*Cyrus*), Ossie Davis (*The Good Rev. Dr Purify*), Samuel L. Jackson (*Gator Purify*). Produced by SL. 132 mins.

1992
MALCOLM X

Script: SL and Arnold Perl. Direction: SL. Photography: Ernest Dickerson. Editing: Barry Alexander Brown. Production Design: Wynn Thomas. Music: Terence Blanchard. Players: Denzel Washington (*Malcolm X*), Angela Bassett (*Betty Shabazz*), Albert Hall (*Baines*), Al Freeman, Jr. (*Elijah Muhammad*), Delroy Lindo (*West Indian Archie*). Produced by Marvin Worth and SL. 201 mins.

1994
CROOKLYN

Script: Joie Susannah Lee, Cinque Lee and SL. Directed by SL. Photography: Arthur Jafa. Editing: Barry Alexander Brown. Production Design: Wynn Thomas. Music: Terence Blanchard and various artists. Players: Alfre Woodard (*Carolyn*), Delroy Lindo (*Woody*), Zelda Harris (*Troy*), Carlton Williams (*Clinton*). Produced by SL. 115 mins.

1995
CLOCKERS

Script: Richard Price and SL, from Price's novel. Direction: SL. Photography: Malik Hassan Hayeed. Editing: Samuel D. Pollard. Production Design: Andrew McAlpine. Music: Terence Blanchard. Harvey Keitel (*Rocco Klein*), Mekhi Phifer (*Strike*), Isaiah Washington (*Victor*), Regina Taylor (*Iris Jeeter*), John Turturro (*Larry Mazilli*). Produced by Martin Scorsese, SL and Jon Kilik. 129 mins.

1996
GIRL 6

Script: Suzan-Lori Parks. Direction: SL. Photography: Malik Hassan Sayeed. Editing: Samuel D. Pollard. Production Design:

Lee promoting CLOCKERS at the 1995 Venice Film Festival
photo: Stephane Fefer

Ina Mahew. Music: Prince. Players: Theresa Randle (*Girl 6*), SL (*Jimmy*), Madonna (*Boss #3*), Quentin Tarantino (*Director #1*). Produced by SL. 100 mins.

1996
GET ON THE BUS

Script: Reggie Rock Bythewood. Direction: SL. Photography: Elliot Davis. Editing: Samuel D. Pollard. Production Design: Ina Mayhew. Music: Terence Blanchard. Players: Ossie Davis (*Jeremiah*),

Charles S. Dutton (*George*), Richard Belzer (*Rick*). Produced by Reuben Cannon, Bill Borden and Barry Rosenbush. 120 mins.

1997
4 LITTLE GIRLS

Direction: SL. Photography: Ellen Kuras. Editing: Samuel D. Pollard. Music: Terence Blanchard. Featuring: Chris McNair, Rev. Jesse Jackson, Coretta Scott King. Produced by SL and Sam Pollard. 102 mins.

1998
HE GOT GAME

Script and Direction: SL. Photography: Malik Hassan Sayeed. Editing: Barry Alexander Brown. Production Design: Wynn Thomas. Music: Aaron Copland and Public Enemy. Players: Denzel Washington (*Jake Shuttlesworth*), Ray Allen (*Jesus Shuttlesworth*), Milla Jovovich (*Dakota Burns*), Rosario Dawson (*Lala*). Produced by Jon Kilik and SL. 131 mins.

1999
SUMMER OF SAM

Script: Victor Colicchio, Michael Imperioli and SL. Direction: SL. Photography: Ellen Kuras. Editing: Barry Alexander Brown. Production Design: Thérèse DePrez. Music: Terence Blanchard. Players: John Leguizamo (*Vinny*), Adrien Brody (*Ritchie*), Mira Sorvino (*Dionna*), Jennifer Esposito (*Ruby*), Michael Rispoli (*Joey T*). Produced by Jon Kilik and SL. 142 mins.

Denzel Washington with Ray Allen on the basketball court in HE GOT GAME

photo: David Lee/The Kobal Collection

David Mamet

by Juliet Fleming

There is a paradox at the heart of David Mamet's film career. As a scriptwriter for hire, he has lent his talents to the service of mainstream entertainment – intellectual employment which sits uneasily with a man whose cultural politics have made him loudly suspicious of the Hollywood system. As an independent director, however, his first five features have worked within conventional genre labels to deny and even affront audience expectations.

DAVID MAMET was born in Chicago in 1947. His parents, Lenore (a teacher) and Bernie (a labour-lawyer, on whom Mamet modelled the main character in his 1992 screenplay *Hoffa*), were middle-class, first-generation American Jews, determined to assimilate. "At home," he has recalled, "everything was defined negatively. Let's stop being poor, let's stop being Russian, let's stop being Jews."

Mamet's relationship with his sister, Lynn, to whom he remains close, forms the basis of his short play *Jolly* (1989). Their childhood (explored in Mamet's 1994 play *The Cryptogram*) was unhappy, and left Mamet with what he has described as "two warring needs – the need to be accepted, and the need to be revenged". In interviews and elsewhere Mamet represents himself – like many before him – as someone whose "artistic vision... arose to accommodate and embrace a deviant personality", one driven to live outside the social orders it admires. Lament for a lost

sense of community, and its brief recovery in unlikely places, has been, to date, the dominant concern of his writing.

Mamet graduated from Goddard College, Vermont, which has no formal entry requirements, and from which he claims to have learned little besides contempt for institutions of higher education. His essay collections, *Writing in Restaurants* (1987), *Some Freaks* (1989), *The Cabin* (1992), *Make-Believe Town* (1996), and *Three Uses of the Knife* (1998), and his writing on technique, *On Directing Film* (1990) and *True or False – Heresy and Common Sense for the Actor* (1997), are governed by their reliance on a small corpus of idiosyncratically-read authors (including Aristotle, Bruno Bettelheim, Freud, Stanislavsky and Thorstein Veblen). Mamet has fashioned a set of passionately-held political and artistic opinions from this reading, which he uses in registers of both earnestness and self-mockery to give voice to the formal intuitions that make him one of the most accomplished dramatists writing today.

Mamet began writing plays in his final year of college. On graduation he moved to Chicago, where he worked for the Second City and Goodman theatres, and began his long friendship and artistic collaboration with theatre director Gregory Mosher. *Sexual Perversity in Chicago* (1974; loosely filmed in 1986 as *About Last Night*, Dir: Edward Zwick), was Mamet's first hit; it was followed by *American Buffalo*, which won an Obie Award and was voted Best Play by the New York Drama Critics Circle (1976, filmed in 1996, Dir: Michael Corrente).

In 1976, Mamet moved to New York and married actress Lindsay Crouse (they divorced in 1991, when he married British actress Rebecca Pidgeon). Mamet has written or adapted nearly 30 plays, including *Lakeboat* (1980, to be filmed by one of Mamet's favourite actors, Joe Mantegna); the Obie-awarded *Edmond* (1982); Pulitzer Prize-winning *Glengarry Glen Ross*, (1984, filmed in 1992 by James Foley); the Hollywood satire *Speed-the-Plow* (1988), the controversial *Oleanna* (1992,

Joe Mantegna and Lindsay Crouse enter the HOUSE OF GAMES   photo: The Kobal Collection

filmed by Mamet in 1994); and four translations from Chekhov, including the 1994 version of *Uncle Vanya* used in Louis Malle's *Vanya on 42nd Street*.

A language all his own

In the 1980s, looking for a more absorbent market for his talents, Mamet embarked on a prolific screenwriting career. He has written scripts as diverse as *The Postman Always Rings Twice* (1981), *The Verdict* (1982, Academy Award nomination for Best Adapted Screenplay), *The Untouchables* (1987), *We're No Angels* (1989), *Hoffa* (1992), *The Edge* (1997) and *Wag the Dog* (1997).

Mamet's plays are short: time, place and action are restricted; the characters are types. Plots typically concern counter-transferential relationships, such as those between student and teacher, brother and sister, a confidence man and his victims. Characters express their desires and commit their crimes within the elastic and often hilarious register of Mamet's language: one that combines invented truisms and an apparently demotic diction within a short but metrically-compulsive spoken line.

Mamet's language appears, on first encounter, as the record of an authentic idiolect (for example, that of the Chicago

mob), while the easy relation between his characters often looks to have originated with the actors in rehearsal. In fact, both language and relationships have been precisely devised by Mamet, whose spare dialogue wise actors follow word for word. Mamet once corrected an interviewer who had suggested that his dramatic language was "inarticulate": "You understand exactly what the character is saying. You can't have a drama with inarticulate people in it." But audiences are brought to understand less what the character is saying, than the dramatic function of each speech.

Mamet's scripts consequently call for an acting style that bases performance on action rather than emotion; and he has gathered a group of actors who can eschew the Method and other motivational performance modes. Mamet regulars (who have included Alec Baldwin, Lindsay Crouse, Ricky Jay, Mike Nussbaum, William H. Macy, Joe Mantegna, Rebecca Pidgeon and Colin Stinton) seek to perform every action, including speech, as simply as possible, adding, if they are following Mamet's own published advice, "nothing to what the playwright has written".

This emotionally uninflected style readily translates from stage to screen, and explains the apparent paradox whereby one of America's foremost "language" playwrights (who argues that "a good play should be able to be done on the radio, just like that"), has created movies that aspire to the minimal dialogue and formal transparency of silent film. For Mamet intends neither plays nor films as

Don Ameche (left) and Joe Mantegna in THINGS CHANGE   photo: Stephen Vaughan/Kobal Collection

personally felt statements, regarding them instead as "designs" within which language and acting should be as gestural as possible, camerawork simple, and the story told in cuts; "which is to say, through a juxtaposition of images that are basically uninflected".

Shrink vs. con man

In 1987 Mamet directed his first film, *House of Games*, for which he also wrote the screenplay. This noirish debut (expressively scored by Alaric Jans, with whom Mamet subsequently worked on *Things Change*, *Homicide* and *The Winslow Boy*) concerns a con-game in which a famous psychoanalyst, Margaret Ford (Lindsay Crouse), falls victim to her equal in affectless desire, confidence-man Mike (Joe Mantegna).

Pitting psychoanalyst against hustler, the film compares the pleasures and dangers of counter-transference as these operate in the clinic and on the street. As Mike explains to Margaret when he invites her to join him in a con: "It's called a confidence game. Why? Because you give me your confidence? No. Because I give you mine. So what we have, in addition to 'Adventures in Human Misery', is a short course in psychology." Having been robbed of $80,000, tricked into believing that she has killed a man, and heard herself cruelly ridiculed, Margaret lures Mike into a game of her own, and shoots him for real. At the end of the movie she is transformed: happy and free to indulge, in fairly harmless ways, her tendency to kleptomania.

House of Games has been critically well-received, but no full account of its ending – and consequently of its argument – has been made. This indeterminacy stems in part from the impossibility of knowing how the film judges its characters and their actions. Is Margaret's murder of Mike a feminist reversal of genre expectations, or a demonstration of the danger that women pose to men? Or is it, as William F. Van Wert has suggested, a therapeutic fantasy that allows Margaret to free herself, without legal consequences or guilt, from her hatred of those who have tricked her?

"All film is", says Mamet, "finally a dream sequence." But who is dreaming what? In spite of the occasional testimony of Mamet's actors, such questions can rarely be answered by reference to characters' motivations. Instead, Mamet sets audiences the more onerous, less familiar, task of affective engagement with the dramatic action itself: "I try to put the audience in the same position as the protagonists: led forth by event, by the inevitability of the previous action." Which is to say that the first thing to ask of a Mamet film is whether or not it is a game of directorial bluff.

Mamet's second movie as director is, however, something of an exception to this rule. While it shares the spare dialogue, theatrical staging and visual thrift of its predecessor, *Things Change* (1988) is freighted by the marked chemistry between Joe Mantegna (Jerry) and Don Ameche (Gino) – performances for which the two actors shared the Volpi Cup for best actor at the 1988 Venice Film Festival.

They centre the film on the growing love between Gino, an elderly shoe-shine man persuaded to take the rap for a Mafia killing, and Jerry, the junior mobster-on-probation who has been appointed as his guard and executioner. Jerry takes Gino to Lake Tahoe, where his gentle equanimity is mistaken for the powerful indifference of a Mafia Don. The two are lavishly entertained, and invited to the house of local Don Joseph Vincent (Robert Prosky). They escape with their lives because Gino's innocent dignity, and his old-world determination to keep his word, earns him the protection of the Don.

Changing sides

Homicide (1991) featured Mantegna, Macy, Jay and other Mamet regulars, introduced Rebecca Pidgeon into her husband's film work and was Mamet's third collaboration with producer Michael Haussman. Beautifully shot by Roger Deakins, the film poses as an action-thriller, describing the professional fall from grace of police officer Bobby Gold (Mantegna).

The only Jew in his unit, Gold is pulled off a manhunt for drug dealer Randolph

Sims (Ving Rhames) and reassigned, to investigate the shooting of a Jewish shopkeeper in a black neighbourhood. Gold's contemptuous response to the suggestion by the victim's family that she is the victim of a hate-crime is changed first to doubt, then to identification and belief: anxious, like so many Mamet characters, to "help", he detonates a bomb in the headquarters of a local neo-Fascist group, only to find himself blackmailed by the underground Jewish organisation for which he acted.

Returning to his unit, Gold sees his partner Sullivan shot dead by Sims, and takes a bullet himself; he survives, but is cast out forever from the police "family". This extraordinary plot posits the existence of a gun-running Jewish terrorist organisation within an unspecified American city, and pays ostentatious but puzzled attention to contemporary anti-Semitism, while endorsing white America's fear of its black underclass. It relies on some heavy-handed symbolism for its articulation, even as it insists that symbols are

unreliable, and that (for characters and audiences alike) the search for meaning is only ever an exercise in transference. The challenge of Mamet's movies is not that sense cannot be made of them – it is that they do not, in themselves, make full sense.

In *Oleanna* (1994), the only film Mamet has adapted from one of his own plays, the indeterminacy that is a consequence of transferential relationships is used to explore (and, as many have argued, to trivialise) the topic of sexual harassment. Mamet's masculine bias has often been noted; he writes very few good parts for women, his work is propelled by the logic of men in communities, and his attempts to defend himself from charges of sexism are ill-judged.

As *Oleanna*'s tag line – "Whatever side you take, you're wrong" – suggested, the film proposes that the relationship between the student, Carol (Deborah Eisensadt) and the teacher, John (William H. Macy), may be characterised by a misprision so thorough that its ethical

Joe Mantegna (far right) is a detective under pressure in HOMICIDE

photo: The Kobal Collection

contours can be neither known nor patrolled. *Oleanna* reverses the terms within which sexual harassment (as a mode of the systematic oppression of one group by another) is usually understood to occur – here a female student manages, with the help of a militant feminist "group", to threaten and endanger her male teacher. The play and the film invite their audiences to identify with the exasperated John, as – in an attempt to punish, if not conquer, female irrationality – he is driven to assault Carol.

Trick, or treat?

The Spanish Prisoner (1997) returns Mamet's concerns with self-delusion to the safer ground of the thriller. Joe Ross (Campbell Scott) has created for his employers a valuable new formula. He confides his concern that he will not be properly rewarded for his work to a newly-acquired friend, Jimmy Dell (Steve Martin, in great form); rightly grows suspicious of Dell; meets with the FBI for a wire-tap; and discovers that their "agents" are part of the scam, and have vanished with the formula. Now wanted for theft and the murder of a colleague, Ross turns to Susan (Rebecca Pidgeon), who has repeatedly warned him not to trust Dell: she too is in on the game, and Ross avoids death only when saved by two US Marhsals posing as Japanese tourists.

The film manages repeatedly to wrong-foot its audience, sometimes by lying, sometimes by luring us in with the truth that "you never know who anybody is": the lesson of this not entirely pleasurable experience is that, however hard it can and should try, film cannot teach people not to trust film.

But Mamet's latest (and some will think best) movie represents a retreat from that distrust of his medium which has dominated his film career (and is written large in *Wag the Dog*). A hugely enjoyable costume drama, with a stout heart and a concern that "Right be Done", *The Winslow Boy* (1999) is a careful realisation of Terence Rattigan's 1945 play (previously filmed in 1948, Dir: Anthony Asquith). The play is based on the true story of a naval cadet

Guy Edwards stands accused in THE WINSLOW BOY
photo: Sony Pictures Classics

wrongly dismissed for stealing a five shilling postal order, and his family's financially-ruinous fight to clear his name.

The import of the case, which concerned the right of a private individual to take the Admiralty to court (and thus became national news) is registered by Violet, the Winslow family's maid: "It was a fuss about nothing and a shocking waste of the Government's time, but... a good thing all the same because it could only happen in England." Rattigan's play understands the case (eventually won by the Winslows) to be an index of the superiority of a governmental system that protects individuals not with a Bill of Rights, but through the operation of its own fine discrimination: a discrimination that it links to the "English" virtue of wit.

Mamet's actors, particularly Nigel Hawthorne (as Arthur Winslow) and Jeremy Northam (as Sir Robert Morton) are well able to give voice to this wit (derived here from Mamet's direction and Rattigan-based script); but the director's own concerns are finally focused on a simplified and rather abstracted, though not unmoving, struggle for "Right". Relying less than usual on rapid editing, permitting and even elaborating the relationships between Rattigan's characters, and unable, for once, fully to resist the visual seduction of his own sets, Mamet has, for the first time as director, broken away from his negative love affair with film.

JULIET FLEMING is a lecturer in the English Faculty at Cambridge University.

Rebecca Pidgeon and Campbell Scott, caught up in the intricate plot of THE SPANISH PRISONER
photo: James Bridges/Kobal Collection

Nigel Hawthorne as the father of THE WINSLOW BOY

photo: Sony Pictures Classics

Mamet Filmography

Scripts: *The Postman Always Rings Twice* (1981, Dir: Bob Rafelson); *The Verdict* (1982, Dir: Sidney Lumet); *The Untouchables* (1987, Dir: Brian de Palma); *We're No Angels* (1989, Dir: Neil Jordan); *Hoffa* (1992; Dir: Danny De Vito; *The Edge* (1997; Dir: Lee Tamahori); *Wag the Dog*, with Hilary Henkin (1997; Dir: Barry Levinson).

1987
HOUSE OF GAMES

Script: DM, based on a story by DM and Jonathan Katz. Direction: DM. Photography: Juan Ruiz Anchia. Editing: Trudy Ship. Music: Alaric Jans. Players: Joe Mantegna (Mike), Lindsay Crouse (Margaret Ford), Mike Nussbaum (Joey), Lilia Skala (Dr Littauer), J. T.Walsh (Business Man). Produced by Michael Hausman for Orion. 102 mins.

1988
THINGS CHANGE

Script: DM and Shel Silverstein. Direction: DM. Photography: Juan Ruiz Anchia. Editing: Trudy Ship. Music: Alaric Jans. Players: Joe Mantegna (Jerry), Don Ameche (Gino), Robert Prosky (Joseph Vincent), J. J. Johnston (Frankie), Ricky Jay (Mr Silver), Mike Nussbaum (Mr Green), Jack Wallace (Repair shop owner), Dan Conway (Butler). Produced by Michael Hausman for Columbia. 100 mins.

1991
HOMICIDE

Script and Direction: DM. Photography: Roger Deakins. Editing: Barbara Tulliver. Music: Alaric Jans. Players: Joe Mantegna (Bobby Gold),William H. Macy (Tim Sullivan), Natalija Nogulich (Chava), Ving Rhames (Randolph), Rebecca Pidgeon (Miss Klein), Vincent Gustaferro (Senna), Lionel Mark Smith (Olcott), Jack Wallace (Frank). Produced by Michael Hausman and Edward R. Pressman for Triumph. 100 mins.

1994
OLEANNA

Script: DM, based on his play. Direction: DM. Photography: Andrzej Sekula. Editing: Barbara Tulliver. Music: Rebecca Pidgeon. Players: William H. Macy (John), Deborah Eisenstadt (Carol). Produced by Patricia Woolff for Samuel Goldwyn/ Hallmark. 101 mins.

1997
THE SPANISH PRISONER

Script and Direction: DM. Photography: Gabriel Beristain. Editing: Barbara Tulliver. Music: Carter Burwell. Players: Campbell Scott (Joe Ross), Steve Martin (Jimmy Dell), Ricky Jay (George Lang), Ben Gazzara (Joe Klein), Rebecca Pidgeon (Susan Ricci), Felicity Hauffman (Pat McCune). Produced by Jean Doumanian for Jasmine Productions/Sweetland Films. 110 mins.

1999
THE WINSLOW BOY

Script: DM, based on the play by Terence Rattigan. Direction: DM. Photography: Benoit Delhomme. Editing: Barbara Tulliver. Music: Alaric Jans. Players: Nigel Hawthorne (Arthur Winslow), Jeremy Northam (Sir Robert Morton), Rebecca Pidgeon (Catherine Winslow), Gemma Jones (Grace Winslow), Colin Stinton (Desmond Curry), Guy Edwards (Ronnie Winslow), Aden Gillet (John Watherstone), Sarah Flind (Violet), Matthew Pigdeon (Dickie Winslow). Produced by Sarah Green for Sony Pictures. 110 mins.

Crowds attending the 1998 International Film Festival of Catalonia at Sitges, which began its career with a focus on horror movies and has now broadened its appeal across other genres

Still from HATHI, directed by Prajna Chowta and Philippe Gautier and produced by Rock Demers for Distribution La Fête, and already selected for 12 major festivals during the past year

By Peter Cowie

Since our last edition, the DVD format has become an established component of the home entertainment scene. In the US, DVD has superseded laser disc, and seems well on the way to burying video cassettes as well. The studios have spent millions of dollars restoring classics and producing and marketing DVDs of all their new releases.

With hardware at reasonable prices, consumers have embraced the new technology for what it offers: razor-sharp imagery, digital sound and the convenience of access to favourite scenes. All the more reason for the studios to maintain a competitive price structure; if DVDs are allowed to drift up to the $35-$40 or £25 mark, they run the risk of languishing at the back of stores as elitist toys.

In Europe, and even the Far East, the picture is less bright. Markets like Japan and Hong Kong offer a plethora of formats to the avid consumer, with VCD the most popular and the least expensive to acquire. In Europe, the launch of digital television has overshadowed the roll-out of DVD. As of June 1999, there were still less than 300,000 DVD players in European households.

Research suggests that a substantial minority of PC users are playing DVDs through their computer monitors, but that by definition denies them the inherent values of the format (surround sound in a reasonably-sized room, and a larger, sharper image).

From the film buff's perspective, and indeed that of the film-maker, the advent of DVD must be seen as a godsend. It will enable the public to experience cinema in the home in an authentic mode, and provide new revenue streams for the movie industry. The option of viewing a film with subtitles, often in numerous languages, is unique to DVD.

Some companies have committed themselves to the revolution with unreserved zeal: Warners in particular, followed by MGM, Sony, Criterion, and even Disney (whose maiden animation transfer to DVD, **A Bug's Life**, set an exquisite standard for others to challenge).

Criterion has simply passed the baton from LD to DVD without a stumble, offering pristine versions of classic movies (and even cult items like **The Most Dangerous Game**) in a context of respect and admiration for their stature. Others - Fox Lorber, for example - have done DVD a disservice by rushing out crude transfers of classic films by Truffaut and Rohmer without any hint of extra ingredients.

For probably the last time, we also note below some laser discs of quality that have been issued in 1998-1999 by the likes of Pioneer and Warners. They will be missed.

Foreign-Language classics

The Criterion Collection continues to hold the inside track where foreign films are concerned. In its first full year of DVD production, the company has published mouth-watering transfers of Fritz Lang's **M**, Kurosawa's **High and Low** and **Seven Samurai**, and Truffaut's **The 400 Blows**. Even more spectacular is the Criterion version of **Black Orpheus**, winner of the

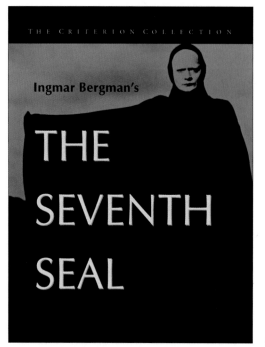

Criterion's DVD of THE SEVENTH SEAL

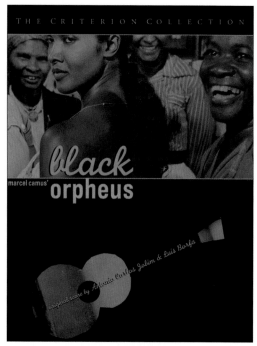

Criterion's DVD of BLACK ORPHEUS

Palme d'Or at Cannes in 1959 and a vivid, mythical evocation of life in Rio. Abbas Kiarostami's tantalising, intense study of a man bent on suicide, **The Taste of Cherry**, shared the same award in 1997, and receives a faultless transfer from the Criterion team.

Pride of place in Criterion's catalogue goes to **The Seventh Seal**, released in an immaculate RSDL dual-layer edition. Transferred digitally from a new 35mm fine-grain master positive, made in its turn from the restored camera negative, Bergman's masterpiece soars again. An intriguing "before and after" section of the disc demonstrates how flecks and streaks in the image were removed using a digital restoration system.

Columbia TriStar's restoration of Wolfgang Petersen's **Das Boot** also sets a benchmark. The sound effects have been enhanced to a remarkable degree, with the foley technicians enjoying a field day: the viewer sits enveloped by the myriad pings, creaks and whispers that characterise a submarine at war. This DVD not only revels in the potential of DVD, it also revives Petersen's magnum opus as probably the finest German film of the past 20 years.

The less said the better about Fox Lorber's treatment of Rohmer's great works of the late 1960s. **My Night at Maud's** fares best, because its black-and-white image is less susceptible to the ageing process. But **Chloe in the Afternoon** and **Claire's Knee** look like fuzzy 16mm copies. Fox Lorber, who have recently acquired a host of Truffaut classics, must include chapter stops and a modicum of liner notes if they are to gain the respect of the foreign film enthusiast.

English-language restorations

Criterion also shine in this field. Their DVD versions of **The Silence of the Lambs** and **A Night to Remember** are stuffed with

Jodie Foster in CONTACT, one of the most spectacular DVD releases from Warners

extra goodies, while the off-screen commentary by director Terry Gilliam and some of the Monty Python team elevates **Time Bandits** almost to the level of **Brazil** (which itself has been issued by Criterion in a mouth-watering 3-disc boxed set).

Less anticipated, however, and therefore more thrilling to discover on DVD, is the latest Criterion transfer of **Picnic at Hanging Rock**. Peter Weir, when shown, in succession, a videocassette version, followed by the same scene on laser disc, and then finally in DVD, is said to have uttered an expletive of delight. Russell Boyd's shimmering photography has never been seen like this outside the film's original run in theatres - nor has the music sounded so atmospheric as it does in this new Dolby Digital 5.1 channel version.

An even older exercise in mood, David Lean's **Summertime** (aka *Summer Madness*), has been given the Criterion treatment, with its Technicolor images of Venice dramatically more sumptuous than they were on the same company's LD, thanks to a new digital transfer under that

Tensions snap in DAS BOOT, issued in its new director's cut on DVD by Columbia-TriStar Home Video

most diligent of telecine supervisors, Maria Palazzola. If only Criterion could do the same for Visconti's *Senso*!

Such DVDs (and Warner's restoration of **Jeremiah Johnson** is another) almost convince the viewer that the film is intrinsically superior to its theatrical release a quarter-century ago. MGM has bestowed on **Gone with the Wind** the best-ever home release with its 1998 DVD, offering a choice between a new Dolby Digital 5.1 track and the original mono track.

Whereas a laser disc would require four sides to cope with this behemoth, DVD needs just one flip of the disc — which occurs logically at the original "Intermission". Even at reel-changes, the Technicolor print looks resplendent, while the French and English subtitles are a bonus often ignored by the studios.

A highlight of the season has been the restored director's cut of **The Last Emperor** (Artisan Entertainment). Bertolucci has integrated a further hour of unseen footage, to bring the film up to 218 minutes. The lush, widescreen transfer offers 2.0 Dolby Surround Audio, as well as production notes and information about cast and crew.

As if to mock this year's remake starring Pierce Brosnan and Rene Russo, a restored DVD of 1968's original **The Thomas Crown Affair** is now available from MGM, with a precise and cogent commentary by director Norman Jewison, and a choice between widescreen and standard

PICNIC AT HANGING ROCK, in a glorious DVD transfer from Criterion

versions. McQueen and Dunaway have never looked more glamorous, and DVD has resurrected their charisma for all time.

Another Steve McQueen classic, **Bullitt**, has at last been rendered in widescreen by Warner Home Video, with the colour contrasts refreshed and the bonus of a short film about the making of the picture, shot in 1968. The previous year **Bonnie and Clyde** had appeared to much acclaim, and the magnificent DVD release from Warners flaunts the photography of Burnett Guffey and the production design of Dean Tavoularis to absolute perfection.

How regrettable that Fox Lorber should have missed the opportunity to revive George Sluizer's macabre tour de force, **The Vanishing**. The DVD is in full-screen, with aggressive yellow subtitles throughout, and washed-out colours that diminish the impact of the verdant countryside near Nîmes that originally contributed so powerfully to the film's atmosphere .

Not every film responds to the DVD format. **Amadeus**, for instance, still looks marginally better on laser disc than it does in the 1998 Warner DVD (although the Dolby Digital sound does improve the musical aspects). Black-and-white classics tend to fare better: that quintessential Joan Crawford thriller, **Sudden Fear**, for example, from Kino on Video; or **The Lady Vanishes**, from Criterion, in which 7,000 blemishes were removed from the original print.

Contemporary releases

While all too many dud movies are given the DVD treatment, only the churlish would deny that the studios have done well by their latter-day hits. PolyGram Video International has issued several excellent films, housed in a most luxurious "jewel-box" casing that deserves to survive but probably will not, given the parsimonious margins of the mass video market.

SEVEN SAMURAI literally hurtles off the screen once again, thanks to a superb transfer on the Criterion DVD

Four Weddings and a Funeral has subtitles in English, French, Spanish, and Dutch as well as optional French and Spanish dubbed dialogue. **Fargo** offers the same facilities, but may at least be viewed in its original widescreen ratio. The most assured British film of recent years, **Trainspotting**, leaps off the screen in PolyGram's razor-sharp transfer, and may be played in either full-screen or widescreen format

David Fincher's underrated **The Game** comes into its own on DVD, with Dolby Digital 5.1 and 'scope proportions ensnaring the viewer in much the same way as did Fincher's *Seven*. **The Usual Suspects** is the only real blot on the PolyGram landscape, for it has been issued in full-screen format, thus robbing the imagery and compositions of so much of their subtlety.

Warners have distinguished themselves with two outstanding releases. **Contact**, a mediocre movie, looks and sounds altogether better than the sum of its parts on the DVD, which comes with off-screen commentaries by Jodie Foster, Robert

BULLITT has been released in wide-screen on DVD by Warners

John Frankenheimer's RONIN proves a spectacular DVD release from MGM

Zemeckis and others, and a bundle of special effects designs and tests.

City of Angels also seems to transcend its original theatrical release, and positively hums with extras: off-screen commentaries, a brace of documentaries, interviews with Alanis Morissette and

Peter Gabriel about the music, five theatrical trailers, and subtitles in English and French.

A two-disc box set from Criterion bestows on the execrable **Armageddon** a dignity it lacked in theatres, and Michael Bay's commentary proves most informative for anyone interested in film technique. The same company has issued **Insomnia**, a Norwegian psychological thriller by Erik Skjoldbjærg that won many admirers on its release in 1997.

Finally, a return to form by that long-lost master of Cold War allegory, John Frankenheimer. His thriller, **Ronin**, takes him back to *French Connection 2* country, and the MGM Home Entertainment DVD brings the relentless car-chase sequences right into the living-room. The director himself delivers an invaluable off-screen commentary, and there's a choice of widescreen and full-screen formats.

A DVD menu from COPLAND, produced by MAWA Film & Medien GmbH, Germany, the largest independent producer and supplier of DVDs in Europe

Laser Discs

Pioneer in the UK have continued their loyalty to Francis Ford Coppola by releasing **The Rainmaker** in widescreen, on three sides in Dolby Surround, and also a digitally restored version of **The Godfather Part II**. The latter includes a mini-documentary on the making of the picture. Anyone awaiting this masterpiece on DVD need look no further than the LD, which delivers a magnificent transfer.

The same applies to **Titanic**, which Pioneer has issued in a two-platter set in the UK. The Dolby Surround, enhanced by a THX environment, conveys the best moments of the film with some intensity (e.g. the rumble through the rear speakers as the ship strikes the iceberg). James Cameron supervised the colour transfer, and this LD belongs on any collector's shelves.

Pioneer's other UK highlights have included **Sliding Doors**, which comes in a sparkling transfer and is supplemented by three trailers; **The Ice Storm**, Ang Lee's ominous foray into what used to be regarded as John Updike turf; and Tarantino's **Jackie Brown**, with its many engaging characters and intricate plotting.

Perhaps the most valuable LD of the year, however, came from DVD's most active proponent, Warner Bros. The studio's Home Video department lovingly restored Jan Troell's twin masterpieces, **The Emigrants** and **The New Land**. Presented uncut, and in the correct aspect ratio, these luminous, lyrical accounts of the Swedish migration to Minnesota in the nineteenth century have a vivid quality that improves with age. LD collectors, search and buy this limited edition; it may be a long time before the DVD becomes available.

Note: for both DVD and LD collectors, Doug Pratt's The DVD-Laser Disc Newsletter remains an indispensable monthly read (P.O. Box 420, East Rockaway, NY 11518, U.S.A.)

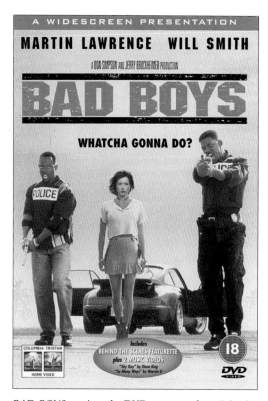

BAD BOYS *receives the DVD treatment from Columbia TriStar*

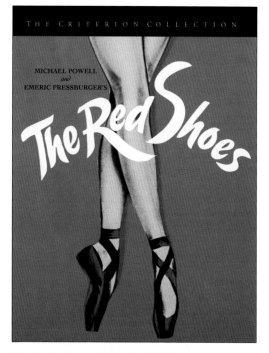

Criterion's release of THE RED SHOES on DVD

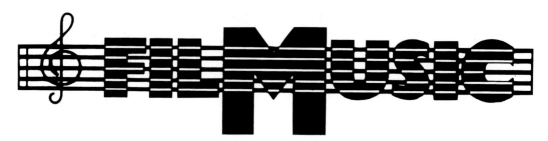

Below is a selection of specialist film music stockists around the world.

AUSTRALIA

Ava & Susan's, Town Hall Arcade, Sydney, NSW 2000. Tel: (61 2) 9264 3179.

BELGIUM

B.F.S., Kon. Astridlaan 171, 2800 Mechelen. Tel: (32) 1541 4107; Fax: (32) 1543 3610. Publishers of *Soundtrack* magazine since 1975; owners of the Prometheus label; European distributors of American labels such as Super Tracks, Intrada, Brigham Young and Screen Archives; wholesale and retail.

Promotion et Diffusion, Boulevard Anspach 49, 1000 Brussels. Tel/Fax: (32 2) 217 5947. Specialising in symphonic music; film merchandise available in store; mail order service provided.

CANADA

Disque-Cinémusic, 4426 Ernest-Gendreau St, Montreal H1X 3J3, Quebec. Tel: (1 514) 522 9590; Fax: (1 514) 522 2607; e-mail: disqcine@ cedep.com; www.disqcine.qc.ca. Specialising in out of print, second-hand items and European imports. Catalogue/mail order service only, with extensive selection of soundtracks on CD.

Song & Script, 1200 Bay Street, Toronto MR5 2A5. Tel: (1 416) 923 3044; Fax: (1 416) 923 7879; e-mail: DANEBDS@aol.com. This business has been running for 36 years and has a very efficient mail order service for CDs. It deals mainly in theatrical soundtracks, although most requests can be met. Sheet music also available.

FRANCE

Ciné Musique, 50 rue de l'Arbre Sec, 75001 Paris. Tel: (33 1) 4260 3030; Fax: (33 1) 4260 3022. Boutique specialising in sound-

Nicola Piovani's Oscar-winning score for LIFE IS BEAUTIFUL has attracted soundtrack buyers throughout the world
photo: Sergio Strizzi/Kobal Collection

Dave Grusin's energetic score greatly added to the tense atmosphere of THE NEGOTIATOR

photo: B.V. & Regency Entertainment

track material. Mail order service provided.

GERMANY

Cinema-Soundtrack Club, Postfach 52 02 65, 22591 Hamburg. Tel: (49 40) 8908 5200; Fax: (49 40) 890 5671; e-mail: contactsound track @edel.de; www.soundtrack-club.de. Main catalogues printed in April and October, with additional catalogues printed monthly. Extensive range of soundtracks available, specialising in Edel label. Small range of film books and DVDs, small collectable items and memorabilia.

Tarantula Records, Pilatuspool 7, 20355 Hamburg. Tel: (49 40) 353 511; Fax: (49 40) 343 407; e-mail: tarantulaR@aol.com; www. tarantula-records.com. About 20,000 titles on CD and LP. Mail order service provided.

ITALY

CAM, Via Cola di Rienzo 152, 00192 Rome. Tel: (39 06) 687 4220; Fax: (39 06) 687 4046; e-mail: cam-ost@uni.net; www.cam-ost.it. Music publishers and independent record label based in Rome. Over the past 38 years,

CAM has produced 2,700 soundtracks for Italian, French, Spanish and American films. Catalogue available.

Intermezzo Media, Piazza Aspromonte 13, 20131 Milano. Tel: (39 02) 7063 5936; Fax: (39 02) 236 3392. Both a mail order business and a label, Legend Records.

JAPAN

Sumiya, 2-15-1 Shibuya, Shibuya Ku, Tokyo 150. Fax: (813) 3409 6091; e-mail: soundtrack@ sumiya.co.jp.

NETHERLANDS

Cinesoundtrack Service, Chopinlaan 30, 6865 EW Doorwerth. Tel: (31 26) 333 3013; Fax: (31 26) 334 2990.

SPAIN

Rosebud Cinema Shop, C/Pelayo, bajo izquierda, 46007 Valencia. Tel/Fax: (34 96) 394 4592; e-mail: saimel@arrakis.es; www.rose budbandasonora.com. A catalogue of more than 5,000 CDs; extensive film merchandise available; mail order service

provided. Also magazine and record publishers for Rosebud Banda Sonora.

Vinilo Soundtrack Club, Pozas 6, 28004 Madrid. Tel: (34 91) 522 6073; Fax: (34 91) 524 0104; www.vinilo.es. A wholesaler/ retailer with its own record label (Vinilo Records). Mail order catalogue provided.

UNITED KINGDOM

Backtrack, The Old Grammar School, Rye, East Sussex, TN31 7PJ. Tel: (44 1797) 222 777; Fax: (44 1797) 222 752; e-mail: sales@backtrackrye.freeserve.c o.uk. Monthly mail order catalogue listing thousands of new releases and rare soundtracks on CD and LP. Film magazines, books, stills and posters available in store.

Discovery Records, Kings Corner, Pewsey, Wiltshire SN9 5BS. Tel: (44 1672) 563 931; Fax: (44 1672) 563 934. Wholesale distributors and importers.

Movie Boulevard, 3 Cherry Tree Walk, Leeds LS2 7EB. Tel: (44 113) 242 2888; Fax: (44 113) 243 8840.

Mail order service available, with catalogue updated monthly. Specialising in new and deleted soundtracks, film memorabilia, magazines, stills and posters.

Rare Discs, 18 Bloomsbury Street, London WC1B 3QA. Tel: (44 171) 580 3516; Fax: (44 171) 788 3809. Europe's oldest soundtrack shop. LPs and CDs available, as well as film books and memorabilia. Mail order service provided.

Soundtrack Deletions, Hillside House, 1 Woodstock Road, Strood, Rochester, Kent ME2 2DL. Tel: (44 1634) 711 053; Fax: (44 1634) 294 176. Specialising in Italian film soundtracks. CDs and LPs available. Catalogue updated several times a year.

Soundtracks Direct, 3 Prowse Place, London NW1 9PH. Tel: (44 171) 428 5500; Fax: (44 171) 482 2385; e-mail: info@silvascreen. co.uk; www.silvascreen.co.uk. The mail order division of Silva Productions Ltd, with an extensive catalogue including many recent releases and best-sellers.

UNITED STATES

Footlight Records, 113 East 12th Street, New York, NY 10003. Tel: (1 212) 533 1572; Fax: (1 212) 673 1496; e-mail: Footlight1@aol. com; www.footlight.com. CD catalogue published on website, but call the store direct with specific inquiries. Film and theatre magazines also available.

Intrada, 2220 Mountain Blvd, Suite 220, Oakland, California 94611. Tel: (1 510) 336 1612; Fax: (1 510) 336 1615; e-mail: intrada@ intrada.com; www.intrada.com. Mail order CDs available, with a catalogue published on the website. Specialising in orchestral and instrumental soundtracks.

Screen Archives Entertainment, PO Box 500, Linden, VA 22642. Tel: (1 540) 635 2575; Fax: (1 540) 635 8554; e-mail: craig@ screenarchives.com; www. screenarchives.com. Strictly mail order service, with monthly catalogue published. Vast quantity of titles available on CD.

Soundtrack Album Retailers, 912 West Main Street, Suite 201, PO Box 487, New Holland, PA 17557- 0487. Tel/Fax: (1 717) 656 0121; e-mail: star@cdsgroup.com; www. soundtrak.com. Worldwide mail order service with monthly catalogues, specialising in soundtracks from film and TV and original cast recordings.

Super Tracks Music Group, PO Box 2791, Orange, CA 92859, Tel: (1 714) 628 9699; Fax: (1 714) 628 9698. Mail order business which also runs its own label (Super Tracks Records). US distributor of *Soundtrack* magazine.

Super Collector, 12072 Brookhurst, Garden Grove, CA 92840. Tel: (1 714) 636 8700; Fax: (1 714) 636 8585; e-mail: supercollector@super collector.com; www.supercol lector.com. Imported and hard-to-find US CDs, soundtracks and movie music available, as well as extensive merchandise, both online and in store.

West Point Records, 24325 San Fenando Road, Newhall, CA 91321. Tel/Fax: (1 805) 253 2190.

John Williams' soundtrack for THE PHANTOM MENACE is bound to be one of the year's top sellers
photo: Keith Hamshere/LucasFilm

Fans of Randy Newman's film work will have enjoyed his soundtrack for A BUG'S LIFE
photo: The Kobal Collection

World Box-Office Survey

ARGENTINA

		Admissions
1.	Titanic	4,593,982
2.	An Argentinean in New York (Argentina)	1,643,709
3.	Godzilla	1,416,168
4.	As Good As It Gets	1,047,477
5.	Armageddon	934,808
6.	The Devil's Advocate	781,433
7.	Lethal Weapon 4	694,580
8.	Mulan	688,218
9.	Cohen vs. Rosi (Argentina)	661,254
10.	Deep Impact	649,562

AUSTRALIA

		$ (millions)
1.	Titanic	30.7
2.	There's Something About Mary	12.5
3.	As Good As It Gets	12.1
4.	Saving Private Ryan	11.7
5.	The Wedding Singer	11.1
6.	Deep Impact	10.9
7.	Dr. Doolittle	10.7
8.	Good Will Hunting	9.5
9.	Armageddon	9.2
10.	Sliding Doors	8.9

$1 = AUS$1.53

AUSTRIA

		Admissions
1.	Titanic	1,389,000
2.	Hinterholz 8 (Austria)	587,000
3.	Armageddon	547,000
4.	As Good As It Gets	371,000
5.	Dr. Dolittle	370,000
6.	Saving Private Ryan	315,000
7.	Deep Impact	295,000
8.	The Truman Show	265,000
9.	The Horse Whisperer	264,000
10.	There's Something About Mary	263,000

BELGIUM

		$ (millions)
1.	Titanic	20.8
2.	Saving Private Ryan	5.6
3.	Armageddon	4.9
4.	Lethal Weapon 4	3.1
5.	Dr. Dolittle	2.9
6.	Les Visiteurs 2 (France)	2.83
7.	Godzilla	2.74
8.	Deep Impact	2.6
9.	Mulan	2.57
10.	The Jackal	2.5

$1 = 37 Belgian francs

BRAZIL

		Admissions
1.	Titanic	16,374,377
2.	Armageddon	2,306,839
3.	Godzilla	2,034,678
4.	The Mask of Zorro	2,016,495
5.	Mulan	1,956,927
6.	The Devil's Advocate	1,856,349
7.	As Good As It Gets	1,658,581
8.	Lethal Weapon 4	1,381,497
9.	City of Angels	1,283,258
10.	There's Something About Mary	1,230,402

(Source: Filme B consultants)

BULGARIA

		$
1.	Titanic	1,057,771
2.	Armageddon	434,032
3.	The Mask of Zorro	332,991
4.	Godzilla	268,679
5.	Lethal Weapon 4	237,358
6.	The Devil's Advocate	186,857
7.	The Jackal	157,021
8.	Bean (UK)	156,285
9.	The X-Files Movie	143,642
10.	The Man in the Iron Mask	140,344

All films are US productions unless otherwise indicated.
All figures are for January to December 1998 unless otherwise indicated.

CHILE

	Admissions
1. Titanic	1,078,882
2. Deep Impact	368,448
3. Godzilla	295,239
4. The Mask of Zorro	250,462
5. Armageddon	220,778
6. Mulan	185,709
7. As Good As It Gets	162, 507
8. George of the Jungle	150,408
9. The Man in the Iron Mask	147,479
10. Lethal Weapon 4	138,437

Figures are for Santiago only and correspond to approximately 75% of national admissions totals.

CZECH REPUBLIC

	Admissions
1. Titanic	1,050,371
2. Armageddon	540,783
3. Godzilla	307,062
4. Seven Years in Tibet	296,885
5. Alien Resurrection	238,144
6. Saving Private Ryan	231,138
7. Bean (UK)	218,610
8. As Good As It Gets	218,332
9. The Time of Debts (Czech)	193,645
10. Deep Impact	166,328

DENMARK

	Admissions
1. Titanic	1,359,000
2. The Celebration (Denmark)	386,000
3. Tomorrow Never Dies	357,000
4. The Full Monty	354,000
5. The Olsen Gang – Final Mission (Denmark)	328,000
6. Mulan	320,000
7. Saving Private Ryan	271,000
8. Armageddon	257,000
9. Lethal Weapon 4	249,000
10. Anastasia	195,000

THE CHAMP won sixth place in Egypt's top ten

EGYPT

1. An Upper Egyptian at AUC (Egypt)	
2. Titanic	
3. Message to the Ruler (Egypt)	
4. Lace (Egypt)	
5. 48 Hours in Israel (Egypt)	
6. The Champ (Egypt)	
7. Armageddon (Egypt)	
8. Hysteria (Egypt)	
9. Home Alone 3	
10. Delicious Killing (Egypt)	

ESTONIA

	Admissions
1. Titanic	130,308
2. The X-Files Movie	35,902
3. Godzilla	35,699
4. Armageddon	32,735
5. Dr. Dolittle	32,718
6. The Mask of Zorro	31,881
7. The Full Monty	31,705
8. Lethal Weapon 4	26,866
9. Deep Impact	25,998
10. The Man in the Iron Mask	23,696

TITANIC: all-time box-office champ, with a global gross of $1.7 billion during calendar year 1998

photo: Fox/Lightstorm

Bruce Willis (left), Will Paton and ARMAGEDDON rocketed to second place in the year's chart, with a global take of $464.3 million

photo: Frank Masie/Touchstone

Gross-out comedy brought huge takings for THERE'S SOMETHING ABOUT MARY, the year's sixth biggest hit with $328 million worldwide   *photo: Fox*

Tea Leoni announces the prospect of DEEP IMPACT, which devastated box-office charts all over the world, taking $350 million   *photo: Myles Aronowitz/Paramount DreamWorks*

FRANCE $ (millions)

1. Titanic	124
2. Le Dîner de Cons (France)	51
3. Les Visiteurs 2 (France)	48
4. Taxi (France)	38
5. Armageddon	27
6. Mulan	26
7. Saving Private Ryan	23
8. Lethal Weapon 4	20
9. Life is Beautiful (Italy)	19
10. The Mask of Zorro	18

LIFE IS BEAUTIFUL, a major success in France and Greece   photo: Sergio Strizzi/Kobal Collection

GERMANY $

1. Titanic	138,391,388
2. Armageddon	37,937,259
3. The Horse Whisperer*	29,461,211
4. Saving Private Ryan	27,283,454
5. Dr. Dolittle	22,596,559
6. Deep Impact	21,112,603
7. Godzilla	20,471,468
8. As Good As It Gets	20,001,588
9. Mulan*	19,129,734
10. There's Something About Mary*	18,865,024

*Still in release in Jan. 1999. $1 = DM 1.76

GREECE   Admissions

1. Asterix and Obelix vs. Caesar (France)	350,000
2. Armageddon	330,000
3. Shakespeare in Love	295,000
4. Life is Beautiful (Italy)	290,000
5. There's Something About Mary	240,000
6. The Horse Whisperer	215,000
7. The Truman Show	200,000
8. Dr. Dolittle	195,000
9. Saving Private Ryan	190,000
10. The Mating Game (Greece)	185,000

Figures are for the Greater Athens area only, September 1998 to May 1999. Statistics are unconfirmed officially and based on information from distribution offices.

HONG KONG $ (millions)

1. The Stormriders (Hong Kong)	5.3
2. Who Am I? (Hong Kong)	5.0
3. Tomorrow Never Dies	3.73
4. Saving Private Ryan	3.71
5. The Lucky Guy (Hong Kong)	3.55
6. Deep Impact	3.06
7. Armageddon	2.75
8. The Replacement Killers	2.72
9. Godzilla	2.70
10. Mulan	2.23

$1 = HK$7.8. Source: MPIA.

ICELAND   Admissions

1. Titanic	124,008
2. As Good As It Gets	47,795
3. Armageddon	47,660
4. There's Something About Mary	45,830
5. Leathal Weapon 4	44,017
6. Godzilla	30,324
7. The Truman Show	29,730
8. Saving Private Ryan	29,424
9. Dr. Dolittle	28,224
10. Six Days Seven Nights	23,842

INDIA

1.	Kuch Kuch Hota Hai
2.	Pyar To Hona Hi Tha
3.	Pyar Kiya To Darna Kya
4.	Ghulam
5.	Satya
6.	Dulhe Raja
7.	Dushman
8.	Titanic
9.	Soldier
10.	China Gate

All films except *Titanic* are Indian. Source: *India Today*, December 1998.

INDONESIA

1.	Titanic
2.	Tomorrow Never Dies
3.	Godzilla
4.	Armageddon
5.	Mouse Hunt
6.	The Man in the Iron Mask
7.	Ever After
8.	A Bug's Life
9.	Mulan
10.	Leaf on a Pillow (Indonesia)

IRAN

		$
1.	The Wrong Man	683,000
2.	The Glass Agency	275,000
3.	The Psychic	192,000
4.	The Sunshine Man	188,000
5.	Help Me!	173,000
6.	Wild Lilacs	157,000
7.	The Visit	150,000
8.	Mercedes	130,000
9.	Life	120,000
10.	Banoo	93,000

All films are Iranian. Figures are for first run in Tehran only. $1 = 6,000 Rials.

IRELAND

		$
1.	Titanic	10.56
2.	There's Something About Mary	3.3
3.	Saving Private Ryan	2.66
4.	Dr. Dolittle	2.52
5.	Armageddon	2.27
6.	Godzilla	1.99
7.	The General (Ireland)	1.9
8.	The Wedding Singer	1.83
9.	The Butcher Boy (Ireland)	1.6
10.	As Good As It Gets	1.58

$1 = IR£0.70

ITALY

		$
1.	That's Life (Italy)	25,620,136
2.	Shakespeare in Love	14,082,782
3.	Saving Private Ryan	13,611,372
4.	There's Something About Mary	12,099,922
5.	The Truman Show	11,928,279
6.	Sliding Doors	11,122,306
7.	The Prince of Egypt	10,563,637
8.	Mulan	10,197,845
9.	Armageddon	10,609,033
10.	You've Got Mail	10,732,683

Source: *Giornale dello Spettacolo*. $ = 1,700 lire

THE GENERAL proved that crime can pay, bagging seventh place in Ireland's chart

JAPAN

	$ (millions)
1. Titanic	133.3
2. Bayside Shakedown (Japan)	41.7
3. Deep Impact	39.3
4. Pocket Monsters (Japan)	34.6
5. Men in Black	29.2
6. Godzilla	25
7. Saving Private Ryan	20
8. Doraemon (Japan)	17.5
9. Air Force One	16.7
10. City of Angels	14.2

Figures are rentals (distribution income), not box-office gross. $1= 120 Yen.

LATVIA

	Admissions
1. Titanic	132,300
2. The Millstones of Fate (Latvia)	84,000
3. The Mask of Zorro	38,700
4. Armagedon	36,200
5. Dr. Dolittle	33,100
6. Tomorrow Never Dies	32,000
7. Home Alone 3	30,000
8. Godzilla	29,200
9. The Fifth Element (France)	29,100
10. Mouse Hunt	28,400

LITHUANIA

	Admissions
1. Titanic	81,380
2. Bean (UK)	25,613
3. Armageddon	25,068
4. Air Force One	20,280
5. Godzilla	20,194
6. The Fifth Element (France)	19,600
7. Kama Sutra (India)	18,638
8. Starship Troopers	17,645
9. Tomorrow Never Dies	15,049
10. The Mask of Zorro	14,691

Figures are from Lietuva, the largest cinema in Vilnius, only.

THE MASK OF ZORRO, a swashbuckling favourite in Latvia and Lithuania
photo: Sam Urdank/Columbia TriStar

MEXICO

	$ (millions)
1. Titanic	22.5
2. Godzilla	11.5
3. Armageddon	9.5
4. A Bug's Life	9.0
5. Deep Impact	8.1
6. Antz	7.0
7. The Mask of Zorro	6.1
8. Mulan	6.0
9. The Prince of Egypt	5.2
10. Dr. Dolittle	4.6

$1 = 10 pesos. Source: Canacine.

NETHERLANDS

	Admissions
1. Titanic	3,424,000
2. Armageddon	747,000
3. Saving Private Ryan	726,000
4. Seven Years in Tibet	555,000
5. Flubber	537,000
6. Deep Impact	527,000
7. Tomorrow Never Dies	521,000
8. Lethal Weapon 4	508,000
9. Abeltje (Netherlands)	497,000*
10. Dr. Dolittle	483,000

*Still in release in Jan 1999

NEW ZEALAND

	$ (millions)
1. Titanic	6.73
2. Saving Private Ryan	2.03
3. There's Something About Mary	2
4. As Good As It Gets	1.7
5. Armageddon	1.6
6. Good Will Hunting	1.5
7. Godzilla	1.25
8. Deep Impact	1.14
9. Tomorrow Never Dies	1.11
10. The Wedding Singer	1.10

$1 = NZ$2

THE WEDDING SINGER won many hearts in New Zealand photo: K. Wright/Entertainment Film

NORWAY

	Admissions
1. Titanic	1,360,505
2. Gurin With the Foxtail (Norway)	674,926
3. Tomorrow Never Dies	619,038
4. As Good As It Gets	389,331
5. There's Something About Mary	346,088
6. Saving Private Ryan	296,267
7. Home Alone 3	274,450
8. Lethal Weapon 4	253,612
9. Armageddon	229,731
10. Good Will Hunting	217,030

PAKISTAN

1. Bangles
2. Love Crazy
3. Titanic
4. Wedding
5. Custodian
6. Burning Scarf
7. Trading Places
8. Fury
9. Showdown
10. Kingmaker

All films except *Titanic* are Pakistani.

POLAND

	$ (millions)
1. Titanic	14
2. Armageddon	2.9
3. Godzilla	1.8
4=. As Good As It Gets	1.4
4=. Young Wolves 1/2 (Poland)	1.4
6. Saving Private Ryan	1.26
7. Alien Resurrection	1.15
8. Killer (Poland)	1.14*
9. Demons of War (Poland)	1.06
10. Flubber	1

*1997 release. $1 = 3.5 zlotys

PUERTO RICO

	$
1. Godzilla	2,170,000
2. Armageddon	2,000,000
3. Deep Impact	1,800,000
4. Dr. Dolittle	1,790,000

ROMANIA

		Admissions
1.	Titanic	1,204,761
2.	Armageddon	273,319
3.	George of the Jungle	263,687
4.	The Fifth Element (France)	191,392
5.	Godzilla	191,149
6.	Home Alone 3	174,158
7.	Alien Resurrection	174,095
8.	The Mask of Zorro	156,399
9.	The Devil's Advocate	149,053
10.	Starship Troopers	144,150

SERBIA & MONTENEGRO

		Admissions
1.	Titanic	166,508
2.	Black Cat, White Cat	159,242
3.	The Powder Keg (Serbia)	142,144
4.	Barking at the Stars (Serbia)	133,360
5.	Three Palms for Two Punks and a Babe (Serbia)	111,154
6.	Wounds (Serbia)	109,184
7.	Hornet (Serbia)	74,673
8.	Tommorow Never Dies	63,402
9.	As Good As it Gets	51,067
10.	Godzilla	43,061

Figures are for Belgrade only. Source: Beograd film.

SINGAPORE

		$ (millions)
1.	Titanic	6.4
2.	Money No Enough (Singapore)	5.8
3.	Who Am I ? (Hong Kong)	3.4
4.	Godzilla	2.9
5.	Armageddon	2.63
6.	Deep Impact	2.62
7.	Saving Private Ryan	2.3
8.	The Replacement Killers	2.05
9.	The Storm Riders (Hong Kong)	2.02
10.	Mulan	1.9

SLOVAKIA

		Admissions
1.	Titanic	524,021
2.	Seven Years in Tibet	184,984
3.	Armageddon	176,695
4.	Godzilla	96,268
5.	Flubber	90,809
6.	Saving Private Ryan	88,638
7.	Deep Impact	85,815
8.	As Good As It Gets	82,777
9.	The Jackal	79,355
10.	Lethal Weapon 4	73,929

SOUTH AFRICA

		$
1.	Titanic*	6,000,000
2.	Tomorrow Never Dies	1,740,535
3.	Armageddon	1,692,246
4.	There's Something About Mary	1,641,686
5.	Deep Impact	1,572,409
6.	City Of Angels	1,451,847
7.	Rush Hour	1,444,003
8.	Dr. Dolittle	1,392,433
9.	Lethal Weapon 4	1,306,110
10.	Godzilla	1,217,144

$1 = 6 rand. * Excludes 1997 gross.

High-school horror: WHISPERING CORRIDORS scared up healthy business in South Korea

SOUTH KOREA

	Admissions
1. Titanic	1,971,780
2. Armageddon	1,170,252
3. Mulan	771,194
4. The Letter (South Korea)	724,747
5. A Promise (South Korea)	661,174
6. Deep Impact	637,387
7. Whispering Corridors (South Korea)	621,032
8. Saving Private Ryan	593,681
9. Alien Resurrection	571,751
10. Tomorrow Never Dies	479,621

SPAIN

	$ (millions)
1. Titanic	40.1
2. As Good As It Gets	13
3. Torrente, the Dumb Arm of the Law (Spain)	11.1
4. Six Days Seven Nights	10.8
5. Saving Private Ryan	9
6. Armageddon	8.8
7. There's Something About Mary	8.7
8. The Man in the Iron Mask	8
9. Godzilla	8
10. The Mask of Zorro	7.7

$1 = Ptas154

THE HORSE WHISPERER: bestselling novel became a top ten movie in Sweden

photo: Elliott Marks/Touchstone

SWEDEN

	Admissions
1. Titanic	2,170,000
2. Fucking Åmål (Sweden)	850,000
3. Mulan	700,000
4. Under The Sun (Sweden)	675,000
5. Armageddon	600,000
6. Saving Private Ryan	440,000
7. As Good As It Gets	400,000
8. There's Something About Mary	399,000
9. The Horse Whisperer	390,000
10. Hamilton (Sweden)	370,000

Figures are for April 1998 to April 1999.

SWITZERLAND

	Admissions
1. Titanic	1,997,083
2. The Horse Whisperer	444,795
3. Armageddon	377,824
4. There's Something About Mary	376,388
5. As Good As It Gets	374,500
6. Saving Private Ryan	343,597
7. Tomorrow Never Dies	319,163
8. Life is Beautiful (Italy)	307,872
9. Dr. Dolittle	300,419
10. Good Will Hunting	292,777

THAILAND

	$
1. Titanic	5,930,000
2. Armageddon	3,760,000
3. Godzilla	3,580,000
4. Tomorrow Never Dies	2,580,000
5. Deep Impact	2,579,000
6. Starship Troopers	2,030,000
7. Lethal Weapon 4	1,540,000
8. Alien Resurrection	1,360,000
9. The Replacement Killers	1,270,000
10. The Mask of Zorro	1,250,000

$1= 40 baht. Figures are based on information from distribution offices and are unconfirmed officially.

TURKEY

		Admissions
1.	Titanic	2,650,000
2.	Everything's Gonna be Great (Turkey)	1,300,000
3.	Propaganda (Turkey)	1,150,000
4.	There's Something About Mary	870,000
5.	My Best Friend's Wedding	860,000
6.	Republic (Turkey)	726,000
7.	Saving Private Ryan	687,000
8.	Armageddon	672,000
9.	You've Got Mail	671,000
10.	Meet Joe Black	585,000

UNITED KINGDOM

		$m
1.	Titanic	114,492,728
2.	Dr. Dolittle	32,958,633
3.	Saving Private Ryan	29,672,932
4.	Armageddon	27,400,964
5.	Godzilla	26,518,062
6.	There's Something About Mary	28,004,541
7.	Sliding Doors (UK)	20,641,627
8.	Lock, Stock and Two Smoking Barrels (UK)	19,123,315
9.	Flubber	18,080,345
10.	Lost in Space	17,702,992

$1 = 1.66

*LOCK, STOCK AND TWO SMOKING BARRELS,
with Sting, shot to Number 8 in the UK chart*
photo: Sebastian

UNITED STATES & CANADA $ (millions)

1.	Titanic	488.2 *
2.	Armageddon	201.6
3.	Saving Private Ryan	190.8
4.	There's Something About Mary	174.4
5.	The Waterboy	147.9
6.	Dr. Dolittle	144.2
7.	Deep Impact	140.5
8.	Godzilla	136.3
9.	Rush Hour	136
10.	Good Will Hunting	134

*Excludes 1997 gross,

Animal magic for DR. DOLITTLE in the UK and the US
photo: Fox

VENEZUELA

		Admissions
1.	Titanic	2,037,701
2.	Godzilla	555,501
3.	Mulan	539,301
4.	Armageddon	536,325
5.	Deep Impact	477,768
6.	Lethal Weapon 4	454,778
7.	The Mask of Zorro	402,361
8.	The Devil's Advocate	381,815
9.	George of the Jungle	348,000
10.	Dr. Dolittle	293,066

WORLD SURVEY

ALGERIA — Roy Armes

While no Algerian fiction features were shown at European festivals in the past year, a fascinating documentary initiative made an impression at festivals and on television in a dozen countries. **The Other Algeria: Views from Within** was produced on video by Internews Europe and funded by the European Commission through its MEDA-Democracy programme.

It comprises five 25-minute films: two made by experienced feature directors (Azzedine Meddour and Rachid Ben Brahim), one by a documentarist (Boualem Kamel) and two by journalists (Abdelkader Ensâad and the team of Abed Charef, Rabah Khoudri and Abdelmajid Sellamna).

The series offers a variety of insights into contemporary Algeria. Meddour's *Silent Suffering* examines children who are the victims of massacres. Ben Brahim's *Birds Always Sing of Freedom* follows the journey of a man who makes his living hunting and selling birds.

The 1001, Train of Hope, made by the team of Charef, Khoudri and Sellamna, focuses on the engine driver who risks his life every day driving the train from Algiers to Oran, and Ensâad's *Echoes of the Stadiums*, looks at the (mainly unemployed) young men for whom the city's football stadium is a place of solidarity and resistance.

Kamel's *The Children of The El Manar* looks at intellectuals who are forced to rethink their lives in the cramped rooms of the former luxury hotel in which they have been condemned to live by violent threats from fundamentalists. All in all, this is a haunting picture of bravery and protest in the face of intolerable violence and social deprivation.

French connections

Film-makers with Algerian roots who are currently based in France continue to produce remarkable work. Merzak Allouache, whose last film in Algeria was *Bab el-Oued City*, in 1994, has completed **Algiers-Beirut: In Remembrance**, which displays the director's customary concern for precise story construction.

It tells of a journalist, Laurence, who returns to Beirut, which she left as a child, and meets Rachid, whom she had previously known in Algiers. They fall in love and she tries to persuade him to seek asylum in France. But instead of accepting, this renewal of emotion merely reminds him of his own guilt and complicity with the fundamentalists, and he goes back to face death in Algiers.

After his study of Vietnamese orphans, *Poussières de vie*, the French-born Rachid Bouchareb has returned to immigrant problems with **My Family's Honour**. This is the story of a liberated young second generation immigrant, Nora, who goes through a conventional arranged marriage after she falls pregnant by her French lover. Events do not turn out as she hoped.

Two striking feature debuts – both dealing with memories of the early years of immigration – have also been made in the past year by directors born in Paris of Algerian descent. Bourlem Guerdjou won the top prize at the Carthage Film Festival (the most prestigious such gathering in the Arab world) with his semi-autobiographical fiction, **To Live in Paradise**. Set in the shanty-town of Nanterre in 1961–62, the film gives a vivid portrait of a world in which families are split by the struggle for existence.

A husband turns to deceit, while his wife chooses militancy, but within the community a true solidarity grows against the background of clashes between FLN supporters and French security forces. Guerdjou is the first European-born director to win the Carthage festival's Tanit d'Or prize.

Equally impressive is Yamina Benguigui's first feature-length documentary for cinema release, **Immigrants' Memories**, which won the top documentary award in San Francisco. This is an in-depth survey of the experiences of people whose lives were transformed by their move to France: the fathers who arrived alone, the mothers whose existence was transformed by the alien French environment, and the children who have to confront the full contradictions of the immigrant situation.

ROY ARMES is the author of several books on film history and specialises in African cinema. He teaches film in London.

Recent Films

L'AUTRE ALGÉRIE: REGARDS INTÉRIEURS (The Other Algeria: Views from Within)

Documentary. Script and Dir: Azzedine Meddour, Abdelmadjid Sellamna, Abdelkader Ensaad, Boualem Kamel, Rachid Ben-brahim. Prod: Internews Europe (France).

ALGER-BEYROUTH, POUR MÉMOIRE (Algiers-Beirut, In Remembrance)

Script and Dir: Merzak Allouache. Phot: Laurent Machuel. Players: Fabienne Babe, Georges Corraface, Paul Matar, Hocine Choukri, Zeina Saab Demelero, Mona Tayeh, Shadi el-Zein. Prod: Cinétévé – La Sept – Arte (France).

L'HONNEUR DE MA FAMILLE (My Family's Honour)

Script: Rachid Bouchareb, Alain Broders and Gilles Adrien. Dir:

Bouchareb. Phot: Youcef Sahraoui. Players: Seloua Hamse, Karole Rocher, Roschdy Zem, Alex Descas, Firmine Richard. Prod: 3B Productions (Paris).

VIVRE AU PARADIS (To Live in Paradise)

Script: Bourlem Guerdjou, Olivier Lorelle and Olivier Douyère. Dir: Guerdjou. Phot: Georges Lechptois. Players: Roschdy Zem, Fadila Belkebia, Omar Belkhaled, Mustapha Adouani, Fethi Akkari, Aziza Boulabiar, Amor Zouite. Prod: 3B Production (Paris)

MÉMOIRES D'IMMIGRÉS (Immigrants' Memories)

Documentary. Script and Dir: Yamina Benguigui. Phot: Virginie Saint Martin and Bakir Belaïdi. Prod: Bandits Production (Paris).

Useful Addresses

Cinémathèque Algérienne
rue Larbi-Ben-M'Hidi
Algiers
Tel: (213 2) 638 301

Centre Algérien pour l'Art et l'Industrie Cinématographique (CAAIC)
Immeuble les Asphodeles
16030 Ben Aknoun
Algiers
Tel: (213 2) 781 657
Fax: (213 2) 784 104

Entreprise Nationale de Production Audiovisuelle (ENPA)
3 avenue d l'Indépendence
BP 76
Didouche Mourad
Algiers
Tel: (213 2) 665 140
Fax: (213 2) 662 520

Agence Nationale des Actualitées Filmées (ANAF)
12 rue Ali
Bedjaoui
El Biar
Algiers
Tel: (213 2) 791 029
Fax: (213 2) 788 349

ARGENTINA

Alfredo Friedlander

With 36 Argentine films released in 1998 (up from 28 in 1997) and the prospect of at least that number reaching cinemas by the end of the year, the upward trend in production is holding firm. The same is true of the total number of new releases: 170 in 1997, 210 in 1998 and a projected total of 250 this year.

Two main reasons explain these trends. The first is the dramatic expansion in the number of screens, due to the construction of several new multiplexes by well-known international companies such as Hoyts, Cinemark and National Amusements. Recoleta, one of the most expensive districts of Buenos Aires, will soon have a multiplex with two VIP theatres charging premium prices for special tickets, which include a glass of champagne.

Another reason behind the increasing number of movies shown locally is the discovery of niche markets by independent distributors. One big surprise was the huge success of Abbas Kiarostami's *The Taste of Cherries* which was seen by almost 150,000 spectators in only two cinemas over the course of 28 weeks, a highly unusual record for this kind of film.

The first International Independent Film Festival of Argentina, held in Buenos Aires in April 1999, was a huge success, with most of the screenings sold out and Francis Ford Coppola the star attraction at one of the press conferences. The festival awarded prizes to the Argentineans Pablo Trapero (Best Director) and Luis Margani (Best Actor) for **Crane World** (*Mundo Grúa*) – well-deserved recognition for this black-and-white 16mm feature about the problems of high unemployment and low salaries in contemporary Argentina.

Positive signs

January 1999 had a good start with the release of the absurdist social satire **Bad Times** (*Mala Epoca*). This movie in four episodes is the second production (after *Moebius*) of the Universidad del Cine and like its predecessor gained several prizes for its four new directors at Mar del Plata's 14th International Film Festival, in November 1998.

Argentina was also in competition for the Oscar for Best Foreign Film with Carlos Saura's **Tango** (co-produced with Spain) and another Argentinean feature, Alejandro Agresti's **The Wind Gone With** (*El viento se llevó lo que*) picked up the Golden Shell for Best Film at San Sebastian in September 1998.

Unlike 1997, when the three top-grossing films in Argentina were local productions, in 1998 *Titanic* was, as in almost every other country of the world, the top hit, with attendance of more than 4.5 million. It was followed by the comedy **An Argentinean in New York** (*Un Argentino en Nueva York*, reviewed in *IFG 1999*). The only other Argentinean movie

Luis Margani in CRANE WORLD

to occupy a position in the top ten list was **Cohen vs. Rosi**, a comedy by the same team which produced *Wild Cards* (*Comodines*), the top-grossing movie in 1997. Now in 1999, they are coming back with what seems certain to be their third hit in a row, **Dear Alma** (*Alma mía*), a

typical boy-meets-girl story starring popular local TV stars.

ALFREDO FRIEDLANDER is a freelance film critic who writes regularly for the monthly *Cinetop* magazine. He also broadcasts on movie history and, above all, is a film buff.

Recent and Forthcoming Films

ALMA MIA (Dear Alma)

Script: Jorge Leyes. Dir: Daniel Barone. Phot: Guillermo Zappino. Music: Ivan Wyszogrod. Players: Araceli González, Pablo Echarri, Héctor Bidonde. Prod: Pol-ka Producciones.

Romantic comedy in which Alma, a confectioner, meets Leo, an architect who is about to get married to another girl.

EL AMATEUR (The Amateur)

Script and Dir: Juan Bautista Stagnaro. Phot: Víctor Quino González. Music: Jaime Roos. Players: Mauricio Dayub, Vando Villamil, Juan Verdaguer, Walter Santa Ana. Prod: Aleph Media, Juan Bautista Stagnaro.

In the suburbs of a provincial town, two friends share a dream: to beat the world cycling endurance record.

MUNDO GRUA (Crane World)

Script and Dir: Pablo Trapero. Phot: Cobi Migliora. Sound: Catriel Bildosola. Players: Luis Margani, Adriana Aizemberg, Daniel Valenzuela, Roly Serrano. Prod: Pablo Trapero Cinematográfica Producciones, Lita Stantic.

Rulo (Margani), 50, gets a job as a crane operator, but soon loses it when he is replaced by a much younger worker. He is obliged to leave Buenos Aires and travel to the south, where he finds a similar but lower paid job. An impressive first picture on the problems of unemployment in today's Argentina.

MALA EPOCA (Bad Times)

Script: Nicolás Saad, Mariano De Rosa, Salvador Roselli, Rodrigo

Moreno, Jorge Goldenberg. Dir: Saad, De Rosa, Roselli, Moreno. Phot: Javier Julia, Lucas Schiaffi. Players: Pablo Vega, Alberto Busaid, Daniel Valenzuela, Martín Adjemián, Carlos Roffé. Prod: Universidad del Cine.

A film divided into four episodes, each featuring an absurd and arbitrary event which changes the fates of the characters. The links between each episode underline the serious social repercusions of Menemism.

COHEN VS. ROSI

Script: Adrián Suar. Dir: Daniel Barone. Phot: Esteban Sapir. Players: Alfredo Alcón, Adrián Suar, Laura Novoa, Pepe Soriano. Prod: Pol-ka & Flehner/Patagonik Film Group/Buena Vista International.

The rivalry between two families, one Jewish, the other Catholic, is overcome when two of their young members fall deeply in love.

EL VISITANTE (The Visitor)

Script: José Pablo Feinman and Javier Olivera. Dir: Olivera. Phot: Víctor Quino González. Players: Julio Chávez, Valentina Bassi, Mariano Bertolini, Elsa Berenguer. Prod: Tercer Milenio, Aries Cinematográfica Argentina.

A traumatised veteran of the Falklands War is 'visited' by a former comrade who was killed in action. Is it really him or only a product of the veteran's disturbed imagination?

COMPLICES (Accomplices)

Script: Gustavo Barrios. Dir: Néstor Montalbano. Phot: Marcelo Iaccarino. Players: Oscar Martínez, Jorge Marrale, Leticia Bredice, Mauricio García. Prod: Raúl J. Naya producciones/Film Suez/Gabriel Díannunzio producciones.

An Argentinean living in the US must fly home to Buenos Aires to sell his mother's

Araceli González and Pablo Echarri in DEAR ALMA

home. While there he meets an old friend who becomes his accomplice in a terrible act.

DIARIO PARA UN CUENTO
(Diary for a Short Story)

Script: Leslie Megahey, Jana Bokova, Gualberto Ferrari. Dir: Bokova. Phot: Alfredo Mayo. Players: Germán Palacios, Silke, Inés Estevez, Héctor Alterio, Ingrid Pelicori. Prod: Kompel Producciones/Aleph Media/Mate Cantero Producciones (Spain).

Drama about a young man who decides to become a writer in 1950s Buenos Aires, where he is surrounded by prostitutes, sailors and gangsters.

YEPETO

Script: Roberto Cossa. Dir: Eduardo Calcagno. Phot: Roberto Mateo and Andrés Mazzon. Players: Ulises Dumont, Nicolás Cabré, Alejandra Flechner, Malena Figo. Prod: Eduardo R. Calcagno Producciones

The fourth collaboration between Calcagno and Dumont, it portrays a mature teacher who falls in love with a young student. His friendship with the girl's boyfriend prevents him from revealing his hidden passion.

LISBOA

Script: Enrique Brasó and Antonio Hernández. Dir: Hernández. Phot: Aitor Mantxola. Players: Carmen Maura, Federico Luppi, Sergi López, Antonio Birabent. Prod: Blue Legend Prods/Sinfonía Otoñal/ G.R.P.C./Alta Films.

Tragic road movie, set on one day and based on the true story of the strange encounter between a salesman (López) and a woman (Maura) escaping from her family.

TRES VERANOS
(Three Summers)

Script and Dir: Raúl Tosso. Phot: Carlos Torlaschi. Players: Fabián Gianola, Nicolás Scarpino, Alberto Busaid, Esteban Prol. Prod: Raúl Tosso/Punto y Aparte.

After 20 years, two friends return to the village by the seaside where they had spent three key summers in their lives and the life of the country: 1973 to 1975, which marked the return of Peronism to power.

EL SECRETO DE LOS ANDES
(The Secret of the Andes)

Script: Bernardo Nante and Alejandro Azzano. Dir: Azzano. Phot: Máximo Munzi. Players: David Keith, Nancy Allen, John Rhys Davies, Betiana Blum, Camilla Belle. Prod: Semana Mágica/Hombre Grande Producciones.

Culture-clash comedy about an American archaeologist and his family searching for part of a pre-Columbian relic in northern Argentina.

AMERICA MIA
(Beloved America)

Script: Gerardo Herrero, Horacio Vázquez Rial. Dir: Herrero. Phot: Alfredo Mayo. Players: José Coronado, Federico Luppi, Maribel Verdú, Peter Lohrmeyer. Prod: Tornasol Films(Spain)/Aleph Producciones/Sogetel (Spain)/ Blue Dahlia Prod (France)/Road Movies Vierte Produktionen (Germany)/Eurimages.

The story of a group of European immigrants in Argentina between 1880 and 1900.

EL SIGLO DEL VIENTO
(Century of the Wind)

Documentary. Script: Eduardo Galeano. Director: Fernando Birri. Phot: Libio Pensavalle, Udo Alberts. Prod: U.C.G. Producciones (Argentina)/Sur Films & Crea Audiovisual (Germany)/ ARTE/TVE/Cinemateca Uruguaya.

Based on the third volume of *Memories of the Fire*, by the Uruguayan Eduardo Galeano, this retraces the main political events in Latin America during the twentieth century.

SABES NADAR?
(Do You Know How to Swim?)

Script: Constanza Novick. Dir: Diego Kaplan. Phot: Ramiro Civita. Players: Juan Cruz Bordeu, Leticia Brdice, Antonio Birabent, Damián Dreizik, Iván González, Patricia Echegoyen. Prod: Bordeu, Echegoyen, Ferrari, Kaplan

Set in Mar del Plata, Argentina's most popular resort, this gloomy story focuses on a surfer and his waitress girlfriend, who dreams of becoming an actress.

LA VENGANZA (Vengeance)

Script and Dir: Juan Carlos Desanzo. Phot: Juan Carlos Lenardi. Players: Diego Torres, Laura Novoa, Paola Krum, Luis Luque, Pepe Novoa, Luis Machin. Prod: Argentina Sono Film, in association with TELEFE.

Pablo (Torres), an ambitious young executive in a major pharmaceuticals corporation must decide whether to expose the fraud within the company, which is revealed by a systems analyst (Novoa).

Producers

Aleph Producciones S.A.
Rivadavia 2358 – 5° Piso
1034 Buenos Aires
Fax: (54 11) 4954 3670/4/5
e-mail: cpustelnik@telefe.com.ar

Argentina Sono Film
Lavalle 1860
1051 Buenos Aires
Fax: (54 11) 4374 9250

Artear Group S.A.
Lima 1261
1138 Buenos Aires
Fax: (54 11) 4370 1309

Imágen Satelital S.A.
Avenida Melián 2752
1430 Buenos Aires
Fax: (54 11) 4546 8001

Kompel Producciones S.A.
Avenida Corrientes 1660
1042 Buenos Aires
Fax: (54 11) 4814 2657

Negocios Cinematográficos
Lavalle 1943
1051 Buenos Aires
Fax: (54 11) 4372 2807/2813

Oscar Kramer Producciones
Figueroa Alcorta 3351 –
Piso 1° Of.104
1425 Buenos Aires
Fax: (54 11) 4807 3254
e-mail: okafilms@overnet.com.ar

Patagonik Film Group S.A.
Godoy Cruz 1540
1414 Buenos Aires
Fax: (54 11) 4778 0046
e-mail: patafilm@intermedia.com.ar

POL-KA Producciones S.A.
Jorge Newbery 3483
1427 Buenos Aires
Fax: (54 11) 4553 0588/0543

Telefe S.A.
Pavón 2444
1248 Buenos Aires
Fax: (54 11) 4308 0054

Tercer Milenio S.A.
Fitz Roy 1940
1414 Buenos Aires
Fax: (54 11) 4771 2752
e-mail: aries@fibertel.com.ar

U.C.G. Producciones S.A.
Lavalle 1619 – 3° Piso E
1048 Buenos Aires
Fax: (54 11) 4373 8208
e-mail: cineojo@interlink.co.ar

Distributors

Alfafilm
Rivadavia 2358 – 5° Piso
1034 Buenos Aires
Fax: (54 11) 4954 3670/4/5
e-mail: alffafilm@topmail.com.ar

Artistas Argentinos Asociados
Lavalle 1977/79
1051 Buenos Aires
Fax: (54 11) 4811 5016/4371 3862

Buena Vista Columbia Tristar Films of Argentina S.A.
Ayacucho 533
1026 Buenos Aires
Fax: (54 11) 4954 3819/4952 9168
e-mail: felix.constanzo@disney.com.ar

Cine3 S.A.
Lavelle 1527 PB 2
1048 Buenos Aires
Fax: (54 11) 4375 5010/4373 7823
e-mail: cine3sa@cotelco.com.ar

Distribution Company S.A.
Ayacucho 595
1026 Buenos Aires
Fax: (54 11) 4372 9945/4371 3662
e-mail: dcazupnik@arnet.com.ar

Eurocine S.A.
Tucumán 1980 – P.B-
1050 Buenos Aires
Fax: (54 11) 4373 0547
e-mail: eurocine@navigo.com.ar

IFA Argentina
Riobamba 339 2° Piso A
1025 Buenos Aires
Fax: (54 11) 4373 7967

Líder Films S.A.
Lavalle 2086
1051 Buenos Aires
Fax: (54 11) 4953 7355

Primer Plano Film Group S.A.
Riobamba 477
1025 Buenos Aires
Fax: (54 11) 4374 0648/8435

UIP (United International Pictures) S.R.I.
Ayacucho 520
1026 Buenos Aires
Fax: (54 11) 4373 5098
e-mail: zrossini@arnet.com.ar

Warner Bros. – Fox
Tucumán 1938
1050 Buenos Aires
Fax: (54 11) 4372 6094/97
e-mail: maicat@ssdnet.com.ar

Useful Addresses

INCAA (Instituto Nacional de Cine y Artes Audiovisuales)
Lima 319
1073 Buenos Aires
Fax: (54 11) 4383 0029

Universidad del Cine
Pasaje Giufre 330
1064 Buenos Aires
Fax: (54 11) 4300 0674
e-mail: ucine@sninter.com.ar

ARMENIA — Sousanna Haroutiunian

Gloomy forecasts of the imminent collapse of Armenian cinema proved, happily, to be inaccurate. Notwithstanding the numerous unfavourable conditions – the general economic crisis in the country, the constant threat of reduced state subsidy for cinema, the destruction of the distribution system and the lack of private investment – the past year can be considered a fruitful one.

State support for film production increased threefold in 1999. This enabled the completion of post-production on some of the films left unfinished in 1998. Among them are *Documentalist* (*Vaveragrogh*), directed by Haroutiun Khachatrian, and *Crazy Angel* (*Khent Hreshtak*), by Souren Babayan (see *IFG 1999*). The funding also allowed two full-length features and one animated film to go into production at the state Hayfilm Studio and about 10 short documentaries to be started at the state Haik Documentary Studio.

The working title of the first feature is **Melody of the Destroyed City** (*Kandvats Kaghaki Meghedy*). Written and directed by well-known Armenian film-maker Albert Mkrtchian, it is set in the aftermath of the devastating earthquake of 1988, which took away thousands of lives and destroyed several towns in north-eastern Armenia, including the country's second biggest city, Leninakan (now called Gyumri), which is where Mkrtchian comes from.

The central characters are a teenage boy and his middle-aged teacher, who have both lost their families and homes in the earthquake. These orphaned people find their safest refuge in a new, improvised family: the teacher eventually decides to adopt the orphaned child, and, ignoring her objections, the boy chooses himself a father – a blind street musician.

Taking over the asylum

Vigen Chaldranian, one of the most successful and energetic film-makers of the middle generation won international festival citations with his debut, *God, Help Us* (*Kyrie Eleyson*, 1997) and at press time was shooting his follow-up at Hayfilm studio. **The Symphony of Silence** (*Lrutsian Simphonia*, working title) tells an unbelievable story: a madman returns to his native land after 20 years away, with a considerable amount of money to spend, and decides to privatise a madhouse. The man is suffering from an incurable disease and has resolved to use his last months to help the desperate and unhappy inmates, by creating a "paradise" for them.

Among his patients is a man who draws pictures on the walls of his ward. The hero organises an exhibition for him, which enjoys great success, and the man imagines himself to be an outstanding painter. There is also a girl who has lost her father, brother and lover during the earthquake, and he finds replacements for all three. However, it all ends when outsiders who want to taste the joy of the "paradise" attack and destroy it, accidentally killing the 'mad' benefactor. The authors have chosen the genre of grotesque tragi-comedy to reveal the problems of contemporary Armenian society.

The young film-maker Edgar Baghdassarian, whose debut, *Outflow*, proved to be a great success, has begun shooting a full-length documentary, **Aratta – The Land of Holy Rituals** (*Aratta – Srpazan Tsesery Erkir*). The story explores pre-Christian culture and the emergence and adoption of Christianity, in 12 chapters. The film will mark the anniversary of the adoption of Christianity in Armenia in 301 AD, which will be officially celebrated in the year 2001.

Another young film-maker, Tigran Xmalian, director of the third Armenian state film studio, Yerevan, has finally obtained funding for his feature-length debut, **Pierlekino**, which will be a lyrical comedy dedicated to Leonid Engibarov, the great Armenian clown and poet.

We are witnessing a slow rehabilitation of the film distribution system as an important component of the industry. Most Armenian cinemas have been privatised but very few are open for business as the new owners cannot arrange regular delivery of new films and doubt whether it is worth investing in new equipment for the cinemas. Yet the first symptoms of revival emerged in the two-week run of *Titanic* in the Moscow cinema, one of the few theatres operating in Yerevan. The run proved to be successful despite obsolete projection and sound equipment.

Titanic was shown three times a day at $1 (500 drams) a ticket and made a healthy profit, demonstrating to other exhibitors that, despite competition from home video and television, the public will still come to the cinema. As a result, the owners of some cinemas have started investing in refurbishment and technical upgrades. While we wait for the revival in production and exhibition to continue, a catalogue, *Armenian Cinema: 1923–1998*, is being prepared by the Armenian Association of Film Critics and Cinema Journalists.

SOUSANNA HAROUTIUNIAN graduated from Moscow's State Cinematographic Institute in 1987. She has contributed to numerous Armenian and Russian publications, such as *Film*, *Kino* and *Sovetskaya Kultura*, and has been film expert of the daily *Respublica Armenia* since 1991. She is president of Armenia's Association of Film Critics and Cinema Journalists.

Producers

Haifilm Studio
50 Gevork Chaush
375088 Yerevan
Tel: (374 2) 343 000

Haik Documentary Studio
50 Gevork Chaush
375088 Yerevan
Tel: (374 2) 354 590
Fax: (374 2) 357 032

Yerevan Studio
47, Nork
375047 Yerevan
Tel: (374 2) 558 022
e-mail: tx-yes@media.internews.am

Distributor

Paradise
18, Abovian
75001 Yerevan
Tel: (374 2) 521 271
Fax: (374 2) 521 302

Useful Addresses

Armenian Union of Cinematographers
18 Vardanats
Yerevan
Tel: (374 2) 570 528
Fax: (374 2) 571 136

Armenian National Cinematheque
25A Tbilisskoye shosse
Yerevan
Tel: (374 2) 285 406

Association of Film Critics and Cinema Journalists of Armenia
5 Toumanian St.
375 001 Yerevan
Tel: (374 2) 521 517
Fax: (374 2) 151 849
e-mail: aafccj@arminco.com

Association of Film Producers of Armenia
15 Armiryan St., Apt. 85
375010 Yerevan
Tel/Fax: (374 2) 535 322
Fax: (374 2) 907 141

Film Department Ministry of Culture
5,Toumanian St.
375 001 Yerevan
Tel: (374 2) 529 319
Fax: (374 2) 523 922

AUSTRALIA — David Stratton

For two years in this section I've been writing about the difficulty the vast majority of Australian films have in finding a substantial local audience, and the situation has, if anything, deteriorated in the last 12 months. Though there has been the occasional surprise, such as the lightweight, well-marketed *The Craic*, most Australian features have again struggled vainly to attract paying customers, in the face of overwhelming competition from the Hollywood films swamping the nation's cinemas.

This at a time when, in other respects, the local film industry would appear to be on a roll. Australians received no less than seven nominations for 1998 Academy Awards (Peter Weir for direction of *The Truman Show*; Cate Blanchett for her performance in *Elizabeth*; David Hirschfelder for *Elizabeth*'s score; Rachel Griffiths and Geoffrey Rush for supporting roles in, respectively, *Hilary and Jackie* and *Shakespeare in Love*; and producer Grant Hill and sound recordist Paul Brincat for *The Thin Red Line*). The fact that none of them won and, indeed, that none was nominated for an Australian film, was something of a disappointment, but nevertheless the industry was proud of the acknowledgement of local talent.

Richard Roxburgh in PASSION   photo: Beyond Films

The Thin Red Line was filmed in north Queensland, an increasingly popular location for producers looking for jungles, beaches and a good rate of exchange; *Sniper*, *Komodo* and Frankenheimer's *The Island of Dr. Moreau* had previously used the same location. The Fox studios in Sydney have, on the other hand, been used for lavishly art-directed city-based sci-fi films, like *Dark City* and the Wachowski Brothers' *The Matrix*.

George Miller's *Babe: Pig in the City* also used studio facilities and the increasingly creative Australian special effects and animatronics craftspeople. But these American-financed films in no way represent the core of the Australian industry; that is made up of modestly-budgeted, story- and character-driven films – the ones which seem to be losing the battle to put bums on seats.

The Thatcherite Liberal government is quite obviously not terribly interested in things artistic. The Arts Minister waged a successful campaign to have Pasolini's *Salo* banned after it had been in release for several years with an adults-only rating. A 10% tax was imposed on all books, and there have been massive cuts to the national broadcaster, the ABC. So there is understandable concern in the film community.

The lesser of two evils

Funding is becoming harder to find and the Film Finance Corporation, as it has done from its inception, insists that some kind of pre-sale be in place before support is given to a film project. But this is usually a Catch-22 situation – never more so than

when two projected films about musician Percy Grainger were under consideration.

Grainger was evidently rather fonder of his mother than he might have been and was heavily into S&M; one screenplay, reportedly, delved more explicitly into this material than the other. The milder project, **Passion**, attracted the required pre-sale and went ahead, under the competent direction of Peter Duncan and with Richard Roxburgh as Grainger and Barbara Hershey as his mother. The other Grainger film, which might well have been more interesting and provocative, was abandoned.

Censorship, as hinted last year, has also begun to have an impact on Australian cinema. In a year when there was a strong push by right-wing politicians, encouraged by the Prime Minister, to ban Adrian Lyne's *Lolita* (which none of the pro-censorship forces had, at that stage, seen) *Passion* was unaccountably given the most restrictive censorship classification (equivalent to America's NC-17) even though the film-makers had been decidedly timid in tackling the more outré elements of the story (some very mild whipping in which blows are heard but not seen, and an equally mild, male nipple-piercing). The R-18 classification suggested a more 'daring' film, but the censorship boards, under pressure, as always, from the government, refused to give it the more appropriate MA rating.

Swell or swill?

For some, the disappointment of the year was the much-anticipated **Babe: Pig in the**

City. Certainly Universal seems to have panicked when they first viewed the film, and George Miller was reportedly required to delete 17 minutes just prior to release. It would be fascinating to see the director's cut one day (perhaps on DVD), because most of the film is quite brilliant.

It was certainly a daring move to eliminate the first film's loveable farmer (James Cromwell) almost completely, and it is also true that the pig's misadventures in the city are a lot more gothic than his farmyard antics the first time around (one wag called it *Babe: Beyond Thunderdome*). But in terms of the extraordinary production design and the special effects, and the wonderful combination of live and animatronic animals, the film is surely a triumph. It was, of course, a box-office calamity once word escaped that it was "too dark".

Perhaps the best film of the year was **Praise**, an exceedingly tough, virtual two-hander, set in a sleazy Brisbane apartment block, about the relationship between an overweight, sexually active young woman with bad skin and a diffident, hopelessly inactive young man. Sacha Horler and musician Peter Fenton are quite wonderful in their very candid roles, and director John Curran, who hails from New York, does a marvellous job with the claustrophobic material, which deservedly won the FIPRESCI Award at Toronto in 1998. *Praise* opened to rave reviews and performed well, though not spectacularly, at the box-office.

At the time of writing, the amiable **Siam Sunset** has had festival success (Cannes, Seattle) but is yet to be tested with paying customers. The film takes a tried and true formula, used, with variations, in such films as Ted Kotcheff's *Wake In Fright* and Stephan Elliott's *Welcome To Woop Woop*. It is a fish-out-of-water tale about a foreigner who finds himself in the unexpectedly hostile environment of central Australia.

British actor Linus Roache plays the recently-widowed designer (the circum-stances of his wife's death provide the film with a truly unforgettable scene) who finds

Linus Roache in SIAM SUNSET

photo: Southern Star Films

romance in the outback with a young woman (Kiwi actress Danielle Cormack) who's escaping the vengeance of her drug-dealer boyfriend after stealing his stash of cash. The clever script is full of humour, actor John Polson's direction is consistently inventive, although the film portrays Australia in a decidedly negative light.

A very similar situation is the basis for **The Craic**, an undernourished comedy about the misadventures of an illegal immigrant from Northern Ireland. Popular stand-up comedian Jimeoin McKeown, who wrote the rather thin screenplay and played the lead, enjoyed box-office success thanks to his loyal followers.

Brown's hash

Gregor Jordan's feature debut **Two Hands** is a fiendishly-structured thriller with rich black comic overtones. Up-and-coming star Heath Ledger is Jimmy, who has ambitions to be a gangster – but his first big assignment from gang boss Pando (a delicious performance from Bryan Brown) goes horribly wrong. In an early cut of the film – the one which premiered at Sundance, unfortunately – a good deal of footage was devoted to the character of Jimmy's ghostly brother; this material was, sensibly, greatly reduced for the theatrical release, and makes for an infinitely better film.

Bryan Brown had a less rewarding role in the dreary **Dear Claudia**, a kind of poor man's *Six Days Seven Nights*, in which he played a besotted mailman delivering letters in remote northern Australia. His plane crashes, stranding him on an idyllic desert island with the eponymous Claudia. The abrasive performance from Aleksandra Vujcic in the latter role dooms this attempt at romantic comedy from the start, and writer-director Chris Cudlipp's stolid handling is no help.

A marginally better attempt at romantic comedy, **Paperback Hero**, by Antony Bowman, featured an attractive pair of leads – Claudia Karvan and Hugh Jackman – saddled with a screenplay which, after establishing a pleasantly loopy situation, quickly ran out of steam. Jackman, who made his name performing in stage musicals in Australia and Britain, is also excellent in **Erskineville Kings**, a beautifully photographed film which unfolds in a run-down inner-Sydney suburb during a very hot summer. Directed by newcomer Alan White, this drama takes place when two brothers are reunited, after a long absence, at their father's funeral. Though a bit over-written and theatrical, the film impresses because of fine performances and an acute eye for the details of inner-city life.

The family reunion theme, so popular in recent Australian films, also crops up in Christina Andreef's debut, **Soft Fruit**, which won the audience prize for best local film at the 1999 Sydney Film Festival. Like *Hotel Sorrento* and *Radiance*, the film features three long-separated sisters, who gather at the family home because mother (Jeanie Drynan) is dying of cancer. The gimmick here is that all three sisters –

splendidly played by Genevieve Lemon, Sacha Horler and Alicia Talbot – are decidedly overweight. Andreef, a former assistant to Jane Campion (who was *Soft Fruit*'s executive producer) borrows from several Australian films, including Campion's own *Sweetie*, *Muriel's Wedding* and *Crackers*; but, amid the clichés, she comes up with some fine scenes.

Island life

The most ambitious film of the year, apart from *Babe 2*, has been Bill Bennett's **In A Savage Land**, a love story set and filmed in the Trobriand Islands, off Papua-New Guinea. Set just before and during the Second World War, when the remote islands were under threat from Japanese invasion. Evelyn (talented newcomer Maya Stange) is an anthropological student who marries her university professor (Martin Donovan) and accompanies him to this remote spot to study the sexual habits of the islanders. There she meets, and eventually falls in love with, an Errol Flynn-like pearl diver (Rufus Sewell). The love story, a rather low-voltage one, takes second place to the documentary-style depiction (stunningly photographed) of life on the islands.

A couple of years ago, Emma-Kate Croghan delighted audiences with her first feature, *Love and Other Catastrophes*; her eagerly-awaited follow-up, **Strange Planet**, provided more of the same: an entertaining, often delightful snapshot of modern twentysomethings looking for love, with a great cast headed by Claudia Karvan,

Still from Alan White's ERSKINEVILLE KINGS

Rufus Sewell in IN A SAVAGE LAND
photo: Beyond Films

Still from Emma-Kate Croghan's STRANGE PLANET
photo: Beyond Films

Still from Brad Hayward's OCCASIONAL COARSE LANGUAGE

Naomi Watts and Alice Garner. But this is really no advance over *Catastrophes*.

Finally, mention should be made of a handful of no-budget films, some shot on video, which managed to find theatrical distribution during the year. Best of them was Jon Hewitt's **Redball**, a bleak depiction of a murder investigation carried out by corrupt police. Also commendable were Neil Mansfield's **Fresh Air**, about three young people sharing an inner-city house, and Brad Hayward's **Occasional Coarse Language**, about a 'plain' girl looking for a relationship.

Ten of the 15 films discussed above were made by first-time directors, which is indicative of a wealth of eager new talent. It is not so easy, however, for the new-comers to make their crucially important second films, and the achievement of continuity is a key goal for an industry which, despite considerable problems, still produces an impressive body of work .

DAVID STRATTON was Director of the Sydney Film Festival (1966–1983) and is co-host of *The Movie Show*, a weekly programme on the SBS TV network. He also contributes reviews to *Variety* and *The Australian*, and lectures on film history at the University of Sydney.

Industry Survey

by Peter Thompson

Will 2000 be an ordinary year? Certainly not in Australia, cursed or blessed with the Olympic Games in September. Caught in an escalating spiral of scandal, massive disruption and reconstruction, Sydney seems to have been living with the preparations forever. Whether anything else can compete remains to be seen. George Lucas will still be working on Episode 2 of *Star Wars* at Rupert Murdoch's new Fox Studios. Free-to-air television networks are supposed to begin broadcasting digital signals and, in the Olympic arts festival, Australian short, documentary and feature films will be paraded before the eyes of the world.

In between the hyperbole and the ephemera, life goes on, but the last 12 months have seen seismic shifts which have left astute observers guessing. Robert Connolly, producer of Rowan Woods' dark drama *The Boys*, suggested: "We live in fear of the government forgetting there's a difference between a film industry in Australia and an Australian film industry."

Elected in 1996 (and re-elected in 1999) on promises of level funding for the arts and for public broadcasters ABC and SBS, John Howard's conservatives have since dismantled the bipartisan cultural policy that prevailed for more than three decades. Convinced that the arts and the media are riddled with left-wingers, Howard embarked on a policy of attrition at best, revenge at worst, which has alienated much of the community.

The most egregious insult came during the recent election campaign. Liberal (conservative) Party advertisements attacked Kim Beazley's Labor Party for promising $26m (Aus$40m) to the "elite arts". The "elite" slur comes easily in Australia but fell hard on the ears of many who find the economic road in their chosen professions perilous indeed. And it wasn't just words. SBS Independent, an important television production entity, was threatened with the axe. Visa restrictions on foreign actors were eased. The sale of Film Australia was contemplated. Happily, these decisions were all reversed in the face of public pressure – but others were not.

The Commercial Television Production Fund was allowed to run out, removing nearly $13m a year from the industry. The ABC suffered swingeing cuts and a campaign of political intimidation. All government-funded cultural organisations were subjected to "efficiency" audits which effectively shrank their spending power. And, as an indication of their mind-set, members of Howard's party campaigned for less permissive censorship.

This reached a farcical stage when the government's own citizen's panels, appointed to review the Office of Film and Literature Classification's decisions, sided with the Office. Not deterred, the government intervened to block the appointment of seven new censors, selected by independent consultants, because they were deemed unrepresentative of the community. In the May 1999 Federal Budget more than $4.5m was pledged to expanding the censorship powers of the broadcasting and Internet watchdogs.

Progress against the odds

The arts, however, do not necessarily wither in an unsympathetic environment. The film and television industry has considerable momentum and production activity has, if anything, increased. More private and foreign investment is finding its way in. Some of this has gone into totally foreign projects such as *The Matrix*, but Australian films are also being fully funded from outside: *Babe: Pig in the City*

(George Miller) by Universal Pictures; *Dark City* (Alex Proyas) by New Line; *Holy Smoke* (Jane Campion) by Miramax; *Me, Myself and I* (Pip Karmel) by Gaumont; *Mr Accident* (Yahoo Serious) by G2 Films; *Moulin Rouge* (Baz Luhrmann) by 20th Century Fox; *Soft Fruit* (Christina Andreef) by Fox Searchlight and the Australian Film Finance Corporation.

In 1997–98, the latest year for which the Australian Film Commission has data, foreign movies worth $85m were shot here. Australian feature film and independent TV drama production reached $275m (38 features and 43 TV dramas) – the highest figure on record. In a trend previously noted on these pages, a growing number (18 features) had budgets of $650,000 or less. This represents a lot of activity – and much greater diversity of funding than we have ever seen. Although Prime Minister Howard has cut direct film and television subsidies by 30%, his new incentive scheme for private investment, the so called FLICs, may see an additional $65m flowing into production in the 1999–2000 fiscal year.

Though Australians are visible internationally, winning Oscar nominations and other prizes, and Aussie movies continue to attract interest, nothing can conceal the sense of wariness, if not outright malaise, within the industry. Of course, this could change with a big popular success or two on the level of *Babe, Shine, Muriel's Wedding* or *The Piano*. But the point is that all of these titles emanated from independent producers, and the going in that sector is tough and getting tougher.

There is a dearth of direct support for producers and, with rare exceptions (such as George Miller) no one has been able to build up the financial resources aggressively and painstakingly to develop new projects on their own. Often the very real returns from big box-office grosses fail to reach them because of the deals done early on with distributors just to get their films made. One obvious result of this financial hardship is that too often films go into production before scripts are ready. Producers simply can't afford to wait.

The bottom line is that the industry is chronically undercapitalised and it is development funding that is hardest to find. Government agencies, federal and state, disperse shrinking dollars on a modest scale but most of their grants go directly to writers after an often laborious and time-consuming assessment process. "I call it a green drought," says seasoned producer Sue Milliken (*Paradise Road, Black Robe*). All the activity diverts people from the truth that the fundamentals are weak. And the basis of a creative industry must always be ideas – ideas honed and strengthened by a rigorous and appropriate development process.

The problems are real, but Australia remains film crazy. Good weather, good cinemas and a surplus of (mostly American) movies sustain the boom, and new technologies and media outlets (such as Pay TV) outstrip predictions. And just to indicate how weird things can be, the favourable exchange rate on the Aussie dollar not only attracts foreign producers to our shores, it's also spawning an export business in film and television equipment rentals!

PETER THOMPSON is a writer, film-maker and critic who appears regularly on Australian national television.

Producers

Arenafilm Pty Ltd
(Robert Connolly,
John Maynard)
270 Devonshire Street
Surrey Hills NSW 2010
Tel: (61 2) 9317 7011
Fax: (61 2) 9319 6906
e-mail: mail@arenafilm.com.au

Artist Services Pty Ltd
(Andrew Knight,
Steve Vizard)
33 Nott Street
Port Melbourne VIC 3207
Tel: (61 3) 9646 3388
Fax: (61 3) 9646 7644
e-mail: artserv@ozemail.com.au

Bazmark Inq. Pty Ltd
(Baz Luhrmann)
PO Box 430
Kings Cross NSW 1340
Tel: (61 2) 9361 6668
Fax: (61 2) 9361 6667
Web: www.bazmark.com

Beyond International
(Mikael Borglund)
53-55 Brisbane Street
Surrey Hills NSW 2010
Tel: (61 2) 9281 1266
Fax: (61 2) 9281 1261
e-mail: beyond.com.au
Web: www.beyond.com.au

Bill Bennett Productions Pty Ltd
(Bill Bennett)
PO Box 117
Castlecrag NSW 2068

Tel: (61 2) 9417 7744
Fax: (61 2) 9417 7601
e-mail: billben@ozemail.com.au

Binnaburra Film Company Pty Ltd
(Glenys Rowe)
PO Box 2124
Clovelly NSW 2031
Tel: (61 2) 9665 6135
Fax: (61 2) 9665 4378

Cascade Films
(David Parker, Nadia Tass)
117 Rouse Street
Port Melbourne VIC 3207
Tel: (61 3) 9646 4022
Fax: (61 3) 9646 6336
e-mail: rasa@cascadefilms.com.au

David Hannay Productions
(David Hannay)
PO Box 175
Leura NSW 2780
Tel: (61 2) 4782 7111
Fax: (61 2) 4782 3711
e-mail: memdah@hermes.net.au

Emcee Films
(Martha Coleman)
24 Bayswater Road
Kings Cross NSW 2011
Tel: (61 2) 9368 7600
Fax: (61 2) 9356 4897
e-mail: marthac@ozemail.com.au

Filmside
(Richard Brennan, Al Clark, Andrena Finlay, Ross Mathews)
33 Riley Street
Woolloomooloo NSW 2011
Tel: (61 2) 9361 4164
Fax: (61 2) 9332 3427

Fox Icon Productions Pty Ltd
(Tim White)
Fox Studios Australia FSA No 24
Driver Avenue
Moore Park NSW 1363
Tel: (61 2) 9383 4600
Fax: (61 2) 9383 4605

Fox Studios Australia
(Kim Williams)
Driver Avenue
Moore Park NSW 1363
Tel: (61 2) 9383 4000
Fax: (61 2) 9361 3106

Great Scott Productions
(Jane Scott)
27 Elizabeth Street
Paddington NSW 2021
Tel: (61 2) 9331 3535
Fax: (61 2) 9360 5875
e-mail: greats@netspace.net.au

House & Moorhouse Films
(Lynda House, Jocelyn Moorhouse)
117 Rouse Street
Port Melbourne VIC 3207
Tel: (61 3) 9646 4025
Fax: (61 3) 9646 6336

Jan Chapman Productions
(Jan Chapman)
PO Box 27
Potts Point NSW 1335
Tel: (61 2) 9331 2666
Fax: (61 2) 9331 2011

Kennedy Miller Pty Ltd
(George Miller)
The Metro Theatre
30 Orwell Street

Kings Cross NSW 2011
Tel: (61 2) 9357 2322
Fax: (61 2) 9356 3162

Matt Carroll Films Pty Ltd
(Matt Carroll)
12 Sloane Street
Newtown NSW 2042
Tel: (61 2) 9516 2400
Fax: (61 2) 9516 2099
e-mail: mcfilms@pop.real.com.au

Palm Beach Pictures Pty Ltd
(David Elfick)
33 Edward Street
Bondi NSW 2026
Tel: (61 2) 9365 1043
Fax: (61 2) 9365 1380
e-mail: palmbeach@infolearn.
com.au

RB Films
(Rosemary Blight)
9 Knox Street
Chippendale NSW 2008
Tel: (61 2) 9281 9550
Fax: (61 2) 9211 2281
e-mail: rbfilms@ozemail.com.au

REP Films
(Richard Becker)
Level 2, 486 Pacific Highway
St Leonards NSW 1590
Tel: (61 2) 9438 3377
Fax: (61 2) 9439 1827

Samson Productions Pty Ltd
(Sue Milliken)
119 Pyrmont Street
Pyrmont NSW 2009
Tel: (61 2) 9660 3244
Fax: (61 2) 9692 8926

Southern Star Group Limited
(Errol Sullivan)
Level 9/8 West Street
North Sydney NSW 2060
Tel: (61 2) 9202 8555
Fax: (61 2) 9925 0849
e-mail: general@sstar.com.au

Stamen Films Pty Ltd
(Jonathan Shteinman)
PO Box 3226
Tamarama NSW 2026
Tel: (61 2) 9365 2284
Fax: (61 2) 9300 0264
e-mail: stamen@ozemail.com.au

Tristram Miall Films Pty Ltd
(Tristram Miall)
270 Devonshire Street
Surrey Hills NSW 2010
Tel: (61 2) 9310 2422
Fax: (61 2) 9318 2542
e-mail: tmfilm@zeta.org.au

Vertigo Productions Pty Ltd
(Rolf de Heer)
3 Butler Drive
Hendon SA 5014
Tel: (61 8) 8348 9382
Fax: (61 8) 8348 9347
e-mail: vertigo@adelaide.on.net

Village Roadshow Pictures
(Michael Lake)
Warner Roadshow Movie World
Studios
Pacific Highway
Oxenford QLD 4210
Tel: (61 7) 5588 6666
Fax: (61 7) 5573 3698
Web: www.village.com.au

Wintertime Films Pty Ltd
(John Winter)
48 Lamb Street
Lilyfield NSW 2040
Tel: (61 2) 9810 5271
Fax: (61 2) 9818 3640
e-mail: nomad@s054.aone.net.au

Working Dog Pty Ltd
(Santo Cilauro, Tom Gleisner,
Michael Hirsh, Jane Kennedy,
Rob Sitch)
PO Box 488
South Yarra VIC 3141
Tel: (61 3) 9826 4344
Fax: (61 3) 9826 4355
e-mail: dog@fox.net.au

Distributors

Note: The Beyond Group and
Southern Star are important
distributors (see producer list for
contact details).

Buena Vista International
Level 4, The Como Centre
650 Chapel Street
South Yarra
Victoria 3141
Tel: (61 3) 9826 5200
Fax: (61 3) 9826 6708

Columbia TriStar Films Pty Ltd
GPO Box 3342
Sydney NSW 2001
Tel: (61 2) 9272 2900
Fax: (61 2) 9272 2991

Dendy Films
19 Martin Place
Sydney NSW 2000
Tel: (61 2) 9233 8558
Fax: (61 2) 9232 3841
dendy@dendy.com.au

Footprint Films Pty Ltd
(same address as
Arenafilm Pty Ltd)

The Globe Film Company
373 Liverpool Street
Darlinghurst NSW 2010
Tel: (61 2) 9332 2722
Fax: (61 2) 9332 2888
e-mail: info@globefilm.com.au

Newvision Film Distributors Pty Ltd
252 Bay Street
Port Melbourne VIC 3207
Tel: (61 3) 9646 5555
Fax: (61 3) 9646 2411

Palace Films
233 Whitehorse Road
Balwyn VIC 3103
Tel: (61 3) 9817 6421
Fax: (61 3) 9817 4921
e-mail: palace@netspace.net.au

Roadshow Film Distributors
GPO Box 1411M
Melbourne VIC 3000
Tel: (61 3) 9667 6666
Fax: (61 3) 9662 1449

Ronin Films
PO Box 1005
Civic Square ACT 2600
Tel: (61 6) 248 0851
Fax: (61 6) 249 1640
e-mail: roninfilms@netinfo.com.au

Sharmill Films
4/200 Toorak Road
South Yarra VIC 3141
Tel: (61 3) 9826 9077
Fax: (61 3) 9826 1935

20th Century Fox Film Distributors Pty Ltd
505 George Street
Sydney NSW 2000
Tel: (61 2) 9273 7300
Fax: (61 2) 9283 2191

United International Pictures
208 Clarence Street
Sydney NSW 2000
Tel: (61 2) 9264 7444
Fax: (61 2) 9264 2499

Universal Pictures International
PO Box 17
Millers Point NSW 2000
Tel: (61 2) 9207 0500
Fax: (61 2) 9251 9654

Useful Addresses

Australian Film Finance Corporation
130 Elizabeth Street
Sydney NSW 2000
Postal address: GPO Box 3886
Sydney NSW 2001
Tel: (61 2) 9268 2555
Fax: (61 2) 9264 8551
www.ffc.gov.au

Australian Film Commission
150 William Street
Wooloomooloo NSW 2011
GPO Box 3984
Sydney 2001
Tel: (61 2) 9321 6444
Fax: (61 2) 9357 3737
e-mail: info@afc.gov.au
www.afc.gov.au

Australian Film, Television and Radio School
PO Box 126
North Ryde NSW 2113
Tel: (61 2) 9805 6611
Fax: (61 2) 9887 1030
e-mail: direct.sales@syd.aftrs.edu.au

Film Australia
101 Eton Road
Lindfield NSW 2070
Tel: (61 2) 9413 8777
Fax: (61 2) 9416 9401

More information can be found via the Web on www.nla.gov.au/oz/gov/. Also www.sna.net.au for Screen Network Australia which is a gateway to more than 250 film and television sites.

AUSTRIA

Beat Glur

The most notable event in Austrian cinema in 1998 was the success of a film that virtually no one has heard about beyond the nation's borders. **Hinterholz 8**, released in autumn 1998, became Austria's first blockbuster. The black comedy about a family's dream of a perfect home that turns into a nightmare, became the biggest ever Austrian box-office hit in Austrian cinema.

If it had not been for *Titanic*, the DOR Film production would have topped the year's box-office chart, with a total of more than 600,000 admissions – 25,000 more than 1997's top hit, *Men in Black*. It beat the previous mark (440,000 admissions) set by *Mueller's Office (Müllers Büro)* 13 years ago.

Director Harald Sicheritz had enjoyed success with his first two features, *Mother's Day (Muttertag*, 1993) and *Replay (Freispiel*, 1995), both comedies. But the popularity of *Hinterholz 8* (the name of the small, remote and run-down farmhouse the family buys) surprised everyone, including the inde-

pendent distributor Filmladen, which was short of prints throughout the film's run.

Though everybody knows how exceptional a domestic hit like this is, and though *Hinterholz 8* did not add much to the artistic reputation of the Austrian film industry, it had a tremendous effect on public opinion, and among government and television executives. Hollywood films still dominate the market, but *Hinterholz 8* has shattered the old stereotype that the public is simply not interested in domestic films, and as a result the amount of trust placed in Austrian productions has grown.

The Austrian film industry depends heavily on state subsidies. Following the amended Film Promotion Act, an automatic merit system launched two years ago which has already proven its value, Austrian chancellor Viktor Klima is pushing for an increase in government arts funding, with additional priority for film production. At the same time the new management of the ORF, the state

Roland Düringer in HINTERHOLZ 8
photo: Petro Domenigg

broadcasting company, has promised to do more for the promotion of Austrian cinema.

Destination Vienna

The promotion of Vienna as a location for foreign film productions has also come along well. Since the reopening of the film studios on the Rosenhügel in November 1995 and the creation of the Filmstadt Wien, the capital of Austria has somewhat regained its reputation as a location for international film-making, and is heading to become number four in German-language cinema after Munich, Cologne and Berlin.

The Vienna Film Financing Fund, launched in 1992 by the city council, attracts foreign productions via conditionally repayable loans. The main conditions are that a Viennese is engaged as co-producer and that at least 30% of the loan is spent in the city. Last year, $8m was spent on films meeting these criteria.

With the huge success of *Hinterholz 8*, the market share of domestic productions rose from a mere 2–3% in recent years to a respectable 8%, an all-time record in new Austrian cinema. Due to the record of *Titanic*, which sold almost 1.4 million tickets, 1998 was, like in many European countries, a very good year for Austria's distributors and exhibitors, too. Total admissions have risen from 12.3 million in 1996, to 13.7 million in 1997 and 15.2 million in 1998. On average, each Austrian went to the movies 1.8 times in 1998, a substantial increase compared with 1.4 annual visits two years ago.

The major increase in admissions may also be due to the number of new cinemas that opened recently. Since 1994, when UCI inaugurated the first nine-screen multiplex in Vienna, there has been a boom in multiplexing in Austria that is set to change the cinema landscape dramatically. The seating capacity in Vienna alone, with four more multiplexes opening in 1999, will increase by more than 50%, to a total of some 25,000 seats.

Encouragingly, *Hinterholz 8* was not the year's only successful domestic production. Nikolaus Leytner's black comedy **Three Gentlemen** (*Drei Herren*), which premiered in November, has sold more than 100,000 tickets, and Reinhard Schwabenitzky's comedy sequel **An Almost Perfect Wedding** (*Eine fast perfekte Hochzeit*) came close to 100,000.

Future films which justify great expectations include Sicheritz's new production, **Wanted**, Thomas Roth's **Way Out** (*Der Baldower*), and Barbara Albert's first feature, **North Side** (*Nordrand*). Austria also has great hopes for the long-awaited, high-budget **Everyman's Feast** (*Jedermanns Fest*), by Fritz Lehner, with Juliette Greco and Klaus Maria Brandauer in the leads, and the new Haneke film, **Unknown Code** (*Code inconnu*), shot in French and produced by MK2, with Juliette Binoche.

BEAT GLUR is a Swiss film and music critic, editor of the cultural department of the Swiss News Agency, a member of the Swiss Federal Film Commission and a member of the Cultural Commission of Suissimage.

FILMCATALOGUES
FILM NEWS
FILMFESTIVALS

AUSTRIAN FILM COMMISSION

STIFTGASSE 6 • A-1070 VIENNA

TEL.(+431)526 33 23 FAX (+431)526 6801

E-MAIL   AFILMCO@MAGNET.AT

WEBSITE WWW.AFC.AT

PRESENTATION
INFORMATION
PROMOTION

Forthcoming Films

EIN FLÜCHTIGER ZUG NACH DEM ORIENT
(A Fast Train to the Orient)

Documentary. Script and Dir: Ruth Beckermann. Phot: Nurith Aviv, Sophie Cadet. Prod: Aichholzer Film

DER BALDOWER (Way Out)

Script: Thomas Roth, Robert Treichler, Martin Daniel. Dir: Roth. Phot: Helmut Pirnat. Players: Marek Harloff, Jürgen Hentsch, Dieter Pfaff. Prod: DOR Film.

DIE JUNGFRAU (The Virgin)

Script and Dir: Diego Donnhofer. Phot: Peter Roehsler. Players: Kirsty Hinchcliffe, Joey Kern. Prod: Nanook Film.

GEBOREN IN ABSURDISTAN
(Born in Absurdistan)

Script: Houchang Allahyari, Darius Allahyari, Agnes Pluch. Dir:

Houchang Allahyari. Phot: Helmut Pirnat. Players: Karl Markovics, Julia Stemberger. Prod: Epo-Film.

NORDRAND (Northside)

Script and Dir: Barbara Albert. Phot: Christine Maier. Players: Nina Proll, Edita Malovcic. Prod: Lotus-Film/zero-Film/Fama Film.

HUNDSTAGE (Dog Days)

Script and Dir: Ulrich Seidl. Phot: Wolfgang Thaler. Players: Alfred Mrwa, Maria Hofstätter. Prod: Allegro Film.

MONDVATER (Moonfather)

Script: Irakli Kvirikadze. Dir: Bakhtiar Khoudoinazarov. Phot: Rotislav Piroumov. Players: Chulpan Khamatova, Moritz Bleibtreu, Merab Ninidse. Prod: Prisma Film/Pandora Film/Les Films de l'Observatoire/Thomas Koerfer Film.

JEDERMANNS FEST
(Everyman's Feast)

Script and Dir: Fritz Lehner. Phot: Gernot Roll, Wolfgang Treu. Players: Klaus Maria Brandauer, Juliette Gréco. Prod: Wega Film/Studio Babelsberg/Star Production.

DER UMWEG
(The Detour)

Script and Dir: Frouke Fokkema. Players: Joachim Bissmeier, Tamara van den Dop. Prod: Sigma Pictures Productions/Lotus-Film/Lichtspiel Filmproduktion.

WANTED

Script: Alfred Dorfer. Dir: Harald Sicheritz. Phot: Helmut Pirnat. Players: Alfred Dorfer, Erwin Steinhauer, Michael Niavarani. Prod: MR-TV Film.

Producers

**Allegro Film
Produktionsges.m.b.H.**
(Helmut Grasser)
Krummgasse 1a
A-1030 Vienna
Tel: (43 1) 712 5036
Fax: (43 1) 712 5036-20

Cult-FilmproduktionsgmbH
Niki List
Spittelberggasse 3/7
A-1070 Vienna
Tel: (43 1) 526 00 06
Fax: (43 1) 526 00 06–16
e-mail: cultfilm@cultfilm.com

Dor Film Produktionsges.m.b.H.
(Danny Krausz/Kurt Stocker)
Neulerchenfelderstrasse 12
A-1160 Vienna
Tel: (43 1) 402 2138
Fax: (43 1) 402 2139
e-mail: dorfilm@magnet.at

Eclypse Filmpartner Gmbh
(Arno Ortmair)
Hietzinger Hauptstrasse 11
A-1130 Vienna
Tel: (43 1) 877 6393
Fax: (43 1) 877 3564
e-mail: 106037,2557@compuserve.
com

Epo-Film Produktionsges.m.b.H.
(Dieter Pochlatko)
Edelsinnstrasse 58
A-1120 Vienna
Tel: (43 1) 812 3718
Fax: (43 1) 812 3718-9
e-mail: office@epo-film.co.at

**Extrafilm Arbeitsgemeinschaft
Film & Video Ges.m.b.H.**
(Bernd Neuburger/Lukas Stepanik)
Grosse Neugasse 44/24
A-1040 Vienna
Tel: (43 1) 581 7896
Fax: (43 1) 587 2743
e-mail: stepanik@aon.at

Fischer Film
Markus Fischer
Scharitzerstraße 12
A-4020 Linz
Tel: (43 732) 600 606
Fax: (43 732) 600 606–3

Lotus-Film Ges.m.b.H.
Erich Lackner
Johnstraße 83

A-1150 Vienna
Tel: (43 1) 786 3387
Fax: (43 1) 786 3387–11
office@lotus-film.co.at

**MR Film Kurt Mrkwicka
Ges.m.b.H.**
Kurt Mrkwicka
Auhofstraße 70
A-1130 Vienna
Tel: (43 1) 876 8715
Fax: (43 1) 876 8715–10
k-mrkwickasr@mr-film.com

Neue Studio Film GmbH
Peter Pochlatko
Hietzinger Hauptstrasse 11
A-1130 Vienna
Tel: (43 1) 877 6253
Fax: (43 1) 877 3564
e-mail: 106037,2557@compuserve.
com

**Nikolaus Geyrhalter
Filmproduktion**
Nikolaus Geyrhalter
Hildebrandtgasse 21
A-1180 Vienna
Tel/Fax: (43 1) 403 0162
nikolaus.geyrhalter@blackbox.at

Prisma Film Produktion GmbH
Heinz Stussak/Michael Seeber
Neubaugasse 8/1
A-1070 Vienna
Tel: (43 1) 522 8325
Fax: (43 1) 522 8325–28
film@prisma-wien.at

**Satel Fernseh- und
Filmproduktions Ges.m.b.H.**
Michael Wolkenstein
Wiedner Hauptstraße 68
A-1040 Vienna
Tel: (43 1) 588 720
Fax: (43 1) 588 72–106
106114.2540@compuserve.com

Teamfilm Produktion
Ges.m.b.H.
Wulf Flemming
Waaggasse 5
A- 1040 Vienna
Tel: (43 1) 587 37 04–0
Fax: (43 1) 587 25 42–75

**Terra Film
Produktionsges.m.b.H.**
Norbert Blecha
Lienfeldergasse 39
A-1160 Vienna
Tel: (43 1) 484 1101-0
Fax: (43 1) 484 1101-27
e-mail: terrafilm@magnet.at

Wega-Filmproduktionsges.m.b.H.
Veit Heiduschka
Hägelingasse 13
A-1140 Vienna
Tel: (43 1) 982 5742
Fax: (43 1) 982 5833

Distributors

Buena Vista (Austria) Gmbh
Ferdinand Morawetz
Hermanngasse 18
A-1071 Vienna
Tel: (43 1) 526 9467
Fax: (43 1) 526 9468-5
e-mail: ferdinand_morawetz@
studio.disney.com

Centfox-Film Ges.m.b.H.
Roman Hörmann
Neubaugasse 35
A-1070 Vienna
Tel: (43 1) 523 2629
Fax: (43 1) 526 7297

**Columbia TriStar Filmverleih
Ges.m.b.H.**
Hermann Hobodides
Wallgasse 21
A-1060 Vienna
Tel: (43 1) 597 1515
Fax: (43 1) 597 1516
e-mail: columbiatristaraustria@
compuserve.com

**Concorde Media Beteiligungs
GmbH**
Herbert Kloiber
Seilergasse 15
A-1010 Vienna
Tel: (43 1) 513 2728

**Constantin-Film Verleih-,
Vertriebs- &
Produktionsges.m.b.H.**
Christian Langhammer
Siebensterngasse 37
A-1070 Vienna
Tel: (43 1) 5212 8122
Fax: (43 1) 5212 8160

Filmladen
Michael Stejskal
Mariahilferstrasse 58
A-1070 Vienna
Tel: (43 1) 523 4362
Fax: (43 1) 526 4749
e-mail: m.stejskal@vip.at

Polyfilm Verleih
Hans König, Christa Auderlitzky
Margaretenstrasse 78
A-1050 Vienna
Tel: (43 1) 581 3900-20
Fax: (43 1) 581 3900-39
e-mail: polyfilm@polyfilm.at

Stadtkino
Franz Schwartz
Spittelberggasse 3
A-1070 Vienna
Tel: (43 1) 522 4814
Fax: (43 1) 522 4815

U.I.P. Filmverleih GmbH. UIP
Steven O'Dell
Neubaugasse 1, P.O.Box 280
A-1071 Vienna
Tel: (43 1) 523 4631
Fax: (43 1) 526 7548

Warner Bros Ges.m.b.H.
Ingeborg König
Zieglergasse 10
A-1070 Vienna
Tel: (43 1) 523 8626-0
Fax: (43 1) 523 8626-31

Useful Addresses

Association of the Audiovisual and Film Industry
Elmar A. Peterlunger
Wiedner Hauptstraße 63
P.O. Box 327
A-1045 Vienna
Tel: (43 1) 501 05–3010
Fax: (43 1) 501 05–276
film@fafo.at

Austrian Broadcasting Corporation (ORF)
Würzburggasse 30
A-1136 Vienna
Tel: (43 1) 87878–0
www.orf.at/orf/home.htm

Austrian Film Commission
Martin Schweighofer
Stiftgasse 6
A-1070 Vienna
Tel: (43 1) 526 3323-200
Fax: (43 1) 526 6801
e-mail: afilmco@magnet.at
www.afc.at

Austrian Film Institute
Mag. Gerhard Schedl
Spittelberggasse 3
A-1070 Vienna
Tel: (43 1) 526 9730-400
Fax: (43 1) 526 9730-440
e-mail: oefi@filminstitut.or.at

Filmstadt Wien Studio
Ges.m.b.H. Speisinger Str. 121–127
A-1230 Vienna
Tel: (43 1) 889 1117
Tel: (43 1) 889 1293
office@filmstadt-wien.com

Location Austria
Austrian Business Agency
Opernring 3
A-1010 Vienna
Tel: (43 1) 588 5836
Fax: (43 1)586 8659
e.unterberger@aba.gv.at

Vienna Film Financing Fund
(Wiener Filmfinanzierungsfonds)
Wolfgang Ainberger
Stiftgasse 6/2/3
A-1070 Vienna
Tel: (43 1) 526 5088
Fax: (43 1) 526 5088-20
e-mail: wff@wff.at

BELGIUM

Patrick Duynslaegher

By winning the Palme d'Or at Cannes with **Rosetta**, director brothers Luc and Jean-Pierre Dardenne (*La Promesse*) achieved a first for Belgian cinema and confirmed their talent for hard-hitting social drama, as poignant and pure as it is uncompromising. Rosetta, intensely played by newcomer Emilie Dequenne (who shared the Cannes Best Actress award) is an 18-year-old living on a trailer park in an industrial wasteland on the outskirts of Liège. While her alcoholic mother has given up all hope of a normal life, Rosetta struggles on.

The film shows her ferocious battle to secure and hold on to a job, and the remarkable sacrifices she is willing to make, including betraying the one man who wishes her well. The Dardenne brothers follow their stubborn heroine – part saint, part madwoman – in a crudely direct, hand-held camera style. The film jumps relentlessly from one emotionally disturbing scene to another, from Rosetta's violent reaction when she gets the sack at the factory, to a shocking suicide attempt.

Another Cannes favourite, in the Directors Fortnight, was **The Carriers Are Waiting** (*Les convoyeurs attendent*), the first feature by documentary film-maker Benoît Mariage. His portrait of a struggling family living on the outskirts of an impoverished

Emilie Dequenne in the Palme d'Or-winning ROSETTA

industrial town (Charleroi) is no less bleak than *Rosetta*. But Mariage counters the sombre outlook with black humour and some bold formal choices: the film is shot in deeply contrasted black-and-white, the widescreen compositions are superb, and the long-held shots are part of a rigorous *mise en scène*.

This family chronicle is dominated by the father, a benevolent tyrant who desperately wants his family to succeed at the dawn of the new millennium. He hopes to reach this goal by training his adolescent son to win a car by setting an absurd record: opening and closing a door 40,000 times in 24 hours.

Belgian cinema's strongest-ever showing at Cannes, with the new Chantal Akerman documentary **South** (*Sud*) hailed as a masterpiece by *Le Monde*, was a triumph for the film policy in the French-speaking community. After many years, the policy of supporting and encouraging auteur cinema, and stimulating film-makers who have strong voices, has finally paid off.

National strife, colonial ghosts

With the ironically-titled **Pure Fiction**, Marion Handwerker offered a fictionalised account of the child murder scandal that sent shockwaves through Belgium in 1996. Her non-sensationalist approach may actually have worked against this deserving film, which disappeared quickly from the cinemas. A very minor affair is **The Wall** (*Le Mur*), Alain Berliner's entry in the series *2000 Seen By*. On the eve of the millennium, Belgian language quarrels have finally split the country neatly in two, dividing the francophones and the Flemish. During the night a wall has been erected, forcing the hero – who runs a French fries stand – to take sides. The few sharp comments in this heavy-handed satire were swamped by the half-baked demagoguery and poetic, surrealist banality.

Two films dealt with our colonial past in the Belgian Congo. In **ID** (*Pièces d'identités*), a mild satire set in Matongue, the Zairian quarter of Brussels, Congolese film-maker Mweze Ngangura shows the remnants of the Belgian colonial past and focuses on a zany cast of characters in search of their African identity. Most of the story is seen through the bemused eyes of a Zairian king searching for his long-lost daughter, and discovering a society which is less paternalistic, but also less comforting, than the one he encountered during his first visit to Brussels, for the World Expo of 1958.

Zaire's former ruler examined in MOBUTU, ROI DU ZAIRE

In **Mobutu, King of Zaire** (*Mobutu, Roi du Zaire*), the documentarist Thierry Michel spins a revealing history lesson about the rise and fall of Mobutu Sese Seko, the journalist-turned-soldier who seized power in the Congo in 1965 and renamed it Zaire. Chronologically told, the film is sometimes overly didactic in explaining the endurance of the long-time African dictator (his Washington-backed reign of oppression lasted until 1997), but offers a wealth of previously-unseen newsreels, plucked from archives in Kinshasa.

Damien: a horror story

While French-language films prosper, Flemish cinema is still struggling to find its own voice, hindered by a government policy as unrealistic as it is megalomaniac. The attempt to create a local film industry with international appeal led to a major disaster: **Father Damien**, an academic biopic about the Flemish priest who devoted his life to missionary work among the lepers deported by the Hawaiian government to Kalaupapa, on Molokai Island, in 1873.

As no other production in recent years, *Father Damien* exposed the incongruities of the Flemish film policy. While officials promote strongly the dubious notion of a cinema reflecting the Flemish cultural identity, what we have here is a $10m international co-production, helmed by the Australian arthouse director Paul Cox, that downplays completely the Flemish origins of the subject matter.

By concentrating the story exclusively on the 16 years Damien spent on Molokai and allowing no flashbacks, the film cuts out the Flemish background of the missionary completely, including the social conditions in nineteenth-century Flanders that shaped Damien's decision to sacrifice himself. Worse still, Damien's proselytising is shown without any critical distance; the well-intentioned depiction of the miserable conditions in the leper settlement plays more as a Monty Python sketch than as religious drama.

Cox's culpability in this mish-mash is difficult to gauge, since he was sidelined in post-production, with his producer and even some of the bankers having their say in the editing. Cox threatened to take his name off the film, and dissociated himself from the results. After a lukewarm reception at the local box-office, there seems to be a new export version in the making, under the title *Molokai*.

Young, gifted and bleak

Happily there were some better and more vital Flemish productions, notably two portraits of rebellious young girls, one directed by promising newcomer Patrice Toye, the other by veteran helmer Guido Henderickx; both films boast strong performances from remarkable child actresses.

In **Rosie: the Devil in My Head**, Toye takes us into the mind of a 13-year old girl, brilliantly played by first-timer Aranka Coppens. In the first scenes, Rosie arrives in a juvenile detention centre; flashbacks explain how she got there. A story of claustrophobic family life, lack of mother love, incest, reckless and sometimes self-destructive behaviour. Rosie escapes her grey surroundings in a rich fantasy life, fed by paperback romances. Inventing a young soulmate increases her self-absorbed, obsessive behaviour, with dire consequences. In spite of the grainy realism and gutsy intimacy, the psychological mystery is quite conventional.

S. is a raw, provocative low-budget production, shot in 13 days in a style as freewheeling as the traumatised young woman at its centre. S. is looking for love, not an easy thing to find in the peep show where she works. Her promiscuous odyssey is full of sexual audacity, her life flashes on the screen as one hallucinogenic, voyeuristic trip – but somehow the director Guido Henderickx avoids the pitfalls of the exploitation genre. This tautly-edited and furiously-paced tale is occasionally inter-cut with S.'s video diary, thus adding to the multi-layered visuals. The nihilistic outlook on life is neither profound nor illuminating, but Henderickx's cinematic flair is undeniable, and debutante actress Natali Broods is terrific.

Eco-fable and children's adventure film meet in **The Ball** (*De Bal*), a promising first feature from Dany Deprez (director) and Jean-Claude Van Ryckeghem (screenwriter-producer). Thanks to a magic ball, lonely

Still from Dany Deprez's THE BALL

eleven-year old Sophia finds new friends, restores her self-confidence and fights the city planners whose projects threaten children and the environment.

Finally, two satirical one-note comedies about film-making, both with international casts. In-jokes abound in **Shades**, a thriller full of twists, which is firmly rooted in the Antwerp film scene. Erik Van Looy plays freely, and ironically, with a handful of stock characters – the has-been director (played by a star who has himself seen better days, Mickey Rourke), the cynical producer and his actress girlfriend, who will do anything to advance her career, and throws an escaped serial killer in the mix.

Jean-Philippe Toussaint's **The Ice Rink** (*La Patinoire*) is a much more stylised affair, its action entirely confined to a film studio, with the titular arena as its central set. Toussaint has a ball with the egomaniac foibles, overwhelming libidos and insecurities of the film world, but his ice-skating concept is also an excuse for some old-fashioned slapstick.

PATRICK DUYNSLAEGHER is film critic for *Knack*, the leading Belgian weekly. His articles have appeared in *Variety, Sight and Sound* and other periodicals. He has written a book on André Delvaux, a guide for films on television and video, and a history, through 2,000 reviews, of a hundred years of cinema.

Recent and Forthcoming Films

THE JUST JUDGES

Script: Guido Van Meir. Dir: Vincent Rouffaer. Phot: Jan Vancaillie. Players: Maria Schneider, Dirk Roofthooft, Johan Leysen. Prod: Eric Kint (Itinera Films).

THE IRON MAN

Script and Dir: Vincent Bal. Phot: Glynn Speeckaert. Players: Ides

Meire, Peter Gorissen, Charlotte de Ruyter. Prod: Dirk Impens, Rudy Verzyck (Favourite Films).

FORGOTTEN STREET

Script: Bob Goossens. Dir: Luc Pien. Phot: Glynn Speeckaert. Players: Mark Peeters, Jos Verbist, Tuur Deweert. Prod: Tharsi Vanhuysse, Grietje Lammertyn (Era Films).

PAULINE AND PAULETTE

Script: Jaak Boon, Lieven Debrauwer. Dir: Debrauwer. Players: Dora vander Groen, Ann Petersen, Chris Lomme. Prod: Dominique Janne (K2).

EVERYBODY FAMOUS!

Script and Dir: Dominique Deruddere. Prod: Otomatic.

SOFT SOAP

Script: Fernand Auwera. Dir: Robbe De Hert. Players: Koen De Bouw, Mike Verdrengh, Willeke van Ammelrooy, Sylvia Kristel. Prod: Ruud den Drijver, Michel Houdmont (Cineventura, Signature Films).

LE DERNIER PLAN

Script: Benoît Peeters, Sandrine Willems, Pierre Drouot. Dir: Peeters. Phot: Ella Van Den Hove. Players: Florin Piersic Jr.,

Manuela Servais, Mihai Dinvale, Pierre Arditi. Prod: Les Piérides.

POURQUOI SE MARIER LE JOUR DE LA FIN DU MONDE

Script: Harry Cleven. Dir: Harry Cleven. Phot: Zvonock. Players: Jean-Henri Compère, Elina Löwensohn, Pascal Gréggory. Prod: Patrick Quinet, Jani Thiltges.

LES SIESTES GRENADINE

Script: Mahmoud Ben Mahmoud.

Dir: Mahmoud Ben Mahmoud. Phot: Gilberto Azevedo. Players: Yasmine Bahri, Hicham Rostom, Loubna Azabaal. Prod: Hassen Daldoul, Luc Dardenne.

UNE LIAISON PORNOGRAPHIQUE

Script and Dir: Ferédéric Fonteyne. Phot: Virginie Saint-Martin. Players: Nathalie Baye, Sergi Lopez, Jacques Viala. Prod: Patrick Quinet, Claude Waringo, Alain Rocca, Laurent Pétin, Rolf Schmid.

Producers

Corsan Productions
J. De Hasquestraat 7
2000 Antwerp
Tel: (32 3) 234 2518
Fax: (32 3) 226 2158

D.D.D. 1867
Avenue de la Jonction
1190 Brussels
Tel: (32 2) 344 0201
Fax: (32 2) 344 0201

Emotion Pictures
Volaardestraat 250
5200 Dendermonde
Tel: (32 52) 413 783

Favorite Films
Vandenbusschestraat 3
1030 Brussels
Tel: (32 2) 242 4510
Fax: (32 2) 242 1408

Fugitive Cinema
Prinsesstraat 35
2000 Antwerp
Tel: (32 3) 234 3674
Fax: (32 3) 232 8684

Independent Productions
Sphere Business Park
Doornveld 1 Box 42
1731 Zellik
Tel: (32 2) 463 1130
Fax: (32 2) 466 9460

Kunst en Kino
Avenue Louise 32/4
1050 Brussels
Tel: (32 2) 511 6341
Fax: (32 2) 512 6874

La Nouvelle Imagerie
Avenue Jacques Pastur 90
1080 Brussels
Tel: (32 2) 646 3946
Fax: (32 2) 646 3946

Lamy Films
Moensberg 57,
1180 Brussels
Tel: (32 2) 375 3442
Fax: (32 2) 375 3271

Les Films de la Drève
Rue de la Victoire 175
1060 Brussels
Tel: (32 2) 537 8894

Man's Films
Avenue Mostinck 65
1150 Brussels
Tel: (32 2) 771 7137
Fax: (32 2) 771 9612

Multimedia
Nieuwstraat 99
1730 Asse
Tel: (32 2) 453 0304
Fax: (32 2) 453 0920

Useful Addresses

Communauté Française de Belgique
Boulevard Léopold II, 44
1080 Brussels
Tel: (32 2) 413 2221
Fax: (32 2) 413 2068

Flanders Image
Handelskaai 18/2
1000 Brussels
Tel: (32 2) 219 3222
Fax: (32 2) 219 3402

Ministry of the Flemish Community
Koloniënstraat 29-31
1000 Brussels
Tel: (32 2) 510 3411
Fax: (32 2) 510 3651

Wallonie Bruxelles Image
Boulevard Adolphe Max 13
1000 Brussels
Tel: (32 2) 233 2304
Fax: (32 2) 218 3424

Still from Benoît Mariage's THE CARRIERS ARE WAITING

BOSNIA & HERZEGOVINA — Rada Šešić

Four years after the end of the war, film production in Bosnia and Herzegovina has yet to be re-established. There is no feature production, and while a few happy film professionals manage to perform their craft under exceptional circumstances, such as the occasional visit by an international film crew, the majority remain out of work.

Two years after it was first given a green light, septuagenarian Croatian director Veljko Bulajić's epic film about the war, **Sarajevo**, had still not begun shooting when this report went to press (the revised start-date was given as August 1999). Although one of the film's co-producers is Bosnia's Bosnafilm, Bulajić's outsider status means he faces ongoing animosity from the majority of the Bosnian film industry.

The most important event of the last season was the production of several shorts by young directors, under the auspices of the International Film Festival of Sarajevo. The main goal was to promote and develop quality in Bosnian cinema. Young local talent could apply to the new Film Festival Fund and eight projects were selected.

Six of them were presented at the Sarajevo Festival in August 1998, and gained exposure at many other festivals, including Rotterdam, where they were shown collectively in a strand called "Made in Bosnia". Each deserves individual attention.

Twin perspectives

Jasmila Žbanić filmed her documentary *We Light the Night* (*Noc jé, mi svijetlimo*) in the month of Ramadan, as twin brothers reflect on their war experiences. Ines Tanović's

Still from THE END OF UNPLEASANT TIMES

Syndrome (*Sindrom*) examines the shifting behavioural boundaries amongst people who have lived through a war, specifically the two young men who terrorise people on a Sarajevan tram late at night. *724*, directed by Dino Mustafić, deals with an actual war situation, but only in the dream of a potential soldier.

Trip to the Moon (*Put na mjesec*), directed by Srdjan Vuletić, is a witty story showing a day in the life of a typical Sarajevan bum. *The End of Unpleasant Times* (*Kraj doba neprijatnosti*), by another gifted director, Pjer Žalica, who did his best work during the war years, is a sensitive love story depicting the loneliness of old people in Sarajevo. Using soft and occasionally over-exposed photography, Žalica created a unique piece of film poetry.

The Man Who Exchanged His Home for a Tunnel (*Čovjek koji je zamijenio kuću za tunel*), Elmir Jukić's second work, differs from the other five shorts because of its classical structure. The documentary tells the story of a man under whose house a tunnel was dug as an escape route from Sarajevo.

Beyond the Looking Glass, the second part of "Made in Bosnia", consisted of videos premiered at the Sarajevo festival. The whole project was financed by the SOROS Foundation and gave film-making opportunities to 15 young visual artists. Also presented at the festival was *Lights and Shadows* (*Sjene i Svjetla*), a compilation of five animated films created by schoolchildren, under the guidance of two instructors from Bosnia and Herzegovina and one from Belgium.

One of the old masters of domestic documentary-making, Vefik Hadžismajlović, compiled a new film from footage shot at the beginning of the war, but edited only recently. *B'ezrat Hašem*, follows the Jewish population of Sarajevo during the war and concentrates on their dilemma: whether to leave or stay.

During the years of destruction, the Bosnian Cinemathek lost hundreds of film reels. Having consolidated its remaining resources, the organisation is now fully operational again and at the Sarajevo festival it presented the ten best Bosnian features of the last 50 years, as voted by the country's film critics.

Absurdity of war

The only Bosnian feature screened at festivals worldwide was **Unexpected Walk** (*Neočekivana šetnja*), directed by Frenchman François Lunel. The film was shot between 1994 and 1997, when the director was living in Sarajevo and sharing the fate of its citizens. His first-hand experience enabled him to show quite provocatively the absurdity of the war situation. In the spirit of Ionesco's theatre, the film unveils the everyday life of three close friends under harsh circumstances. The main role was brilliantly played by Senad Basić, whose wife Jasna produced the film.

Provocateur (*Provokator*), an animated short directed by Nedžad Begovič, had its premiere at the Oberhausen Short Film Festival. Using a style similar to his first success, *EKG*, in which he draws only simple lines and creates very rich and imaginative sound effects, Begovič focuses on a man who tries to provoke everybody with his brutality. The drawings were made during the war – on the last unbroken window panes in Begovič's house.

The government still cannot find the means to fund regular production, but the Ministry of Culture of Kanton Sarajevo sponsored a very big and important project: a published Filmography of all films and videos produced during the war years, 1992–1995. It describes in English and Bosnian more than 100 works, mainly war testimonies and personal expressions documenting the tragedy.

The domestic cinema repertoire does not differ much from that of other European countries, consisting largely of mainstream American films. But now and then independent films do find their way to the smaller theatres, especially when they are promoted at the Sarajevo Festival. Indeed, the arthouses are where most Serbian, Croatian and Slovenian films are released.

RADA ŠEŠIĆ is a film critic and director. Since leaving Sarajevo in 1992 she has lived in the Netherlands, writing for film magazine *Skrien* and lecturing at Utrecht University. She is currently working on two short films from her own scripts.

Producers

SAGA Film Production
Hakije Kulenovića 7
71 000 Sarajevo
Fax: (387 71) 666 811
e-mail: saga@sagafilm.com

Stop Film
Buka 5
71 000 Sarajevo
Tel/Fax: (387 71) 665 393

Ton-Light Film
R. Abazovića 2
71 000 Sarajevo
Tel/Fax: (387 71) 520 897

Kaleidoskop
Kevrin potok 18–1
71 000 Sarajevo
Tel: (387 71) 678 233
Fax: (387 71) 202 273

HEFT prod. comp.
71 000 Sarajevo
Tel/Fax: (387 71) 133 568

Sarajevo International Production Company
Maršala Tita 54–1
71 000 Sarajevo
Tel: (387 71) 200 392
Fax: (387 71) 211 972

Useful Addresses

National Film Archive of BiH
Alipašina 19
71 000 Sarajevo
Tel/Fax: (387 71) 668 678

Association of Film Workers
Štrosmajerova 1
71 000 Sarajevo

SINEAST Film Magazine
Strosmajerova 1
71 000 Sarajevo
Phone: (387 71) 212 377
Fax: (387 71) 470 029

Sarajevo Film Festival
Obala Kulina Bana
71 000 Sarajevo

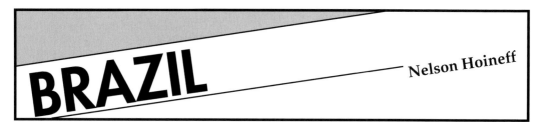

BRAZIL — Nelson Hoineff

The huge international success of **Central Station** (*Central do Brasil*) did not necessarily reflect the mood of the Brazilian film industry in 1998–99. Walter Salles' movie won a total of more than 40 awards at home and abroad, including the Golden Bear at Berlin and the British Academy Award for Best Foreign Film, and was nominated for two Oscars (Best Foreign Language Film and Best Actress, for Fernanda Montenegro).

Yet *Central Station* was one of the few Brazilian movies to do well at the local box-office. In fact, this has been a disappointing period for most Brazilian producers, as local audiences failed to respond to local films, and investors more than halved their contributions to production budgets. The Rouanet and Audio-Visual laws, on which the Brazilian industry depends so heavily, allow for a maximum of $120m to be invested in film production each year, but in 1998 only $35m was spent, compared to $75m in 1997.

The laws, which allow deductions of up to 3% in the income tax payable by companies investing in films, are currently under fire from producers and investors. Producers claim that companies tend to invest only in politically correct projects, because they do not want to see their names associated with potentially controversial themes.

On the other hand, companies such as Fiat and Gessy-Lever, are refraining from further film investment because in the majority of cases they have not even had a chance to recoup their money at the box-office, with film projects abandoned at the pre-production stage, or completed but never released. According to a survey by *Cultural Marketing* magazine, of 624 projects approved under the Audio-Visual law between 1995 and 1998, only 72 were actually released.

Globo's world

Last year, however, saw the creation of Globofilmes, the movie arm of the giant Brazilian media conglomerate, Globo. Globofilmes co-produced films that were in some cases spin-offs of popular TV shows, like **Simao the Troublesome Ghost** (*Simao, o Fantasma Trapalhao*), with popular comedian Renato Aragao, and **Fooling Around on TV** (*Zoando na TV*), starring TV host Angelica. Globofilmes was also an important partner of Rio Vermelho Filmes in the production of Cacáa Diegues' **Orfeu**.

Based on the play *Orfeu do Carnaval* by Vinicius de Moraes (which also inspired Marcel Camus' *Black Orpheus*), this adaptation has Orfeu as a Samba composer who falls in love with the beautiful Euridice. As they plan to escape from the violence of the last day of the Rio Carnival, Euridice is killed by a drug dealer, who was once Orfeu's best friend. Beautifully photographed by Affonso Beato and featuring a remarkable production design and a fine original score by Vinicius and Tom Jobim, *Orfeu* was the first Brazilian picture released by Warner Bros and sold more than a million tickets domestically.

The first three Globofilmes productions accounted for 75% of the total attendance for Brazilian films in 1998, around four million, but that figure represents less than 5% of the total attendance for all titles. Cinema owners are obliged by law to show Brazilian films for a minimum of 49 days a year but most Brazilian titles reached less than 60,000 viewers and many were seen by only 2,000–3,000 – a cause for huge concern in an industry where average feature budgets are around $2m.

However, forthcoming films by Salles (*O Primeiro Dia / Midnight*, co-directed with Daniela Thomas), Sergio Rezende (*Maua, the Emperor and the King*), Ruy Guerra (*Estorvo*), Zelito Vianna (*Villa-Lobos*), Bruno Barreto (*Miss Simpson*) and Miguel Farias (*Xango de Baker Street*) are expected to boost attendance for Brazilian films in 1999–2000.

Other important developments include the growth of the distributor Lumiere, which picked up some of the most important local films and secured exclusive rights to Miramax titles, and the construction of new multiplexes. Major players like Cinemark and UCI have made their first forays into Brazil, forcing traditional exhibitors, like Severiano Ribeiro and Art Films, to close many old cinemas, open new ones and establish partnerships with the newcomers, dramatically changing the habits of film viewing in Brazil.

NELSON HOINEFF is film critic of *O Dia* newspaper in Brazil, president of the Association of Film Critics of Rio de Janeiro and a regular contributor to *Variety*.

Recent and Forthcoming Films

PRIMEIRO DIA (Midnight)

Script: Emmanuel Carneiro, Walter Salles. Dir: Daniela Thomas and Salles. Phot: Walter Carvalho. Players: Fernanda Torres, Carlos Vereza.

Producers and Distributors

Rio Vermelho Filmes
(Cacá Diegues)
Rua Ataulfo de Paiva 527 s.702
22420-030 Rio de Janeiro
Tel: (55 21) 259 2289

Cinédia
(Alice Conzaga)
Estrada do Soca, Jacarepagua
Rio de Janeiro
Tel: (55 21) 445 6868
Fax: (55 21) 445 8215

Comunicacao Alternativa
(Marcos Rezende)

VILLA-LOBOS

Script: Joaquim Assis, Zelito Viana and Eduardo Coutinho. Dir: Viana. Players: Marcos Palmeira, Antonio Fagundes, Marieta Severo, Leticia Spiller.

Rua do Russel, 450
22210-010 Rio de Janeiro
Tel: (55 21) 558 2825
Fax: (55 21) 557 5848
e-mail:comalt@ibm.net

Filme B
(Paulo Sergio Almeida/Andrea Queiroga)
Rua Alcindo Guanabara 24 s.801
20038-900 Rio de Janeiro
Tel/Fax: (55 21) 240 8439

Grupo Novo de Cinema e TV
(Antonio Urano/Tarcisio Vidigal)
Rua Marechal Neimeyer 24
22251-060 Rio de Janeiro
Tel: (55 21) 266 3637

XANGO DE BAKER STREET

Script: Patricia Mello, based on the book by Jô Soares. Dir: Miguel Faria Jr. Players: Joaquim de Almeida, Maria de Medeiros, Candido Damm, Marco Nanini.

L. C. Barreto
(Luiz Carlos Barreto)
Av. Franklin Roosevelt, 194
Rio de Janeiro
Tel: (55 21) 240 8161

Morena Filmes
(Marisa Leão)
Rua Visconde de Pirajá, 596/204
Rio de Janeiro
Tel/Fax: (55 21) 511 0754

HB Filmes
(Hector Babenco)
Rua Emmanoel Kant, 39
Jardim Paulista – S. Paulo
Tel: (55 11) 883 7755

BULGARIA — Pavlina Jeleva

After lengthy discussion at the end of 1998, Bulgaria's parliament finally passed its new Media Law and the creation of a specialised body, the National Council for Television and Radio, followed. But there is still no new legislation governing cinema. That is a great shame, especially since the past three years have been particularly difficult for the Bulgarian film industry. In 1998-99, state subsidy decreased by more than 65% and only two features were produced.

Director Ivan Nichev finally completed **After the End of the World**, about the breakdown of ethnic tolerance in the beautiful town of Plovdiv. The masterful Nitchev blended a love story between a beautiful Armenian girl and a Bulgarian Jewish boy with amusing images from the communist 1950s. The film was selected in the Panorama section at Berlin in 1999 and was well-received by the international press and the German audience.

The other feature, Andrei Slabakoff's debut, **Wagner**, gave Bulgarian audiences this 40-year-old director's take on the communist past: a black-and-white absurdist drama.

Turning to TV

In April 1998 a much-needed Television Films Production Centre was created by Bulgarian National Television. As state subsidy for film rarely exceeded 25% of the whole budget, the Centre's initial purpose was to provide supplementary feature funding. In fact the TV support slowly went to films intended only for TV – and this in comparatively small amounts.

As a result, some of the country's most important film directors such as Ivan Andonov and Gueorgui Duilgerov offered their creativity to television. Andonov's **Danube Bridge** (*Dunav Most*), focused on three young couples living in the fictional Bulgarian town of Stari Han.

With the surprising **Sand Watch** (*Piassachen Chassovnik*), Duilgerov (who won a Silver Bear at Berlin for *Advantage* in the 1970s) transferred a story by Polish writer Liudmila Petrushevskathe from Second World War Russia to present-day Bulgaria. Total state support for TV films in 1999 was officially announced as equal to $1.4m (2.5 billion Bulgarian levas).

In spite of these limitations, there have been some success stories. Nikolay Volev's **Emergency**, about the current state of Sofia's medical services, won the documentary "Grand Prix" at the 1999 conference of the International Co-operative for International Communications Research, in Croatia, ahead of competing films from more than 100 TV channels. Boyan Papazov's **Where the Souls Rest**, about the ancient minority Karakachans, attracted the attention of London's Jane Balfour sales company.

Several Eurimages-supported co-productions have filmed in Bulgaria over the past year, including French *Est-Ouest*, directed by Régis Wargnier and co-produced by Bulgaria's Gala Film Ltd, which used locations in Plovdiv, Varna and Bourga.

Greek director Panos Karkanevatos came to Sofia to shoot parts of *Earth and Water* (co-produced by Bulgarian Geopoly Ltd.). Michael Cacoyannis's version of Chekhov's *The Cherry Orchard* was entirely shot in the ex-Bulgarian monarch's beautiful Vrana residence, near Sofia. With varied locations, adequate supplies of equipment and well-trained, inexpensive crews, Bulgaria remained one of the cheapest shooting countries in Europe.

PAVLINA JELEVA has been a film critic since 1978. A former national representative on the Eurimages Board and FIPRESCI, she is now artistic and foreign relations director of her own film company. She takes over from Ivan Stoyanovich, who died in 1998 after a distinguished career in film, television and animation, as well as more than 20 years as our correspondent in Bulgaria.

Recent and Forthcoming Films

PIASSACHEN CHASSOVNIK (Sand Watch)

Script: Liudmila Petruchevska. Dir: Gueorgui Diulgerov. Phot: Gueorgui Bogdanov and Boris Missirkov. Players: Vladimir Penev, Maria Sapoundjieva. Prod: Bulgarian National Television.

DUNAV MOST (Danube Bridge)

Script: Gueorgui Mishev. Dir: Ivan Andonov. Phot: Dimo Minev. Players: Petar Popiordanov, Ioana Boukovska, Ivan Lasskin, Stefka Ianorova. Prod: Bulgarian National Television.

GOLEMITE IGRI (The Big Plays)

Script: Gueorgui Danailov. Dir: Ivanka Grabcheva. Prod: Bulgarian National Television.

STAKLENI TOPCHETA (Glass Bulls)

Script and Dir: Ivan Cherkelov. Phot: Emil Hristov.

Producers

Bulgarian Film Producers Association
67 Dondukov Blvd
Sofia 1504
Tel: (359 2) 447 326
Fax: (359 2) 463 676

Borough Film Ltd
13 Krakra Street
Sofia 1000
Tel: (359 2) 445 880
Fax: (359 2) 445 880
e-mail: borough@mbox.cit.bg

Gala Film Ltd
3 Uzundjovska Street
Sofia 1000
Tel: (359 2) 981 4209
Fax: (359 2) 804 434

Geopoly Ltd
16 Kapitan Andreev Street
Sofia 1421
Tel: (359 2) 9630 661
Fax: (359 2) 9630 661
e-mail: geopoly@mail.techno-link.com

Klas Film
156 Kniaz Boris I Street
Sofia 1000
Tel: (359 2) 523 580
Fax: (359 2) 527 451

Paralax Ltd
67 Dondukov Blvd
Sofia 1504
Tel: (359 2) 447 326
Fax: (359 2) 463 676
e-mail: dimo@omega.bg

Distributors

Alexandra Film
17 Naycho Tzanov Street
Sofia 1000
Tel: (359 2) 980 6070
Fax: (359 2) 981 0715

Duga Entertainment
141 Kniaz Boris I Street
Sofia 1304
Tel: (359 2) 981 9584
Fax: (359 2) 980 8842

Sofia Film
26 Maria Luiza Blvd
Sofia 1000
Tel: (359 2) 835 584
Fax: (359 2) 833 707

Sunny Films
17-a Tzar Osvoboditel Blvd
Sofia 1000
Tel: (359 2) 943 4849
Fax: (359 2) 943 3703

Useful Addresses

Ministry of Culture
17 Stamboliiski Street
Sofia 1000
Tel: (359 2) 861 11
Fax: (359 2) 877 339

National Film Centre
2-a Dondukov Blvd
Sofia 1000
Tel: (359 2) 803 134
Fax: (359 2) 873 626

Union of Bulgarian Film Makers
67 Dondukov Blvd
Sofia 1504
Tel: (359 2) 946 1068
Fax: (359 2) 946 1068

Bulgarian National Television
29 San Srefano Street
Sofia 1000
Tel: (359 2) 985 591
Fax: (359 2) 871 871

BURKINA FASO
Judy
Kendall

The theme for the 16th edition of FESPACO (1999), the biannual film festival of Burkina Faso, was Cinema and Distribution Channels in Africa. Distribution is a crucial issue for African cinema, as Baba Hama, Permanent Secretary General of FESPACO, highlighted in *FESPACO News* when he referred to "the paradox of a film industry which is cut off from its audience".

In the years 1994–97, nearly 60% of the films screened in Burkina Faso were from America, whereas African films accounted for just 0.4% of the total. According to Hama, it seems as if this trend is continuing, due to "a lack of distribution structures, absence of promotion, a badly-structured market, very few cinema halls available and so on."

Despite these drawbacks, the 1999 FESPACO and the concurrent MICA International Market of African film and television, saw more than 100 films screened for more than 5,000 guests from 60 countries.

The big film from Burkina Faso in 1999 is Pierre S. Yameogo's **Whirlwind** (*Silmande*). 'Silmande' is Mossi for whirlwind, and the film has certainly caused a stir since its release. This urban story is about two brothers, rich Lebanese businessmen living in Burkina Faso, and it deals with the themes of corruption and elitism.

Produced by Afix Productions, the company founded by Yameogo in Paris and responsible for work by other young African directors, *Whirlwind* caused a furore amongst the African Lebanese community, and the Lebanese owners of several cinema halls in Abidjan (Ivory Coast) refused to screen it, despite its record-breaking box-office success in Burkina Faso. It was in the running for the 1998 M-Net All Africa Film Awards and won an award at FESPACO 1999.

Success on the circuit

Amongst movies made for television, last year's co-production by the National Film Board and National TV, **The Secret** (*Le Secret*), directed by Tiendrebeogo Raymond, has done well on the festival circuit, winning an award as the Best TV Fiction Film in FESPACO 1999. It was bought by Canal France International. The series continues with two more films, *The Last of the Bozos* (*Le Dernier des Bozos*), by Abdoulaye Dao, and *The Two Adorable Rivals* (*Les Deux Adorables Rivales*).

Fanta Regina Nacro won an award for her short film *Konte's Thing* (*Le Truc de Konte*) at Vues d'Afrique 1999 (15th African and Caribbean Festival, Montreal) as well as at FESPACO. This film deals with a misunderstanding in a village woman's life when she returns home after a short stay in town. *Souko, Le Cinématographe en Carton*, by Issiake Konate, is about a group of children who get swept up into a magic world of fantasy when they make their own film projector. This film received the French co-operation prize for cinema at Cannes 1998.

Garba, by Rouamba Adama, also won a prize at FESPACO 1999, and in the 1999 Milan Festival of African Cinema was awarded the Air Afrique prize. This is a film about the problems of street urchins, and is to be the first in a trilogy by this director about abandoned children. *Garba* was selected for festivals in Montreal, Angers and Cannes.

At press time, Idrissa Ouedraogo's UNESCO/Noe productions-funded film about Moi Boukari Koutou, the nineteenth-century Emperor of the Mossi people, perceived as a hero of Burkina Faso for his resistance to the French, was still in production.

JUDY KENDALL is a freelance writer on theatre and film, and has spent some time in Southern Africa.

Useful Addresses

Centre National du Cinéma du Burkina Faso
Ministère de la Communication et de la Culture
Ouagadougou 01
Tel: (226) 302 551/557

African Film Library and Baba Hama, FESPACO Secretary General
Ardiouma SOMA
01 BP 2505
Ouagadougou 01
Tel: (226) 307 538
Fax: (226) 312 509
soma@fespaco.bf

Télévision Nationale de Burkina Faso (TNB)
BP 2530
Ouagadougou 01
Tel: (226) 306623

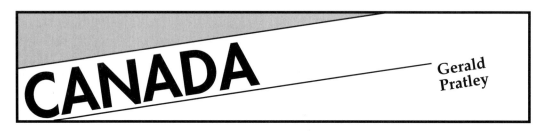

CANADA — Gerald Pratley

In the past year it has actually been suggested by the small minds in the tourist trade and on local councils in Nova Scotia that Disney should be given tax breaks and subsidies to encourage its executives to make films there. This continuing belief in official circles that US companies filming on Canadian soil gives the nation worthwhile international exposure defies all logical explanation. However, it is satisfying to report that almost all Canadian-produced features have been released in all of the larger cities, including *The Red Violin*, *Last Night*, *eXistenZ* and *Such a Long Journey*.

In Quebec, of course, almost all French-language productions get wide distribution and make money, the best among them being *Les Boys II*, *Laura Cadieux*, *Two Seconds* and *August 32nd on Earth*. Cinema exposure for Quebec film in the rest of Canada is limited, with some political pundits suggesting that the virtual rejection of Quebec films outside the province is one way by which English-Canadians can show their disapproval of the Quebec government's continued attacks on the English language and its

tiresome talk of independence. So much for a happy Millennium!

The improvement in distribution and exhibition is due largely to Cineplex and to the independent owners of specialised cinemas, whose numbers sadly decrease over the years. Famous Players (owned by Paramount-Viacom), which has almost always resisted showing anything but American films, has gone into partnership with Alliance Atlantis and Leonard Schein of Vancouver to create a small circuit of mini-plexes primarily for the showing of Canadian and other non-American movies. AMC shows whatever the other two circuits show.

But any thoughts of new, single auditoria being built in the new century should be banished. There has been a feverish, $1 billion rush by Sony-owned Cineplex Odeon and Famous Players to build multiplexes throughout the country, mainly in the suburbs. As the multiplexes open, so the old single and twin cinemas close. The major exhibitors have said that as far as is practical (i.e. profitable) one auditorium per multi-screen site will be set aside for Canadian and foreign films. But who would want to see them in such a gaudy, noisy atmosphere? Only the younger generation, it appears, who follow Hollywood films and relish attending these complexes to become intoxicated with the whoop-it-up sense of excitement.

Fear of flying

Some 20 Canadian features were released least year, most of them inconsequential and with little public appeal. Easily the best of the year, despite being ignored by the public, was **Today or Never** (*Aujourd'hui ou jamais*), co-written and directed by Jean Pierre Lefebvre. This is yet another of Lefebvre's quiet, beautiful portraits of individuals who have known sadness and joy and survived emotional and physical torments.

Abel, who has wanted to fly since he was a child, runs a small airfield but cannot bring himself to fly after the death of his best friend and co-pilot in a plane crash. The arrival of a bright and attractive young aviatrix changes his outlook on life. There is nothing forced or false in the telling of this gossamer-like story, with its sunny, spring background, and one is enveloped in Lefebvre's characteristic warmth and compassion.

Thom Fitzgerald's docudrama **Beefcake** looks like a faded scrapbook about the 1950s, as it tries to recreate the heyday of the American "muscle magazine" *Physique Pictorial*, and its editor, Bob Mizer, who brought male models into the world of advertising via more than 500,000 photographs. Financed largely by the UK's Film Four, *Beefcake* evokes interest in recalling a time when homosexuality was a crime and censorship was draconian. Nevertheless, the awfully healthy young men capering about in posing pouches seem to have distracted the director from keeping track of his narrative. The Hollywood setting, mocked up in Halifax, Nova Scotia, looks like the tourist postcards of the time.

Elaine Cassidy and Bob Hoskins in FELICIA'S JOURNEY

Lesbian love in Vancouver is the theme of **Better Than Chocolate**, a comedy written and directed by Anne Wheeler and based partly on the real-life difficulties of The Little Sisters Bookshop and its struggles with Canadian Customs over importing books about lesbian and homosexual life. Well-made and well-acted, it would have been more enjoyable if the characters' sexual activity had been left to the imagination, and more time devoted to the issues.

Jerry Ciccoritti's **Boy Meets Girl**, set in Toronto's Little Italy, is a ghastly concoction. A supposedly romantic tale, complete with songs and music, about a jaded photo-caption writer and a waitress, it drags in every love-struck cliché known to cinema and becomes a painful pastiche of supposedly loveable, Fellini-esque characters, who are sadly lacking in genuine *amore*.

Women on a mission

Based on a novel by William Trevor, Atom Egoyan's latest, **Felicia's Journey**, is a story of unrequited love and murder, centred around a young Irish girl who has been impregnated by a British soldier and sets out to England to find him. She becomes enmeshed in the evil deeds of a serial killer, making this one of the most morally repugnant movies in an age of cinematic ugliness.

Stylishly adapted from a play about Alberta's enforced sterilisation policies, Francis Damberger's **Heart of the Sun** is a sympathetic and compelling story about a simple-minded young woman, happily married, who yearns for a family. Through a series of flashbacks we discover why she will never carry her own child. Filmed not far from Medicine Hat, the beauty of the landscape is striking to behold.

Charles Biname delivers dark yet touching drama in **Streetheart** (*Le Cœur au poing*), the story of two sisters, one who is not quite of this world and offers herself to strangers for one hour. Some people react in disbelief and reject her, others show compassion and there are those who think only of sex. This is a woman who feels too deeply and expects too much from life, and the film depicts her struggle with understanding and sensitivity.

Such a Long Journey, written by Sooni Taraporevala and directed by Sturla Gunnarsson, is based on the novel by Rohinton Mistry and set in Bombay, 1971, the year when India went to war over the creation of Bangladesh. The social upheaval is seen through the eyes of an honest, industrious bank clerk, a man dedicated to his family and whose principles are compromised by terrorist activities. An excellent cast of Indian players, set against authentic backgrounds, make this a thoughtful and honest film, but lacking the empathy an Indian film-maker would have brought to it.

Jeremy Podeswa's **The Five Senses** is composed of five interconnected stories inspired by the five senses and linked by the search for a missing girl. Love, sex and self-discovery among neurotic characters are the chief themes

Best of the rest

The year's crop also included **Angel in a Cage**, written and directed by Mary Jane Gomes, a likeable first film inspired by the director's own family history in Trinidad (the angel is a long-suffering wife and mother). **Clutch**, directed by Chris

Still from Mary Jane Gomes' ANGEL IN A CAGE

Grismer, offers a tattered tale of love and crime involving a thief, a mechanic and a dead body, while Bruce Sweeney's **Dirty** takes us into a household of individuals who have all but given up on life.

Extraordinary Visitor, from John Doyle, is a very funny Newfoundland comedy which pokes fun at religion and the media: John the Baptist returns to the City of St John's and becomes a popular talk-show guest. Designed as a light-hearted romantic comedy, Jack Kalangis' **Jack and Jill** tumbles haplessly downhill from start to finish.

When I Will Be Gone (*Líage de braise*), directed by Jacques Leduc, is the sad tale of an elegant and deeply troubled woman at odds with life and preparing herself for death; Paul Tana's operatic **Mr Aiello** (*La deroute*) follows a wealthy Italian businessman in Montreal as he becomes increasingly isolated from his family; **Rupert's Land**, directed by Jonathan Tammuz, brings together two half-brothers, one from England, on a road trip through northern British Columbia to attend the funeral of their father. It flounders after a promising start.

The Falling begins as an intriguing account of a love affair told from three diverse points of view, before director Raul Sanchez Inglis allows the narrative to become too complicated for its own good; **The Fishing Trip**, a remarkable first film from Ammon Buchbinder, follows two sisters and a friend on a trip up to Northern Ontario to confront the father who abused them in childhood.

Finally, Peter Lynch's **The Herd** is an over-the-top docudrama about the six-year trek of reindeer across the Arctic, from Alaska into the Yukon Territories, which began in 1919. Films on the way when this article went to press included the long-awaited *15 Moments*, Denys Arcand's first feature for five years, and an adaptation of Leonard Cohen's novel *The Favourite Game*.

Lies, damned lies and ...

It has become almost impossible to keep up with the statistics which flood the media these days, or with the bewildering sums of money made available by funding agencies, with "who spent what and where" tables, tax credits, subsidies and bi-lingual services making the financial picture both murky and contradictory. To pick some of the choicest figures: there were 656 cinemas operating in 1998. Receipts from admissions (excluding taxes) amounted to $440.8m, from 91.8 million paid admissions. The Federal Government's Canadian Film Development Corporation (generally known as Telefilm) lost $150m last year, the largest taxpayers' loss among 48 Crown corporations; domestic movie and TV productions brought in $1.3 billion up 4.8% over the previous year (15% of that came from features).

But Hollywood is growing restless and threatens to bite back on "runaway production" in Canada. This year, the exceptionally low Canadian dollar, combined with labour tax credits, good crews and subsidies have made Canada such good value that production costs are 35% lower than in the US. The US Directors and Screen Actors guilds claim that 23,500 film jobs were lost to runaway production in 1998, 81% to Canada, which collected $2.5 billion worth of production, of which British Columbia claimed an estimated $1 billion. There is increasing recognition that bloated costs in LA must be cut down to bring production back home.

Amongst the leading Canadian cinema figures to pass away in the last year was 89-year-old Gratien Gelinas, whose 1948 play *Ti-Coq*, about a betrayed soldier, was a huge success in English and French; his screen version became a landmark in Quebec film-making. Winnipeg-born Osmond "Bordie" Borradaile, died aged 100. He was better known in Britain than in Canada, for his pioneering on-location cinematography on Sir Alexander Korda films such as *The Scarlet Pimpernel*, *The Four Feathers* and *The Thief of Bagdad*. Alberta-born William McCauley, who has died aged 82, was one of Canada's earliest film composers. For Crawley Films, in Ottawa, he scored some 125 documentaries and several features.

GERALD PRATLEY has been reporting on the Canadian scene for *Variety* since 1956. He teaches film history at Ryerson Polytechnic University, Toronto.

Recent Films

AUJOURD'HUI OU JAMAIS
(Today or Never)

Script: Jean Pierre Lefebvre, Marcel Sabourin. Dir: Lefebvre. Players: Marcel Sabourin, Claude Blanchard, Julie Menard, Micheline Lanctot, Jean-Pierre Ronfard. Prod: Vent d'Est Films.

BEEFCAKE

Script and Dir: Thom Fitzgerald. Players: Daniel MacIvor, Joshua Peace, Carroll Godsman, Jonathan Torrens. Prod: Alliance Atlantis.

BETTER THAN CHOCOLATE

Script and Dir: Anne Wheeler. Players: Wendy Crewson, Karyn Dwyer, Christina Cox, Ann-Marie MacDonad, Peter Outerbridge. Prod: Alliance Atlantis.

BOY MEETS GIRL

Script and Dir: Jerry Ciccoritti. Players: Sean Astin, Emily Hampshire, Kate Nelligan, Joe Mantegna. Prod: Artopelli Motion Pictures.

LE COEUR AU POING
(Streetheart)

Script: Charles Biname, Monique Proulx. Dir: Biname. Players: Pascale Montpetit, Anne-Marie Cadieux, Guy Nadon, Guylaine Tremblay. Prod: Cite-Amerique.

FELICIA'S JOURNEY

Script: Atom Egoyan, based on a novel by William Trevor. Dir: Egoyan. Players: Bob Hoskins, Elaine Cassidy, Arsinee Khanjian, Peter McDonald. Prod: Alliance Atlantis.

THE FIVE SENSES

Script and Dir: Jeremy Podeswa. Players: Mary-Louise Parker, Molly Parker, Philippe Volter, Marco Leonardi, Gabrielle Rose, Daniel MacIvor. Prod: Alliance Atlantis.

HEART OF THE SUN

Script: Kim Hogan. Dir: Francis Damberger. Players: Christianne Hirt, Shaun Johnston, Michael Riley. Prod: Dancing Stone Films.

SUCH A LONG JOURNEY

Script: Sooni Taraporevala, based on the novel by Rohinton Mistry. Dir: Sturla Gunnarsson. Players: Roshan Seth, Om Puri, Soni Radzan, Naseeruddinn Shah, Pearl Padamsee, Ranjit Chowdhry. Prod: The Film Works (UK/Canada).

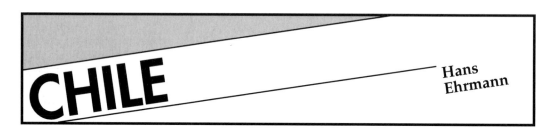

CHILE — Hans Ehrmann

In Chile, as elsewhere, *Titanic* ruled the waves, passing the unprecedented million spectator mark in Santiago. This mega-hit provides one explanation for 1998's 50% increase in total spectators, to six million. The other reason is the multiplex explosion which climaxed in May 1999 with Hoyts opening a 16-screener (Chile's largest), bringing the capital to a total of 150 screens.

Growth is even larger in the provinces. A year ago there was only one regional multiplex and now there are half a dozen, with a total of 38 screens. Provincial box-office now amounts to approximately 25% of the country's total. Three international chains are responsible for this growth. Nationwide, Hoyts has five complexes (51 screens), Boston's National Amusements International has two (24) and Texas-based Cinemark has 11 complexes (89).

Local company Conate had been the undisputed ruler of Chilean exhibition for many years and, in a 50/50 joint venture with Cinemark, initially shared in the market's growth. However, it could not keep up with the investment required by Cinemark's rapid expansion and in 1998 sold back its multiplex share. Conate still owns 19 Santiago screens, plus six in the provinces, but several of these are doing poorly.

More surprising than multiplexing, which is of course a global phenomenon, is the growth of outlets for alternative cinema. Santiago now has ten arthouses, fed by independent distributors and some of the majors' specialist outlets. Reliable statistics for this sector are unavailable, but they are doing reasonably well and have led to the capital's cinemagoers being offered a good range of international films to contrast with standard multiplex fare.

Low-budget bombs

Three local films unfortunately shared the fate of sinking at the box-office. Nicolás Acuña's opera prima **Blind Heaven** (*Cielo Ciego*) deals with small-time punks, has traces of Tarantino-esque violence and some visually arresting moments, but tends to be somewhat hermetic.

Carmen Maura and Alvaro Escobar in Ricardo Larraín's ENTHUSIASM

Claudio Sapiain's **The Man Who Imagined** (*El hombre que imaginaba*) presents a disenchanted view of present-day Chile, applying an absurdist viewpoint to a range of characters and issues: from a girl who disappears without trace, to private health insurance, soccer fans, an attractive prostitute and an ice-cream salesman on his lunch break. Some items work individually, but the wrap-around framework of a TV host in search of original stories is not sustained and is largely responsible for the film's inconsistencies and fragmented feel.

Both of these cost less than $500,000, in contrast to Ricardo Larraín's **Enthusiasm** (*El Entusiasmo*), a Chilean-Spanish co-production budgeted at close to a million and a half, whose cast included Spanish stars Carmen Maura and Maribel Verdú.

The success of Larraín's first film, *The Frontier* (1991), at the local box-office and also on the festival circuit (including a Silver Bear at Berlin) made *Enthusiasm* the most eagerly awaited of the year's crop

and it obtained an unprecedented (for a Chilean film) 17-screen Christmas opening. Given these precedents its return of 17,000 spectators was definitely disappointing.

Technically solid and with visually stunning scenes shot in the Atacama desert, *Enthusiasm* follows a youngster's career twists and turns, partially suggesting parallels to Chile's development in recent years. An excessively elliptical screenplay was to a large extent responsible for leaving local audiences and critics emotionally uninvolved.

One major problem faced by practically all of Chile's recent films has been their screenplay structure; subject matter poses an additional problem. The country is still too polarised regarding Pinochet and the 17-year military dictatorship for this period to be faced head-on. Attempts to make escapist entertainment have not succeeded.

An interim alternative which may well bring dividends lies in the adaptation of some of the country's literary classics, a trend which seems to be taking root with forthcoming adaptations: Silvio Caiozzi's *Coronation* (based on a José Donoso novel) and Miguel Littín's *Tierra del Fuego* (from a Francisco Coloane novel).

HANS EHRMANN is a columnist and the film critic for Santiago's daily *La Nación*. He passed away shortly after filing this report, and will be much missed after ten years as *IFG's* correspondent in Chile

Useful Addresses

Arauco Film
(production facility)
Silvina Hurtado 1789
Santiago
Tel: (56 2) 209 2091
Fax: (56 2) 204 5096

Asociación de Productores de Cine de Chile
Federico Froebel 1755
Providencia
Santiago
Tel: (56 2) 209 9031
Fax: (56 2) 204 8988

Conate and Chile Films
(studio, lab, distributor and exhibitor)

La Capitania 1200
Santiago
Tel: (56 2) 220 3086
Fax: (56 2) 211 9826

Filmocentro
(production facility)
Jorge Washington 302
Santiago
Tel: (56 2) 341 3100
Fax: (56 2) 209 1671

Oficina de Difusión de la Cinematografia Chilena
Villavicencio 352
Santiago
Tel: (56 2) 632 6565 or 632 6607
Fax: (56 2) 632 6389

Roos Films
(production facility)
Ricardo Matte Pérez 0216
Santiago
Tel: (56 2) 341 1188

Augusto Ubilla
(distributor)
General del Canto 10, 3°
Santiago
Tel: (56 2) 223 7685
Fax: (56 2) 235 2399

Unicine
(producers and directors union)
Huérfanos 587, Of.918
Santiago
Tel/Fax: (56 2) 273 1462

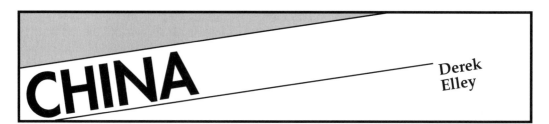

CHINA — Derek Elley

There is a generational change underway in China that showed concrete results during 1998-99, even though the financial underpinnings of the film industry still remain extremely shaky. It is now more than 15 years since the so-called Fifth Generation of directors, who put China on the international cinema map, began making movies; and even though most festival selectors (who play a vital role in defining a country's film profile) still remain in thrall to that generation, it is time to acknowledge that names like Chen Kaige and Zhang Yimou no longer represent current trends in Chinese film-making.

Both Chen and Zhang, now middle-aged, have reached career plateaux, operating largely on reputations forged a decade ago. Following the decidedly mixed reception to *Temptress Moon*, Chen initially planned to make a smaller feature, but ended up making the mammoth **The Emperor and the Assassin** (*Jing Ke ci Qin wang*), which devoured three years of his life and was finally unveiled at the 1999 Cannes festival.

Zhang, after the befuddled foreign reception to his contemporary comedy *Keep Cool*, lay quiet for a while, finally shooting two small features: **Not One Less** (*Yige dou bu neng shao*), about a teenage supply teacher who struggles to control her class in a country school, and **The Road Home** (*Wode fuqin muqin*), a 1950s-set love story told through the eyes of the man's son. Both were shot in 1998, either side of Zhang remounting his 1997 Italian production of *Turandot* in Beijing's Forbidden City.

Neither of Zhang's films turned up at Cannes: the first was offered a slot in Un Certain Regard, which Zhang turned down (Chen's "rival" film had already been accepted into Competition), and the second was rejected. Zhang then went public with a letter to Cannes head Gilles Jacob in which he "withdrew" his films and accused the festival of politicising its selection process for Chinese films (i.e. only being interested in those that were banned or sensitive). Whatever the merits of Zhang's two films – the first of which was later accepted by Venice – his letter to Jacob, couched in respectful but firm language, raised a valid point about western festivals' hidebound attitude to Mainland movies. Unfortunately, Zhang's outburst was dismissed in the West as petulant, and back home the publicity did not much help the April release of *Not One Less*, which performed poorly.

An imperial failure

Meanwhile, Chen's *The Emperor and the Assassin* met a very mixed response at Cannes. Costing an enormous (by Chinese standards) $15m, raised from Japanese, Chinese and French sources, the film had already premiered in Japan the previous autumn in a 176-minute version that died on commercial release. In October, a 160-minute cut had a glitzy premiere in Beijing's Great Hall of the People, again generating poor word-of-mouth. During the next six months, Chen totally reworked the film, even bringing back previously discarded footage, and this version, also running 160 minutes, was the one premiered at Cannes.

The movie is based on the same historical material from which Zhou Xiaowen wove the much more gripping *The Emperor's Shadow* (1996): the story of united China's first emperor (known for his huge tomb at Xi'an), the man sent to murder him, and the woman they both love. Chen's film is a consistent visual treat, but is more a series of impressive moments than an involving drama; and the plot is desperately over-complicated. As the lover, Gong Li is little more than a clothes horse, though Zhang Fengyi, as the assassin (a role originally begun by Jiang Wen), has his moments. It is one of the

Still from Chen Kaige's THE EMPEROR AND THE ASSASSIN

ironies of his career that Chen, basically a gifted miniaturist, has ended up making three big-budget period dramas in a row.

Emperor seems to exist in a time warp that has little to do with the main currents of contemporary Chinese cinema, best exemplified by the growing slate of Beijing-based company Imar Film, masterminded by young, American-born producer Peter Loehr. Loehr set the standard in 1998 with Zhang Yang's collection of vignettes about love and marriage, *Spicy Love Soup* (see *IFG 1999*), and has continued to work with young talent on modern stories set in urban China that are accessible to and aimed at a young, native audience, rather than tailored simply for film festivals or western arthouses.

Shi Runjiu's **A Beautiful New World** (*Meili xin shijie*) is a funny, touching and beautifully played tale of a country bumpkin (Jiang Wu, younger brother of Jiang Wen) who arrives in Shanghai to claim an apartment he has won, and ends up in a love-hate relationship with a distant relative, the young, streetwise Jinfang (Tao Hong). Loehr's third production, **Shower** (*Xizao*), directed by Zhang Yang, is a less boisterous but equally touching study of a father-son relationship set around a traditional Beijing bath house threatened with demolition. Both productions remain totally true to modern Chinese life without dressing it up in rural exoticism or period dress. Imar's fourth feature is set to shoot in autumn 1999 – a criss-crossing road movie, *The End of the Line*, directed by Shi Runjiu.

Talking 'bout their generation?

Though *Shower* is Imar's "artiest" production to date, it still has none of the introverted anomie (seemingly borrowed from Taiwan) that some of the so-called Sixth Generation directors exhibit – a trait best exemplified by **Scenery**, a moody story about a lawyer hired by a taxi driver to track down a passenger who raped her. Independently made by He Jianjun under

Shi Yu and Wang Tong in SO CLOSE TO PARADISE

the pseudonym Zhao Jisong, it exhibits the same baffling obscurity and emotional desiccation as his earlier *Postman*, though without that film's interesting grace notes.

Far more interesting was Wang Xiaoshuai's **So Close to Paradise** (*Biandan, guniang*), which started life four years ago as *Vietnam Girl* (*Yuenan laide guniang*) and, after lengthy problems with the Film Bureau, and re-editing and re-shooting, was briefly shown in Hong Kong in December 1998 under the title *Take Me Off*, before emerging at Cannes 1999 under its present, rather meaningless handle. Pitched somewhere between mainstream and arthouse, the film shows signs of reworking but is still very interesting, as two country friends in the big port city of Wuhan become involved with its sleazier elements, in particular a bar-girl (striking singer Wang Tong) who may or may not be Vietnamese.

Most young directors now shrug off the "Sixth Generation" tag as meaningless and self-limiting: if the industry is to win back local audiences, rather than cater to foreign festivals, films must be set in a recognisable world for the average viewer, just as western movies are. One of the most impressive of the past year was Shanghai-based Li Hong's **Tutor** (*Ban wo gao fei*), a beautiful, sensitively told story of a young student teacher's friendship with a boy he gives lessons to at home. There's a simple, poetic flavour to her first feature, with a wisp of Truffaut, that marks Li as a talent to watch.

Beijing takes the lead

Despite newcomers like Li – and the occasional well-made commercial movie, like the glossy thriller **Ghost in the Computer** (*Linghun chu qiao*), by the pseudonymous Hai Da – the core of the country's film-making talent remains in Beijing. Mainstream director Feng Xiaogang followed up his 1998 Chinese New Year box-office success *Party A, Party B*, which grossed $2.75m (RMB 22m) with another vehicle for top comedian Ge You, the far more superior and often very moving romantic comedy **Be There or Be Square** (*Bu jian bu san*). Glossily directed, the movie teams Ge, as a crafty Beijinger living on the edge of the law in Los Angeles, with leggy beauty Xu Fan, as a fellow Mainlander who's always threatening to return home.

One of the big attractions at Christmas 1998, *Be There or Be Square* performed well for a local movie – and was far better than the much-publicised melodrama **A Time to Remember** (*Hongse lianren*), a fabricated "international" production, half in English, with Hong Kong star Leslie Cheung playing a doomed revolutionary. Directed by Ye Daying, it was produced by the semi-independent Beijing Forbidden City Film Co., which has previously done more interesting work.

One film that need not worry about home box-office is **Mr. Zhao** (*Zhao xiansheng*), the directing debut of cinematographer Lü Yue (*To Live*; *Shanghai Triad*), which has yet to be released in China. A trenchantly observed study of a habitual womaniser, shot through with a delicious sense of irony and genuine warmth for its characters, it is also a structurally bold exercise whose opening 40 minutes are devoted to two sequences of Ken Loach-like docudrama, before broadening out into an elliptical narrative that cleverly shuffles its main characters. True to contemporary life, but played with restraint by a terrific cast, *Mr. Zhao* was one of the most rewarding movies of the past year for viewers prepared to stay the course.

After a healthy-looking year during 1998, there then came a box-office drought during the first half of 1999 that even affected US releases (still limited to about 10 titles a year). Apart from being criticised for being too American, Disney's *Mulan*, based on a famous Chinese yarn, performed feebly compared with *The Lion King*, despite the lead role being voiced by well-known singer Ai Jing and another character, General Li, by Jackie Chan; even Chan's *Rush Hour* earned far less than usual for his films.

The phenomenon puzzled local observers, and cannot simply be blamed on the regular problems: dilapidated cinemas, sub-standard product, rampant piracy and distribution difficulties. The likeliest reason, as in Hong Kong, is that China's newly-affluent urban populations now have many ways in which to spend their money, and traditional filmgoing is only one of their many entertainment options.

In 1998, some 120 features were officially released – 80 local, and 40 imported via China Film (of which *Titanic* and *Saving Private Ryan* were the year's biggest hits). To give some idea of the size of the market, between January and October 1998 total grosses in Beijing alone were $14.5m (RMB 117m), but with only seven local features doing significant business, among them *Party A, Party B* (the most successful, with almost $1.5m), *A Time to Remember* ($825,000), the Hong Kong co-production *Eighteen Springs* ($400,000) and *Going to School with Dad on My Back* ($390,000).

Box-office prospects look little better for the second half of 1999, which will be dominated by movies-on-command celebrating the 50th anniversary of the People's Republic. But there is certainly enough right-minded talent out there to make the high-quality mainstream movies needed to attract large audiences, so long as film-makers are supported by more indie producers like Imar.

DEREK ELLEY has been associated with *IFG* for more than 25 years, during which time he has written extensively on East Asian cinema. Currently Senior Film Critic of *Variety*. He is also editor of the annual *Variety Movie Guide*, a distillation of the paper's reviews of the past 90 years.

The 18th Golden Rooster Awards

The awards were made in Chongqing on November 22, 1998, alongside those for the 21st Hundred Flowers Awards (voted by readers of *Popular Cinema*, the large-circulation monthly). Main prizes:

Best Film: *Live in Peace.*
Best Director (shared): Hu Bingliu (*Live in Peace*), Saifu Mailisi (*Genghis Khan*).
Best Script: Lu Zhuguo (*The Big March: Sweeping across the Southeast*).
Best Actor: Feng Gong (*Having Fun*).
Best Actress: Tao Hong (*Colours of the Blind*, aka: *Black Eyes*).
Best Supporting Actor: Ge Cunzhuang (*Zhou Enlai: A Great Friend*).
Best Supporting Actress: Bao Xueyun (*Live in Peace*).
Best Photography: Mu Deyuan (*Genghis Khan*).
Best Art Direction: Chen Yaogong (*The Long March*).
Best Costume Design: Ru Meiqi (*Genghis Khan*).
Best Editing: Cheng Long (*A Time to Remember*).

Best Music: Zhang Shaotong (*Romance in Xishuangbanna*).
Best Sound: Zhang Wen (*Genghis Khan*).
Best First Work by a Director: Zhang Yang (*Spicy Love Soup*).
Best Documentary: *Zhou Enlai's Diplomatic Troubles.*
Best Musical: no award.
Best Children's Film: *Flower Season, Rain Season.*
Best Feature Film Co-production: *Eighteen Springs* (Dir: Ann Hui).
Special Jury Prizes: *The Big March: Sweeping across the Southeast*, and actress Pan Yu (*Live in Peace*).

21st Hundred Flowers Awards

Best Films: *Party A, Party B, The Opium War, The Long March.*
Best Actor: Ge You (*Party A, Party B*).
Best Actress: Liu Bei (*Party A, Party B*).
Best Supporting Actor: Li Baotian (*Keep Cool*).
Best Supporting Actress: Zhang Lu (*This Woman's Life*).

Forthcoming Films

YIGE DOU BU NENG SHAO (Not One Less)

Script: Shi Xiangsheng. Dir: Zhang Yimou. Prod: Guangxi Film Studio.

WODE FUQIN MUQIN (The Road Home)

Script: Bao Shi. Dir: Zhang Yimou. Prod: Guangxi Film Studio.

GUIZI LAILE

Dir: Jiang Wen. Phot: Gu Changwei. Players: Jiang Wen, Jiang Hongbo, Yuan Ding.

XIYANG JING (Shadow Magic)

Dir: Ann Hu. Cast: Jared Harris, Xia Yu. Prod: Beijing Film Studio (China)/CMPC (Taiwan)/Hollywood Partners (US).

Jared Harris in Ann Hu's SHADOW MAGIC

Useful Addresses

August First Film Studio
A1, Beili
Liuliqiao
Guanganmenwai
Beijing 100073
Tel: (86 10) 6681 2329
Fax: (86 10) 6326 7324

Beijing Film Institute
4 Xitucheng Rd
Haidian District
Beijing 100088
Tel: (86 10) 6201 8899
Fax: (86 10) 6201 3895

Beijing Film Studio
77 Beisanhuan Central Rd
Haidian District
Beijing 100088
Tel: (86 10) 6201 2067
Fax: (86 10) 6201 2312

Changchun Film Studio
20 Hongqi St
Changchun 130021

Tel: (86 431) 595 3511
Fax: (86 431) 595 2747

China Film Archive
3 Wenhuiyuan Rd.
Haidian District
Beijing 100088
Tel: (86 10) 6225 4422
Fax: (86 10) 6225 0362

China Film Corp.
(import, export)
25 Xinjiekouwai St
Beijing 100088
Tel: (86 10) 6225 4488
Fax: (86 10) 6225 0652

China Film Coproduction Corp.
5 Xinyuan South Rd
Chaoyang Distruct
Beijing 100027
Tel: (86 10) 6466 3330
Fax: (86 10) 6466 3983

Guangxi Film Studio
26 Youai North Rd

Nanning 530001
Tel: (86 771) 313 4261
Fax: (86 771) 313 3739

Imar Film Co.
No. 8, Jian'an Xi Lu
Haidian district
Beijing 100088
Tel: (86 10) 6207 3032
Fax: (86 10) 6207 3117

Pearl River Film Production Co.
352 Xingang Central Rd
Guangzhou 510311
Tel: (86 20) 8420 2238
Fax: (86 20) 8420 9584

Shanghai Film Studio
595 Caoxi North Rd
Shanghai 200030
Tel: (86 21) 6438 7100
Fax: (86 21) 6439 1650

Xi'an Film Studio
70 Xiying Rd
Xi'an 710054
Tel: (86 29) 552 2526
Fax: (86 29) 552 2611

CROATIA — Tomislav Kurelec

These are dire days for Croatian cinema, as the industry struggles with the national economic crisis. Zagreb-based Kinematografi, the largest distributor of foreign films, and owner of the Zabreb cinemas which generate over 60% of the box-office market, is in financial difficulty. So too is Croatian Television (HRT), which has co-produced nearly all Croatian films in the eight years since independence. The popularity of Croatian films at home has been in steady decline. Cinemas in several towns have been closed down; 117 new films were shown in Croatia in 1998, 21 fewer than in 1996.

Two films from the 1996–97 season were huge successes, Vinko Brešan's comedy, *How the War Started on My Island*, with more than 300,000 admissions, and Milan Blažeković's feature length animation, *The Strange Adventures of Apprentice Hlapić* (200,000-plus). Since then, features which attract 10,000 or 15,000 viewers have been regarded as successful. None of this, however, has stopped new features from being made and at the 1998 Croatian Film Festival in Pula, six new films were shown – the average annual output for Croatia.

The two most successful films at the festival were both comedies, Snježana Tribuson's **Melita and Her Three Men** (*Tri muskarca Melite Zganjer*) and Krsto Papić's *When the Dead Start Singing* (*Kad mrtvi zapjevaju*). Tribuson's script has our heroine, Melita, battling problems with her weight and her love life, and the story is told with warmth and sympathy. First, she wants to have an affair with the star of her

Krsto Papić directing WHEN THE DEAD START SINGING

Still from Neven Hitrec's MADONNA

favourite Latin American soap opera while he is in Zagreb to star in a co-production. Next she tries to get it together with the womanising police inspector who only shows an interest in her because he needs a place to stay after being thrown out by his wife. Finally, she hits it off with the young pastry-cook who's been in love with her for ages, but has not managed to tell her because he is shy and stammers.

Born in 1957, Tribuson had previously directed eight television films and a feature, *Recognition* (1996), which also won awards at the national film festival. She has drawn on the 1960s Czech comedy tradition of Forman and Menzel, while visually she is akin to Pedro Almodóvar, especially when she explores kitsch. Yet she blends these influences with a fine representation of female concerns in contemporary Croatian society. Local audiences respond well to Croatian comedy (while turning to Hollywood fare for suspense and action), and *Melita* attracted 36,000 viewers, as many as went to see Michael Douglas in *The Game*.

Homecoming heroes?

Krsto Papić, now in his late sixties, is one of the most successful Croatian directors of all time. **When the Dead Start Singing**, his eighth film, is a road movie. It is the story of two Croatian emigrants, one having left for political reasons, the other to seek better economic prospects, who return to their homeland. The one who emigrated for economic reasons plays dead because he wants his family to get his German pension. They return just in time for the first Serb attacks. Some 22,000 viewers enjoyed Papić's mix of the humorous and the grotesque.

The year's other films were less successful, mostly because their attention was devoted more to ideology than human destinies – though they are not without cinematic merit. Mladen Juran's **Transatlantic** deals with pre-First World War emigration in the US. Two directors dealt with the Croatian struggle for independence at the beginning of the 1990s: the veteran Željko Senečić, in **Delusion** (*Zavaravanje*), and the talented newcomer Neven Hitrec, in **Madonna** (*Bogorodica*), whose none-too successful script was by his father Hrvoje Hitrec.

Real-life war veterans have not been happy with these films, and a group of them starred in **Encircled**, which was written, produced and directed, on video, by their comrade-in-arms Stjepan Sabljak. With a budget of just $5,000, the soldiers-turned-actors had to use real bullets – leftovers from the war – for the action scenes in a film reminiscent of John Boorman's *Deliverance*. Despite containing many beginner's mistakes its sincerity is captivating. The *Encircled* team plan to undertake more no-budget projects – let us hope that the economic situation does not deteriorate so far that all Croatian films have to be made this way.

TOMISLAV KURELEC has been a film critic since 1965, mostly on radio and television, and has directed five short films and many TV features.

Recent and Forthcoming Films

TRANSATLANTIC

Script: Mladen Juran (with Božidar Violić and Mate Matišić). Dir: Mladen Juran. Phot: Goran Trbuljak. Players: Melita Jurišić, Filip Šovagović, Alen Liverić, Boris Dvornik, Josip Genda, Matija Prskalo. Prod: Jadran film/HRT.

KAD MRTVI ZAPJEVAJUI (When the Dead Start Singing)

Script: Mate Matišić, Krsto Papić. Dir: Krsto Papić. Phot: Vjekoslav Vrdoljak. Players: Ivo Gregurević, Iveca Vidović, Mirjana Majurec, Ksenija Pajić, Djuro Utješanović. Prod: Jadran film/HRT.

ZAVARAVANJE (Delusion)

Script and Dir: Željko Senečić. Phot: Enes Midžić. Players: Sandra Lončarić, Božidar Orešković, Filip Šovagović, Loby Dimitrijević. Prod: Patria film/HRT.

AGONIJA (Agony)

Script: Georgij Paro, Jakov Sedlar. Dir: Sedlar. Phot: Karmelo Kursar. Players: Ena Begović, Sven Medvešek, Božidar Alić. Prod: Patria film/HRT.

TRI MUŠKARCA MELITE ŽGANJER (Melita and Her Three Men)

Script and Dir: Snježana Tribuson. Phot: Goran Mećava. Players: Mirjana Rogina, Goran Navojec, Suzana Nikolić, Sanja Vejnović, Ena Begović, Filip Šovagović. Ivop Gregurević, Ljubomir Kerekeš. Prod: Kvadar d.o.o.

KANJON OPASNIH IGAR (The Canyon of Dangerous Games)

Script: Hrvoje Hitrec, Vladimir Tadej. Dir: Tadej. Phot: Šime Strikoman. Players: B. Dvornik, S. Martinčević Mikić, D. Boljičak, G. Tadej, A. Ćagalj, I. Lukić, J. Genda. Prod: HRT/Zagreb film.

BOGORODICA (Madonna)

Script: Hrvoje Hitrec. Dir: Neven Hitrec. Phot: Stanko Herceg. Players: ljubomir Kerekeš, lucija Šerbedžija, Ivo Gregurević. Prod: Maxima film/HRT

GARCI (Garcia)

Script and Dir: Dejan Šorak. Phot: Vjekoslav Vrdoljak. Players: Ksenija Pajić, Dubravko Šimić. Prod: Ban film/HRT.

NEBO, SATELITI (Sky, Satellites)

Script and Dir: Lukas Nola. Phot: Darko Šuvak. Players: Filip Nola, Barbara Nola, Ivo Gregurević, Lucija [G]erbedžija. Prod: Ban film/HRT.

CRVENA PRAŠINA (Red Dust)

Script: Goran Tribuson. Dir: Zrinko Ogresta. Phot: Davorin Gecl. Players: Josip Kučan, Ivo Gregurević, Marko Matanović, Kristijan Ugrina. Prod: Inter film/HRT.

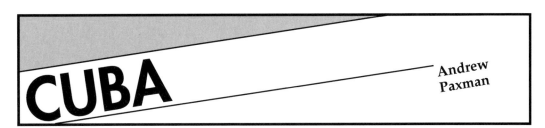

CUBA — Andrew Paxman

The problem with Oscar nominations is that they can give a misleading impression of a nation's film industry. Such was the case in 1994, when *Strawberry & Chocolate*, from Tomas Gutiérrez Alea and Juan Carlos Tabío, led many to believe that Cuban film was the next hot thing. Yet with the local economy enduring a dire "special period" following Russia's withdrawal of support, Cuba was barely eking out two films a year. At Havana's 1996 film festival, not one Cuban feature debuted.

The scenario today is much brighter. The ragged Cuban economy is growing again, thanks in part to European and Canadian investment in tourism and mining, and Europeans – notably the Spanish – are also keen to come to film. Some are simply making their own pictures, such as Wim Wenders' musical documentary, *Buena Vista Social Club* (Germany, 1999); others engage in co-production. Cubans bring little or no finance to such ventures, but can offer well-trained crews and a celebrated ability to stretch scant resources.

The December 1998 Havana fest – officially, the 20th Festival of New Latin American Cinema – gave clear indications of a revival in Cuban film. Local helmer Fernando Pérez took the top award for **Life is to Whistle** (*La Vida es Silbar*), which only the previous January had won a screenwriter's prize at Sundance, and long-absent veteran Humberto Solas (*Lucía*) won the prize for best unfilmed script, with his Chile-set *Horcón*.

Life is to Whistle is a beautifully-shot meditation on life in today's Cuba, more of a cinematic poem than a narrative, which studies denial and reconciliation in Havana. The film is notable for its gentle jokes at the expense of the Castro regime, some of them admittedly too subtle for foreign audiences, and also for the captivating debut of Claudia Rojas, as a nymphomaniac ballerina who takes a vow of chastity to secure the role of Giselle.

Two other local features premiered at the event, period piece **Mambi** and the docudrama **Che**, though to little acclaim. Better things may develop from scripts awarded subsidies by Ibero-American film fund Ibermedia: of the 15 Latin projects Ibermedia announced during the festival, four were due to be directed by Cubans.

Gains from Spain

Also last December, Spanish producers were thick on the ground, talking up greenlit co-productions or seeking new ones. Madrid-based Wanda Films, which co-produced *Life is to Whistle*, went on to co-produce Gerardo Chijona's Ibermedia-supported **Paraiso Bajo las Estrellas** (literally, *Paradise Under the Stars*), a comedy of errors set at Havana's famous Tropicana nightclub, complete with production numbers.

Another Spanish company, San Sebastián-based Igeldo, has co-produced Pastor Vega's **Las Profecías de Amanda**, again supported by Ibermedia. This stars Daisy Granados as a woman able to look into the past, present and future of people's lives. Meanwhile Argentina's Alberto Lecchi has helmed **Operación Fangio**, a

Still from Fernando Pérez's LIFE IS TO WHISTLE

Cuban-Argentine-Spanish collaboration about the kidnapping of motor-racing champion Juan Manuel Fangio in Havana in 1958.

All co-productions, like all native pictures, are handled by the national film institute, the ICAIC, under long-running president Alfredo Guevara. Production chief Camilo Vives is the institute's deal-maker. The ICAIC is very keen to co-produce, not least because of the impossibility of recouping at home, where the standard cinema ticket price is 10 cents. Havana's movie palaces mostly show foreign fare, including US films (often several years after their original release), using prints apparently donated by Spanish and independent distributors.

Despite the domestic revival, top Cuban thespians are finding more work in foreign pictures. Jorge Perugorría, who played the gay aesthete in *Strawberry*, has been most in-demand, recently appearing in Betty Kaplan's *Doña Bárbara* (Argentina-US, 1998) and Bigas Luna's *Volavérunt* (Spain, 1999). Mirta Ibarra, the widow of Gutiérrez Alea, and another *Strawberry* alumna, has also been very active, lately starring in Fernando Colomo's *Havana Quartet* (Spain, 1998).

Simultaneously, US actors and directors seem keener than ever to visit Cuba. In 1998, Jack Nicholson and Leonardo DiCaprio made special trips, and the Havana fest drew Coppola, the Coen brothers, Frances McDormand, Terry Gilliam and Randa Haines. Some are

Still from PARAISO BAJO LAS ESTRELLAS

clearly attracted because they think Cuba is fashionable, while others evince a genuine love for Latin cinema – and a desire to build bridges until Cubans and Americans can work together on a film set.

ANDREW PAXMAN led *Variety* coverage of Latin American TV and film from 1994–99, chiefly from Mexico City. He is co-author of a biography of Mexican media mogul Emilio Azcarraga Milmo.

Recent and Forthcoming Films

OPERACION FANGIO
(Operation Fangio)

Script: Claudia Furiati, Orlando Senna, Manuel Pérez. Dir: Alberto Lecchi. Phot: Hugo Colacé. Players: Dario Grandinetti, Ernesto Tapia. Prod: ICAIC, Aleph [TK] (Argentina), El Paso Prods. (Spain).

PARAISO BAJO LAS ESTRELLAS
(literally, **Paradise Under the Stars**)

Script: Gerardo Chijona, Luis Agüero, Senel Paz. Dir: Chijona. Phot: Raúl Pérez Ureta. Players: Thaís Valdés, Vladimir Cruz, Luis Alberto García. Prod: ICAIC, Wanda Films (Spain).

LAS PROFECIAS DE AMANDA
(literally, **The Prophecies of Amanda**)

Script: Aaron Vega, Pastor Vega. Dir: Pastor Vega. Phot: Rafael Solís. Players: Daisy Granados, Marisela, Berti, Adolfo Llaurado. Prod: ICAIC, Igeldo (Spain), Alter (Venezuela).

LA VIDA ES SILBAR
(Life is to Whistle)

Script: Fernando Pérez , Eduardo del Llano. Dir: Pérez . Phot: Raúl Pérez Ureta. Players: Luis Alberto García, Claudia Rojas, Isabel Santos. Prod: ICAIC, Wanda Films (Spain).

Useful Addresses

ICAIC
Calle 23 – 1111
Entre 8 y 10, Vedado,
La Habana
Tel: (537) 348 26/302 425
Fax: (537) 333 281
e-mail: productora@icaic.inf.cu
Contact: Camilo Vives

Festival del Nuevo Cine Latinoamericano
Calle 23 – 1155
Entre 8 y 10, Vedado
La Habana
Tel: (537) 552 841/552 849
Fax: (537) 334 273/333 078
e-mail: sitcine@icaic.inf.cu
Contact: Ivan Giroud

CZECH REPUBLIC
Eva Zaoralová

How does Czech cinema look ten years after film-makers eagerly demolished its state-controlled monopoly? Each year sees the advent of between 15 and 20 features, funded by various private producers and Czech Television, which has become the most important producer of documentaries and features. Contributions from the state, allocated according to somewhat unstable principles, represent an inconspicuous percentage of the ever-increasing budgets and, though audiences have remained reasonably faithful to Czech cinema, only very rarely can those budgets be recovered, as happened with the Oscar-winning *Kolya*.

Though still in the draft stage, the new law on audio-visual production and the state fund for cinematography should, among other things, lead to the founding of a national audio-visual centre and secure more stable film funding. With so few Czech films being picked up for international distribution (*Kolya* and Petr Zelenka's *The Buttoners* are the most recent examples) domestic directors' only exposure to international critics and audiences is at small festivals, or during the Karlovy Vary International Film Festival each July.

It is rare for a Czech film to appear at a large international festival, even rarer for one to be screened in competition. According to foreign film critics, this problem stems not only from the inherent handicap of a small film industry, but also from the attitude of Czech film-makers, who set their films in the present, but tend to neglect the most pressing contemporary themes, such as poverty, unemployment and racism.

The film which won more of the national Film Academy's Czech Lion awards for 1999 than any other, was Vladimír Michálek's **Sekal Has To Die** (*Je třeba zabít Sekala*). However, the public gave a lukewarm reception to this parable of the duel between good and evil. Conversely, Irena Pavlásková's **A Time of Debts** (*Čas dluhù*), vehemently condemned by the critics, worked its way into the box-office top ten. The film is a loose sequel to her debut, *Time of the Servants*, which described the cynical rise of an ambitious woman and was included in Critics' Week at Cannes in 1991.

1968 and all that

The Best Film award at the 12th Finale, a festival of Czech films held in Plzeò in the spring of 1999, went to **Return of the Idiot** (*Návrat idiota*). Talented director Sasa Gedeon, inspired by Dostoyevsky's novel, tells the contemporary story of a "pure" man who finds it hard to orient himself in an intricate maze of human relationships

Still from Jan Hrebejk's COZY DENS   *photo: Ivan Malý*

based on love, lies and hypocrisy. This masterful work, however, has been less popular with audiences than **Cozy Dens** (*Pelíšky*), the retro-comedy by another young film-maker, Jan Hrebejk. Set shortly before the Soviet invasion of August 1968 and played out to a soundtrack of pop hits, it succeeds in recreating the relaxed atmosphere of the Communist regime during the Prague Spring, before it was crushed by the arrival of the "friendly armies".

Experienced director Jaromil Jireš, one of the representatives of the "New Wave" of the 1960s, decided to try his hand at psychological science-fiction in **Double Role** (*Dvojrole*). The brain of an intelligent and principled old woman is transplanted into the body of an attractive young girl who is drawn towards doubtful company. The film is dominated by the performance of Tereza Brodská, the daughter of former star of Czechoslovak film Jana Brejchová and excellent stage and film actor Vlastimil Brodský.

Another experienced director from the younger generation, Zdeněk Troška, showed great professionalism in his fairytale **Helluva Good Luck** (*Z pekla Štìstí*). Well-known Czech animation director Michaela Pavlátová, turned to live action for the first time with *Absolute Love* (*Absolutní láska*), the most fascinating of three Prague-set tales in the portmanteau film, **Prague Stories** (*Praha oèima…*).

There were mixed reviews for Ivo Trajkov's **The Past** (*Minulost*), an attempt to capture reality as perceived by someone with severe hearing difficulties. The film-maker uses an unusual combination of documentary shots, feature performances by totally unknown actors and marked stylisation (suppressed or exaggerated sounds alternating with silence).

Critics and audiences rejected another experiment, **Rapid Eye Movement** (*Rychlé pohyby oèí*), the second film by recent FAMU graduate Radim Špacec, which he characterises as "an existential anti-story about love and bad dreams".

Still from PRAGUE STORIES

Field of dreams

Two debuts were well-received at the 12th Festival of Czech Films. The bitter comedy **What you Catch in the Rye** (*Co chytneš v žitě*) by recent FAMU graduate Roman Vávra comprises four tales whose common link is a field of rye transformed by the changing seasons. Though written by various screenwriters, the stories all share a poetic vision and cross the fragile border between reality and fantasy. The other debut, **Agatha** (*Agáta*) was written and directed by Prague Drama Academy graduate Dan Krameš. Based on stories by Chekhov, it was a film poem addressing the timeless theme of love.

Another debut scheduled for release in the second half of 1999 is **All My Loved Ones** (*Všicni moji blízcí*), written by competent dramatist Jiří Hubač and directed by Matěj Mináč. The film describes the life of a Jewish family on the threshold of the Second World War and a key character is the Englishman Nicholas Winton (still alive today) who saved several hundred Jewish children from the Holocaust. Jaroslav Brabec, a cinematographer who made his debut as a film director in 1993 with the parody *The Bloody Novel* (*Krvavy román*) is preparing his second feature, *Melancholy Chicken* (*Kure melancholik*), loosely based on the book by a well-known naturalist.

Good news for the industry came with the reopening of the Zlín film studios (formerly Gottwaldov). The Bonton Zlín

Studios will continue to focus chiefly on films for children and animation, although a new film aimed at adults has also been shooting there: an autobiographical work by experienced film-maker Vladimír Drha entitled *The Conception of My Younger Brother* (*Poèetí mého mladšího bratra*).

EVA ZAORALOVÁ is a Czech film critic and editor of the magazine *Film a doba*. The author of many essays and books on Italian, French and Czech cinema, she taught film history for ten years at FAMU in Prague, and is artistic director of the Karlovy Vary International Film Festival.

Recent and Forthcoming Films

CO CHYTNEŠ V ŽITE
(What You Catch in the Rye)

Script: Jaroslav Pozzi, Martin Ryšavý, Roman Vávra. Dir: Vávra: Phot: David Ployhar, Antonín Chundela, Miro Gábor. Players: Andrea Elsenerová, Ladislav Frej jr., Klára Issová, Iva Janžurová, Karel Brožek. Prod: Verbascumm/ Czech TV.

ČAS DLUHU (A Time of Debts)

Script and Dir: Irena Pavlásková. Phot: Yuri Sokol. Players: Karel Roden, Lucie Bílá, Ivana Chýlková, Tatian Vilhelmová, Jiří Labus. Prod: Eydelle Film/ČNTS s.r.o. – TV Nova.

DVOJROLE (Double-Role)

Script: Jaroslava Moserová, Jaromil Jireš. Dir: Jireš. Phot: Josef Víšek. Players: Tereza Brodská, Jan Hartl, Karel Roden, Slávka Budínová. Prod: Czech TV-Studio Brno.

KUŘE MELANCHOLIK
(Melancholy Chicken)

Script: Vladimí Körner, Jarooslav Brabec. Dir: Brabec. Phot: Martin Čech, Jiří Macát, Jarooslav Brabec. Players: Radko Chromek, Karel Roden, Anna Geislerová, Vilma Cibulková, Vlasta Chramostová, Lubomír Kostelka. Prod: Belt Film/Czech TV.

MINULOST (The Past)

Script and Dir: Ivo Trajkov. Phot: Klaus Fuxjaeger. Players: Karel Zima, Madla Zimová, Peter Georgiev, Klára Melíšková. Prod: The World Circle Foundation/ Czech TV (in cooperation with the Deaf and Hard of Hearing Union in the Czech Republic.

NÁVRAT IDIOTA
(Return of the Idiot)

Script and Dir: Saša Gedeon. Phot: Štěpán Kučera. Players: Pavel Liška, Anna Geislerová, Tatiana Vilhelmová, Jiří Langmajer. Prod: NEGATIV/Czech TV.

PELÍŠKY (Cozy Dens)

Script: Petr Jarchovský. Dir: Jan Hřebejk. Phot: Jan Malíř. Players: Jiří Kodet, Miroslav Donutil, Simona Stašová, Emilia Vašáryová, Eva holubová. Prod: Czech TV/Total Helpart.

VŠICNI MOJI BLÍZCÍ
(All My Loved Ones)

Script: Jiří Hubač. Dir: Matěj Mináč. Phot: Dodo Šimončlč. Players: Jiří Abrhám, Libuše Šafránková, Jiří Bartoška, Ondřej Vetchý, Ladislav Chudík. Prod: InFilm/Dting/Titanic/Markiza/ Czech TV.

ZPEKLA ŠTESTÍ (Close Thing)

Script and Dir: Zdeněk Troška. Phot: Juraj Fandli. Players: Michaela Kuklově, Miroslave Šimůnek, Daniel Hůlka, Vladimír Brabec, Sabina Laurinová. Prod: Frona Film/Whisconti.

Producers

Ateliéry Bonton Zlín
Filmová 174
761 79 Zlín
Tel: (420) 6752 7200
Fax: (420) 6752 7527

Barrandov Biografia
(also distributor)
Kříženeckého nám. 322
151 00 Praha 5
Tel: (420 2) 6707 1111
Fax: (420 2) 6707 2273

BUC Film
Krízeneckého nám. 332
152 00 Praha 5
Tel: (420 2) 581 9441
Fax: (420 2) 6707 2125

CINEART Productions
Vzdušná 817
140 00 Praha 4
Tel: (420 2) 6171 1108/6171 1044
Fax: (420 2) 6171 1048

Czech TV Productions
Kavcí hory

140 70 Praha 4
Tel: (420 2) 6121 2945
Fax: (420 2) 5121 1354

Febio, Ltd
Růžová ul. 13
110 00 Praha 1
Tel: (420 2) 2421 3933
Fax: (420 2) 2421 4254

NEGATIV
Svédská 21
150 00 Praha 5
Tel: (420 2) 5732 6042

Nova TV
Vladislavova 20
110 00 Praha 1
Tel: (420 2) 2421 3933
Fax: (420 2) 2421 4254

Space Films s.r.o.
(also distributor)
Karlovo nám. 19
120 00 Praha 2
Tel: (420 2) 2491 3043
Fax: (420 2) 2491 3045

VaC – Vachler Art Company
Na Žertvách 40
180 00 Praha 8
Tel: (420 2) 683 2600

Whisconti Production
Odbora 4
120 00 Praha 2
Tel/Fax: (420 2) 296 930

Distributors

Bonton Films
Národní tř. 28
1120 00 Praha 1
Tel: (420 2) 2110 5248
Fax: (420 2) 2422 5263

CINEMART a.s.
Národní 28
110 00 Praha 1
Tel: (420 2) 2110 5235
Fax: (420 2) 2110 5220

FALCON
Stroupežnického 6
150 00 Praha 5
Tel: (420 2) 538 085
Fax: (420 2) 533 194

Filmexport Prague
Na Moráni 5
128 00 Praha 2
Tel: (420 2) 2491 5239
Fax: (420 2) 293 312

Gemini Film
V jámě 1
110 00 Praha 1
Tel: (420 2) 2416 2471
Fax: (420 2) 2422 6562

**Intersonic Taunus
Prod. Ltd**
Palackého 15
110 00 Praha 1
Tel/Fax: (420 2) 2422 9007

Useful Addresses

Ministry of Culture
Milady Horákové 139
160 00 Praha 6
Tel: (420 2) 5708 5111
Fax: (420 2) 2431 8155

**FITES (Association of
Czech Film Artists)**
Pod Nuselskými schody 3
120 00 Praha 2
Tel: (420 2) 691 0310
Fax: (420 2) 691 1375

**Union of Czech
Distributors**
U Rajské zahrady 14
130 00 Praha 3
Tel: (420 2) 9000 2651

**Association of Producers
in the Audiovisual Industry
c/o SPACE Film**
Karlovo nám. 19
120 00 Praha 2
Tel: (420 2) 2491 3043

DENMARK — Ebbe Iversen

Astrong sense of optimism and confidence pervades the Danish film community on the brink of the new millennium. Parliament has allocated more money for film production than ever before, the domestic audience is keener to watch Danish films than it has been for decades, and the movies are receiving international attention, especially thanks to the Dogma movement, born in Copenhagen in 1995.

The Danish Film Institute (DFI), which is financially involved in the production of almost all Danish features, had a total budget of $36m (DKK 255m) for 1999, which can be seen in relation to 18 feature films – the number of Danish films released in 1998 – at an average cost of $1.8m. A comfortable parliamentary majority has decided to allocate an extra $7m to the DFI in 1999, $14m in 2000 and $21m per year in 2001 and 2002. According to DFI chief executive Henning Camre this should make it possible in four years' time to increase annual production to around 25 features.

The domestic cinema circuit is expanding rapidly. In 1998, Denmark had 166 cinemas with a total of 328 screens and 50,634 seats and the average Dane went to the cinema 2.07 times that year. Several new multiplexes are in the pipeline, the largest being built in Copenhagen by the

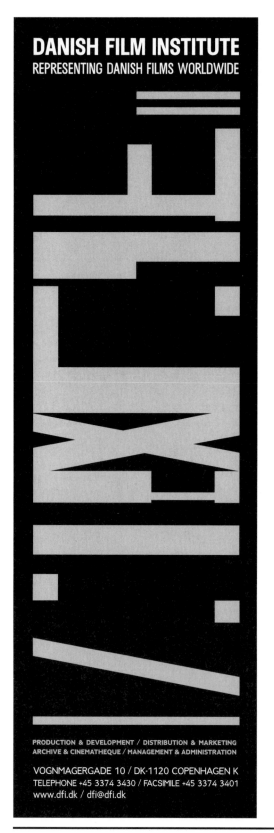

German company CinemaxX (ten screens), which also intends to build new multiplexes in the three largest provincial towns: Århus, Odense and Aalborg.

The growing commercial success of domestic films is reflected by the fact that in April this year a record 46% of total admissions were secured by Danish films, with Søren Kragh-Jacobsen's Dogma instalment **Mifune** (*Mifunes sidste sang*) and Susanne Bier's witty romantic comedy **The One and Only** (*Den eneste Ene*) simultaneously drawing large crowds.

In spite of such success, a much-publicised conflict erupted in the film world in the spring of 1999, the main protagonists being the DFI and Zentropa, which – run by Lars von Trier and Peter Aalbæk Jensen – is Denmark's most active production company. Jensen accused the DFI, and in particular Thomas Stenderup, who heads its production and development division, of favouring director Bille August with a debatable grant for a planned film, and trying to sabotage von Trier's new project, the $14m musical *Dancer in the Dark*.

The DFI denied the accusations, and the conflict reached a head when about 30 of Denmark's most prominent film-makers – among them Kragh-Jacobsen, Thomas Vinterberg, Nils Malmros, Henning Carlsen and Nicolas Winding Refn – publicly criticised the DFI for centralising all decisions and dismantling the film-makers' democratic influence. The DFI subsequently arranged a large conciliatory meeting, which seemed to settle matters – at least temporarily. Camre and Stenderup admitted they had not been sufficiently receptive when dealing with the film-makers.

Of mice, men and vampires

Among new features, veteran director Henning Carlsen's **I Wonder Who's Kissing You Now** (original title) is a light, charming comedy about a paranoid husband tormented by jealousy, while Christian Braad Thomsen's first feature in 15 years, **The Blue Monk** (*Den Blå Munk*), describes in fine psychological detail the hopes, frustrations and dreams of the regulars in a Copenhagen bar, while paying homage to the music of Thelonious Monk.

In **Mimi & The Movers** (*Mimi & Madammerne*), Linda Wendel tells the not very original story of the reunion of a handful of former female friends – a sort of feminist *The Big Chill*. Torben Skjødt Jensen, previously known for experimental shorts, in his first feature **The Man Who Would Live Forever** (*Manden som ikke ville dø*) employs striking black-and-white CinemaScope images to recount the weird fable of a man, who after losing his wife and son in a fire, decides to spite God by living forever. The film is symbolic and ambitious, but also frustratingly incoherent and rather pointless.

First-time director Thomas Borch Nielsen's **Webmaster** (*Skyggen*) is a technically impressive cyberspace-thriller, which was a commercial failure domestically, but was sold to a large number of territories. Children were pleased to watch Jørn Faurschou's good-

Still from THE BLUE MONK
photo: Ole Kragh-Jacobsen

humoured **Albert** and Jannik Hastrup's charming cartoon **Circleen – City Mice** (*Cirkeline – Storbyens mus*).

Shaky González's debut, **Angel of the Night** (*Nattens engel*), is a wild and bloody vampire horror film, not to be taken seriously, whereas serious ambitions are intelligently executed in Morten Henriksen's handsome and thought-provoking **The Magnetist's Fifth Winter** (*Magnetisørens femte vinter*), about a nineteenth-century hypnotist (inspired by

Paprika Steen and Sidse Babett Knudsen in THE ONE AND ONLY
photo: Ole Kragh-Jacobsen

Ole Lemmeke and Johanna Sällström in THE MAGNETIST'S FIFTH WINTER

Franz Anton Mesmer), who may or may not be a fraud. Ole Christian Madsen's **Pizza King** tells a vivid, dynamic and highly realistic story of young immigrant hustlers in Copenhagen.

A tragic farewell

The beloved Olsen Gang, who amused Danes in 13 films between 1968 and 1981, made one last appearance in **The Olsen Gang – Final Mission** (*Olsen Bandens sidste stik*). More nostalgic than funny, the project was hit by a double tragedy when both director Tom Hedegaard and actor Poul Bundgaard died during shooting. Nevertheless, the film was finished, and was, as expected, a commercial success.

Nicolas Winding Refn, whose debut *Pusher* was a huge domestic success, has made a very different film with the uncompromising social drama **Bleeder** (original title) about the tragic results of a man not being able to cope with his wife's pregnancy. Another sophomore effort, **Possessed** (*Besat*), by Anders Rønnow-Klarlund (*The Eighteenth*), is an occult

thriller about Satan's appearance in Denmark – quite entertaining in all its morbid absurdity. Katrin Ottarsdóttir's **Bye Bye Bluebird** is a rare item, a comic, poignant road movie from the remote North Atlantic Faroe Islands about two hip young girls returning from abroad to visit their narrow-minded families.

Former stunt expert Lasse Spang Olsen's crazy crime story **In China They Eat Dogs** (*I Kina spiser de hunde*) is clearly influenced by Quentin Tarantino in its playful mixture of black humour and shocking violence. The film is wittily scripted by Anders Thomas Jensen, who also co-wrote *Mifune*, and who having twice been nominated for an Academy Award for Best Short Fiction Film (for *Ernst & the Light* and *Wolfgang*), this year collected the coveted award for the satirical, very funny *Election Night* (*Valgaften*) about a man (Ulrich Thomsen from Vinterberg's *The Celebration*) who is forced to confront various forms of racial intolerance, as he hurries to cast his vote. *Election Night* is an outstanding example of the large number of excellent shorts produced by Dansk Novellefilm .

Among films currently in production, pre-production or post-production, the greatest expectations are linked to von Trier's **Dancer in the Dark**, which was shot in the summer of 1999 in Sweden. Catherine Deneuve, Sweden's Peter Stormare and Icelandic singer Björk head the cast in the story of an Eastern European immigrant (Björk) in the United States who struggles hard to provide for her child, while in danger of going blind. *Dancer in the Dark* is scheduled to have its world

Catherine Deneuve, Björk and Lars von Trier rehearsing DANCER IN THE DARK   *photo: Rolf Konow*

premiere at Cannes in 2000. Also on the way is **Katja's Adventures** (*Falkehjerte*), in which Lars Hesselholdt tells the story of a Danish girl who falls asleep in a truck and wakes up in Italy. With a budget of $3m this is the most expensive Danish film for children ever made.

Finally, the Dogma movement is alive and well. After *The Celebration*, *Idiots* and *Mifune*, director Kristian Levring shot the fourth official Dogma film, **The King is Alive**, during the summer of 1999 in Namibia, with Jennifer Jason Leigh heading the cast. At Cannes, Zentropa's Peter Aalbæk Jensen struck deals with producers in a number of European countries, among them England, Germany and Holland, to co-produce 16 Dogma films over the next two years. At press time, the names of the directors had yet to be revealed.

EBBE IVERSEN has been a professional journalist since 1966. He has been film critic of *Berlingske Tidende* since 1973, and is a former co-editor of the magazine *Kosmorama*.

Producers

ASA Film Production ApS
Mosedalvej
DK-2500 Valby
Tel: (45) 3618 8200
Fax: (45) 3116 8502

Crone Film Produktion A/S
Blomstervænget 52
DK-2800 Lyngby
Tel: (45) 4587 2700
Fax: (45) 4587 2705

Danish Film Studio
Blomstervænget 52
DK-2800 Lyngby
Tel: (45) 4587 2700
Fax: (45) 4587 2705
Telex: 37798 (studio dk)

Domino Film & TV Production
Langebrogade 6 A
København N
DK-1411
Tel: (45) 3296 6644
Fax: (45) 3296 0644

Film & Lyd Produktion A/S
Bredgade 63A
DK-1260 København K
Tel: (45) 3312 1050
Fax: (45) 3312 1093

Grasten Film, Regner
Lykkevej 6
DK-2920 Charlottenlund
Tel: (45) 3163 4424
Fax: (45) 3163 4823

Holst Film A/S, Per
Klampenborg 50
DK-2930 Klampenborg
Tel: (45) 3963 8866
Fax: (45) 3963 5575

Lense-Møller Film ApS, Lise
Fortunvej 56
DK-2920 Charlottenhund
Tel: (45) 3164 2284
Fax: (45) 3164 2269

Locomotion Kofod Schiller Film
Nannasgade 28
DK-2200 København N
Tel: (45) 3183 8900
Fax: (45) 3582 1737

Madsen, Kenneth Filmproduktion A/S
Guldbergsgade 29 F
DK-2200 København N
Tel: (45) 3536 0036
Fax: (45) 3536 0011

Mandart Production
H. P. Ørumsgade 47
DK-2100 København

Metronome Productions A/S
Søndermarksvej 16
DK-2500 Valby

Nimbus Film
Ryesgade 106A
DK-2100 København Ø
Tel: (45) 3526 1110
Fax: (45) 3526 1182

Nordisk Film Production A/S
Mosedalvej
DK-2500 Valby
Tel: (45) 3630 1033
Fax: (45) 3116 8502

Panorama Film International Ltd.
The Old Mill, London Road, Hook,
Hants AG27 9EH, England
Tel: (44) 256 766868
Fax: (44) 256 768747

Penta Film
Strandgade 4 B
DK-1401 København K
Tel: (45) 3296 6230
Fax: (45) 3296 0014

Ravn Film og Media Aps
Mosedalvej 11 B
DK-2500 Valby
Tel: (45) 3645 5800
Fax: (45) 3645 0808

Such Much Movies ApS
Blomstervænget 52
DK-2800 Lyngby
Tel: (45) 4587 2700
Fax: (45) 4587 2705

Superfilm Productions
Forbindelssvej 5
DK-2100 København Ø
Tel: (45) 3142 4611
Fax: (45) 3142 4611

Vestergaard Film, Jørgen
Gadekøret 24, Sennels
DK-7700 Thisted
Tel: (45) 9798 50020
Fax: (45) 9798 5020

Victoria Film
Frederiksberggade 16
DK-1459 København K
Tel: (45) 6260 1595
Fax: (45) 6260 1534

Zentropa Entertainment ApS
Avedøre Tværvej 10
DK-2650 Hvidovre
Tel: (45) 3686 8776/3678 0055
Fax: (45) 3678 0077

Distributors

AB Collection
Hirsemarken 3
DK-3520 Farum
Tel: (45) 4499 6200
Fax: (45) 4295 1786

Camera Film
Mikkel Bryggers Gade 8
DK-1460 København K
Tel: (45) 3313 6112
Fax: (45) 3315 0882

Constantin Film ApS
Skelbækgade 1
DK-1717 København V
Tel: (45) 3325 2424
Fax: (45) 3325 0707

Still from THE OLSEN GANG – FINAL MISSION

Egmont Audio Visual A/S
Skelbækgade 1
DK-1717 København V
Tel: (45) 3325 4000
Fax: (45) 3325 4002

Holland House
Vesterbrogade 26, 2
DK-1620 København V

Gloria Film
Vesterbrogade 149
DK-1620 København V
Tel: (45) 3327 0022
Fax: (45) 3327 0099

Nordisk Film Distribution A/S
Skelbøkgade 1
DK-1717 København V
Tel: (45) 3123 2488
Fax: (45) 3123 0488

Scala Film
Centrumpladsen
DK-5700 Svendborg
Tel: (45) 6221 8866
Fax: (45) 6221 0821

20th Century Fox
Skelbækgade 1, 3
DK-1717 København V
Tel: (45) 3325 4000
Fax: (45) 3325 4002

**United International Pictures
(UIP)**
Hauchsvej 13
DK-1825 Frederiksberg C
Tel: (45) 3131 2330
Fax: (45) 3123 3420

Warner & Metronome ApS
Søndermarksvej 16
DK-2500 Valby
Tel: (45) 3146 8822
Fax: (45) 3644 0604

Useful Addresses

Danish Film Institute
Vognmagergade 10
DK-1120 København K
Tel: (45) 3374 3430
Fax: (45) 3374 3435
Tlx: 31465 dfilm dk

The Danish Film Studio
Blomstervænget 52
DK-2800 Lyngby
Tel: (45) 4587 2700
Fax: (45) 4587 2705

Risby Studios
Ledøjevej 1
DK-2620 Albertslund
Tel: (45) 4262 9646

Danish Film Institute Workshop
Vognmagergade 10
DK-1120 København V
Tel: (45) 3374 3480
Fax: (45) 3374 3490

National Film Board of Denmark
Statens Filmcentral
Film House Denmark
Vognmagergade 10
DK-1120 København K
Tel: (45) 3374 3500
Fax: (45) 3374 3565

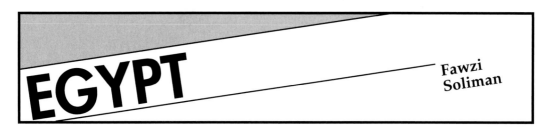

EGYPT

Fawzi
Soliman

The wheels of the Egyptian film industry are grinding once again. The two giant companies recently founded by a group of entrepreneurs are starting to bring dividends. Sho'aa (Cultural Media Co.) is creating good opportunities for budding directors and Egyptian Renaissance has built new cinemas, boasting up-to-date equipment, in Alexandria, Cairo and the Cairo suburbs.

Subsidiaries of Egyptian Television have been active in film production, making 13 films which have covered their costs. Nile Thematic Channels Film Production (TV) hopes to introduce a new generation of film-makers, beginning with Ahmad Maher's **April Signs**. Complaints against cinemas which were screening filmed stage productions led the Chamber of Film Industry to halt such action. Meanwhile the prime minister has issued a decree whereby taxes on foreign films are to decrease from 40% to 10%, and those on Egyptian films from 20% to 5%. That is a positive move, but there is still a need for reducing taxes on all equipment and raw materials imported for film production.

An Upper Egyptian at AUC, a comedy starring Mohamed Heneidy, has become the biggest box-office hit in the history of Egyptian Cinema. Huge audiences rooted for the hero, who leaves Upper Egypt on a scholarship to the American University in Cairo and must rely on old-style Southern values to help him cope in the complicated, metropolitan community. The brilliant script is by producer Medhat El-Adl, and smoothly directed by Sudanese-born Said Hamed.

Less commercially successful was **"Smile, the Photo Will be Nicer"**, which showed director Sherif Arafam and scriptwriter Waheed Hamed working in perfect harmony. It features three generations of a middle-class family courageously confronting various life events. Superstar Ahmed Zaki won numerous awards in the lead role, as a rural photographer who moves to Cairo to look after his daughter while she attends university.

Approaching 60 years of age, and after almost 50 films, Nadia El-Guindy remains one of the biggest box-office draws, her movies carefully tailored to accommodate her staple role: the attractive, athletic and powerful woman who always emerges victorious. The latest examples are **The Empress** (in which she battles a drug lord) and **Security Case** (this time the enemies are international terrorists).

Another major star, Adel Imam, takes comical pot-shots at contemporary politics in **Mahrous – The Minister's Boy**. London-based Syrian director Anwar El-Kawadri's **Nasser**, co-written with Britain's Erich Selders, was not as successful a biopic as *Nasser '56* (See *IFG 1996*). It chronologically traces the major events in the life of the Egyptian leader from 1935 until his death in 1970.

Still from Anwar El-Kawadri's NASSER

Still from Daoud Abdel Sayed's LAND OF FEAR

Masters of their art

In his new film, **The Other** (*Al-Akhar*), the great Youssef Chahine presents another joint co-production with France (and for the first time on a Chahine film, Egyptian Television was also involved). The movie's love story, augmented by music and song, touches on an array of important issues, including globalisation, extremism and terrorism; ultimately it is an appeal for humans to understand one another better.

Another great director back on the scene is Daoud Abdel Sayed, with **Land of Fear** (*Ard El-Khouf*), which delves controversially into the intricate relationships and loyalties of the criminal underworld, and explores a generation torn between principles and reality. **Date Wine** (*Arack Ek-Balah*), the second film of Radwan El-Kashef, had won eight prizes at international film festivals before being released at home. It describes daily life in a small village in the South, where the men have emigrated to Gulf countries, leaving behind their women, an old man and an adolescent who has to take all responsibility. This is a fine study of the complexity of male-female relationships in a region built on rigid tradition.

Two Egyptian films participated in the Cairo International Film Festival: **The Disappearance of Gaafer El-Masry** (*Iktifaa Gaafer El-Masry*), directed by Add El-Aasar and based on a Spanish play, shared the Ministry of Culture prize, and **Concerto darb Saada**, a second film from Asmaa El-Bakri, won the jury prize, for its attempt to address inter-cultural relations. The National Film Centre has produced 11 shorts in various genres, including *The Last Scene*, by Saad Hendawi, which took part in many festivals.

FAWZI SOLIMAN is Vice-President of the Egyptian Film Critics Association. He has contributed to magazines and newspapers in Egypt and the Arab world.

Recent and Forthcoming Films

EDHAK EL-SOURA TETL'A HELWA ("Smile, the Photo Will Be Nicer")

Script: Waheed Hamed. Dir: Sherif Arafa. Phot: Ramses Marzouk. Players: Ahmad Zaki, Laila Elwy, Sana'a Gamil. Prod: Waheed Harned Films and TV.

GAMAL ABED NASSER (Nasser)

Script: Anwar El-Kawadri, Erich Sclders, Dir: El-Kawadri. Phot: Mohsen Nasr. Players: Khaled El-Sawi, Hesham Selim, Gamil Rateb, Abla Kamel. Prod: Al-Batrik Art Production.

AL-AKHAR (The Other)

Script: Yousef Chahine, Khalikd Youssef. Dir: Chahine. Phot: Mohssen Nasr. Players: Nabila Ebeid, Mahmoud Hemeda, Hani Salama, Hanan Truki. Prod: Misr International/ Radio & T.V. Union (France).

ARD EL-KHOUF (Land of Fear)

Script and Dir: Daoud Abdel Sayed. Phot: Samir Bahzan. Players: Ahmed Zaki, Farah, Safwa, Hamdy Gheiss. Prod: Sho'aa.

ARACK EL-BALAH (Date Wine)

Script and Dir: Raadwan El-Kashef. Phot: Tarek El-Telmessani. Players: Sherihan, Mohamed Nagati, Fayza Amasaib. Prod: Misr International.

CONCERTO DARB SAADA

Script: Hossam Zalkarya, Rafik El-Sabban. Dir: Asma El-Bakri. Phot: Mohsen Nasr. Players: Nagla Fathi, Salah Ek-Saadani, Salwa Khattab, Hassan Kami. Prod: Misr International.

Still from Raadwan El-Kashef's DATE WINE

Still from THE DISAPPEARANCE OF GAAFER EL-MASRY

IKTIFAA GAAFTER EL-MASRY (The Disappearance of Gaafer El-Masry)

Script: Bassyouni Osman. Dir: Adel Al Aasar. Phot: Mohsen Nasr. Players: Nour El-Sherif, Hussein Fahmy, Raghda. Prod: Egyptian Union of Radio & Television.

FATAT MEN ISRA'IL (A Girl from Israel)

Script: M. Moharam, R Sabban, F. Abdel Khalek, Ihab Radi. Dir: Radi. Phot: Maher Radi. Players: Mahmoud Yassin, Raghda, Farouk El-Feshaoui, Khaled El-Nabawi. Prod: Shoaa & Radi Films.

Producers and Distributors

Al-Alamia for TV & Video
10 Naguib El-Rehani St
Cairo
Tel: (20 2) 577 0259
Fax: (20 2) 577 029

Egyptian Radio & TV Film
Kornish El-Nil, Maspero
Cairo
Tel: (20 2) 769 584/575 9313
Fax: (20 2) 574 6989

Egyptian Renaissance Co.
162 (B) 26th July St.
Agouza, Cairo
Tel: (20 2) 303 8422/3/4
Fax: (20 2) 303 4307

El-Sultan Film
102 Al Aharam Av.
Giza
Tel: (20 2) 385 5561
Fax: (20 2) 386 000

Hani Fawzi Film
40 Talaat Garb St.
Cairo
Tel: (20 2) 576 7430
Fax: (20 2) 575 6840

Misr Al Arabiya Films
12 Soliman El-Halaby St.
Cairo
Tel: (20 2) 574 8879
Fax: (20 2) 574 8878

Misr International
35 Champollion St.
Cairo
Tel: (20 2) 578 8034/578 8038
Fax: (20 2) 578 8033

El Adl Film
4 Oraby Sq.
Cairo
Tel: (20 2) 579 0290
Fax: (20 2) 579 5295

Shoa'a Cultural & Media Arab Co.
28 Yathreb St.
Dokki
Giza
Tel: (20 2) 336 9510
Fax: (20 2) 336 9511

Studio 13
Soliman El-Halaby St.
Cairo
Tel: (20 2) 574 8807
Fax: (20 2) 578 1406

Sultan Film
102 Al-Ahram Ave.
Giza
Tel: (20 2) 340 1523'25
Fax: (20 2) 304 7744

Useful Addresses

Academy of Arts
City of Arts
Gamal El-Din El-Afghany St.
Giza
Tel: (20 2) 561 3995
Fax: (20 2) 561 1034

Chamber of Film Industry
33 Oraby St.
Cairo
Tel: (20 2) 574 1677
Fax: (20 2) 575 1583

Cultural Development Fund
Opera Area, Gezira
Cairo
Tel: (20 2) 340 4234/7001
Fax: (20 2) 341 4634

National Film Centre
City of Arts
Al Ahram Ave.
Giza
Tel: (20 2) 585 4801
Fax: (20 2) 585 4701

ESTONIA
Jaan
Ruus

The state production subsidy provided through the Estonian Film Foundation increased by 10% in 1998 to $1.33m (17.6 million crowns), and the Estonian Cultural Endowment (funded by tobacco and alcohol taxes) gave $640,000 to film projects. To set these grants in context, minimal feature budgets are around $380,000 per film. Since the domestic film industry was saved from collapse by the doubling of state subsidies in 1996, novice producers have become over-reliant on state support, instead of seeking private finance at home and abroad. Rules state that a feature must be at least 20% equity-financed but, to the anger of many, some films end up wholly government-funded.

During Soviet times, three features were made every year in Estonia, but in 1998 just two were completed. One of them, **Georgica**, had taken director Sulev Keedus five years and $600,000 to bring to the screen. This starkly-beautiful film is visually and philosophically ambitious. A mute boy is sent away for rehabilitation to a remote Estonian island and left in the care of a former missionary who, years after returning from Africa, dreams of translating Virgil's poem *Georgica* into Swahili. The old man notes, as Virgil did 2,000 years ago, that a peasant can see happiness in everyday farm labour.

Georgica's words and images are an attempt to counter destructive forces. Its lyrical, dreamy cinematography and slow, rather monotonous rhythm reminded festival programmers of Tarkovsky or Sokurov. At the festival in Naples, Virgil's

Evald Aavik as Jakub in Sulev Keedus' GEORGICA

home city, the film won the Jury's Grand Special Prize and Eevald Aavik's tour de force as the ex-missionary brought him best actor prizes at Russia's Kinoshok Festival and France's 12th Nordic Film Festival.

Dear Mister Moon (*Kallis härra Q*) is a very rare bird: an Estonian film for children. Director Rao Heidmets, previously known for his work in animation, has two half-sisters 'steal' their beloved granny from her old people's home. While these main roles are treated seriously, the supporting parts are disappointingly caricatured. Children are also the target audience of *Tom & Fluffy*, a comical TV animation series about the adventures of two dogs. Estonian animation took three of the five main prizes at the Ottawa Animation Festival in 1998, with the humorous *The Night of the Carrots* taking the Grand Prix.

Newcomers make their mark

A lot can be expected from the first graduates of the audiovisual department of Tallinn Pedagogical University. Internationally, the most valued is Jaak Kilmi, whose diploma short *Came to Visit* (*Külla tuli*) won the Grand Prix at Poitiers in 1998 and the main award at Oberhausen in 1999. The film debunks countryside cliché as the hero, Leopold, finds that rural life can be just as violent as the city existence he is trying to escape.

In 1998, two film festivals were born in Estonia, both showing a distinguished programme. Sadly, the Tallinn Film Festival suffered great financial loss and may not continue, but the Black Nights Film Festival is ready to proceed, cooperating with Helsinki's Love and Anarchy. We have also had the 12th Visual Anthropology Festival, in the seaside resort of Pärnu.

The slump in cinemagoing appears to have ended, with total attendance in 1998 up 9% on the previous year, at 1,060,485. Box-office was up 40% to $3.51m thanks to a staggering 29% rise in the average ticket price, to $3.3 (44 crowns), the most expensive in Eastern Europe. In 1998, 177 films were screened in Estonian cinemas, 141 of which were American. There are still only three cinemas in Tallinn, the capital city of 400, 000 inhabitants and 110 cinemas in Estonia as a whole, only a dozen of which are open full-time.

Video rentals are gradually becoming better-regulated, as the choice of legally-distributed films has grown. However, the battle with video piracy continues; Finnish tourists visiting Tallinn continue to buy pirate videos in large quantities

JAAN RUUS is film critic for the biggest Estonian weekly, the Tallinn-based *Eesti Ekspress*. In the Estonian Film Foundation he serves as a Member of the Board and the Chairman of the Commission of Experts.

Recent and Forthcoming Films

KARU SDA (The Heart of the Bear)

Script: Nikolai Baturin, Rustam Ibragimbekov, Arvo Valton, Arvo Iho. Dir: Arvo Iho. Phot: Rein Kotov. Players: Rain Simmul, Lembit Ulfsak, Merle Palmiste, Dinara Drukarova, Julia Men, Arvo Kukumägi. Prod: Cumulus Project, Faama Film (Estonia)/ Komifilm (Russia).

A romantic drama of love, adventures and the search for spiritual harmony of a hunter living in Siberia.

DOOMINO (Domino)

Script: Maria Avdjushko, William Aldridge, Jüri Sillart, Graham Dallas, Tiina Lokk. Dir: Sillart. Phot: Allan Trow. Prod: Filmimax (Estonia)/Movie Makers (Sweden)/ Albafilm (UK).

Esoteric thriller about the deadly forces let loose when a former Soviet nuclear plant is used for suspicious commercial purposes.

LURJUS (An Affair of Honour)

Script and Dir: Valentin Kuik. Phot: Arko Okk. Players: Taavi Eelma, Elina Reinold, Andres Puustusmaa, Arvo Kukumägi, Vello Janson. Prod: OnFilm.

What would happen in today's world if men solved questions of honour with a duel? Based on the story by Vladimir Nabokov.

SAATAN JA ARLEKIIN
(The Devil and the Harlequin)

Script: Aleksandr Borodianski, Mati Päldre. Dir: Päldre. Prod: Lege Artis Film (Estonia)/Fora Film (Russia).

An opera singer is struck down by a fatal disease at the peak of his career, when he is singing Don Giovanni. Based on the life of popular Estonian singer Georg Ots (1920–1975).

KOLM KIUSATUST
(Me, Myself and I)

Script: Jaak Kilmi, Peter Herzog, Rainer Sarnet, Taavi Eelma. Dir: Kilmi, Peter Herzog, Rainer Sarnet. Prod: Exitfilm (Estonia)/ Zentropa (Denmark).

A compilation of three picaresque short stories following Jan the adventurer, Florian the playboy and Paul, a singer.

FORCE MAJEURE

Script: Priit Pärn. Dir: Rao Heidmets. Prod: Heidmetsa Filmistuudio, Nukufilm, Eesti Joonisfilm.

Grotesque, absurd comedy about extreme situations.

PAGULAS ROMANSS
(Romance to Refugee)

Script and Dir: Peeter Urbla. Prod: EXITfilm (Estonia)/Zentropa (Denmark).

A story of two exiled Estonian brothers struggling to survive in Stockholm.

DESINTEGRAATOR
(Disintegrator)

Script: Oskar Kurganov, Mati Unt. Dir: Tünu Virve. Prod: Freyja Film (Estonia)/Fora Film (Russia).

Drama based on the true story of sensational inventor Johannes Hint (1914–1985).

UNISTUSTE VALGE LAEV
(The White Ship of Dreams)

Script: Toomas Sula, Toomas Muru. Dir: Toomas Sula. Phot: Mait Mäekivi. Players: Friedrich Fromm, Maarja Jakobson, Peeter Volkonski, Marko Matvere, Linnar Priimägi, Eduard Toman. Prod: Nikodemus Film.

Second World War drama with touches of love, honour and betrayal.

K'IK MOONID ON PIKAD
(All Poppies Are Tall)

Script and Dir: Aare Tilk. Prod: Aristo.

Tragi-comic tale of a rock band in a little Estonian market town in the late 1960s.

LEND (The Flight)

Script: Indrek Ude, Toomas Sula, Toomas Muru. Prod: Nikodemus Film.

A romantic comedy about the validity of Lobatchevsky's geometry concerning the images of a man and a woman.

Producers

A Film
Kaare 15
EE 0016 Tallinn
Tel: (372 2) 670 6485
Fax: (372 2) 670 6433
e-mail: afilm@online.ee

Allfilm
Saue 11
EE 0006 Tallinn
Tel: (372 2) 654 1030
Fax: (372 2) 642 7115
e-mail: allfilm@datanet.ee

Cumulus Project
Köleri 32-2
EE 0010 Tallinn
Tel: (372 2) 426 645
Fax: (372 2) 640 9118
e-mail: iho@dpu.ee

Eesti Joonisfilm
Laulupeo 2
Tallinn 10121
Tel: (372 2) 601 0275
Fax: (372 2) 641 9047
e-mail: joonis@online.ee

EXITfilm
Kaupmehe 6
EE 0001 Tallinn
Fax: (372 2) 660 4121
Fax: (372 2) 448 416

Faama Film
Pärnu mnt 67 A
EE 0001 Tallinn
Tel: (372 2) 646 2027
Fax: (372 2) 646 2028
e-mail: faama@ index.ee
http:// www.ee/faama

FilmiMAX (also distributor)
Nafta 1
Tallinn 10152
Tel: (372 2) (2) 425 939
Fax: (372 2) 643 1351
e-mail: filmimax@ pb.uninet.ee

Freyja Film
Regati 8
Tallinn 11911
Tel/Fax: (372 2) (2) 238 682

F-Seitse
Narva mnt 63
Tallinn 10152
Tel: (372 2) 642 1808
Fax: (372 2) 642 1803
E-mail: fseitse@online.ee

Gaviafilm
Kivila 42–61
Tallinn 13814
Tel: (372 2) 523 2554
Fax: (372 2) 641 1629

Kairiin
Säpruse pst 175-53
Tallinn 13413
Tel: (372 2) (2) 520 182
Fax: (372 2) (2) 520 182
e-mail: jyri@datanet.ee

Lege Artis Film
Narva mnt 5
Tallinn 10117
Tel: (372 2) (2) 437 733
Fax: (372 2) 648 8014
E-mail: lehtmets@ uninet.ee

Myth Film
Kuhlbarsi 1–410B
Tallinn 10128
Tel: (372 2) 620 7573
Fax: (372 2) 620 7573
e-mail: helle@ coolbars.ee

Nikodemus Film
Kaupmehe 6
Tallinn 10114
Tel: (372 2) 642 6682
Fax: (372 2) 642 6682
e-mail: niko@online.ee

Nukufilm
Kaupmehe 6
Tallinn 10114
Tel/Fax: (372 2) 660 4040
e-mail: nukufilm@ online.ee

OMAfilm
Vene 14
Tallinn 10123
Tel: (372 2) 646 6249
Fax: (372 2) 646 6249
e-mail: omafilm@online.ee

ONfilm
Lasnamäe 24-12
Tallinn 11413
Tel: (372 2) (2) 215 296

Polarfilm
Suur-Sıjamäe 10
Tallinn 11415
Tel: (372 2) 638 1052
Fax: (372 2) 638 1052
e-mail: polarfilm@anet.ee

Q-film
Mäe talu, Neeme küla,
Harju mk. 74203
Tel: (372 2) 642 1808
Fax: (372 2) 642 1803

Raamat-film
Tähe 5–3
Tallinn 11619
Tel: (372 2) 670 0778
Fax: (372 2) 670 0778

Rao Heidmets Filmstudio
Müürivahe 31–16
Tallinn 10140
Tel: (372 2) 646 4299
Fax: (372 2) 646 4299
e-mail: raoheidmets@ hotmail.com

Weiko Saawa Film
Nikolai 15–4
Pärnu 80011
Tel: (372 2) 443 0772
Fax: (372 2) 443 0774
e-mail: docfest@chaplin.ee

Distributors

BDG
Vana-Posti 8
Tallinn 10146
Tel: (372 2) 699 7830
Fax: (372 2) 699 7855
e-mail: bdg@bdg.ee

MPDE
Pärnu mnt 45
Tallinn 10119
Tel: (372 2) 631 4546
Fax: (372 2) 631 3671
e-mail: lauri@ mpde.ee

Useful Address

Estonian Film Foundation
Harju 9
Tallinn 10146
Tel: (372 2) 641 1120
Fax: (372 2) 644 2356
e-mail: film@ efsa.ee

FINLAND
Antti
Selkokari

The most important news from Finland in 1998–1999 is that the Finns are going to the cinema again. After a decade of depressing box-office figures – between 5.4 and 5.9 million admissions a year throughout the 1990s – there was a huge leap in 1998 to 6.4 million. That a major reason for this is the newly-found success of domestic films only strengthens the happy mood within the country's movie industry.

The Finns flocked to see *Titanic* in the same mass numbers as in the rest of the world and, perhaps, the epic functioned as a wake-up call, its enormous power as a crowd-pleaser somehow making it easier for Finns to head to the movies; cinemagoing was suddenly sexy again. The most encouraging evidence of the new drawing power of domestic films is that they accounted for almost 50% of ticket sales in the first four months of 1999.

Another factor is the opening of new multiplexes in Helsinki and other key cities. The biggest is Finnkino's Tennispalatsi, with 2,697 seats and 14 screens, one of which is the widest in Scandinavia (180 square metres). Finnkino now controls about 60% of the market in Helsinki, but is facing tough competition from Sandrews, the Norwegian/Swedish-owned exhibitor, whose 10-screen Kinopalatsi multiplex sold a quarter of a million tickets in its first three months.

One of the local crowd-pleasers was Markku Polonen's **A Summer by the River** (*Kuningasjätkä*), in which a father and son must survive in the masculine world of log-floaters in the 1950s. With its nostalgic touch, Polonen's film reflects the confusion felt by the Finns, confronted by the post-modern world which no longer needs brutes to carry out heavy physical

Young soldiers in Olli Saarela's hugely successful Second World War drama, AMBUSH

labour and instead demands suave behaviour.

The same confusion fuels Aleksi Mäkelä's **The Tough Ones** (*Häjyt*), in which two ex-cons return to their small home town only to discover their old partner in crime has become the local police chief. The pair continue their family's tradition of bootlegging and have to face the consequences of selling moonshine to minors.

An inevitable tragedy – with violent deaths – ensues. The relentless pace must derive from Mäkelä's taste for action movies. The somewhat populist and racist undertones of the protagonists leave you wondering: what does this film (well on its way making the Top Ten list of 1999) tell us about the Finnish psyche?

Screening history

Timo Koivusalo's **The Swan and the Wanderer** (*Kulkuri ja Joutsen*) examines Finnish identity by dramatising the friendship and career of the most popular singer and songwriter duo of the post-war era in Finland. The songwriter, Repe Helismaa, was a musician with a flair for rhyming, and the singer, Tapio Rautavaara, was also a movie star and winner of the javelin gold medal at the London Olympic Games.

The film draws its emotional power from the eternal love Finns feel for booze, and from the duo's rhymes and melodies, familiar to virtually every Finn. As Helismaa, Martti Suosalo once again demonstrates what a good, versatile actor he is.

Another film dealing with Finnish history is Olli Saarela's **Ambush** (*Rukajärven tie*), the story of a young lieutenant and his squad as they enter a village in Soviet Karelia during the Second World War. He reaches a personal heart of darkness after hearing that his fiancée has been killed in an ambush, and goes berserk. The impressively shot film has reached its audience tremendously well, and at press time was on its way to becoming the most popular Finnish film of the 1990s.

Another film showing the booze-loving Finns at their best was Pekka Milonoff's **Love and Crime** (*Rikos ja rakkaus*), a comedy fuelled by Arctic fury. The murder of a small-time criminal proves to be too chaotic an event to be solved by the deceased's friends, each a more disorganised criminal than the next. If

Finnish machismo exists, here it is on show in all its pathetic hilarity.

An interesting film aiming for family audiences is Raimo O. Niemi and Ville Suhonen's **Tommy and the Wildcat** (*Poika ja Ilves*). A 12-year-old boy moves with his father to live near an Arctic wildlife park. The boy befriends a captive lynx, whom he sets free, because the park has decided to sell the lynx abroad. The local reindeer herders fear the predator and set up a mob to capture it. Cue lots of running through the snow and close shaves.

This should appeal to a large audience, with its universal animal-protecting theme embellished by enough suspense and chases to push the entertainment buttons.

The beautiful shots of Arctic nature and wildlife should make this acceptable fare for parents as well.

Finally, Aki Kaurismäki did what he has been on his way to doing for a long time: he made a film without any spoken dialogue. **Juha**, the story of a cabbage farmer deserted by his wife for a city slicker, shows the director's love of cinema history and his pursuit of a cinematic language cleansed of the compromises of commercial film-making.

ANTTI SELKOKARI is a film critic for Tampere-based daily newspaper *Aamulehti* and the president of the Finnish section of FIPRESCI.

Recent and Forthcoming Films

KUNINGASJÄTKÄ
(A Summer by the River)

Script and Dir: Markku Pölönen. Phot: Kari Sohlberg. Players: Pertti Koivula, Simo Kontio, Esko Nikkari, Anu Palevaara, Peter Franzén, Sulevi Peltola, Heikki Kujanpää, Ilkka Koivula, Hannu Virolainen. Prod: Fennada-filmi.

TULENNIELIJÄ (Fire-Eater)

Script: Pirkko Saisio. Dir: Pirjo Honkasalo. Phot: Kjell Lagerroos. Players: Tiina Weckstrom, Jordi Borrell, Tiina Makkonen, Richard Einhorn, Elina Hurme, Elsa Saisio, Elena Leeve. Prod: Marko Rohr Productions.

SÄÄDYLLINEN
MURHENÄYTELMÄ
(A Respectable Tragedy)

Script: Michael Baran. Dir: Kaisa Rastimo. Phot: Tuomo Virtanen. Sound: Pietari Koskinen. Players: Ville Virtanen, Päivi Akonpelto, Kyllikki Forssell, Timo Jurkka, Henriikka Salo. Prod: Kinotauros oy.

GOING TO KANSAS CITY

Script: Morrie Ruvinsky, Pekka

Mandart and Tony McNabb. Dir: Mandart. Phot: Pini Hellstedt. Players: Michael Ironside, Mikko Nousiainen, Melissa Galianos. Prod: Mandart Entertainment.

EROS JA PSYKHE
(Eros and Psyche)

Script: Timo Linnasalo and Ilpo Tuomarila, based on the play by Eeva-Liisa Manner. Dir: Linnasalo. Phot: Tahvo Hirvonen. Players: Antti Reini, Heli Takala, Markku Blomqvist, Matti Onnismaa. Prod: Reppufilmi.

JUHA

Script and Dir: Aki Kaurismäki. Phot: Timo Salminen. Players: Sakari Kuosmanen, Kati Outinen, Andre Wilms, Esko Nikkari, Elina Salo, Matti Peltola, Ona Kamu, Outi Mäenpää, Helka Viljanen. Prod: Sputnik Films.

POIKA JA ILVES
(Tommy and the Wildcat)

Script and Dir: Raimo O. Niemi and Ville Suhonen. Phot: Kari Sohlberg. Players: Konsta Hietanen, Antti Virmavirta, Kristiina Halttu, Jarmo Makinen, Vaiski the Lynx. Prod: Wildcat Production.

KULTALA (Gold)

Script: Heikki Vuento. Dir: Åke Lindman. Phot: Pauli Sipiläinen. Players: Vesa Vierikko, Pirkka-Pekka Petelius, Lasse Pöysti, Jarmo Mäkinen, Ville Haapasalo. Prod: Hanna Hemilä/Åke Lindman Film-Productions.

RUKAJARVEN TIE (Ambush)

Script: Antti Tuuri. Dir: Olli Saarela. Phot: Kjell Lagerroos. Players: Peter Franzén, Irina Björklund, Kari Heiskanen, Taisto Reimaluoto. Prod: Matila & Röhr MR Productions.

SOKKOTANSSI
(Blindfolded)

Script and Dir: Matti Ijäs. Phot: Kari Sohlberg. Players: Mikko Vanhala, Walter Grohn, Martti Suosalo, Pirkka-Pekka Petelius, Vesa-Matti Loiri, Johanna Kerttula. Prod: Omnia/Mea Ars.

MUSTA KISSA LUMIHANGELLA
(Black Cat on the Snow)

Dir: Anu Kuivalainen. Phot: Marita Hällfors. Prod: Lasse Saarinen/Kinotar.

HÄJYT (The Tough Ones)
Script: Aleksi Bardy. Dir: Aleksi Mäkelä. Players: Samuli Edelman, Teemu Lehtilä, Juha Veijonen, Kalevi Haapoja. Prod: Markus Selin/Solar Films.

HISTORY IS MADE AT NIGHT
Script: Patrick Amos. Dir: Ilkka Järvi-Laturi. Players: Bill Pullman, Irène Jacob, Isaiah Washington. Prod: Upstream Pictures/Ilkka Järvi-Laturi.

KULKURI JA JOUTSEN
(The Swan and the Wanderer)
Script: Timo Koivusalo and Juha Numminen. Dir: Koivusalo. Phot: Timo Heinänen. Players: Tapio Liinoja, Martti Suosalo, Heikki Nousiainen. Prod: Koivusalo/Artista Filmi.

PELON MAANTIEDE
(The Geography of Fear)
Script: Auli Mantila, from a novel by Anja Kauranen. Dir: Mantila. Phot: Heikki Färm. Players: Tanja Lotta Raikka, Leea Klemola. Prod: Zentropa Productions APS & Blind Spot Pictures /Tero Kaukomaa.

PIKKUSISKO (Little Sister)
Script: Raija Talvio. Dir: Taru Makela. Phot: Jouko Seppälä. Players: Vera Kiiskinen, Kai Lehtinen, Seela Sella, Pirkko Hamäläinen, Tarmo Ruubel. Prod: Bueno Pictures.

Producers

Artista Filmi Oy
Friitalantie 11
FIN 28400 Ulvila
Tel: (338 2) 538 3665
Fax: (358 2) 538 3663
e-mail: artista@pekko.com

Blind Spot Pictures Oy
Merimiehenkatu 27
FIN 00150 Helsinki
Tel: (358 9) 622 2144
Fax: (358 9) 622 2307
e-mail: blind@spot.pp. fi

Dada-Filmi Oy/
Fennada-filmi Oy
Kolmas linja 5
FIN 00530 Helsinki
Tel: (358 9) 737 788
Fax: (358 9) 730 734
e-mail: kari.sara@dada.pp. fi

Filmikonttori/Wildcat
Productions Oy
Katajanokan laituri 11 B, K 13
FIN 00160 Helsinki
Tel: (358 9) 658 799
Fax: (358 9) 658 414
e-mail: filmikonttori@co.inet.fi

GNUfilms Oy
Aleksis Kiven katu 26 C
FIN 00500 Helsinki
Tel: (358 9) 726 1525
Fax: (358 9) 726 1536
e-mail: gnu@gnufilms.fi

Kinoproduction Oy
Katajanokankatu 6
FIN 00160 Helsinki
Tel: (358 9) 63 217
Fax: (358 9) 662 048
e-mail: niina.otva@kolumbus.fi

Kinotar Oy
Meritullinkatu 33
FIN 00170 Helsinki
Tel: (358 9) 135 1864
Fax: (358 9) 135 7864
e-mail: kinotar@kaapeli.fi

Kinotaurus Oy
Lemuntie 7 A
FIN 00510 Helsinki
Tel/Fax: (358 9) 753 6506

Marianna Films Oy
Pursimiehenkatu 25
FIN 00150 Helsinki
Tel: (358 9) 622 1811
Fax: (358 9) 622 3855
e-mail: mika@marfilm.fi

MRP
Matila & Rohr Productions Oy
Tallberginkatu 1A/141
FIN 00180 Helsinki
Tel: (358 9) 685 2227
Fax: (358 9) 685 2229
e-mail: mrp@surfnet.fi

Seppa Callahanin Filmimaailma
Oy/Blacksmith Callahan's
Filmworld
Telakkakatu 2
FIN 00150 Helsinki
Tel: (358 9) 278 4078
Fax: (358 9) 278 4035

Solar Films Oy
Kiviaidankatu 1, 4.krs
FIN 00210 Helsinki
Tel: (358 9) 682 3622
Fax: (358 9) 682 3410
e-mail: jukka.helle@solarfilms.com

Sputnik Oy
Pursimiehenkatu 25
FIN 00150 Helsinki
Tel: (358 9) 622 1811
Fax: (358 9) 622 3855

Villealfa Filmproductions Oy
Pursimiehenkatu 25
FIN 00150 Helsinki
Tel: (358 9) 622 1811
Fax: (358 9) 622 3855

Talent House
Tallberginkatu 1A/141
FIN 00180 Helsinki
Tel: (358 9) 685 2227
Fax: (358 9) 685 2229
e-mail: johannes.talent@surfnet.fi

Åke Lindman Film-Productions
Oy
Elimaenkatu 14–16 C
FIN 00510 Helsinki
Tel: (358 9) 736 300
Fax: (358 9) 737 700
e-mail: hemila@kulta.com

Distributors

Buena Vista Int. Finland Oy
Kaisaniemenkatu 1 C 110
FIN-00100 Helsinki
Tel: (358 9) 2530 3200, 2530 3224
Fax: (358 9) 2530 3220

Cinema Mondo Oy
Unioninkatu 10
FIN-00130 Helsinki
Tel: (358 9) 629 528/177 501
Fax: (358 9) 631 450

Columbia TriStar Egmont Film
Film Distributors
Runeberginkatu 60 B
FIN-00260 Helsinki
Tel: (358 9) 4764 460
Fax: (358 9) 4764 4660

Finnkino Oy
Koivuvaaranjuja 2
FIN-01640 Vantaa
Tel: (358 9) 131 191, 1311 9323
Fax: (358 9) 852 7206

Kamras Film Group Oy
Mikonkatu 19
FIN-00100 Helsinki
Tel: (358 9) 6220 0260
Fax: (358 9) 6220 0261

Kinoscreen Oy
Katajanokankatu 6
FIN-00160 Helsinki
Tel: (358 9) 663 717
Fax: (358 9) 622 048

Scanbox Finland Oy
Vapaalantie 2 B 26
FIN-01650 Vantaa
Tel: (358 9) 854 5560
Fax: (358 9) 8545 5611

United International
Pictures Oy
Kaisaniemenkatu I C 98
FIN-00100 Helsinki
Tel: (358 9) 684 1007
Fax: (358 9) 6841 0010

Warner Bros Finland Oy
Kaisaniemenkatu 1 b
FIN-00100 Helsinki
Tel: (358 9) 8624 5806, 8624 5808
Fax: (358 9) 8624 5810

Useful Addresses

Central Organisation of Finnish
Film Producers
Kaisaniemenkatu 3 B 29
FIN-00160 Helsinki
Tel: (358 9) 636 305
Fax: (358 9) 176 689

Finnish Film Foundation
Kanavakatu 12
FIN-00160 Helsinki
Tel: (358 9) 622 0300
Fax: (358 9) 6220 3060, 6220 3050
Internet: lumo@kaapeli.fi

Finnish Cinema Association
Finnish Film Chamber
Kaisaniemenkatu 3 B
FIN-00100 Helsinki
Tel: (358 9) 636 305
Fax: (358 9) 176 689

FRANCE — Michel Ciment

At Cannes in 1999, Unifrance Film president Daniel Toscan du Plantier, the man in charge of promoting French cinema abroad, enthused about the eccentric list of award winners chosen by David Cronenberg's jury, seeing it as a message sent by people "at the heart of the Hollywood system" to the French: "Hold on, resist. We are with you".

Besides smacking of anti-Americanism, a pet subject for the French, this statement is partly untrue, since Cronenberg is hardly an ambassador of the Hollywood majors. It is true, however, that the highly controversial verdicts were a paean to European cinema (and for that matter to French producers and co-producers) with five films, out of 22 in competition,

collecting all the jury prizes: one French-Belgian, *L'humanité*; one Belgian, the Palme d'Or winner *Rosetta*; one Spanish-French, *All About My Mother*, one Russian-German (*Molokh*) and one French-Portuguese, *La Lettre*.

The Cannes endorsement came as welcome support for an industry which continues to enjoy vital government support, but still has to endure strong progress by American films, which claimed 64% of the box-office market, while witnessing a decline in its own market share to 27.4% – though compared to other European countries, French films did very well. Thirty of the 40 films to attract more than a million spectators were American and six were French.

There was much cause for celebration amongst exhibitors and some distributors, with attendance up 14% to 170 million (149 million in 1997), the best for 13 years, and total box-office hitting $1 billion (6 billion francs). The French are still Europe's most avid cinemagoers, with three per capita visits a year, compared to 2.8 in Spain and 2.3 in Britain. Worryingly, however, the public increasingly spends its money only on the big hits, to the detriment of smaller films: out of 448 films released during the year (up from 354 in 1997), 100 accounted for 86% of the total audience. Of the 448, 173 were French and 159 American. The number of cinemas rose by 101 to 4,762. Because of the Hollywood hegemony, foreign markets are not easy to penetrate but French cinema holds its own abroad better than other countries.

Production continues to flourish: 183 films were shot, 20 more than in 1997, 50 more than in 1996, and the highest total since 1980 (185). Television provided about 40% of the $850m invested in production (up 7% on 1997), and more films were made on a medium budget (45 for between $2.5m and $4.2m). As usual, there was an important renewal of talent (or lack of talent!), since half of the new films were first or second features (58 debuts, compared to 46 in 1997). Belgium has been the most important partner in co-production, with 18 films (10 in 1997), then Spain (16), Italy (12) and Switzerland (10). Documentary production increased by 27% and the programme of French animated films for television by 43%.

Gauls vs. Hollywood

Commercially, the biggest French success of the year was **Asterix and Obelix**, a hugely expensive screen version by Claude Zidi of the famous comic strip. This not only gained an immense response from the public, but also an unashamedly positive reaction from the media, who supported the film as the last rampart against Hollywood imperialism. Whether it is appropriate to praise such a mediocre film as representative of a French industry assailed by foreign forces is debatable. It is also ironic that such an ideological label

Christian Clavier and Gérard Depardieu as ASTERIX AND OBELIX

should be attached to a story which shows French villagers willingly accepting Roman occupation because it means they will no longer have to pay tax!

There was less cause to rejoice at the state of French cinema in Zidi's ugly, broadly-acted epic than in a batch of impressive first or second features. **Voyages**, for instance, by Emmanuel Finkiel, is not only a subtle and poignant portrayal of elderly Jews and their relationship with the past, but also a structurally inventive movie which reveals the emotional undercurrents beneath everyday conversation. Built as a triptych, it tells of three journeys: Riwka, a concentration camp survivor, returns to Auschwitz by bus 50 years on, with a group of fellow victims; an adopted Parisian welcomes her father from Lithuania; finally, and perhaps most poignant of all, an 80-year-old Russian woman feels lost on a visit to a cousin in Israel.

Nos vies heureuses, by Jacques Maillot, evokes convincingly the intertwined destinies of six friends in their thirties. Contemporary sexual, emotional and social issues are embodied by fine performances in a lively piece marred by its excessive length and occasional clichés. The weird humour of **Peau Neuve**, by Emilie Deleuze, helped it win the FIPRESCI prize at Cannes. It follows a thirtysomething husband and father who abandons his family to work on a building site. The director (daughter of a famous philosopher) has a fine sense of the absurd, which endows a rather banal story with real charm.

In **Haut les cœurs**, Solveig Anspach cast probably the finest actress of her generation, Karin Viard, to depict the daily life of a woman struck by cancer – and managed to avoid both pathos and an overly clinical, documentary approach; humorous, trivial details blend in with more serious aspects, such as the woman's loss of sexual desire. Melancholy and nostalgia give **Plus qu'hier et moins que demain**, by Laurent Achard, its tense emotional atmosphere. When the eldest daughter of a provincial family returns home, a string of long-hidden secrets suddenly emerge, including an incestuous relationship, the devastating effects of alcoholism and a suicide attempt.

In **Karnaval**, Thomas Vincent shows a debt to Loach and Frears with his vivid sense of reality and his capacity to blend individual stories against strong spatial backgrounds. The love story of Corbi, an Algerian worker, and Bea, a married woman splendidly acted by Sylvie Testud, takes place during the Dunkirk carnival – a time when pent-up emotions are given free rein, and the film has an almost Breughelian vitality.

Dead of night

The most radical of the year's seven very promising debuts was Philippe Grandrieux's **Sombre**. For nearly two hours, a hand-held camera follows a serial killer at night as he stalks and murders prostitutes and has a chance encounter with a woman who will offer him a brief respite from his neurotic destiny. The film mixes an almost documentary style with an expressionist mood. Nocturnal nature – bushes, forests, lakes- is almost a character in itself in this disturbing, obsessional, and, for some, revolting poem of the darker side of the human psyche, which demonstrates astonishing bravura.

Good debuts are frequently followed by less successful follow-ups, so it is nice to note the high quality of Dominique Cabrera's second feature, **Nadia et les Hippopotomes**, which benefits from the director's vast documentary experience to evoke the big railway strike of 1995. The strike is the background for the story of Nadia, a mother in search of the father of her child, a penniless lost soul whose solitude is set against the solidarity of the workers on strike. Ariane Ascardie, muse of Robert Guediguia, brings all her warmth and sensitivity to the heroine, and, like Cabrera, avoids all sentimentality.

Bruno Dumont's **L'Humanité** confirms the promise of La vie de Jésus. Once again, he sets his story in a bleak northern landscape, magnifies nature with outstanding camerawork in cinemascope, and casts non-professional actors. Sometimes indulgently slow, the film is nevertheless a haunting, profound portrayal of a policeman who carries the suffering of humanity on his shoulders, almost a reincarnation of Dostoyevsky's idiot. Though his style is not to everyone's taste, Dumont has imposed himself as one of the few major talents of his generation.

More modestly, Catherine Corsini's **La Nouvelle Eve** is a mordant comedy in which Karin Viard again shines, this time as a screwball heroine in a world of men who take themselves too seriously. In the same vein, former screenwriter Pascal Bonitzer, who has worked for André Téchiné, Raoul Ruiz and others, has concocted a pleasant comedy, **Rien sur Robert**, about a paranoid critic (played with unusual restraint by the brilliant Fabrice Luchinii). The intellectual as victim of women and society is a theme perfectly fitted to the cerebral inspiration of this director who, with partial success, attempts a cross between late Buñuel and Rohmer.

Hard-core, and caution

Middle generation directors proved less daring, as if past experiences had made them more cautious towards an audience less and less prone to welcome off-beat film. The exception was probably Catherine Breillat's **Romance**, which created some scandal because of its explicit depiction of sex. The journey of a married woman (excellently played by newcomer Catherine Ducey) into the lower depths of sex, encountering on her way porn star Rocco Siffredi, takes on a spiritual dimension with a final redemption through childbirth.

Though the controversial subject matter helped it reach a much wider audience than Breillat's previous films, this is not as deeply provocative as, say, *Virgin*, and fails to avoid all of the clichés of the hard-core genre.

After many years of absence, Leos Carax made a comeback with his long-awaited **Pola X**, a very free adaptation of Herman Melville's *Pierre or the Ambiguities*. Though at times visually stunning, this proved to be largely an exercise in narcissistic pretension, as if Carax, intoxicated by the praise lavished on him for so long, was seeking a lyrical romantic style without thematic substance.

Robert Guédiguian, after many years of critical neglect and scarce public attendance, reached fame and success with *Marius et Jeanette* two years ago. His latest effort, **A la place du cœur**, proved disappointing. He returns once again to the same warm community of working-class people in a Marseilles suburb, still portrayed by pretty much the same cast, but also ventures into new territory as a mother (Ariane Ascaride) searches for the woman her son is accused of raping, a journey which leads her to Sarajevo. The film lacked the vitality of its predecessors.

Oliver Assayas' **Fin Avril, début Septembre** confirmed the director's talent with actors, and attempted to give his work a more novelistic dimension, rather in the manner of Claude Sautet, with its criss-crossing of individual destinies in modern Paris. It is inside a beauty salon that Tonie Marshall, with **Venus Beauté (Institut)**, reaches also for a choral work, a comedy with Nathalie Baye at its centre, surrounded by colleagues, clients, lovers and family. It has charm and wit, but its commentary on appearances does not go far beyond a seductive veneer.

Pierre Jolivet offered two new films in the space of a year. **En plein cœur**, a remake of Claude Autant-Lara's *En cas de Malheur* (with Gabin and Bardot), is an attempt at more commercial cinema from a director who has hitherto had devotees but no mainstream audience. His characters, as usual, are fragile beings almost destroyed by emotional whirlwinds, but there is something improbable in the affair between a well-known Paris lawyer (Gérard Lanvin) who cheats on his wife (Carole Bouquet) and a young suburban girl (Virginie Ledoyen).

Much more satisfying was Jolivet's latest film, **Ma Petite Entreprise**, in which his sense of comedy, his witty dialogue and his superb use of actors (François Berleand, Roshdy Zem, Vincent Lindon) are at their best in a social comedy about a factory owner entangled in a fraudulent insurance deal.

Cheating hearts

Films by the seven newcomers singled out earlier were matched by seven established directors. Claude Chabrol's **Au Cœur du mensonge** showed the director at his most convincing and on his favourite territory: a murder investigation in a French provincial town highlights the mystery of human behaviour and the ambiguity of marital relationships. Jacques Gamblin is a tortured painter, his wife Vivian (the always impressive Sandrine Bonnaire) a nurse who visits patients in their home and Antoine de Caunes a pretentious writer from Paris with whom she has an affair. The investigation by a female police inspector into the murder of a little girl by a paedophile is an excuse for the more serious study of the lies – as the title of the film makes clear – that govern this small society on the Brittany coast.

Vincent Lindon in MA PETITE ENTREPRISE

Still from Chabrol's AU CŒUR DU MENSONGE

'Scope frame from Philippe Garrel's LE VENT DE LA NUIT

Bertrand Tavernier also explores provincial France in **Ça Commence Aujourd'hui**, this time the northern region (frequently featured in contemporary cinema) whose population suffers severely from unemployment and precarious economic conditions. Through the eyes of a primary school headmaster (the formidable Philippe Torreton, Tavernier's new pet actor) we are offered an angry look at France today, as the hero struggles against educational administrators and helps to solve the parents' problems. Tavernier's lyricism and use of cinemascope to enhance the arid beauty of the landscape, the poetic quality of the teacher's voice-over commentary and the film's sheer energy transcend what might have been just another slice-of-life drama.

A similar energy is at work in **Petits Frères**, by Jacques Doillon, a chronicle of teenagers from various origins – Arab, African, Jewish – in the Paris suburbs.

Still from Tavernier's CA COMMENCE AUJOURD'HUI

Doillon elicits remarkably spontaneous performances from the youngsters and generates powerful emotions through the confrontation between a young girl whose dog has been stolen and a gang of petty thieves .

In **Le vent de la Nuit**, Philippe Garrel, once a hero of French underground cinema, has become more accessible thanks to some remarkable films such as *J'entends plus le guitare*, plumbs the core of man's solitude. Shot in superb widescreen, this is a meditation, 30 years later, on the loss of May '68 dreams. An architect (Daniel Duval), who has remained a rebel, but whose disillusionment drives him to suicide, and a young man hardly aware of the political past, while a wounded, ageing woman (Catherine Deneuve) drifts between the two. The purity and silence of Garrel's film make it a unique visual and emotional experience.

Patrice Leconte likes to change themes, experiment with different forms, and surprise critics and audiences. **La fille sur la pont** is a black-and-white tragi-comic fable about a knife thrower (Daniel Auteuil) who gets involved with a young girl (Vanessa Paradis) as she tries to commit suicide by throwing herself from a bridge. Their journey into the world of music-hall is a ballad at once moving, poetic and entertaining.

Through foreigners' eyes

Foreign directors in France have always enriched and broadened the artistic

Vanessa Paradis in Patrice Leconte's LA FILLE SUR LE PONT

landscape. For example, the Chilean Raoul Ruiz mesmerisingly integrated Proust's spirit into his own baroque world view. It is possible that no adaptation of *A la recherche du temps perdu* can be totally satisfactory, but in concentrating on the final part, **Le Temps Retrouvé**, Ruiz has produced a fascinating interpretation. The social dimension, the humour and the metaphorical and aesthetic strands are all present in this complex work, superbly cast, with a particularly convincing narrator (Proust himself) played by Marcello Mazzorella.

The same capacity to blend into a foreign culture is evident in **Adieu, plancher de vaches** which Georgian director Otar Iosseliani shot in Paris and nearby countryside. The fluid camerawork of William Lubtchovsky follows two groups of eccentrics: a manor's idle or snobbish aristocrats (including a wine-addicted father played by the director) on one side, on the other the modest people of the town – café waiters or tramps who are cousins of the citizens in René Clair's or Jacques Tati's worlds. Tender comic touches, playful fantasy and irony make this one of Iosseliani's supreme achievements.

Finally, one must mention the vitality of French documentaries and animation. Two cartoon features managed to attract audiences in spite of formidable competition from Disney, Fox and DreamWorks. Michel Ocelot's **Kirikou et la sorcière** takes its inspiration from African culture, with a child hero whose quest is both a rite of passage and a fight against evil, while Jean François Laguinoie's **Le château des Singes** uses the world of apes to deliver a fable about the relativity of the notion of "civilisation" and the fight against intolerance. Both works are entertaining without ever stooping to mindless escapism.

The best film essays of the year included **Grand comme le monde**, in which Denis Gheerbrandt follows a year in the lives of young school pupils, eliciting confident responses by creating a feeling of mutual trust. Equally impressive was **Un spécialiste**, in which Eyal Sivan condensed hundreds of hours of video taken during the trial of Adolf Eichmann in Jerusalem and, following Hannah Arendt's thesis on the benality of evil, gives us an impressive, chilling account of the opinionated civil servant who just "did his job".

MICHEL CIMENT is one of France's most eminent critics and commentators on cinema. An editor of *Positif*, and a lecturer on film at universities in France and abroad, he has also made documentaries on various directors. He has recently published an updated edition of his book on Kubrick.

Producers

Alexandre Films
14 rue de Marignan
75008 Paris
Tel: (33 1) 44 95 89 89
Fax: (33 1) 42 89 26 89

Alter Films
4 Rue Treilhard
75008 Paris
Tel: (33 1) 42 56 12 97
Fax: (33 1) 42 56 45 74

Caméra One
38 rue du Bac
75007 Paris
Tel: (33 1) 45 49 09 79
Fax: (33 1) 45 49 93 69

Cinéa
87 rue Taitbout
75009 Paris
Tel: (33 1) 44 91 94 14
Fax: (33 1) 40 16 19 11

Film Par Film
10 avenue George V
75008 Paris
Tel: (33 1) 40 73 84 20
Fax: (33 1) 47 23 95 68

Films Alain Sarde
17 rue Dumont d'Urville
75116 Paris
Tel: (33 1) 44 43 43 70
Fax: (33 1) 47 20 61 50

Films Christian Fechner
39 Rue des Tilleuls
92100 Boulogne
Tel: (33 1) 46 99 02 02
Fax: (33 1) 46 99 03 43

Flach Films
47 rue de la Colonie
75013 Paris
Tel: (33 1) 44 16 40 00
Fax: (33 1) 45 80 40 01

Gaumont
30 avenue Charles de Gaulle
92200 Neuilly
Tel: (33 1) 46 43 20 00
Fax: (33 1) 46 43 21 68

Hachette Première
10 rue de Marignan
75008 Paris
Tel: (33 1) 42 25 19 70
Fax: (33 1) 42 56 00 81

IMA Productions
3 rue de Liège
75009 Paris
Tel: (33 1) 40 23 48 10
Fax: (33 1) 40 82 97 01

MACT Productions
27 Rue de Fleurus
75006 Paris
Tel: (33 1) 45 49 10 10
Fax: (33 1) 45 59 30 60

MK2 Productions
55 rue Traversière
75012 Paris
Tel: (33 1) 44 67 30 00
Fax: (33 1) 43 41 32 30

Les Productions Lazennec
5 rue Darcet
75017 Paris
Tel: (33 1) 43 87 71 71
Fax: (33 1) 43 87 17 74

Renn Productions
10 rue Lincoln
75008 Paris
Tel: (33 1) 40 76 91 00
Fax: (33 1) 42 25 12 89

Le Studio Canal+
17 rue Dumont d'Urville
75116 Paris
Tel: (33 1) 44 43 98 00
Fax: (33 1) 47 20 13 58

Téléma
26 rue Danton
92300 Levallois Perret
Tel: (33 1) 47 58 67 30
Fax: (33 1) 47 58 81 16

UGC Images
24 avenue Charles de Gaulle
92200 Neuilly
Tel: (33 1) 46 40 44 00
Fax: (33 1) 46 24 37 28

Distributors

A.M.L.F.
10 rue Lincoln
75008 Paris
Tel: (33 1) 40 76 91 00
Fax: (33 1) 42 25 12 89

Bac Films
10 Avenue de Messine
75008 Paris
Tel: (33 1) 53 53 52 52
Fax: (33 1) 53 53 52 53

Diaphana Distribution
50 rue de Paradis
75010 Paris
Tel: (33 1) 44 79 92 92
Fax: (33 1) 42 46 54 48

Gaumont/BVI
5 rue du Colisée
75008 Paris
Tel: (33 1) 46 43 24 53
Fax: (33 1) 46 43 20 47

Mars Films
95 Bd Haussmann
75008 Paris
Tel: (33 1) 44 94 95 00
Tel: (33 1) 44 94 95 01

Metropolitan Filmexport
116 bis avenue des
Champs Elysées
75008 Paris
Tel: (33 1) 45 63 45 60
Fax: (33 1) 45 63 77 31

MKL
55 rue Traversière
75012 Paris
Tel: (33 1) 43 07 15 10
Fax: (33 1) 43 44 20 18

Pyramide Film
5 rue Richepanse,
75008 Paris
Tel: (33 1) 42 96 01 01
Fax: (33 1) 40 20 02 21

UFD
2 avenue Montaigne
75008 Paris
Tel: (33 1) 53 67 17 17
Fax: (33 1) 53 67 17 00

UGC
24 avenue Charles de Gaulle
92200 Neuilly
Tel: (33 1) 46 40 44 00
Fax: (33 1) 46 24 37 28

Useful Addresses

**Centre National de la
Cinématographie (CNC)**
12 rue de Lubeck
75116 Paris
Tel: (33 1) 44 34 34 40
Fax: (33 1) 47 55 04 91

Unifrance Film International
4 Villa Bosquet
75007 Paris
Tel: (33 1) 47 53 95 80
Fax: (33 1) 47 05 96 55

GERMANY — Jack Kindred

German film had a disappointing 1998, with home-grown movies trailing far behind American blockbusters – mainly as a result of the *Titanic* effect. While total admissions soared to 154 million and *Titanic* broke all records (more than 18 million), only two domestic productions attracted more than two million patrons, and neither made the year's box-office top ten.

Early in the year, Josef Vilsmaier's **Comedian Harmonists** held its own for weeks in second place on the ladder. The dramatic, true story musical set in Nazi Germany in the 1930s wound up with a respectable 2.7 million visitors, still far behind Hollywood mega-budget movies like *Armageddon* (5.3 million), and *The Horse Whisperer* (4 million).

The quirky love story **Run Lola, Run** (*Lola Rennt*) surprised with two million admissions, which boosted but could not rescue German film from a disastrous year overall. Nevertheless, Tom Tykwer's low-budget ($1.7m) opus recalled the excitement sparked by the 1960 release of Jean-Luc Godard's debut, *A Bout de Souffle*.

Tykwer achieved his visual fireworks with rapid camera movements, jump cuts and split-screen techniques, using variable video animation and real film for character presentations. Franka Potente, a rising new star on the German cinema scene, plays Lola, who is in love with Manni (Moritz Bleibtreu). Manni acts as a money courier for black market car dealers, but when he inadvertently leaves the money in a plastic bag in the subway, the gang gives him 20 minutes to find the cash.

Lola's frenzied marathon run through the streets of Berlin begins. Tykwer shot the film with three endings, one where Lola is shot dead, another when Manni is run over by an ambulance and the third when Lola wins the money at a casino, making for a happy ending for the lovers.

Reality flops

Lola aside, whenever a younger generation of German film-makers attempted a new, non-commercial approach, they failed to win audiences and, overall, German film slumped to a dismal 9.5% market share. Entertainment-hungry burghers prefer Hollywood blockbusters, or the domestic popular comedies that saw German films' market share hit 17.3% in 1997.

Many directors latched on to the "new realism", a trend reflecting such themes as angst, loneliness and alienation in a cold society and the resort to immediate "kicks" as a remedy. Screened with great fanfare at Munich's 1998 International Film Festival, Hans-Christian Schmid's **23** was typical of

Moritz Bleibtreu and Franka Potente in Tom Tykwer's smash hit RUN LOLA, RUN

this movement, featuring a computer hacker, his head filled with conspiracy theories. Wanted by the CIA, he seeks solace in cyberspace and drug-induced highs. The thriller failed to click with film buffs.

Actor-turned director Rolf Peter Kahl's first movie, **Angel Express**, combined a round of fleeting encounters in Berlin with quick sex and Russian roulette and met a similar fate. And despite a sterling cast, led by major stars Götz George and Corinna Harfouch, director Nico Hofmann's **Solo for Clarinet** also flopped, pulling in only 420,000 visitors.

The gruesome detective story opened with a mutilated corpse whose killer had "bitten off" part of the victim's private parts. George, as the hard-nosed chief inspector, falls in love with the main suspect, a mysterious young woman in a red raincoat. Caught in a labyrinth of his own emotions, Bernie loses control of his life.

Another quick fallout came from stunt-man turned director Hardy Martins, a product of LA's International Stunt Association, who cranked out **Cascadeur – The Search for the Amber Room**, an action film full of land, water and air stunts. Despite much ballyhoo at the Munich fest, the movie was box-office disasterville, lasting only a couple of weeks in release.

Another gloomy, intellectual costume drama directed by erstwhile art historian Dagmar Knöpfel, **Requiem for a Romantic Woman** (*Requiem für eine romantische Frau*), quickly disappeared from the cinemas. Its title alone was doubtless enough to discourage average movie fans. The film's lofty themes, involving literature, art and life, revolve around the love affairs of the nineteenth-century poet Clemens Brentano.

Back on track?

Despite the false starts, however, German film-makers now appear to be heading in the right direction again, with a number of excellent productions released in the first half of 1999 or scheduled to be out by year's end. Topping the list is Andreas Kleinert's **Paths in the Night** (*Wege in die Nacht*), which was the first German film to open the Directors Fortnight at Cannes for more than two decades, and the only German feature film screened at the 1999 festival.

This existential psycho-drama was well received at Cannes, though it failed to garner any awards. The plot centres around Walter (Hilmar Thate), a hapless, unemployed 55 year-old, who, having lost a position of power, seeks to find meaning in his life through a personal crusade for human rights. But turned down by society, he becomes a danger to others and himself. His wife Sylvia (Cornelia Schmass), the only person who loves him, is unable to save him from a tragic end.

The only other German film at Cannes was the documentary **My Best Fiend** from director Werner Herzog of New German Cinema fame. Film buffs should be pleased with Herzog's account of his years with the late eccentric actor Klaus Kinski, who acted in Herzog's *Aguirre the Wrath of God*, *Nosferatu*, *Fitzcarraldo* and *Cobra Verde*. Herzog revisited some of the South American locations used in *Fitzcarraldo* and *Cobra Verde*, rendering a tender and sometimes scornful portrait of the difficult actor, whose fame was based as much on his outlandish behaviour as his thespian prowess.

A German film had the honour of opening the 1999 International Film Festival in Berlin. **Aimee and Jaguar** explores lesbian passion as Germany confronts its Nazi past. A true story, the plot concerns a young Jewish lesbian in wartime Berlin who falls in love with a mother of four, while the latter's Hitler-worshipping husband is away at the Eastern front.

The jury gave Best Actress awards to the film's stars, Maria Schrader and Juliane Köhler. Helped by the publicity generated by the festival, the film topped one million visitors, the benchmark for a highly successful film in Germany.

Although it was a German-French-Italian co-production, **Asterix and Obelix** is worth mentioning since some of its interiors were shot at Bavaria Film, in Munich, and it drew more than three million visitors in Germany.

The Late Show, another spoof by writer-director Helmut Dietl, this time on television, disappointed with less than a million admissions when compared with Dietl's earlier and more successful *Rossini*, a satire on Munich's "schicki-micky" film community. The movie features a top cast, including TV entertainer Thomas Gottschalk and talk show host Harald Schmidt.

Forthcoming attractions

A number of promising German productions are in the distribution pipeline. One of the most interesting could be director Roland Suso Richter's **After the Truth**, starring Götz George and Kai Wiesinger. When none of Germany's film-funding organisations would support the project, focusing on the notorious death camp doctor Josef Mengele, the cast, led by George, paid back their upfront salaries to keep it alive. The film's script asks what would happen if Mengele, who died in 1979, were brought to trial today.

Upcoming is Rainer Kaufmann's romantic thriller **Long Hello and Short Goodbye**, starring Nicolette Krebitz as an undercover agent who falls in love with an ex-con safecracker (Marc Hosemann). Also slated for fall release is **The Great Bagarozy** (*Der Grosse Bagarozy*), written, directed and produced by Bernd Eichinger. The psychological drama toplines Til Schweiger and Cornna Harfouch in a storyline revolving around the anti-hero Stanislaus Nagy (Schweiger), who believes himself to be responsible for the rise and fall of opera singer Maria Callas, and his sessions with Cora Dulz, a therapist (Harfouch).

Sönke Wortmann's new film, **A Night on the Town** (*St Pauli Nacht*), will take audiences into Hamburg's red light district, and watch for writer-director Doris Dörrie's **Erleuchtung garantiert**, a working title translating as "Enlightenment Guaranteed". The film stars Uwe Ochsenknecht and Gustav Peter Wöhler as a pair whose spiritual quest takes them to a Japanese monastery.

Lastly, Rolf Schübel's **Gloomy Sunday** is a romantic drama starring Joachim Król

and Stefano Dionisi and based on the popular song that set off a wave of suicides in Budapest during the 1930s.

JACK KINDRED, former *Variety* bureau chief and college professor, covers the media scene in Munich from his outpost at Charles Schumann's American bar, favourite watering hole of the film community.

Recent and Forthcoming Films

ABSOLUTE GIGANTEN (Gigantic)

Script and Dir: Sebastian Schipper. Phot: Frank Griebe. Players: Frank Giering, Florian Lukas, Antoine Monot Jr., Julia Hummer. Prod: X-Filme Creative Pool, Berlin.

AIMÉE & JAGUAR

Script and Dir: Max Fäberböck. Phot: Tony Imi. Players: Maria Schrader, Juliane Köhler, Johanna Wokalek, Heike Makatsch, Detlev Buck. Prod: Senator Film Production.

ASTERIX & OBELIX

Script and Dir: Claude Zidi. Phot: Tony Pierce-Roberts. Players: Christian Clavier, Gérard Depardieu, Roberto Benigni, Gottfried John, Laetitia Casta, Marianne Sägebrecht. Prod: Renn Productions, Paris/Bavaria Film, Munich/Melampo Cinematografica, Rome.

BIS ZUM HORIZONT UND WEITER (To the Horizon and Beyond)

Script: Oliver Bukowski. Dir: Peter Kahane. Phot: Gero Steffen. Players: Wolfgang Stumph, Corinna Harfouch, Nina Petri, Gudrun Okras. Prod: Polyphon Film-und Fernseh, GmbH, Hamburg.

COMEDIAN HARMONISTS

Script: Klaus Richter. Dir: Joseph

Vilsmaier. Phot: Vilsmaier. Players: Ulrich Noethen, Ben Becker, Heino Ferch, Kai Wiesinger, Max Tidof, Heinrich Schafmeister. Prod: Senator/Bavaria/Iduna.

DEALER

Script and Dir: Thomas Arslan. Phot: Michael Wiesweg. Players: Tamer Yigit, Idil Üner. Prod: Trans-Film, Berlin.

DIE BRAUT (The Mask of Desire)

Script and Dir: Egon Günther. Phot: Peter Brand. Players: Veronica Ferres, Herbert Knaup, Sybille Canonica, Christoph Waltz. Prod: Tellux Film, Dresden, Studio Babelsberg Independents, Potsdam.

EINE FRAGE DER WAHRHEIT (After the Truth)

Script: Johannes W. Betz. Dir: Roland Suso Richter. Phot: Martin Langer. Players: Götz George, Kai Wiesinger, Maria Schrader, Doris Schade. Prod: Helkon Media, Munich, Studio Babelsberg, Potsdam.

ERLEUCHTUNG GARANTIERT (Enlightenment Guaranteed)

Script: Doris Dörrie and Ruth Stadler. Dir: Dörrie. Phot: Hans Karl Hu. Players: Uwe Ochsenknecht, Gustav Peter Wöhler, Anica Dobra, Ulrike Kriener, Heiner Lauterbach. Prod: Megaherz, Munich.

GEORGIA O'KEEFFE "TILL THE END OF TIME"

Script: Hans-Jörg Weyhmüller. Dir: Jeremy Kagan. Phot: Igor Luther. Players: Sean Young, Christopher Walken, Jan Niklas, Barbara Auer. Prod: ArtOko, Munich.

GLATTEIS (Black Ice)

Script and Dir: Michael Gutmann. Phot: Johannes Geyer. Players: Günter Lamprecht, Gottfried John, Hilde van Mieghem, Elfriede Irrall. Prod: Colon Filmproduktion, Cologne.

HELDEN WIE WIR (Heroes Like Us)

Script and Dir: Sebastian Peterson. Phot: Peter Przybylski. Players: Gojko Mitic, Volkmar Kleinert, Daniel Borgwardt, Xenia Snagowski. Prod: Senator Film, Berlin.

I LOVE YOU BABY

Script: Ron Peer. Dir: Nick lyon. Phot: Eckehart Pollack. Players: Mark Keller, Jasmin Gerat, Maximilian Schnell, Burkhard Driest. Prod: Two Guys and a Girl Entertainment/Warner Bros.

JIMMY THE KID

Script: Martin Rauhaus, Peter Wohlgemuth. Dir: Wolfgang Dickmann. Phot: Dickmann. Players: Rufus Beck, Herbert Knaup, Christiane Hörbiger, Sophie Moser. Prod: Wohlgemuth Filmproduktion.

KISS ME!

Script and Dir: Alexander Kunja. Phot: Björn Kurt. Players: Margret Völker, Zacharias Preen, Anouschka Renzi, Max Herbrechter. Prod: Zitro Film, Berlin.

LATE SHOW

Script and Dir: Helmut Dietl. Phot: Gernot Roll. Players: Thomas Gottschalk, Harald Schmidt, Veronica Ferres, Jasmin Tabatabai, Otto Schenk. Gaby Dohm. Prod: Constantin, Munich.

LOLA RENNT (Run Lola Run)

Script and Dir: Tom Tykwer. Phot: Frank Griebe. Players: Franka Potente, Moritz Bleibtreu, Herbert Knaup, Joachim Krol. Heino Ferch. Prod: X Filme Creative Pool, Berlin.

LONG HELLO AND SHORT GOODBYE

Script and Dir: Rainer Kaufmann. Players: Til Schweiger, Nicolette Krebitz, Katja Riemann. Prod: Studio Hamburg Filmproduktion.

MESCHUGGE

Script and Dir: Dani Levy. Phot: Carl Friedrich Koschnick. Players: Maria Schrader, Dani Levy, David Straithairn. Nicole Heesters. Prod: X-Filme Creative Pool, Berlin.

OSKAR UND LENI

Script and Dir: Petra Katharina Wagner. Phot: Peter Polsak. Players: Christian Redl, Anna Thalbach, Elisabeth Trissenaar, Reiner Heise, Nadja Engel. Prod: Indigo Film und Fernseh Produktion, Berlin.

PÜNKTCHEN UND ANTON (Annaluise and Anton)

Scipt and Dir: Caroline Link. Phot: Torsten Breuer. Players: Elea Geissler, Max Felder, Juliane Köhler, August Zirner. Prod: Bavaria Filmverlieh, Lunaris Film.

Still from Andreas Kleinert's PATHS IN THE NIGHT

SCHNEE IN DER NEUJAHRSNACHT (Snow on New Year's Eve)

Script: Stefan Kolditz. Dir: Thorsten Schmidt. Phot: Klaus Eichhammer. Players: Jürgen Tarrach, Tamara Simunovic, Lisa Martinek, Barbara Rudnick. Prod: Ufa Film & TV Produktion/Buena Vista Productions/Mr Brown Entertainment Filmproduction.

REQUIEM FÜR EINE ROMANTISCHE FRAU (Requiem for a Romantic Woman)

Script and Dir: Dagmar Knöpfel. Phot: Igor Luther. Players: Sylvester Groth, Janina Sachau, Felix von Manteuffel, Anne Bennert. Prod: Dagmar Knöpfel Filmproduktion.

ST. PAULI NACHT (A Night on the Town)

Script: Frank Göhre. Dir: Sönke Wortmann. Phot: Thomas Fährmann. Players: Armin Rhode, Benno Fürmann, Florian Lukas, Peter Stattman. Prod: Hager Moss Film, Munich.

STRAIGHT SHOOTER

Script and Dir: Thomas Bohn. Phot: Peter von Haller. Players: Dennis Hopper, Heino Ferch, Katja Flint. Prod: Perathon Film- und Fernseh, Senator Film Produktion, Berlin.

SOLO FÜR KLARINETTE (Solo for Clarinet)

Script: Susanne Schneider. Dir: Nico Hofmann. Phot: Hans-Günther Bücking. Players: Götz George, Corinna Harfouch, Tim Bergmann, Barbara Auer. Prod: Regina Ziegler Filmproduktion.

UMNACHTUNG (Deranged)

Script and Dir: Oskar Roehler. Phot: Hagen Bodgdanski. Players: Hannelore Eisner, Vadim Glowna, Mathieu Carrière, Tonio Arrango. Prod: Distant Dreams, Munich.

WEGE IN DIE NACHT (Paths in the Night)

Script: Johann Bergk. Dir: Andreas Kleinert. Phot: Jürgen Jürges. Players: Hilmar Thate, Cornelia Schmaus, Henriette Heinze, Dirk Borcharft. Prod: Ö-Filmproduktion, Berlin.

WER LIEBT, DEM WACHSEN FLÜGEL (Wings of Love)

Script and Dir: Gabriel Barylli. Phot: Achim Poulheim. Players: Lisa Martinek, Heio von Stetten, Maximilian Schell, Gudrun Landgrebe, Verona Feldbusch. Prod: Tele-München Film und Fernseh, Munich.

Producers

Allianz Filmproduktion GmbH
Leibnitzstr. 60
10625 Berlin
Tel: (49 30) 323 9011
Fax: (49 30) 323 1693

Anthea Film GmbH
Widenmayerstr. 4
80538 Munich
Tel: (49 89) 226 194
Fax: (49 89) 221 251

Bavaria Film GmbH
Bavariafilmplatz 7
80336 Geiselgasteig
Munich
Tel: (49 89) 6499 2389
Fax: (49 89) 649 2507

BioSkop-Film GmbH
Türkenstr. 91/111
80799 Munich
Tel: (49 89) 394 987
Fax: (49 89) 396 820

Capitol Film + TV International GmbH & Co. Vertriebs KG
Harvestehuder Weg 43
20149 Hamburg 13
Tel: (49 40) 411 79-0
Fax: (49 40) 411 70-199

Constantin Film GmbH
Kaiserstr. 39
47441 Munich
Tel: (49 89) 3860 9221/2
Fax: (49 89) 3860 9242

Franz Seitz Produktions GmbH
Beichstr. 8
80802 Munich
Tel: (49 89) 391 1123
Fax: (49 89) 340 1291

Willy Bogner Film GmbH
Sankt Veitstr. 4
81673 Munich
Tel: (49 89) 436 06-0
Fax: (49 89) 436 06 429

CCC Filmkunst GmbH
Verlangerie Daumstr. 16
13599 Berlin
Tel: (49 30) 334 200-1
Fax: (49 30) 334 0418

CineVox Film GmbH
Bavaria Filmplatz 7
80336 Geiselgasteig
Tel: (49 89) 641 80-0
Fax: (49 89) 649 3288

Manfred Durniok Produktion
Hausotterstr. 36
13409 Berlin
Tel: (49 30) 491 8045
Fax: (49 30) 491 4065

Hermes Film GmbH
Kaiserplatz 7
47441 Munich
Tel: (49 89) 394 368
Fax: (49 89) 344 363

Oko-Film GmbH
Mauerkircherstr. 3
81679 Munich
Tel: (49 89) 987 666
Fax: (49 89) 987 602

Olga Film GmbH
Tengstr. 16
80798 Munich
Tel: (49 89) 271 2635
Fax: (49 89) 272 5768

Regina Ziegler Filmproduktion
Budapesterstr. 35
10789 Berlin
Tel: (49 30) 261 8071
Fax: (49 30) 262 8213

Rialto Film GmbH
Bismarckstr. 108
13469 Berlin
Tel: (49 30) 310 0000
Fax: (49 30) 3100 0559

Roxy-Film GmbH
Schützenstr. 1
80335 Munich 2
Tel: (49 89) 555 341
Fax: (49 89) 594 510

Studio Hamburg
Tonndorfer Hauptstr. 90
22045 Hamburg
Tel: (49 40) 66 880
Fax: (49 40) 665 601
(49 40) 6688 4370

Tele-München GmbH
Kaufingerstr. 25
80331 Munich
Tel: (49 89) 290 930
Fax: (49 89) 290 93129

Vision Film GmbH
Kurfürstenplatz 4
80796 Munich
Tel: (49 89) 390 029
Fax: (49 89) 395 569

Von Vietinghoff Filmproduktion
Potsdamerstr. 199
10783 Berlin
Tel: (49 30) 216 8931
Fax: (49 30) 215 8219

Distributors

Advanced Film Verleih
Raiffeinsenallee 16
82041 Oberhaching
Tel: (49 89) 273 7610
Fax: (49 89) 273 76173

Ascot Filmverleih GmbH
St. Annastr. 16
80538 Munich
Tel: (49 89) 296 995
Fax: (49 89) 331 839

Columbia TriStar Filmgesellschaft GmbH
Ickstattstr. 1
80469 Munich
Tel: (49 89) 236 90
Fax: (49 89) 264 380

Concorde Filmverleih GmbH
Rosenheimerstr. 143 B
81671 Munich
Tel: (49 89) 4506 100
Fax: (49 89) 4506 1014

Futura/Filmverlag GmbH
Rambergstr. 5
80799 Munich
Tel: (49 89) 381 701
Fax: (49 89) 3817 0020

Helkon Media Filmvertrieb GmbH
Widenmayerstr. 36
80538 Munich
Tel: (49 89) 2916 0490
Fax: (49 89) 291 3720

Jugend Film Verleih GmbH
Reichsstrasse 15
14052 Berlin
Tel: (49 30) 300 6970
Fax: (49 30) 3006 9711

Kinowelt Filmverleih GmbH
Schwere-Reiterstrasse 35
Building 14
80797 Munich
Tel: (49 89) 307 960
Fax: (49 89) 3079 6701

Nil Film GmbH
Bnd Brunnthal 3
81657 Munich
Tel: (49 89) 9980 5800
Fax: (49 89) 9980 5810

Progress Film Verleih
Burgstrasse 27
10178 Berlin
Tel: (49 30) 2400 3400
Fax. (49 89) 2400 3459

ScotiaFilm GmbH
Possartstr. 14
81679 Munich
Tel: (49 89) 413 0900
Fax: (49 89) 470 6320

SenatorFilm GmbH
Kurfürstendamm 65

10707 Berlin
Tel: (49 30) 8809 1700
Fax: (49 30) 8809 1790

20th Century Fox of Germany GmbH
Postfach 70 11 22
60561 Frankfurt am Main
Tel: (49 69) 609 020
Fax: (49 69) 627 716

TiMe Filmverleih GmbH
Brüsselerstr. 89–93
50672 Cologne
Tel: (49 221) 952 9680
Fax: (49 221) 19529 6866

Transit Film GmbH
Dachauerstrasse 35
80335 Munich
Tel: (49 89) 555 261
Fax: (49 89) 596 122

United International Pictures GmbH
Hahnstr. 31-35
60528 Frankfurt am Main

Tel: (49 69) 669 8190
Fax: (49 69) 666 6509

Warner Bros Film GmbH
Hans-Henny-Jahn-Weg 35
22085 Hamburg
Tel: (49 40) 226 500
Fax: (49 40) 2265 0259

Useful Addresses

Verband der Filmverleiher e.V (49 VDI)
(49 Assn. of Distributors)
Kreuzberger Ring 56
65205 Wiesbaden
Tel: (49 611) 778 920
Fax: (49 611) 778 9212

Export Union
Türkenstr. 93
80799 Munich
Tel: (49 89) 390 095
Fax: (49 89) 395 223

GREECE
Yannis Bacoyannopoulos

Despite box-office receipts which dipped after 1998's *Titanic*-fuelled boom, Greek cinemagoing continued its dynamic upward course. More multiplexes were completed or are under construction (in greater numbers, perhaps, than are justified by forecasts of the potential audience). Already, many traditional movie theatre owners are complaining of a dramatic fall in business.

Moviegoers (chiefly the young) continue to show a marked preference for American cinema. Hollywood films again dominated the list of top-grossing films, though France's *Asterix and Obelix* took the number one spot and Italy's *Life is Beautiful* also made it to the top ten. Attendance for Greek films remained poor. Apart from Olga Malea's **The Mating Game**, the one domestic film in the year's Top Ten, and Theo Angelopoulos award-winning **Eternity and a Day**, which neared the 80,000 admissions mark, none of the other eight Greek films exceeded 100,000 admissions.

The presence of Greek cinema, chiefly on a cultural level, was more notable abroad, where sales, especially to television networks, increased by 134%. Greek films participated in a large number of international festivals, winning several awards, while major retrospectives devoted to Theo Angelopoulos, Michael Cacoyannis and Greek Cinema in general were held in London, Kiev, Ankara, Karlsroy, Erevan, Boston, Chicago, Stockholm, Oslo and Helsinki.

Alan Bates and Charlotte Rampling in Michael Cacoyannis' adaptation of THE CHERRY ORCHARD

Taking advantage of increased state funding, the Greek Film Centre (GFC) undertook initiatives that are already starting to bear fruit and should bring about significant results in the future. It has already created a broader and more stable production base, particularly for young film-makers. There is now greater investment from the television sector, with the private SKY station joining state network ERT in the production and promotion of Greek cinema. The pre-production stage has been improved by the creation of a Script Workshop and there is now also greater market research for Greek films, and producers are exploring new sources of finance and sponsorship.

Of course the greatest challenge in sustaining the revitalisation of Greek cinema remains the need to sway audiences at home and abroad, a predicament faced by most European countries.

YANNIS BACOYANNOPOULOS is one of Greece's best-known film critics. Since 1960, he has worked for many newspapers and magazines, and for the past 20 years has been film critic of the Athens daily *Kathimerini* and Greek State Television ET-1.

Recent and Forthcoming Films

EARTH AND WATER

Script and Dir: Panos Karkanevatos. Players: Giorgos Karamichos, Fotini Papadodima, Lena Kitsopoulou, Vassia Eleftheriadis, Katerina Karayianni, Michalis Mitroussis. Prod: Greek Film Centre/Greek TV ET-1/ Cinergon/Geopoly/Monipoly Productions/Panos Karkanevatos, with Thessaloniki Cultural Capital of Europe 1997 Organisation and EURIMAGES.

Nicolas is a young lyre player and a devotee of the Dionysiac rites, the Macedonian ceremonies in which initiates walk on burning coals. He is young, innocent and in love with Constantina, a girl with whom he has nothing in common.

THE CHERRY ORCHARD

Dir: Michael Cacoyannis. Players: Alan Bates, Charlotte Rampling.

Adaptation of the Chekhov play.

INNOCENT

Script and Dir: Costas Natsis. Phot: Giorgos Arvanitis. Players:

Still from Costas Kapakas' PEPPERMINT

Jacques Bonnafe, Laura Schiffman, Etienne Chicot, François Berleand, Caroline Ducey, Elizabeth Depardieu, Jean-Pierre Leaud. Prod: Blue Films, Love Streams Productions, Le Bureau, Canal +, CNC (France)/Lumiere Productions, S.A. and GFC (Greece).

Maxim, a loner,becomes a taxi driver and the windscreen of his cab becomes the personal cinema screen through which he experiences city life in Paris.

FEMALE COMPANY

Script: Nikos Perakis and Katerina Bey. Dir: Perakis. Players: Nikos Kaloyeropoulos, Maria Georgiadou, Christina Theodoropoulou, Emilios Hilakis, Alekos Sissovitis. Prod: Odeon/GFC/SKAI/Stefi Films.

Six women are blackmailed by a crooked ex-cop and their actions devastate an entire community in a country town.

BACK DOOR

Script: Yorgos Tsemberopoulos, Deni Iliadi. Dir: Tsemberopoulos. Prod: Ideefixe Ltd. (Greece)/JBA Production (France)/FILMEX (Romania).

Coming-of-age story, set in Athens in 1966, a period of transformation and destruction when Greeks giddily sought role models in both East and West. A

major building contractor dies suddenly of a heart attack when the new government forces him to stop building his life's work, a 12-storey skyscraper. His 13-year-old son, Dimitris, must suddenly grow up very fast.

BEWARE OF GREEKS

Script: Tom Galbraith. Dir: John Tatoulis. Players: Lakis Lazopoulos, Tasso Kavadia, Titos Vandis, Noni Ioannidou. Prod: Mythos, Mega Channel, GFC (Greece) Media World (Australia).

Romantic comedy about a vendetta that spans three generations. A quiet schoolteacher (Poulakis) sets out to avenge a wrong committed almost 60 years ago.

TOO EARLY TO FORGET

Dir: Dionyssis Gregoratos. Prod: Gregoratos/Hyperion S.A./GFC/ERT.

Drama set in the near future, in a harbour threatened by an ecological catastrophe.

GOLDEN FIELDS OF WHEAT

Script: Giorgos Zafiris and Christos Koulinos. Dir: Zafiris. Prod: Notos/GFC/ERT.

A young man who returns to his homeland and finds it radically altered makes a wager with himself that he can rebuild the lost landscape of his memory.

PEPPERMINT

Dir: Costas Kapakas. Prod: Kappa Films, P.P.V./Stefi Films/ Cinegramm/Giannikos/Prooptiki/ Focus Films (Hungary)/Spectra '92 (Bulgaria)/Greek TV ET-1/GFC.

When his mother dies, a 45 year-old man starts remembering his childhood and adolescence, reliving the emotions and the atmosphere of his 1960s youth in a series of flashbacks.

THE YELLOW BICYCLE

Script: Dimitris Stavrakas, Stavros Tsiolis, Vassilis Spiliopoulos. Dir: Stavrakas. Players: George Halaris, Manos Vakoussis, Alexandra Pandelaki, Thanos Grammenos. Prod: Hyperion S.A./GFC/ERT/Tonicon Ltd./Alekos Papageorgiou.

Fact-based drama about a semi-literate boy and the teacher who helps him find social acceptance.

DRUMMER

Dir: Thanassis Scroubelos. Players: Phillippos Lazaris. Prod: Scroubelos/GFC.

The story of 'Drummer', a hit man from the former Soviet Union who takes on a new contract without knowing that the target is a long-lost member of his family.

THE FLOWER OF THE LAKE

Script and Dir: Stamatis Tsarouchas. Players: Lakis Komninos, Yannis Kasdaglis, Vangelis Kourikis, Evri Sofroniadou, Katerina Moutsatsou, Akis Machairas.

Drama set in Northern Greece at the turn of the century, when people struggled to survive in harsh economic conditions.

EVERY SATURDAY

Script and Dir: Vassilis Vafeas. Players: Costas Voutsas, Nikos Poursanidis. Prod: Sigma Film/GFC/ERT.

Drama about the relationship between a teenage son and his divorced father, who see each other once a week.

BLACK MILK

Script: Christos Chomenidis, Nikos Triantafyllidis. Dir: Triantafyllidis. Players: Michael Marmarinos, Myrto Alikaki, Ieroclis Michailidis. Prod: Yannis Koutsomitisí/Astra Films/ERT/GFC.

Alekos, a young writer who has the power to travel across space and time at will, is caught up in the cogs of the mass media machine.

I'LL SEE YOU IN HELL, DARLING

Dir: Nikos Nikolaidis. Players: Pchalis Tsarouchas, Vicky Harris, Valeria Christodoulidou. Prod: Nikolaidis/ERT/GFC.

Supernatural romance in which two women begin a night-time journey to hell, full of hallucinations and desperate violence. They try to kill each other in a quest for their former lover.

A NIGHT TO REMEMBER

Script: Thanos Alexandris, Nikos Panayotopoulos. Dir: Panayo-topoulos. Players: Nikos Kouris, Athena Maximou. Prod: Marianna Film/ERT/GFC.

The love affair between two young people unfolds in Athenian coffee shops and on rooftops and snowy mountains.

HONG KONG — Derek Elley

Industry jitters in Hong Kong have increased during the past year, with the prophets of doom having a field day. An end to Hong Kong production as we knew it? Maybe. The death of the Hong Kong film industry? Hardly likely. The plain truth is that, despite omens to the contrary, just as many Hong Kong films were released in 1998 as the previous year: 84, compared with 82 in 1997.

However, the total gross was considerably smaller – around $53m (HK$407m), against $71m in 1997. Only one movie broke the magical $5m (HK$40m) mark, Andrew Lau's swordplay fantasy *The Storm Riders*, with Jackie Chan's *Who Am I?* in second place with $4.9 million. The period from August 1998 to January 1999 was particularly bleak, and the two big Chinese New Year 1999 releases – Jackie Chan's *Gorgeous* and Stephen Chiau's *King of Comedy* – failed to top even $4m each.

The only hopeful sign for local producers was that US imports fared little better. *Deep Impact*, *Godzilla*, *Armageddon* and *A Bug's Life* hovered around the $2.5m mark, and the Jackie Chan vehicle, *Rush Hour*, managed a lame $2m. All of this suggests a theatrical market in overall decline, with people spending their more limited leisure money on ancillary products (VCD, DVD), and other things besides movies.

The past year saw several high-profile demonstrations and pronouncements by industry people against piracy, though the phenomenon is nothing new in Hong Kong and did not seem to worry anyone when the cinema market thrived. Video piracy is well-organised and of a high quality in Hong Kong; the irony is that most of its revenues go to the underworld, which is still responsible for much film financing.

However, for a territory used to prosperity, all of this caused major jitters throughout the industry, with some observers predicting a further fall in production to 40 titles in 1999. In fact, by July 1999, 40 local titles had already been released, with – to everyone's surprise – the biggest half-year grosser being a modestly-budgeted Japanese psychodrama, **The Ring**, with $4m, trampling US blockbusters like *The Matrix*. Following the success of *The Ring*, a host of other Japanese movies flooded into the market.

Final curtains

In the summer of 1999, two long-running industry sagas drew to a close. Shaw Bros.' massive library of more than 700 titles, which it had jealously guarded since virtually withdrawing from production during the 1980s, was sold for $50m to two Taiwanese entities, cable channel HBO and Central Motion Picture Corp. Representing a huge chunk of Hong Kong cinema's post-war history, and with only a handful of titles released on video, the library had been on the block for some time, though what condition the prints and negatives are in is anyone's guess.

Golden Harvest – begun 30 years ago as a rival to Shaw Bros., and long rumoured to be financially overstretched – announced the liquidation of its production arm. The GH group, which includes cinema chains, will continue, but the effective end of Hong Kong's last "major studio", even though it had been retreating from production for some time, was another psychological blow to the industry.

Such developments mean the old days are over, and Hong Kong is going through a slow transition – exacerbated by the East Asian economic meltdown – into a much more diversified talent centre, forcing it to look outside for production finance rather than relying on local conglomerates. There is still no sign that any other centres – Beijing, Shanghai, Taipei or Singapore – will replace it as a fulcrum for Chinese production. And even its stars, whose inflated salary demands contributed to the present "crisis", are now publicly reducing their price tags – reportedly by 70% in comedian Stephen Chiau's case, and around a third in others'.

Commercial wizard Wong Jing rose to these new challenges in 1998, producing, writing or directing some 15% of the year's movies – many of them schlockers, but at least they kept the industry's wheels turning. Top of his quality titles was former Peter Chan scriptwriter James Yuen's third feature, **Your Place or Mine!**, a wonderfully warm and enjoyable relationships comedy, well cast, about an ad executive (Tony Leung Chiu-wai) who just can't keep a regular woman. Best of his schlockers was the return to form of Clarence Fok (*Naked Killer*) with the trashy **Cheap Killers**, about two assassins' downward death spiral.

Notable directing debuts included renowned art director Yee Chung-man with the romantic triangle **Anna Magdalena**, uniting pop star Kelly Chan with male pinups Takeshi Kaneshiro and Aaron Kwok; and actor Francis Ng with a flawed but interesting rogue cop drama, **9413....**

Action men

After finishing off his *Young and Dangerous* series with **Young and Dangerous: The Prequel**, one of the best of the six, Andrew Lau changed stride with the big-budget, special effects-laden *The Storm Riders*, a swordplay yarn adapted from a long-running manga, that was wobbly on structure but highly entertaining. He immediately went into production on a follow-up, *A Man Called Hero*.

Ringo Lam, following his tenebrous underworld drama *Full Alert*, also changed tack with **The Suspect**, an ambitious gangster spectacle shot in the Philippines, that was weakened by a sappy male lead (Louis Koo) but featured some classic Lam set-pieces. Flawed by a lack of variety in tone, but very ambitious on a small budget, was action star Donnie Yen's second directorial outing, **Ballistic Kiss**, a dark killer's nocturne, starring himself and Taiwanese starlet Annie Wu, with parallels to *Leon* and *The Collector*.

Also of interest were Raymond Yip's *Young and Dangerous* spin-off, **Portland Street Blues**, with Sandra Ng excellent as a female gang leader, and former art director Daniel Lee's **...Till Death Do Us Part**, a psychological drama with Anita Yuen as a devoted wife traumatised by her husband's infidelity.

Johnnie To's company, Milkyway Image, continued to foster its family of talent – including director Patrick Yau, writer-director Wai Fa-fai and actor Lau Ching-wan – and came up with one its best productions, Yau's **Expect the Unexpected**, a crime drama with the same storytelling texture and oblique atmosphere as Yau's *The Longest Nite*, but a completely different visual style (rain instead of sweltering Macau heat, day instead of night). To signed his own name as director of **A Hero Never Dies**, an operatic, Leone-ish gangster movie about two betrayed gunmen.

After a false step with the twentieth-century saga *The Soong Sisters*, Mabel Cheung recovered some of her old form with **City of Glass**, an unashamedly romantic vehicle for stars Leon Lai and Shu Qi, with an almost Chabrol-ian approach to interweaved narrative and the impact of chance on people's lives. Another New Wave veteran, Ann Hui, came up with the very ambitious but structurally confused **Ordinary Heroes**, a portrait of Hong Kong society – and disillusioned activism – spread over a decade.

Taiwanese actress Shu Qi was the best thing in Jackie Chan's **Gorgeous**, directed by Vincent Kuk, about a romantic young dreamer who travels to Hong Kong in search of the man who sent her a message in a bottle. This was a very enjoyable change of style and pace for Chan, with fewer death-defying stunts and more charm. Chan's box-office competitor during Chinese New Year, the Stephen Chiau/Li Lik-chi-directed **King of Comedy**, was not among the comic's best, but contained some fine moments in its first half, with Chiau as a wannabe actor who just can't seem to get a job (the film was only loosely based on Scorsese's *The King of Comedy*)

The year's most ambitious film was Fruit Chan's long-awaited follow-up to *Made in Hong Kong*. **The Longest Summer** is a very different piece of work, an epic portrait of the city prior to and after its handover to China in July 1997, through the stories of a group of people who turn to organised crime when they need something to believe in. Beginning in a jumbled way, but slowly developing a strong emotional pull, the film establishes Chan, 40, as one of the territory's most original and provocative talents.

During the past year, Hong Kong cinema lost two veterans. Actor Roy Chiao died in the US in April 1999, aged 72, and Yueh Feng, a leading Mandarin director of the 1950s and 1960s, died in July 1999, aged 90.

The 18th Hong Kong Film Awards

The following awards were presented on April 24, 1999, for Hong Kong films released the previous year:

Best Film: *Beastcops*.
Best Directors: Gordon Chan, Dante Lam (*Beastcops*).
Best Script: Chan Hing-kai, Gordon Chan (*Beastcops*).
Best Actor: Anthony Wong (*Beastcops*).
Best Actress: Sandra Ng (*Portland Street Blues*).
Best Supporting Actor: Tam Yiu-man (*Beastcops*).
Best Supporting Actress: Shu Qi (*Portland Street Blues*).
Best Photography: Arthur Wong (*Sleepless Town*).
Best Art Direction: Yohei Taneda (*Sleepless Town*).

Best Costume Design: Lee Pik-kwan (*The Storm Riders*).
Best Action Design: Jackie Chan (*Who Am I?*).
Best Editing: Mak Chi-sin, Pang Fat (*The Storm Riders*).
Best Acting Newcomer: Nicholas Tse (*Young and Dangerous: The Prequel*).
Best Original Music: Chan Kwong-wing (*The Storm Riders*).
Best Original Song: "This Life Comes Only Once" (from *City of Glass*).
Best Sound Effects: *The Storm Riders*.
Lifetime Achievement Award: producer/exhibitor Leonard K.C. Ho.

Producers

Bob & Partners Co.
22/F, 83 Austin Rd.
Tsimshatsui
Tel: (852) 2314 7198
Fax: (852) 2314 7120

Chang-Hong Channel Film & Video Co. (HK)
5/F, Blk A, Full View Bldg.
3-7 Liberty Ave.
Kowloon
Tel: (852) 2762 2689
Fax: (852) 2762 2692

China Star Entertainment Group
Unit 503C, Miramar Tower
1-23 Kimberley Rd.
Tsimshatsui
Tel: (852) 2313 1888
Fax: (852) 2191 9888

Eastern Production
Kimberley Mansion, GA
15 Austin Ave.
Tsimshatsui
Tel: (852) 2367 3328
Fax: (852) 2367 5797

Golden Harvest/Golden Communications
8 King Tung St.
Hammer Hill Rd.
Kowloon
Tel: (852) 2352 8222
Fax: (852) 2351 1683

Impact Films Production
6/F, Blk 2, Tien Chu Centre
1E Mok Cheong St.
Tokwawan, Kowloon
Tel: (852) 2715 6545
Fax: (852) 2713 3390

Ko Chi Sum Films Co.
Room 617, Hewlett Centre
52-54 Hoi Yuen Rd.
Kwun Tong
Tel: (852) 2793 1123
Fax: (852) 2793 1134

Long Shong Pictures (H.K.)
G/F, Blk D, 272 Prince Edward Rd.
West Kowloon
Tel: (852) 2338 2211
Fax: (852) 2336 9911

Mandarin Films (Singapore)
1801-2 Westlands Centre
20 Westland Rd
Quarry Bay
Tel: (852) 2579 1718
Fax: (852) 2579 1707

Media Asia Films
Rm 412-416, 4/F, World Commercial Centre
11 Canton Rd
Tsimshatsui
Tel: (852) 2314 4288
Fax: (852) 2314 4247

Mei Ah Films Production Co.
Unit 15-28, 17/F, Metro Centre, Phase 1
32 Lam Hing St
Kowloon Bay
Tel: (852) 2754 2855
Fax: (852) 2799 3643

Milkyway Entertainment Group
22/F, Remington Centre
23 Hung To Rd
Kwun Tong
Kowloon
Tel: (852) 2718 8128
Fax: (852) 2718 8122

Mobile Film Production
Flat C, 2/F, Dorfu Court
5-6 Hau Fook St
Tsimshatsui
Tel: (852) 2301 3008
Fax: (852) 2732 5315

Pineast Pictures
Flat B, 8/F, Beauty Mansion
69-71 Kimberley Rd
Kowloon
Tel: (852) 2722 0896
Fax: (852) 2311 4167

Salon Films (H.K.)
6 Devon Rd
Kowloon Tong
Tel: (852) 2338 0505
Fax: (852) 2338 2539

Seasonal Film Corp.
12/F, Flat H, Kim Tak Bldg
328 Nathan Rd
Kowloon
Tel: (852) 2385 6125
Fax: (852) 2770 0583

Southern Film Co.
Rm 1902, Dominion Centre
43-59 Queen's Rd East
Hong Kong
Tel: (852) 2528 4787
Fax: (852) 2865 1449

Tomson (H.K.) Films Co.
Suite 1406-09, 14/F,
China Resources Bldg
26 Harbour Rd
Hong Kong
Tel: (852) 2848 1668
Fax: (852) 2877 0590

United Filmmakers Organisation
Unit B, 11/F, Prosperous Centre
1 Knutsford Terrace
Tsimshatsui
Tel: (852) 2336 3298
Fax: (852) 2339 0972

Win's Entertainment
2A Kimberley Mansion
15 Austin Ave
Tsimshatsui
Tel: (852) 2739 2877
Fax: (852) 2369 0981

Wong Jing's Workshop
PO Box 99093
Tsimshatsui
Tel: (852) 2314 7198
Fax: (852) 2314 7120

Useful Addresses

Hong Kong Film Archive
Rm 176, 7/F, Camplex
123A Fa Yuen St
Mongkok
Tel: (852) 2739 2139
Fax: (852) 2311 5229

Hong Kong Film Directors Guild
2/F, 35 Ho Man Tin St
Kowloon
Tel: (852) 2760 0331
Fax: (852) 2713 2373

Hong Kong Film Academy
PO Box 71311
Kowloon
Tel: (852) 2786 9349
Fax: (852) 2742 7017

Hong Kong Film Institute
6/F, 295 Lai Chi Kok Rd
Kowloon
Tel: (852) 2728 2690
Fax: (852) 2728 5743

Hong Kong Theatres Assn.
21/F, Hongkong-Chinese Bank
42 Yee Woo St
Causeway Bay
Tel: (852) 2576 3833
Fax: (852) 2576 1833

Performing Artists Guild of H.K.
145 Waterloo Rd
Kowloon
Tel: (852) 2794 0388
Fax: (852) 2338 7742

HUNGARY — Derek Elley

The introduction of multiplexes to Hungary, which began in 1996, continues to fuel the cinemagoing revival in the country, and the past year has seen the trend spreading outside the capital. This has not, of itself, done a great deal to help local production, which continues to deliver a few local hits every year alongside thinly-attended art movies, but it has at least created, a filmgoing climate which can only help, as and when Hungarian directors get their act together and start making audience-pleasing movies in bulk.

In September 1998 a 10-screen multiplex opened in Györ, followed in the next six months by others in Debrecen, Sopron and Kecskemét. In Budapest, a Hollywood Multiplex opened in a shopping centre in October 1998. Most of the country's box-office now comes from these new theatres, putting further strain on small regional cinemas supported by local government.

In 1998, 13 Hungarian movies were released, with total admissions of just over 404,000 and total box-office of some $715,000 (143 million forints); this compares with 16 titles, 1.4 million admissions and $1.9m the previous year. Much of the 1997 figure was accounted for by two titles (*Dollybirds* and *Out of Order*); in 1998 two comedies by the same directors also dominated admissions, though not on the same scale. *Dollybirds* director Péter Tímár again produced the box-office champ, the madcap **Feri's Gang**, which drew 176,960 admissions; in second place was *Out of Order* co-director Róbert Koltai's *Professor Albeit*, with 144,100 tickets.

The only other Hungarian films to make even a meagre impression were Tamás Sas' **Espresso** (35,387) and veteran Károly Makk's costume drama **The Gambler** (21,274). Most other films scraped a few thousand admissions each. The leading distributor of local movies was Budapest Film, with eight titles and a 60% share of the market.

The country's long-delayed Film Law still shows no signs of being implemented, and state funding through the Motion Picture Foundation of Hungary remains fixed at around $2m a year. Of more concern is that, yet again, there is no definitive sign of a breakthrough in film-makers' attitudes towards the market. The new crop of movies on display at the 30th Hungarian Film Week in February 1999 was the familiar mix: a few well-crafted titles with obvious audience appeal, a larger number of art movies with no regard for the realities of the market, plus a scattering of titles by veterans.

Koltai's **Professor Albeit** (*Ámbár tanár úr*) is a strictly local comedy, about a middle-aged high-school teacher (played by Koltai himself) dealing with unruly students and dreams of romancing a gorgeous student (Kata Dobo). After Koltai's earlier hits like *We Never Die*, and even the energetically plotted farce *Out of Order*, the film seems lethargic to foreign eyes and rather tired in its humour.

Far livelier, and with a degree of marketability, was Tamás Sas' **You or Me** (*Kalózok* – literally, *Pirates*), which, though less stylised than his previous *Espresso*, continued to demonstrate this noted cinematographer's talent as a director. An infectiously enjoyable musical comedy centred on a group of young people who run a pirate radio station by day and hang out in a singing club by night, the film has a catchy soundtrack, likeable leads and a bright rhythm. As the beautiful flautist who comes between two of the men (Attila Király, Viktor Bodó), Gabi Gubás is delightful.

Péter Tímár's latest comedy, 6:3, is a clever idea which does not quite realise its potential, despite some good individual sequences. A time-travel movie, in which a modern-day soccer fan finds himself transported back 45 years to a legendary Hungary vs. England game during the darkest days of communism, it makes funny play with running jokes like differences in prices ("The forint used to be a strong currency!") and partly trades on local audiences' nostalgia for old-fashioned certainties, but the script lacks overall sharpness in the dialogue, despite a likeable performance from Károly Eperjes as the hapless, working-class hero.

Sas and Tímár's films were among the most enjoyable in the Film Week, alongside a real curio from veteran Márta Mészáros, now in her late sixties, that is often like a glossy, softcore sex film. The Polish-Hungarian-German co-production **Daughters of Luck** (*Cory szczescie*), shot in Warsaw with dialogue in Russian and Polish, focuses on a Russian wife (the stunning Olga Drozdova) who travels abroad in search of work and ends up as a high-class hooker. The movie, which contains several sex scenes shot in fetishistic detail, can be read as an elaborate table-turning exercise between two former communist "partners": in this instance, the formerly dominant Russians get royally screwed by the Poles instead. As a sheer piece of cinema, it is excellently acted, always striking to look at, and filled with small ironies.

Fellow veteran Miklós Jancsó, 77, came up with a similarly playful, but mind-bendingly obscure movie in **The Lord's Lantern in Budapest** (*Nekem lámpást adott kezembe az Úr Pesten*), a collection of five vignettes featuring the same two characters in different guises. and Jancsó himself (plus his long-time scriptwriter Gyula Hernádi) functioning as a kind of ironic chorus. Broadly centred on life's little ironies, changing fortunes, the weight of history, and the capacity for violence in

Still from Tamás Sas' YOU OR ME

the Hungarian character, the film – Jancsó's first feature in seven years – is playful and spry, with none of his technical trademarks, such as long, elaborate takes, and seems like an end-of-career jape.

In the area of solid, well-crafted festival pleasers, Can Togay's **One Winter behind God's Back** (*Egy tél az Isten háta mögött*) was the year's standout. An examination of life in a mountain backwater during the final years of communism, it is a neatly observed study of a community centred on a bar and a cinema. When a film fails to arrive at the onset of winter, a young film buff pieces together bits of classic movies and provides his own storyline to entertain the villagers. A tribute to the power of cinema, and its ability to stir emotions, this is a small gem.

The year's most interesting debut came from Csaba Bollók, whose 67-minute **North by North** (*Észak, észak*), essentially a graduation film, was one of the most confident calling cards in Hungarian cinema for several years. A nicely shot tale of a girl (Laura Ruttkay), her bike and the wintry landscape through which she rides and encounters several adventures, it manages to hold the viewer without stretching its wafer-thin content beyond breaking point.

Equally intriguing in its delicate handling of atmosphere and tone is András

Salamon's **Close to Love** (*Kösel a szerelemhez*), a charming, almost fairytale-like love story between a rookie Budapest policeman (Ferenc Hujber) and a mysterious Chinese girl. Japanese actress Tsuyu Shimizu is unconvincing as the woman, but the film is otherwise well cast, conveying the passion of the pair's attraction (even though neither speaks the other's language) and everyday racism, without getting on any cross-cultural soapbox.

The past year came up with its usual collection of clinkers that seem not to have been made for any audience beyond the director's friends – and do not even work on their own terms. The most high profile was Ildikó Enyédi's **Simon Magus**, which to everyone's amazement won three top prizes from the local jury – which declined to give any movie in the Week the Best Film prize. Following her remarkable debut 10 years ago with *My Twentieth Century*, Enyédi has seen her career follow a long slide, and *Simon Magus* is another stab at magical realism that is even more embarrassing than her previous flop, *Magic Hunter*. Actor Péter Andorai sleepwalks through the title role as a Hungarian mystic in present-day Paris who is called in by the police to solve a murder and becomes embroiled in a challenge by a rival mystic (Péter Halász) to repeat a Houdini stunt.

Other failures included Gábor Dettre's English-language **The Hurdy-Gurdy Man** (with Brad Dourif as a narcissistic

Hungarian film-maker in New York), that is essentially a long-winded vanity production; Gábor Tompa's stolid and obscure **Chinese Defence** (*Kinai védelem*), about a mysterious returnee from a Siberian labour camp who finds himself a displaced person in Romania; Zoltán Kamondi's muddled melodrama about a modern-day mad scientist-cum-womaniser, **The Alchemist and the Virgin** (*Az alkimista és a szüz*); and Péter Gábor's **Popcorn** (*Pattogatott kukorica*), a downbeat thriller about a street-seller embroiled in Budapest's sleazy underworld.

Though of minimal commercial value, at least without major pruning, maverick Ferenc Grunwalsky, who also shot Jancsó's *Lord's Lantern*, fielded one of his most straightforward but hardest-edged films with **Homecoming: Little but Tough Part 2** (*Visszatérés: kicsi, de nagyon no. 2*), a follow up to his 1989 movie. A quirky, often nasty little movie that nonetheless stays in the memory, it follows the same anti-hero, now out of jail, who is determined to find out what happened to some jewellery he left in the care of his three sisters, as well as deal with his vicious former partner, who is terrorising the village. The film has a slow-burning tension, aided by claustrophobic photography, that effectively sketches the small community and ever-present sense of danger, with excellent performances.

Budapest's Atlantic Press has published *Shoot in Hungary 1999/2000*, a beautifully-illustrated reference guide, with a useful index, to the country's film organisations, studios, locations, talent, technicians and service companies: indispensable for anyone interested in Hungarian cinema or production ($63, by major credit cards, from Atlantic Press, Németvölgyi út 5, 1126 Budapest, Fax +36 1 212 2444).

Finally, veteran director Ferenc Kardos died in Budapest in March, 1999, aged 62. Best known for *Grimaces* (1967, co-directed with Jénos Rózsa), *Red-Letter Days* (1968) and *Petofi '73*, he was latterly head of Budapest Film Studio. Kardos' last feature was the 1997 drama, *The Smallest Foundation in the World*.

Still from Péter Gábor's thriller POPCORN

30th Hungarian Film Week Awards

Best Film: no award.
Best Director: Ildikó Enyédi (*Simon Magus*).
Best Actress: Ágnes Csere, Klára Varga (*Homecoming*).
Best Actor: Péter Andorai (*Simon Magus*), Károly Eperjes (*6:3, One Winter behind God's Back*).
Best Script: András Salamon (*Close to Love*).
Best Photography: Tibor Mathé (*Simon Magus*).

Special Prize: Péter Tímár (*6:3*).
Gene Moskowitz Prize (foreign critics): Miklós Jancsó (*The Lord's Lantern in Budapest*).
Best Documentary: *The Danube Exodus* (Péter Forgács), Poppies (Ágnes Tölgyesi).
Best Documentary Director: János Zelki (*It's All Just a Game*).
Special Documentary Prizes: d.p. Sándor Csukás (*Koko, A Ship Has Flown Away in the Wind*), Livia Gyarmathy (*Our Stork*), László Mihályfy (*Justice*).
Audience Award: *6:3* (Péter Tímár).
Assn. of Hungarian Cinemas Award: *Out of Order* (Róbert Koltai, András Kern).

Producers

Béla Balázs Studio
Bajcsy-Zsilinszky ut 36-38
1054 Budapest
Tel/Fax: (36 1) 111 2809

Budapest Film Studio
Róna utca 174
1045 Budapest
Tel: (36 1) 251 8568
Fax: (36 1) 251 0478

Focus Film
Pasaréti út 122
1026 Budapest
Tel: (36 1) 176 7484
Fax: (36 1) 176 7493

Forum Film
Róna utca 174
1145 Budapest
Tel/Fax: (36 1) 220 5413

Hunnia Studio
Róna utca 174
1145 Budapest
Tel: (36 1) 252 3170
Fax: (36 1) 251 6269

InterPannonia
(animation, also distribution)
Gyarmat utca 36
1145 Budapest
Tel: (36 1) 267 6514, 267 6515
Fax: (36 1) 267 6516

Magic Media
Róna utca 174
1145 Budapest
Tel: (36 1) 163 3479
Fax: (36 1) 263 3479

Movie Innovation Partnership (MIP)
Kinizsi utca 28
1092 Budapest
Tel: (36 1) 218 3600, 218 0983
Fax: (36 1) 216 3601

Novofilm
(also services)
Hajógyárisziget 131
1033 Budapest
Tel: (36 1) 188 9304
Fax: (36 1) 155 9177

Objektiv Film Studio
Róna utca 174
1145 Budapest
Tel: (36 1) 252 5359
Fax: (36 1) 251 7269

Pannonia Film
(animation)
Hüvösvölgyi út 64

1021 Budapest
Tel: (36 1) 176 3333
Fax: (36 1) 176 3409

Transatlantic Media Associates (TMA)
(also services)
Táltos utca 4
1123 Budapest
Tel: (36 1) 155 3200
Fax: (36 1) 175 2444

Satellit-Film/Europe 2000
(also services)
Finkenstrasse 48
8130 Stamberg
Germany
Tel: (36 1) 8151 3551
Fax: (36 1) 8151 28544
ALSO
Róna utca 174
1145 Budapest
Tel/Fax: (36 1) 183 5930

Still from Ferenc Grunwalsky's HOMECOMING: LITTLE BUT TOUGH PART 2

Varga Studio
(animation, F/X)
Raktár utca 25-31
1035 Budapest
Tel: (36 1) 168 8296
Fax: (36 1) 168 6418

Distributors

Budapest Film
Báthori utca 10
1054 Budapest
Tel: (36 1) 132 8198
Fax: (36 1) 111 2687

Flamex
Labanc utca 22B
1021 Budapest
Tel: (36 1) 176 1534
Fax: (36 1) 176 0596

Hungarofilm
(also production services)
Báthori utca 10
1054 Budapest
Tel: (36 1) 111 0020, 131 4746
Fax: (36 1) 153 1850

InterCom
Bácskai utca 28-36
1145 Budapest
Tel: (36 1) 467 1400
Fax: (36 1) 252 2736

UIP-Dunafilm
Hüvosvolgyi ut 54
1021 Budapest
Tel: (36 1) 274 2180
Fax: (36 1) 274 2177

Useful Addresses

Assoc. of Hungarian Film & TV Artists
Városligeti fasor 38
1068 Budapest
Tel/Fax: (36 1) 342 4760

Assoc. of Hungarian Film Distributors
Karolina út 65
1135 Budapest
Tel/Fax: (36 1) 295 5001

Filmunio Hungary
(festivals, foreign promo)
Városligeti fasor 38
1068 Budapest
Tel: (36 1) 351 7760 351 7761
Fax: (36 1) 268 0070 351 7766

Hungarian Film Institute
Budakeszi út 51B
1012 Budapest
Tel: (36 1) 176 1018, 176 1322
Fax: (36 1) 176 7106

Motion Picture Foundation of Hungary (MMA)
Városligeti fasor 38
1068 Budapest
Tel: (36 1) 351 7696
Fax: (36 1) 268 0070

Mafilm Corp.
(studio complex)
Róna utca 174
1145 Budapest
Tel: (36 1) 252 2870
Fax: (36 1) 251 1080

S-media 2000
Szemlöhegy 28-30
1022 Budapest
Tel/Fax: (36 1) 326 0698

ICELAND — Ásgrímur Sverrisson

Aftter years of intense lobbying by the film-making community, the government finally relented at the end of 1998 and agreed to address the dire financial situation of the Icelandic Film Fund. Over the next four years the money allocated to the fund will increase to around $3m a year, a vast improvement on the $1m annual subsidy that has applied for many years. Icelandic producers will have to rely a little less on foreign investors, who, increasingly, have been asking themselves why they were supporting Icelandic-language films when such a small proportion of the budgets were coming from Iceland.

Furthermore, the government announced a special benefits plan to attract foreign productions to Iceland, with a tax rebate of up to 12% on productions spending more than $1m in the country. These measures have already attracted several international (mainly American) features to the country.

Things are looking up at last, and Icelandic film-makers can now put the years of moaning behind them and turn to the important matter of producing good movies. It is inevitable that, with an improved financial climate, the focus now shifts to the question of what kind of films we should be making; an issue that has

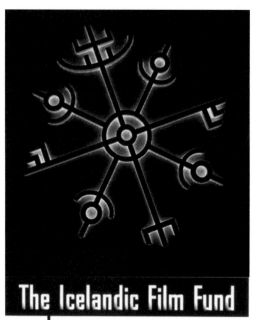

The Icelandic Film Fund

Túngata 14 • 101 Reykjavík • Iceland
tel: (+354) 562 3580 • fax: (+ 354) 562 7171
e-mail: iff@iff.is • http://www.iff.is

generally been sidelined. Indeed, a healthy debate now exists throughout Europe, with the British production boom in full swing, the Danish Dogma movement spreading to other countries and an increasing emphasis on the distribution of European films.

Icelandic producers have been very efficient in securing offshore investment, with various co-production deals and successful "raids" on European film funds. But while this indicates that Icelandic films are regarded as potentially interesting and "different", their quality has remained very inconsistent, with too many film-makers not delivering on their initial promise. Perhaps this is due to the inability of most local film-makers to work regularly and build up a body of work.

Another contributing factor is probably the relative lack of a frank exchange of views, ideas and approaches to film-making. Icelandic film-makers are experts in justifying public spending on their films, but shy away from discussions on artistic direction. This comes as no surprise, since

loud proclamations and innovative insults are the prevailing forms of discussion in Icelandic society, with healthy debate usually frowned upon.

Icelandic film-makers have the potential to make interesting cinema, which will be noticed on the world scene, but only if they manage to create a dynamic environment which encourages exploration and strong self-criticism.

No Trace - and no point

The last quarter of 1999 will see the release of several new Icelandic films, including the latest works from veteran directors Hrafn Gunnlaugsson and Friðrik Thór Friðriksson and several promising debuts. This is an improvement on 1998, when only two films were released. One of these, **No Trace**, was a pointless exercise in genre film-making. Directed by Hilmar Oddsson (who a few years ago made the ambitious *Tears of Stone*, a biopic about a composer who has to choose between his career in Nazi Germany and his Jewish wife) and written by Sveinbjörn I. Baldvinsson, it was commissioned by The Nordic Film Fund under a scheme designed to attract a younger audience to Nordic films. Sadly it failed on every level.

Its dull and at times incomprehensible plot revolved around a celebrity swimmer who wakes up after a wild night out to find a dead girl in his bed, and soon becomes involved in an incredible quest for stolen diamonds, helped along by his motley group of friends. The mostly under-developed and uninteresting characters do not help and the unenthusiastic execution suggests that Oddsson was having an off day. The icing on the cake is the music, by classical composer Hjálmar H. Ragnarsson, which resembles circus tunes, but has no business in a film that purports to be about intrigue and suspense.

The Dance, by Ágúst Guðmundsson, was an altogether happier experience, a charming comedy in the Celtic vein. Based on a short story by renowned Faroese writer William Heinesen, it depicts colourful

Still from Ágúst Guðmundsson's Faroese comedy, THE DANCE

she really loves. But he has not yet given up hope and tries to lure the fickle bride away. The hypnotic traditional "vikivaki" dance provides the rhythm of the story, which is enlivened by a shipwreck, some looting and supernatural occurrences.

This is clearly a labour of love for Guðmundsson and his co-writer / producer Kristín Atladóttir, and a welcome return to prominence for this pioneer of the Icelandic cinema after a 14-year absence (his 1980 debut, *Land and Sons*, remains one of the best Icelandic films). The proceedings are handled with affection and wit and the cast is excellent, although a couple of underwritten characters and an ending which fails to tie up all the loose ends convincingly, hold the film back from the first rank.

events during a wedding party on a small island in the North Atlantic in 1913. The bride has chosen to marry a man of importance instead of the passionate sailor

ASGRÍMUR SVERRISSON is a director and writer.

New and Forthcoming Films

ÓSKABÖRN (Plan B)

Script and Dir: Jóhann Sigmarsson. Prod: Sigmarsson/ Friðrik Þór Friðriksson

Petty criminals and drug addicts seek escape from the seedy underworld.

MYRKRAHÖF INGINN (Witchcraft)

Script: Hrafn Gunnlaugsson, Þórarinn Eldjárn. Dir: Gunnlaugsson. Prod. Gunnlaugsson/ Friðrik Þór Friðriksson.

An idealistic seventeenth-century priest is determined to save his flock from the devil, only to find demons raging within himself.

ENGLAR ALHEIMSINS (Angels of the Universe)

Script: Friðrik Þór Friðriksson, Einar Már Guðmundsson, from his Nordic Council Award-winning novel. Dir: Friðriksson. Prod. Friðriksson/The Icelandic Film Corporation.

The tragi-comic story of a mentally ill man, told with humour and vitality.

FÍASKÓ (Fiasco)

Script and Dir: Ragnar Bragason. Prod. Þórir Snær Sigurjónsson/ The Icelandic Film Corporation.

A funny look at the trials of a hapless family in downtown Reykjavík.

101 REYKJAVIK

Script and Dir: Baltasar Kormákur. From the novel 101 Reykjavík, by Hallgrímur Helgason. Prod. Ingvar Þórðarson/101 Productions.

A nihilistic thirtysomething man who still lives with his mother falls in love with her new lesbian lover.

UNGFRÚIN GÓ A OG HÚSI (Honour of the House)

Script and Dir: Guðný Halldórsdóttir. From a short story by Halldór Laxness. Prod: Halldór Þorgeirsson/Umbi Films/Nordisk Film.

Two sisters torture each other at the turn of the century, because both are in love with the man who has fathered the younger sister's child.

IKINGUT

Script: Jón Steinar Ragnarsson. Prod: Friðrik Thór Friðriksson/The Icelandic Film Corporation.

In the late seventeenth century, a small eskimo boy drifts on an iceberg from Greenland to Iceland, where the superstitious locals regard him as an evil spirit. Only young Boas, the priest's son, befriends him.

VILLILJÓS (Dramarama)

Script: Huldar Breiðfjörð. Dir: Dagur Kári Pétursson, Inga Lísa Middleton, Ragnar Bragason, Ásgrímur Sverrisson, Einar Thor Gunnlaugsson. Prod: Thorir Snaer Sigurjónsson, Skuli Malmquist/Zik Zak Filmworks.

Five darkly comic stories intertwine into one as Reykjavík suffers a power cut during a cold winter night.

SÓLON ÍSLANDUS

Script and Dir: Margrét Rún. Prod.: The Icelandic Dream Factory/Edgar Reitz Filmproduktiongesellschaft mbH.

A historical drama about the eccentric nineteenth-century painter and philosopher Sölvi Helgason.

Producers

The Icelandic Film Corporation

Contact: Friðrik Thór Friðriksson, Ari Kristinsson
Hverfisgata 46
101 Reykjavík
Tel: (354) 551 2260
Fax: (354) 552 5154
e-mail: amk@vortex.is
www.saga.is/ifc

Pegasus Pictures

Contact: Snorri Thórisson
Sóltún 24
105 Reykjavík
Tel: (354) 511 4590
Fax: (354) 511 4595
e-mail: pegasus@islandia.is
www.pegasus-pictures.com

Ísfilm

Contact: Ágúst Guðmundsson
Oðinsgata 20
101 Reykjavík
Tel: (354) 561 3395
Fax: (354) 552 3395

Umbifilm

Contact: Halldór Thorgeirsson, Guðny Halldórsdóttir
Melkot
270 Mosfellsbær
Tel: (354) 566 6874
Fax: (354) 566 8002

Distributors

Association of Icelandic Film Distributors

Laugarásbíó, Laugarási
104 Reykjavík
Tel: (354) 553 8150
Fax: (354) 568 0910

Useful Addresses

Icelandic Film Fund

Túngata 14,
101 Reykjavík
Tel: (354) 562 3580
Fax: (354) 562 7171
e-mail: iff@iff.is
www.iff.is/

Association of Icelandic Film Producers

Pósthússtraeti 13
PO Box 476
121 Reykjavík
Tel: (354) 562 8188
Fax: (354) 562 3424

Land & synir
(bi-monthly film magazine)
Contact: Sigurjón Baldur
Hafsteinsson, editor
Tel: (354) 566 7264
e-mail: sbh@reykjavik.is

**Ministry of Culture and
Education**
Sölvhólsgötu 4
101 Reykjavík
Tel: (354) 560 9500
Fax: (354) 562 3068

**The Icelandic Film Makers'
Association**
PO Box 5162
121 Reykjavík
Tel: (354) 552 1202
Fax: (354) 562 0958
e-mail: fk@isholf.is

**The Association of Icelandic
Film Directors**
Laugarnestangi 65
105 Reykjavík
Tel/Fax: (354) 588 1706

**The Icelandic Producers
Association**
PO Box 5357
125 Reykjavík

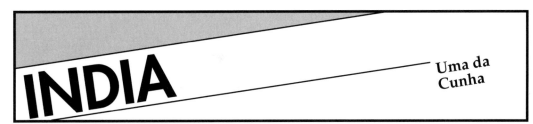

INDIA

Uma da
Cunha

Top star Aamir Khan, playing a street-smart city kid, lounges seductively in jeans, T-shirt and jaunty beret. Eyeing his rich, mini-skirted girlfriend he bursts into song and invites her to "sing, dance and chill out" with him in Khandala, a fashionable hill-resort near Bombay. This number from **Slave** (*Ghulam*) kept all of India humming for months and helped make the film one of the year's biggest hits. The film and the song are indicative of the furious pace of change in India's gargantuan, time-warped movie business. The industry just might be entering the new millennium with a new tune and style, something which will affect the way it functions in the early years of the twenty-first century.

The most obvious change lies in the years and wrinkles that scripts and casts are shedding. Movie audiences are getting younger. Filmgoing is not the family outing that it once was, with elders policing their brood. The young are ditching their chaperones. They have more money and leisure time. They are beginning strongly to identify with the rest of the world, specifically with the MTV generation and the American way of life. Film-makers have listened and acted accordingly.

Yet, as ever, India is choosing the middle path ahead of revolution. The new Indian movie does a balancing act between the demands of youth and those of tradition. Public opinion and censorship have still to be taken into account, too. But there is a more important, cash-driven motive. Traditional values matter even more to the sizeable Indian markets in the UK, US, the Middle East and Africa. The Indian movie of 1999 caters to both worlds – the restless, US-influenced youth at home, and the millions of nostalgia-driven Indians abroad, longing for contact with their roots.

The angry young men who dominated Indian cinema in the early 1990s no longer appeal. Increasingly, the movie model is the college-educated yuppie who uses foreign words ("dude" and "Yo!" are becoming commonplace) and dallies with

Madhur Jaffrey and Greta Scacchi in COTTON MARY

nubile ladies, but remains respectful of conventions and his traditional up-bringing. For example, **The First Wife** (*Biwi Number One*), a hit in mid-1999, is about a vamp who menaces a marriage. The Good Wife, in the mould of the new no-nonsense young movie heroine, goes all out to prove to her rival that she is no match and is unsuitable. Decent Husband chooses to stay with her, Sacred Marriage Vows hold firm and the Good Woman wins. A minority believe that such films are retrogressive, even a harmful influence on the country's gullible, poor masses. But their views count for little.

Breaking records

Last year's outstanding money-spinner was **Kutch Kutch Hota Hai**, an idiomatic phrase that translates as "When the heart flutters". A young girl and boy become friends over college basketball games. He falls for the Principal's sexy daughter and marries her. The wife, on her deathbed, plans to unite her husband with his old flame, knowing that they still care for each other. Songs and dance abound in this make-believe India of goodies and joy. *Kutch Kutch* marked the debut of 26-year-old Karan Johar (son of veteran producer Yash Johar). As in many of today's movies, his actors wear Western designer clothes, the sets wear an imported look, music boasts the latest disco sounds – and high standards are maintained in every technical field.

Kutch Kutch had a record-breaking success in England, becoming the highest Hindi grosser ever there when it took $1.9m in its first five weeks. It was also the first English-subtitled Indian film to attract non-ethnic audiences. *The First Wife* and Mani Ratnam's eagerly-awaited **Dil Se** (which had flopped badly at home) also broke into England's box-office top ten. The reason put forward for such successes is that Indians abroad are more appreciative of technical quality and camera aesthetics.

Kutch Kutch also embodies another new trait in Indian movie-making. The senior citizens of yore who had held positions of power for years are being replaced by a new generation of young people (actually, they are mostly the children of the old guard), who are market-savvy and boast MBAs. These well-qualified, sophisticated youngsters are laying down new tracks for the industry to run on.

Multiplexes ahoy!

India's diminishing production roster still remains the world's largest, although that claim rests as precariously as the business does at home. Of the 693 films censored in 1998, 85% failed at the-box office. In that total, Hindi is ahead with 153 films (30 dubbed from other languages). The South Indian languages follow, with 133 films in Tamil, 124 in Telugu, 72 in Kannada and 69 in Malayalam. Bengali follows with 48 films, while there were just five English releases.

In a country that boasts an annual film production turnover of $1.4 billion, and where movies are a manic obsession, the abject neglect of the exhibition circuit seems inexplicable. India's static base of 13,000 cinemas creates a vicious circle: the exhibitor is disproportionately powerful, particularly in controlling large, first-run theatres in the big cities. Distributors gamble for theatre time at huge cost and risk, in an industry bedevilled by sky-high production and heavy taxation.

In March 1999, however, Maharashra State, whose capital is Bombay, announced it would start promoting multiplexes as part of its tourism plan. It offered several concessions, notably exemption on sales and purchase taxes on projection equip-ment, and entertainment tax exemption for five years. Wholly Indian, joint ventures and foreign-owned multiplexes would have access to similar concessions. The policy extended to existing cinemas converted into multiplexes and there is now frantic screen-building activity. Leading distributor and cinema manager Shravan Shroff confidently predicts that India will have about 500 new screens within two years. That will give distributors breathing space and should assist the growing niche market for minority films.

Still from Rituparna Ghosh's LANDLADY

Since 1998, the government has been gradually softening its attitude towards the industry, a move attributed to pressure exerted by film star members of parliament. In May 1998, film was granted industry status, giving it certain financial advantages, such as obtaining accountable funding from reliable sources. However, that concession has achieved little, besides the hype surrounding Subhash Ghai's **Taal** (due for a mega release in September 1999), which became the first Indian production to be insured (against natural disasters) for as much $4.5m. The following January, another sanction permitted export concessions of software in film, music and television.

The Yanks are coming

In January 1999, the government allowed foreign investment in India's film industry. This had immediate results, namely the entry of Columbia TriStar into Hindi film distribution and production in India and worldwide, a move that could have a far-reaching impact. Columbia generated great hype around the mid-1999 release of its first venture, a musical college romp called **When in Love** (*Pyar Mein Kabhie Kabhie*).

Despite its two-year back-log of bad business running into 1999's first quarter, India's ever-optimistic movie world perked up at the odd summer release doing well and at press time was readying itself for a stream of major openings in the remaining months of the year. Even leading directors lost temporarily to television or theatre have returned reassuringly to film-making.

In Calcutta, Aparna Sen, Buddhodeb Dasgupta and Nabyendu Chatterjee were completing films. In the south, Girish Karnad was at work on a major film. Mani Ratnam had made a quickie. Kamal Hassen was at work on two epics. In Maharashtra, Shyam Benegal, Amol Palekar and Govind Nihalani had new films ready. Octogenarian painter M F Hussein had completed his debut film. Another eagerly awaited film is Mahesh Mathai's **Bhopal Express**. India's crowning glory was Murali' Nair winning the Caméra d'Or for **Throne of Death**, while Shaji's **The Last Dance** was also well-received at Cannes.

The success in India of the previous year's English language films made on Indian themes, Nagesh Kukunoor's *Hyderabad Blues* and Kaizad Gustad's *Bombay Boys*, encouraged others to follow suit. Kukunoor is ready with his next film, **Rockford**, while Sunheil Sippy debuts with **SNIP!** In the US, the South Asian community is producing its own India-

Still from Murali Nair's debut, THRONE OF DEATH

Rohan Dey in Nagesh Kukunoor's ROCKFORD

The presiding guru of the trans-India movie, Ismail Merchant, completed his third feature as a director. **Cotton Mary**, shot in South India's Cochin city, will be release through Universal Pictures in India and worldwide. The release precedes a tribute to Merchant-Ivory at the Calcutta Film festival in mid-November.

UMA DA CUNHA heads Medius (India) Services Private Ltd, a company that provides promotional and executive services for films shot in India, specialising in casting Indian actors. She is *Variety*'s correspondent in India and a consultant on film programming and events for festivals in India and abroad.

connected scripts, among them Nisha Ganatra's *Chutney Popcorn*, Krutin Patel's *ABCD* and Darshan Bhagat's *Karma Local*.

Recent and Forthcoming Films

ROCKFORD

Lang: English. Dir, Story and Script: Nagesh Kukunoor. Phot: Ram Prasad. Players: Rohan Dey, Suhail Bajaj, Ricci Mandelia, Nandita Das, Gerson da Cunha. Prod: Sic Films & Padmini Films.

Kukunoor's second feature (after *Hyderabad Blues*) deals with 13-year-old Rajesh, who leaves home for a new life as a boarder at Rockford, the sequestered and selective Roman Catholic public boys' school in South India. He experiences joys, fears, awakening sexuality and the inevitable legacy of British colonial life on India.

SPLIT WIDE OPEN

Lang: English. Script: Farrukh Dhondy. Story: Dev Benegal and Upamanyu Chatterjee. Dir: Benegal. Phot: Sukumar Jatania. Players: Rahul Bose, Laila Rouass, Shivaji Satham, Farida Haider Mulla. Prod: Manmohan Shetty and Suresh Thomas.

Benegal follows up *English August* with this second feature, set in Bombay 1999, a city of extremes buzzing towards globalisation. Young hustler KP, who sells tap water for a living, and falls foul of his mafia don boss. He returns home to find his adopted kid sister missing. His search leads him to the bizarre world of Nandita, hostess of a TV sex-confession show.

SNIP!

Lang: English. Story, Script and Dir: Sunhil Sippy. Phot: Ravi K Chandran. Players: Archana Puran Singh, Zohra Sehgal, Sohrab Ardeshir, Makarand Deshpande, Noor Mohommed. Prod: Mercury Films.

A dark and sexy comedy set in contemporary Bombay. The film follows six characters, each living in their own urban microcosm, over three unusual days.

BHOPAL EXPRESS

Lang: Hindi/English. Dir and Phot: Mahesh Mathai. Story: Piyush/Prasoon Pandey. Players: Kay Kay, Nehtra Raghuraman, Naseerudin Shah, Zeenat Aman. Prod: Deepak Nayar, Philip Von Alvensleben, Tabrez Noorani for the Bhopal Express Company.

This film is linked to the 1984 Bhopal gas disaster which killed and mutilated several thousands. The film centres around a rickshaw puller (Naseeruddin Shah), an unlikely prophet of doom and nemesis around the impending incident. A first feature.

SHADOWS IN THE DARK

Lang: Hindi. Script and Dir: Pankaj Butalia. Phot: Ranjan Palit. Players: Kitu Gidwani, Srivardhan, Subroto, Naseeruddin Shah Mandeep, Mandakini Goswami. Prod: NFDC/Vital Films/JBA Productions (France).

Feature debut, about the impact of Partition on the people who were driven away from one side of the border and on their children who grew up on the other side. The first part of the film deals with the period just after Partition while the second part takes place about 20 years later.

MARANA SIMHASANAM
(Throne of Death)

Lang: Malayalam. Script: Bharathan Njarakkal. Dir and Story: Murali Nair. Phot: M J Radhakrishanan. Players: Lakshmi Raman, Vishwas Njarakkal, Master Jeevan Mitra, Suhas Thayat and the villagers. Producer: Preeya Nair. Prod: Flying Elephant Films.

In a backward island off Kerala, a seasonal labourer arrested for theft is accused of a long-unsolved murder. The villagers, dazzled by the electric chair that is soon to replace hanging as the local form of capital punishment, demand that the murderer be the chair's first victim.

Still from M.F. Hussain's debut, GAJA GAMINI

Kishore Kadam (left) and Rajeshwari Sachdev in CONFLICT

SAMAR (Conflict)

Lang: Hindi. Script: Ashok Mishra. Dir: Shyam Benegal. Phot: Rajen Kothari. Players: Rajat Kapur, Rajeshwari Sachdev, Ravi Jhankal, Raghuvir Yadav, Kishore Kadam, Seema Biswas. Prod: NFDC.

A film unit is riven by prejudices while re-creating a true-life 1991 incident in Madhya Pradesh, when a village leader became furious at a hand pump being installed in the low-caste Dalit hut settlement on his land. His brutal castigation of the repressed community leaves the judiciary as their only recourse. The film uses local dialect, folk music and dance forms.

KANOORU HEGADITHI (The Lady of Kanooru)

Lang: Kannada and Hindi versions. Story: K V Puttappa. Dir: Girish Karnad. Phot: S Ramachandra. Players: Girish Karnad, Tara, Arundhati Nag, Riju Bajaj, P Suchendra.

In Karnataka in the early 1900s, two women, two generations apart, struggle for self-reliance in a rigidly chauvinist society. Subbamma, widow of a land owner, is ruined by an illicit affair. Seethe, forced to marry against her will, flees to live alone and celibate, before returning as a widow to wed the man of her choice.

BARIWALI (Landlady)

Lang: Bengali. Script and Dir: Rituparna Ghosh. Photo: Vivek Shah. Players: Kiron Kher, Chiranjeet Chakraborty, Rupa Ganguly, Abhishek Chatterjee. Prod: Radical Entertainment.

The landlady of a mansion resists the loss of human values in a world torn apart by self-interest and greed.

PARAMITAAR EK DIN (A Day in Paramitaar's Life)

Lang: Bengali. Scipt, Story and Dir: Aparna Sen. Phot: Abhik Mukhopadhyay. Players: Aparna Sen, Rituparna, Soumitra Chatterjee.

A mother-in-law and daughter-in-law develop an unlikely closeness in a traditionally fraught relationship. But when the younger woman divorces and remarries, the bereft mother-in-law's social conditioning forces her to give up this cherished friendship.

GAJA GAMINI

Script and Dir: M F Hussain. Phot: Ashok Mehta. Players: Madhuri Dixit, Shabana Azmi, Naseeruddin Shah, Shahrukh Khan. Prod: Riku Rakesh Nath for Daksha Films.

First feature by renowned octogenarian painter Hussain, in which his muse, leading actress and dancer Madhuri Dixit, plays different roles in three avatars as she tells the story of a perfect woman traversing time and space. The title roughly denotes a woman who walks with the grace and gait of an elephant.

KAIREE (The Raw Mango)

Lang: Marathi. Script: Chitra and Amol Palekar. Dir: Amol Palekar. Phot: Debu Deodhar. Players: Yogita Deshmukh, Shilpa Navalkar, Mohan Gokhale, Sonali Kulkarni. Prod: Vijay Shirke for Ministry of Health and Family Welfare.

Orphaned ten-year-old Kairee, uprooted from a decent, loving home, is sent to live with her childless maternal aunt, who raises her with great care, ensuring that the child is not psychologically scared or stunted by her brutish husband.

KAL KA AADMI (Man Beyond Time)

Lang: Marathi and Hindi versions. Dir: Amol Palekar. Script: Chitra Palekar. Phot: Deodhar. Players: Ashok Kadam, Seema Biswas, Sanjay Pawar. Prod: Vijay Chandra/Amol Palekar for the Minsitry of Health and Family Welfare.

A film on the Maharashtra social crusader R D Karve who as a progressive young man in the 1930s fought for reformist practices such as family planning and women's education.

DAYA

Lang: Malayalam. Dir: Venu. Script: M T Vasudevan Nair. Photo: Sunny Joseph. Players: Nedumudi Venu, Lal, Manju Warrior and Narayanan. Prod: C K Gopinath for Devapriya Prods.

Mansoor, scion of an ageing, wealthy nobleman, loses his riches and mansion when he falls prey to scheming gamblers. His father dies and everyone forsakes him except for the lively, intelligent slave-girl, Daya.

HEY! RAM

Lang: Hindi and Tamil versions. Script and Dir: Kamal Haasan. Phot: Thiru. Players: Kamal Haasan, Shah Rukh Khan, Hema Malini, Girish Karnad, Rani Mukherji, Nasser, Mohan Gokhale, Sourabh Shukla ad Valle. Prod: RaajKamal Films International.

India's freedom struggle is explored through the experiences of a Brahmin youth from orthodox South India and his best friend Amjad Khan, a Pathan from Baluchistan. The film spans the years

1946 to 1996. The title denotes the last words uttered by Mahatma Gandhi as he was felled by his assassin's bullets.

TAPISH (Burning Desire)

Script: Pradeep. Story and Dir: Jai Prakash. Ghatak/Nayeem Ejaj. Phot: Prem Ningoo. Players: Ellora Patnaik, Tara Deshpande, Praveen Davar, Bobby Pooniya. Prod: Dr Yatinder Singhal (US) for N.S. Films Int.

The story of two young Bombay women from contrasting backgrounds and the choices they must make as they are caught between principle and passion.

MANSUR MIANR GHODA (Mansur's Horse)

Lang: Benagli. Scritp and Dir: Nabyendu Chatterjee. Story: Amerendra Sanyal. Players: Arun Mukhopadhyay, Rias-ul-Islam Azad, Master Toofan, Archana Bannerjee. Prod: NFDC.

An old-world man is passionately attached to his ancestral horse and carriage but changing times are making both redundant. His son pesters him to sell both and buy a taxi; a wedding party discards the traditional carriage for a decorated car and, finally, the horse dies and the man gives in.

NAUKAR KI KAMEEZ (A Servant's Shirt)

Lang: Hindi. Story: Vinod Kumar Shukhla. Dir: Mani Kaul. Photo: K U Mohanan. Players: Pankaj Sudheer Mishra, Anu Joseph, Om Prakash Diwedi. Prod Co: Miryam van Lier and Ant Carry The Mountain Films.

Set in 1960s India, this near-farcical film explores hierarchicahal small-town life. The Sahib and his wife live in a colonial bungalow, the alcoholic head clerk spends his time looking for a domestic for the Sahib, and Sanju, the junior hero of the film and his wife struggle with a leaking roof. It won the Netpac award at Rotterdam and Best Director at Kerala.

Tara Deshpande (left) and Ellora Patnaik in BURNING DESIRE

VANAPRASTHAM (The Last Dance)

Lang: Malayalam. Direction/Story/Phot: Karun N Shaji. Players: Mohanlal and Suhasini. Producer: Pierre Assouline for Euro American Films.

Selected for Un Certain Regard at Cannes 1999, this is the story of a classical Kathakalli dancer who feels he is losing his identity, torn between his different roles as a person, an actor and the part he is enacting on stage. This film is a co-production between France and India with additional help from the Locarno Film Festival.

Useful Addresses

Ministry of Information and Broadcasting

Joint Secretary (Films)
Shastri Bhavan
New Delhi
Fax: (91 11) 338 3513
(for government permissions on shooting feature films in India)

Film Federation of India

Everest Building (8th floor)
Tardeo
Fax: (91 22) 495 2062

National Film Development Corporation of India

Discovery of India Building
6th and 7th floors
Nehru Centre
Dr Annie Besant Road
Worli
Bombay 400018
Fax: (91 22) 495 9753/0591/1455

Children's Film Society

c/o Films Division (see below)
Fax: (91 22) 387 5610
(organisers of the International Children's Film Festival of India, November 1999)

Films Division

24 Dr G Deshmukh Road
Mumbai 400026
Fax: (91 22) 380 1008
(organisers of the Bombay International Film Festival of Documentaries and Shorts, February 2000)

Calcutta Film Festival

(November)
Director: Ansu Sur
Nandan Festival Complex
1/1 AGC Bose Road
Calcutta 700020
Fax: (91 33) 223 5744

INDONESIA

Marselli Sumarno

Following the collapse in 1998 of President Suharto's 32-year regime, and the appointment of President Habibie as leader of the transitional administration, the winds of change are blowing strongly. But does this mean a revival in Indonesia's film industry? Unfortunately not.

The ongoing monetary crisis in this nation of 205 million people means that the government has many social problems to tackle ahead of cultural matters such as film-making. But the film community has not been completely forgotten. On National Film Day in March, President Habibie presented four awards for professional dedication, with recipients including actress Christine Hakim and writer Asrul Sani.

More significantly, he announced the revocation of the tax on domestic film receipts. The government has also funded the manufacture of prints of some 20 films which had languished in the labs since the end of 1997 – but ironically most of them were erotic dramas of doubtful merit.

There is also irony in the fact that the president admitted never having seen an Indonesian film! The film community believes his commitment to be symbolic rather than genuine and is lobbying for further reform. Directors and producers are calling for the abolition of the film censor bureau and questioning the use of the funds accumulated from the tax on imported films, asking why more of the money has not been granted, as the law intends, as subsidy for talented Indonesian film-makers.

Despite these problems, a new generation of film-makers is emerging, to replace the senior directors who have died

or retired. The IKJ Film and Television School has played a key role in this development, with more and more graduates emerging every year. About 300 alumni of the school are now working in the audio-visual industry. Some have directed short films, but the majority make their living in television, advertising, corporate videos and public service films.

Art imitating life

The dire economic situation meant that in 1998 only eight Indonesia features were produced, three of which very deliberately made use of recent events. **The 1998 Reform** (*Reformasi 1998*) dwelt on the year's socio-political turbulence, while **The Banyuwangi Tragedy** (*Tragedi Banyuwangi*) and **The Banyuwangi Mystery** (*Banyuwangi Misteri*) dramatised politically-motivated assassinations in East Java.

Two serious dramas were well-received by moviegoers. **Leaf on a Pillow** (*Daun Di Atas Bantal*), directed by Garin Nugroho, is about street children who are looked after by a foster mother (Christine Hakim). Despite a story that is sometimes hard to follow, it won Best Film in the 43rd Asia-Pacific Film Festival in Bangkok and the Special Jury Prize in Tokyo. Incessant promotion helped it become the only Indonesian film in the domestic box-office top ten for 1998.

Cul-de-sac, about young people who feel lost and pessimistic about their futures, was comprised of four segments of variable quality, directed by Riri Riza, Mira Lesmana, Rizal Mantovani and Nan T.Achnas. Achnas was at press time working on a new feature, **Sand House**, about a mother's obsessive love for her daughter during the upheavals of 1960s

A poster advertises the erotic drama GAIRAH PERAWAN

Indonesia. She has noted: "This story could not possibly have been made in the days of Suharto, because of its political inclination."

Your correspondent is preparing to direct a new film, **Good Morning, The Unemployed** (*Selamat Pagi, Penganggur*), about a man who, after being fired by his company because of the economic crisis, becomes so frustrated that he almost kills his pregnant wife.

Finally, the gradual collapse of the Film Importers Association should bring to an end the long-standing distribution monopoly in Indonesian cinemas. It is hoped that new importers will emerge and be able to do business in a much freer market than has existed for the past 15 years.

MARSELLI SUMARNO is a film critic, screenwriter and director. He is a chairman of the Department of Cinema Studies at his alma mater, Faculty of Film and Television IKJ.

Recent and Forthcoming Films

MISTERI BANYUWANGI
(The Banyuwangi Mystery)

Script and Dir: Walmer Sihotang. Phot: Max Parkusi. Players: Erni Melati, Anton Yanuar, Rengga Takengon, Yunus Takara. Prod: Andalas Kencana Film.

TRAGEDI BANYUWANGI
(The Banyuwangi Tragedy)

Script and Dir: Steady Rimba. Phot: D.Hasanuddin Rate. Players: Ibra Azhari, Rika Herlina. Prod: Sinema Abadi Utama.

REFORMASI 1998
(The 1998 Reform)

Script: Joko Supriyono. Dir: Kaonawan S. Phot: Budi Wahyudi. Players: Eichal, Yeni. Prod: Diwangkara Citra Film.

Producers

Star Vision
Jalan Cempaka Putih Raya 116 A–B
Jakarta Pusat 10510
Tel: (62 21) 425 3390
Fax: (62 21) 425 5477

Diwangkar Citra Film
Jalan Kayu Putih VI B/28
Jakarta Timur
Tel: (62 21) 489 6434

Eka Praya Film
Jalan Pahlawan no. 4
Rempoa
Jakarta Selatan
Tel/Fax: (62 21) 743 0146

Cinevisi
Gedung PSKD
Jalan Kramat IV
Jakarta 10330
Tel: (62 21) 334 333/361 824
Fax: (62 21) 310 2133

Pancaran Indra Cine
Jalan KS Tubun 75B
Jakarta 10260
Tel: (62 21) 571 0998/571 1003
Fax: (62 21) 573 1636

Miles Production
Jalan Pelita 18
Cipete
Jakarta Selatan
Tel: (62 21) 720 7341
Fax: (62 21) 722 6569

Rapi Film
Jalan Cikini II/7
Jakarta Pusat
Tel: (62 21) 357 135/332 860

Parkit Film
Roxi Mas
Blok C–2, no. 31-34
Jakarta
Tel: (62 21) 386 7315/7316

Elang Perkasa Film
Jalan Kayu Putih 4/48
Jakarta Timur
Tel: (62 21) 470 0801
Fax: (62 21) 489 4574

Prasidi Teta Film
Jalan Dr. Sahardjo 149 J
Jakarta Selatan
Tel: (62 21) 828 2740/1324

Bola Dunia Film
Jalan Pintu Air 51C
Jakarta Pusat
Tel: (62 21) 384 3983/8721

Sepakat Bahagia Film
Jalan Mangga Besar Raya 107
Blok D–7
Jakarta Pusat
Tel: (62 21) 649 6657

Virgo Putra Film
Jalan KH Hasim Ashari Dalam 111
Jakarta Pusat
Tel: (62 21) 363 308

Studio 41
Jalan Kapten P. Tendean 41
Mampang
Tel: (62 21) 520 4356
Fax: (62 21) 520 1493

Distributors/ Importers

Satrya Perkasa Estetika
(European/American importer)
Subentra Building
Jalan Gatot Subroto Kav.21
7th Floor
Jakarta
Tel: (62 21) 522 0022

Suptan Film
(Mandarin importer)
Subentra Building
Jalan Gatot Subroto Kav.21
7th Floor
Jakarta
Tel: (62 21) 522 0022

Buanavista Indah Film
(Asia non-Mandarin importer)
Jalan Pintu Air 51C
Jakarta
Tel: (62 21) 384 3983/8721

Useful Addresses

Faculty of Film and Television – The Jakarta Institute of the Arts
Jalan Cikini Raya 73
Jakarta 10330
Tel: (62 21) 316 1258
Fax: (62 21) 323 603

Directorate for Film and Video Development
Ministry of Information
Gedung Film
Jalan MT Haroyono
Kav. 47–48
Jakarta
Tel: (62 21) 7919 6086/6087
Fax: (62 21) 7919 6085

National Film Advisory Board
Jalan MT Haryono
Kav. 47–48
Jakarta Selatan
Tel: (62 21) 790 2974/2975
Fax: (62 21) 790 2973

State Film Production Centre
Jalan Otto Iskandardinata 125–127
Jakarta Timur
Tel: (62 21) 819 2508
Fax: (62 21) 819 0339

Indonesian Film Producers Association
Pusat Perfilman H. Usmar Ismail
Jalan Rasuna Said
Jakarta 12940
Tel: (62 21) 526 8461
Fax: (62 21) 526 8460

Association of Film and TV Technicians
Pusat Perfilman H. Usmar Ismail
Jalan Rasuna Said
Jakarta 12940
Tel: (62 21)526 8459/8457
Fax: (62 21) 526 8457

Sinematek Indonesia
Pusat Perfilman H. Usmar Ismail
Jalan Rasun Said
Jakarta 12940
Tel: (62 21) 526 8455/527 8841
Fax: (62 21) 526 8454

Inter Pratama Studio & Lab
Jalan Raya Pasar Ragunan
Jakarta 12550
Tel: (62 21) 780 6030
Fax: (62 21) 780 6230

Televisi Republic Indonesia
(TVRI, state-owned TV network)
Jalan Gerbang Pemuda
Senayan
Jakarta
Tel: (62 21) 570 4720/4732
Fax: (62 21) 531 1195

IRAN

Jamal
Omid

A new record was set for Iranian cinema in 1998, with domestic films bringing home a total of 60 prizes from international festivals, including Venice, Thessaloniki and San Sebastian. For the first time, an Iranian film, Majid Majidi's *The Children of Heaven*, was nominated for Best Foreign-Language Film at the Oscars, while Abbas Kiarostami's *The Taste of Cherries* was named Film of the Year by the American Society of Film Critics.

Since the appointment of film-maker Seifollah Daad as deputy minister for film affairs in 1997, a certain degree of legal freedom has been granted, allowing film-makers to get closer to the type of social issues which had been almost impossible to address for about 20 years. Consequently, a number of films previously banned for their social content have been granted exhibition licences, among them Davud Mirbaqeri's *The Snowman* (1994) and Mohammad Reza Honarmand's *The Visit* (1994), which were among the top-grossing releases of 1998–99.

The domestic box-office was dominated by **The Wrong Man**, directed by Mohammad Reza Honarmand. This strange tale – a dead scientist's brain is transplanted into the skull of a businessman who has suffered a stroke, with remarkable consequences – reached a final tally of more than $1.6m (10 billion rials), making it the most successful picture in Iranian history. Though these figures were the highlight of an encouraging year for cinemagoing, after a decade of falling admissions and cinema closures, the fact that *The Wrong Man* took as much as 24 other Iranian releases combined shows that many well-made films are struggling to reach substantial audiences.

The year's more notable films included the fifth feature of the last decade from former film critic Tahmine Milani. In **Two Women** she demonstrates her increasing mastery of cinematic techniques. She examines the relationship of two women architects who meet again 15 years after studying at the same college. While she has taken advantage of the new liberality allowing film-makers to address feminist concerns at Iran's male-dominated society, Milani refrains from indulging in superficial rhetoric, and this is an intelligent, balanced work.

Alireza Davudnezhad has sustained two differing strands within his career, on the one hand serious pictures like *The Need*, presented at numerous international festivals, on the other purely commercial productions. His latest, **Sweet Affliction**, belongs to the former group. The director brings fine performances from members of his own family (all but one of them non-professional actors) in a domestic drama which boldly examines of the age-old tradition whereby boys and girls are betrothed in childhood.

Post-war stories

In **The Red Ribbon**, Ebrahim Hatamikia once again takes up the war theme which has dominated his career, this time presenting an innovative vision of post-war Iran which focuses on just three characters in a vast landscape, including Qasem, a man responsible for the grim task of defusing mines. Rasul Mollaqolippor, who fought at the front in the Iran-Iraq war, ventures onto similar ground with **Shiva**, the tale of a woman who, 15 years after the disappearance of her husband, revisits the house she shared with him. Mollaqolippor skilfully interweaves memories of the past

Mohsen Rezai as the blind schoolboy hero of Majid Majidi's THE COLOR OF GOD   *photo: Hashem Attar*

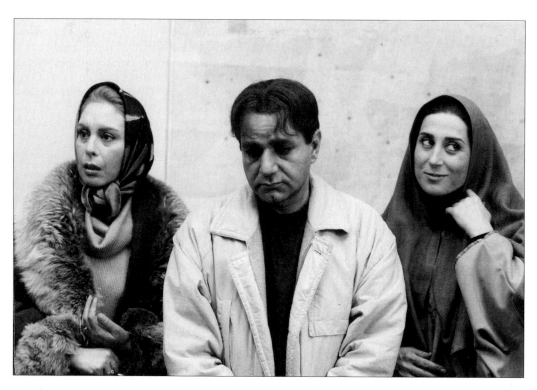

Parviz Parastui (centre) stars in the phenomenally successful THE WRONG MAN   *photo: Shahrokh Sakhui*

with images of the present in a delicately structured reflection on the sacrifices made by so many in wartime.

Majid Majidi's new film, **The Color of God**, follows an eight-year-old blind boy who leaves Tehran on a journey to his birthplace in the mountains of northern Iran. Majidi creates a tender, poetical picture of the boy's return to nature, ending in a profound revelation. As in his previous films, this masterful director again depicts the delicacies of the human spirit with great insight.

Parviz Kimiavi returned to directing for the first time in 20 years with **Iran is My Homeland**, the story of Sohrab, a young author, who gets lost in the desert and encounters the ghosts of five renowned Iranian poets. This is a fine work, though it lacks the spontaneity which characterised Kimiavi's previous works. In **Red**, Freidun Jeirani deals with a psychological theme which could only have been addressed in the present climate: a widow remarries, choosing as her new husband a much younger man, and the difference between them in age and social status leads to catastrophe.

Announcing his plans for the film industry in the new Iranian year 1378 (March 1999-March 2000), Seifollah Daad said he wanted Iran to have "a culturally powerful cinema that can stand on its own feet without the crutch of government support" – a declaration which brought ineffectual complaints from commercial producers who felt they were being penalised; though they continued to churn out run-of-the-mill movies. Film production has, encouragingly, been given the status of an industrial enterprise, and now qualifies for credit assistance from the banking system.

JAMAL OMID has worked in Iranian cinema for 35 years, as the author of 15 books, as a screenwriter and as director of the Fajr and Tehran international film festivals. He is working on volumes two and three of his history of Iranian Cinema and was project manager for a new, 30-episode TV series, *The Trial*.

Forthcoming Films

THE MIX

Script and Dir: Dariush Mehrjui. Phot: Mahmud Klari. Players: Khosro Shakibai, Negar Foruzande, Fersows Kaviani. Prod: Hassan Frazmand/D. Mehrjui.

THE WIND AND THE WILLOW

Script: Abbas Kiarostami. Dir: Mohammad Ali Talebi. Phot: Farhad Saba. Players: Amir Janfedah, Hadi Alipoor. Prod: Mohammad Mehdi Dadgu,/CMI Co.

THE CRY

Script and Dir: Masud Kimia'ie. Phot: Alireza Zarrindast. Players: Mohammad Reza Forutan, Mitra Hajjar. Prod: Naser Shafaq/ Avishan Film Co.

THE WIND WILL CARRY US AWAY

Script and Dir: Abbas Kiarostami. Phot: Mahmnud Klari. Players: Behzad Dorani, and residents of Siah Darre village in Kurdistan. Prod: Kiarostami.

THE HEMLOCK

Script and Direction: Behruz Afkhami. Phot: Nemnat Haqiqi. Players: Fariborz Arabnia, Athene Faqih Nasiri. Prod: Seyed Zia Hashemi/Soore Film. Development Organization.

THE GIRL IN THE SNEAKERS

Script and Dir: Rasul Sadr Ameli. Phot: Dariush Ayari. Players: Pegah Ahangarani, Majid Hajizade, Akram Mohammadi, Abdolreza Akbari, Mahmud Azizi. Prod: Milad Film.

BORN IN OCTOBER

Script and Dir: Ahmad Reza Darvish. Phot: Hassan Puya. Players: Niki Karimi, Reza Kianian. Prod: A. R. Darvish/Soore Film Development Organization.

STAINED HANDS

Script: Tirdad Sakhaie. Dir: Sirus Alvand. Phot: Ali Allahyari. Players: Abolfazl Poorarab, Hedye Tehrani, Asal Badi'ie. Prod: Hassan Kaffash Araqi.

THE RAIN MAN

Script: Davud Mirbaqeri, Abolhassan Davudi. Dir: A. Davudi. Phot: Bahram Badakhshani. Players: Framarz Qaribian, Mahtab Karamati, Roya Teimurian. Prod: A. Davudi/Soore Film Development Organization.

ADOLESCENCE

Script and Dir: Masud Jafari Jozani. Phot: Alireza Zarrindast. Players: Vishka Asayesh, Hossein Yari. Prod: Abbas Haqiqi/Jozan Film.

TAHER'S LOVE

Script: Nader Talebzade. Dir: Mohammnad Ali Najafi. Phot: Saeed Sadeqi. Players: Behnaz Jafari, Manuchehr Ahmadi, Fanny Kasraiyan. Prod: MA. Najafi/Seyed Jamal Sadatian.

THE NIGHT IT RAINED

Script and Dir: Homayun As'adian. Phot: Farhad Saba. Players: Parviz Parastui, Fateme Motamed Aria. Prod: Namadin Co.

THE FRIENDS

Script: Naser Abdollahi. Dir: Ali Shah-Hatami. Phot: Reza Banki. Players: Mohammad Saleh Ala, Mahmud Azizi, Jalal Pishvaiyan, Hassan Rezai. Prod: Puya Film.

MR. 212

Script and Dir: Reza Heidarnezhad. Phot: Farhad Saba. Players: Parviz Parastui, Mahnaz Afzali. Prod: Nadushan Cinema Organization/Ezzatollah Jame'ie.

SIAVOSH

Script and Dir: Saman Moqaddam. Phot: Mahmud Klari. Players: Hedye Tehrani, Mehdi Zia'ie. Prod: Morteza Shayeste/Hedayat Film.

DAUGHTERS OF THE SUN

Script and Dir: Maryam Shahriar. Phot: Homayun Pivar. Players: Atinai Qeilich-Taqai, Habibollah Haddad. Prod: Jahangir Kosari.

LOVE IS NOT ENOUGH

Script: Asghar Abdollahi, Dir: Mehdi Sabbaghzade. Phot: Hassan Qolizade. Players: Abolfazl Poorarab, Framarz Sediqi, Shaqayeq Frahani. Prod: Nimruz Cinema Institute/Late Film.

EVE'S RED APPLE

Script: Mohammad Hadikarimi. Dir: Saeed Asadi. Phot: Mehrdad Fakhimi. Players: Niki Karimi, Amin Hayaie. Prod: Amir Hossein Sharifi/Afaq Film.

THE BLUE TRIANGLE

Script and Dir: Hadi Saber. Phot: Turaj Mansuri. Players: Mohammad Saleh Ala, Homeira Riazi. Prod: Davud Rashidi/Film Emruz.

THE TELEPHONE

Script: Jafar Hassan. Dir: Shafi Aqa Mohammnadian. Phot: Gholamreza Azadi. Players: Fateme Gudarzi, Reza Ashtiani. Prod: Magic Lantern Cinema Institute.

ARBABA OAKS

Script and Dir: Bahman Qobadi. Phot: Saed Nikzat. Players: Ayyub Ahmadi, Rozhin Yunosi. Prod: Farabi Cinema Foundation.

DAWN OF VICTORY

Script and Dir: Hossein Bolande. Phot: Hossein Maleki. Players: Jafar Dehqan, Habib Allahyari, Reza Safaipoor, Kazem Afrandnia. Prod: Habib Allahyari.

HIDDEN FEAR

Script: Mehdi Ahmadi. Dir: Qodratollah Solh Mirzai. Phot: Mahmud Kushan. Players: Framarz Qaribian, Mahshid Afsharzade. Prod: Ebrahim Banki/Sepahan Cinema Organization.

DAUGHTERS OF EXPECTATION

Script: Mohaminad Hadi Karimi. Dir: Rahman Rezai. Phot: Mojtaba Rahimi. Players: Parsa Piruzfrir, Farhad Zare'ie. Prod: R. Rezai.

LONE RIDER

Animation, Script and Dir: Abolfazl Razani. Phot: Mohsen Shamsara. Prod: Saba Cultural, Art Institute.

Producers/ Distributors

Abgun Cultural Center
(Ali Akbar Saqafi)
No. 401 Avarez, Shariati Ave
Tehran
Tel: (98 21) 762 047

Afaq Film
(Amir Hussein Sharifi)
No. 23 Shalid Amini (Frahbod) St
Vali-e Asr Ave
Tehran
Tel: (98 21) 879 8588
Fax: (98 21) 8884 5141

Ama Medium
(Mohammad Mehdi Dadgu)
No. 138 Shahid Beheshti Ave
Tehran
Tel: (98 21) 874 4694
Fax: (98 21) 875 2976

Andishe Film Workshop
(Seyed Mohsen Vaziri)
No. 728 Shariati Ave
Tehran
Tel: (98 21) 845 398

Arman Film
(Ali Akbar Erfani)
No. 5 Ghaffari Alley, Fajr (Jam) St
Motahhari Ave
Tehran
Tel: (98 21) 882 2117
Fax: (98 21) 884 4025

Arta Film
(Tahmine Milani, Abolhassan Davudi)
No. 1/1 Etehad Alley
South Shiraz St, Molla Sadra Ave
Tehran
Tel/Fax: (98 21) 803 1193

7th Art Cultural Institute
(Karim Atashi)
No. 334, Khaje Nasir Tusi St
Shariati Ave
Tehran
Tel: (98 21) 750 3797

Atlas Film
(Mohsen Shayanfar)
No. 26 Khorram Alley, Ansari St,
Jomhuri Ave
Tehran
Tel: (98 21) 646 6131

Avishan Film
(Naser Shafaq)
No. 5 Fast Láal Alley
Parvin Etesami St
Dr. Fatemi Ave
Tehran
Tel: (98 21) 654 415
Fax: (98 21) 885 1720

Basir Film
(Habibollah Bahmani)
No. 12 J. St Moqaddas Ardabili
Vali-e Asr Ave
Tehran
Tel/Fax: (98 21) 204 0545.

Cadre Film
(Majid Modarresi)
No. 39 Ashqian (Nilufar) St
Khorramshahr Ave
Tehran
Tel: (98 21) 876 6110
Fax: (98 21) 876 0488

Children of Iran
(Mohammad Reza
Sarhangi)
No. 1 Sirus Alley, Shariati Ave,
Qolhak.
Tehran
Tel: (98 21) 267 708
Fax: (98 21) 269 496

Didar Film
(Shabanali Eslami)
No. 24 Behruzi Alley
North Kargar Ave
Tehran
Tel/Fax: (98 21) 928 034

Dohol Film
(Mohammad Baqer Khosravi)
No. 246 (Opposite Mir Emad St)
Motahhari Ave
Tehran
Tel: (98 21) 882 5519

Fajr Cinema Organization
(Abdolreza Sa'atchifard)
No. 52 Shahin Alley, Shoa Sq.
Qaem
Maqam Farahani St
Tehran
Tel: (98 21) 882 5650
Fax: (98 21) 883 7991

Fanus Khiyal
(Gholamreza Azadi)
No. 75 Bakhtyar St, 7th of Tir Sq.
Tehran
Tel: (98 21) 883 4678
Fax: (98 21) 884 7795

Film Baharan
(Akbar Sadeqi)
No. 101 Baharmastian Alley
7th of Tir Sq
Jami St
Tehran
Tel: (98 21) 670 6473

Film Emruz
(Davud Rashidi Haeri)
No. 27, Sohrevardi Ave
Tehran
Tel: (98 21) 862 621/862 583

Film Noor
(Fuad Noor)
No. 9 Azarshahr Alley, Iranshahr St
Tehran
Tel: (98 21) 834 889
Fax: (98 21) 272 310

Gol Film
(Majid Ashtianipoor)
No. 2 Maraghe St, Villa St
Tehran
Tel: (98 21) 880 2151
Fax: (98 21) 881 0150

Hedayat Film
(Morteza Shayeste)
No.15 7th St
Khaled Eslamboli Ave
Tehran
Tel: (98 21) 872 7188/9
Fax: (98 21) 871 4220

Hamrah Cooperative
(Hassein Zandbaf)
No. 40 Baharmastian Alley
7th of Tir Sq.
Tehran
Tel: (98 21) 883 4612
Fax: (98 21) 843 212

**Institute of Film Affairs of
Mostazafan Foundation**
(Alireza Sarbakhsh)
Bldg. No. 343, Shahid Beheshti Ave
Tehran
Tel: (98 21) 871 6666
Fax: (98 21) 872 7330

Iran Film Development
(Alireza Raisian)
No. 5 Arbabi Alley, Nesa St
Dastgerdi Ave
Tehran
Tel: (98 21) 222 1600
Fax: (98 21) 225 5621

Iran Film Mansion
(Alireza Beheshti)
Tavakkol Bldg., Jomhuri Ave
Tehran
Tel: (98 21) 671 247
Fax: (98 21) 649 7106

Iran-Milad
(Bizhan Emkanian)
No. 1 Marivan St, South Sohreverdi
Tehran
Tel: (98 21) 831 549
Fax: (98 21) 752 4881

Jozan Film
(Masud Jafari Jozani)
No. 20 Razmandegan Alley
Ghaffari, Fajr (Jam) St,
Motahhari Ave
Tehran
Tel: (98 21) 883 7271/884 4010
Fax: (98 21) 882 6876

Kowsar Cinema Organization
(Ruhollah Khoshkam)
No. 363 Motahhari Ave
Tehran
Tel/Fax: (98 21) 872 5809

Lale Film
(Gholamhasan Bolurian)
No. 41 Amir Soleinani,
Enqelab Ave
Tehran
Tel: (98 21) 649 4562
Fax: (98 21) 645 5518

Mahab Film
(Seyed Zia Hashemi)
No. 85 Bakhtyar Alley,
7th of Tir Sq.
Tehran
Tel: (98 21) 837 547
Fax: (98 21) 883 4332.

Mahed Film
No. 27, Third Goldis, Danesh Blvd.
Gendarmerie Town.
Tehran
Tel: (98 21) 821 3042
Fax: (98 21) 228 009

Mehrab Film
(Jamal Shurle)
No. 86, 25th St, Jahan-Ara
Shahid Gomnam Express Way
Tehran
Tel/Fax: (98 21) 800 0076

Milad Film
(Rasul Sadr-Ameli)
No.3 Fourth St, Asadabadi Ave
Tehran
Tel: (98 21) 872 7673
Fax: (98 21) 885 7119

Mina Film
(Mohammad Reza Alipayam)
No. 9, 11, Bldg. No. 1317, Vanak Sq.
Tehran
Tel: (98 21) 887 9314
Fax: (98 21) 879 9803

Misaq Film
(Hussein Yaryar)
No. 101 North Sohreverdi Ave
Tehran
Tel: (98 21) 875 7517

Nahid Film
(Hojjatollah Seifi)
No. 27 Sharif Alley, Sheikh Hadi St
Jami St
Tehran
Tel: (98 21) 670 6473

Namaye Awal
(Mohammad Reza Sarhangi)
No. 75, Madayen Alley, Tisfun St
Khaje Abdollah Ansari St,
Shariati Ave
Tehran
Tel: (98 21) 285 1857/284 2367
Fax: (98 21) 285 1858

National Iranian Film Archive
Director: Mohammad Hassan
Khoshnevis
Baharestan Square
Tehran
Tel: (98 21) 342 1601

**Negin Film Production
Cooperative**
(Fariborz Arabnia)
Unit 103, 2nd Block,
Chehelstun Bldg.
South Bahar St
Tehran
Tel: (98 21) 753 1961

Nemayesh Film Co.
(Habibollah Sahranavard)
No. 2, Mirmotahari
Seyed Khandan Bridge
Shariati Ave
Tehran
Tel: (98 21) 868 703/866 638

Nimruz
(Mehdi Sabbaghzade)
No. 1 Mohammadi Alley
North Bahar St
Tehran
Tel: (98 21) 753 6727
Fax: (98 21) 753 6727

Novin Film
(Hushang Nurollahi)
No. 15 48th Passage, Jomhuri Ave
Tehran
Tel/Fax: (98 21) 640 3697

Ofoq Cinema Organisation
(Rasul Mollaqolipoor)
No. 23 Mansur Alley
(adjacent to Tehran Grand Hotel)
Motahhari Ave
Tehran
Tel: (98 21) 872 1871
Fax: (98 21) 872 1781

Omid Film
(Sirus Taslimi)
No. 23 Tajbakhsh Alley, Nesa St
Mirdamad Ave
Tehran
Tel: (98 21) 227 6746
Fax: (98 21) 227 2310

Oruj Film
(Mohammad Shariati)
No. 335 Darband, Tajrish.
Tehran
Tel: (98 21) 801 8414
Fax: (98 21) 602 2193

Pakhshiran
(Harun Yashayaie)
No. 8 Somaye St, Bahar St
Tehran
Tel: (98 21) 882 4052
Fax: (98 21) 883 7684

Peyman Film
(Abolhassan Sanamari)
No. 11 Mehrzad Alley
South Iranshahr St
Tehran
Tel: (98 21) 883 9163
Fax: (98 21) 883 3789

Purika Film
1st Floor, No. 105 Somaye St
Tehran
Tel: (98 21) 882 8442

Puya Film
(Hussein Farahbakhsh,
Abdollah Alikhani)

No. 10 Tavakko 1 Bldg., Jomhuri Ave
Tehran
Tel: (98 21) 673 574

Resane Filmsazan
(Seyed Gholamreza Musavi)
No. 7, Ghaffari Alley
Baharmastian St, 7th of Tir Sq
Tehran
Tel: (98 21) 830 676/883 2839

Roshan Film
(Ali Mazinani)
No. 97 Arbab Jamshid, Kushk St
Ferdowsi Ave
Tehran
Tel: (98 21) 645 2975

Sahra-Film Cultural Institute
(Majid Modaresi)
No. 39 corner of 6th Alley, Eshqyar
St, Khorramshahr Ave
Tehran
Tel: (98 21) 876 5392/876 6110

Sepahan Film
(Mohammad and Asghar Banki)
No. 126 Razi Alley, Sheikh Hadi St
Jomhuri Ave
Tehran
Tel: (98 21) 673 047
Fax: (98 21) 670 6268

Shahr Film
(Jalal Qazal-Ayaq)
No. 1/36 Kabkanian (Homa) St
Keshavarz Blvd.
Tehran
Tel: (98 21) 658 181
Fax: (98 21) 652 480

Shekufa Film
(Dariush Babaiyan)
No.18 Amir Parviz, Abureyhan St
Enqelab Ave
Tehran
Tel: (98 21) 641 6939
Fax: (98 21) 640 2202

Shiraz Film
(Mohammad Hashem Sabuki)
No. 1/56 Neauphle-le-Chateau St
Tehran
Tel: (98 21) 677 952
Fax: (98 21) 672 985

Sima Film
(Mohammad Mehdi Heidarian)
No. 53 Kuhyar Alley, Fereshte St

Tehran
Tel: (98 21) 221 8118
Fax: (98 21) 221 5889/802 8853

Sobhan Film
(Saeed Hajimiri)
No. 45 Zay Alley, Vali-e Asr
Tehran
Tel: (98 21) 641 0816
Fax: (98 21) 641 5098

Soore Film Develepment Organization
(Mohammad Ah Hussein-Nezhad)
No. 213 Sornaye St
Nejatollahi Ave
Tehran
Tel: (98 21) 881 0270
Fax: (98 21) 889 3530

Tamasha Cultural Institute
(Taqi Aliqolizade)
No. 1, 14th Alley, Eshqyar St
Khorramshar Ave
Tehran
Tel: (98 21) 873 3843/873 3844

Tuba Film Co.
(Ruhollah Braderi)
No. 505, Corner of 51st Alley
Asadabadi Ave
Tehran
Tel: (98 21) 878 7515/878 7516

Yaran Film
(Samuel Khachikian)
No. 78, 1st Haeri, Shahid Adibi St
Shariati Ave
Tehran
Tel: (98 21) 870 2552

Vara Honar
(Mehdi Karimi)
No.168 Avang Alley
Parvin Etesami St
Dr. Fatemi Ave
Tehran
Tel: (98 21) 800 0345

Zeitun Cultural Institute
(Mojtaba Faravarde)
No. 47, Haj Hosseini Alley
North Sohrevardi Ave
Tehran
Tel: (98 21) 876 1339

IRELAND — Michael Dwyer

Within the local film industry, some pessimists – or realists, as many of them style themselves – never believed that Ireland would attain the level of feature production successfully achieved in recent years. As soon as the boom became reality, these pessimists began wondering when the bubble would burst, and an unexpected downturn in production during the summer of 1999 will have had many preparing their "I told you so"s.

Many within the industry point to coincidence rather than incipient crisis, suggesting that a number of movies which were likely to shoot in Ireland in the summer were simply not ready to roll, for creative and/or financial reasons, and that the lull would just mean a much busier autumn.

Anxiety was eased when the future of the tax incentive scheme known as Section 481 (formerly Section 35) for investors in film production was secured. Thanks to a good deal of active lobbying and the support of the arts minister, Sile de Valera, and despite opposition from the Department of Finance, the scheme has been renewed for several years.

Another factor causing a degree of anxiety has been the competition offered by the Isle of Man with its financial and production support schemes. Isle of Man

David Kelly (left) and Ian Bannen in WAKING NED

scenery has doubled for Ireland in recent movies such as *Waking Ned*, *Love and Rage* and *Shergar*.

To ensure that the pessimists are proved wrong and that Ireland holds its own against the Isle of Man, the one-year-old Screen Commission of Ireland, under chief executive Roger Greene, is promoting Ireland internationally as a film location and assisting production companies visiting Ireland. Chaired by Mary Leonard, the commission's board includes the Irish actors Pierce Brosnan and Sinead Cusack, among its members.

Battling for release

Irish film-makers and financiers are becoming increasingly aware that getting a movie made is only part of the battle, and that movies must compete fiercely in the distribution and exhibition fields if, in these days of wide releases, they are not to suffer sudden death at the box-office after a single weekend. Such is the case all over the world, but it has been a particularly hard fact to accept for Irish industry figures whose euphoria at getting into production has been significantly dampened by their movies' subsequent commercial fates.

The hardest pill to swallow has been the outright rejection of some films by distributors at home and abroad, with the result that some Irish productions will never get a cinema release and some others have to make do with very short runs at the two-screen Dublin arthouse, the Irish Film Centre.

Nevertheless, homegrown films did make an impact in a year when, boosted by *Titanic*'s record-breaking success, overall Irish admissions increased by 7.8% to 12.39 million. Of the 12 Irish features released during 1998 and the seven which opened in the first half of 1999, six made a sizeable impact on the box-office.

While only one Irish film took more than $700,000 (500,000 Irish punts) in 1997 (the comedy-thriller *I Went Down*) four comfortably exceeded that figure in 1998:

John Boorman's *The General* took a very solid $1.9m, Neil Jordan's adaptation of Pat McCabe's apparently unfilmable *The Butcher Boy* $1.6m, Jim Sheridan's timely Northern Ireland drama, *The Boxer*, chalked up $1.1m, while Pat O'Connor's *Dancing at Lughnasa* grossed more than $900,000.

The huge success of **Waking Ned** surprised many observers who believed that the movie's relentless stereotyping of an imagined notion of the country would not find favour with Irish audiences. Yet, even though it delivers the hoariest of stage-Irish clichés and ladles on the blarney in its twee and slender tale of villagers trying to secure their dead neighbour's lottery winnings, it paid off handsomely.

Family affairs

Most of the popular indigenous Irish movies were period dramas, the most distinguished of which was O'Connor's superbly crafted and deeply moving film of Brian Friel's Tony award-winning play **Dancing at Lughnasa**. The story of five sisters whose lives are changed irrevocably during an eventful summer in 1936, it is graced by an excellent ensemble cast led by Meryl Streep as the eldest sister: outwardly strong and inwardly brittle.

A melancholy meditation on the status and prospects of women in the patriarchal society of those times, the film draws a warm and enthralling picture of the close bonds which link the five sisters while cataclysmic events unfold. O'Connor's long-evident skill with actors has never been demonstrated to such dramatic effect, with the exemplary ensemble led by Streep also including Kathy Burke, Catherine McCormack, Brid Brennan and Sophie Thompson.

Set just three years later, **This Is My Father** is a true 'family' film: written and directed by Paul Quinn, it stars his brother, Aidan, features their sister, Marion, in a minor role, and was shot by their cinematographer brother, Declan. It opens in present-day Chicago, where a middle-

Meryl Streep with her screen sisters in Pat O'Connor's screen adaptation of DANCING AT LUGHNASA

aged, world-weary teacher and widower (James Caan), prompted by the discovery of an old photograph, decides to explore his personal history.

Travelling to Ireland, he hears a story (told in flashback) of first love between the spirited 17-year-old (Moya Farrelly) who would become his mother, and a naive, hard-working farm-hand (Aidan Quinn, remarkably subtle and affecting) who incurs the wrath of her bitter, alcoholic mother (Gina Moxley) and the stern local priest (Eamonn Morrissey). Making an assured directing debut, Paul Quinn employs a firm narrative control and an effective low-key approach to his material which eschews histrionics and over-statement: his reward early in 1999 was a box-office take of $700,000.

A simple man

The accomplished Irish actor Brendan Gleeson (*I Went Down* and *The General*) continues to demonstrate his range in Stephen Bradley's first feature, **Sweety Barrett**, an engagingly offbeat morality

fable set in a strange, timeless world: a run-down port populated mostly by dishevelled eccentrics. Gleeson plays Barrett, a shambling, bewildered-looking man, one of life's innocents, who turns up in the town and finds himself working for smugglers, who are ruled by a ruthless, sadistic and wholly corrupt detective (Liam Cunningham).

In a role which offers him minimal dialogue, Gleeson is remarkably expressive as a simple, innately good man with a

Brendan Gleeson as SWEETY BARRETT

Liam Cunningham is led away in A LOVE DIVIDED

Aidan Quinn and Moya Farrelly in THIS IS MY FATHER

strong survival instinct. Displaying an evident cinematic flair, Bradley places this story of good versus evil in a surreal world, heightening the intriguing, moody atmosphere.

Cunningham turns up again, playing an altogether more sympathetic character, in Syd Macartney's meaty social drama, **A Love Divided**, a factually-based and impeccably-acted drama set in a small Irish town in 1957. It builds with a simmering power as it chronicles the story of a mixed-marriage couple – Catholic husband, Protestant wife – who incur the wrath of the parish priest when the wife (impressive Orla Brady) resists the priest's insistence that their daughter be sent to a Catholic school. The priest is played with hair-raising self-righteousness by Tony Doyle. Originally made for television, it was picked up for release by Buena Vista (as were *This Is My Father* and *Sweety Barrett*) and grossed more than $420,000 in its first month on release.

The most eagerly awaited recent productions include Alan Parker's film of

Frank McCourt's immensely successful memoir, **Angela's Ashes,** featuring Emily Watson and Robert Carlyle; the prospect of Ewan McGregor playing the young James Joyce in Pat Murphy's long-in-gestation **Nora**; and John MacKenzie's **When the Sky Falls**, in which the American actress Joan Allen plays a character loosely based on the Irish journalist, Veronica Guerin, a crime reporter murdered by criminals in Dublin in 1996.

In other developments, the multiplex boom continued in the suburbs of Dublin over the summer of 1999, with the South African company Sten Kinekor opening Ireland's largest complex to date, containing 14 screens. Leo Ward, Ireland's leading indigenous exhibitor, is adding a 12-screen complex to his outlets.

MICHAEL DWYER has been film correspondent of *The Irish Times* since 1988. He is the co-founder and former programme director of the Dublin Film Festival.

Recent and Forthcoming Films

ACCELERATOR

Script: Mark Stewart, Vinny Murphy. Dir: Murphy. Phot: Seamus Deasy. Players: Mark Dunne, Aisling O'Neill, Gavin Kelty, Stuart Sinclair Blyth. Prod: Two For the Show.

AGNES BROWNE

Script: John Goldsmith and Brendan O'Carroll. Dir: Anjelica Huston. Phot: Tony Richmond. Players: Anjelica Huston, Marion O'Dwyer, Arno Chevrier, Ray Winstone, Tom Jones. Prod: Hell's Kitchen.

ALL ABOUT ADAM

Script and Dir: Gerard Stembridge. Phot: Bruno De Keyser. Players: Stuart Townsend, Kate Hudson, Frances O'Connor, Charlotte Bradley, Rosaleen Linehan. Prod: Venus Film Productions.

ANGELA'S ASHES
Script: Laura Jones and Frank McCourt, from McCourt's memoir. Dir: Alan Parker. Phot: Michael Seresin. Players: Emily Watson, Robert Carlyle, Ciaran Owens. Prod: Dirty Hands.

CRUSH PROOF
Script: James Mathers. Dir: Paul Tickell. Phot: Reinier Van Brummelen. Players: Darren Healey, Jeff O'Toole, Viviana Verveen. Prod: Liquid Films.

DANCING AT LUGHNASA
Script: Frank McGuinness, from Brian Friel's play. Dir: Pat O'Connor. Phot: Kenneth McMillan. Players: Meryl Streep, Sophie Thompson, Brid Brennan, Catherine McCormack, Kathy Burke, Michael Gambon. Prod: Ferndale Films.

THE LAST SEPTEMBER
Script: John Banville. Dir: Deborah Warner. Phot: Slawomir Idziak. Players: Fiona Shaw, Maggie Smith, Lambert Wilson, Michael Gambon, Jane Birkin. Prod: Scala Thunder.

LOVE AND RAGE
Script: Brian Lynch. Dir: Cathal Black. Phot: Slawomir Idziak. Players: Greta Scacchi, Daniel Craig. Prod: Cathal Black Films.

A LOVE DIVIDED
Script: Stuart Hepburn. Dir: Syd Macartney. Phot: Cedric Culliton. Players: Liam Cunningham, Orla Brady, Tony Doyle. Prod: Parallel Films.

MAD ABOUT MAMBO
Script and Dir: John Forte. Phot: Ashley Rowe. Players: Keri Russell, Willaim Ash, Brian Cox, Rosaleen Linehan. Prod: First City Features.

NIGHT TRAIN
Script: Aodhan Madden. Dir: John Lynch. Players: John Hurt, Brenda Blethyn. Prod: Subotica Films.

NORA
Script: Pat Murphy, Gerard Stembridge. Dir: Murphy. Phot: Jean-Francois Robin. Players, Ewan McGregor, Susan Lynch. Prod: Volta/NaturalNylon.

ORDINARY DECENT CRMININAL
Script: Gerard Stembridge. Dir: Thaddeus O'Sullivan. Players: Kevin Spacey, Linda Fiorentino, Peter Mullan, Stephen Dillane. Phot: Andrew Dunn. Prod: Little Bird/Icon.

PARK
Script: John Carney. Dir: Carney, Tom Hall. Phot: Mark Waldron. Players: Claudia Terry, Des Nealon, Jayne Snow. Prod: High Hat Productions.

SALTWATER
Script and Dir: Conor McPherson. Phot: Oliver Curtis. Players: Brian Cox, Peter McDonald, Brendan Gleeson. Prod: Treasure Films.

SWEETY BARRETT
Script and Dir: Stephen Bradley. Phot: Thomas Mauch. Players: Brendan Gleeson, Lynda Steadman, Liam Cunningham. Prod: Temple Films.

THIS IS MY FATHER
Script and Dir: Paul Quinn. Phot: Declan Quinn. Players: Aidan Quinn, Moya Farrelly, Stephen Rea, Colm Meaney, John Cusack. Prod: Filmline International/ Hummingbird Communications.

WHEN THE SKY FALLS
Script: Michael Sheridan, Ronan Gallagher, Colum McCann. Dir: John MacKenzie. Phot: Seamus Deasy. Players: Joan Allen, Patrick Bergin, Pete Postlethwaite, Liam Cunningham. Prod: Irish Screen.

Producers

Ferndale Films
4 Harcourt Terrace
Dublin 2
Tel: (353 1) 676 8890
Fax: (353 1) 676 8874

Hell's Kitchen Productions
92 Merrion Road
Ballsbridge
Dublin 4
Tel: (353 1) 667 5599
Fax: (353 1) 667 5592

Irish Screen
34 Lower Baggot Street
Dublin 2
Tel: (353 1) 662 3505
Fax: (353 1) 662 3507

Little Bird Productions
122 Lower Baggot Street
Dublin 2
Tel: (353 1) 661 4245
Fax: (353 1) 660 0351

Merlin Films Group
16 Upper Pembroke Street
Dublin 2
Tel: (353 1) 676 4373
Fax: (353 1) 676 4368

Parallel Film Productions
14-15 Sir John Rogersons Quay
Dublin 2
Tel: (353 1) 671 8555
Fax: (353 1) 671 8242

Samson Films
The Barracks
76 Irishtown Road
Dublin 4
Tel: (353 1) 667 0533
Fax: (353 1) 667 0537

Temple Films
4 Windmill Lane
Dublin 2
Tel: (353 1) 671 9313
Fax: (353 1) 671 9323

Treasure Films
Shamrock Chambers
Dame St
Dublin 2
Tel: (353 1) 670 9609
Fax: (353 1) 670 9612

Distributors

Abbey Films
35 Upper Abbey Street
Dublin 1
Tel: (353 1) 872 3422
Fax: (353 1) 872 3687

Buena Vista International
12 Parliament Street
Dublin 2
Tel: (353 1) 677 3484
Fax: (353 1) 671 0098

Clarence Pictures
13 Denzille Lane
Dublin 2
Tel: 661 4022
Fax: 661 4186

Columbia TriStar Films
Seagrave House
20 Earlsfort Terrace
Dublin 2
Tel: (353 1) 616 3200
Fax: (353 1) 616 3210

20th Century Fox
14/15 Kildare Street
Dublin 2
Tel: 661 7171
Fax: 661 7228

Warner Bros
9 Townyard Lane
Malahide
Co Dublin
Tel: (353 1) 845 1844
Fax: (353 1) 845 1858

United International Pictures
D'Olier Chambers
D'Olier Street
Dublin 2
Tel: (353 1) 679 2433
Fax: (353 1) 679 8801

Useful Addresses

Ardmore Studios
Herbert Road
Bray
Co Wicklow
Tel: (353 404) 286 2971
Fax: (353 404) 286 1894

The Arts Council
70 Merrion Square
Dublin 2
Tel: (353 1) 661 1840
Fax: (353 1) 676 0436

Espace Video Européen
(EVE)
6 Eustace Street
Dublin 2
Tel: (353 1) 679 5744
Fax: (353 1) 679 9657

Film Institute of Ireland
6 Eustace Street
Dublin 2
Tel: (353 1) 679 5744
Fax: (353 1) 679 9657

Film Makers Ireland
19 Duke Street
Dublin 2
Tel: (353 1) 671 3525
Fax: (353 1) 671 3505

Irish Film Board
Rockfort House
St Augustine Street
Galway
Co Galway
Tel: (353 91) 561398
Fax: (353 91) 561405

Irish Film Centre
6 Eustace Street
Dublin 2
Tel: (353 1) 679 5744
Fax: (353 1) 679 9657

Irish Film & Television Academy
43/44 Temple Bar
Dublin 2
Tel: (353 1) 670 7535
Fax: (353 1) 670 7168

Radio Telefis Eireann
(RTE)
Donnybrook
Dublin 4
Tel: (353 1) 208 3111
Fax: (353 1) 208 3080

Screen Commission of Ireland
16 Eustace Street
Dublin 2
Tel: (353 1) 672 7252
Fax: (353 1) 672 7251

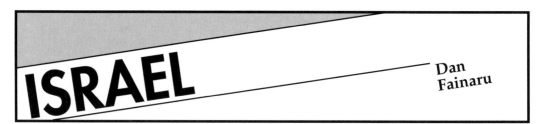

ISRAEL — Dan Fainaru

Up until May 1999, the 1998-1999 film-making year looked like going down as one of the worst in the history of Israeli features. Government subsidies were cut by half and the few Israeli films that were made all failed miserably at the box-office: attendance for local movies dropped to about 1% of the 12 million annual admissions. As for production, it dwindled to a trickle, with some of the titles listed under Forthcoming Films in last year's *IFG* having barely been finished in the past 12 months, and precious little having started since.

Then, against all expectations, Amos Gitai's **Kadosh** became the first Israeli picture for 25 years to be featured in competition at Cannes. Though it failed to win an award, Gitai's blistering portrait of the disgraceful conditions endured by women in Jerusalem's ultra-orthodox Jewish community grabbed the attention of many international viewers.

Not long afterwards, in Karlovy Vary, another Israeli film did even better. Arik Kaplun's debut feature, **Yana's Friends**, a bitter-sweet, sensitive, well-cast and ultimately crowd-pleasing portrait of Russian emigrants in Israel during the Gulf War, won Best Film and Best Actress (for Evlyn Kaplun, the director's wife), as well as an Ecumenical Special Mention. One week later, in Jerusalem, Kaplun walked away with the Jack Wolgin Prize for Best Israeli Feature, after which he immediately boarded a plane for Moscow, where his film was due to open the Panorama section. It is difficult to remember any other Israeli film doing so well in so short a time.

Kadosh and *Yana's Friends* have very little in common in their approach to cinema and characters, but they are in a league of their own compared with the rest of the year's crop – a mass of disappointments which included Eyal Halfon's helpless political metaphor, **Circus Palestine**, Shemi Zarhin's vacuous thriller, **Dangerous**, and the embarrassingly clumsy **Release the Princess**, which cannot really make up its mind what it wants to be. Only Jonathan Segal's **Urban Feel**, screened in competition at Berlin, showed some promise, despite its murky bi-sexual plot, climaxing in a pointless, surrealistic orgy .

Unjustly rejected

Kadosh is as manipulative and militant a film as one would expect of Gitai, a director who has always worn his political convictions on his sleeve. But it achieved its purpose, that of drawing attention to a

society ruled by rituals and obsolete customs, which treats women as "baby-makers" at best. *Yana's Friends*, cinematically more conventional, is far more humane and sympathetic to its characters, and makes no bones about the flaws in the massive Russian emigration. But it delivers a warm, compassionate image of a displaced population, still uncertain about its present conditions and future prospects.

Both films had encountered considerable resistance before their release. The Fund for the Promotion of Israeli Quality Films turned down Gitai's *Kadosh* (partly financed by European money) not once but several times. They did it before and after it was accepted for Cannes, claiming the film did not qualify for a $100,000 completion subsidy, usually granted to most international productions shot in the country.

The Fund, without whose assistance it is practically impossible to make any Israeli film nowadays, does not have to provide reasons for its decisions, so the motivations for this blunder were veiled in mystery. But anonymous sources suggest the anti-religious thrust of *Kadosh* upset some of the bureaucrats on the Fund's Board of Directors, who proved to have more leverage than any of its film professionals. The recent decision to give co-productions a practically automatic subvention may mean *Kadosh* still receives about half the amount originally requested, but that will come too late to repair the damage done to the Fund's public image.

With *Yana's Friends*, Kaplun was told by the Fund that, among other criticisms, his film's unflattering portrait of new emigrants was too offensive. He was sent back several times for re-writes and was about to give up when the Fund's script-reading commission changed, and the new team approved the first draft that had previously been rejected as unsatisfactory.

The new boss

These are prime examples of the problems the Fund's newly appointed director, Katriel Schori, will have to deal with, as he becomes 'the Last Resort' for the local industry. A successful producer, Schori left his company in the hands of his wife, Naomi, in order to take up the post. His first actions have already indicated the kind of policies he favours. First, at his suggestion, the Fund has been renamed Israeli Film Fund, deleting the word 'Quality' from the title: an open invitation for commercial ventures of no artistic pretensions to apply for help.

Second, and no less important, instead of granting its subsidies on the basis of scripts only, the Fund will consider full packages, i.e. scripts with a producer, director and perhaps even a cast already attached to them. Schori also hopes to obtain from the two leading cinema chains, Israeli Theatres and Globus Group (both addicted almost exclusively to Hollywood fare) a guaranteed minimum number of windows for domestic productions. For he believes the theatrical performance of home products has been seriously inhibited in recent years by the exhibitors' lack of co-operation.

Unlike fiction, documentary film-making continues to flourish. A separate, much smaller but far more aggressive Fund, and commissions from television channels, provide a constant flow of new productions and fresh talent. A recently-created Forum of the Documentary Film is battling for better working conditions. A new documentary festival, Doc Aviv, drew unexpectedly large Tel Aviv audiences and critical approval, and there is already competition in sight, with another docu showcase scheduled to take place in 2000 in a small Galilee town, Rosh Pina.

The wealth of fascinating stories circulating in this young country – once suggested as a rich source of inspiration for fiction writing – is finally being successfully tapped by the documentarists. Some recent examples include Danny Wachsman's moving **Menelik**, the story of an Ethiopian emigrant going back home to look for his non-Jewish mother, and Irit Gal's **Harmed Forces**, on the plight of shell-shocked soldiers.

Finally, no one really knows what to make of the biggest story rumbling through the film industry. In late 1998, parliament approved a new cinema law, pledging that all government royalties from commercial TV broadcasts – terrestrial, cable and satellite – would be used to finance the Israeli film industry. At first glance there was much to celebrate, since early estimates indicated that this subsidy would be in the vicinity of $15m, almost three times the budget currently dedicated to film support.

But the draft law suggested this sum would have to cover not just production, but every related film activity: film schools, festivals, cinematheques, institutes, university departments and other initiatives. To distribute the budgets, a Film Council is to be created, consisting of public figures, government officials and film professionals.

However, since the project was voted in, a new government has been voted in, and the new regime's stance on the film industry was unclear when this article went to press. Moreover, there is serious concern that any council fashioned to please the law-makers will once again be ruled by forces alien to cinema interests and insiders remain sceptical about the successful implementation of the film law.

DAN FAINARU is an Israeli film critic and journalist, and Editor-in-Chief of *European Film Review*. A former director of the Israeli Film Institute, he is a familiar face at the world's major and minor festivals.

Nir Levi (left) and Evlyn Kaplun in her husband Arik's award-winning YANA'S FRIENDS

Recent and Forthcoming Films

SHKARIM LEVANIM (White Lies)
Script and Dir: Itzhak Rubin. Phot: Ron Katzenelson. Players: Orna Porath, Sharon Alexander, Arieh Elias, Selim Dow, Semadar Kiltchinski, Alex Munte. Prod: Avishai Kfir, Itzhak Rubin.

**SHAKHRER ET HA'NSIKHA
(Release the Princess)**
Script and Dir: Oron Adar. Phot: Ofer Harari. Players: Giuliano Mer, Liat Gluck, Ma'ayan Keret, Maor Cohen, shraga Harpaz. Prod: Eyal Shirai, Haim Sharir, with Paolo Branco (Gemini Films).

**MASHEHU TOTALI
(Total Love)**
Script: Etgar Keret, Gur Bentwich. Dir: Bentwich. Phot: Sharon Meir. Players: Bentwich, Maor Cohen, Tinkerbell, Zohar Dinar, Gteodora Pachkov, Shira Gefen. Prod: Eyal Shirai, Ran Tal.

PERE (Wild)
Script and Dir: Yoram Gal. Phot: Eitan Riklis. Players: Omer Barnea, Dor Peles, Adi Ezroni, Lanny Shahaf, Bahat Kalachi. Pro: Nili Dotan.

**HAGAR'IN HAKASHE
(Last Resort)**
Script: Tal Silberstein, Aner Preminger. Dir: Preminger. Phot: Itai Waldman. Players: Micha Selectar, Sharon Malki-Shemesh, Ygael Zachs, Orna Katz, Eyal Nachmias.

**KIKAR HAMEYUASHIM
(Desperado Square)**
Script and Dir: Benny Torati. Phot: Dror Moreh. Players: Yona Elian, Mukhamad Bakri, Yossef Shiloakh, Nir Levi, Sharon Regginiani, Ayelet Zorer. Prod: Amir Harel, Haim Manor.

Producers

Marek Rosenbaum
22, Nahmani St Tel Aviv 65201
Tel: (972 3) 566 1484
Fax: (972 3) 566 1450

Screen Entertainment
Eitan Even and Effi Atad
Merkaz Baalei Melacha 40
Tel Aviv 63824
Tel: (972 3) 528 1191
Fax: (972 3) 528 1192

Paralite Productions
Uri Sabbag and Einat Bikel
57, Nahmani St
Tel Aviv
Tel: (972 3) 560 8217
Fax: (972 3) 560 7947

Cinema Factory
11, Hayei Adam St
Tel Aviv
Tel: (972 3) 691 4279
Fax: (972 3) 691 3982

Distributors

Globus Group (UIP, Warner)
10, Glickson St
Tel Aviv
Tel: (972 3) 526 6333
Fax: (972 3) 526 6373

A.D. Matalon & Co. (Columbia, TriStar, Fox)
13, Yona Hanavi St
Tel Aviv
Tel: (972 3) 5162020
Fax: (972 3) 5161888

Forum/Israeli Theatres
(Buena Vista)
91, Medinath Hayehudim
PO Box 12598
Herzlyia Pituakh
Tel: (972 9) 952 6200
Fax: (972 9) 956 1581

Shapira Films
34, Allenby St
Tel Aviv
Tel: (972 3) 517 2923
Fax: (972 3) 510 1370

Shani Films
Lev Cinemas
Dizengoff Center
Tel Aviv
Tel: (972 3) 528 8282
Fax: (972 3) 620 4749

Useful Addresses

Israel Film Centre
Ministry of Industry and Trade
PO Box 299
Jerusalem
Tel: (972 2) 6220608
Fax: (972 2) 6236303

Israeli Film & TV Producers Association
PO Box 20486
Tel Aviv
Tel: (972 3) 5613919
Fax: (972 3) 5612529

Jerusalem Cinematheque & Israeli Film Archive
11, Hebron Rd
Jerusalem
Tel: (972 2) 672 4131
Fax: (972 2) 671 3044

Tel Aviv Cinematheque
2, Shprintzak St
PO Box 20370
Tel Aviv 61203
Tel: (972 3) 691 7181
Fax: (972 3) 696 2841

Israeli Film Fund
(new title for the Fund for the Promotion of Israeli Quality Films)
12, Judith Blvd.
Tel Aviv 61203
Tel: (972 3) 562 8180
Fax: (972 3) 562 5992

The New Fund for Cinema and Television
113, Hashmonaim St
Tel Aviv
Tel: (972 3) 561 5786
Fax: (972 3) 562 7991

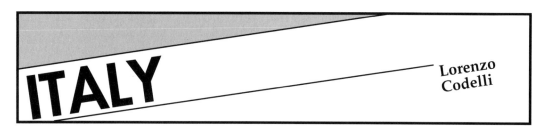

ITALY

Lorenzo
Codelli

The triumph of Roberto Benigni's **Life Is Beautiful** at the Oscars improved the morale, but not the international reputation of Italian cinema, which was represented by just one feature at Cannes and remains largely absent from most European screens.

National output settled at around 100 features, with just a few dozen lucky enough to get a decent release during the commercially fruitful Christmas-Easter season. A slight rise in attendance for Italian movies (27.8% of the gross, compared with 57.5% for US imports) was mostly due to a handful of comic blockbusters.

Powerful producer-distributor Vittorio Cecchi Gori was once again the leader of the pack when it came to the long-standing tactic of exploiting popular TV clowns in tailor-made big-screen vehicles. His recent divorce from his wife, Rita Rusic, regarded by many as the hands-on manager of their business, might shake the company's artistic foundations: made up of many comedians, but also of auteurs like Gianni Amelio, Carlo Mazzacurati and Daniele Luchetti.

Silvio Berlusconi, Cecchi Gori's major competitor – in the political arena, too – gave free rein to his own Medusa firm, which dared to finance high-budget projects such as Giuseppe Tornatore's *The Legend of the Pianist on the Ocean* and Franco Zeffirelli's *Tea with Mussolini*. A third pillar of the production system, state broadcaster Rai, was more active than in recent years, partly in response to the burgeoning pay-TV sector (dominated by the Telepiù network), which has started to invest in the movie business.

Audiences flocked to THE LITTLE SEAGULL AND THE CAT

Millions laughed

Seasonal hits did provide some easy laughs. Aldo, Giovanni and Giacomo's **That's Life** (*Così è la vita*) pulled almost four million customers to the talky escape of the gritty trio from jail to heaven. Carlo Verdone's **Capercaillie** (*Gallo cedrone*, attendance of 1.6 million) updated this Roman *vitellone's* aggressive humour. Neri Parenti's **Paparazzi** (1.6 million) featured a bunch of Northern and Southern funnymen in a farcical media frenzy. Brisk business amongst families enabled **The Little Seagull and the Cat** (*La gabbianella e il gatto*, 1.2 million), an elegiac animated musical by Enzo D'Alò, to come fourth in the domestic hit parade.

Riding the wave of Benigni's charisma, a cohort of Tuscan compatriots made their mark. The most promising, 37-year-old Giorgio Panariello, concocted the madcap beach romp **Bain-marie** (*Bagnomaria*), in which he played four hilarious characters. Massimo Ceccherini directed and starred in **Lucignolo** as a sex-obsessed boor.

Florentine Leonardo Pieraccioni had his comic track record marred by **My West** (*Il mio west*), directed by his pal, screenwriter

Giovanni Veronesi, a rather lame Western set in the Tuscan hills. Francesco Nuti directed and acted in **Mr Fifteeenballs** (*Il signor Quindicipalle*), a billiard table vaudeville.

Paolo Virzì, among the most original film-makers of the 1990s, directed **Hugs and Kisses** (*Baci e abbracci*), a bittersweet satire about self-made capitalists, played by an ensemble of fresh Tuscan faces. Masterful Tuscan veteran Mario Monicelli's **Dirty Linen** (*Panni sporchi*), was another ensemble grotesquerie on a similar theme. Zeffirelli evoked some episodes of his own youth in Fascist Florence in **Tea with Mussolini**.

Giuseppe Tornatore's **Legend of the Pianist on the Ocean**, an overlong jazz session starring a perplexed Tim Roth, which made nods to *Ragtime, America America* and *Titanic*, was at press time awaiting a foreign release in a re-edited version

The Venice Festival Golden Lion was not a blessing for Gianni Amelio's **The Way They Laughed** (*Così ridevano*), an uninspired attempt to explore industrial Turin's boom era through the eyes of two Sicilian brothers immigrants – mimicking Luchino Visconti's masterful *Rocco and His Brothers* (1960). Contemporary Albanian immigrants' sad destinies were brilliantly underlined by Matteo Garrone's **Guests** (*Ospiti*).

Odd couples

With his TV movie **Besieged** (*L'assedio*), Bernardo Bertolucci portrayed an African girl who finds happiness in exile by betraying her roots. This water-colour of a multiracial, implosive Roman neighbourhood is one of Bertolucci's finest achievements. Francesca Archibugi's **The Pear Tree** (*L'albero delle pere*) turns a droll eye on a Roman family set apart by drugs and indolence. Many of the capital city's social evils were highlighted by Ettore Scola's **The Dinner** (*La cena*), a mural starring a stream of players, including Vittorio Gassman in top form as a *trattoria* prophet.

Still from Ettore Scola's THE DINNER

The Taviani brothers and Marco Bellocchio drank deep from the fountain of Luigi Pirandello's short stories. The two parts of the brothers' **You Laugh** (*Tu ridi*) include sparks of characteristic Taviani skill, whereas **The Wet Nurse** (*La balia*) confirms Bellocchio's stylistic fossilisation. Dario Argento's **The Phantom of the Opera** celebrated hip diva Asia Argento's coolness, while Alberto Sordi celebrated his seventy-eighth birthday with the biting **Forbidden Meetings** (*Incontri proibiti*), about the fatal attraction between an old bourgeois and a sexy vamp.

Symposia, festivals and official inquiries were all trying to analyse why the new generation of film-makers seem so remote from reality. Take Giuseppe Piccioni's **Out of This World** (*Fuori dal mondo*), about a romance between a nun and a laundry owner, or Enzo Monteleone's **It's Done Now!** (*Ormai è fatta!*), on a gentle bandit's imprisonment, or Carlo Mazzacurati's **Davide's Summer** (*L'estate di Davide*),

Kim Rossi Stuart (centre) in THE GARDEN OF EDEN

describing a working boy's hard holidays – they all had interesting, contemporary plots, but were unable to catch an audience.

Some say their failure occurred because of their visual under-nourishment, or their similarities to too many TV serials. Daniele Luchetti tried an epic approach with **Little Masters** (*I piccoli maestri*), on a group of intellectual Resistance fighters; unfortunately his half-baked script and inexperienced actors doomed this unusually brave enterprise.

Alessandro D'Alatri should have been less respectfully hagiographic with **The Garden of Eden** (*I giardini dell'Eden*), though it was still an above-par biblical saga. **Radiofreccia**, renowned singer Luciano Ligabue's debut, was a very welcome revelation, a personal ode to the 1970s, set in and around a provincial radio station.

The Philip Morris Association sponsored more restorations of Italian classics, co-publishing with Edizioni Lindau large volumes on them: *Antonio Pietrangeli's 'Io la conoscevo bene'* and *Francesco Maselli's 'I delfini'* and *'Gli sbandati'*, edited by Lino Miccichè. I recommend a new quarterly exploring bizarre Italian genres: *Nocturno Cinema* (noct@uninetecom.it). It was also responsible for *99 donne*, a fascinating gallery of female stars.

Gremese Editore of Rome published a vital double dictionary of Italian screen performers, *Attori & Attrici*. Fellini's astounding heritage was far from forgotten, thanks to *Luci del varietà* (Cineteca Italiana/Editrice Il Castoro), *Federico Fellini da Rimini a Roma, 1937–1947* (Fondazione Fellini, fellini@comune.rimini.it), plus the late Tazio Secchiaroli's *Fellini 8½* (Motta Fotografia, Milan).

LORENZO CODELLI has written for many periodicals, including *Positif*. He is a member of the board of the Cineteca del Friuli, of the Pordenone Silent Film Festival, and of Udine Incontri Cinema.

Recent Films

L'ALBERO DELLE PERE (The Pear Tree)

Script and Dir: Francesca Archibugi. Phot: Luca Bigazzi. Players: Valeria Golino, Sergio Rubini, Stefano Dionisi. Prod: 3 Emme Cinematografica/Istituto Luce/RAI Cinemafiction.

L'AMICO DEL CUORE (The Best Friend)

Script and Dir: Vincenzo Salemme. Phot: Italo Petriccione. Players: Vincenzo Salemme, Eva Herzigova. Prod: Cecchi Gori Group Tiger.

L'ASSEDIO (Besieged)

Script: Clare Peploe, Bernardo Bertolucci, from James Lasdun's short story. Dir: Bertolucci. Phot: Fabio Cianchetti. Players: Thandie Newton, David Thewlis. Prod: Fiction/Navert Film/Mediaset.

BACI E ABBRACCI (Hugs and Kisses)

Script: Francesco Bruni, Paolo Virzô. Dir: Virzô. Phot: Alessandro Pesci. Players: Francesco Paolantoni, Edoardo Gabriellini, Paola Tiziana Cruciani. Prod: Cecchi Gori Group Tiger/Tele+.

BAGNOMARIA (Bain-Marie)

Script: Giorgio Panariello, Leo Benvenuti, Piero De Bernardi. Dir: Panariello. Phot: Danilo Desideri. Players: Panariello, Manuela Arcuri. Prod: Cecchi Gori Group Tiger.

LA BALIA (The Wet Nurse)

Script: Marco Bellocchio, Daniela Ceselli, from Luigi Pirandello's short story. Dir: Bellocchio. Phot: Giuseppe Lanci. Players: Fabrizio Bentivoglio, Valeria Bruni Tedeschi. Prod: Filmalbatros, Istituto Luce, RAI Cinemafiction.

LA BALLATA DEI LAVAVETRI (The Ballad of the Windscreen Washers)

Script: Peter Del Monte, Sergio Bazzini, from Edoardo Albinati's novel. Dir: Del Monte. Phot: Pasquale Mari. Players: Kim Rossi Stuart, Agata Buzek. Prod: P.F.A. Films.

LA CENA (The Dinner)

Script: Ettore Scola, Furio Scarpelli, Silvia Scola, Giacomo Scarpelli. Dir: Ettore Scola. Phot: Franco Di Giacomo. Players: Vittoro Gassman, Stefania Sandrelli, Fanny Ardant, Giancarlo Giannini. Prod: MassFilm, Medusa Film (Rome), Les Films Alain Sarde, Filmtel (Paris).

IL CIELO IN UNA STANZA (The Sky in One Room)

Script: Enrico and Carlo Vanzina. Dir: Carlo Vanzina. Phot: Carlo Tafani. Players: Elio Germano, Gabriele Mainetti. Prod: Filmauro.

COSÌ È LA VITA (That's Life)

Script: Aldo [Baglio], Giovanni [Storti] & Giacomo [Poretti], Massimo Venier, Gino & Michele, Giorgio Gherarducci, Graziano Ferrari. Dir: Aldo, Giovanni & Giacomo and Massimo Venier. Phot: Giovanni Fiore Coltellacci. Players: Aldo, Giovanni & Giacomo, Marina Massironi. Prod: A.GI.DI/Medusa Film/Kubla Khan/Rodeo Drive.

COSÌ RIDEVANO (The Way They Laughed)

Script and Dir: Gianni Amelio. Phot: Luca Bigazzi. Players: Enrico Lo Verso, Lillo Jacolino. Prod: Cecchi Gori Group Tiger.

DEL PERDUTO AMORE (Of Lost Love)

Script: Domenico Starnone, Michele Placido. Dir: Placido. Phot: Blasco Giurato. Players: Giovanna Mezzogiorno, Fabrizio Bentivoglio, Enrico Lo Verso. Prod: Clemi Cinematografica.

L'ESTATE DI DAVIDE (Davide's Summer)

Script: Carlo Mazzacurati, Claudio Piersanti. Dir: Mazzacurati. Phot: Alessandro Pesci. Players: Stefano Campi, Patrizia Piccinini. Prod: Tangram Film, RAI Cinemafiction.

LA FAME E LA SETE (Hunger and Thirst)

Script: Antonio Albanese, Vincenzo Cerami. Dir: Albanese. Phot: Massimo Pau. Players: Albanese, Lorenza Indovina. Prod: Cecchi Gori Group Tiger.

IL FANTASMA DELL'OPERA (The Phantom of the Opera)

Script: Gérard Brach, Dario Argento, from Gaston Leroux's novel. Dir: Argento. Phot: Ronnie Taylor. Players: Asia Argento, Julian Sands, Andrea Di Stefano. Prod: Opera Film/Medusa Film.

FERDINANDO E CAROLINA

Script: Lina Wertmuller, Raffaele La Capria. Dir: Wertmuller. Phot: Blasco Giurato. Players: Sergio Assisi, Gabriella Pession. Prod: Immagine e Cinema/Medusa Film (Rome)/Le Studio Canal+ (Paris).

FUORI DAL MONDO (Out of this World)

Script: Giuseppe Piccioni, Gualtiero Rosella, Lucia Zei. Dir: Piccioni. Phot: Luca Bigazzi. Players: Margherita Buy, Silvio Orlando. Prod: Lumière & Co./RAI Cinemafiction.

LA GABBIANELLA E IL GATTO (The Little Seagull and the Cat)

Script: Enzo D'Alò, Umberto Marino, from Luis Sepùlveda's novel. Dir: D'Alò. Animation: Walter Cavazzuti, Michel Fuzellier, Silvio Pautasso. Prod: Cecchi Gori Group Tiger.

GALLO CEDRONE (Capercaillie)

Script: Carlo Verdone, Leo Benvenuti, Piero De Bernardi, Pasquale Plastino. Dir: Verdone. Phot: Danilo Desideri. Players: Verdone, Regina Orioli. Prod: Cecchi Gori Group Tiger.

I GIARDINI DELL'EDEN (The Garden of Eden)

Script: Alessandro D'Alatri, Miro Silvera. Dir: D'Alatri. Phot: Federico Masiero. Players: Kim Rossi Stuart, Said Taghmaoui. Prod: Medusa Film/Rete Italia/Magic Moments.

IL GUERRIERO CAMILLO (Camillo the Warrior)

Script and Dir: Claudio Bigagli. Phot: Paolo Carnera. Players: Bigagli, Carlo Croccolo, Marco Messeri. Prod: Lucky Red.

HAREM SUARE'

Script: Gianni Romoli, Ferzan Ozpetek. Dir: Ozpetek. Phot: Pasquale Mari. Players: Marie Gillain, Alex Descas, Lucia Bosé. Prod: R & C Produzioni (Rome)/Les Films Balenciaga/ (Paris)/A.F.S. Films (Istanbul).

INCONTRI PROIBITI (Forbidden Meetings)

Script: Rodolfo Sonego, Alberto Sordi. Dir: Sordi. Phot: Armando Nannuzzi. Players: Sordi, Valeria Marini. Prod: Filmauro/Aurelia Cinematografica.

LA LEGGENDA DEL PIANISTA SULL'OCEANO (The Legend of the Pianist on the Ocean)

Script: Giuseppe Tornatore, from Alessandro Baricco's novel. Dir: Tornatore. Phot: Lajos Koltai. Players: Tim Roth, Pruitt Taylor Vince, Melanie Thierry. Prod: Sciarlò/Medusa Film.

LUCIGNOLO

Script: Massimo Ceccherini, Giovanni Veronesi. Dir: Ceccherini. Phot: Mauro Marchetti. Players: Ceccherini, Claudia Gerini, Tinto Brass. Prod: Cecchi Gori Group Tiger.

MATRIMONI (Marriages)

Script: Roberta Mazzoni, Cristina Comencini. Dir: Comencini. Phot: Roberto Forza. Players: Diego Abatantuono, Francesca Neri, Claude Brasseur. Prod: Filmauro/Tele+/Cattleya/(Rome)/ Carrère Télévision (Paris).

IL MIO WEST (My West)

Script: Giovanni Veronesi, Leonardo Pieraccioni, from Vincenzo Pardini's novel. Dir: Veronesi. Phot: José Luis Alcaine. Players: Pieraccioni, Harvey Keitel, David Bowie. Prod: Pacific Pictures/Cecchi Gori Group Tiger.

L'ODORE DELLA NOTTE (The Smell of the Night)

Script: Claudio Caligari, from Dido Sacchettoni's novel. Dir: Caligari. Phot: Maurizio Calvesi. Players: Valerio Mastandrea, Alessia Fugardi. Prod: Sorpasso Film.

ONOREVOLI DETENUTI (Men Behind Bars)

Script and Dir: Giancarlo Planta. Phot: Luigi Verga. Players: Massimo De Francovich, Gianni Cavina. Prod: Indipendent Tv-Movie.

ORMAI E FATTA! (It's Done Now!)

Script: Enzo Monteleone, from Horst Fantazzini's story. Dir: Monteleone. Phot: Arnaldo Catinari. Players: Stefano Accorsi, Antonio Catania, Emilio Solfrizzi. Prod: Hera International Film, RAI Cinemafiction.

OSPITI (Guests)

Script: Attilio Caselli, Matteo Garrone. Dir: Garrone. Phot: Marco Onorato. Players: Corrado Sassi, Pasqualino Mura. Prod: Archimede.

PANNI SPORCHI (Dirty Linen)

Script: Suso Cecchi D'Amico, Masolino D'Amico, Margherita D'Amico, Mario Monicelli. Dir: Monicelli. Players: Ornella Muti, Michele Placido, Luigi Proietti. Prod: Clemi Cinematografica.

PAPARAZZI

Script and Dir: Neri Parenti. Phot: Carlo Tafani. Players: Christian De Sica, Massimo Boldi, Diego Abatantuono. Prod: Filmauro.

RADIOFRECCIA

Script: Luciano Ligabue, Antonio Leotti, from Ligabue's novel. Dir: Ligabue. Phot: Arnaldo Catinari. Players: Stefano Accorsi, Francesco Guccini, Luciano Federico. Prod: Fandango.

LA SECONDA MOGLIE (The Second Wife)

Script: Ugo Chiti, Nicola Zavagli. Dir: Chiti. Phot: Raffaele Mertes.

Useful Addresses

Adriana Chiesa Enterprises
Via Barnaba Oriani, 24/A
00197 Roma
Tel: (39 06) 808 6052
Fax: (39 06) 8068 7855

Agis
Via di villa Patrizi, 10
00161 Roma
Tel: (39 06) 884 731
Fax: (39 06) 4423 1838

Anica
Main Italian producers association
Viale Regina Margherita, 286
00198 Roma
Tel: (39 06) 442 5961
Fax: (39 06) 440 4128

**Banca Nazionale del Lavoro –
Sezione Credito**
Cinematografico
Via degli Scipioni, 297
00192 Roma
Tel: (39 06) 4702 0940
Fax: (39 06) 4702 0970

CAM
Via Cola di Rienzo, 152
00192 Roma
Tel: (39 06) 687 4220
Fax: (39 06) 687 4046

Carol Levi Company
Via pisanelli, 2
00196 Roma
Tel: (39 06) 3600 2430
Fax: (39 06) 3600 2438

Cecchi Gori Group
Via Valadier, 42
00193 Roma
Tel: (39 06) 324 721
Fax: (39 06) 3247 2300

Cinecittà Holding
Via Tuscolana, 1055
00173 Roma
Tel: (39 06) 722 861
Fax: (39 06) 722 1883

Clemi Cinematografica
Via Salaria, 292
00198 Roma
Tel: (39 06) 854 8821
Fax: (39 06) 841 9749

**Dipartimento dello
Spettacolo – Presidenza del
Consiglio dei Ministri**
Via della Ferratella in Laterano,
45/51
00184 Roma
Tel: (39 06) 77321

DueA Film
Piazza Cola di Rienzo, 69
00192 Roma
Tel: (39 06) 321 4851
Fax: (39 06) 321 5108

Filmalbatros
Via di Villa Ada, 10
00199 Roma
Tel: (39 06) 855 4700
Fax: (39 06) 855 5280

Filmexport Group
Via Polonia, 7/9
00198 Roma
Tel: (39 06) 855 4266
Fax: (39 06) 855 0248

Fininvest/Mediaset/Rete Italia
Viale Europa, 48
20093 Cologno Monzese
Tel: (39 06) 25141
Fax: (39 06) 2514 9091
Via Aurelia Antica, 422/424
00165 Roma
Tel: (39 06) 663 901
Fax: (39 06) 6639 0409

Filmauro
Via XXIV Maggio, 14
00187 Roma
Tel: (39 06) 699 581
Fax: (39 06) 6995 8410

International Recording
Via Urbana, 172
00184 Roma
Tel: (39 06) 476 701
Fax: (39 06) 474 5246

Istituto Luce
Via Tuscolana, 1055
00173 Roma
Tel: (39 06) 729 921
Fax: (39 06) 722 1127

Italia Cinema
Voa Anreliana, 63
00187 Roma
Tel: (39 06) 4201 2539
Fax: (39 06) 4200 3530

Lucky Red
Via Baiaonti, 10
00195 Roma
Tel: (39 06) 3735 2296
Fax: (39 06) 3735 2310

Magica
Master Europeo in Gestione di
Impresa
Cinematografica e Audiovisiva
Via Lucullo 7, int. 8
00187 Rome
Tel: (39 06) 420 0651
Fax: (39 06) 4201 0898

Medusa Film
Via Aurelia Antica, 422/424
00165 Roma
Tel: (39 06) 663 901
Fax: (39 06) 6639 0450

**Rai – Radiotelevisione
Italiana**
Viale Mazzini, 14
00195 Roma
Tel: (39 06) 3678
Fax: (39 06) 372 5680

Rai Trade
Via Novaro, 18
00195 Rome
Tel: (39 06) 3749 8269
Fax: (39 06) 370 1343

RCS Editori
via della Mercede, 37
00187 Rome
Tel: (39 06) 688 281
Fax: (39 06) 6882 8860

RCS Film & TV
Via Mecenate, 91
20138 Milano
Tel: (39 02) 50951
Fax: (39 02) 5095 5575

Sacher Film
Via Annia Faustina, 25
00153 Roma
Tel (39 06) 574 5353
Fax (39 06) 638 5720

Tele+
Via Piranesi, 46
20137 Milan
Tel: (39 02) 700 271
Fax (39 02) 7002 7201

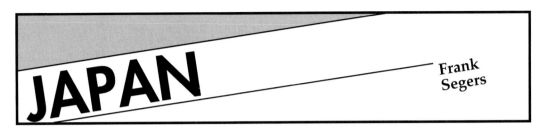

JAPAN — Frank Segers

An official statement from UniJapan Film, in March 1999, noted: "Since box-office receipts of Japanese films other than animation increased in 1998, it can be said that the Japanese film industry has been in good condition." In May 1999 an executive of a major Japanese studio said: "I am afraid that Japan will soon be under the direct control of the American film industry." Somewhere between these two views lies the truest picture of Japanese cinema.

Sure, 1998 produced nine domestic titles (two more than in 1997) which each yielded distribution rentals at or above the blockbuster one billion yen mark ($8.3m), and these hits were not just drawn from the animation or special effects genres. Total cinema admissions increased by almost 10%, from 140 million in 1997 to 153 million in 1998.

However, the share of total market revenues claimed by Japanese films dropped to an embarrassingly low 36.2%, down 5% on the previous year, thus stoking fears that foreign films (read American titles) are at last taking over Japan.

The fact is that Japanese cinema has survived far more rigorous years than 1998, and has reason to be hopeful. The nation's economy appears at long last to have turned several significant corners. Some of Japan's most venerable directors – Shohei Imamura, Kon Ichikawa, Takeshi Kitano, Yoji Yamada and Nagisa Oshima – were at work, making up to a certain extent for the loss of the irreplaceable Juzo Itami and Akira Kurosawa. And fresh helmers were commanding attention from critics, and even from mainstream filmgoers. Not a bad state of affairs.

Cops and monsters

Of Japan's three major film studios, Toho, Toei and Shochiku, only Toho, the strongest, thrived in 1998. For the fourteenth consecutive year, Toho's releases pulled cumulative film rentals of more than $83m. It distributed **Bayside Shakedown** (*Odoru Daisosasen*), Katsuyuki Motohiro's feature film adaptation of a popular TV series, and the jocular policier became the biggest domestic hit of the year.

Bayside Shakedown features a white-collar drone-turned detective, and neatly stands the crime drama form on its head by insinuating comedy and wry social observation into familiar police sleuthing, set in Tokyo's trendy bayside area. A sequel is planned.

Toho also benefited from its production interest in Roland Emmerich's *Godzilla*, the sixth most popular film of the year in Japan, and the company is reclaiming the monster franchise with **Godzilla 2000**, from director Takao Ohgawara, to be released on December 11.

Toei's 1998 film rentals dropped some 30% from the previous year, although the company came up with one of the year's most curious entries: Shunya Ito's **Pride** (*Puraido – Unmei no Toki*), a revisionist look at the war crimes trial of Hideki Tojo, the general who ran Japan's Pacific campaign in the Second World War.

The film argues that Tojo really wasn't such a bad sort, since he fought to "maintain Japan's prestige as a sovereign state". Despite howls from foreigners about Japan's penchant for sugar-coating its history, *Pride* became the sixth most popular domestic film of the year. The bad news for Toei was a significant operating loss, plus an announcement that its workforce would be reduced by 20% by 2001.

Shochiku had one of the most challenging periods of its 104-year history. The company's 8.6% decrease in film rentals was the least of it. Shochiku president Nobuyoshi Otani's radical moves included the closure of the company's Kamakura Cinema World theme park, south of Tokyo, plus a downsizing programme aimed at a 30% workforce reduction and a reduction in the number of films the studio produces annually to two in 1999, down from a dozen in 1997.

Samurai in love

Nagisa Oshima's return to feature directing after a 13-year hiatus is thus hugely important for Shochiku. One of the company's two projects for 1999 is **Forbidden** (*Gohatto*), Oshima's adaptation of Ryotaro Shiba's historical novel *Shinsengumi Keppuroku*, about friendship and love amongst a band of renegade samurai warriors in the late 1800s.

Scheduled to be released at the end of 1999, *Forbidden*'s $7.5m budget is unusually high for a domestic production and its marvellous cast includes Takeshi Kitano as the vice-commander of the warriors and Yoichi Sai, director of the much-praised *All Under The Moon*, as the commander. The score will be by Ryuichi Sakamoto and costumes by Emi Wada, who won an Oscar for her work on Kurosawa's *Ran*. Oshima's handling of the novel's homoerotic elements is bound to arouse great interest.

After the acclaimed *Hana-Bi*, Kitano seemed to coast a bit with **Kikujiro**. An amiably sweet road movie pairing an ageing loser (Kitano) and a lonely boy travelling around Japan, it hardly made a competitive dent at the much-bad-mouthed 1999 Cannes Film Festival.

The festival was kinder to Nobuhiro Suwa's second film, **M/Other**, which won a

Takeshi Kitano (left) instructs Ryohei Matsuda in Nagisa Oshima's FORBIDDEN

FIPRESCI Award. Suwa works in long takes, encourages actors to improvise and adopts a distanced approach to his material that is hard to warm to. *M/Other* is another look at traditional family life gone awry, focusing on a divorced father, his girlfriend and his eight-year-old son.

On a more upbeat note was the festival's Directors Fortnight showing of Kiyoshi Kurosawa's **Charisma**, starring the magnetic Koji Yakusho (star of *The Eel* and *Shall We Dance*). The script tells of a cashiered police detective who finds refuge in a mysterious forest; weirdness and violence ensue (not uncommon in Kurosawa's work).

Among the year's most heralded films was Hideyuki Hirayama's **Begging For Love** (*Aiwo Kouhito*), which dominated the voting at the 22nd Japan Academy Awards in March 1999. The film picked up eight awards, including Best Picture, Best Director, Best Actress (Mieko Harada) and Best Cinematographer (Kozo Shibasaki). The film, based on Harumi Shimoda's novel, is a gruelling mother versus daughter drama, tracing inter-family conflicts over two generations, complete with screams, punches, slaps – and satisfying reconciliation.

A skilled, tough, multi-layered work, Hirayama's film beat off competition from Kitano's *Hana-Bi*, Shohei Imamura's **Dr. Akagi** (an amiable but not terribly good work about an intrepid Second World War doctor who makes an exceptional number of house calls) and Yoji Yamada's **The New Voyage** (*Gakko III*), the third in his series of school stories. This is a warm, humane look at a kind woman who attends a retraining school for unemployed, middle-aged (and older) workers. In spring 1999, Japan's Ministry of Cultural Affairs made a rare acknowledgement of film as art, awarding Yamada a richly deserved citation for promoting Japanese culture.

International acclaim

Japanese films from lesser-known directors drew notice overseas. Hirokazu Kore-Eda's **After Life**, in which the newly-deceased

are asked to make a film based on their fondest single memories, caught the attention of critics at the Sundance Festival.

The Toronto Film Festival in 1998 devoted an entire section to recent Japanese output, including **Cannot Live** (*Ikinai*), a first feature from a Takeshi Kitano protégé, Hiroshi Shimizu; Shimizu was an assistant director on Kitano's last four films. The influence shows: Ikinai tells the tale of a dozen Japanese who hire a tour bus in order to effect ensemble suicide.

In an arresting development, in light of the concerns over US domination of the market, Japanese film companies are joining counterparts in South Korea, Hong Kong and Taiwan in co-productions of films for the Asian market. Among those involved on the Japanese side are Pony Canyon, Nippon Herald, Toho-Towa and the Hakuhodo advertising giant. Feature films to be jointly underwritten include works from directors Shunji Iwai of Japan, Stanley Kwan of Hong Kong and Edward Yang of Taiwan.

The newly-revived Nikkatsu studio announced the production of **Dora Heita**, to be directed by Kon Ichikawa (his first film in four years). What makes this special is that the material was co-scripted 30 years ago by Akira Kurosawa. The plot is vintage Kurosawa: a samurai magistrate cleans up a corrupt and lawless castle town.

Finally, Nagaharu Yodogawa, perhaps Japan's most recognisable film critic, died last November, aged 89. At heart a populariser, he had been a fixture on Sunday night film broadcasts on TV Asahi since 1966. His commentaries on a broad range of films were carried off with style, humour and scholarship.

FRANK SEGERS is a freelance writer who for many years specialised in Far Eastern entertainment issues for *Variety*.

Producers/ Distributors

Daiei Co. Ltd.
1-1-16 Higashi
Shimbashi, Minato-ku
Tokyo 105
Tel: (81 3) 3573 8716
Fax: (81 3) 3573 8720

Nikkatsu Corp.
3-28-12 Hongo
Bunkyo-ku
Tokyo
Tel: (81 3) 5689 1002

Shochiku Co.
13-5 Tsukiji 1-chome
Chuo-ku
Tokyo
Tel: (81 3) 5550 1623
Fax: (81 3) 5550 1654

Shochiku Co. Ltd.
4-1-1 Tsukiji, Chuo-ku
Tokyo 104–8422
Tel: (81 3) 5550 1623
Fax: (81 3) 5550 1654

Toei Co.
2-17, 3-chome
Ginza, Chuo-ku
Tokyo
Tel: (81 3) 3535 7621
Fax: (81 3) 3535 7622

Toho International Co.
Hibiya Park Building
8-1 Yukucho, 1-chome
Chiyoda-ku
Tokyo
Tel: (81 3) 3213 6821
Fax: (81 3) 3213 6825

Distributors/ Sales Agents

Asmik Ace Entertainment, Inc.
5-24-5 Hongo
Bunkyo-ku
Tokyo 113
Tel: (81 3) 3817 6717
Fax: (81 3) 3817 6718

GAGA Communications Inc.
East Roppongi Building
3-16-35 Roppongi
Minato-ku
Tokyo 106
Tel: (81 3) 3589 7503
Fax: (81 3) 3589 7499

Nippon Herald Films Inc.
5-11-1 Ginza
Chuo-ku
Tokyo 104
Tel: (81 3) 3248 1162
Fax: (81 3) 3248 1169

Shibata Organisation Inc.
(France Eigasha)

2-10-8 Ginza
Chuo-ku
Tokyo
Tel: (81 3) 3545 3411
Fax: (81 3) 3545 3519

Tohokushinsha Film Co. Ltd.
4-17-7 Akasaka
Minato-ku
Tokyo 107
Tel: (81 3) 3582 0211
Fax: (81 3) 3589 4504

Toho-Towa Co. Ltd.
Playguide Building 3F
2-6-4 Ginza
Chuo-ku
Tokyo
Tel: (81 3) 3562 0109
Fax: (81 3) 3535 3656

UniJapan Film
Ginza 1-6-5, Chuo-ku
Tokyo 104–0061
Tel: (81 3) 3538 0621
Fax: (81 3) 3538 0622

Useful Address

Association for the Diffusion of Japanese Films Abroad
Nakamura Building 3F
Ginza 5-9-13
Tokyo
Tel: (81 3) 3572 5106
Fax: (81 3) 3572 8876

KAZAKHSTAN
Eugene Zykov

The domestic film industry has, like other sectors, been hit by the struggles of the Kazakh economy. Early in 1999 the state halted financing of new films and the National Production Center (NPC) had to "freeze" its funding to seven of the ten previously approved projects. Only two features which might qualify as "commercial" hit the screens in the summer of 1999: Abai Karpykov's **Fara** and Satybaldy Narymbetov's **Ompa**. Both made a strong debut in, respectively, the main programme and the sidebar at the 1999 Moscow Film Festival, and *Fara*'s Farkhad Abrdaimov won the Best Actor award.

In this situation, the industry is turning an enthusiastic eye towards independent projects, according to Max Smagulov, First Secretary of the Kazakh Film-Makers' Union, and several Kazakh indies are grabbing their opportunities. Gala-TV, whose stunning documentary **The**

Experience of the Cross won a dozen international festival awards, is making a $1m drama, *Vocal Parallels*, by prominent Russian expatriate director Rustam Khamdamov. It also produced a controversial documentary by Vladimir Tyulkin, **Lady with Dogs**, comparing the fates of pets who live in a comfortable house with an elderly woman and those who are awaiting extermination in a dog shelter.

Rik Corp., an up-and-coming Almaty-based independent, has teamed up with Khabar, the major TV producer and broadcaster, for a high-tech computer animation, **Aldar Khasym**, which boasts an exotic storyline and lots of traditional music. Its financing received a fortuitous boost when Kazakh president Nursultan Nazarbaev, after completing a televised interview at Khabar's studios, visited an editing room to watch the pilot and enjoyed it so much that he gave the project a personal endorsement.

In 1998 an average Kazakh viewer watched nearly 75 hours' worth of feature films on television (70% of them American), but only one or two features in cinemas, though local distributors predict a rise in admissions in 2000, thanks largely to the mini cinema-building boom sparked by the success of the first Eurasian Film Festival in Almaty in October 1998.

The republic's first Dolby-equipped cinema, a 250-seat theatre in Almaty's giant Ramstore shopping centre opened in May 1999, followed by three more screens and a multiplex, in Almaty and the new capital, Astana. The new theatres are different from other European cinemas: the Kazakhs like oval-shaped halls, which resemble the traditional "yurta", where nomadic tribes lived. The average admission rate is $4 to $5. Almaty's first drive-in was scheduled to open in the autumn.

In May 1998, the Kazakh film-makers' union elected as its president Max Smagulov, a former heavyweight independent producer, who set off the Kazakh "new wave" in the early 1990s before disappearing from view. He

Kazakh crowd-pleaser OMPA inspires romantic brotherhood

promised: "We shall not turn a deaf ear to the needs of the industry. We plan to change the situation to benefit producers and crews. We'll expand our contacts world-wide, produce and show more films and upgrade production facilities."

He believes that as a location for domestic and international projects, the republic "should not resemble an unhappy Cinderella. On the contrary, we hope to convert the market into a small Paradise, offering nearly 300 sunny days and eight climatic zones within 50 miles of Almaty."

EUGENE ZYKOV is Moscow-based East European Bureau Chief for *Channel 21 International* (UK).

Recent Films

SHANKHAI

Script and Dir: Alexander Baranov. Phot: Fyodor Aranyshev. Players: Vladimir Tolokonnikov, Dimash Akhimov, Beken Rimova, Artur Zagidullin. Prod: Kazakhfilm Studios/National Production Center.

ABAI

Script: Ardak Amirkulov, Leila Akhinzhanova, Alexander Baranov, with Serik Aprymov. Dir: Amirkulov. Phot: Aubakir Suleyev, Khasan Kydyralyev. Players: Gabiden Turykbayev, Tungyshbai Al-Tarazi, Bolot Beishenalyev. Prod: Kazakhfilm Studios/A.S.S. (France)

POSLEDNYE KANIKULY

Script: Alyena Gordyeva, Amir Karakulov. Dir: Amir Karakulov. Phot: Murat Nugmanov. Players: Shalva Gogoladze, Sanzhar Iskakov, Anatoly Gapchyuk. Prod: Dank Video.

AKSUAT

Script and Dir: Serik Aprymov. Phot: Boris Troshev. Players: Sabid Kurmanbekov, Inessa Rodionova, Nurzhuman Ihtynbayev. Prod: Kazakhfilm Studios/Firma Kino/ Film Factory.

KHSRONIKA YUNNOGO AKKORDEONISTA (Chronicles of a Young Accordionist)

Script: Istule Izmagambetova, Saty-Baldy Narymbetov. Dir:

Narymbetov. Phot: Khasan Kydyraliev. Players: Daulet Daniev, Petya Khaitovich. Prod: Miras/ Kazakhfilm Studios.

TOT KTO NEZHNEYE (The Tender One Will Win)

Script: Leila Akhinzhanova, Abai Karpykov. Dir: Karpykov. Phot: Alexei Berkovich, Georgii Gid, Nikolai Kiriyenkov. Players: Ksenia Kachalina, Nikolai Stotskyi, Andrei Rostotsky, Farkhad Abdraimov. Prod: Fora-Film/ Roskomkino/Kazakhkino/ Kazakhinfilm/RTPO Kazakhfilm.

FARA

Script: Leila Akhinzhanova. Dir: Abai Karpykov. Phot: Alexei Berkovich. Players: Farkhad Abdraimov, Kristina Arabkaite, Bopesh Zhandayev. Prod: Karpykov/National Production Center.

KILLER

Script: Darezhan Omirbayev, Gaziz Shaldybayev. Dir: Omirbayev. Phot: Boris Troshev. Prod: Kadam Studios

DESANT (Paratroopers)

Script: Alexander Baranov, Rafad Samigullin. Dir: Leila Oranysheva. Phot: Valerii Mulgaut. Prod: Firma-Kino Studios.

OMPA

Script and Dir: Saty-Baldy

Narymbayev. Players: Alexander Pankratov-Chernyi, Doskhan Zholzhaksymov. Prod: National Production Center.

Useful Addresses

Caravan/BG Productions
017 11 Chaikovsky St
480004 Almaty
Tel: (7 3272) 329 735
Fax: (7 3272) 399 895
e-mail: root@caravan alma-ata.su

Firm-Kino
176 Al-Farabi Ave
480067 Almaty
Tel/Fax: (7 32 62) 630 901

Gala-TV
23A Tole Bi
480100 Almaty
Tel: (7 3272) 617 613
Fax: (7 3272) 616 816
e-mail: galatv@galatv.almaty.kz

National Production Center
176 Al-Farabi Ave
480067 Almaty
Tel: (7 32 62) 482 323
Fax: (7 32 62) 656 069

Orken Film Distribution
10 Abai Ave
Suite 308
Almaty
Tel/Fax: (7 32 62) 407 980/425 450

Rik Corp.
76 Zhibek Zholy St
Suite 603
Almaty
Tel: (7 3272) 47 91 54
e-mail: radiorik1@kazmail.asdc.kz

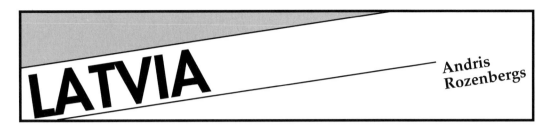

LATVIA

Andris Rozenbergs

For the Latvian film industry, 1999 began disastrously, with more than $180,000 cut from the state support for film production. It was an unjust blow, albeit an understandable one given the knock-on effects of the financial crisis in Russia and the economic instability in South East Asia. The Consultative Film Board, the independent body which decides which projects receive state funding, is very keen for Latvia to enter Eurimages, but there is insufficient government funding on offer, thus excluding Latvia for at least another year from participation in European support networks.

The board was able to support a handful of shorts, and two fiction feature projects, by well-known directors Janis Streics and Laila Pakalnina. Streics made the national hit, *The Millstones of Fate* (121,000 admissions) and received the bulk of the state funding allocation for **The Mystery of the Old Mayoralty**, about a former KGB man whose nights are haunted by the ghosts of his victims.

Pakalnina, who previously wrote and directed the internationally-acclaimed *The Shoe*, has moved on to **Tusya**, a story about an adolescent's love affair during the first years of this century. She received 5% of the film's budget through subsidy, with her German production partner, Schlemmer Film, ready to cover the rest. They will hold the rights and Latvia will have to put up with gratitude in credits written in tiny characters.

Despite the lack of resources, the film community is working intensively, and one interesting trend is the attempt to perceive our national identity in a broader international context, with film-makers exploring the destinies of people who have experienced cross-cultural influences. In **Spanish Capriccio**, Janis Ozolins-Ozols, a student of the Madrid film school, interviewed three Latvian artists whose lives have been influenced by Spanish culture: a dancer, a painter and a flamenco musician.

In **Gavrila**, Romualds Pipars investigated a particular type, within Latvia's traditional Russian orthodox minority. The Gavrila are a bizarre brand of Russian artisans who can build anything and everything: a tractor, or a wind turbine, even an aeroplane. Pipars enjoys searching for interesting characters: his **Shocking Aija** is the story of a Latvian woman who has spent 25 years in Yugoslavia. She graduated from Moscow and Belgrade universities, married a Serb composer and during the collapse of Yugoslavia and the conflicts in Bosnia and Kosovo has worked as a correspondent for Radio Liberty.

Increasingly, producers are looking to set up international partnerships, and even without access to the official European networks, some are succeeding. Guntis Trekteris, the manager of Kaupo Filma, is finishing a Swedish-Latvian co-production, *Follow Me*, directed by Una Celms. Gatis Upmalis of the F.O.R.M.A. studio, achieved an even more difficult task, by setting up a pan-Baltic co-production, **Three Love Stories**. It is a tough business for Riga producers to talk with their counterparts in Latvia and Lithuania – because three poor partners do not make one rich team.

Upmalis' next project, **To Hell with Wagner**, will deal with an episode from the youth of Richard Wagner, who in 1830 became a "Kapellmeister" of the Riga City Orchestra. In Riga, he encounters a young woman but this is not a love story. The legend has it that every Latvian woman in those bygone times was a kind of sorceress. The script is by an emigrée Latvian author and stage director, Baiba Rubesais. How ironic that every European producer who takes the slightest interest in investing in this story immediately asks the same question: "Is Latvia a member of Eurimages?

ANDRIS ROZENBERGS has directed seven fiction films and a dozen documentaries. He is Deputy Director of the National Film Centre, in charge of International Relations.

Recent and Forthcoming Films

BAIGA VASARA
(Summer of Terror)

Script: Pauls Bankovskis, Guntars Gabranovs, Andrejs Ekis, Aigars Grauba. Dir: Grauba and Ekis. Phot: Gints Berzins. Players: Inese Caune, Arturs Skrastins, Uldis Dumpis. Prod: PLATFORMA Filma.

SEKO MAN (Follow Me)

Script: Lauris Gundars. Dir: Una Celma. Phot: Robert Nordström. Players: Baiba Broka, Samuel Fröle. Prod: KAUPO Filma (Latvia)/ Bjerking Production AB (Sweden).

PASLEPES (Hide and Seek)

Script: Lauris Gundars. Dir: Janis Putnins. Phot: Janis Eglitis. Players: Elita Klavina, Vigo Roga. Prod: KAUPO Filma.

Useful Adresses

National Film Centre
Elizabetes 49
Riga LV-1010
Latvia
Tel: (371 7) 505 074
Fax: (371 7) 505 077
e-mail: nfc@com.latnet.lv

Latvian Filmmaker's Union
Elizabetes 49
Riga LV-1010
Latvia
Tel: (371 7) 288 536
Fax: (371 7) 240 543

Riga Film Studio
Smerla 3
Riga LV-1006
Latvia
Tel: (371 7) 755 1706
Fax: (371 7) 782 8408
e-mail: rks@parks.lv

LITHUANIA — Gražina Arlickaite

After the disappointment of 1998, when no Lithuanian films were released, three new features will have been completed by the end of 1999. Valdas Navasaitis, who has won international awards for his documentaries, including *Autumn Snow* (1992) and *Spring* (1996) finished his feature debut, the Lithuania-France co-production **Yard** (*Kiemas*), just in time for it to be shown in the Directors Fortnight at Cannes.

Navasaitis focuses on a socially diverse group of people living together in the same house in the 1980s, during a period of dashed hopes and mental stagnation. Using young, amateur actors and working from a resolutely uncommercial aesthetic, he uses his documentary experience to make us feel the importance of every minute and every object, no matter how small.

Yard continues the tradition of Lithuanian auteur cinema, which is represented most completely by young director Šarūnas Bartas, better-known internationally than at home for *Three Days*

(1991), *Corridor* (1995) and *The House* (1997). Bartas was the first Lithuanian director to enter into co-production and, like his previous two features, his new film **Freedom** (*Laisvé*) is a Lithuanian-French-Portuguese production. At press time he was still shooting *Freedom* in Morocco, and we can expect the new film once again to bring out the individuality of character and situation, using a very understated style of acting.

Elze of the Sands (*Elzé is smelynu*) is the fifteenth film of middle-generation director Algimantas Puipa. Its script was adapted from a classic story by German author Ernst Wichert (1851–1902) by Vytautas Žalakevičius, one of Lithuania's most famous directors and screenwriters, who died recently. Unlike his younger colleagues, Puipa is making a traditional film with a strong story, taking us to East Prussia in the nineteenth century, where the love between the children of two fishermen, one a rich German and the other a poor Lithuanian, causes great drama.

We are promised storms, historical authenticity, some interesting supporting characters and strong lead actors (Kostas Smoriginas and Antanas Šurna). The sensitive cameraman Viktoras Radzevičius

Still from ELZE OF THE SANDS

is certain to provide beautiful images of the Lithuanian coast. In contrast to the films of Navasaitis and Bartas, Puipa's work is likely to have a much wider appeal with the public.

Dr GRAŽINA ARLICKAITE is Head of International Relations and Sales Service at the Lithuanian Film Studio, and Director of Information Antenna. She is also a lecturer in the Film and Theatre Department of the Lithuanian Music Academy and a film researcher.

Production Companies

Lithuanian Film Studio
Nemenčinės pl. 4
2016 Vilnius
Lithuania
Robertas Urbonas – Director
Tel: (370 2) 763 444
Fax: (370 2) 764 254

Kinema
Grybautojų g. 30
2000 Vilnius
Lithuania
Daiva Vaitiekūnaitė – Producer
Tel: (370 2) 770 148/769 594
Fax: (370 2) 619 507

Film and Video Studio 'Kopa'
P.O. Box 2581
2015 Vilnius
Lithuania

Alicija Žukauskienė – Producer
Tel: (370 2) 223 451

Film Studio Nominum
Nemenčinės pl. 4
2016 Vilnius
Lithuania
Arūnas Matelis – Producer
Tel/Fax: (370 2) 700 337

Studija 2000
Nemenčinės pl. 4
2016 Vilnius
Lithuania
Kęstutis Petrulis – Producer
Tel: (370 2) 768 909
Fax: (370 2) 483 690

Filmfocus
Birutės g. 18
2004 Vilnius
Lithuania
Audrius Kuprevičius – Producer

Tel: (370 2) 230 803
Fax: (370 2) 223 769

Litnek
Nemenčinės pl. 4
2016 Vilnius
Lithuania
Arūnas Stoškus – Producer
Tel: (370 2) 768 381
Fax: (370 2) 727 702

Distributors

Lietuvos Kinas
Ozo g. 4
2600 Vilnius
Lithuania
Stasys Karamza – General Director
Tel: (370 2) 772 696
Fax: (370 2) 770 994

BDG
B. Radvilaitės g. 1-309
2026 Vilnius
Lithuania
Tel: (370 2) 610 935
Fax: (370 2) 611 141

Cinemark
Birutės g. 18
2004 Vilnius
Algis Šemeševičius – President
Tel: (370 2) 220 730
Fax: (370 2) 223 716

Bombos filmai
Žygimantų g. 6
2600 Vilnius
Lithuania
Gintaras Plytnikas – Manager
Tel: (370 2) 223 358/312 837
Fax: (370 2) 225 715

Amfiteatro filmai
Pylimo g. 17
2001 Vilnius
Lithuania
Tel: (370 2) 313 118
Fax: (370 2) 313 119

Useful Addresses

The Ministry of Culture of the Republic of Lithuania
Basanavičiaus g. 5
2683 Vilnius
Bonifacas Gintalas – Head of
Cinema Division
Tel: (370 2) 611 830
Fax: (370 2) 220 886

Lithuanian State Archive of Vision and Sound
O. Milašiaus g. 19
2016 Vilnius
Dainius Narvydas – Director
Tel: (370 2) 768 209 /762 587
Fax: (370 2) 764 489

Information Antenna
Nemenčinės pl. 4
2016 Vilnius
Tel/Fax: (370 2) 763 463
Gražina Arlickaitė – Director

Lithuanian Union of Cinematographers
Birutės g. 18
2004 Vilnius
Gytis Lukšas – President
Tel/Fax: (370 2) 220 759

The Association of Independent Producers
Nemenčinės pl. 4
2016 Vilnius
Tel: (370 2) 762 881
Fax: (370 2) 762 882

MALAYSIA
Baharudin A. Latif

The Multimedia Development Corporation (MDC), which is overseeing the development of the much-touted Multimedia Super Corridor (MSC), Malaysia's answer to Silicon Valley, has done good work to revive interest in the country as a location for international film-making. In 1998–99, two big Hollywood movies shot here: *Entrapment* and *Anna and the King*. The former sees Sean Connery and Catherine Zeta-Jones carrying out a daring heist at the Petronas Twin Towers, the world's tallest building. The second sees Jodie Foster reprise the Deborah Kerr role in a remake of *The King and I*. The last international film shot here which went on to make waves was *Indochine*, which won the Oscar for Best Foreign Film in 1994.

Flushed with its success in attracting the two Hollywood films, the MDC plans to build a $60m Entertainment Village within the MSC, which is the centrepiece of an ambitious plan to turn the country into a fully industrialised nation by the year 2020. Spread across 270 square miles, it will be a high-tech but distinctly green environment, where people live, work and study, interacting with other technologically advanced countries.

Construction of the E-Village is scheduled to begin towards the end of 1999 and the aim is for it to be fully operational by 2002, with a digital studio offering several sound stages, a colour processing lab and a theme park. It will be situated on a 480-hectare site near Cyberjaya, the new government headquarters.

There is great enthusiasm for the plan, as previous schemes to establish Universal

Amy Mastura in DREAM PRINCESS 2

A scene from the animated MAN SPIDER

Studios-style theme parks have been announced before without coming to fruition, killed off by the economic downturn. The MSC has already achieved a tremendous response internationally, with 94 companies signed up to the project, including Microsoft and Siemens Multimedia.

Profitable clichés

On our screens, producer-directors Yusof Haslam and Aziz M. Osman dominated the scene with their films **Dream Princess 2** (*Puteri Impiran 2*) and **Maria Mariana 2**, which played profitably. Both were romances in the classic, cliché-ridden tradition, following teenagers' romantic teething troubles on the route to true love, with plenty of pop music and a cast of pretty actor-singers such as Amy Mastura and Erra Fazira. Yusof's most recent film, **Embers** (*Bara*), also in the same vein, raked in $650,000 (RM2.4m) before fizzling out. Aziz's **Senaria – The Movie** a zany, Three Stooges-style slapstick comedy did far better, taking more than $1.3m. Yusof has a unique record as director, producer and actor, since all seven films produced by his Skop Productions have made a profit.

Shaws, which practically started the Malay movie industry back in the 1940, tried to make a comeback by joining forces with Astro, the 22-channel satellite station which began broadcasting in 1996. But despite featuring Awie, a regular in the hits of Yusof Haslam, their joint venture, the youth film **Breath Of Love** (*Nafas Cinta*), flopped miserably.

According to figures released by the National Film Development Corporation, total cinema attendance in 1998 was 14 million, down from 16 million in 1997. Total box-office gross was $25m, of which only $1.8m was taken by 11 local films. Attendance is expected to be severely down again by the end of 1999, yet more multiplexes continue to go up. Golden Screen Cinemas are scheduled to open an 18-screen site late in 1999, while Tanjung Golden Village and Smile-UA Cineplex Holdings are also building new screens.

BAHARUDIN A. LATIF is a professed film buff and historian and has written extensively on Malaysian cinema since the mid-1960s for more than 100 publications, including *Variety*, *Asiaweek*, *Movie/TV Marketing* and *Asia Magazine*.

Vanida Imran in THE LAST MALAY WOMAN

Recent and Forthcoming Films

PUTERI IMPIAN 2
(Dream Princess 2)

Script, Dir and Edit: Aziz M. Osman. Phot: Badarudin Azmi. Players: Amy Mastura, Hairie Othman, Chiko, Harahap Rashid, NorAliah Lee. Prod: Paradigm/Grand Brilliance.

MARIA MARIANA 2

Script and Dir: Yusof Haslam. Phot: Badarudin Azmi. Players: Erra Fazira, Ziana Zain, Awie. Prod: Skop/Grand Brilliance.

SENARIO THE MOVIE

Script and Dir: Aziz M. Osman. Phot: Badarudin Azmi. Players: Wahid Senario, Mazlanpet Pet, Azlee Jaafar, Shamsul Shamsuddin, Saifulazam. Prod: Paradigm/Grand Brilliance.

PEREMPUAN MELAYU TERAKHIR
(The Last Malay Woman)

Script: Syed Azidi, Syed Abd Aziz. Dir: Erma Fatima. Phot: Teoh Gay Hian. Players: Aizlan Yusof, Vanida Imran, Ahmad Yatim, Azri

Iskandar, Nanu Baharuddin. Prod: Grand Brilliance

BARA (Ember)

Script and Dir: Yusof Haslam. Phot. Omar Man. Players: Awie, Nasha Aziz, Rosyam Noor, Zamani. Prod.: Skop/Grand Brilliance.

Producers, Importers and Exhibitors

Grand Brilliance Sdn. Bhd.
99L, Jalan Tandak, off Jalan Bangsar
59100 Bangsar
Kuala Lumpur
Tel: (603) 284 6900
Fax: (603 284 6864

Golden Screen Cinemas Sdn. Bhd.
1 Jalan SS22/19, Damansara Jaya
47400 Petaling Jaya
Sellangor D.D.
Tel: (603) 719 5666
Fax: (603) 712 1655

Mega Pavilion Cinemas Sdn. Bhd.
Kompleks Bukit Jambul
3A-06-01 Jalan Rumbia
11900 Penang
Tel: (604) 646 7888
Fax: (604) 646 4113

Keris Motion Sdn. Bhd.
18B Jalan Tun Mohd. Fuad 1
Taman Dun Dr. Ismail
60000 Kuala Lumpur
Tel: (603) 716 6162
Fax: (603) 716 6167

Tanjung Golden Village Sdn. Bhd.
17th Floor, Menara Boustead
Jalan Raja Chulan
50200 Kuala Lumpur
Tel: (603) 244 3388
Fax: (603) 244 3301

Useful Address

FINAS
(The National Film Development Corporation Malaysia)
Studio Merdeka Complex
Lot 1661, Hulu Kelang
68000 Selangor D.E.
Tel: (603) 408 5722
Fax: (603) 407 5216

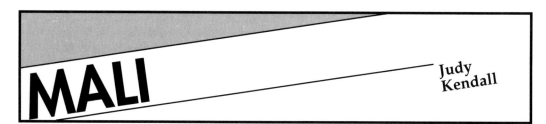

MALI

Judy Kendall

Despite the fact that Mali only produces a small trickle of films, they always seem to fare extremely well. **The Mother of the Sands** (*Faraw! Une Mère Des Sables*), by Abdoulaye Ascofaré, is still scooping up awards two years afters its initial release, winning the 1998 M-Net All Africa Film Awards. Ascofare's film and Adama Drabo's **Skirt Power** (*Taafe Fanga*), also from 1997, are frequently shown on international festival circuits.

This year, two Malian films have once again achieved notable international success. Chieck Oumar Sissoko's **Genesis** (*La Genèse*) graced the opening of the 1999 FESPACO in Burkina Faso and then went on to win the Prix de meilleur décor. It was also selected for Cannes 1999 in Un Certain Regard, one of only two African films to be so represented. *Genesis*, set in the timeless landscape of Mali, is an adaptation of chapters 23 to 37 of "Genesis", when, three hundred years after the flood, three clans are tearing each other apart.

The rivalry between animal-raisers, headed by Jacob, nomads, headed by Esau, and farmers, led by Hamor, mirrors almost perfectly current struggles between people leading different ways of life in rural Mali. The feud is deepened by Esau's hatred for Jacob for usurping his place in the family. As Jacob shuts himself away, mourning the supposed death of his much-loved son, Joseph, Hamor's son Sichem kidnaps Dina, Jacob's daughter.

The cast includes the two local superstars, Sotigui Kouyate and Balla Moussa Keita, as well as the internationally renowned musician Salif Keita, as Esau.

In **Life on Earth** (*La Vie sur Terre*), émigré Abderrahmane Sissako, returns, camera in hand, from France to his father's hometown in an isolated village in Mali, to record the passage of life to the year 2000.

Technology has almost passed this village by (the post office boasts the only, unreliable telephone) – and yet the film is full of activity as it catches moments in the lives of the villagers.

Sissako has chosen to work with a small crew and no script, producing a vibrant portrait of everyday life in rural Mali, which remains largely untouched by the millennial pressures and expectations of the "modern" world. This part-auto-biographical, part-fictional and largely improvised film is accompanied by the powerful music of Salif Keita. Visually stunning, it won first prize at Milan's 1999 Festival of African Cinema and received a special mention at FESPACO.

For the future, Malian directors have been asked to join in a series called **Being 50 in The Year 2000** (*Avoir 50 Ans en An 2000*), co-produced with Canada, though at press time this was still at the synopsis stage.

Recent Films

LA GENESE (Genesis)

Script: Jean-Louis Sagot Duvauroux. Dir: Chieck Oumar Sissoko. Phot: Lionel Cousin. Players: Sotigui Kouyaté, Balla Moussa Keita, Salif Keita. Prod: KORA FILMS, French Cinema Public Films.

LA VIE SUR TERRE (Life on Earth)

Script and Dir: Abderrahmane Sissako. Phot: Jacques Besse. Players: Abderrahmane Sissako, Nana Baby, Mohamed Sissako, Bourama Caulibaly. Prod: LaSept ARTER, Haut et Court.

Producer

Kora Films
114 avenue Merlin
BP 2337 Bamako
Tel: (223) 215 913
Fax (223) 217 762

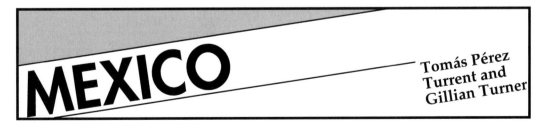

MEXICO

Tomás Pérez Turrent and Gillian Turner

O verall, 1998 was a slightly better year than 1997, in terms of the volume of film production and Mexican films' performance at the domestic box-office, although in general the new features were only of average quality.

Exceptions included **The First Night** (*La primera noche*), the third film by Alejandro Gamboa, which folowed the sexual initiation of a group of middle-class teenagers in Mexico City. **Optic Fiber** (*Fibra Optica*), Francisco Athie's second film, was an excellent, complex thriller about the murder of a union leader. Released in December, 1998, its box-office success was poorer than expected.

Carolos Markovich's **Who The Devil Is Juliet?** (*¿Quien diablos es Julieta?*), about the remarkable journey of two 16-year-old girls, one Mexican and one Cuban, deservedly awoke great interest and lasted for over three months in the cinemas. Finally, Arturo Ripstein's **No One Writes to the Colonel** (*El Coronel no tiene quien le*

escriba), an adaptation of a short novel by Gabriel García Marquez, was in competition at Cannes. Ripstein remains Mexico's best-known director, both at home and in Europe.

TOMÁS PÉREZ TURRENT has been awarded a scholarship from Mexico's Sistema Nacional de Creadores. During 1997 he gave courses on scriptwriting in various Mexican cities. His latest film script, *Birds Die of Fatigue*, was filmed in 1999.

Recent and Forthcoming Films

AVE MARIA (Hail Mary)

Script: Camille Thomasson. Dir: Eduardo Rossoff. Phot: Henner Hofmann. Players: Tere Lopez Tarin, Damian Alcazar, Ana Torrent, Alfredo Sevilla, Juan Diego Botto. Prod: Eduardo Rossoff, Andrea Kreuzhage, Lestes Films, IMCINE, Manga Films.

Jealous enemies cause Maria, the beautiful half-breed daughter of a Spanish duke, to lose all her property. She leaves the mission where she has been living and travels to her Indian grandmother's village, where she becomes a defender and protector of the villagers, and invokes her enemies' anger. Beautiful photography does not make up for the numerous errors and confusions in this first-time feature from .

Juan Carlos Rulfo, director of JUAN, I FORGOT I DON'T REMEMBER

COMO A VECES LLUEVE EN MAYO (Rain Falls in May)

Script: Sergio Vejar. Dir: Juan Antonio de la Riva. Phot: Angel Goded. Players: Luis Fernando, Claudia Goytia, Ignacio Guadalupe, Jorge Acuña, Enrique Guerrero. Prod: Roberto Gomez Bolaños, Televicine.

Juanito, aged eight, and his mother Hilaria are persecuted by the cruel, ignorant neighbours who will not accept that the child can see into the future. Only the village storekeeper will help them. De la Riva returns to the mountainous rural landscape he knows best, though this latest feature is not as effective as his first three movies.

DEL OLVIDO AL NO ME ACUERDO (Juan, I Forgot I Don't Remember)

Script, Dir and Editing: Juan Carlos Rulfo. Phot: Federico Barbabosa. Players: Justo Peralta, Rebeca Jimenez, Jesus Ramirez, Juan Jose Arreola. Prod: Maria Fernandez Suarez, La Media Luna Producciones, IMCINE, Producciones por Marca, Secretaria de Cultura del Estado de Colima, Rockefeller Foundation, Mexican Ministry of Tourism.

Rulfo's feature debut tells of the reminiscences and forgetfulness of old men from the Southern part of the State

of Jalisco. Everyone talks about Juan, but nobody remembers who he was. This is a fresh, original movie from the son of Juan Rulfo, one of the greatest Mexican writers. Despite some lapses, Rulfo shows himself to be a film-maker of whom much may be expected.

UN DULCE OLOR A MUERTE (A Sweet Scent of Death)

Script: Edna Necoechea, from the novel by Guillermo Arriaga. Dir: Gabriel Retes. Phot: Claudio Retes. Players: Karra Elejalde, Ana Alvarez, Diego Luna, Ignacio Retes, Gabriel Retes, Alvaro Carcaño. Prod: Miguel Necoechea, Pablo Barbachano,

Mirador Films, Ivania Films, Lola Films, FPCC-Aleph, Media-IMCINE, INCAM-Via Digital, Mexico-Spain-Argentina.

The secret lover of a murdered young woman sets out to kill her killer. In this typical thriller, Retes once again demonstrates the ease with which he juggles humour and tension.

UN EMBRUJO (Under a Spell)

Script: Martin Salinas, Carlos Carrera. Dir: Carrera. Phot: Rodrigo Prieto. Players: Blanca Guerra, Daniel Acuña, Mario Zaragoza, Luisa Huertas, Elpidia Carrillo, Guillermo Gil. Prod: Berta Navarro, Guillermo del Toro, Salamandra Producciones, Tabasco Films, IMCINE, Pueblo Viejo Producciones, FFCC.

In his fourth film, Carrera follows the love affair between a school teacher and one of her adolescent pupils. Blanca Guerra is always convincing as the teacher but the rest of the performances are far from believable.

BAJO CALIFORNIA: EL LIMITE DEL TIEMPO (Under California: the Edge of Time)

Script: Carlos Bolado, Ariel Garcia. Dir: Bolado. Phot: Claudio Rocha and Rafael Ortega. Players: Damian Alcazar, Jesus Ochoa, Gabriel Retes, Claudette Maille, Fernando Torre Lapham. Prod: Carlos Bolado, Salvador Aguirre, IMCINE, Producciones Sincronia.

The starting point of young film editor Carlos Bolado's directorial debut is a reflection on the meaning of life, as provoked by ancient rock paintings discovered in caves in the Baja California peninsula. An original film, full of unusual elements and a magical, sometimes violent atmoshpere.

LA OTRA CONQUISTA (The Other Conquest)

Script, Dir and Edit: Salvador Carrasco. Phot: Arturo de la Rosa. Players: Damian Delgado, Jose Carlos Rodriguez, Elpidia Carrillo, Josefina Echanove, Lourdes Villarreal, Honorato Magaloni. Prod: Placio Domingo, Enrique Gonzalez Torres and Alvaro Domingo for Carrasco and Domingo Films, Mexican Ministry of Social Development, FONCA-IMCINE, Tabasco Films, 20th Century Fox Mexico.

The action takes place in the years following the fall of Tenochtitlan, as Mexico gropes its way towards a new religious and political identity, and concerns the Aztec scribe Topiltzin. Though it is a slightly confusing tale, its distribution by Fox gives it opportunities seldom afforded domestic productions.

SANTITOS

Script: Maria Amparo Escandon. Dir: Alejandro Springall. Phot: Xavier Perez Grobet. Players: Dolores Heredia, Demian Bichir, Alberto Estrella, Ana Berta Espin, Fernando Torre Lapham. Prod: Alejandro Springall, Claudia

Florescano, Springall Pictures, IMCINE, Tabasco Films, Fonds Sud Cinema, Goldheart, Digital Pictures, Sogepaq (Mexico, United States, France, Canada, Spain).

The faith of Esperanza, a young widow mourning the death of her only daughter, is confirmed when St Jude appears before her and shows her the way to redeem her loss. She sets out on a journey which will take her from the deepest sorrow to a joyful reconciliation with life. Springall, yet another first-time director, who trained at film school in London, delivers a comedy with an almost faultless rhythm and shows that he has a fine way with actors.

SEXO, PUDOR Y LAGRIMAS (Sex, Shame and Tears)

Script: Antonio Serrano, based on his own stage play. Dir: Serrano. Phot: Xavier Perez Grobet. Players: Demian Bichir, Susana Zabaleta, Monica Dionne, Jorge Salinas, Cecilia Suarez, Angelica Aragon. Prod: Matthias Ehrenberg, Christian Valdelievre for Titan and S.L.P., IMCINE, Argos Cine.

Carlos, his wife Ana, and their friend Tomas live in an apartment in Mexico City. Across the street live Andrea and her husband Miguel. Andrea is tired of putting up with Miguel's infidelities and the foursome begin swapping partners. Screen version of a very successful stage comedy.

Producers

Alameda Films
Av. Division del Norte 2462-501
03300, Mexico D.F.
Tel: (52 5) 688 0330/5085/7318
Fax: (52 5) 605 8911

Amaranta Films
Eje 10 Sur,
Henriquez Urena 395
Col. Santo Domingo
Coyoacan
04369, Mexico D.F.
Tel: (52 5) 610 1037/1772/1171
Fax: (52 5) 610 1725

Direccion de Cortometraje (formerly Didecine)
Av. Division del Norte 2462, 3 piso
03300, Mexico D.F.
Tel: (52 5) 688 7614/7079
Fax: (52 5) 688 7611

Estudio Mexico/Altavista
CIE, Palmas 1005
Col. Lomas de Chapultepec
11000, Mexico D.F.
Tel: (52 5) 201 9000
Fax: (52 5) 201 9384

IMCINE
Tepic 40
Col. Roma Sur
06760, Mexico D.F.
Tel: (52 5) 574 2144/3155
Fax: (52 5) 574 1705/0712

Rio Mixcoac, S.C.L.
Morelos 33-4
Col. Torriello Guerra
Tlalpan
14060, Mexico D.F.
Tel: (52 5) 665 6417/8998
Fax: (52 5) 665/9123

Tabasco Films
Cuernavaca 17
Col. Condesa
06140, Mexico D.F.
Tel: (52 5) 286 1860/1890
Fax: (52 5) 286 2063

Distributors

Cine Alternativo
Pereferico Sur 4121
Col. Fuentes de Pedregal
14141, Mexico D.F.
Tel: (52 5) 420 1309, 645 4080
Fax: (52 5) 645 5704

Columbia TriStar/Buena Vista
Edif. Plaza Reforma
Prol. Paseo de la Reforma 600, PH-331
Col. Santa Fe Pena Blanca
01210, Mexico D.F.
Tel: (52 5) 258 2700/2702
Fax: (52 5) 570 1012/0957

Gussi (Artecinema/Videomax)
Gob. Ignacio Esteva 70
Col. San Miguel Chapultepec
Mexico D.F.
Tel: (52 5) 277 8999, 271 0955
Fax: (52 5) 516 5729

Latina, S.A.
Estudios Churubusco
Atletas 2
Col. Country Club
04220, Mexico D.F.
Tel: (52 5) 544 7805
Fax: (52 5) 549 1820

Twentieth Century Fox
Queretaro 65B, 2 piso
Col. Roma
06700, Mexico D.F.
Tel: (52 5) 574 2869/7068
Fax: (52 5) 574 6150; 564 8111

United International Pictures
Apartado Postel No. 70 B.I.S.
0600, Mexico D.F.
Tel: (52 5) 589 5727
Fax: (52 5) 589 7022

Videocine (incorporating Televicine)
America 173
Col. Parque San Andres
04040, Mexico D.F.
Tel: (52 5) 544 4405/549 3100
Fax: (52 5) 549 2911

VideoVisa
Av. Acoxpa 444
Col. Vergel del Sur
14340, Mexico D.F.
Tel: (52 5) 229 3100/3110
Fax: (52 5) 230 3332

Useful Addresses

Asociacion de Productores y Distribuidores de Peliculas Mexicanas
Av. Division del Norte 2462, 8 piso
03300, Mexico D.F.
Tel: (52 5) 688 7251/8705
Fax: (52 5) 688 7378

Camara Nacional de Cine (CANACINE)
Gen. Anaya 198
Col. San Diego Churubusco
04120, Mexico D.F.
Tel: (52 5) 688 0442/3258
Fax: (52 5) 688 8810

Cinemex
Montes Urales no 723
Col. Lomas de Chapultepec
México D.F. C.P. 11000
Tel: 540 6954/520 5184

Direccion General de Actividades Cinematograficas, UNAM
San Ildefonso 43
Col. Centro
06020, Mexico D.F.
Tel: (52 5) 704 3700/702 4454
Fax: (52 5) 702 4503

MOROCCO — Roy Armes

Thanks to the generous government funding administered by the Centre Cinématographique Marocain, under the leadership of Souheil Ben Barka, Morocco remains the most flourishing of the North African film industries, with seven features released in the last year.

The scheme whereby young film-makers are expected to have made three short films before receiving funding for a feature has shown its value with the production of **Goodbye, Travelling Showman**, the debut of photographer-turned director Daoud Aoulad Syad.

This is a nostalgic look at passing traditions, tracing the last trip to the South made by Kacem, a veteran showman, who is accompanied by his surly son and a young transvestite dancer, Rabii. As so often in North African cinema, we are offered a tale of frustrated dreams of escape and success, told here with understatement and a sharp eye for detail.

Less successful is the debut of another newcomer, the former television and film producer Mohamed Ismaïl, whose **Aouchtam** is a melodramatic story charting the rivalries between a blind autocrat and his two sons in a remote Berber community.

Quantity and quality

Hakim Noury has established himself as the most prolific Moroccan director of the 1990s, with his two latest features bringing his total for the decade to five. **A Simple News Item** looks back to the 1970s, with the story of a young journalist who pursues a corrupt, high-ranking official. Strenuous efforts are made to silence the writer, but none is successful. Then, one day, his death at the hands of 'a burglar' is announced in the papers – just another news item.

In Noury's **A Woman's Fate**, the protagonist is a woman who thinks she is happily married, but finds to her horror that her husband is jealous of her success and wants to take control of her inheritance. Even when he beats and humiliates her, she is unable to obtain a divorce until she can discover proof of his adultery. Both films are in the social realist style of which Noury, along with Jilali Ferhati, is a leading Moroccan exponent.

Abdelkader Lagtâa, who made an enormous reputation with his first feature, *A Love Affair in Casablanca* (one of the first local films to reach a mass audience in Morocco), has completed his third film, **The Casablancans**.

This interweaves three stories: a bookseller is terrified of the police, fearing that they may find something 'subversive' in his store; a woman comes to the notice of the authorities when she applies for a passport and is harassed by an official obsessed with her good looks; and a young boy – little more than a child – has his head filled with weird illusions by a fundamentalist teacher and is driven to attempt suicide. As in Noury's work, a vivid picture of life in contemporary urban Morocco emerges.

In contrast, **Cairo Street**, directed as his first solo film by the veteran Moroccan cinematographer Mohamed Abdelkrim Derkaoui, looks at the struggle for the emergence of a new society in Morocco in the years immediately after independence.

Women on top

Farida Benlyzid, one of Morocco's handful of female directors, made her first feature, *Gateway to Heaven*, in 1987. Since then, she has scripted two very different features for Mohamed Abderrahmane Tazi: *Badis*, a tale of female victims, and the highly successful comedy *In Search of My Wife's Husband*. She has made a welcome return to direction with **Keid Ensa**.

She spins a variation on a traditional tale of a rich merchant's daughter who, after much suffering, wins the love of a handsome but cruel prince, who insists that she admit the innate superiority of men over women.

Elegantly shot and well acted, this is a fascinating attempt at reinvigorating traditional story forms, although the first half, in which the future lovers play tricks on each other, works more effectively than the later repetitions essential to a fairy tale (three encounters with the prince, the birth of three children); these translate awkwardly to film.

In My Father's House, which mixes documentary and fiction, marks the equally welcome debut of another Moroccan-born female director, Fatima Jebli Ouazzani, who emigrated with her parents to the Netherlands at the age of 11, in 1970, and has lived there ever since.

In My Father's House looks at the highly controversial issue of virginity before marriage in Moroccan society, mixing memories and personal experiences. The greatest surprise at the Fifth Moroccan National Film Festival in Casablanca was that this film, made by a director with no firm links to the Moroccan production system, outclassed all the Moroccan fictional features of the past three years to take the top prize.

Recent Films

ADIEU FORAIN
(Goodbye, Travelling Showman)

Script: Ahmed Bouanani and Youssef Fadel. Dir: Daoud Aoulad Syad. Phot: Thierry Lebigre. Players: Hassan Esskalli, Mohamed Bastaoui, Abdellah Didane, Nezha Rahile, Mohamed Miftah. Prod: Les Films du Sud (Morocco).

AOUCHTAM

Script and Dir: Mohamed Ismaïl. Phot: Thierry Lebigre. Players: Mohamed El Kalfi, Hassan Esskalli, Fatima Ouchay, Abdellah Chakiri, Ghanim Sennak. Prod: MIA Production (Morocco).

LES CASABLANCAIS
(The Casablancans)

Script and Dir: Abdelkader Lagtaâ. Phot: Michel Laveaux. Players: Aziz Saadalah, Khadidja Assad, Salaheddine Ben Moussa, Mohamed Benbrahim. Prod:

Ecrans du Maroc (Morocco)/ Arcadia Films/POM Films (France)/ Les Films de l'Ile (Canada).

DANS LA MAISON DE MON PERE (In My Father's House)

Script and Dir: Fatima Jebli Ouazzani. Phot: Martin Kramer. Players: Non-professionals. Prod: NOS Sales (Netherlands)

DESTIN DE FEMME
(A Woman's Fate)

Script and Dir: Hakim Noury. Phot: Kamal Derkaoui. Players: Amal Ayouch, Amina Rachid, Rachid El Ouali, Hassan El Fad. Prod: Prod'Action (Morocco).

KEID ENSA

Script and Dir: Farida Benlyazid. Phot: Serge Palatsi. Players: Samira Akariou, Rachid El Ouali, Fatma Bensaïdane. Prod: Tingitania Films (Morocco).

RUE LE CAIRE (Cairo Street)

Script: Larbi Batma and Abderrahmane Khayat. Dir:

Mohamed Abdelkrim Derkaoui. Phot: Derkaoui and Gilles Moizon. Players: Siham Assif, Naîma El Mcherqui, Touria Jabrane, Amina Rachid. Prod: Cinescene International (Morocco).

UN SIMPLE FAIT DIVERS
(A Simple News Item)

Script and Dir: Hakim Noury. Phot: Kamal Derkaoui. Players: Rachid El Ouali, Hamid Zoughi, Mouna Fettou, Hamadi Amor. Prod: Prod'Action (Morocco).

Useful Addresses

Centre Cinématographique Marocain
Quartier industriel
avenue Al-Majd
BP 421
Rabat
Tel: (212 7) 798 110
Fax: (212 7) 798 108

Chambre Marocaine des Distributeurs de Films
36 boulevard d'Anfa
Casablanca
Tel: (212 5) 272 081

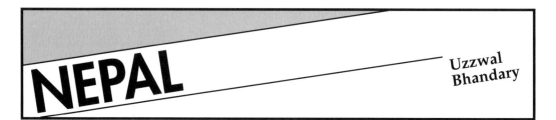

NEPAL

Uzzwal Bhandary

Nepalese cinema began in 1963, with Hrs Sin Khatai's *Mother* (*Aama*), starring Shiva Shanker and Bhuvan Thapa. Before that, the only Asian film to have been shown locally was *Satya Haris Chanrs*, an Indian film dubbed into Nepalese. In those days there were very few cinemas in the country, almost all situated in the capital, Kathmandu. With at most one or two Nepalese films produced each year, the screens were dominated by imported Indian (Hindi) films.

Today, the cinemas still show mostly Indian films, but we can now see their influence on our own film-makers, who imitate slavishly the Hindi films' formulaic plots and brash story-telling. The results are mostly of poor quality, but there are some impressive films being made, such as **Token of Love** (*Prem Pinda*), produced and directed by Yadav Kharel, and **Borderline** (*Sims Rekha*).

Bhanubhakta: First Poet (*Aadi Kabi Bhanubhakta*), directed by Yadav Kharel, was in post-production as this article went to press. It will be a landmark in Nepalese cinema, as the first film about the nation's history. It tells the life story of Nepal's first

Still from the first-ever film about Nepalese history, BHANUBHAKTA: FIRST POET

great poet, widely considered to have been the man who unified Nepal culturally and linguistically. However, having viewed a rough cut, I would say the film's commercial prospects may be uncertain at best. The choice of this historical subject, though, is encouraging, as the best thing that could happen to Nepalese cinema would be for its film-makers to shrug off the influence of Indian films and concentrate on national concerns.

UZZWAL BHANDARY has been an actor in Nepalese film and television for 16 years. He also works as a tour guide and travel consultant.

NETHERLANDS
Pieter van Lierop

In the spring of 1999, a minor miracle occurred in the Netherlands. The children's film **Abel, The Flying Liftboy** (*Abeltje*), which cost $5m to make, took the same amount at the box-office, attracting 900,000 viewers. Ben Sombogaart's effects-heavy film thus exceeded the combined gross of Disney's *Mulan* and DreamWorks' *The Prince of Egypt*. The video release and foreign sales can only increase the satisfaction of writer-producer Burny Bos.

This was exactly the kind of success the Netherlands film industry had been waiting for, since Dutch feature films regularly win awards at festivals but seldom recoup their costs. Mike van Diem won the 1998 Oscar for Best Foreign-Language Film, with *Character*, repeating the success of Marleen Gorris with *Antonia's Line* in 1996 and Fons Rademakers' with *De Aanslag* in 1987, a run of success unequalled by any other non-English-speaking country in the same period, yet the bitter truth is that none of these films broke even. In fact, *Character* sold only 140,000 tickets on home turf.

Admittedly, the Dutch are not fanatical cinemagoers. In 1998, the 15.6 million inhabitants bought 20 million tickets – the lowest per capita ratio in Europe. Recent years have seen a certain amount of growth, but the first half of 1999 showed a slight fall on the previous year.

The government bodies which provide film production grants have for a long time been convinced that film-makers have taken too little account of the tastes and interests of the (predominately young) cinema audience. A more commercial approach is required, they argue.

During the past ten years, Dutch producers have developed a tendency to act more as intermediaries than businessmen. They have concentrated too much on the acquisition of subsidies and budget management, and guaranteeing themselves a hefty fee. They have taken too little trouble to sell films once they are finished – the point at which, for an American producer, there is still much work to be done.

The state steps in

One of those urging a drastic change in mentality is Rick van der Ploeg, Dutch Junior Minister of Culture, who is responsible for the implementation of an ambitious plan initiated by his predecessor. The Nederlands Fonds Voor De Film (Dutch Film Fund), which subsidises homegrown films, has had its annual budget increased from $8.7m (17.3m guilders) to $10.4m.

More importantly, there are now greater incentives for private concerns to invest in the film industry. Alongside fiscal measures, an intermediary agency (FINE

Still from the hugely popular children's adventure, ABEL, THE FLYING LIFTBOY

BV) with a start-up capital of $7.5m has been running since 1997, as a magnet to attract venture capital. FINE has a committee of experts providing advice on the commercial potential of projects, and a manager, Richard Woolley, has been appointed at the Filmfonds to guide film-makers in a commercial direction.

It is also important that the production volume increases and that Dutch TV companies participate more actively. The new 'Telefilmplan' has been designed to produce a steady stream of 'Movies of the Week'. An initial series of six films has been completed and broadcast, and a second series is in production.

The government initiatives have been received with great enthusiasm in the Dutch film world. A number of films have subsequently been made that fitted the profile supported by the Ministry pretty well; films aimed at young people, making use of popular actors from Dutch TV soaps.

But when, in the autumn of 1998, Warner Brothers and UIP provided big releases for two Dutch features, **The 14th Chick**, by Hany Abu-Assad, and **Siberia**, by Robert Jan Westdijk (a well-acted tale about two petty thieves who seduce and rob foreign female backpackers in Amsterdam youth hostels), the results were disappointing.

Early in 1999 the situation worsened. Lodewijk Crijns's **Jesus Is A Palestinian** (set in the Amsterdam youth scene) and Jos Stelling's **No Trains, No Planes** (an overlong, unoriginal tragi-comedy set in a pub) were met by audience indifference, despite large publicity campaigns by Warner. Such setbacks may make it difficult for FINE to find private investors for Dutch productions. Co-productions, with minority Dutch participation, such as recent films by Peter Greenaway and Paul Cox, may be the best we can hope for.

Up, up and away!

A happier example is provided by the remarkable success of *Abel, The Flying Liftboy*. Based on a well-known children's book from notorious Dutch writer Annie Schmidt, it is about a boy who hates school and takes a job as a lift boy. In the elevator he pushes the forbidden green button and immediately flies away, together with a colourful bunch of passengers, to adventures in New York and Latin America.

It is a striking spectacle with, by Dutch standards, great special effects, and its success gave a huge boost to the already lively Dutch children's film scene. Ineke Houtman (*Scratches on the Table*) and Ger Poppelaars (*The Missing Link*) have also provided meritorious entertainment for the young in recent times, while new films by Martin Lagestee (*The Red Swan*) and Maria Peters (*Little Crumb*) are on the way.

The slim chance of reaching a substantial audience is not deterring some young film-makers from taking almost heroic initiatives. Will Wissink and Zebi Damen recently made their debut with the impressive **Dropouts**, made initially with

Still from Will Wissink's DROPOUTS

no subsidised support. Their film about urban nomads in Amsterdam is distinguished by both its artistic inspiration and social commitment, a rare combination in contemporary Dutch cinema.

Director Eddy Terstall is also something of a special case. Each year, without making use of subsidies, this director makes a graceful, low-budget film and, in the exceptionally witty **Based On The Novel**, focuses on the problematical situation of film in the Netherlands. After winning the Golden Calf for Best Experimental Film, a young director is hired to make a mainstream film based on a bestseller. He uses his fresh prestige to screen-test three actresses for a leading role – and shamelessly attempts to get them into bed.

But they outsmart the self-indulgent artist, who finally loses his directing job when the producer suddenly has a preference for Mike van Diem. This is a smartly-written and intriguing picture, which succeeds both as a sparkling comedy of manners and as a satire on opportunism in Dutch cinema. The three actresses are convincing, with Nadja Hupscher in particular an endearing discovery.

Another highly self-willed film-maker is Peter Delpeut, who at press time was

completing **Diva Dolorosa**, having last year picked up two awards for *Felice ... Felice ...* at the Nederlands Film Festival, where *The Polish Bride* (by Karim Traïdia) also took double honours. In Chicago, *Felice ... Felice ...* was awarded a Golden Plaque for best visuals.

The even greater honour of the Special Jury Award in Chicago went to *Wind with the Gone*, directed by Dutch-Argentine Alejandro Agresti, who had already picked up the Golden Shell at San Sebastian with his superior Patagonian satire. In Utrecht, Agresti's film was wrongly ignored, as was Danniel Danniel's excellent *Winter '89*, which was evidently seen as a basically Czech film, in the same way that *Wind with the Gone* was probably seen as insufficiently Dutch.

Such considerations did not seem to apply to documentaries, however, as the Golden Calf in this discipline went to **The House of My Father**, directed by Fatima Jebli Ouazanni from Morocco. Sonia Herman Dolz won the Special Jury Award won for her sublime documentary **Lagrimas Negras**, about elderly Cuban musicians on a concert tour.

It is interesting that, at a time when film-makers such as George Sluizer, Marleen Gorris, Jeroen Krabbé, Dick Maas and Mike Van Diem are following in the footsteps of Paul Verhoeven and Jan de Bont and looking towards the English-language film industry, Dutch cinema is at the same time receiving fertile input from directors born outside the Netherlands.

Nadja Hüpscher in BASED ON THE NOVEL

Finally, Paul Verhoeven has been named as 'Dutch film-maker of the millennium', in a poll of more than 1,000 voters which included many prominent members of the film industry. His films *Soldier of Orange* and *Turkish Delight* topped the poll.

PIETER VAN LIEROP has written about film since 1974 and is film editor of the Netherlands Press Association GPD (18 syndicated daily papers). He has been a correspondent for *IFG* since 1981.

Recent and Forthcoming Films

ABELTJE
(Abel, The Flying Liftboy)

Script: Burny Bos. Dir: Ben Sombogaart. Phot: Reinier van Brummelen. Players: Ricky van Gastel, Soraya Smith, Marisa van Eyle, Frits Lambrechts, Annet Malherbe. Prod: Burny Bos for Bos Bros.

DE BOEKVERFILMING
(Based on the Novel)

Script and Dir: Eddy Terstall. Phot: Willem Nagtglas. Players: Dirk Zeelenberg, Femke de Brouwer, Alette Dirkse, Nadja Hüpscher. Prod: Wim Louwrier for DKP Amsterdam.

THE DELIVERY

Script: David Hilton. Dir: Roel Reiné. Phot: Jan van den Nieuwenhuijzen. Players: Freddy Douglas, Esmée de la Bretonière, Rik Launspach. Prod: Roel Reiné and Thijs Bayens for Two Independent Films.

DO NOT DISTURB

Script and Dir: Dick Maas. Phot: Marc Felperlaan. Players: William Hurt, Francesca Brown, Jennifer Tilly. Prod: Laurens Geels for First Floor Features.

DROPOUTS

Script: Zebi Damen. Dir: Will Wissink. Phot: Willem Helwig. Players: Peter Gorissen, Ashwin Mohanpersad, Zebi Damen. Prod: Wissink and Damen for Dropouts Film Productions.

JEZUS IS EEN PALESTIJN
(Jesus is a Palestinian)

Script and Dir: Lodewijk Crijns. Phot: Menno Westendorp. Players: Hans Teeuwen, Kim van Kooten, Dijn Blom, Peer Mascini. Prod: Martin Lagestee for Lagestee Film BV.

LEF (Guts)

Script and Dir: Ron Termaat. Phot: Maarten Kramer. Players: Viggo Waas, Alice Reys, Rick Engelkes, Kees Geel. Prod: Ron Termaat and Marijke Kloosterman for C.V. Lef.

NO TRAINS NO PLANES

Script: Jos Stelling and Hans Heesen. Dir: Stelling. Phot: Goert Giltaij. Players: Dirk van Dijck, Gene Bervoets, Ellen ten Damme, Katja Schuurman. Prod: Anton Kramer for Jos Stelling Films BV.

DE PIJNBANK
(Pain is the Name of the Game)

Script: Justus van Oel. Dir: Theo van Gogh. Phot: Tom Erisman. Players: Paul de Leeuw, Jack Wouterse, Roeland Fernhout, Eric van Sauers. Prod: Dave Schram, Hans Pos en Maria Peters for Shooting Star Filmcompany.

REGRETS

Script and Dir: Erik Lieshout and Arno Hagers. Phot: Reinier van Brummelen. Cast: Thom Hoffman, Jonna Koster. Prod: Roland Wigman for Outcast Pictures.

DE RODE ZWAAN
(The Red Swan)

Script: Sjoerd Kuyper. Dir: Martin

Lagestee. Phot: Lex Wertwijn. Players: Rufus Heikens, André van den Heuvel, Annet Nieuwenhuijzen, Sanne Himmelreich. Prod: Laurens Geels and Dick Maas for First Floor Features.

SHABONDAMA ELEGY

Script and Dir: Ian Kerkhof. Phot: Tsuji Thomohiko. Players: Thom Hoffman, Hoshino Mai, Ito Kiyomi, Yamazaki Thomoyuki, Tanak Yohji. Prod: Suzuki Akihiro for Stance Company.

SOMBREMAN'S ACTION

Script: Casper Verbrugge and Hans Heesen. Dir: Verbrugge. Phot: Tom Erisman. Players: Dirk Roofthooft, Serge Henri Valcke, Oda Spelbos, Frits Lambrechts. Prod: Hans de Weers and Hans de Wolf for Egmond Film & Television.

VAARWEL PAVEL
(Farewell Pavel)

Script and Dir: Rosemarie Blank. Phot: Martin Gressmann. Players: Valery Kuchareschin, Boris Khvoles, Isil Zabludowsky, Vlatka Simac. Prod: René Scholten for Studio Nieuwe Gronden.

WINTER '89

Script and Dir: Danniel Danniel. Phot: Vladimir Smutny. Players: Markéta Hrubesova, Petr Motloch, Juliana Johanidesova. Prod: Harry de Winter and Anton Smit for IDTV and Etamp Filmproduction Praha.

Producers

Added Films International
Lange Muiderweg 616
1398 PB Muiden
Tel: (31 29) 426 3277
Fax: (31 29) 426 4868

Argus Film Productions
PO Box 58188
1040 HD Amsterdam
Tel: (31 20) 693 1379
Fax: (31 20) 597 4412

Ariel Film Produkties
Prinsengracht 770
1017 LE Amsterdam
Tel: (31 20) 638 8199
Fax: (31 20) 638 0149

Belbo Film Productions BV
Sarphatikade 11
1071 WV Amsterdam
Tel: (31 20) 638 7999
Fax: (31 20) 638 8209

Cilia van Dijk
Ged. Voldersgracht 20
2011 WD Haarlem
Tel: (31 23) 531 4273
Fax: (31 23) 542 1097

CinéTé Film Prods.
Elisabeth Wolffstraat 45
1053 TR Amsterdam
Tel: (31 20) 685 5339
Fax: (31 20) 689 1954

Cine Ventura
Hudsonstraat 52
1057 SN Amsterdam
Tel: (31 20) 683 7439
Fax: (31 20) 616 0500

DNU Film BV
Rolf Orthel/Evelyn Voortman
Zoutkeetsgracht 116-1
1013 LC Amsterdam
Tel: (31 20) 622 0255
Fax: (31 20) 626 1885

Ecco Films
Orlow Seunke
PO Box 53223
1007 RE Amsterdam
Tel: (31 20) 623 9457
Fax: (31 20) 623 7900

Egmond
Keizersgracht 382
1018 GA Amsterdam
Tel: (31 20) 638 7886
Fax: (31 20) 427 2020

First Floor Features
PO Box 30086
1303 AB Almere
Tel: (31 36) 532 7003
Fax: (31 36) 532 7940

Graniet Film
Marc van Warmerdam/
Ton Schippers
Anjeliersstraat 470
1015 NL Amsterdam
Tel: (31 20) 421 2820
Fax: (31 20) 625 1024

Grote Broer Filmwerken
Clea de Koning/
Robert Jan Westdijk
PO Box 58141
1040 HC Amsterdam
Tel: (31 20) 616 1879/622 4705
Fax: (31 20) 616 1879

IJswater Films
Kromme Mijdrechtstraat 110–4
1079 LD Amsterdam
Tel: (31 20) 442 1760
Fax: (31 20) 442 1727

Lagestee Film BV
Martin Lagestee
Maarlemmer Houttuinen 307
Tel: (31 20) 627 3374
Fax: (31 20) 626 1049

Linden Film BV
Chopinstraat 25
1077 GM Amsterdam
Tel: (31 20) 679 3128
Fax: (31 20) 664 1046

Lowland Productions
Duivendrechtsekade 82
1096 AJ Amsterdam
Tel: (31 20) 668 0492
Fax: (31 20) 694 1018

Lucid Eye Productions
Oude Schans 69 A
1011 KW Amsterdam
Tel: (31 20) 623 0354
Fax: (31 20) 638 2968

MGS Film Amsterdam BV
Golden Egg Film
Singel 64
1015 AC Amsterdam
Tel: (31 20) 623 1593/662 9960
Fax: (31 20) 624 3181

Movies Film Productions BV
Postbus 432
1200 AK Hilversum
Tel: (31 35) 261 500
Fax: (31 35) 248 418

Nico Crama Films
Nico Crama
Stevinstraat 261
2587 EJ The Hague
Tel: (31 70) 354 4964

Odusseia Films
Eddy Wijngaarde
Stadhouderskade 6
1054 E5 Amsterdam
Tel: (31 20) 607 1199
Fax: (31 20) 607 1198

Pieter van Huystee Film & TV
Keizersgracht 784
1017 EC Amsterdam
Tel: (31 20) 421 0606

Rolf Orthel Film Prods.
Zoutkeetsgracht 1161
1013 LC Amsterdam
Tel: (31 20) 622 0255
Fax: (31 20) 626 1885

Roeland Kerbosch Film Prods. BV
Keizersgracht 678
1017 ET Amsterdam
Tel: (31 20) 623 0390
Fax: (31 20) 627 9879

Shooting Star Filmcompany BV
Prinsengracht 546
1017 KK Amsterdam
Tel: (31 20) 624 7272
Fax: (31 20) 626 8533

Sigma Film Productions BV
Bolensteinseweg 3
3603 CP Maarssen
Tel: (31 34) 657 0430/0431
Fax: (31 34) 656 9764

Jos Stelling Film Prods. BV
Springweg 50-52
3511 VS Utrecht
Tel: (31 30) 313 789
Fax: (31 30) 310 968

Studio Nieuwe Gronden
Van Hallstraat 52
1051 HH Amsterdam
Tel: (31 20) 686 7837
Fax: (31 20) 682 4367
Telex: 12682 sngfp

Distributors

Cinemien
Entrepotdok 66
1018 AD Amsterdam
Tel: (31 20) 627 9501/623 8152/
625 8357
Fax: (31 20) 6209857

Columbia TriStar Films (Holland) BV
PO Box 533
1000 AM Amsterdam
Tel: (31 20) 573 7655
Fax: (31 20) 573 7656

Contact Film Cinematheek
PO Box 3100
6802 DC Arnhem
Tel: (31 85) 434 949
Fax: (31 85) 511 316

Express Film
Heemraadschapslaan 13
1181 TZ Amstelveen
Tel: (31 20) 641 2331

Filmtrust BV
Molenkade 57A
1115 AC Duivendrecht
Tel: (31 20) 695 7719/695 5503
Fax: (31 20) 695 6625

Holland Film Releasing BV
De Lairessestraat 111-115
1075 HH Amsterdam
Tel: (31 20) 575 1751
Fax: (31 20) 662 2085

Hungrey Eye Pictures BV
Duivendrechtsekade 82
1096 AJ Amsterdam
Tel: (31 20) 668 6126
Fax: (31 20) 668 3452

Indies Filmdistribution
Regentesselaan 20–26
1217 EG Hilversum
Tel: (31 35) 538 5300
Fax: (31 35) 538 5301

Still from Jos Stelling's NO TRAINS, NO PLANES

photo: Felix Kalkman

International Art Film
Vondelpark 3
1071 AA Amsterdam
Tel: (31 20) 589 1418/589 1426
Fax: (31 20) 683 3401

Melior Films BV
Steynlaan 8
1217 JS Hilversum
Tel: (31 35) 245 542
Fax: (31 35) 235 906

Paradiso Entertainment Nederland
Anthony Fokkerweg 1
1057 CM Amstelveen
Tel: (31 20) 615 9222
Fax: (31 20) 614 2027

RVC Entertainment BV and Argus Film BV
PO Box 142
1200 AC Hilversum
Tel: (31 35) 625 1200
Fax: (31 35) 624 7483

Shooting Star Film Distributors
Prinsengracht 546
1017 KK Amsterdam
Tel: (31 20) 624 7272
Fax: (31 20) 626 8533

United International Pictures Netherlands
Willemsparkweg 112
1071 HN Amsterdam
Tel: (31 20) 662 2991
Fax: (31 20) 662 3240

Universal Pictures
Postbus 432
1200 AK Hilversum

Tel: (31 35) 261 500
Fax: (31 35) 248 418

Warner Brothers Holland
De Boelelaan 16 III
1083 HJ Amsterdam
Tel: (31 20) 541 1211
Fax: (31 20) 644 9001

Useful Addresses

Ministry of Education, Culture and Science Department of Film
PO Box 3009
2280 ML Rijswijk
Tel: (31 70) 340 6148
Fax: (31 70) 340 5742

COBO Fund
Jeanine Hagen
Postbus 26444 (NOS TV)
1202 JJ Hilversum
Tel: (31 35) 775 348

Dutch Film and Television Academy
(Nederlandse Film en Televisie Academie)
Ite Boeremastraat 1
1054 PP Amsterdam
Tel: (31 20) 683 0206
Fax: (31 20) 612 6266

Maurits Binger Film Instituut
Nieuwezijds
Voorburgwal 4-10
1012 RZ Amsterdam
Tel: (31) 20 421 2048
Fax: (31) 20 638 3002

Dutch Film Fund
(Stichting Nederlands Fonds voor de
Film)
Jan Luykenstraat 2
1071 CM Amsterdam
Tel: (31 20) 664 3368
Fax: (31 20) 675 0398

Holland Film
Jan Luykenstraat 2
1071 CM Amsterdam
Tel: (31 20) 664 4649
Fax: (31 20) 664 9171

KNF (Dutch Film Critics Circle)
Prinsengracht 770
1017 LE Amsterdam
Tel: (31 20) 623 0221
Fax: (31 20) 627 5923

MEDIA Desk/AV Platvorm
PO Box 256
1200 AG Hilversum
Tel: (31 35) 238 641
Fax: (31 35) 218 541

**Netherlands Institute for
Animation Film**
Bachlaan 640

5011 BN Tilburg
Tel: (31 13) 562 925
Fax: (31 13) 562 428

Sources
(Stimulating Outstanding Resources
for Creative European
Screenwriting)
Jan Luykenstraat 92
1071 CT Amsterdam
Tel: (31 20) 672 0801
Fax: (31 20) 672 0399

**Association of Dutch Film
Theatres**
(Associated with the Netherlands
Cinematographic Assn.)
Prinsengracht 770
1017 LE Amsterdam
Tel: (31 20) 626 7602
Fax: (31 20) 627 5923

Europe Cinema Nederland
PO Box 75242
1070 AE Amsterdam

GNS
(The Film-makers Society of the
Netherlands)

PO Box 581
1000 AN Amsterdam
Tel: (31 20) 676 5088
Fax: (31 20) 676 5837

KNF
(Circle of Dutch Film Critics)
Snelliuslaan 78
1222 TG Hilversum
Tel: (31 35) 856 115

**The Netherlands
Cinematographic Foundation**
(Nederlandse Federatie van
Cinematografie)
Jan Luykenstraat 2
1071 CM Amsterdam
Tel: (31 20) 679 9261
Fax: (31 20) 675 0398

NBF
(The Association of Film and TV
Directors)
Jan Luykenstraat 2
1071 CM Amsterdam
Tel: (31 20) 664 6588
Fax: (31 20) 664 3707

NEW ZEALAND — Peter Calder

A long time ago, in a country far, far away, a young man called Peter Jackson spent all his weekends shooting a no-budget splatter picture in the hills above the seaside community north of Wellington where he was raised. *Bad Taste* it was called, an aptly-named alien invasion extravaganza of exploding latex heads. But it was the first film in a career that has led to a project with a budget roughly equivalent to the combined cost of all the films made locally in the quarter-century since the modern era of New Zealand film-making began, with Roger Donaldson's *Sleeping Dogs*.

The unquestionable sensation of the New Zealand film world this past year was the announcement that Jackson (whose biggest previous outing was to direct the Michael J. Fox vehicle *The Frighteners*) will make three films based on the classic fantasy trilogy *The Lord Of The Rings*.

At press time, big names were being batted around. Wellington was abuzz with suggestions that Sean Connery might be cast – he was spotted lunching in the suburb where Jackson has his headquarters and high-tech studio – and separate reports in Australia and America had it that Keanu Reeves and Bruce Willis had asked Jackson to consider them. Principal photography is slated to start this southern spring on the New Line production, which will feature 65 speaking parts and thousands of extras.

The three-film budget is well under $150 million and local talent is delighted at Jackson's prediction that 90 per cent of the money will stay here. But the project is a testament to America's growing interest in this country as a location. In August Martin Campbell was scheduled to start shooting *The Vertical Limit*, a mountain rescue drama starring Chris O'Donnell, and Renaissance Pacific, which has made the *Xena* and *Hercules* television shows here, has announced plans for two more action projects.

In February, representatives of seven major Hollywood enterprises toured the country getting to know what could become American film-making's most remote backlot. The group included heads of production or finance from DreamWorks, Disney, Sony and MGM.

Raising the standard

All this occurs against the background of the most productive year since the mid-1980s for the local film industry. The New Zealand Film Commission (a film bank which provides script development support and some production finance, and also acts as a sales agent) took no fewer than eight new titles to Cannes this year, compared with last year's three. And if the quality did not always match the quantity – of some titles, the less said the better – it was nevertheless a cheering sign of an industry in its best heart for some time, not least because of the presence of seven first-time directors.

The commission has conspicuously lifted its game under the stewardship of chief executive Ruth Harley, who is now well into her third year at its helm and its ScreenVisionNZ project, established to provide complete finance for low-budget features, is beginning to bear fruit.

Its first success, **Via Satellite**, was an adaptation of a successful stage play about skeletons rattling in the family closet of an Olympic swimmer who is about to be joined, via satellite, with her nearest and dearest on the other side of the world. A genial and genuinely indigenous comedy,

it was directed with considerable flair by its writer, Anthony McCarten.

More consciously stylish – in fact, sometimes nonsensical and pretentious – was Niki Caro's debut feature, **Memory and Desire**, the story of a Japanese couple who elope to New Zealand, where the man tragically drowns on the honeymoon. It enjoyed only moderate success at the local box-office but, for all its flaws, was an impressive debut which showcased a talent of considerable promise.

Return of the Maori

The highest-profile local release was **What Becomes of the Broken-Hearted**, the sequel to Lee Tamahori's gut-wrenching 1994 urban ghetto drama, *Once Were Warriors*. Temuera Morrison reprised his role as the volcanically violent Jake Heke – the film focuses much more on him than on his ill-used wife Beth (Rena Owen), as he seeks redemption when his estranged son becomes embroiled in a gang war.

Temuera Morrison in WHAT BECOMES OF THE BROKEN-HEARTED?

Behind the camera, none of the *Warriors* crew was at work: the script was by Alan Duff, the author of the original novel, and the hand of Ian Mune, the doyen of loyally local directors, was on the helm. And if it lacked the emotional punch of its predecessor it was still distinguished by the biggest opening weekend ever for an indigenous film, taking more than $500,000 off 40 prints in its first five days. Duff, incidentally, tried to raise production finance for a third film of one of his novels, *One Night Out Stealing*, but sold only half of a $3 million equity issue before heading back to the drawing board.

The rest of the slate the commission took to Cannes was less memorable, although special mention should be made of Annie Goldson's **Punitive Damage**, a potent and poignant documentary about the murder of a young New Zealander by Indonesian troops in the infamous Dili massacre in East Timor in 1991. The film, steadied by the veteran talent of Gaylene Preston (who made 1989's quirky comedy, *Ruby and Rata*, and the excellent documentary *War Stories*) enjoyed a successful nationwide cinematic release which coincided with the Indonesian elections. **When Love Comes**, a drama about a fading singing star who returns to New Zealand to revisit her roots, offered Rena Own her first starring role since *Warriors* and earned itself an invitation to Sundance.

Will bust follow boom?

Local filmgoing, which has undergone a decade of double-digit growth in the 1990s (much of which has simply made up for the stagnation resulting from years of neglect by a complacent exhibitor duopoly) seems finally to have reached a plateau. Attendance was up two per cent, but industry observers took the view that without the extraordinary box-office success of *Titanic* and *There's Something About Mary*, attendance would actually have fallen for the first time since the 1980s.

Some distributors are warning that the multiplex boom has saturated the market: in 1990 there were 140 screens nationwide, many of them in tatty condition, but we will enter the new millennium with more than 300 screens servicing a population of less than four million.

Meanwhile a $40m development in the centre of the largest city, Auckland, which incorporates a 12-screen multiplex, an Imax cinema, New Zealand's first Planet Hollywood and Australasia's second branch of Borders bookstore, will be welcome, not least because it has included a complete refurbishment of the Civic, one of the hemisphere's finest deco picture palaces.

More significantly, the Civic centre heralds a pioneering joint venture between the two major exhibition chains, Hoyts, the Australian giant recently acquired by media magnate Kerry Packer, and Force

Corporation, the local property developer which operates under the banner of the other Australian market leader, Village. The two exhibitors have hitherto competed fiercely but hope to save on overheads by co-operating.

Force is expanding its operations in Argentina (Recoleta in Buenos Aires) and in Fiji's second city Lautoka, with new 'plexes in both sites. Fijians are among the world's most enthusiastic cinemagoers – Suva's 300,000 people buy a million tickets a year.

PETER CALDER is a columnist and feature writer for the *New Zealand Herald*, where he has been a film critic since 1985.

Recent and Forthcoming Films

WHAT BECOMES OF THE BROKEN-HEARTED

Script: Alan Duff. Dir: Ian Mune. Players: Temuera Morrison, Rena Owen, Clint Eruera, Nancy Brunning. Prod: Bill Gavin.

PUNITIVE DAMAGE

Documentary. Dir: Annie Goldson. Phot: Leon Narbey. Prods: Goldson, Gaylene Preston.

SAVAGE HONEYMOON

Script and Dir: Mark Beesley.Players: Nicholas Eadie, Perry Piercy, Sophia Hawthorne. Prod: Steve Sachs.

Earthy romantic comedy set among the motorcycle and hot-rod set in working-class west Auckland.

SCARFIES

Script: Robert Sarkies, Duncan Sarkies. Dir: Robert Sarkies. Players: Willa O'Neill, Neill Rea. Prod: Lisa Chatfield.

Black comedy about university students who become mixed up in crime.

Sophia Hawthorne and Craig Hall in SAVAGE HONEYMOON

VIA SATELLITE

Script: Anthony McCarten, Greg McGee. Dir: McCarten. Players: Danielle Cormack, Rima Te Wiata, Tim Balme, Jodie Dorday. Prod: Philippa Campbell.

WHEN LOVE COMES

Script: Garth Maxwell, Peter Wells, Rex Pilgrim. Dir: Maxwell. Players: Rena Owen, Dean O'Gorman, Simon Prast. Prod: Jonathan Dowling, Michele Fantl.

Producers

Ample Films
PO Box 90 227
Auckland
Tel: (64 9) 378 9839
Fax: (64 9) 376 3999

Communicado Ltd
PO Box 5779
Wellesley Street
Auckland
Tel: (64 9) 379 3734
Fax: (64 9) 377 7419

Fiona Copland
PO Box 47632
Ponsonby
Auckland
Tel: (64 9) 413 8405
Fax: (64 9) 413 8403
e-mail: fcopland@ibm.net

Essential Productions Ltd
45A Crummer Road
Ponsonby
Auckland 1002
Tel: (64 9) 378 9754
Fax: (64 9) 303 1630
e-mail: jonathan@esspro.co.nz

Frame Up Films Ltd
PO Box 46 065
Herne Bay
Auckland
Tel: (64 9) 360 0509
Fax: (64 9) 360 0278

Gibson Group
PO Box 6185
Te Aro
Wellington
Tel: (64 4) 384 7789
Fax: (64 4) 384 4727

Hampster Films
15 Wesley Road
Kelburn
Wellington
Tel: (64 4) 934 4730
Fax: (64 4) 934 4731
e-mail: hampster@compuserve.com

Kahukura Productions
PO Box 31444
Lower Hutt
Wellington
Tel: (64 4) 619 0759
Fax: (64 4) 619 0944
e-mail: 100351.2475@compuserve.
com

M F Films
23 Curran Street
Herne Bay
Auckland
Tel: (64 9) 376 0876
Fax: (64 9) 376 9675
e-mail: fantl@ihug.co.nz

Meridian Film Productions
PO Box 19 043
Wellington
Tel: (64 4) 384 6405
Fax: (64 4) 384 7406

Messenger Films
PO Box 90 056
Auckland Mail Centre
Auckland
Tel: (64 9) 378 0529
Fax: (64 9) 378 1662

Motion Pictures Limited
PO Box 9668
Wellington
Tel: (64 4) 385 0767
Fax: (64 4) 384 5840

Nightmare Film Productions
PO Box 6809
Wellington
Tel: (64 4) 801 9581
Fax: (64 4) 801 9564

Oceania Productions Ltd
PO Box 78–128
Grey Lynn
Auckland
Tel: (64 9) 443 2404
Fax: (64 9) 443 2414
e-mail: denave@ibm.net

Pacific Films
PO Box 6249
Wellington
Tel: (64 4) 938 7526
Fax: (64 4) 382 9916

Plumb Productions
PO Box 2070
Wellington
Tel: (64 4) 385 1283
Fax: (64 4) 382 8787

Preston Laing Productions
PO Box 9175
Wellington
Tel: (64 4) 384 6405
Fax: (64 4) 384 7406

Rocket Pictures
PO Box 78 076
Grey Lynn
Auckland
Tel: (64 9) 360 0877
Fax: (64 9) 360 0079
e-mail: ssrocket@compuserve.com

Satellite Films
PO Box 6757
Wellington
Fax: (64 4) 802 5738
e-mail:
philippa.campbell@xtra.co.nz

South Pacific Pictures
PO Box 35 656
Browns Bay
Auckland
Tel: (64 9) 444 3000
Fax: (64 9) 443 5900

Southern Light Pictures
PO Box 37 177
Parnell
Auckland
Tel: (64 9) 529 1004
Fax: (64 9) 524 0926

Trevor Haysom Enterprises
PO Box 7015
Wellesley Street
Auckland
Tel: (64 9) 307 0036
Fax: (64 9) 366 0503
e-mail: the@iconz.co.nz

James Wallace Productions Ltd
PO Box 5508
Wellesley Street
Auckland
Tel: (64 9) 302 5271
Fax: (64 9) 302 5272

Distributors

2 Brothers Films
PO Box 5653
Wellesley Street
Auckland
Tel: (64 9) 378 2123 or (09) 376 1544
Fax: (64 9) 378 1005

Blue Angel Films
The Bridgeway Theatre
122 Queen Street
Northcote Point
Auckland
Tel: (64 9) 418 3308
Fax: (64 9) 418 4183
e-mail: matthew@blueangel.co.nz

Buena Vista International (NZ)
PO Box 37524
Parnell
Auckland
Tel: (64 9) 302 7565
Fax: (64 9) 302 0201

Columbia TriStar (New Zealand) Ltd
PO Box 68 041
Newton
Auckland
Tel: (64 9) 366 9499
Fax: (64 9) 366 9488

Essential Films
PO Box 47045
Ponsonby
Auckland
Tel: (64 9) 376 3682
Fax: (64 9) 376 3293
e-mail: kellyrogers@rialto.co.nz

Everard Entertainment Ltd
PO Box 3664
Auckland 1
Tel: (64 9) 302 1193
Fax: (64 9) 302 1192
e-mail: everard@nznet.gen.nz

Footprint Films
PO Box 1852
Auckland
Tel: (64 9) 309 8388
Fax: (64 9) 373 4722

Hoyts Cinemas
PO Box 6445
Wellesley Street
Auckland
Tel: (64 9) 303 2739
Fax: (64 9) 307 0011

REP Film Distributors
30 Prosford Street
Ponsonby
Auckland
Tel: (64 9) 360 2360
Fax: (64 9) 360 2920

Roadshow Film Distributors
PO Box 68 246
Newton
Auckland
Tel: (64 9) 377 9669
Fax: (64 9) 377 9449

Twentieth Century Fox
PO Box 6923
Auckland
Tel: (64 9) 309 0955
Fax: (64 9) 309 0967

United International Pictures
PO Box 105 263
Auckland
Tel: (64 9) 379 6269
Fax: (64 9) 379 6271

Village Force
PO Box 2384
Auckland
Tel: (64 9) 309 9137
Fax: (64 9) 307 2522

Useful Addresses

Screen Producers and Directors Association
PO Box 9567
Wellington
Tel: (64 4) 802 4931
Fax: (64 4) 385 8755
e-mail: info@spada.co.nz

New Zealand Film Commission
PO Box 11546
Wellington
Tel: (64 4) 382 7680
Fax: (64 4) 384 9719
e-mail: marketing@nzfilm.co.nz

NZ On Air
PO Box 9744
Wellington
Tel: (64 4) 382 9524
Fax: (64 4) 382 9546

Film New Zealand
(assists overseas producers)
PO Box 24 142
Wellington
Tel: (64 4) 802 4594
Fax: (64 4) 385 8755
e-mail: info@filmnz.org.nz

NZ Federation of Film Societies
(the film festivals)
PO Box 9544
Wellington
Tel: (64 4) 385 0162
Fax: (64 4) 801 7304
e-mail: enzedff@actrix.gen.nz

NORWAY — Trond Olav Svendsen

The 1990s have brought great changes to the Norwegian film industry. Almost all of its institutions – private and public – have acquired their present form during the last decade. The Film Institute swallowed the National Film Board and became a large body handling archive work, the distribution of films and educational material to schools, and film funding, with consultants replacing the old endowment committee.

The Foundation for Audiovisual Productions became the third source of government subsidies for feature films (in addition to the Film Institute and the state-owned production company, Norsk Film), with increased co-operation between film and television as one of its objectives.

TV2, a second TV channel, financed through commercials, was established in Bergen. Finally, a Film School was

Sophie´s World
director Erik Gustavson

Norwegian Film Institute presents
feature films worldwide

Misery Harbour
director Nils Gaup

The Promter
director Hilde Heier

Bloody Angels
director Karin Julsrud

NORWEGIAN FILM INSTITUTE

For further information please contact Stine Oppegaard
Norwegian Film Institute, Department of Production and
International Relations, P.O.Box 482 Sentrum, N-0105 Oslo
Tel: +47 22 47 45 75/00 or +47 90 85 96 38 Fax: +47 22 47 45 97

established at Lillehammer and a Film Museum in Oslo – the government's way of saying that the future of Norwegian cinema, as well as its history, is now taken seriously.

Despite all the improvements, the situation is far from stable. In fact, the production, distribution and exhibition sectors are all on the boil. On the production side, much discussion followed the winter release of a report by a management consultancy hired by the Department of Culture. They proposed that government spending on film should be administered by one large institution, differentiating between projects (low-budget, high-budget), and demanding that producers find a larger private share of a budget than is currently the case.

This seemed to imply that the Film Institute would split in two, with the archives and educational work going to one side and the film production and marketing to the other. While the proposal met some opposition, at press time the general consensus was that some of the recommendations would be implemented.

Public vs. private

There is also conflict between distributors and Oslo Cinema, the sole exhibitor in Norway's only big city, and by far the country's largest exhibitor. During the 1980s home video revolution, distributors' profit margins decreased, small distributors lost ground, and the market became dominated by a handful of large companies, several of them under foreign ownership and operating in both the theatrical and video markets.

The unique municipal cinema system survived, with 90% of the cinemas remaining local monopolies under the control of town and village councils. The law regulating this system was, however, softened, and Oslo Cinema became a company (though still owned by the municipality).

Oslo is obviously the key to most films' profitability. Its 31 up-to-date screens exhibit a varied programme co-ordinated by a central management, and Oslo's citizens are avid cinema patrons. But when distributors feel their films are not offered the maximum opportunity here, they have no alternatives.

As a result, private interests are closing in. In Sandvika, to the west of Oslo, there is already a privately-owned multiplex. The renowned Swedish company Svensk Filmindustri is building a cinema on Oslo's back doorstep at Lillestrøm, and has plans for cinemas in Trondheim and Tromsø. Private companies also bid for shares in the Oslo Cinema. The result may be the first major change in movie exhibition in Norway since the 1920s.

Bird-brained detective

The 1998–99 season was a mixed bag, but it started well with the animated feature **Gurin with the Foxtail** (*Solan, Ludvig og Gurin med reverompa*), based on the self-consciously homely universe of writer Kjell Aukrust.

The plot, concerning a private detective – a cigar-smoking, brandy-swilling blackbird – solving cases in a mythical rural Norway, was not much to write home about, and the comedy was uneven. But Aukrust's wacky universe (also the source for the all-time Norwegian box-office winner, the puppet animation *Flåklypa Grand Prix*, from 1976) has the kind of loveable, fallible characters that Norwegian audiences love. The attractive, accessible animation style, developed by newcomer Nille Tystad and veteran producer John M. Jacobsen, helped the film finish second only to *Titanic* in the year's box-office chart.

Torun Lian's film about unbearable sorrow, **Only Clouds Move the Stars** (*Bare skyer beveger stjernene*), was another hit. A 10-year old girl loses her little brother to cancer, and has to struggle with profound grief, and her mother's depression. Her return to normality begins when she makes friends with a boy her own age. Lian makes the young characters come to life, although the grown-ups are somewhat muted. This is perhaps intentional, since her real subject is the healing possibilities of the relationship between the two children, whose confidence in front of the camera alleviates the gloom.

Schpaaa (from a foreign-derived slang word meaning "OK") provoked some discussion. First-time director Erik Poppe has made a sort of *Pulp Fiction* among 15-year old delinquents in Oslo. They are an ethnic mix of Yugoslav, Pakistani and Norwegian and carry out minor chores for criminals, slowly graduating to extortion and violence. One day they beat up the wrong person and find themselves in harm's way. The camerawork and editing are more fluid than the acting, and Poppe does not pause to let us get properly involved with the characters. But this film did connect with young audiences, and also offered grown-ups an uncensored update on the subject of juvenile delinquency.

An impressive compilation of very interesting footage was Stig Andersen and Kenny Sanders' **Frozen Heart** (*Frosset hjerte*), a documentary on the polar explorer Roald Amundsen, whose expeditions were more successful than his affairs with various women.

The second portmanteau film in a series from Norsk Film, **Thirst – Crimes of the Future** (*Tørst – fremtidens forbrytelser*),

Delinquents in Erik Poppe's SCHPAAA

provided three female directors with the opportunity to make their first feature. It consists of three narratives based on short stories by novelist and Nobel Prize-winner Knut Hamsun (1859–1952), whose work has received a lot of attention from film-makers in the 1990s.

Unsurprisingly, *Thirst* did not make waves at the box-office, perhaps because of the uncompromising narrative style. The first episode, directed by Maria Fuglevaag Warsinski, features an icon from Russia that turns out to be radioactive, and is a bit too heavy on the symbolism. Karoline Frogner makes a strong comment on the exploitation of women in her episode, about a man making a documentary on a woman who falls on hard times.

The greatest visual flair and a fine way with the actors is evident in the last episode, by Nathilde Overrein Rapp. This is an amoral tale of a young woman's spiralling madness. When rejected by her husband she has him murdered on their yacht in Cannes, then picks up the killer's unsuspecting friend. The film's complex sense of past and present and its mood of sexual alienation are well done.

There have been 54 first-time directors in Norway since 1984 – a very large number in a country that produces 10 films per year. Some people refer to Norwegian film history, jokingly but not without foundation, as a history of "one-timers".

Of the five most praised newcomers of the 1990s, Marius Holst (*Cross My Heart and Hope to Die*, 1995), Bent Hamer (*Eggs*, 1996), Pål Sletaune (*Junk Mail*, 1997), Erik Skjoldbjærg (*Insomnia*, 1997) and Emil Stang Lund (*Batwings*, 1992), only Hamer and Stang Lund have made second films. Now it is time to look back and decide which talents must be given new opportunities; the trio from *Thirst* should certainly be considered.

TROND OLAV SVENDSEN has a history degree from the University of Oslo. He works as a critic and film historian, and has published a *Theatre and Film Encyclopaedia*, and other books on film.

Still from THIRST – CRIMES OF THE FUTURE, adapted from short stories by Knut Hamsun

Recent and Forthcoming Films

SOLAN, LUDVIG OG GURIN MED REVEROMPA
(Gurin with the Foxtail)

Animated feature. Script: Kjell Aukrust and Vibeke Idsøe, based on Aukrust's novel. Dir: John M. Jacobsen. Prod: Filmkameratene A/S.

CELLOFAN (Cellophane)

Script: Leidulv Risan. Dir: Eva Isaksen. Phot: Erling Thurmann-Andersen. Players: Andrine Sæther, Sverre Anker Ousdal, Kelly Tainton. Prod: Yellow Cottage A/S (Aage Aaberge).

JUNKIES

Documentary. Dir: Trond Kvist. Phot: Knut Aas and Bjørn Bøthun. Prod: Subfilm A/S (Svend Aavitsland Wolf).

DEI MJUKE HENDENE
(In the House of Angels)

Documentary. Script and Dir: Margreth Olin. Phot: Svein Krøvel. Prod: Speranza Film A/S (Thomas Robsahm).

BARE SKYER BEVEGER STJERNENE
(Only Clouds Move the Stars)

Script: Torun Lian, based on her novel. Dir: Lian. Phot: Svein Krøvel. Players: Thea Sofie Rusten, Jan Tore Kristoffersen, Anneke von der Lippe, Jørgen Langhelle. Prod: Filmkameratene A/S (John M. Jacobsen).

DESPERATE BEKJENTSKAPER
(Desperate Acquaintances)

Script: Svend Wam and Dag Anders Rougseth. Dir: Wam.

Phot: Anders Leegaard. Players: Bjarte Hjelmeland, Anders Dale, Bjørnar Teigen. Prod: Mefistofilm A/S (Svend Wam).

SCHPAAA

Script: Hans Petter Blad and Erik Poppe. Dir: Poppe. Phot: John Christian Rosenlund. Players: Maikel Andressen Abou-Zelof, Sharjil Arshed, Mickael Marman, Jalal Zahedjekta. Prod: BulBul Film A/S (Finn Gjerdrum).

1732 HØTTEN – MARERITTET HAR ET POSTNUMMER (Bloody Angels)

Script: Kjetil Indregard. Dir: Karin Julsrud. Phot: Philip Øgaard. Players: Reidar Sørensen, Gaute Skjegstad, Trond Høvik, Stig Henrik Hoff. Prod: Norsk Film A/S (Tom Remlov).

OLE ALEKSANDER FILLIBOM-BOM-BOM (Ollie Alexander Tiddly-Om-Pom-Pom)

Script: Gudny Hagen, based on the books by Anne-Cath Vestly. Dir: Anne-Marie Nørholm. Phot: Bjørn Lien. Players: Jakob Kirsebom Lanto, Nina Woxholtt, Sigve Bøe. Prod: Norwegian Broadcasting Corporation.

FROSSET HJERTE (Frozen Heart – a film about Roald Amundsen)

Documentary. Script: Stig Andersen and Kenny Sanders, based on the biography by Tor Bomann-Larsen. Dir: Andersen and Sanders. Phot: Hallgrim Ødegård. Prod: Motlys A/S (Sigve Endresen).

ABSOLUTT BLÅMANDAG (Absolute Hangover)

Script: Axel Hellstenius, based on a play by Karl Sundby. Dir: Petter Næss. Phot: Svein Krøvel. Players: Ingar Helge Gimle, Brit Elisabeth Haagensli, Gard Eidsvold, Anette Hoff. Prod: Monolith Production A/S (Dag Nordahl), Moviemakers AS.

TØRST – FREMTIDENS FORBRYTELSER (Thirst – Crimes of the Future)

Compendium of 3 episodes. Script: Maria Fuglevaag Warsinski and Hans Petter Blad; Karoline Frogner and Håvard Rem; Nathilde Overrein Rapp and Vigdis Hjorth; all based on short stories by Knut Hamsun. Dir: Warsinski, Frogner, Rapp. Phot: Svein Krøvel. Players: Eindride Eidsvold, Igor Sklyar, Bjørn Sundquist, Vanja Riksfjord, Alexia Stresi, Philippe Volter. Prod: Norsk Film A/S (Tom Remlov).

SUFFLØSEN (The Prompter)

Script and Dir: Hilde Heier. Phot: Harald Paalgard. Players: Hege Schøyen, Sven Nordin, Philip Zandén, Anne-Lise Berntsen. Prod: Wildhagen Produksjon A/S (Christian Wildhagen).

SOFIES VERDEN (Sophie's World)

Script: Petter Skavlan and Erik Gustavson, based on the novel by Jostein Gaarder. Dir: Gustavson. Phot: Kjell Vassdal. Players: Silje Storstein, Tomas von Brömssen, Andrine Sæther, Bjørn Floberg. Prod: Norwegian Broadcasting Corporation (Oddvar Bull Tuhus), Filmkameratene A/S (John M. Jacobsen).

S.O.S.

Script and Dir: Thomas Robsahm. Phot: Gaute Gunnari. Players: Gianmarco Tognazzi, Jacqueline Lustig, Kjersti Holmen. Prod: Speranza Film A/S (Thomas Robsahm).

MISERY HARBOUR

Script: Kenny Sanders and Sigve Endresen, based on a novel by Aksel Sandemose. Dir: Nils Gaup. Phot: Erling Thurmann-Andersen. Players: Nikolaj Coster Waldau, Stuart Graham, Anneke von der Lippe, Graham Green, Bjørn Floberg. Prod: Motlys A/S (Sigve Endresen).

NÅR MØRKET ER FORBI (Passing Darkness)

Script: Alf R. Jacobsen and Knut Erik Jensen, based on a novel by Jacobsen. Dir: Jensen. Phot: Svein Krøvel. Players: Stig Henrik Hoff, Gørild Mauseth, Nicholas Hope, Snorre Tindberg, Gunnel Lindblom. Prod: Barentsfilm A/S (Jan-Erik Gammleng).

EVAS ØYE (Eva's Eye)

Script: Berit Nesheim, based on a novel by Karin Fossum. Dir: Nesheim. Phot: Erling Thurmann-Andersen. Players: Andrine Sæther, Bjørn Sundquist, Gisken Armand, Sverre Anker Ousdal. Prod: Northern Lights A/S (Axel Helgeland).

FOMLESEN I KATTEPINE (Fumblebody in a Cat's Jam)

Script: Arthur Johansen. Dir: Petter A. Fastvold. Phot: Philip Øgaard. Players: Lars Vik, Sverre Anker Ousdal, Henriette Steenstrup, Mia Gundersen, Mikkel Gaup. Prod: Yellow Cottage A/S (Aage Aaberge).

BALLEN I ØYET (Eye Ball)

Script: Beate Grimsrud. Dir: Catrine Telle. Phot: Peter Mokrosinski. Players: Laila Goody, Bjørnar Teigen, Marit Adeleide Andreassen, Kristin Kajander. Prod: Norsk Film A/S (Tom Remlov).

ABERDEEN

Script: Kristin Amundsen and Hans Petter Moland. Dir: Moland. Phot: Philip Øgaard. Players: Lena Headey, Stellan Skarsgård. Prod: Norsk Film A/S (Tom Remlov).

Producers

AS Film 21
Solligt. 2
N-0254 Oslo
Tel: (47) 2256 0590
Fax: (47) 2256 1210
Contact: Olav Øen

Barentsfilm A/S
PO Box 4383 Torshov
N-0402 Oslo
Tel: (47) 8800 3230
Tel: (47) 8800 3234
Contact: Jan Gammleng

BulBul Film A/S
Fossvn. 24A, bygn. 4
N-0551 Oslo
Tel: (47) 2242 2227
Fax: (47) 2242 2299
Contact: Bent Hamer

Filmhuset A/S
President Harbitz gt. 22 A
N-0259 Oslo
Tel: (47) 2256 2100
Fax: (47) 2255 1540
Contact: Egil Ødegård

Filmkameratene A/S
Dronningens gf. 8
N-0152 Oslo
Tel: (47) 2200 7880
Fax: (47) 2233 2797
Contact: John M. Jacobsen

Magdalena Film A/S
President Harbitz gt. 21
N-0259 Oslo
Tel: (47) 2256 2278
Tel: (47) 2256 2279
Contact: Bente Erichsen

Mefistofilm A/S
Gyldenløves gt. 41
N-0260 Oslo
Tel: (47) 2243 8260
Fax: (47) 2255 7777
Contact: Svend Wam

Merkurfilm A/S
Munkedamsvn. 61
N-0270 Oslo
Tel: (47) 2283 2270
Fax: (47) 2283 2271
Contact: Petter Vennerød

Motlys A/S
Islandsgt. 6
N-0658 Oslo
Tel: (47) 2303 5560
Fax: (47) 2303 5561
Contact: Sigve Endresen

MovieMakers A/S
PO Box 6858 St. Olavs plass
N-0130 Oslo
Tel: (47) 2246 3200
Contact: Dag Nordahl

Nordic Screen Production AS
Wedel Jarlsbergs vei 36
N-1342 Jar
Tel: (47) 6752 5460
Fax: (47) 6712 3773
Contact: Petter J. Borgli

Norsk Film A/S
PO Box 4
N-1342 Jar
Tel: (47) 6752 5300
Fax: (47) 6712 5108
Contact: Tom Remlov

Northern Lights A/S
PO Box 104
N-1342 Jar
Tel: (47) 6752 5330
Fax: (47) 6752 5340
Contact: Axel Helgeland

National Broadcasting Corporation
Drama
N-0340 Oslo
Tel: (47) 2304 8921
Fax: (47) 2304 5350
Contact: Oddvar Bull Tuhus

Parabel Film A/S
Parkveien 71
N-0254 Oslo
Tel: (47) 2243 6300
Fax: (47) 2256 3650
Contact: Emil Stang Lund

Speranza Film A/S
Dronningens gt. 16
N-0152 Oslo
Tel: (47) 2282 2470
Fax: (47) 2282 2471
Contact: Thomas Robsahm

Studio Regin A/S
Lofotgt. 2
N-0458 Oslo
Tel: (47) 2238 2223
Fax: (47) 2235 4699
Contact: Sverre Pedersen

Unni Straume Filmproduksjon A/S
Corso Anita Garibaldi 45
I-040 19 Terracina
Italy
Tel: (39) 773 7001 83
Contact: Unni Straume

ViPro A/S
PO Box 238
N-6101 Volda
Tel: (47) 7007 8194
Fax: (47) 7007 8819
Contact: Jørn Brente

Wildhagen Produksjon A/S
Kragsvei 9B
N-0391 Oslo
Tel: (47) 2214 8366
Fax: (47) 2214 8344
Contact: Christian Wildhagen

Yellow Cottage AS
Wedel Jarlsbergs vei 36
N-1342 Jar
Tel: (47) 6752 5345
Fax: (47) 6752 5349
Contact: Aage Aaberge

Distributors

Arthaus
Dronningens gt. 16
N-0152 Oslo
Tel: (47) 2247 4685
Fax: (47) 2247 4692
Contact: Svend B. Jensen

BV Film A/S
PO Box 17
N-4262 Avaldsnes
Tel: (47) 5284 2210
Fax: (47) 5284 3575
Contact: Bjørg Veland

Egmont Columbia Tristar Filmdistributors A/S
Kristian Augusts gt. 14
N-0164 Oslo
Tel: (47) 2336 6680
Contact: Bjørn Hoenvoll

Europafilm A/S
Stortingsgt. 30
N-0161 Oslo
Tel: (47) 2283 4290
Fax: (47) 2283 4151
Contact: Åge Hoffart, Erik Sælen

AS Fidalgo
PO Box 2054 Posebyen
N-4602 Kristiansand
Tel: (47) 3802 4004
Fax: (47) 3802 2354
Contact: Arild Frøyseth

Kommunenes Filmcentral AS
PO Box 411 Sentrum
N-0103 Oslo
Tel: (47) 2236 9530
Fax: (47) 2242 1469
Contact: Bjørn Jacobsen

Sandrew Metronome Norge AS
PO Box 1178 Sentrum
N-0107 Oslo
Tel: (47) 2282 7800
Fax: (47) 2282 7810
Contact: Frida Ohrvik

Scandinavian Entertainment Group
President Harbitz' gt. 22A
N-0259 Oslo
Tel: (47) 2256 2100
Fax: (47) 2255 1540
Contact: Egil Ødegård

SF Norge A/S
Box 6868 St. Olavs pl.
N-0130 Oslo
Tel: (47) 2200 7800
Fax: (47) 2200 7801
Contact: Guttorm Petterson

Tour de Force AS
Georgernes V. 3
N-5011 Bergen
Tel: (47) 5532 2590
Fax: (47) 5532 3740
Contact: Tor Fosse

United International Pictures
PO Box 7134 Majorstua
N-0307 Oslo
Tel: (47) 2256 6115
Fax: (47) 2256 7181
Contact: Liv Jacobsen

Useful Addresses

Foundation for Audiovisual Production
Dronningens gt. 16
N-0152 Oslo
Tel: (47) 2247 4650
Fax: (47) 2247 4691
Contact: Elin Erichsen

The National Association of Municipal Cinemas
Dronningens gt. 16
N-0152 Oslo
Tel: (47) 2247 4610
Fax: (47) 2247 4699
Contact: Lene Løken

National Centre for Screen Studies
PO Box 904 Sentrum
N-0104 Oslo
Tel: (47) 2282 2400
Fax: (47) 2282 2422
Contact: Kjersti Alver

The Norwegian Federation of Film Societies
Dronningens gt. 16
N-0152 Oslo
Tel: (47) 2247 4680
Fax: (47) 2247 4692
Contact: Jon Iversen

Norwegian Film and TV Producers' Association
Dronningens gt. 16
N-0152 Oslo
Tel: (47) 2247 4644
Fax: (47) 2247 4688
Contact: Tom G. Eilertsen

Norwegian Film Critics' Association
Dronningensgt. 16
N-0152 Oslo
Tel: (47) 2247 4648
Fax: (47) 2242 0356

Contact: Osman Kibar

Norwegian Film Distributors' Association
Øvre slottsgt. 12
N-0157 Oslo
Tel: (47) 2242 4844
Fax: (47) 2242 3093
Contact: Kristin Hoenvoll

Norwegian International Film Festival
PO Box 145
N-5501 Haugesund
Tel: (47) 5273 4430
Fax: (47) 5273 4420

The Norwegian Film Institute
PO Box 482 Sentrum
N-0105 Oslo
Tel: (47) 2247 4571
Fax: (47) 2247 4597
Contact: Jan Erik Holst

Norwegian Film Workers' Association
Dronningens gt. 16
N-0152 Oslo
Tel: (47) 2247 4640
Fax: (47) 2247 4689
Contact: Rolv Håan

PAKISTAN — Aijaz Gul

The biggest news from Pakistani cinema in 1999 has been the enormous, unbelievable critical and commercial success of Punjabi low-budget musical romance **Bangles** (*Choorian*). Released in October 1998, the film ran to capacity crowds in many cities (especially interior Punjab) for months. Yet the most remarkable thing about this smash is neither its shoestring budget – five million rupees, compared to an average of about seventy-five million – or even that it has it has made some 200m rupees ($4m) at the box-office.

What's really mind boggling is the fact that many exhibitors have made so much from Bangles in cities like Gujranwala, Rawalpindi, Gujrat and Faisalabad that they have been able to start their own film productions – this despite the fact that

Humayun Saeed (left) and Resham in EXTREME

producer Haji Faqeer Mohammad (a dairy billionaire) was levying huge weekly rental payments on all *Bangles* prints. Never before in the history of Pakistani cinema has a film made so much money from such a small investment in such a short time.

Directed by Syed Noor and scripted by his journalist-poetess wife Rukhsana Noor, with charming Saima and Moammar Rana in the leads, *Bangles* deals with a fatherless brat whose mother can no longer handle him and sends him off to live with her brother in a village. In his tight jeans and trainers, guitar in hand, the brat instantly falls for his cousin. She has been living an unhappy life with her step-family and finds new life and love with the hero.

Romantic musical encounters, carnivals and green pastures are the order of the day, the cousins are married, but the consumation must wait until after a bloody climax which includes too many dead bodies, bullet-ridden horses and colourful explosions.

Bangles not only left *Titanic* miles behind in the box-office stakes, but also managed to win 17 out of 19 nominations for the prestigious National Film Awards, including Best Picture, Actress, Actor, Supporting Actor, Director, Composer, Editor and Song. It is a well-crafted film with good music and a well-knit script. Syed's treatment of the main plot is excellent, brisk and beautifully composed.

Producers tried quickly to emulate the film's success. Masood Butt's **Consent** (*Niki Jai Haan*), released in March 1999, followed *Bangles* in plot and spirit but despite impressive production effects, a popular musical score, bankable leading pair and heavy newspaper and TV publicity it lasted only a few weeks.

Marital strife

Among the 51 features released in 1998, **Wedding** (*Nikah*), produced by Shahzad Rafiq and directed by Sangeeta, was another hit, about a bickering couple whose rows cause a child's death. Sangeeta also impressed with **Aware** (*Ehsas*) and **Betrayal** (*Herjai*), the latter based on *Indecent Proposal*. Other good films included the prolific Syed Noor's **Burning Scarf** (*Dupatta Jal Raha Hai*), **Hurdles** (*Dewarain*) and **Precious** (*Zever*). Noor was the outstanding director of 1998–1999, while Saima was the most bankable actress, followed by Resham, Meera and Reema. Moammar Rana and Shan were the leading heroes.

Eighteen titles bowed in the first quarter of 1999. Actress-producer-director Samin Pirzada made her debut with a smash, **Extreme** (*Inteha*), the most distinguished film of 1999. It deals with two boys who love the same girl. One of them is forced to marry her and tortures her as his father had tortured his mother (we learn this through sepia flashbacks). Samina's beautifully-directed film was recalled by the Government for sex and nudity but the producer quickly got a Court order supporting its continued release.

Syed has continued his fine run of form with **Bandit** (*Daku Rani*), while actor Shan stunned everyone with his violent directorial debut **Guns and Roses**, visually impressive but with a script that three different writers failed to salvage, condemning the film to box-office failure after three weeks.

The National Film Development Corporation held a successful one-day film conference in March this year where more than 150 delegates discussed subjects like video piracy, the establsihment of Pakistan's first film academy, a reduction in taxes and duty on film stock and equipment and Pakistani involvement in international film festivals.

With an additional 15% duty levied on film imports in 1999 and the government demanding arrears from previous years, many importers went out of business and fresh imports virtually came to a standstill. MPAA officials visited Islamabad to voice their concern over the new duty and the widespread piracy of American films. Since Pakistan is a member of the World Trade Organisation it will sooner or later have to take action to deal with such complaints.

With releases such as *The Rock, Con Air* and *Air Force One* only reaching cinemas long after they became available on video, filmgoers showed considerable indifference to Hollywood imports. Another import, *Jinnah*, a biopic about Pakistan's founder, was more of a prestige success than a box-office winner. Finally, the film community mourned the death of Shaukat Hussain Rizvi, who left Bombay at the peak of his career to settle in Lahore and lay the foundation of Pakistan's film industry at Shahnoor Studios.

AIJAZ GUL earned his MA in Cinema from the University of Southern California, Los Angeles. He has written three books and numerous articles on film. He is presently working for Egypt's National Film Development Corporation and resides in Islamabad.

Recent Films

INTEHA (Extreme)

Script: Dr Dannis Isaac. Dir: Samina Pirzada. Phot: Azhar Burki. Players: Meera, Humayun Saeed, Zeeshan, Resham. Prod: Samina Pirzada.

CHOORIAN (Bangles)

Script: Rukhsana Noor. Dir: Syed Noor. Phot: Naseeruddin. Players: Saima, Moammar Rana, Shafqat Cheema, Bahar. Prod: Pak Nishan Films.

GUNS AND ROSES

Script: Shan, Babar Iqbal, Pervaiz Kaleem. Director: Shan. Phot: Waqar Bukhari. Players: Shan, Faisal, Farooq Zamir, Resham, Meera. Producer: Riaz Shahid Films & X'9 Production.

Producers/ Distributors

Evernew Pictures
(Producer-Distributor-Studio)
2 Abbott Road
Lahore
Tel: (92 42) 631 7063/631 6929
Fax: (92 42) 571 2743/783 10831

Eveready Pictures
(Producer-Distributor)
Eveready Chambers
4th Floor
I.I. Chundrigar Road
Karachi
Tel: (92 21) 263 4817/4818
Fax: (92 21) 262 7843

Pak Nishan Films
(Producer-Distributor)
Royal Park
Lahore
Tel: (92 42) 631 0129

Mandviwalla Entertainment
(Producer-Distributor-Exhibitor-Importer)
Nishat Cinema Building
M. A. Jinnah Road
Karachi'74400
Tel: (92 21) 721 9101/9505
Fax: (92 42) 722 7259
e-mail: nishat@www.fascom.com

Useful Addresses

Ministry of Culture, Sports, Tourism & Youth Affairs,
Block 'D', Pak Secretariat
Islamabad
Secretary: Syed Roshan Zamir
Tel: (92 51) 9213121/1790
Fax: (92 51) 922 1863

National Film Development Corporation Limited
56'F Jinnah Avenue
Blue Area
Islamabad
Chairman: Ahad Malik
Tel: (92 51) 920 3548
Fax: (92 51) 922 1863

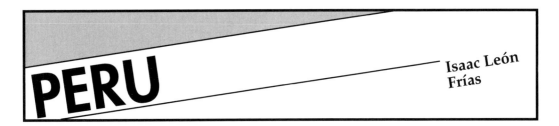

Isaac León
Frías

After the disappointment of 1997, when for the first time in 20 years no Peruvian features were released, 1998 saw a re-activation of domestic production, thanks to two local films: *Don't Tell Anyone* (*No se lo digas a nadie*), directed by Francisco J. Lombardi, and Alberto Durant's *Courage* (*Coraje*).

Don't Tell Anyone, based on the novel by young Peruvian writer Jaime Bayly, attracted the largest audience for a Peruvian movie in many years: more than 600,000 saw it in Lima, putting it second behind *Titanic* in the year's box-office chart. Lombardi's ninth film, co-produced with Spain, is perhaps his least personal. Although he has tried to accentuate the dramatic oppositions of the novel, which explores the contradictory sexual identity of a high-class Peruvian young man, the results are weak.

The film demonstrates Lombardi's narrative skills, but falls into superficiality when depicting the escapist universe of sex and drugs in which the young characters move. There is no doubt that the film's commercial success owed a good deal to the scenes of homosexual relations and the abuse of cocaine, as well as the casting of two popular young Peruvian TV actors, Santiago Magill and Christian Meier.

By contrast, **Courage** was made on a smaller budget and drew a much smaller audience: about 70,000 people. Its story is inspired by the last months of the life of María Elena Moyano, a popular Peruvian leader murdered by the terrorist group Shining Path in 1992. Alberto Durant's fourth and most conventional film, its small budget and weak script give it the appearance of a modest TV movie. The story should have made for powerful drama.

Rejected *Bait*

Early 1999 saw the release of **The Bait** (*La carnada*), the third film directed by Norwegian-born Marianne Eyde, who enjoyed success with *It's Only One Life* (*La vida es una sola*). The script, which won second prize in the Second Feature Film Contest organised by Consejo Nacional de Cinematografía (CONACINE) in 1998, sets the action in a small fishing bay on the northern coast of Peru.

It follows the search for personal affirmation of a young pregnant woman, against a background of mythological elements familiar from the Latin American tradition of "magical realism". Sadly, weak direction and a poorly-handled release meant that *The Bait* had perhaps the worst critical and audience reception of any Peruvian film in recent years.

At the end of 1998 there was a third CONACINE feature film script contest. The three scripts awarded production funding were Edgardo Guerra's **Dead from Love** (*Muerto de amor*), the veteran Armando Robles Godoy's **Impossible Loves** (*Amores imposibles*) and Alvaro Velarde's **Destiny Has No Favourites** (*El destino no tiene favoritos*).

In the first months of 1999, Francisco Lombardi shot a new feature, *Pantaleón and the Visitors* (*Pantaleón y las visitadoras*), based on the novel by Mario Vargas Llosa, and at press time already had plans for his next project, *Bad Mood* (*Mala onda*), adapted from a novel by the young Chilean, Alberto Fuguet.

Remarkably, given the difficult climate for feature projects, the volume of short film production continues to increase, largely thanks to the work of film school students. Finally, although new screens continue to go up around Peru, the country's serious recession has slowed the multiplex-building boom.

ISAAC LÉON FRÍAS is a film critic and Professor of Language and Film History at the University of Lima. From 1965 to 1985 he was director of *Hablemos de Cine* magazine and is now a member of the editorial council of *La gran ilusión* magazine and director of Filmoteca de Lima.

Recent and Forthcoming Films

A LA MEDIA NOCHE Y MEDIA
(At Half-Past Midnight)

Script and Dir: Marité Ugaz and Mariana Rondón. Phot: Micaela Cajahuaringa. Players: Salvador del Solar, María Fernanda Ferro, Constanza Morales. Prod: Imagen Latina (Perú)/Sudaca Films (Venezuela).

LA CARNADA (The Bait)

Script and Dir: Marianne Eyde. Phot: César Pérez. Players: Mónica Sánchez, Orlando Felices, Miguel Medina, Ana Cecilia Natteri. Prod: Kusi Films.

CORAJE (Courage)

Script: Alberto Durant and Ana Caridad Sánchez. Dir: Durant. Phot: Mario García Joya. Players: Olenka Cepeda, María Teresa Zúñiga, Ana Ponce, Jorge Chiarella. Prod: Agua Dulce Films, Pontificia Universidad Católica, Fernando Colomo P.C. (Spain).

NO SE LO DIGAS A NADIE
(Don't Tell Anyone)

Script: Giovanna Pollarolo and Enrique Moncloa. Dir: Francisco J. Lombardi. Phot: Carlos Gusi. Players: Santiago Magill, Christian Meier, Hernán Romero, Carmen Elías, Lucía Jimenez,

Giovanni Ciccia. Prod: Inca Films (Peru)/Lola Films (Spain).

EL BIEN ESQUIVO
(The Elusive Good)

Script: Augusto Tamayo and Alejandro Rossi. Dir: Tamayo. Phot: Juan Durán. Players: Jimena Lindo, Diego Bertie. Prod: Argos Interactiva (Peru).

PANTALEÓN Y LAS VISITADORAS
(Pantaleón and the Visitors)

Script: Giovanna Pollarolo and Enrique Moncloa. Dir: Francisco J. Lombardi. Phot: Teo Delgado. Players: Salvador del Solar, Angie Cepeda, Mónica Sánchez, Pilar Bardem. Prod: América Producciones, Inca Films, Televisión Española.

Useful Addresses

Asociación de Cineastas del Perú
Calle Manco Capac 236
Miraflores
Lima
Tel: (51 14) 470 041

Casablanca Films
Malecón Grau 967
Chorrillos
Lima
Tel: (51 14) 670 722
Fax: (51 14) 300 603/408 550

CONACINE
Museo de la Nación
Av. Javier Prado 2465
8° Piso
Lima
Tel: (51 14) 377 607/769 892
Tel/Fax: (51 14) 225 6479

Filmoteca de Lima
Paseo Colón 125
Lima
Tel: (51 14) 331 0126
Fax: (51 14) 251 101

Kusi Films
Godofredo García 140
San Isidro
Lima
Tel: (51 14) 226 005

Producciones Inca Films
La Florida 180
San Isidro
Lima
Tel: (51 14) 221 427
Fax:(51 14) 406 390

Sociedad Peruana de Directores y Productores Cinematográficos (SOCINE)
Tel/Fax: (51 14) 791 722

PHILIPPINES — Agustin Sotto

eature production dropped sharply to a low of 130 titles in 1998, from 204 in the previous year. Censorship controls have been loosened, allowing brief frontal nudity, and cheap sex films now dominate our screens, squeezing out more legitimate genres. The industry has been scampering to tackle this situation, and to many directors and producers, expanding the narrow domestic market offers the best solution.

'Globalisation' has become the rallying cry, with Filipino films once again playing at international festivals. However, insular practices have kept the industry from making a successful bid for co-production finance. The situation could be termed precarious. Even prime-time television is short of new TV films, and is forced to repeat films from the early 1990s. Piracy and bootleg screenings on local cable channels have forced many provincial cinemas to close.

One ingenious new development is the *pito-pito* production. Literally translated as "seven-seven", each film has a seven- to ten-day shooting schedule and a shoe-string budget. Originally developed by a local studio as the best way to comply with its existing television contract, the low-cost production plan has resulted in some fine films, which have launched new talent – although the scrimping and saving sometimes shows through the seams.

One such production is Mario O'Hara's **Woman on a Hot Tin Roof** (*Babae sa Bubungang Lata*), an expansion of a one-act play about a stuntman whose superstar ambitions force him to undergo extreme physical and mental humiliation. To make ends meet, his wife secretly works as a neighbourhood hooker. The material was one of the late Lino Brocka's dream projects; he had been prevented from shooting it because its steamy sex scenes were unacceptable under the stringent censorship which operated during the martial law years.

Killing time

First-time director Lav Diaz's **Serafin Geromino, the Criminal of Bo. Concepcion** won its lead player Raymond Bagatsing the Urian award for Best Actor from the nation's film critics. He plays a journalist whose search for a killer unearths some startling truths about an infamous murder case, and the corruption at the base of society. The film was a wake-up call to an industry that has for a long time failed to give breaks to unknown young talent.

Gil Portes' **The Kite** (*Saranggola*) is loosely based on a real-life case in which a policeman, disturbed in his sleep by suspicious noises, shot a toddler who was flying a kite from his roof. Many reasons are proffered for his impulsive action, particularly his stinging rebuke at the hands of his district's congressman, yet, sadly, the movie puts the social agenda to one side and settles into standard thriller mode, as a police detective investigates the murder.

I Wish It Were Love (*Sana Pag-ibig Na*), a first film from Jeffrey Jeturian, handles with sensitivity the posthumous revelations of a dead husband's infidelities. Jeturian coaches the actors to winning performances: subtle in the grand moments and poignant in the smaller gestures. The film collected numerous local film awards and within months Jeturian was working on **Queuing for Water** (*Pila-Balde*), a snapshot of life amongst slum dwellers who live close to more affluent tenement homes. The class tensions are sharply delineated in the desperation of the poor, who try to rise above their status, only to see their dreams exploited by their slightly better-off neighbours.

AGUSTIN SOTTO is an archivist and film critic who chairs Manunuri ng Pelikulang Pilipino, the Philippine film critics' circle.

Recent and Forthcoming Films

SARANGGOLA (The Kite)

Script: Butch Dalisay. Dir: Gil Portes. Players: Ricky Davao, Llester Lansang, Jennifer Sevilla. Prod: GMA Films.

HUBAD SAS ILALIM NG BUWAN (Naked Under the Sun)

Dir: Lav Diaz. Players: Joel Torre, Elizabeth Oropesa. Prod: Good Harvest.

PILA-BALDE (Queuing for Water)

Dir: Jeffrey Jeturian. Players: Ana Capri, Harold Pineda, Estrella Kuenzler. Prod: Good Harvest.

Useful Addresses

Film Academy of the Philippines
Sampaguita Compound
Gilmore
Quezon City

Film Committee
National Commission for Culture and the Arts
Intramuros
Manila

Film Division
Cultural Center of the Philippines
Roxas Blvd
Manila

Mowelfund Film Institute
66 Rosario Drive
Quezon City

Society of Film Archivists
C63A Gueventville II
Libertad
Mandaluyong

UP Film Center
University of the Philippines
Diliman
Quezon City

POLAND

Rick Richardson

I n years to come, 1999 may well be cited as a benchmark for Polish cinema. It certainly has been a year unlike any other. As this post-communist country enters the new millennium, there are huge changes in progress on all fronts - after a decade of unprecedented developments that have virtually transformed production, distribution and exhibition from cottage industries into a fully-fledged motion picture business.

Apart from the welcome renovation of old cinemas, and what might be termed, without too much irony, the "multiplex miracle", producers like Studio Zebra and Studio Zodiak, and local distributors such as Syrena and ITI have filled their coffers on a diet of Polish hits. American

blockbusters no longer dominate the scene. For proof, just study the box-office returns for the first six months of 1999, in which two Polish films did half as much business as all films combined in the previous year. Juliusz Machulski's *Killer 2* and Jerzy Hoffman's *With Fire and Sword* earned a cool $3.5m and $20m respectively.

In **Killer 2**, Cezary Pazura reprises his role from 1996's smash hit, *Killer*, in which he was a cabdriver mistaken for a hitman. In this year's instalment, Pazura plays a national hero whose richly endowed do-gooder foundation is the target of a Mafia takeover which, of course, will require the murder of our hero. Audiences loved the film, though not as much as the original *Killer*, which did twice as well, with three million admissions, and so impressed Disney that they bought the re-make rights, for a reported $650,000.

But *Killer 2* seems like small beer next to **With Fire and Sword** (*Ogniem i Mieczem*), vet helmer Jerzy Hoffman's final tribute to the epic, late nineteenth-century trilogy by Polish novelist Henryk Sienkiewicz (Hoffman had already filmed parts two and three in 1968 and 1974). *With Fire and Sword*, which tells the story of a seventeenth-century Ukrainian uprising within the Polish kingdom, has been to Poles what *Gone with the Wind* is to Georgians in the US - an historical epic which has become buried deep in the collective consciousness.

Made on a budget of $10m, the film doubled that in Polish box-office alone. Between them, the two *Killer* films and *With Fire and Sword* brought roughly 12 million people to the nation's cinemas - a huge number for domestic productions. Now, inevitably, the push is on to make copycat historical Polish epics and light,

even zany comedies, while conventional action films continue to lose their popularity with Poland's audiences.

Waiting for a master

During the summer, Polish filmgoers were anticipating the autumn premiere of Andrzej Wajda's **Pan Tadeusz**, based on the nineteenth-century work of Polish national icon, Adam Mickiewicz, the poet who gave Poland its messianic complex. By all accounts, *Pan Tadeusz* marks Wajda's return to form, offering a large-scale, deeply patriotic theme, well-suited to this inimitable master's talents. The film's release was timed for exactly one month after the release of *Star Wars* - an indication that distributors in Poland are becoming ever more cautious about release dates and print runs. Such competitive savvy is obligatory for those who want to succeed in this increasingly competitive market.

Happily, several films notable for their content rather than their box-office gross have demonstrated that artistry is not

Location filming for Jerzy Hoffman's hugely successful WITH FIRE AND SWORD

being abandoned in the gold rush. State funds still support fine directors whose films do not attract large audiences. Notables are Polish industry award-winners Jacek Bromski (Best Director, 1998), Jan Jakub Kolski (Best Film, 1998) and Jerzy Stuhr. Bromski uses an ensemble cast of little known actors to breathe comic life into a story of small town Polish life in his **In Heaven As It Is On Earth** (*U Pana Boga za Piecem*).

Kolski, who has consistently won awards in Poland over the last ten years without ever finding much of an audience, continues to purvey his eccentric brand of magic realism in **The Story of the Cinema in Popielawach**. Written, produced and directed by Jerzy Stuhr, **Love Stories** (*Historie Milosne*) garnered the Press Award in 1998 in Venice, as well as a Felix for Stuhr as best actor.

There is an encouraging crop of young scriptwriters emerging, with the most successful undoubtedly being the young man who wrote *Killer*, Piotr Weresniak. In the last year he has directed his first film, **In Love** (*Zakochany*), seen the belated production of his first ever script, **Before Winter Comes**, written dialogue for Wajda's *Pan Tadeusz*, and won the Hartley-Merrill prize for eastern European screenwriting.

Commercial breaks

Other signs of the times include the preoccupation of Polish film stars with doing commercials. It is hard to find a major Polish star who has not committed his or her name and face to some kind of advertising. The kind of ads that American stars would only do in Japan - or that British stars would never do - pop up on billboards and television sets across the land: Star X chomping on a Big Mac, Star Y grinning over a cup of coffee, Star Z urging you to buy a pension.

The main event of the Polish film industry continues to be the annual Gdynia Festival of Feature Films in early October. But, increasingly, the most significant film festival is Camerimage, which takes place in Torun in December. According to the directors of photography themselves, this is now the leading event focusing on their talents. Last year's winner of the Lifetime Achievement award, Laszlo Kovacs, remarked that his "Golden Frog" was more important to him than an Oscar.

RICK RICHARDSON is *Variety*'s correspondent in Warsaw.

Producers

Film Studio Dom
Puławska 61
02595 Warsaw
Tel: (48 22) 455 065

Film Studio Kadr
Puławska 61
02595 Warsaw
Tel: (48 22) 454 923

Film Studio Oko
Puławska 61
02595 Warsaw
Tel: (48 22) 454 041, ext. 222

Film Studio Perspektywa
Puławski 61
02595 Warsaw
Tel: (48 22) 455 494

Film Studio Tor
Puławska 61
02595 Warsaw
Tel/Fax: (48 22) 455 303

Film Studio Zebra
Puławska 61
02595 Warsaw
Tel/Fax: (48 22) 455 484

Film Studio Zodiak
Puławska 61
02595 Warsaw
Tel: (48 22) 452 047

Karol Irzykowski Film Studio
Mazowiecka 11
02595 Warsaw
Tel: (48 22) 276 653, 276 656

Film Studio Kronika
Chełska 21
00724 Warsaw
Tel/Fax: (48 22) 416 221

S.F. Semafor
Pabianicka 34
93513 Łódź
Tel/Fax: (48 42) 814120

Studio Indeks
Targowa 61/63
90323 Łódź
Tel: (48 42) 205 126

Łódź Film Centre
Łąkowa 29
90554 Łódź
Tel: (48 42) 367 500
Fax: (48 42) 360 487

WFDiF (Wytwórnia Filmów Dokumentalnych i Fabularnych)
Chełmska 21
00724 Warsaw
Tel: (48 22) 411 211
Fax: (48 22) 415 891

Independent Producers

Apple Film Production Ltd
Pl. Konstytucji 3/10
00647 Warsaw
Tel/Fax: (48 22) 290 754

Ekran Bis
Łąkowa 29
90554 Łódź
Tel: (48 42) 372 577
Fax: (48 42) 362 046

Feniks Film
Chełmska 21
00724 Warsaw
Tel/Fax: (48 22) 413 821

Figaro
Chełmska 21
00724 Warsaw
Tel/Fax: (48 22) 635 6130

Focus Producers Ltd
Ryżowa 42
02495 Warsaw
Tel: (48 22) 662 7586
Fax: (48 22) 662 7083

Fokus Film Ltd
Okrąg 4/45
Łódź
Tel: (48 42) 297 003

Gambit Productions
Przemysłowa 7
02496 Warsaw
Tel/Fax: (48 2) 667 4596

Heritage Films
Marsałkowska 2/6
00581 Warsaw
Tel: (48 22) 625 2601
Fax: (48 22) 625 2693

Marek Nowowiejski Film Productions
Chełmska 21
00740 Warsaw
Tel/Fax: (48 22) 644 3400

MS Film
Chełmska 21
00724 Warsaw
Tel: (48 22) 405 056
Fax: (48 22) 405 935

N (Independent Studio "Niezalezni")
Lajkonika 5
04110 Łódź
Tel: (48 42) 861 394

Pleograf Ltd
pl. Mirowski 18
00138 Warsaw
Tel/Fax: (48 22) 208 342

MM Potocka Productions
Puzonistów 4
02876 Warsaw
Tel: (48 22) 643 9556
Fax: (48 22) 643 9553

Skorpion Film
Chełmska 21
00724 Warsaw
Tel/Fax: (48 22) 416 171

Distributors

Film Agency Silesia-Film
Kościuszki 88
40519 Katowice
Tel/Fax: (48 832) 512 284
and
al. Ujazdowskie 20/10
00478 Warsaw
Tel/Fax: (48 22) 628 4518

Gentrum Filmowe Graffiti Ltd
Sw. Gertrudy 5
31046 Krakow
Tel: (48 12) 211 628
Fax: (48 12) 211 402

Fundacja Sztuki Filmowej
Andersa 1
00174 Warsaw
Tel: (48 22) 311 636
Fax: (48 22) 635 2001

MAF – Mlodziezowa Akademia Filmowa
Marsałkowska 28
00639 Warsaw
Tel/Fax: (48 22) 628 9698

Black Cat
Magnoliowa 2
20208 Lublin
Tel/Fax: (48 81) 774 654

Iti Cinema
Marsałkowska 138
00004 Warsaw
Tel: (48 22) 826 9862
Fax: (48 22) 826 8552

Solopan Film Centrum
Krakówskie Przedmiescie 21/23
00071 Warsaw
Tel/Fax: (48 22) 635 0044

Syrena Entertainment Group
Marsałkowska 115
00102 Warsaw
Tel: (48 22) 273 503
Fax: (48 22) 275 648

Vision
Rydygiera 7
01793 Warsaw
Tel: (48 22) 390 753
Fax: (48 22) 391 367

Imp Poland
Hoża 66/68
00950 Warsaw
Tel/Fax: (48 22) 628 7691

Imperial Entertainment
Kolska 12
01045 Warsaw
Tel: (48 22) 472 052
Fax: (48 22) 430 585

Artvision
Jerolimskie 125/127
01017 Warsaw
Tel: (48 22) 628 9315
Fax: (48 22) 467 239

Useful Addresses

Committee for Cinema
Krakowskie Przedmiescie 21/23
00071 Warsaw
Tel: (48 22) 826 7489
Fax: (48 22) 276 233

Film Polski
Mazowiecka 6/8
00048 Warsaw
Tel: (48 22) 826 8455
Fax: (48 22) 826 2370

PORTUGAL

John Hopewell

Portuguese cinema has never enjoyed such prosperity in terms of box-office success at home or recognition abroad. In 1998–99, there were three major local hits, all backed by the leading private broadcaster, SIC. The most successful was **Zona J**, with 239,446 admissions. Directed by Leonel Vieira and produced by Tino Navarro, this is a tough, *Romeo and Juliet*-style story, set in one of Lisbon's most run-down neighbourhoods. The film clicked with young audiences who identified with the slang-speaking characters, and the vivid portrayal of drugs, racism and social exclusion.

The nation's second biggest hit, **Jaime** (190,000 admissions), was set in Portugal's northern capital, Oporto, and marked the directorial return of Antonio Pedro Vasconcelos after a ten-year absence. This unevenly-plotted feature makes Oporto look like Naples in a 1950s Italian neo-realist film. It boasts some fine performances, notably from Vitor Norte as a gangsterish businessman. The third main local success, **Sweet Nightmare** (185,472 admissions), by Fernando Fragata, is an ultra-light pop movie, shot in English, whose local success was mainly due to the long legs of hot TV presenter Catarina Furtado.

At the main international film festivals, Portuguese auteurs continue to be much in demand. João Botelho's **Traffic** was included in official selection in Berlin, 1998. The film is much more upbeat than Botelho's

Leonel Vieira's ZONA J was Portugal's biggest domestic hit of 1998–99

other work, venturing into the world of kitsch, and Almodóvar-style parodies of modern Portugal, a nation in which, Botelho suggests, "money now circulates far more easily than ideas". One of the strongest scenes is a high society party in which the guests dance around the swimming pool in co-ordinated shades of pastel pink.

João Mario Grilo's **Far from View** (Official Selection, Venice 1998) returns to the auteur's key recurrent theme: men in prison. The jail setting transmits the idea of Portugal as a claustrophobic cul-de-sac, in which the only escape is writing letters under a false name to rich emigrants in the United States. The film is low-key and downbeat but boasts fine character performances, notably that of stage actor Canto e Castro.

Film editor Manuela Viegas' debut, **Gloria** (Official Selection, Berlin 1999), is a slow mosaic of short episodes in the lives of characters who are always on the brink of departure but who never quite depart; it's a sequence of contrasting moments which leave the audience either spellbound or profoundly irritated. João Cesar Monteiro provides a further glimpse into his private life and obsessions in **God's Wedding** (Un Certain Regard, Cannes 1999), a slightly more chaste version of his previous outin⸢ as "John of God".

The crowning glory of Portu u e auteur cinema was the award of the S⸢ ⸢cial Jury Prize in Cannes 1999 to Manoe. de Oliveira for **The Letter**, which features a⸢ of the 91-year old director's hallmarks: exquisite photography, a story adapted from literary classic, and the deification of his central female characters, notably Chiara Mastroanni and his muse, Leonor Silveira.

Fighting on the home front

The relative success of Portuguese films at home and abroad failed, however, to satisfy local film critics. Many of the local hits are considered to be TV-movies at best, and the films selected internationally are criticised by many as being outdated

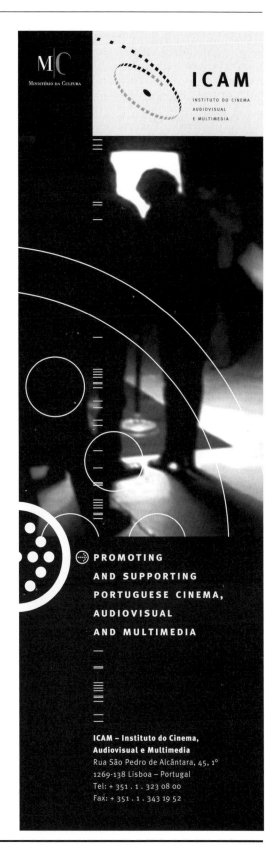

PROMOTING AND SUPPORTING PORTUGUESE CINEMA, AUDIOVISUAL AND MULTIMEDIA

ICAM – Instituto do Cinema, Audiovisual e Multimedia
Rua São Pedro de Alcântara, 45, 1°
1269-138 Lisboa – Portugal
Tel: + 351 . 1 . 323 08 00
Fax: + 351 . 1 . 343 19 52

visions of Portugal, charming to foreign elites but with little to say about contemporary domestic issues. These disputes have been further ignited by a lack of consistency in the government policy for the sector.

Extraordinary events have engulfed the national Institute of Cinema, Audiovisual and Multimedia (ICAM). The seeds were sown when Minister of Culture Manuel Maria Carrilho announced a "revolution" for the sector in 1998, based on diversifying financing sources and creating a new public investment fund – Conteúdos S.A. (Contents plc).

These measures were severely criticised by some leading Portuguese auteurs, including João Mario Grilo and João Botelho, who accused the Minister of making a U-turn from his previous commitment to auteur cinema. By the end of 1998 Conteúdos S.A. had finally been created and ICAM president José-Carlos de Costa Ramos and Conteúdos managing director Martin Dale provided interviews to the national press identifying a new strategy intended to reinforce the international potential of Portuguese production companies.

The launch of the new initiative prompted articles by João Mario Grilo, who described the company and its employees as "The Thing", and announced that he did not want to make films about "contents", but only about "ideas and forms". The row really took off when the Minister of Culture announced in February 1999 that the company was a "pure fiction". Two months later, national newspaper *Público* proved that the company did exist and had been discussing the publicly-announced projects.

After these revelations, Costa Ramos resigned and was replaced by his deputy, Pedro Behran da Costa. A month later the new law for cinema, audiovisual and multimedia was revoked by Parliament and the future of ICAM, Conteúdos SA and audio-visual legislation is now likely to be decided only after the general election in October 1999.

Still from Manoel de Oliveira's THE LETTER, a prize-winner at Cannes

Movers and shakers

In the meantime, leading Portuguese producers try to consolidate their activity. Paulo Branco is an increasingly prestigious international producer, above all as a result of his French company Gemini Films, which unveiled at Cannes 1999 the $20m *Le Temps Retrouvé*, directed by Raoul Ruiz. Tino Navarro increasingly has his eyes set on the US market and is preparing the next outing by local box-office champ Joaquim Leitão, while Rosi Burguette continues to produce interesting shorts. Antonia Seabra's AS Produções produces interesting shorts and features, including Manuel Mozos' magic realist **When it Thunders**. Last but not least, veteran producer Antonio da Cunha Telles is preparing ten TV movies for a new joint venture established by ICAM and SIC.

The main media groups, Lusomundo, SIC, RTP and Portugal Telecom increasingly view cinema, audiovisual and multimedia as priority investment areas. There is also a rising level of international co-productions, the most notable recent example being Maria de Medeiros' tale of the 1974 revolution, **Captains of April**, co-produced by France's Jacques Bidou and budgeted at over $5m – Portugal's most ambitious production to date. Some of these new ventures are criticised in certain quarters as attempts to undermine the very fabric of Portuguese culture. In such a climate, a balanced evolution combining traditional ventures *and* innovation seems impossible to achieve.

JOHN HOPEWELL is *Variety's* bureau chief for Spain and Portugal and the author of two books on Spanish film-making.

Recent and Forthcoming Films

A CARTA (The Letter)

Script and Dir: Manoel de Oliveira. Photo: Emmanuel Machuel. Players: Chiara Mastroianni, Leonor Silveira, Pedro Abrunhosa. Prod: Madragoa Filmes (Portugal)/ Gemini Films (France).

AS BODAS DE DEUS
(God's Wedding)

Script and Dir: João Cesar Monteiro. Phot: Mário Barroso. Players: João Cesar Monteiro, Luis Miguel Cintra, Joana Azevedo, Rita Durão. Prod: Madragoa Filmes.

TRAFICO (Traffic)

Script and Dir: João Botelho. Phot: Olivier Gueneau. Players: Rita Blanco, Adriana Luz. Prod: Madragoa Filmes.

LONGE DA VISTA
(Far from View)

Script: João Mario Grilo, Paulo Filipe Monteiro. Dir: Grilo. Phot: Laurent Machuel. Players: Canto e Castro, Henrique Viana. Prod: Madragoa Filmes.

GLORIA

Script: Manuela Viegas, Joaquim Sapinho. Dir: Sapinho. Phot: João Gil, Artur Costa. Players: Jean-Christophe Bouvet, Francisco Relvas. Prod: Rosa Filmes.

ZONA J

Script: Rui Cardoso Martins. Dir: Leonel Vieira. Phot: Carlos Gusi. Players: Félix Fontoura, Núria Madruga, Ana Bustorff, José Pedro Gomes. Prod: MGN Filmes.

JAIME

Script: Antonio Pedro Vasconcelos, Carlos Saboga. Dir: Vasconcelos. Phot: Edgar Moura. Players: Saul Fonseca, Vitor Norte, Fernanda Serrano. Prod: Fado Filmes.

PESADELO COR DE ROSA
(Sweet Nightmare)

Script and Dir: Fernando Fragata. Phot: Rui Poças. Players: Catarina Furtado, Diogo Infante. Prod: Virtual Audiovisuais.

QUANDO TROVEJA
(When it Thunders)

Script: Manuel Mozos, Jeanne Waltz. Dir: Mozos. Phot: José António Loureiro. Players: Miguel Guilherme, José Wallenstein, Raquel Dias. Prod: AS Produções.

THE WINDOW IS NOT THE LANDSCAPE

Script and Dir: Edgar Pêra. Phot: Luís Branquinho. Players: Lúcia Sigalho, José Wallenstein, Nuno Melo. Prod: Akademya Lusoh Galaktika.

CAPTAINS OF APRIL

Script: Maria de Medeiros, Eve Duboise. Dir: de Medeiros. Phot: Michel Abramowitz. Players: Stefano Accorsi, Joaquim de Almeida, Emmanuel Salinger. Prod: JBA Production.

Producers

Akademya Lusoh-Galaktika
Beco de Galheta, 26
1200–676 Lisboa
Tel: (351) 1 395 22 10
Fax: (351) 1 395 22 09

Animanostra
Av. Cinco Outubro, 10, 7°, sala 2
1000 Lisbon
Tel: (351 1) 315 7692
Fax: (351 1) 353 4194

Animatógrafo
Rua de Rosa, 252, 2°
1200 Lisbon
Tel: (351 1) 347 5372
Fax: (351 1) 347 3252

AS Produções
Rua Jacinto Nunes, 18–1 E
1170 Lisboa
Tel: (351) 1 813 20 90
Fax: (351) 1 812 44 04

David & Golias
Rua da Madalena 91, 3ºD
1100 Lisboa
Tel: (351 1) 888 2028
Fax: (351 1) 888 2046

Fábrica de Imagens
Largo do Contador Mor, 3
1100 Lisbon
Tel: (351 1) 888 1102
Fax: (351 1) 886 0 23

Filmógrafo
Rua Duque de Loulé, 141 R/C
4000 Oporto
Tel: (351 2) 208 6780
Fax: (351 2) 208 6861

Madragoa Filmes
Av. D. Manuel 1, nº 3
2890 Alcochete
Lisbon
Tel: (351 1) 234 2185/2225/2233
Fax: (351 1) 234 2202

MGN Filmes
Rua de S. Bento, 644, 4º Esq.
1200 Lisbon
Tel: (351 1) 388 7497
Fax: (351 1) 388 7281

Mutante Filmes
Rua Imprensa Nacional, 48, 3'E
1250 Lisbon
Tel: (351 1) 395 2975
Fax: (351 1) 395 2975

Produções Off/Rosi Burguete
Rua da Barroca, 72-3'
1200 Lisbon
Tel: (351 1) 347 0378
Fax: (351 1) 347 0370

Rosa Filmes
Campo de Cebolas, 17, 2º, Esqº
1100 Lisbon
Tel: (351 1) 882 0160
Fax: (351 1) 882 0169

S.P. Filmes
Rúa Das Pracas, 60, 1º DTº
Lisbon
Tel: (351 1) 396 4222
Fax: (351 1) 397 1352

Virtual Audiovisuais
Avenida de Roma, 72, 8 D
1700 Lisboa
Tel: (351) 1 846 3891
Fax: (351) 1 846 3898

Distributors

Filmes Castelo Lopes
Rua de Sto Amaro à Estrêla, 17A
1200 Lisbon
Tel: (351 1) 392 9750
Fax: (351 1) 395 5924

Filmes Lusomundo
Av. Liberdade, 266
1250 Lisbon
Tel: (351 1) 318 7300
Fax: (351 1) 352 3568

Atalanta Filmes
Rua Tomás Ribeiro 8, 2º
1050 Lisbon
Tel: (351 1) 353 1585/9
Fax: (351 1) 353 1636

Useful Addresses

Cinemateca Portuguesa
Rua Barata Salgueiro, 39
1250 Lisbon
Tel: (351 1) 354 6279
Fax: (351 1) 352 3180

IPACA/ICAM – Instituto da Cinema, Audiovisual e Multimedia
Rua São Pedro de Alcântara, 45-1'
1250 Lisbon
Tel: (351 1) 323 0800
Fax: (351 1) 343 1952

Media Desk, Portugal
Rua S. Pedro de Alcântara, 45, 1º
1200 Lisbon
Tel: (351 1) 347 8644
Fax: (351 1) 347 8643

Radiotelevisao Comercial (RTC)
Av. Fontes Pereira de Melo, 17-19, 2º-3º
1050 Lisbon
Tel: (351 1) 352 8835
Fax: (351 1) 355 7076

Radiotelevisao Portuguesa (RTP)
Av. 5 de Outubro, 197
1094 Lisbon Codex
Tel: (351 1) 757 5070/793 1774
Fax: (351 1) 796 6227

Sociedade Independente de Comunicaçao (SIC)
Estrada da Outurela, 119
Linda-A-Velha
2795 Carnaxide
Tel: (351 1) 417 3138/71
Fax: (351 1) 417 3119/20

Televisão Independente (TVI)
Rua Mário Castelhano, 40
Queluz de Baixo
2745 Queluz
Tel: (351 1) 435 5181
Fax: (351 1) 435 8747

Tobis Portuguesa
Praça Bernardino Machado
1700 Lisbon
Tel: (351 1) 759 5425
Fax: (351 1) 758 9622

PUERTO RICO — José Artemio Torres

Every year, the film-making environment in Puerto Rico varies so much that even when production levels are down, some new development takes place. As reported in last year's *IFG*, 1998 was quite a busy year, with the premiere of seven locally-produced films; yet the tail end of 1998 and the first half of 1999 have produced only three new films.

The first to be finished and screened is a Spanish-language film for children, **My Little Angel** (*Angelito mío*). This must be the most heavily marketed Puerto Rican film ever, with a soundtrack CD, a doll, a colouring book and other tie-ins; yet the production style harks back to the 1960s. A child television star, the Mexican Luz Clarita, plays an angel who comes down to earth looking for God, to persuade Him to go back to heaven to straighten things up there. Songs and dance routines abound under the direction of Cuban Enrique Pineda Barnet and the film did well at the local box-office. The producers anticipate distribution in Mexico and other Latin American territories.

Flight of Fancy is the debut of Puerto Rican Noel Quiñones. It took him five years to raise the $3m budget for this romantic comedy about a pilot who crashes his biplane in a mountainous town, setting off a chain of events that send its inhabitants' tranquility into a tailspin. It stars Talisa Soto, from *Don Juan de Marco* and *The Living Daylights*, and Dean Cain, television's Superman.

Star-studded remake

This year, **Under Suspicion** becomes the biggest Hollywood film to be entirely shot in Puerto Rico. Based on the French film *Garde à vue*, it stars Morgan Freeman and Gene Hackman, who has wanted to make this new version for 15 years. Then Freeman agreed to do it through his own production company, Revelations Entertainment. The film is a thriller that takes place on one night in which a powerful lawyer (Hackman) is investigated for murder by the local police captain (Freeman). The director is Stephen Hopkins (*Lost in Space*, *The Ghost and the Darkness*), who insisted that Old San Juan was selected as the location because of its mix of Spanish and American cultures, although local investment and tax breaks also influenced the decision.

Although *Flight of Fancy* and *My Little Angel* also got production money from two local film funds, there is talk of the tap running dry. That seems true at least of Banco Popular, Puerto Rico's largest bank, whose Motion Pictures and Allied Services division is currently inactive, for the simple reason that none of the films it has sponsored have made any money. Film finance will, it seems, be harder to come by in the near future.

Gene Hackman and Monica Beluchi filming UNDER SUSPICION

On the other hand, the flow of American films using Puerto Rico (mainly Old San Juan) to double for Cuba shows no signs of drying up. This year it was *The Company Man*, a CIA/Castro comedy starring Doug McGrath, Sigourney Weaver and John Turturro. In exhibition, the number of screens keeps growing, along with the shopping malls. In the first half of 1999, 22 new screens were added.

JOSÉ ARTEMIO TORRES is a film-maker and writer. He heads La Linterna Mágica, a film and video production and distribution company.

Producers

Guede Films
PO Box 194140
San Juan, Puerto Rico 00919-4140
Tel: (1 787) 783 5656
Fax: (1 787) 782 8600
e-mail: guedpost@icepr.com

Paradiso Films
PO Box 11894

San Juan, Puerto Rico 00922-1894
Tel (1 787) 782 0020
Fax: (1 787) 783 8394
e-mail: lux1@caribenet.com

Distributors

Premiere Films
PO Box 8598
San Juan, Puerto Rico 00910-8598

Tel (1 787) 724 0762
Fax: (1 787) 723 4562
e-mail: premiere@caribe.net

La Linterna Magica, Inc.
667 Ponce de Leon Ave.
Box 132
San Juan, Puerto Rico 00907
Tel: (1 787) 723 2362
Fax: (1 787) 723 6412
e-mail: llmagica@.tld.net

Tropical Visions Entertainment Group
954 Ponce de Leon Ave.
Suite 208
San Juan, Puerto Rico 00907
Tel: (1 787) 725 3565
Fax: (1 787) 724 4333
e-mail: tvegsjpr@prtc.net

Useful addresses

Corporación para el Desarrollo del Cine en Puerto Rico
(Government organisation. Director: Manuel A. Biascoechea)
Apartado Postal 2350
San Juan
Puerto Rico 00936-2350
Tel: (1 787) 754 7110
Fax: (1 787) 756 5806

Asociación de Productores
(President: Ana María García)
PO Box 190399
San Juan
Puerto Rico 00919-0399
Tel: (1 787) 764 1589
Fax: (1 787) 764 1204

Archivo de Imágenes en Movimiento (Film archive)
(Director: Nelly V. Cruz Rodríguez)
Archivo General de Puerto Rico
PO Box 4184
San Juan
Puerto Rico 00901
Tel: (1 787) 722 2113/0331
Fax: (1 787) 722 9097

San Juan Cinemafest
PO Box 9020079
San Juan
Puerto Rico 00902
Tel: (1 787) 721 6125
Fax. (1 787) 724 4187
Director: Gabriel Suau
October 1999

Puerto Rico International Film Festival
Calle Mayagüez 17
Suite B-1
San Juan, Puerto Rico 00918
Tel: (1 787) 763 4997
Fax: (1 787) 753 5367
Director: Juan Gerard González
November 1999

ROMANIA — Cristina Corciovescu

The director Lucian Pintilie has noted: "Exceptions keep Romanian cinema alive." Before the 1989 revolution, about 25 to 30 Romanian features were produced each year, but very few were shown abroad (and then mostly in the socialist countries). Nowadays there are two or three films made annually, but they are selected for and even receive awards at prestigious festivals, and get international distribution. Which situation is preferable? The answer should be an average of 20 movies per year, mostly worthy to participate in international competitions.

That is the aim of the two-year-old National Film Office (NFO), which has begun to finance projects chosen on a competitive basis. The competitions are held twice a year, and, through 50% NFO financing per project, have resulted in the completion of several full-length features, shorts and documentaries. Perhaps the most positive sign is the decreasing average age of active Romanian film-makers, with talented young people likely soon to attract the interest of critics and audience: the likes of Cristian Mungiu, Andrei Morosanu, Hano Hoffer, Cristi Puiu and Thomas Ciulei.

For the time being, however, we are still depending on the "exceptions". The most prestigious in the past year have been two Romanian-French co-productions. The first was Pintilie's **Terminus Paradis**, winner of the Silver Lion at Venice. As usual, Pintilie's screen universe is a dark one, and his characters scream in vain, for the society they live in is deaf to their grief. Such is the fate of Mitu, son of an ex-communist dignitary, whose dream of escaping to the Western world has failed. The young man rebels hysterically against everything (family, army, country), soothed only by the presence of Norica, a young waitress who sleeps with her boss in exchange for the promise of a better life. Mitu kills the boss, but this tragic event is lightened by a wave of warmth and gentleness between

Still from Lucian Pintilie's Silver Lion-winning
TERMINUS PARADIS

the youngsters that is unheard of in Pintilie's films.

If Benigni can do it ...

At the opposite pole stands Radu Mihaileanu, writer-director of **Train of Life** (*Trenul vietii*), an artist who demonstrated his extraordinary comic abilities through the tragedy of the Holocaust. During the Second World War, a Jewish community from South-Eastern Europe tries to avoid the death camps by organising a false deportation, with Jews playing the parts of the prisoners and the guards on a train that is actually heading towards Palestine. There follows a chain of unexpected incidents, confrontations and, of course,

gags – supported by sparkling dialogue. In the year of Benigni, Mihaileanu (now working on his second film) matched the Tuscan clown, winning the FIPRESCI Award at Venice, the Audience Award at Sundance and a Best Screenplay nomination at the Césars.

Last year also saw debut films from Bogdan Cristian Dragan with **The Tent** (*Cortul*), a drama set against the background of the 1989 revolution, and Marius Theodor Barna, with **Face to Face** (*Fata in fata*), a family drama analysing the secret police's devastating interference in the lives of an ordinary couple.

Finally, two Romanian names were noticed on the world's screens in 1998: Nae Caranfil (writer-director of the Italian-French-Belgian co-production *Dolce far niente*, which won the Best Screenplay award at the Namur Film Festival) and Rona Hartner, who starred in Tony Gatlif's Romanian-shot *Gadjo Dilo* (she received a Best Actress Award at Locarno and a César nomination).

CRISTINA CORCIOVESCU is a film critic, author of several cinema dictionaries and chief editor of the magazine *ProCinema*.

Recent and Forthcoming Films

FAIMOSUL PAPARAZZO
(The Famous Paparazzo)

Dir: Nicolae Margineanu. Players: Marcel Iures, Maria Ploae.

Determined to catch a member of parliament having illicit sex, and destroy his political career, a journalist moves in to the apartment of a prostitute, who briefly deludes herself that she is having a normal relationship.

TRIUNGHIUL MORTII
(Deadly Triangle)

Dir: Sergiu Nicolaescu. Players: Nicolaescu, Stefan Velniciuc, Maia Morgenstern.

First World War drama set during the bloody battles of Marasti, Marasesti and Oituz on the Romanian front.

ALLEGRO ALLARMATO

Dir: Mircea Daneliuc. Players: Cecilia Birbora, Horatiu Malaele.

Titi and Marius, two friends who fought together during the revolution of 1989, follow very different social and political paths in its aftermath.

Producers

Atlantis Film
Cal. Giulesti nr. 16, sector 6
Bucharest
Tel: (401) 221 0079
Fax: (401) 221 0535

Castel Film
Str. Episcop Timus nr. 25, sector 1
Bucharest

Tel: (401) 211 6282/7291
Fax: (401) 211 6135

Domino Film
Str. Dr. Felix nr. 59, et.1
Bucharest
Tel: (401) 210 3713/223 4669
Fax: (401) 312 9609

Filmex
Str. Pictor Verona nr. 2, sector 1
Bucharest
Tel: (401) 615 8913/615 9038
Fax: (401) 312 1388

Sc. Rofilm SA
Bd. M.Kogalniceanu nr. 11, sector 5
Bucharest
Tel: (401) 311 2710
Fax: (401) 311 3080

Still from Nicolae Margineanu's THE FAMOUS PAPARAZZO

photo: Cos Aecenei

Distributors

Glob Com Media
Str. Brezoianu nr. 57A, et 2, sector 1
Bucharest
Tel. (401) 315 4707
Fax. (401) 315 4506

Guild Film Romania
Str. Arcului nr. 14A, et.1, ap.7
Bucharest
Tel: (401) 210 5359/211 4880
Fax: (401) 210 7699

Independenta
Bd. Nicolae Balcescu nr. 24
sc C, et. 7, ap. 9,
Sector 1
Bucharest
Tel/fax: (401) 311 32 08

RoIMAGE 2000
Sos. Mihai Bravu nr. 85–93, bl.C16
sc.C, ap. 8
Bucharest
Tel: (401) 252 60 66
Tel/fax: (401) 252 76 61

Vision PM
Sos. Cotroceni nr. 7–9
Bucharest
Tel: (401) 638 4045
Fax: (401) 222 1551

Useful Addresses

Oficiul National al Cinematografiei
Str. Dem I Dobrescu nr. 4–6
Bucharest
Tel: (401) 310 4301
Fax: (401) 310 4300

Romania Film
Str. Thomas Massaryk nr. 25
70231 Bucharest
Tel: (401) 210 7398/7835
Fax: (401) 611 7660

Uniunea Cineastilor
Str. Mendeleev nr. 28–30, sector 1
70169 Bucharest
Tel: (401) 650 4265
Fax: (401) 311 1246

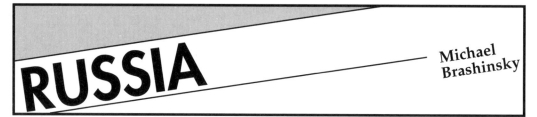

RUSSIA

Michael Brashinsky

In Russia, 1998 saw the death of hopes for a revival in the national cinema. Or so it seemed. The August 1998 economic crisis marked the end of the "virtual capitalism" phase, during which money poured into cultural image-making (while the economy remained largely unproductive), and ushered in the period of "new stagnation".

The industry mechanism that only recently began to function properly has stalled on the verge of breakdown. As private investments in the industry waned, the state supplied only 8% of what had been promised in the Domestic Film Development federal programme adopted a year earlier, and only one third of the sum reflected in the federal budget. The equivalent of $5.3m – instead of an expected $18m – was the total government input for all branches of the film industry (including distribution, exhibition, film preservation, capital projects and education), with only $1.8m of the projected $7.5m going to film production.

Dropping all pretence of enlightened patronage, the state provided no more than one fifth of the industry's accumulated budget. The film, TV and video distribution markets shrunk overnight, essentially destroying the newly-born distribution infrastructure. Without it, new Russian films could be made, but not seen.

According to the official statistics, 45 features were produced in 1998, which was a consequence of the 1997 production boom (the biggest in a decade), rather than a sign of good health. Illness could be easily diagnosed from a single symptom: no new production contracts had been signed by the end of 1998. With the state's debt to the industry from the previous year outgrowing the new year's allowance, it could make no promises, and no one dared venture into the thankless production business without state support. Some 64 films were not financed as contracted in 1998.

By the summer of 1999, however, things had begun to look somewhat brighter. The reconstruction of big cinemas in major cities signalled a new interest in quality exhibition. Film-makers began to shave again: work, they sensed, might be out there after all. In film-making, as in the economy, the crisis seemed to be receding.

Capital ideas

Films continued to be made, although, in many cases, this was the only good news about them. The weakest outing was from Mosfilm. The country's main studio attempted to package several features into a demonstration of the vitality of the old Soviet film-making system, but failed to convey a positive message because of the appalling quality of the product.

The desire for popular cinema (or "people's cinema" as it is better known here) translated into Vladimir Grammatikov's dull children's melodrama **Hello From Charlie the Trumpeter** (*Privet ot Charlie-trubacha*); Victor Titov's chaotic folk comedy **Quadrille**; Valery Priemykhov's uncertain problem-kids "message" pic **Who If Not Us** (*Kto, esli ne my*); Vitaly Moskalenko's inept

costume con-comedy **China Set** (*Kitaiskyi serviz*); and Alexander Surin's laughable adaptation of E.M. Remarque's *The Three Comrades*, **Flowers From the Winners** (*Tsvety ot pobeditelei*).

Petersburg offered a better, if thinner, selection. Sergei Snezhkin's **Marigold Blossoms** (*Tsvety kalenduly*) was an ironic elegy to the Soviet intelligentsia (imagined here as a dying, Chekhovian breed), and Vyacheslav Sorokin's **Totalitarian Romance** (*Totalitarnyi roman*) was a love triangle KGB drama set in 1968. Both proved that a solid dramatic tradition has not yet completely deteriorated. Alexander Rogozhkin's **Peculiarities of the National Fishing** (*Osobennosti natsionalnoi rybalki*) pleased the numerous fans of Rogozhkin's comic *Peculiarities* cycle, which lovingly mocks Russians' legendary alcoholism, in various habitats: the woods (*Peculiarities of the National Hunting*), a hospital ("*Happy New Year*" *Operation*) and, this time, on the water.

The same director's **Checkpoint** (*Blockpost*), a light ensemble piece, focused on a squad of draftees bored to death at the margins of the Chechen war, became the most well-received film of the year, voted the best at the Kinotaur National film festival in Sochi. Rogozhkin was truly the film-maker of the year, as he also stood behind **Cops** (*Menty*), the nation's most popular TV police drama.

Indy deeds

Independent producers, who suffered as badly as anyone from the effects of the

Bored soldiers in Alexander Rogozhkin's CHECKPOINT

Yevgeny Mironov in Dennis Yevstigneev's MOMMA

economic crisis, tried twice as hard to keep the show on the road. NTV-Profit, the major of the minors, unveiled two high-profile projects. Dennis Yevstigneev's **Momma** (*Mama*) was a melodrama based on a real-life case involving a young folk band, whose members were all brothers. Led by their mother (played by veteran actress Nonna Mordyukova), they attempted to highjack a Soviet aeroplane in the 1980s.

Stanislav Govorukhin's **Sharpshooter** (*Voroshilovskyi strelok*) was an earnest political parable made by a director who is also a Communist congressman. Its hero (played by veteran Mikhail Ulyanov) is an old man who, deprived of everything but his dignity and a rifle, assumes a Charles Bronson role to avenge the rape of his grand-daughter. Both films looked very promising in their synopses but were quite disappointing as finished products. The gloss of expensive mainstream cinema could not conceal the dramatic incoherence and poor direction.

A smaller Slovo production company

presented the first two instalments of an ongoing project, The Russian Decameron, a series of feature-length romantic anecdotes. Dmitry Meskhiev's **Women's Property** (*Zhenskaya sobstvennost'*) was a half-successful attempt at middle-class melodrama, undermined by script problems – writing is undeniably the weakest aspect of new Russian cinema.

Tests for Real Men (*Testydlya nastoyashchikh muzhchin*), by Andrei Razenkov, stylishly created a mystery where one did not exist, but fell victim to its plot's impenetrable silliness. This debut showed there are young forces ready to join the mainstream and make clean, conservative, pleasant films (all that is missing is a mainstream for them to join).

Other notable debuts took greater risks. Gennady Konstantinopolsky's **$8½** made Fellini's torn alter ego a chewing-gum commercials director bankrolled by the mafia, and his story became a cheerfully long music video. In **Private Chronicles: A Monologue** (*Chastnye khroniki: Monolog*), Vitaly Mansky, a documentary film-maker, debuted in a peculiar genre of "fictionalised non-fiction". His montage of a single Soviet life-story from hundreds of 8mm home-movies, synchronised with a poignant voice-over monologue, became a sensation at the National film festival. It created a portrait of a life lived in oblivion that many here could relate to.

The most accomplished and controversial debut came from popular screenwriter Piotr Lutsik. **Outskirts** (*Okraina*) envisioned contemporary Russia as a stark black-and-white Neverland of mutated Soviet myths, heroic Stalinist movies and low-budget slasher-flicks. Lutsik played imaginatively on the most sensitive strings of the new Russian soul, those that tie it to its own national identity. The critics accused the director of reactionary politics.

Clash of the titans

As if to prove that crises are for mortals, Nikita Mikhalkov and Alexander Sokurov, the country's two leading auteurs – and also the most commercial and esoteric –

unveiled major new works. Mikhalkov's $40m **The Barber of Siberia** (*Sibirskiy tsiryulnik*) played poorly with the Russian critics and at Cannes, where it opened the fest (the first Russian movie ever to do so), but did much better at the European box-office.

This convoluted English-language epic about Russian imperial history is low on dramatic sense but rich on the lush sensuality that has long been this director's trademark. The shadows of Boris Pasternak (who, like Mikhalkov, loved winter and cheap melodrama) and David Lean (who glued history to carnality in the vast space of *Doctor Zhivago*) linger over *The Barber of Siberia*, informing it with a nobler and deeper meaning than the story should have allowed.

Sokurov's **Molokh** is much more controversial than Mikhalkov's film, or, perhaps, any film this year: it dares to imagine Hitler as a man and a lover. Set in the Fuhrer's Alpine residence in 1942, *Molokh* focuses on Hitler's relationship with Eva Braun and his inner circle, but is more a mystic meditation on the nature of evil than a chamber piece. Impressive acting and, especially, Sokurov's hand-crafted mise-en-scène make *Molokh* a singular achievement.

MICHAEL BRASHINSKY is a contributing editor of *Seance* film magazine and a regular contributor to *Vogue* (Russia). He is co-author of *The Zero Hour: Glasnost and Soviet Cinema in Transition* and co-editor of *Russian Critics on the Cinema of Glasnost* (both with Andrew Horton). He divides his time between New York and St Petersburg.

Recent and Forthcoming Films

$8½

Script: Grigory Konstantinopolsky, Dunya Smirnova, with Sergei Krylov. Dir: Konstantinopolsky. Phot: Yuri Lyubshin, with Yevgeny Korzhenkov. Players: Ivan Okhlobystin, Olesya Potashinskaya, Natalya Obmanutaya (Andreichenko), Fyodor Bondarchuk, Igor Vernik. Prod: The Gorky Studio with Goskino, Premier Film.

BELYI TANETS (White Dance)

Script: Rauf Kubayev, from an idea by Rano Kubayeva. Dir: Kubayev. Phot: Sergei Onufriev. Players: Olga Tsirsen, Nikolai Dobrynin, Alexander Domogarov, Boris Gafurov, Victor Bakin. Prod: SADR.

BLOCKPOST (Checkpoint)

Script and Dir: Alexander Rogozhkin. Phot: Andrei Zhigalov. Players: Roman Romantsov, Andrei Krasko, Dennis Moisseev, Alexander Ivanov. Prod: ORT-TV, STV Studio with Soyuzkino, Goskino

CHASTNYE KHRONIKI: MONOLOG (Private Chronicles: A Monologue)

Script and Dir: Vitaly Mansky. Narration: Igor Yarkevitch, narrated by Alexander Tsekalo. Prod: MV-Studio, Ren-TV.

CINEMA, CINEMA, ILI NEOTVRATIMAYA VESNA (Cinema, Cinema, or The Inevitable Spring)

Script and Dir: Misha Beberashvili. Phot: Yevgeny Shermergor. Players: Zhenya Alexeenkova, Marina Pavlova, Igor Volkov, Marina Malikova, Gennady Spiridenkov. Prod: MMB Film.

KHOCHU V TYURMU (I Want To Go To Jail)

Script: Vladimir Yeremin. Dir: Alla Surikova. Phot: Grigory Belenky. Players: Vladimir Ilyin, Alla Klyuka, Natalya Gundareva, Alexander Kuznetsov, Sergei Batalov. Prod: NTV-Profit.

KITAISKYI SERVIZ (China Set)

Script and Dir: Vitaly Moskalenko. Phot: Yuri Nevsky. Players: Anna Samokhina, Oleg Yankovsky, Bogdan Stupka, Sergei Nikonenko, Alexander Rezalin. Prod: Genre (Mosfilm).

KLASSIK (The Classic)

Script: Yelena Karavaeshnikova, Georgy Shengelia, Pavel Chukhrai. Dir: Shengelia. Phot: Ilya Demin. Players: Yuozas Budraitis, Sergei Nikonenko, Valentina Telichkina, Vladimir Etush, Alexei Guskov. Prod: Kinomost, with the participation of Slovo (Mosfilm).

KTO, ESLI NE MY (Who, If Not Us)

Script and Dir: Valery Priemykhov. Phot: Alexander Nosovsky. Players: Artur Smolyaninov, Zhenya Krainov, Valery Priemykhov, Tatyana Yakovenko. Prod: Courier (Mosfilm).

MAMA (Momma)

Script: Arif Aliyev. Dir: Dennis Yevstigneev. Phot: Pavel Lebeshev, Sergei Kozlov. Players: Nonna Mordyukova, Oleg Menshikov, Vladimir Mashkov, Yevgenyi Mironov, Mikhail Krylov. Prod: NTV-Profit, Russian Project Studio.

MOLOKH

Script: Yuri Arabov. Dir: Alexander Sokurov. Phot: Alexei Fyodorov, Anatolyi Rodionov. Players: Yelena Rufanova, Leonid Mozgovoi, Leonid Sokol, Yelena Spiridonova, Vladimir Bogdanov. Prod: Lenfilm, Goskino, Fusion Product (Japan), Zero Film (Germany).

NA BOIKOM MESTE
(In a Busy Place)

Script: Alexei Sakharov, Dmitry Sukharev. Dir: Sakharov. Phot: Nikolai Nemolyaev. Players: Nikolai Rastorguyev, Alexei Kortnev, Olga Drozdova, Valdis Pelsh, Nadezhda Gorelova. Prod: Kinomost, with the participation of Ritm (Mosfilm).

NEBO V ALMAZAKH
(Sky of Diamonds)

Script: Maria Khmelik. Dir: Vassily Pichul. Phot: Andrei Makarov. Players: Nikolai Fomenko, Anjelika Varum, Alla Sigalova, Valentin Gaft, Garik Sukachev, Anna Mikhalkova. Prod: Soyuzkino, InterCinema-Art, Parnasse Internation (France).

NOVOSTI (The News)

Script: Stas Preobrazhensky, Ilya Khotinenko. Dir: Khotinenko. Phot: Andrei Naidenov. Players: Yana Lvova, Svetlana Timofeeva, Andrei Merzlikin, Boris Estrin, Dennis Krokhin. Prod: Roy, VGIK.

OKRAINA (Outskirts)

Script: Piotr Lutsik, Alexei Samoryadov. Dir: Lutsik. Phot: Nikolai Ivasiv. Players: Yuri Dubrovin, Nikolai Olyalin, Alexei

Vanin, Rimma Markova, Alexei Pushkin, Victor Stepanov. Prod: Morning of the XXI Century Film Company with Goskino.

PEREVODY S VOSTOCHNOGO
(Translations from Eastern Languages)

Script and Dir: Nina Shorina. Phot: Georgy Krymov, Sergei Ivanov, Alexander Kazarenskov. Players: Vassily Nemirovich-Danchenko, Nina Shorina, Andrei Vyatkin. Prod: Nina Shorina Film with Goskino.

PRIVET OT CHARLIE-TRUBACHA
(Hello From Charlie the Trumpeter)

Script: Georgy Danelia, Sergei Dernov. Dir: Vladimir Grammatikov. Phot: Alexander Antipenko. Players: Alesha Zotov, Valery Yaremenko, Irina Rozanova, Sergei Koltakov, Yuri Stepankov. Prod: Ritm (Mosfilm).

PRO URODOV I LYUDEI
(On Freaks and People)

Script and Dir: Alexei Balabanov. Phot: Sergei Astakhov. Players: Sergei Makovetsky, Victor Sukhorukov, Ahjelica Nevolina, Dinara Drukarova, Igor Shibanov, Alexander Mazantsev. Prod: STV Studio, Soyuzkino with Goskino.

QUADRILLE (Tanets s obmenov partnerami)
(Changing Dance Partners)

Script: Vladimir Gurkin, Victor Titov. Dir: Titov. Players: Oleg Tabakov, Stanislav Lyubshin, Valentina Telichkina, Nina Usatova, Lyubov Polishchuk. Prod: Genre (Mosfilm).

S DNEM ROZHDENIYA!
(Happy Birthday!)

Script and Dir: Larissa Sadilova. Phot: Irina Uralskaya, Alexander Kazarenskov. Players: Goulya Stolyarova, Irina Proshina, Lyubov Starkova, Mourad Ibragimbekov, Yevgeniya Tourkina, Masha Kuzmina. Prod: Film Support Fund.

SIBIRSKIY TSIRYULNIK
(The Barber of Siberia)

Script: Nikita Mikhalkov, Roustam Ibragimbekov, in collaboration with Rospo Pallenberg. Dir: Mikhalkov. Phot: Pavel Lebeshev. Players: Julia Ormond, Oleg Menshikov, Richard Harris, Alexei Petrenko, Vladimir Ilyin, Marat Basharov, Nikita Tatarenkov, Georgy Dronov, Artem Mikhalkov, Anna Mikhalkova, Marina Neelova, Daniel Olbrykhsky, Nikita Mikhalkov. Prod: Camera One (France), Tri-T.

SOCHINENIYE KO DNYU POBEDY (A Term Paper for the Victory Day).

Script: Gennady Ostrovsky, Alexei Zernov. Dir: Sergei Ursulyak. Phot: Misha Suslov. Players: Mikhail Ulyanov, Vyacheslav Tikhonov, Oleg Efremov, Zinaida Sharko, Vladimir Mashkov. Prod: Gorky Studios.

TAINA NARDO, ILI SON BELO SOBAKI (The Mystery of Nardo, or The Dream of the White Dog)

Script: Tonino Guerra, Vladimir Naumov, Grigory Kushnir. Dir: Naumov. Phot: Victor Shestoperov. Players: Nataliya Belokhvostikova, Armen Dzhigarkhanian, Valentin Gaft, Anatolyi Romashin, Liudmila Savelyeva. Prod: Soyuz (Mosfilm), Profilm, Navona, with participation of Goskino.

TESTY DLYA NASTOYASHCHIKH MUZHCHIN (Tests for Real Men)

Script: Valentin Chernykh. Dir: Andrei Razenkov. Phot: Masha Solovyova. Players: Anna Kamenkova, Elvira Bolgova, Alexei Serebryakov, Vitaly Solomin, Nikolai Yeremenko, Jr. Prod: Slovo, Soyuz-Video.

TOTALITARNYI ROMAN
(Totalitarian Romance)

Script: Marina Mareyeva. Dir: Vyacheslav Sorokin. Phot: Sergeu Astakhov, Valery Mironov.

Players: Galina Bokashevskaya, Sergei Yushkevich, Svetlana Kryuchkova, Olga Volkova, Alexander Lykov. Prod: AKV Studio with Goskino.

TSVETY KALENDULY
(Marigold Blossoms)

Script: Mikhail Konovalchuk, Sergei Snezhkin. Dir: Snezhkin. Phot: Arto Melkumian. Valery Yurkevitch. Players: Era Ziganshina, Marina Solopchenko, Kseniya Rappoport, Yuliya Sharikova, German Orlov. Prod: Lenfilm.

TSVETY OT POBEDITELEI
(Flowers from the Winners)

Script: Alla Surina (Krinitsina). Dir: Alexander Surin. Phot: Tatyana Loginova. Players: Aurelia Anuzhite, Alexander Nosik, Pavel Safonov, Vladimir Zaitsev, Olga Budina, Alexei Kravchenko. Prod: Krug (Mosfilm).

UPOTREBIT' DO ...
(Best before ...)

Script: Pyotr Tochilin with Veronika Vozniak. Dir: Tochilin. Phot: Dmitry Skladov. Players: Yevgeny Oreshin, Lyubov Zemtsova, Irina Zharkova. Prod: STV Studio.

VOROSHILOVSKYI STRELOK
(Sharpshooter)

Script: Alexander Borodyansky, Stanislav Govorukhin, Yuri Polyakov. Dir: Govorukhin. Phot: Gennady Engstrem. Players: Mikhail Ulyanov, Anna Sinyakina, Ilya Drevnov, Alexei Makarov, Marat Basharov, Alexander Porokhovschikov, Irina Rozanova. Prod: NTV-Profit.

ZHENSKAYA SOBSTVENNOST'
(Women's Property)

Script: Yuri Korotkov. Dir: Dmitry Meskhiev. Phot: Yuri Shaigardanov. Players: Yelena Safonova, Amalia Mordvinova, Konstantin Khabensky, Nina Usatova, Tatyana Lyutayeva. Prod: Slovo Studio, Soyuz-Video.

Useful Addresses

Arc-Film
(Production, distribution)
1 Mosfilmovskaya St
Moscow 119858
Tel: (0 95) 143 4935
Fax: (0 95) 938 2083

Double D Agency
7 Maly Gnezdnikovsky per
Suite 604
Moscow 103877
Tel: (0 95) 229 7921
Fax: (09 5) 369 1815
(sociological research, publishing)

Intercinema Agency (distribution, production)
Contact: Raissa Fomina at Kinocentre (see below)

East-West
9 Voznesensky Per., Str. 4
Moscow 103009
Tel: (0 95) 229 6991
Fax: (0 95) 200 4249
Distribution

Filmmakersí Union
13 Vassilyevskaya St
Moscow 123825
Tel: (0 95) 251 5106

The Gorky Film Studio
8 Sergei Eisenstein St
Moscow, 129226
Tel: (0 95) 181 0434/181 1418
Fax: (0 95) 188 9871

Gosfilmofond (Central film archives)
Belye Stolby,
Moscow District 6, 142050
Tel: (0 95) 546 0505/546 0513
Fax: (0 95) 546 0525

Goskino
7 Malyi Gnezdnikovsky per
Moscow 103877
Tel: (0 95) 229 3704/229 4522
Fax: (0 95) 229 2248

Higher Courses of Screenwriters And Directors
12 Bolshoy Tishinsky Per
Moscow 123557
Tel: (0 95) 253 6488
Fax: (0 95) 253 8709

Iskusstvo Kino Film Magazine
9 Ussievicha St
Moscow 125319
Tel: (0 95) 151 5651
Fax: (0 95) 151 0272
e-mail: kinoart@glasnet.ru

Konotaur Film Festival (domestic & international)
35 Arbat, Suite 533
Moscow 121835
Tel: (0 95) 248 3498
Fax: (0 95) 248 0966
Also: Faces of Love Festival (films about love)

Lenfilm
10 Kamennoostrovsky Pr
St. Petersburg 197101
Tel: (812) 232 8359
Fax: (812) 232 8881
Production, distribution

Message To Man
Tel/Fax: (0 95) 310 9992
Nonfiction International Film Festival held in St. Petersburg

Moscow International Film Festival
10 Khokhlovske Per., Str. 1
Moscow 109028
Tel: (0 95) 917 2486
Fax: (0 95) 916 0107

Mosfilm
1 Mosfilmovskaya St
Moscow 119858
Tel: (0 95) 143 9100
Fax: (0 95) 143 9290

Museum of Film
15 Druzhinnikovskaya St
Moscow 123242
Tel: (0 95) 255 9886, 255 9189
Fax: (0 95) 255 9096

NTV-Profit
4 Pereyaslavsky Per
Moscow 129110
Tel: (0 95) 284 1338
Fax: (0 95) 971 1279
Production, distribution

Premiere Film Magazine
35 Myasnitskaya St
Suite 742, Moscow, 101959
Tel: 204 1787
Fax: (0 95) 204 1583.
e-mail: premiere@hfm.ru

Seance Film Magazine
10 Kamennoostrovsky Pr
St Petersburg 197101
Tel: (812) 237 0842
Fax: (812) 232 4925
e-mail: seance@spb.cityline.ru

Slovo Production Comopany
1 Mosfilmovskaya St
Moscow 119858
Tel/fax: (0 95) 143 4917
e-mail: chumbon13@glasnet.ru

STV Studio
10 Kamennoostrovsky Pr
St Petersburg 197101
Tel: (812) 326 8330; 326 8331
Production, distribution

Tri-T Studio
11 Maly Kozikhinsky Per
Moscow, 103001
Tel/fax: (0 95) 299 4068; 299 3102

VGIK (Film School)
3 Wilhelm Pik St
Moscow 129226
Tel: (0 95) 181 0605
Fax: (0 95) 187 7174

SERBIA & MONTENEGRO

Goran
Gocić

The Kosovo conflict has left the people of Serbia with many more important concerns than cinema – although cinema was caught up in the crisis. At the beginning of the NATO air raids, in March, all foreign films were promptly withdrawn from Belgrade's cinema repertoire. Radio Television of Serbia (RTS) remained patriotic, screening old partisan movies and the occasional, "politically correct" US product, such as *Wag the Dog*, which became an even more painfully credible tale about Balkan reality. However, RTS was promptly punished by NATO, which included Yugoslav state television on the list of "legitimate military targets", and bombed its transmitters and offices, killing 16 people.

Presumably, not a lot of films are going to be produced by RTS, or for that matter, anyone else in Yugoslavia in the near future. Prominent Serbian actresses Mirjana Joković and Branka Katić have already sought opportunities abroad; the former stars in the BBC drama *Peacekeepers*, and the latter in US comedy *Side Streets*.

If we are to have a long wait for new features, then at least the 1998–99 season has provided a good vintage – even without the arrival of anxiously-awaited

works from the patriarchs of Serbian cinema: Emir Kusturica, Goran Paskaljević and Živojin Pavlović. The standard combination – one quickie, one student omnibus and a lot of brooding over our miserable destiny – was again delivered, but the exceptional aspect was that three comedies were also released in 1998, alongside the political and human tragedy.

The extremely black humour of Goran Paskaljević's **The Powder Keg** (*Bure baruta*) is indicative of the suicidal despair felt in the Balkans. It consists of loosely-connected, violent vignettes set one evening just before the Dayton peace agreement. Those who saw Dejan Dukovski's original play rated it more highly than this screen adaptation. Nevertheless, *The Powder Keg* remained a powerful, contemporary statement about the vicious circle of cruelty that currently rages in the Balkans. This was probably the best work of the season.

Srdjan Dragojević's **Wounds** (*Rane*) is even more cynical. This was an account of delinquents in Serbia, people who looked impoverished, bitter and war-weary even before the Kosovo crisis. Little did the film-makers know what was coming next. The film follows the unhappy existence of three

Left to right: Vojislav Brajović, Toni Mihajlovski and Mirjana Joković in the blackly comic THE POWDER KEG

teenagers growing up in Belgrade in the 1990s. With strong performances from the three leads, all making their screen debuts, *Wounds*, like *The Powder Keg*, left viewers with a bitter taste in their mouths.

Crooks and Gypsies

As in last season's Serbian films *Three Summer Days* and *Three Palms for Two Punks and a Babe*, crooked "pyramid" bankers who run off with impoverished European customers' money struck again in **Thief's Comeback** (*Povratak Lopova*). This was the most serious attempt so far to explore the workings of the 'novelties' in eastern European banking, yet cinematically the least successful of the three films so far made on the subject, and in the opus of director Miroslav Lekić.

Belgrade Faculty of Dramatic Arts' student omnibus **Crossroads** (*Raskršće*), like the 1997 Macedonian feature *Gypsy Magic*, indicated that Gypsies are back in vogue. Both of those preceded **Black Cat, White Cat** (*Crna mačka, beli mačor*),

Kusturica's most accessible film in years. It is a further exploitation of the Gypsy baron motif on which, having made the genre's masterpiece, *Time of the Gypsies*, Kusturica can justifiably claim the copyright. Some commentators criticised him for abandoning conspicuous political statement, and producing a more digestible cinematic product. Indeed, the exaggerations of *Wounds* evoke *Underground* more directly than Kusturica did in *Black Cat, White Cat*. Perhaps Kusturica's least ambitious film, it was still good enough to earn Venice's Silver Lion for direction in 1998.

Barking at the Stars (*Lajanje na zvezde*) is a more conventional comedy, based on Milovan Vitezović's 1975 novel about his post-Second World War school days (there have been so many recent wars in the former Yugoslavia that the adjective 'post-war' is no longer specific enough). True, today's teenagers still face similar emotional dilemmas, but *Barking at the Stars* felt dated. Audiences, notoriously short of laughs, and not very choosy when it comes to comedies, loved it.

After an inexplicably long absence, **Buy Me Eliot** (*Kupi mi Eliota*) marked the return of Dejan Zečević. His understanding of comedy is quite different, offering us a tale of a criminal gang whose outrageous, cartoonish behaviour is by turns comic and grotesque. The content was expected from the unconventional Zečević, an avid fan of obscure horror films, but a total shock coming from the pen of Gordan Mihić, who scripted *Black Cat, White Cat*. The screenwriter himself was also shocked with what ended up on screen, and disavowed the project.

Finally, with his new feature – prophetically entitled *Land of the Dead* – still to be released, the last active veteran of Serbian cinema, Živojin Pavlović, died in Belgrade, aged 65.

GORAN GOCIĆ is a freelance journalist. He writes for various publications in Yugoslavia and abroad and is currently working on an MSc degree in Media & Communications. He has co-written five books on cinema and visual arts, including *A Light in Dark*, *Pop Vision* and *When I'm Dead and White*.

Recent and Forthcoming Films

BELO ODELO (White Suit)

Script and Dir: Lazar Ristovski. Phot: Milorad Glušica. Players: Ristovski, Radmila Sogoljeva, Dragan Nikolić. Prod: British Screen (UK)/Zillion Films, Belgrade.

NA KRAJU PUTA
(At the End of the Road)

Script: Predrag Perišić. Dir: Predrag Velinović. Phot: Radoslav Vladić. Players: Velimir-Bata Zivojinović. Prod: RTV Serbia, Belgrade.

NOŽ (Knife)

Script: Igor Bojović, Miroslav Lekić, based on a novel by Vuk Drašković. Dir: Lekić. Phot: Predrag Todorović. Players: Žarko Lausević, Bojana Maljević. Prod: Metrofilm/Monte Royal Pictures/Srpska Reč, Belgrade.

TOČKOVI (Wheels)

Script and Dir: Djordje Milosavljević. Phot: Dušan Ivanović. Players: Dragan Micanović, Anica Dobra. Prod: Sinema dizajn, Belgrade.

U IME OCA I SINA
(In the Name of the Father and the Son)

Script: Željko Mijanović, Božidar Nikolić. Dir and Phot: Nikolić. Players: Danilo Bata Stojković, Sonja Jauković. Prod: Montenegro Art-Film / Union film, Belgrade.

Useful Addresses

Beograd film
(Chain of theatres)
Terazije 40
11000 Beograd
Tel: (381 11) 688 940
Fax: (381 11) 687 952

First Production
(Independent distributor)
Kumodraška 176/6
11040 Beograd
Tel: (381 11) 471 403
Fax: (381 11) 473 207

Institut za film
(Yugoslav Film Institute)
Čika Ljubina 15
11000 Beograd
Tel: (381 11) 625 131
Fax: (381 11) 634 253

Still from Dejan Zečević's BUY ME ELIOT

Metrofilm International
(Independent producer/distributor)
Trg Nikole Pašića 8
11000 Beograd
Tel: (381 11) 334 0318
Fax: (381 11) 323 5221

Monte Royal Pictures
(Independent producer)
Skerlićeva 30
11000 Beograd
Tel: (381 11) 431 726
Fax: (381 11) 444 1951

Sinema Dizajn
(Producer)
Ustanicka 125/1
11000 Beograd
Tel: (381 11) 488 2377
Fax: (381 11) 488 8011

Tuck
(Independent distributor)
Velikomoravska 11-15
11000 Beograd
Tel: (381 11) 424 666
Fax: (381 11) 413 177

Vans
(Independent producer and
distributor)
Njegoševa 84
11000 Beograd
Tel: (381 11) 432 492
Fax: (381 11) 434 226

SINGAPORE — Yvonne Ng

Film production in Singapore seems to be growing in leaps and bounds. While only one Singapore feature was made in 1996, three in 1997 and four in 1998, about a dozen homegrown films should have hit the screens by the end of 1999.

One reason for this dramatic rise is the government's growing interest in building a local film industry. That policy was manifested in the formation of the Singapore Film Commission in April 1998. To encourage and support indigenous film talents, the Commission awarded a total of $227,000 (S$392,000) to 11 short and two feature film projects in February 1999 – the first time local film production has been funded by the state.

In addition, in July 1999, Singapore's Ngee Ann Polytechnic extended its film curriculum to include the Advanced Diploma in Film Production, a two-year programme that will provide local and regional students with advanced training in narrative film-making.

The impressive number of films being made now can also be attributed to the boost in confidence to local investors when the local Hokkien comedy **Money No Enough** (1998), about the impact of the Asian economic crisis on ordinary

Singaporeans, became the second highest-grossing film in the republic after *Titanic*.

Made for $490,000, *Money No Enough* collected a total of $3.4 million at the local box-office, becoming the most profitable Singapore feature since film production was revived in the 1990s. It also did well in Malaysia. Not surprisingly, the movie's commercial success triggered an outbreak of clones, and six of the eight local features released in 1998 and the first five months of 1999 have been comedies.

Sorry, wrong *Number*

The first to jump on the *Money No Enough* bandwagon was **Lucky Number,** a predictable tale about two jobless friends who are saved through the purchase of a "wrong" number in a lottery. The film was directed by Hong Kong film-maker Gao Lin Pao, with a cameo role by the well-known Hong Kong actor Law Kar Ying, but neither of them succeeded in redeeming the film's technical crudity, shallow characterisation and base humour. *Lucky Number* was produced by local exhibitor Overseas Movie for $290,000 but took in only $220,000 in its five-week run.

Where Got Problem (1999) is the debut feature of J.P. Tan, the producer of *Money*

No Enough. Although a social drama rather than a comedy, this is another variation on the *Money No Enough* theme, highlighting the financial crises of the rich instead of the public housing crowd. Budgeted at $490,000, the film offers credible perform-ances, but the sense of optimism in this riches-to-rags-to-riches story is pushed to ludicrous heights in the heavy-handed finale.

Plans for a fourth film in the same vein, called *I Strike it Rich*, were aborted when the film's creators suffered an unmitigated disaster with **Tiger's Whip** (1998). Directed and produced by local entertainer Victor Khoo, the film tells the kitsch-ridden tale of a struggling Hollywood actor who travels to Singapore in search of a cure for a rare male genital disease. The $870,000 movie took a woeful $35,000 in ticket sales.

Cross-dressed for success

A new benchmark in marketing strategy for local productions was set this year by **Liang Po Po – The Movie**. Its publicity blitz began two months before its theatrical release, which coincided with the Chinese New Year, and involved the screening of teasers and trailers, and a steady stream of promotional tie-ins.

Liang Po Po is the maiden project of Raintree Pictures, the newly-formed film-making subsidiary of the Television Corporation of Singapore, and was made for $460,000 in association with film-maker Eric Khoo's Zhao Wei Films. Based on a popular, elderly TV character played by a cross-dressing Jack Neo, the film's comic-book perspective is saved by subversive humour. It is directed by Teng Bee Lian and stars *Money No Enough*'s potent team: Neo, Mark Lee and Henry Thia.

In line with Raintree Pictures'objective to make films that travel, Hong Kong stars Eric Tsang, Shereen Tang and Malaysian singer Ah Niu were drafted in to lend glamour to the movie. *Liang Po Po* made a modest profit, with box-office takings of $1.75m after a two-month run.

Still from the comedy LIANG PO PO – THE MOVIE

Neo, Lee and Thia reappear in Neo's directorial debut **That One No Enough** (1999), which he also penned. Lee is particularly funny in this well-paced, farcical exposition of three men's romantic, marital and sexual dilemmas, told in a vernacular mix of Hokkien, Mandarin and English.

At press time, the first feature film funded by the Singapore Film Commission was also slated for a 1999 release. Directed by Jasmine Ng and *Straits Times* film critic Kelvin Tong, **Eating Air** (loosely translated from the Chinese term for "joyride"), was made for $320,000, of which $87,000 came from the Film Commission. The directors, both in their twenties, call it "a motorcycle-gongfu-love story".

Though 1999 seems to be an *annus mirabilis* for Singapore film production, film-makers and critics know that if the fledgling film industry is to survive in this city with a population of less than four million, it is not enough for local films to gain acceptance at home, they must also succeed internationally.

YVONNE NG was born in Singapore and graduated in film studies from the University of Waterloo, Ontario. She has written on contemporary mainland Chinese cinema and is on the editorial board of *KINEMA* (published at the University of Waterloo). She is currently co-authoring a book on the development of cinema in Singapore.

Recent and Forthcoming Films

BAILIU LIBAI (Lucky Number)
Dir: Gao Lin Pao. Players: Lin Yisheng, Wu Jianhua, Law Kar Ying. Prod: D.S. Movies.

BUTTERFLY EFFECTS
Dir: Yim Ho. Players: Tony Leung Kar Fai, Michelle Yeoh. Prod: Raintree Pictures.

EATING AIR
Dir: Kelvin Tong, Jasmine Ng. Prod: Multi-Storey Complex.

GHOST STORIES
Dir: Jeffrey Chiang. Players: Thomas Ong, Edmund Chen, Michelle Goh. Prod: Chinarunn Pictures.

NA GE BU GOU (That One No Enough)
Script and Dir: Jack Neo. Phot: Tung Sei Kwong. Players: Jack Neo, Mark Lee, Henry Thia. Prod: Cathay Asia Films.

LIANG PO PO CHONG CHU JIANG HU (Liang Po Po – The Movie)
Script: Jack Neo. Dir: Teng Bee Lian. Phot: Ho Yoke Weng. Players: Neo, Mark Lee, Henry Thia, Patricia Mok, Shereen Tang, Eric Tsang. Prod: Raintree Pictures, Zhao Wei Films.

SEVENTH MOON
Script: Johnny Lau, Lee Chee Keng, Jack Neo. Dir: Jeffrey Chiang. Players: Neo, Mark Lee, Patricia Mok. Prod: Chinarunn Pictures.

SHAONU DANG (Street Angels)
Script: Wong Kai Gay. Dir: David Lam. Phot: Ardy Lam. Players: Melody Chen, Grace Ip. Prod: ACT Venture.

THE STORY OF JANE AND SAM
Script and Dir: Derek Yee Tong Sheng. Players: Fann Wong, Peter Ho, Qian Jia Le, Zheng Pei Pei, Zhang Tong Zhu. Prod: Raintree Pictures.

TIGER'S WHIP
Script and Dir: Victor Khoo. Phot: S. Mohan. Players: David Calig, R. Chandran, Andrea De Cruz, C.K. Cheong. Prod: River Films.

WENTI BU DA (Where Got Problem)
Dir: J.P. Tan. Players: Edmund Chen, Neo Swee Lin, Lim Kay Siu, Sherry Tan. Prod: Sunnez.

Producers

Chinarunn Pictures
96 Club Street
Singapore 069464
Tel: (65) 324 2770
Fax: (65) 324 0721
e-mail: jeff_chiang@chinarunn.com
www.chinarunn.com

Monster Films
53B Boat Quay
Singapore 049842
Tel: (65) 536 9140
Fax: (65) 536 9154
e-mail: monster@monsterfilms.com
www.monsterfilms.com

The Moving Visuals Company
10-A Loke Yew Street
Singapore 179229
Tel: (65) 333 3051/2
Fax: (65) 339 6329
e-mail: galenyeo@singnet.com.sg
www.movingvisuals.com

Oak 3 Films
73A Pagoda St.
Singapore 059232
Tel: (65) 226 2338
Fax: (65) 226 2339
e-mail: oak3films@pacific.net.sg

Raintree Pictures
Caldecott Broadcast Centre
Andrew Rd
Singapore 299939
e-mail: davidlgh@raintree.com.sg

Sunnez
106B Amoy St.
Singapore 069926
Tel: (65) 221 1488
Fax: (65) 221 1955

Zhao Wei Films
22 Scotts Rd, Unit 01–28
Singapore 228221
Tel: (65) 730 1809
Fax: (65) 737 8195
e-mail: zhaowei@pacific.net.sg
www.zhaowei.com

Distributors and Exhibitors

Cathay Organisation
2 Handy Rd,
#05–00 Cathay Building
Singapore 229233
Tel: (65) 337 8181
Fax: (65) 334 3373

Eng Wah Organisation
400 Orchard Road
#16–06 Orchard Towers
Singapore 238875
Tel: (65) 734 0028
Fax: (65) 235 4897

Golden Village Entertainment
2 Handy Rd
#15–04 Cathay Building
Singapore 229233
Tel: (65) 334 3766
Fax: (65) 334 8397
www.golden-village.com.sg/homepage.html

Overseas Movie Distribution
1 Park Rd
#04–21, People's Park Complex
Singapore 059108
Tel: (65) 535 0555
Fax: (65) 535 0783
e-mail: oegroup@pacific.net.sg

Shaw Organisation
1 Scotts Rd
#14–01, Shaw Centre
Singapore 228208
Tel: (65) 235 2077
Fax: (65) 235 2860
www.shaw.com.sg

United International Pictures
1 Scotts Rd
#15–05, Shaw Centre
Singapore 228208
Tel: (65) 737 2484
Fax: (65) 235 3667
e-mail: roger_pollock@uipham.com

Useful Addresses

Centre for Film and Media Studies
Ngee Ann Polytechnic
Block 23, #01–01
535 Clementi Rd
Singapore 599489
Tel: (65) 460 6992
Fax: (65) 462 5617
e-mail: vtv@np.edu.sg
www.np.edu.sg

Singapore Film Commission
460 Alexandra Road
#30–00, PSA Building
Singapore 119963
Tel: (65) 375 7825
Fax: (65) 375 7860
www.sfc.org.sg

Singapore Film Society
Golden Village Marina
5-A Raffles Avenue
#03–01 Marina Leisureplex
Singapore 039801
Fax: (65) 737 1543
e-mail: ktan@sfs.org.sg
www.sfs.org.sg

Singapore International Film Festival
45A Keong Saik Rd
Singapore 089 136
Tel: (65) 738 7567 Fax: (65) 738 7578
e-mail: filmfest@pacific.net.sg
www.filmfest.org.sg

SLOVAKIA
Hana Cielová

Although the political situation in Slovakia has improved since the election of the new democratic government, the country's economy remains far from rosy. State funding is in short supply for health and social security, so it is no wonder that the only public source of film finance, Pro Slovakia, can only invest about $2m (70m Slovak crowns) a year. With the budgets of average, low-budget Slovak films at between $500,000 and $800,000, that subsidy does not go far.

Slovak Television, the state broadcaster, is also quite poor and cannot finance ambitious projects or work by young film-makers. The private television station, Markíza, though better-resourced, does not invest in domestic production. So the only current solution seems to be international co-production.

This applied to Slovakia's most prolific and successful young director, Martin Šulík. His latest work is called *Pictures from a Trip* (*Obrázky z vyletu*), one of the four parts of **Prague Stories** (*Praha oèima*), financed completely with French money and premiered at the Rotterdam Film Festival. The other three parts are directed by equally successful young Czech director Vladimír Michálek's *The Cards Are Dealt / Karty jsou rozdany*), young, but already well-known Czech animator Michaela Pavlátová's *Absolute Love* (*Absolutní láska*) and Prague-based French producer-director Artemio Benki's *Risk* (*Riziko*).

Benki and his co-producer Joel Farges wanted to make a similar film as *Paris vu par ...* , and all four stories were supposed to be about love in Prague. Even though the film does not work especially well as a feature, Martin Šulík's story about a conservative Slovak mother from the countryside visiting her "liberal", single daughter living in Prague – and having an affair with a married man – is very refreshing and definitely the most original of the quartet. Especially enjoyable is the humour which arises from the clash of two completely different cultures.

Behind the camera on this and two of the other stories was Sulík's regular director of photography, Martin Strba, another Slovak. He also shot the Czech-Polish-French-Slovak co-production, *Sekal Has to Die*, directed by the young Czech Vladimír Michálek.

Šulík was at press time seeking finance for his new project, **Landscape** (*Krajinka*), based on a script by well-know Slovak writer Dušan Dusek. Another well-known Slovak director, Dusan Hanák, is still preparing his documentary feature about communist crimes, **Intolerance** (*Intolerancia*), while in complete contrast Dušan Rapoš' **Fountain for Susannah III** (*Fontána pre Zuzanu III*) is the third in a series of commercial teen dramas. It was in post-production when this article went to press.

State secrets

What has happened to the plans for five nationalistic film projects, which were in line with the cultural policy of the former government? Some ended up on television and some were not made at all, even after the state pumped more than $2.8m into them during the last few years. Another recent development which very probably will also be investigated is the privatisation of the former state film studio, Koliba. There are muddy waters to be cleared.

The Slovak film school, VŠMU (Academy of Art, Film and TV Faculty) is very short of money, but not talent: *Swimming* (*Plávanie*) by FAMU's Martin Repka was chosen by Kodak for its annual Showcase of young European talent at Cannes. And Repka is by no means the only promising director out there.

Amongst local film festivals, the seven-year-old Trenčianske Teplice International Art Film Festival continues to expand and gain prestige. This spa town has already hosted such famous guests as Peter Greenaway, Krzysztof Zanussi, Erland Josephson, Geraldine Chaplin, Franco Nero and Gina Lollobrigida. Its award winners include Scott Hicks' *Shine*, Mika Kaurismäki's *Tigrero* and Peter Zelenka's cult Czech hit, *The Buttoners* (*Knoflíkáři*). The June festival has become the annual meeting point of the Slovak film crowd.

HANA CIELOVA is a freelance writer. She writes for *Rolling Stone*, has a monthly TV show about film on Czech Television and also works as a programmer for the Karlovy Vary International Film Festival.

Producers

ALEF
Uršulínka 9
811 01 Bratislava
Tel: (421 7) 533 4812
Fax: (421 7) 531 9406

Ars Media
Odeská 13
821 06 Bratislava
Tel/Fax: (421 7) 552 4617

Atan Film
Rovniakova 1
824 95 Bratislava
Tel: (421 7) 838421
Fax: (421 7) 838486

Attack
Karpatská 2
811 05 Bratislava
Tel: (421 7) 392 520

Barok Film
Konventná 8
811 03 Bratislava
Tel: (421 7) 531 9480
Fax: (421 7) 531 9372

Charlie's
Špitálska 4
811 08 Bratislava
Tel: (421 7) 363 430/363 396
Fax: (421 7) 323 678

Davay
Trnavská cesta 68
821 01 Bratislava
Tel: (421 7) 572 1498
Fax: (421 7) 572 1497

JMB Film and TV Production
Korničova 12
811 03 Bratislava
Tel: (421 7) 531 1041
Fax: (421 7) 531 5778

Štúdio Koliba
Brečtanová 1
833 14 Bratislava
Tel: (421 7) 371 368, 378 8213
Fax: (421 7) 372 224

Distributors

Asociácia Slovenských Filmových Klubov
Grosslingova 32
811 09 Bratislava
Tel/Fax: (421 7) 325 533

Bioscop
Hviezdoslavovo nám. 17
811 02 Bratislava
Tel: (421 7) 533 5815

Butterfly
Trenèianska 53
821 09 Bratislava
Tel: (421 7) 521 8682
Fax: (421 7) 521 8383

Continental Film
Vajanského nábr. 17
P.O. Box 124
810 00 Bratislava
Tel: (421 7) 363 354, 325 427
Fax: (421 7) 536 1363

Gemini Film
Stefánikova 47
8121 04 Bratislava
Tel: (421 7) 391 127
Fax: (421 7) 396 361

Intersonic Taunus Productions
Staré Grunty 36
842 25 Bratislava
Tel: (421 7) 721 011
Fax: (421 7) 722 070

Tatra Film
Priemyselná 1
821 09 Bratislava
Tel: (421 7) 526 7681
Fax: (421 7) 521 5685

Saturn
Podháj 19
841 03 Bratislava
Tel: (421 7) 731 151
Fax: (421 7) 731 150

Solarfilm
Priemyselná 1
821 09 Bratislava
Tel: (421 7) 211 301
Fax: (421 7) 521 5685

Useful Addresses

Academy of Art, Film and TV Faculty
Ventúrska 3
800 00 Bratislava
Tel: (421 7) 5443 2182
Fax: (421 7) 5443 0125

Intl. Art Film Festival Trenčianske Teplice
Konventná 8
811 03 Bratislava
Tel: (421 7) 5441 9480/9372
Fax: (421 7) 5441 1679
e-mail: festival@artfilm.sk
www.artfilm.sk

National Centre for Audiovisual Arts
Grosslingova 32
811 09 Bratislava
Tel: (421 7) 321 789/ 361 232
Fax: (421 7) 363 461
e-mail: aic@aic.sk

SOUTH AFRICA — Martin Botha

At the 3rd Southern African International Film and Television Market and the 22nd Cape Town International Film Festival the real strength of post-apartheid cinema was clearly demonstrated: our short films and documentaries, which won numerous international awards during 1998 and 1999, overshadowed our features.

Two documentaries towered above the rest: Greta Schiller and Mark Gevisser's lovely historical over-view of gay lives under apartheid, **The Man Who Drove with Mandela**, and François Verster's magnificent portrait of the homeless, **Pavement Aristocrats: The Bergies of Cape Town**. Schiller and Gevisser's film received the Documentary Teddy prize at the 49th Berlin International Film Festival for its unique contribution to gay history, while Verster's grim study of marginalised people won a major documentary award in South Africa.

Wynand Dreyer's trilogy of documentaries about ordinary lives on the Cape Flats, **Ravensmead, A Piece of Life, A Piece of Death** and **Steel upon Steel** is a lyrical and moving document, much praised at home. His work deserves to be seen by international audiences.

Another multi-award winner is Zola Maseko's **The Life and Times of Sara Baartman**, which deals with the tragic true story of a young South African woman who was exhibited as a freak in London and Paris in the early nineteenth century. Maseko's short *The Foreigner*, a heart-breaking indictment of current xenophobia in South Africa, also won various international awards, including a second prize at the African Film Festival in Milan.

Among other shorts, Gavin Hood's *The Storekeeper* stood out, winning awards in Nashville and Houston. It is a devastating portrait of the culture of violence in South Africa. Without relying on dialogue, Hood tells the story of an elderly man who owns a small, isolated shop in rural South Africa. After several burglaries he takes the law into his own hands – with shocking consequences. Hood's feature debut, *A Reasonable Man*, was at the time of writing in post-production.

The small renaissance in documentary and short films has been made possible by funding from the Department of Arts, Culture, Science and Technology – more than $330,000 (R2m) from its Interim Film Fund for documentaries in 1998–99, and about $165,000 for shorts.

Full length, slim pickings

Post-apartheid feature production, however, remains disappointing. We have yet to repeat the small renaissance in independent film-making of the late 1980s and early 1990s. For example, the less said the better about Bernard Joffe's **Letting Go**, a poorly-made account of a black woman's return from exile.

Russell Thompson's **The Sexy Girls**, about gangs on the Cape Flats, suffers from a poor script and weak characterisation. Herman Binge's **Pride of Africa**, about intrigues on a luxury steam train in 1925, is a boring affair. Even worse, Robert Benjamin's sentimental ghost story, **The Ghost**, merely imitates aspects of the far superior American movie, *Ghost*.

Only two recent features were worth noting: Neal Sundstrom's **Inside Out**, a reasonable romantic comedy about a

Still from the documentary PAVEMENT ARISTOCRATS

Jewish South African bit-part actress who ends up directing a Nativity play in a small rural town, and Ntshaveni Wa Luruli's delightful Sowetan comedy, **Chikin Biznis – The Whole Story**. This celebrates the ordinary experiences of black South Africans, especially those who are trying to make a living in the informal market as chicken salesmen. Fats Bookholane's performance in the lead and Mtutuzeli Matshoba's witty script deservedly won prizes at Burkina Faso's FESPACO.

The prospects for feature directors, however, are great. The National Film and Video Foundation, which will support and promote the local film industry, has finally been established and a council of 14 members was appointed in April 1999. On a regional level, the Cape Film Commission is being developed to promote and market the film industry within the Western Cape, which has become a vibrant base for short and documentary production, as well as commercials.

The forming of significant financial power blocks in the film industry, such as Africa Media Entertainment (AME) and Primedia, is evidence of new foundations for a post-apartheid film industry. According to a report by the government's arts' department, South Africa's expanding film industry is worth about $1 billion in assets and annual revenue.

Our most prominent film producer, Anant Singh, who received the Distinguished Producers Award at the 12th Wine Country Film Festival, secured the rights to Nelson Mandela's autobiography, *Long Walk to Freedom*. The film version will be directed by Shekhar Kapur (*Elizabeth*) and is scripted by William Nicholson.

A film version of Kuki Gallman's book, *I Dreamed of Africa*, was shot in northern KwaZulu. Director Hugh Hudson's film deals with the story of an Italian woman who moved to a farm in Kenya with her two small children after her husband was killed in a car accident. Another 20 features were shot in 1998 and 1999, but still await local release.

Lastly, James Polley, who directed the Cape Town International Film Festival for 21 years, passed away in 1999. Trevor Steele Taylor took over the reigns and presented a huge collection of international cinema for the 22nd festival.

Dr MARTIN BOTHA is a member of the Council of the South African National Film and Video Foundation. He also serves on the Steering Committee of the Cape Film Commission. His latest book on South African cinema examines the oeuvre of the late Manie van Rensburg.

Recent and Forthcoming Films

CAPE OF RAPE

Documentary. Dir and Prod: Derek Antonio Serra, New Film Makers Forum.

CHIKIN BIZNIS – THE WHOLE STORY

Script: Mtutuzeli Matshoba. Dir: Ntshaveni Wa Luruli. Phot: Rod Stewart. Players: Fats Book-holane, Connie Chiume, Sello Motloung. Prod: M-Net.

DEATH

Documentary. Dir: Luiz DeBarros. Prod: Marc Schwinges (Under-dog Productions).

ERNEST COLE

Documentary. Dir and Prod: Jurgen Schadeberg.

THE FURIOSUS

Documentary. Dir and Prod: Liza Key (Key Films Productions).

THE GHOST

Script and Dir: Robert Benjamin. Players: Gavin van den Berg, Bo Petersen, Vuyisile Bojana, Kevin Otto. Prod: M-Net.

HILLBROW KIDS

Documentary. Dir: Michael Hammon.

INSIDE OUT

Script: Neal Sundstrom, Gilda Blacher. Dir: Sundstrom. Phot: Paul Gilpin. Players: Tobie Cronje, Philip Moolman, Lizz Meiring, Gilda Blacher, Gys de Villiers, Val Donald Bell. Prod: Roberta Durrant (Penguin Films), SABC, African Media Entertainment.

THE LIFE AND TIMES OF SARA BAARTMAN

Documentary. Dir: Zola Maseko. Phot: Guilio Bicarri. Prod: Dola Bill Productions, SABC, France3, Mail & Guardian TV, Dominant 7 (France).

THE MAN WHO DROVE WITH MANDELA

Documentary. Script: Mark Gevisser. Dir: Greta Schiller. Prod: Beulah Films.

PAVEMENT ARISTOCRATS: THE BERGIES OF CAPE TOWN

Documentary. Dir and Prod: François Verster.

PLACE OF LIONS

Script: John Loy. Dir: Audrey Cooke. Players: Guy Edwards, Hugh Laurie, Miriam Margolyes, Alfred Molina, Thabekile Mkhwanazi. Prod: Michael Bird.

THE SEXY GIRLS

Script and Dir: Russell Thompson. Players: Jamie Bartlett, Tina Schouw, Ivan Lucas. Prod: M-Net.

WHAT HAPPENED TO MBUYISA?

Documentary. Dir and Prod: Feizel Mamdoo (Primedia).

Producers

African Media Entertainment
Roberta Durrant
PO Box 3189
Parklands 2121
Johannesburg
Tel: (27 11) 483 2006
Fax: (27 11) 483 2037
e-mail: penguin@icon.co.za

African Mirror
Wynand Dreyer
PO Box 226
Cape Town 8000
Tel/Fax: (27 21) 928 673

Beulah Films
Mark Gevisser
PO Box 28938
Kensington 2101
Tel/Fax: (27 11) 6148047
e-mail: gevisser@wn.apc.org

Endemol Entertainment International/
Endemol Productions
Carl Fischer
PO Box 71917
Bryanston 2021
Tel: (27 11) 799 2200
Fax: (27–11) 465 6001
e-mail: endemol.sa@iafrica.com

M-Net
New Directions
Richard Green
PO Box 1237
Ferndale
Randburg 2160
Tel: (27 11) 329 5279
Fax: (27 11) 329 5474
e-mail: newdirections@mnet.co.za

Naked Grail Productions
Naas Ferreira
PO Box 12402
Elspark 1418
e-mail: ngrailpro@gem.co.za

Primedia Pictures
Jeremy Nathan
PO Box 652110
Benmore 2010
Johannesburg
Tel: (27 11) 784 3466
Fax: (27 11) 884 1707
e-mail: pictures@primedia.co.za
www.primepix.com

SABC
Molefe Mokgatle
Chief Executive: Television
Private Bag x 41
Auckland Park 2006
Johannesburg
Tel: (27 11) 714 2414
Fax: (27 11) 714 3341
e-mail: swartes@sabc.co.za

Videovision Enterprises
Sanjeev Singh
134 Essenwood Road
Berea
Durban 4001
Tel: (27 31) 204 6000
Fax: (27 31) 202 5000
e-mail: info@videovision.co.za

Underdog Productions
Marc Schwinges
PO Box 78965
Sandton 2146
Tel: (27 11) 325 5252
Fax: (27 11) 325 6252
e-mail: info@underdog.co.za
www.underdog.co.za

Distributors

Nu-Metro Entertainment
Sid Morris
PO Box 392026
Bramley 2018
Johannesburg
Tel: (27 11) 880 7040
Fax: (27 11) 442 7030
e-mail: sid@numetro.co.za

Ster-Kinekor
Mike Ross
PO Box 76461
Wendywood 2144
Tel: (27 11) 455 7700
Fax: (27 11) 444 0659

UIP Warner
7 Junction Avenue
Castrol House
Parktown
Johannesburg 2000
Tel: (27 11) 484 4215
Fax: (27 11) 484 3339

Useful Addresses

The Camera Guild
Antoinette Steinhobel

11 Frenschhoek Bergbron
Northcliff x.19
1709
Tel/Fax: (27 11) 706 0775

Cape Film Commission
Kevin Hosking
22nd floor
2 Long Street
Cape Town 8001
Tel: (27 21) 418 6464
Fax: (27 21) 418 2323
e-mail: capefilm@wesgro.org.za

Cape Town International Film Festival
Trevor Steele Taylor
University of Cape Town
Private Bag
Rondebosch
Cape Town 7700
Tel: (27 21) 238 257
Fax: (27 21) 242 355
e-mail: filmfest@hiddingh.uct.ac.za

Commercial Producers Association of SA (CPA)
Bobby Amm
PO Box 678
Parklands 2121

Department of Arts, Culture, Science and Technology
(For information on the National Film and Video Foundation)
Themba Wakashe
Private Bag x894
Pretoria 0001
Tel: (27 12) 337 8132
Fax: (27 12) 324 2720

Film Resource Unit (Mike Dearham)
Training, Distribution and Resource Centre
Gate 2, Newtown Cultural Precinct
1 President Street
Newtown
Johannesburg 2001
Tel: (27 11) 838 4280/1/2
Fax: (27 11) 838 4451
e-mail: fru@wn.apc.org

Independent Producers' Organisation of South Africa
Qetello Zeka
PO Box 2631
Saxonwold 2132
Tel/Fax: (27 11) 482 2187
e-mail: ipo@yebo.co.za
www.ipo.org.za

National Film, Video and Sound Archives
Brenda Kotze
Private Bag x236
Pretoria 0001
Tel: (27 12) 343 9767/323 5300 ext 204
Fax: (27 12) 344 5143

National Television and Video Association of Southern Africa (NTVA)
Glynn O'Leary
Western Cape
Tel: (27 21) 480 3100
Fax: (27 21) 424 7580
e-mail: ntva@iafrica.com
www.ntva.org.za

Out in Africa: Gay and Lesbian Film Festival
Nodi Murphy
808 Dumbarton House
1 Church Street
Cape Town
Tel: (27 21) 424 1532
www.oia.co.za

Performing Arts Workers' Equity (PAWE)
Ramolao Makhene
PO Box 30802
Braamfontein 2017
Tel: (27 11) 403 6234/5/6
Fax: (27 11) 403 1681

Screen Africa
Angela van Schalkwyk
PO Box 706
Strathavon
Sandton 2031
Tel: (27 11) 884 3162
Fax: (27 11) 883 9281

Showdata
Alan Hammond: Showdata
Webmaster
PO Box 15756
Vlaeberg
Cape Town 8018
Tel: (27 21) 683 7280
e-mail: admin@showdata.org.za
www.showdata.org.za

South African Guild of Editors
Micki Stroucken
PO Box 66105
Broadway
Kensington
Johannesburg 2020

South African Society of Cinematographers
Duane Rogers
PO Box 81251
Parkhurst 2120
Tel/Fax: (27 11) 788 0802
e-mail: sasc@mweb.co.za

Southern African International Film & Television Market (Sithengi)
Dezi Rorich
PO Box 1176
Auckland Park 2006
Tel: (27 11) 714 3229
Fax: (27 11) 714 3275
e-mail: saftvm@hot.co.za
www.sithengi.org.za

South African Screenwriter's Laboratory
Liza Key
Tel: (27 11) 442 6379
Fax: (27 11) 442 6391
e-mail: scrawl@iafrica.com

South African Scriptwriters' Association
Etienne van den Heever
PO Box 91937
Auckland Park 2006
Tel/Fax: (27 11) 482 7171

Women in Film
Merrilee Kick
PO Box 130982
Bryanston 2021
Tel: (27 11) 483 2006
Fax: (27 11) 483 2037
e-mail: homekey@icon.co.za

SOUTH KOREA
Frank Segers

The resilience of Korean cinema was vividly demonstrated over the last year against the backdrop of the nation's nightmarish economic situation. Some of the conglomerates, or *chaebols*, pressured by President Kim Dae-Jung to get back to basics or face bank loan cut-offs, shed film and television-related subsidiaries and took other stringent measures. The Grand Bell Awards ceremony, roughly equivalent to the Oscars, was dropped in 1998 for lack of sponsorship (though it was reinstated in 1999).

But the most drastic alteration was also the most basic. Total production was reduced markedly: 1998's output of Korean features was 43, a startling 37% decline from 1997, and the lowest number in recent history in a movie-mad country. And yet, proving once again that hard times invite treks to the cinema, total 1998 attendance jumped 5.6% to 50.2 million. Total box-office registered a surprisingly strong 8.4% increase from the 1997 tally, winding up at $215m (258 billion won), the highest figure in nearly a generation. Auteurists howled, but general audiences had no complaints.

Much of this, of course, is due to the ever-increasing dominance of American films. Cinema attendance has been steadily rising since 1981, mostly for Yank films and other popular titles from abroad; there were eight foreign titles released in Korea in 1998 for each domestic title. In 1985, three years before the market opened up to films distributed by the American majors, a mere 30 foreign titles played in Korea; in 1998, the total was 342. Yet domestic titles are also benefiting from the general trend.

Market forces

Combining box-office and festival kudos most conspicuously was director Lee, Kwangmo's **Spring in My Hometown**, a languidly-paced but moving tale of a young boy who discovers that his mother and father are doubling as prostitute and pimp, servicing American GIs in 1952. Lee, a product of UCLA's film studies program, spent eight years developing the script for his debut feature, envisioned in part as a tribute to his late father's generation.

In the words of critic Lee Yong-Kwan, "*Springtime* combines the aesthetics of the long take with the distance of the long shot, in order to reproduce not only the Korean landscape but a sense of its painful history as well." It won the Gold Prize at the 1998 Tokyo International Film Festival, three Grand Bell Awards, including Best Film and Best Director, and on home turf played to some 250,000 patrons.

The year's number one domestic success, Lee Jung-Gook's **The Letter**, was a multiple hankie melodrama about the fateful affair between two graduate school students. There is much here that is formulaic, including an idyllic courtship, and a young wife receiving a heart-rending letter written by her husband before his demise. Lee Jung-Gook is a facile director and the huge success of *The Letter* (attendance of some 725,0000 besting the likes of *Deep Impact* and *Saving Private Ryan*) proved the enduring clout of the so-called "soft melodrama".

Still from Lee, Kwangmo's award-winning SPRING IN MY HOME TOWN

That lesson was not lost on many film-makers during a hard-pressed year. The economic crisis spurred a renewed emphasis on tailoring films closely to audience taste. Standard practice in Hollywood, this market-bound concept seems out of place in Korea's free-wheeling production climate.

One who followed the mass-market route with great success was Park, Ki-Hyung. His **Whispering Corridors** worked the horror genre on the cheap, providing enough stylish chills to scare 620,000 filmgoers. The third biggest commercial domestic hit of 1998 is set in a high school full of winsome female students and features the obligatory hanging of the class teacher, the ominous presence of a whacko dubbed "crazy dog" and an eerie phone message from a student presumed dead.

Brief lives

Short films flourished. The more pure-minded cineastes, resisting the pressures of the marketplace, turned to shorts to express themselves and make the most of limited production money. They had an incentive. Korea's Motion Picture Promotion Corp. (KMPC) disclosed in

September that it would provide funds for the support of "small-scale" shorts, and some 215 film students and directors lined up for assistance.

This turned out to be one of the KMPC's last initiatives, as in May 1999 it was replaced by a new body, the Korean Film Commission (KOFIC). This was officially described as "a non-governmental, self-regulating organisation made up of 10 professionals from the Korean film industry", which "will take on all major responsibility for the promotion of Korean film, including the writing of a new film production policy".

Before this change, the renewed emphasis on shorts (even cinema chains are setting aside time for their exhibition) had already yielded admirable results. Such 35mm and 16mm shorts as *Crack of the Halo, Bitter Sushi* and *Mirror* won festival awards in, respectively, Clermont-Ferrand, Houston and New York. One ambitious distributor, Miro Vision, packaged together seven shorts at the 1999 Cannes market as part of an effort to sell Korean films abroad.

Miro Vision, established in October 1998 by Seoul-based Jason Chae, is currently the most aggressive foreign seller of Korean titles. Among the features it took to Cannes was Kim, Sion's **Fly Low**, a low-budget, three-part exploration of two groups drawn to an abandoned rural schoolhouse. Also in the Miro Vision larder: Lee, Jeong-Hyang's **Art Museum by the Zoo**, a romantic comedy that was the Christmas season's number one draw, winding up ninth in the 1998 box-office chart.

The scars left by Japan's brutal occupation of Korea from 1910 to 1945 have now healed sufficiently to permit for the first time what was previously unthinkable: the officially-sanctioned import of Japanese-made films. The embargo was broken with a

Formulaic romance in THE LETTER

trio of Japanese titles, with the government tacking on a stipulation that the films must arrive attached to a sufficiently credible festival award. The government plans to expand the quota of Japanese film imports to about 15 annually, and has no objection to the import of Korean/Japanese co-productions. Finally, the most topical film of the year was director Kang, Woo-Suk's **Bedroom and Courtroom**, which cleverly exploited the economic malaise of 1998 in a comic melodrama. The plot? A disgruntled wife sues her overworked husband's *chaebol* employer, demanding alimony to compensate for her poor love life.

Grand Bell Awards 1999

Best Film: *Spring in My Hometown.*
Best Director: Lee, Kwangmo for *Spring in My Hometown.*
Best Screenplay: Oh, Seung-Wook for *Christmas in August.*
Best Actor: Choi, Min-Sik for *Swirl.*
Best Actress: Shim, Eun-Ha for *Art Museum by the Zoo.*
Best Supporting Actress: Lee, Mee-Yeon for *Whispering Corridors.*
Best Cinematography: Kim, Hyung-Koo for *Spring in My Hometown.*
Best New Director: Hur, Jin-Ho for *Christmas in August.*

Useful Addresses

Korean Film Commission
206–46 Chongnyangni-dong
Tongdaemun-gu
Seoul, Korea
Tel: (82 2) 958 7582
Fax: (82 2) 958 7550

Miro Vision
4th Floor
Kyounghee Bldg.
1–153 Shinmunro 2-Ga
Chongro-Gu
Seoul 110–062
Tel: (82 2) 737 1185
Fax: (82 2) 737 1184

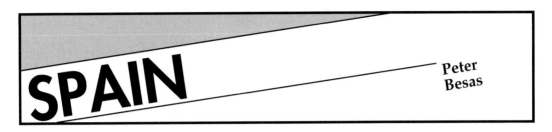

SPAIN

Peter
Besas

The number of features shot in Spain over the past year was up slightly to 79, and of these a handful evinced the quality, inventiveness and diversity which have become the hallmarks of modern Spanish cinema, presently one of the most dynamic in Europe. Production is expected to remain at about 80 features a year, culling in the region of 10% of the domestic box-office (that figure has varied between 7% and 14% over the past years; in 1998 it was 12%).

The effervescence is being provided by a mixture of veteran directors, such as Carlos Saura, Bigas Luna, Luis García Berlanga, Vicente Aranda and Pedro Almodóvar, together with a wave of relatively new talent – young writer-directors heading into their second, third or fourth films.

Four recent films, for example, bear witness to the vigour of the local scene. Julio Medem's **The Lovers of the Arctic Circle** (*Los Amantes del Círculo Polar*) was a sensitive, inventive and idiosyncratic treatment of a love story between two children that is carried on into maturity, narrated in a fresh manner that made the film a critical success both in Spain and abroad.

Alejandro Almenábar's **Open Your Eyes** (*Abre Los Ojos*) was, indeed, an eye-opener, for the director of *Thesis* limned a fantasmagoric "virtual reality" tale whose endless twists may have lost a few spectators along the way, but which ultimately succeeded as a powerful and disturbing psychological thriller. It consecrated Alemenábar as one of Spain's top new talents.

Neighbourhood (*Barrio*), a first film by Fernando de León Aranoa, about a group of youths in the Basque area, was a real revelation, widely acclaimed first at the San Sebastian festival, and later with audiences around the country. Another surprising effort was Iciar Bollain's **Flowers from Another World** (*Flores de Otro Mundo*), which won the Critics' Prize in Cannes.

Berlin games

Sweeping the Goya awards was a historical pseudo-comedy, **The Girl of Your Dreams** (*La Niña de Tus Ojos*), popular also at Spanish box-offices. The rather silly story concerns a troupe of actors in 1938, during the Spanish Civil War, who are sent by the Franco regime to Berlin to shoot a folk lore film in the UFA studios.

Writer-director Fernando Trueba throws into the bathetic goings-on a love-smitten Dr Goebbels, who falls for a half-Gypsy singer/dancer (Penélope Cruz), while comical mishaps on the sound-stage are grimly offset by a group of Jewish extras about to be deported to concentration camps, with uniformed guards and police dogs mingling in the studio with the actors. The oafish Spaniards are portrayed as witty, the Germans, from the German film director to the brownshirts, as *dummköpfe*.

Director Carlos Saura (left) with Francisco Rabal (leading actor in GOYA), and cinematographer Vittorio Storaro

Still from THE UGLIEST WOMAN IN THE WORLD, with Elia Galera

More sombre was José Luis Garci's **The Grandfather** (*El Abuelo*), based on Pérez Galdó's classic novel, superbly acted by Fernando Fernán Gómez, which was the year's Spanish Oscar nominee. Also at the Oscars was Carlos Saura's **Tango**, a jejune story inter-cut with dance sequences, which drew yawns and blah reviews in both Spain and Argentina. The indefatigable Saura has already completed his next, **Goya**. Francisco Rabal is cast as the painter in old age in Bordeaux, with flashbacks to the younger artist played by José Coronado. Saura avers that this is his "personal vision" of Goya during the last years of life.

Meanwhile the 73-year-old Vicente Aranda, after the flop of his recent *Another's View* (*La Mirada de Otro*) is filming **Jealousy** (*Celos*), with Aitana Sánchez Gijón and Mexican actor Daniel Giménez Cacho, about a steamy affair between a truck driver and an orange packer. Also back behind the camera is veteran film-maker Luis García Berlanga, who has completed **Paris – Timbuctu**, with Michel Piccoli, Concha Velasco and Juan Diego.

Mother love

Pedro Almodóvar's **All About My Mother** (*Todo sobre mi madre*) culled the Best Director's prize in Cannes and drew large audiences in Spain and France. In this lachrymose melodrama, the Spanish wunderkind mostly spurns comedy and opts for a virtually all-distaff marathon of hand-wringing and plangent overacting, which some may take to be a sly take-off on Latino soap-operas, but may pass with others as acting in the grand tradition.

Weaving into his story constant references to *All About Eve* and *A Streetcar Named Desire*, with plenty of hospital scenes and the inevitable transvestites and prostitutes mixed in, Almodóvar traces the fate of a middle-aged woman whose husband dies, whose teenage son dies, whose bosom pseudo-daughter dies – all of it played to squeeze out the ultimate on-screen, "tragic" teardrop.

Numerous high-priced co-productions are on the way, with financing from major sources such as Lolafilms (Andrés Vicente Gómez), backed by Spain's telephone company. Lolafilms set up a division in London last May to make English-language films slanted at the international market, which has always been one of Gómez's elusive goals. The Sogepaq/Sogetel group, bankrolled by the powerful PRISA media group, also remains active in production, as does a group headed by Enrique Cerezo, who has close links to domestic television.

Among the smaller films is **Yoyes**, based on the life of a famous terrorist whose death at the hands of the Basque extremists became a cause célèbre in the early 1980s. First-time director is Helena Tabernera, with Ana Torrent playing the lead. Another youthful effort is **Kilometre Zero** (*Kilómetro Cero*), a comedy about a group of people who decide to meet in Madrid's Puerta del Sol square, officially designated in Spain as the starting point for the measurement of all highway distances. And newcomer Miguel Bardem made his offbeat **The Ugliest Woman In the World**

Aitana Sánchez-Gijón (centre) in Bigas Luna's VOLAVÉRUNT

(*La Mujer Más Fea del Mundo*) with Elia Galera cast in the eponymous part.

Bigas Luna's **Volavérunt** (a Latin word meaning 'They flew'), is based on a bestselling historical whodunit involving the mysterious death of the Duchess of Alba, the putative subject of Goya's "Nude Maja". Two of Spain's most popular actresses, Penélope Cruz and Aitana Sánchez Gijón are cast, along with Cuban heart-throb Jorge Perugorría. Luna can be expected to give the film the proper erotic twists.

Thespians in their twenties, such as Cruz, Sanchez-Gijón, Carmelo Gómez, Santiago Segura, Eduardo Noriega, Najwa Nimri, Karro Elejalde and Jordi Mollá have connected with young Spanish audiences, as have the new generation of writers and directors. With substantial continued economic backing from television networks, the Culture Ministry and Euro-funding, Spanish cinema can be expected to remain one of the most provocative in Europe.

PETER BESAS has lived in Madrid since the mid-1960s and for over 25 years was chief of *Variety*'s Madrid bureau. He has written various books, including *Behind the Spanish Lens*, a history of Spanish cinema.

Goya Awards 1998

Best Film: *The Girl Of Your Dreams.*
Best Director: Fernando León de Aranoa (*Neighborhood*).
Best Actor: Fernando Fernán-Gómez (*The Grandfather*).

Fernando Colomo directing HAVANA QUARTET

Best Actress: Penélope Cruz (*The Girl of Your Dreams*).
Best Supporting Actor: Tony Leblanc (*Torrente*).
Best Supporting Actress: Adriana Ozores (*The Hour of the Valiant*).

Best Foreign Film In Spanish: *The Lighthouse of the South* (Dir: Eduardo Mignogna, Argentina).
Best European Picture: *The Boxer* (Dir: Jim Sheridan, Ireland).

Recent and Forthcoming Films

CASBAH

Script: Mariano Barroso and Luis Marías. Dir: Barroso. Players: José Coronado, Emma Surez, José Sancho. Prod: Tornasol Films and Sogetel.

GOYA

Script and Dir: Carlos Saura. Phot: Vittorio Storaro. Players: Francisco Rabal, José Coronado, Dafne Fernandez, Maribel Verdú, Eulalia Ramón. Prod: Lolafilms.

CELOS (Jealousy)

Script: Vicente Aranda and Alvaro del Amo. Dir: Aranda. Phot: José Luis Alcaine. Players: Aitana Sánchez Gijón, Candela Peña. Prod: Calle Cruzada for Sogecine.

THE PAPER BOY

Script: Pete Dexter, based on his novel. Dir: Pedro Almodóvar. Prod. El Deseo (Spain)/Blue Tulip Productions (US).

VOLAVERUNT

Script: Bigas Luna and Cuca Canals, based on the novel by Antonio Larreta. Dir: Luna. Photo: José Luis Alcaine. Players: Aitana Sánchez Gijón, Jorge Perugorría, Penélope Cruz. Prod: Mate Productions and UGC.

YOYES

Script: Helena Tabernera and Andrés Martoreli. Dir: Tabernera. Phot: Federico Ribas. Players: Ana Torrent, Ion Gabella, Florence Pernell. Prod: CIPI (Enrique Cerezo), in co-production with Italy and France.

SALSA!

Script: Joyce Buñuel and Jean-Claude Carrière. Dir: Buñuel. Phot: Javier Aguirresarobe. Players: Alexis Valdés, Naim Thomas, Vincent Lecoeur. Prod: Mate Production (Madrid)/Vertigo Productions (Paris).

LA MUJER MAS FEA DEL MUNDO (The Ugliest Woman in the World)

Script: Nacho Faerna. Dir: Miguel Bardem. Phot: Nestor Calvo. Players: Elia Galera, Héctor Alterio, Roberto Alvarez. Prod: Aurum Producciones.

CUARTETO DE LA HABANA (Havana Quartet)

Script: Julio Carrillo and Fernando Colomo. Dir: Colomo. Phot: Livio Delgado. Players: Ernesto Alterio, Mirtha Ibarra, Javier Cámara, Laura Ramos. Prod: Aurum Producciones and El Paso Films.

Producers

Aurum Films
Avda. de Burgos, 12
Madrid 28036
Tel: (34 91) 768 4800
Fax: (34 91) 302 5764

Avanti Films
Rda. Sant Pere, 46, 5è
08010 Barcelona
Tel: (34 93) 268 1233
Fax: (34 93) 268 1617

Bailando en la Luna
Plaza de España 18, piso 13, Of.11
28008 Madrid
Tel: (34 91) 548 3090
Fax: (34 91) 547 9821

Boca a Boca Producciones
Marqués de Valdeiglesias 5, 2 Izqa
28004 Madrid
Tel: (34 91) 701 4580
Fax: (3491) 701 4588

Cartel
Lanzarote 4
Polígono Ind. "Los Alamillos"
San Sebastián de los Reyes
28700 Madrid
Tel: (34 91) 654 2857
Fax: (34 91) 654 3455

El Deseo SA
Ruiz Perelló, 15, bajo centro
28028 Madrid
Tel: (34 91) 725 0106/7
Fax: (34 91) 355 7467

Elías Querejeta PC
Maestro Lasalle 21
28016 Madrid
Tel: (34 91) 345 7139
Fax: (34 91) 345 2811

Els Films de la Rambla
Casp, 59, 3er, 2°
08010 Barcelona
Tel: (34 93) 265 3026
Fax: (34 93) 232 2870

Enrique Cerezo PC
Ferrán González 28
28009 Madrid
Tel: (34 91) 431 4790
Fax: (34 91) 431 7555

Esicma
Maestro Lasalle 15
28016 Madrid
Tel: (34 91) 345 8708
Fax: (34 91) 359 6683

Fernando Colomo PC
Génova 7, 2°, escalera interior
28004 Madrid
Tel: (34 91) 310 3834
Fax: (34 91) 310 4613

Fernando Trueba PC
Antonio Cavero, 37
28043 Madrid
Tel: (34 91) 759 6264
Fax: (34 91) 300 0104

Igeldo Komunikazioa
Aldamar 9, 5° izda.
20003 San Sebastián
Tel: (34 43) 431 252/3
Fax: (34 43) 427 794

Lolafilms
Velázquez 12, 7°
28001 Madrid
Tel: (34 91) 431 4246
Fax: (34 91) 435 5994

Mate Producciones
Hortaleza 59, 1A
28004 Madrid
Tel: (34 91) 532 0225
Fax: (34 91) 532 9450

Sogetel
Gran Vía 5
28013 Madrid
Tel: (34 91) 523 9960
Fax: (34 91) 522 2297

Samarkanda
Capitán Haya, 51, 3°, 2 (Portal)
28020 Madrid
Tel: (34 91) 571 5334
Fax: (34 91) 571 5620

Starline
Principe de Vergara, 39
Madrid
Tel: (34 91) 431 5908
Fax: (34 91) 575 1181

Tornasol
Plaza Emilio Jiménez Millás, 2, 1°B
28008 Madrid
Tel: (34 91) 542 9564
Fax: (34 91) 542 8710

Distributors

Alta Films
Martin de los Heros 12
28008 Madrid
Tel: (34 91) 542 2702
Fax: (34 91) 542 8777

Araba Films
Avenice del Doctor Arce, 13
28002 Madrid
Tel: (34 91) 564 9498
Fax: (34 91) 564 5738

Buena Vista International (BVI)
José Bardasano Baos, 9.
(Edif. Gorbea 3)
28016 Madrid
Tel: (34 91) 384 9400
Fax: (34 91) 766 9341

Columbia TriStar Films de España
Hernández de Tejada, 3
28027 Madrid
Tel: (34 91) 377 7100
Fax: (34 91) 377 7129

Cine Company
Zurbano 74, 2 dcha
28010 Madrid
Tel: (34 91) 442 2944
Fax: (34 91) 441 0098

Cine Mussy
Quintana 1 – 2° B
28008 Madrid
Tel: (34 91) 542 0036
Fax: (34 91) 559 9069

Filmax
Miguel Hernández 81–87
Pol. Pedrosa
L'Hospitalet de Llobregat
Barcelona 08908
Tel: (34 93) 336 8555
Fax: (34 93) 263 4778

Filmayer
Edificio Bronce
Avda. de Burgos, 8A, 10°-1
28036 Madrid
Tel: (34 91) 383 1572
Fax: (34 91) 383 0845

Golem Distribución
Corazón de María 56 – 9° A
Madrid 28002
Tel: (34 91) 519 1737
Fax: (34 91) 416 3626

Lauren Films
Balmes 87, principal
08008 Barcelona
Tel: (34 93) 496 3800
Fax: (34 93) 323 6155

Lider Films
Avda. de Burgos, 12
Madrid 28036
Tel: (34 91) 768 4800
Fax: (34 91) 302 5764

Musidora Films
Princesa 17, 2
28008 Madrid
Tel: (34 91) 541 6869
Fax: (34 91) 541 5482

Sogepaq
Gran Via 32, 1°
28013 Madrid
Tel: (34 91) 524 7220
Fax: (34 91) 521 0875

Tripictures
Doce de Octubre, 28
28009 Madrid
Tel: (34 91) 574 9007/8
Fax: (34 91) 574 9005

20th Century Fox Films
Avda. de Burgos, 8A, Pl.11
28036 Madrid
Tel: (34 91) 343 4640
Fax: (34 91) 343 4655

U Films
Via Lactea, 30
Pozuelo
Madrid 28223
Tel: (34 91) 715 2010
Fax: (34 91) 715 1757

United International Pictures (UIP)
Plaza Callao 4, 6°
28013 Madrid
Tel: (34 91) 522 7261
Fax: (34 91) 532 2384

Vertigo
Silva 2, 4°, officina 4
28013 Madrid
Tel: (34 91) 542 2225
Fax: (34 91) 541 6985

Wanda Films
Avda. Europa 9, Portal 3 bajo
Pozuelo 28224
Tel: (34 91) 352 8376
Fax: (34 91) 352 8371

Warner Sogefilms
Cardenal Marcelo Spinola, 8
Madrid 28016
Tel: (34 91) 768 8800
Fax: (34 91) 768 8829

Useful Addresses

**Academia de Artes y Ciencias
Cinematográficas**
Sagasta 20 – 3° dcha.
Madrid 28004
Tel: (34 91) 593 4648
Fax: (34 91) 593 1492

Catalan Films & TV
Portal Santa Madrona, 68
08001 Barcelona
Tel: (34 93) 412 5640
Fax: (34 93) 412 1958

**Federación de Asociaciones de
Productores Audiovisuales
Espanoles (FAPAE)**
Capitán Haya, 50, 6° D
28020 Madrid
Tel: (34 91) 571 1682
Fax: (34 91) 571 1841

Filmoteca Nacional
Ctra. Dehesa de la Villa s/n
Madrid 28040
Tel: (34 91) 549 0011
Fax: (34 91) 549 7348

**Instituto de la Cinematografia
y de las Artes Audiovisuales
(ICAA)**
Plaza del Rey, 1
28071 Madrid
Tel: (34 91) 532 5089
Fax: (34 91) 522 9377

SRI LANKA — Amarnath Jayatilaka

In May 1999, Sri Lanka's president, Chandrika Bandaranaike Kumaratunga, announced a new National Film Policy, which, according to the official media release "seeks to restore the industry to make it viewer-friendly and to ensure that cinema artistes are lucratively employed." The new scheme is designed "to restore the industry to its pristine glory through far-reaching policy changes". The new reforms will end the monopoly of the National Film Corporation (NFC) in the distribution of both local and imported films. The laws and regulations governing the import and distribution of films will also be liberalised.

The new policy acknowledges that cinema has suffered greatly from the onset of cable and satellite television in Sri Lanka. Also, in the absence of any regulatory body, Sri Lanka has become a thriving market for video pirates, with unlicensed rental outlets all over the island. Pornographic videos are freely available without any control or censorship.

This lack of regulation has been in stark contrast to the strict trade and censorship controls imposed by the NFC on the import and exhibition of films for cinema. The dilapidated condition of the island's cinemas was another audience deterrent.

Thirdly, the island has no modern film studio with the equipment and trained technicians needed to produce quality Sinhala films that might compete with the imported Hindi and Tamil films.

The reforms thus come at a time when the film industry was heading rapidly for ultimate destruction. President Kumaratunga responded four years ago, by personally taking charge of the NFC. However, the Film Commission of Enquiry appointed in 1996 failed to come up with concrete proposals and was replaced by several committees representing the industry. It was their recommendations which formed the basis of the new film policy.

All three leading exhibitors, Antony A. Page of Ceylon Theatres, Asanka Edirisinghe of EAP Films and Theatres, and Imthiaz A. Cader of Ceylon Entertainment have been unanimous in their praise for the new policy. They have watched a once profitable business run into deep trouble, with only 130 cinemas open today, compared to 365 in the 1970s, before the introduction of state controls. According to Cader, treasurer of the National Film Exhibitors Association, the NFC's import tariffs had become so high that US majors were not prepared to negotiate with Sir Lankan exhibitors.

The most notable consequence of this stand-off remains the absence of *Titanic* from Sri Lankan screens. Thousand of people have seen the film on video, initially on pirated tapes but, more recently, on authentic copies, and there is now a huge audience clamouring to see the film on the big screen. The video exposure has fuelled a massive trade in *Titanic* merchandise, which is sold in shops, on the streets – just about everywhere.

While the legal framework for the new policy is finalised, there is great hope within the industry that, with the aid of sufficient private sector investment, Sri Lanka can look forward to a cinema revival at the start of the new century.

AMARNATH JAYATILAKA is a filmologist and one of the leading personalities in Sri Lankan cinema. He has been the country's *IFG* liaison for the last 25 years.

Useful Addresses

Ceylon Entertainment Ltd.
Liberty Cinemas Ltd.
35 Sri Anagarika Dharmapala
Mawata
Colombo 7
Tel: (94 1) 325 764
(Importer/exhibitors)

Ceylon Theatres Ltd.
8 Sir C. Gardner Mawata
Colombo 2
Tel: (94 1) 431 243/431 109
(Producer/importer/exhibitor)

EAP Films & Theatres Ltd.
122 Ward Place
Colombo 7
Tel: (94 1) 694 517/694 608
Fax: (94 1) 694 845
(Producer/importer/exhibitor)

Film Location Services Ltd
Taprobane Pictures Ltd
790 Kotte Road, Etul Kotte
Tel: (94 1) 864 928/875 120
Fax: (94 1) 875 119
(Producer/importer/services)

National Film Corporation
224 Bauddhaloka Mawata
Colombo-07
Tel: (94 1) 580 247
Fax: (94 1) 585 526

SWEDEN

Bengt Forslund

Last year I complained about the large quantity and low quality of Swedish films. A tougher economic climate for production in 1998 resulted in just 20 films (including seven feature-length document-aries!) being made, compared to 30 in 1997, and it was no surprise that the overall standard was much better; tough conditions mean stronger competition and, often, stronger results.

Thanks to *Titanic* and some successful Swedish movies, exhibitors and video dealers had a good year. The turnover for cinema takings increased by 12% in 1998 and by 24% for video rentals.

The surprise hit of the year was debutant Lukas Moodysson's **Fucking Åmål** about lesbian love amongst kids in their early teens (Åmål is the name of a small provincial Swedish town). Though in my view rather overrated, thanks to its smart title and up-to-date-theme, the film was loved by critics and the public – and as a youth film in the good Scandinavian tradition it certainly had its moments, with fresh, natural kids and a realistic setting. The film was chosen as Sweden's entry for the Oscars, but had to change its title to the more decent *Show Me Love* to be accepted.

Rebecca Liljeberg and Alexandra Dahlström in Lukas Moodysson's FUCKING ÅMÅL

Best film of the year was Colin Nutley's mature love story **Under the Sun** (*Under solen*), based on a short story by English writer H.E. Bates about a middle-aged farmer looking for love. Rolf Lassgård was magnificent in the main part, well supported by Bo Widerberg's son, Johan Widerberg, who shows that his part in his late father's Oscar-nominated *All Things Fair* was no fluke.

English-born Nutley has been the most successful "Swedish" director during the 1990s, since his breakthrough with *House of Angels* (*Änglagården*) in 1992. All four of his films since then have reached a theatrical audience of between 500,000 and one million, outstanding figures for Swedish films these days.

Original sins

Richard Hobert presented number five in his series of films based on the seven deadly sins, this time a thriller on jealousy, **The Eye** (*Ögat*). Too contrived to be completely realistic, it had its flaws, but popular stars Lena Endre and Samuel Fröler were convincing enough as a couple killed by their love. In any case it was a more original film than the Hollywood-inspired action movies **Hamilton** and **The Last Contract** (*Sista kontraktet*), the latter based on the murder of Swedish Prime Minister Olof Palme.

Anders Grönros' fairytale **The Glass-blower's Children** (*Glasblåsarens barn*) became the children's film of the year, beautifully made but a bit too artistic and

artificial. The same can be said of Lisa Ohlin's feature debut **Waiting for a Tenor** (*Veranda för en tenor*), a buddy film about the friendship between an author and an alcoholic actor. Krister Henriksson, making a tour de force of the latter part, was an easy choice for the Golden Bug as Best Actor.

Three remarkable documentaries with festival appeal are also worth mentioning. Documentary master Stefan Jarl made a beautiful homage to Bo Widerberg, who succumbed to cancer in 1997, with **Life At Any Cost** (*Liv till varje pris*). Peter Cohen followed up his famous *Architecture of Doom* (1989) with **Homo Sapiens 1900**, a film about racial hygiene in Nazi Germany and the Soviet Union, and wildlife cameraman Mikael Kristersson made a fascinating close-up on kestrels, **Kestrel's Eye** (*Falkens öga*).

Encouragingly, five new Swedish films were in the box-office top 20 in March this year. Best among them were two debuts, the comedy **The Way Out** (*Vägen ut*), by Daniel Lind Lagerlöf (hailed by local critics as a Swedish *The Full Monty*), and the children's film **Star-sisters** (*Stjärnsystrar*), by Tobias Falk, who picked up the Grand Prix at the Montreal Children's Festival in March.

Lena Endre and Samuel Fröler in Richard Hobert's THE EYE

Helena Bergström and Rolf Lassgård in Colin Nutley's UNDER THE SUN

A new deal at last

In May 1999 a new agreement for the Swedish Film Institute was finally signed by the government and the various trade organisations, producers, distributors, exhibitors and television companies. It looks good on paper: more money, but with a new board and a new boss to decide how funds are distributed.

Film company Sandrews has been expanding into Norway and Denmark. Since late 1997, Sandrews – with former Film Institute head Klas Olofsson as its dynamic boss – has been in a 50/50 partnership with Norwegian company Shipsted, who had earlier bought Danish Metronome. Now Sandrew Metronome has daughter companies and cinemas in all the Nordic countries except Iceland. No wonder Sandrew Metronome was chosen as Sweden's Exhibitor of the Year for 1998.

The situation for Svensk Filmindustri (SF), once the big production centre and still the main cinema owner, is less certain, after they decided to close their new studios after just five years and to change their boss, for the third time in just three years! Since February, the Norwegian Rasmus Ramstad has been in charge. We wait to see what his leadership will bring.

BENGT FORSLUND was a well-known film producer for 30 years at Svensk Filmindustri, the Swedish Film Institute and Nordic Film and TV Fund. He is also a film historian and author of several books on cinema, including the definitive study of Victor Sjöström, and a volume on Sven Nykvist.

The Golden Bugs 1999

Best Film: *Show Me Love.*
Best Direction: Lukas Moodysson (*Show Me Love*).
Best Actress: Alexandra Dahlström & Rebecca Liljeberg (*Show Me Love*).
Best Actor: Krister Henriksson (*Waiting for a Tenor*).
Best Script: Lukas Moodysson (*Show Me Love*).
Best Camera: Philip Øgaard (*The Glassblower's Children*).
Best Supporting Actress: Ia Langhammar (*Love Fools*).
Best Supporting Actor: Thommy Berggren (*The Glassblower's Children*).
Best Foreign Film: *Festen* (Denmark).

Recent and Forthcoming Films

DET BLIR ALDRIG SOM MAN TÄNKT SIG
(Never What You Expected)

Script and Dir: Måns Herngren/Hannes Holm. Phot: Mats Olofson. Players: Bibi Andersson, Josefin Nilsson, Marie Richardson, Gösta Ekman. Prod: Herngren, Holm & Ryborn/SVT/DR/NRK/Canal+/ Buena Vista/Swedish Film Institute/Nordic Film & TV-Fund.

DÄR REGNBÅGEN SLUTAR
(Where the Rainbow Ends)

Script and Dir: Richard Hobert. Phot: Lars Crépin. Players: Lena Endre, Rolf Lassgård, Göran Stangertz. Prod: Cimbria Film/SVT/Film på Österlen, Swedish Film Institute.

DÖDLIG DRIFT (Deadly Instinct)

Script and Dir: Rolf Börjlind. Phot: Esa Vuorinen. Players: Mikael Persbrandt, Stefan Sauk, Kjell Bergqvist. Prod: CinemaArt Prod/Svensk Filmindustri/Swedish Film Institute.

FUCKING ÅMÅL (Show Me Love)

Script and Dir: Lucas Moodysson. Phot: Ulf Brantås. Players: Alexandra Dahlström, Rebecca Liljeberg, Mathias Rust. Prod: Memfis Film/Zentropa Prod/SVT/Film i Väst/Swedish and Danish Film Institutes.

HAPPY END

Script: Sony Jörgensen. Dir: Christina Olofson. Phot: Robert Nordström. Players: Harriet Andersson, Stefan Norrthon, Alexander Skarsgård. Prod: CO Film/Sandrew Metronome/GF Studios/Swedish Film Institute.

HELA HÄRLIGHETEN
(Love Fools)

Script: Håkan Lindhé. Dir: Leif

Magnusson. Phot: Ian Wilson. Players: Tomas von Brömsen, Ia Langhammar, Mikael Persbrandt, Anna Wallander. Prod: Memfis Film/Zentropa Prod/Film i Väst/SVT/Swedish and Danish Film Institutes/Nordic Film & TV Fund.

KNOCKOUT

Script: Peter Birro/Agneta Fagerström-Olsson. Dir: Agneta Fagerström-Olsson. Phot: John O Olsson. Players: Örjan Landström, Reine Brynolfsson, Igor Chernevich. Prod: Giraff Film/Svensk Filmindustri /SVT/ Filmpool Nord/Swedish Film Institute/Nordic Film & TV-Fund.

LUSTEN TILL ETT LIV
(Yearning for a Life)

Script: John O. Olsson. Dir: Christer Engberg. Phot: Anders Bohman. Players: Matthias Barthelsson, Lotta Ernryd. Prod: Giraff Film/Svensk Filmindustri/ SVT/Filmpool Nord/Swedish Film Institute.

NOLL TOLERANS
(Zero Tolerance)

Script: Anders Nilsson/Joakim Hansson. Dir: Anders Nilsson. Phot: Jacob Jorgensen. Players: Jacob Eklund, Marie Richardson, Peter Andersson. Prod: Sonet Film/TV4/TV 1000/Sandrew Metronome/Film i Väst/Nordic Film & TV-Fund.

SJÖN (The Lake)

Script: Hans Iveberg. Dir: Hans Åke Gabrielsson. Phot: Björn Blixt. Players: Regina Lund, Fredrik Hammar, Björn Gedda. Prod: Omega Film & TV/Sonet/Nordisk Film & TV/Film i Väst/ Swedish Film Institute.

STJÄRNSYSTRAR (Starsisters)

Script: Johan Bogaeus. Dir: Tobias Falk. Phot: Per Källberg. Players: Teresa Niva, Vania Lundmark, Fanny Kivimäki, Mona Malm. Prod: Filmlance /Swedish, Danish and Finnish Film Institutes/Nordic Film & TV-Fund.

STRAY DOGS

Script: Hans Renhäll. Dir: Daniel Alfredson. Phot: Peter Mokrosinski. Players: Kevin Knapman, Sarah Jane Potts, Mark Bagnall, Michael Legge. Prod: Vildhundarna/Swedish Film Institute.

SÅ VIT SOM SNÖ
(As White as Snow)

Script: Jacques Werup/Jan Troell. Dir and Phot: Jan Troell. Players: Amanda Ooms, Rickard Wolff. Prod: SVT/Nordisk Film & TV/Swedish and Danish Film Institutes.

SÅNGER FRÅN ANDRA VÅNINGEN
(Songs from the Second Floor)

Script and Dir: Roy Andersson. Phot: Istvan Berbas. Players: Lars Nordh, Stefan Larsson, Lugio Uucina, Fredrik Sjögren. Prod: Studio 24/SVT/ Swedish Film Institute/Nordic Film & TV Fund.

TOMTEN ÅR FAR TILL ALLA BARNEN
(Father Christmas is Every Child's Father)

Script: Monika Rolfner. Dir: Kjell Sundvall. Phot: John-Christian Rosenlund. Players: Katarina Ewerlöf, Peter Haber, Leif André, Jessica Zandén. Prod: FilmLance/Swedish Filminstitute

TSATSIKI

Script: Ulf Stark/Moni Nilsson Brännström. Dir: Ella Lemhagen. Phot: Anders Bohman. Players: Samuel Haus, Alexandra Rapaport, Jonas Karlsson, Helge Jordal. Prod: Felicia Film/Film i Väst/Norsk Film/Per Holst Film/DR/Swedish Institute/Nordic Film & TV Fund/Eurimages.

UNDER SOLEN (Under the Sun)

Script and Dir: Colin Nutley. Phot: Jens Fischer. Players: Rolf Lassgård, Helena Bergström, Johan Widerberg. Prod: Sweetwater/Svensk Filmindustri/ SVT/Film i Väst.

VUXNA MÄNNISKOR (Grown-Ups)

Script: Fredrik Lindström. Dir: Felix Herngren/Fredrik Lindström. Phot: Göran Hallberg. Players: Felix Herngren, Karin Bjurström, Mikael Persbrandt. Prod: Svensk Filmindustri, SVT/FLAB & Fix/Swedish Film Institute.

VÄGEN UT (The Way Out)

Script: Malin Lageröf. Dir: Daniel Lind Lagerlöf. Phot: Jens Fischer. Players: Björn Kjellman, Peter Haber, Thomas Hanzon. Prod: Sonet Film/SVT/Sandrew Metronome/TV 1000/Swedish Film Institute.

ZINGO

Script: Santiago Gil. Dir: Christjan Wegner. Phot: Henrik Jongdahl. Players: Björn Kjellman, Thomas Hellberg, Per Morgerg, Helena af Sandeberg. Prod: Soren Staermose AB/SVT/Canal+, Swedish Film Institute.

ÖGAT (The Eye)

Script and Dir: Richard Hobert. Phot: Lars Crépin. Players: Lena Endre, Samuel Fröler, Göran Stangertz, Camilla Lundén. Prod: Cimbria Film/SVT/Filmhus Ateljéerna/Film på Österlen/ Swedish Film Institute.

Producers

Cimbria Film
Östra Parkskolan
S-272 31 Simrishamn
Tel: (46) 4141 6660
Fax: (46) 4141 6661

Cinema Art Productions
Box 20105
S-161 02 Bromma
Tel: (46) 8555 24860
Fax: (46) 898 1005

FilmLance International
Box 27156
S-102 52 Stockholm
Tel: (46) 8665 1100
Fax: (46) 8662 0444

Memfis Film & Television
Upplandsgatan 35
S-113 28 Stockholm
Tel: (46) 833 5576
Fax: (46) 830 9934

MovieMakers Sweden
Råsundavägen 150
S-171 30 Solna
Tel: (46) 8730 2850
Fax: (46) 8730 2853

Moviola Film
Box 20102
S-161 02 Bromma
Tel: (46) 8799 6900
Fax: (46) 829 1386

Omega Film & Television
Box 20105
S-16102 Bromma
Tel: (46) 8555 24800
Fax: (46) 8555 24810

Sandrew Metronome
Box 5612
S-114 86 Stockholm
Tel: (46) 8762 1700
Fax: (46) 810 3850

Spice Produktion
Box 20105
S-161 02 Bromma
Tel: (46) 8555 24000
Fax: (46) 890 3002

Svensk Filmindustri
S-127 83 Stockholm
Tel: (46) 8680 3500
Fax: (46) 8710 4460

Sveriges Television/Drama
S-105 10 Stockholm
Tel: (46) 8784 0000
Fax: (46) 8664 5418

Sweetwater
Grev Turegatan 21
S-114 38 Stockholm
Tel: (46) 8662 1470
Fax: (46) 8662 1471

Viking Film
Sturegatan 8
S-114 35 Stockholm
Tel: (46) 8679 9115
Fax: (46) 8679 9120

Distributors

Atlantic Film
Box 21112
S-100 31 Stockholm
Tel: (46) 830 5230
Fax: (46) 830 5280

Buena Vista International
Box 181
S-10220 Stockholm
Tel: (46) 8555 44500
Fax: (46) 8555 44580

Columbia TriStar Films
Box 9501
S-102 74 Stockholm
Tel: (46) 8555 79000
Fax: (46) 8555 79050

Folkets Bio
Box 2068
S-103 12 Stockholm
Tel: (46) 8566 26100
Fax: (46) 8566 26149

Fox Film
S-127 83 Stockholm
Tel: (46) 8680 3500
Fax: (46) 8710 4460

Novemberfilm
Nidarosgatan 4, 2tr.
S-164 34 Kista
Tel: (46) 8751 5144
Fax: (46) 8632 0185

Polfilm
Östra Rönneholmsvägen 4
S-211 47 Malmö
Tel: (46) 4012 4044
Fax: (46) 4012 4044

Sandrew Film
Box 5612
S-114 86 Stockholm
Tel: (46) 8762 1700
Fax: (46) 810 3850

Scanbox Sweden
Box 1447
S-17128 Solna
Tel: (46) 8444 7600
Fax: (46) 8444 7610

Sonet Film
Box 20105
S-161 02 Bromma
Tel: (46) 8555 24800
Fax: (46) 828 5834

Svensk Filmindustri
(see Producers)

Triangel film
Box 285
S-201 22 Malmö
Tel: (46) 4012 5547
Fax: (46) 4012 9099

United International Pictures
Box 9502
S-102 74 Stockholm
Tel: (46) 8616 7400
Fax: (46) 884 3870

Warner Bros
Box 9503
S-102 74 Stockholm
Tel: (46) 8658 1050
Fax: (46) 8658 6482

Willmar Andersson Film
Box 5612
S-114 86 Stockholm
Tel: (46) 823 4700
Fax: (46) 810 3850

Useful Addresses

The National Archive of Recorded Sound and Moving Image
Box 27890
S-115 93 Stockholm
Tel: (46) 8783 3700
Fax: (46) 8663 1811

The Swedish Film Distributors' Association
Box 23021
S-10435 Stockholm
Tel: (46) 8441 5570
Fax: (46) 8343 810

Swedish Film Institute
Box 27126
S-102 52 Stockholm
Tel: (46) 8665 1100
Fax: (46) 8661 1820

Swedish Film Producers' Association
Blasieholmsg. 4B
S-10329 Stockholm
Tel: (46) 8762 7798
Fax: (46) 8762 7760

The Swedish Institute
Cultural Film Events
Box 7434
S-103 91 Stockholm
Tel: (46) 8789 2000
Fax: (46) 820 72 48

SWITZERLAND
Cécile Küng

S witzerland's seven million inhabitants love cinema. In 1998 there were 15.7 millions tickets sold, but only about 330,000 were for Swiss movies. The five-year-old process of government reforms aimed at improving the prospects of domestic productions has had some success, but, as almost everywhere else, the one big winner in the cinema business here is Hollywood.

The appeal of local documentaries remains extraordinary. In 1997, the top Swiss film was the documentary *Das Wissen vom Heilen*, with 120,000 admis-sions. Running in 1997 and 1998, *Die Salzmänner von Tibet* attracted more than 50,000, and this year's *Steps of Mindfulness* is heading for a similar total.

It was a surprise to see **F. is a Son of a Bitch** (*F. est un salaud*), a very "in" novel written in Swiss-German in the early 1970s, adapted for the screen by young film-maker Marcel Gisler. Yet his considerable talent and the personal distance he had from the 1970s helped him make a striking film. It charts the passionate and painful relationship of a young gay couple, one somehow the 'dog', the other somehow his master. Gisler worked with two outstanding young actors, Hans-Peter Remund and Frédéric Andrau. His film was invited to many festivals and won numerous prizes, among them the Swiss Film Award 1998 for Best Feature Film.

Pastry, Pain and Politics is a wonderful 30-minute comedy by young Stina Werenfels. An elderly Jewish American couple plan a vacation. She refuses to go to Switzerland, which denied her shelter as a refugee; he refuses to go to Israel, because it's too hot and full of Arabs. But he suffers a heart attack and ends up in a Swiss hospital – where a Palestinian nurse saves his life. Werenfels shows us that, with courage, sensibility and craft, very delicate situations like this can make us laugh. Her film won several prizes at international film festivals and the Swiss Film Award for Best Short.

Follow the guru

The well-received documentary **Steps of Mindfulness** is the first film by Thomas Lüchingers, an artist and writer. It follows one of the world's great spiritual leaders, the Vietnamese Zen master Thich Nhat Hanh, on a journey through India. Thich Nhat Hanh, who lives in France, developed a new form of committed Buddhism during the Vietnam war. He teaches this discipline, and demonstrates the inevitable relationship between the development of inner peace and peace in the outside world. As well as doing good business in domestic cinemas, the film has been sold to several other countries.

Still from BERESINA

At press time, the release of Richard Dindo's sixteenth feature documentary, **Genet in Chatila**, was eagerly awaited. It is about the French poet Jean Genet and his relationship with the people of Palestine. A day after the September 1982 massacre at the refugee camp of Chatila, Genet visits the camp. Close to death from throat cancer, and having written nothing for years, he begins to write about this disturbing new experience. It leads to his last book, entitled *Un captif amoureux*, in which Genet reflects on the Palestinian revolution, its failure, and the loss of one's homeland. A young French woman of Algerian origin reads the book and returns in search of Genet.

Beresina, Daniel Schmid's new film, had its world première at Cannes in Un Certain Regard. This is a fairytale, a thriller, a comedy and a musical all rolled into one, about Irina, a young, beautiful Russian call-girl who brings the Cold War to an end in Switzerland. Schmid has her sing Swiss

The Film Department of PRO HELVETIA
Arts Council of Switzerland

promotes Swiss cinema. We arrange and coordinate seasons, retrospectives and other special film events around the world. We specialize in bilateral exchange with film archives, universities, arthouses, ministries of cultural affairs, etc.

**Hirschengraben 22, P.O. Box, CH-8024 Zurich
Phone: ++41 (1) 267 71 71, Fax: ++41 (1) 267 71 08,
E-mail: phmail@pro-helvetia.ch.**

---

hits from the 1930s and 1940s in a stroke of wonderful, sophisticated cinema. The photography by Renato Berta is sensual, the actors, especially young Elena Panova and Geraldine Chaplin, are unforgettable. Schmid looks at life with curiosity, with the spirit of a historian, a precise sense of the absurd and a readiness to adore beauty wherever he can find it.

CÉCILE KÜNG was for many years head of the film department of Pro Helvetia, the arts council of Switzerland. She now works as a freelance organiser of film events.

Recent and Forthcoming Films

BERESINA – OR THE LAST DAYS OF SWITZERLAND

Script: Martin Suter. Dir: Daniel Schmid. Phot: Renato Berta. Players: Elena Panova, Martin Benrath, Geraldine Chaplin, Ulrich Noethen. Prod: T&C Film/Pandora/Prisma.

BILL DIAMOND

Script and Dir: Wolfgang Panzer. Phot: Edwin Horak. Players: Marek Kondrat, Kati Tastet. Prod: Claudia Sontheim Filmproduction/ Broken Silence Productions/Ciné Film/Tumbleweed.

D'OR ET D'OUBLIS
(Of Gold and Forgetting)

Script: Anne Cuneo. Dir: Yvan Butler. Phot: Denis Jutzeler. Players: Anne Richard, Jacques Roman, Patricia Bopp, Philippe Mathey. Prod: Ciné Manufacture/ TSR.

EMPORTE-MOI (Bring Me Away)

Script: Léa Pool, with Nancy Houston, Monique Messier. Dir: Pool. Phot: Jeanne La Poirie.

Players: Miki Manojlovic, Pascale Bussières, Karine Vanasse. Prod: Catpics/Cité-Amérique/Haut et Cour/SF DRS.

F. EST UN SALAUD !
(F. is a Son of a Bitch)

Script: Marcel Gisler, Rudolf Nadler, based on the novel by Martin Frank. Dir: Gisler. Phot: Sophie Maintigneux. Players: Frédéric Andrau, Vincent Branchet, Urs-Peter Halter, Martin Schenkel, Jean-Pierre von Dach. Prod: Vega Films, Arena Films, Avventura Films.

DIE HOCHZEITSKUH
(The Wedding Cow)

Script: Ela Thier, Tomi Streiff. Dir: Streiff. Phot: Johannes Hollmann. Players: Isabella Parkinson, Oliver Reinhard, Maria Schrader, Dani Levy. Prod: SWR/SF DRS/arte.

MONDIALITO

Script: Nicolas Wadimoff, Moussa Maaskri. Dir: Wadimoff. Phot: Thomas Hardmeier.

Players: Maaskri, Antoine Maulini, Anton Kouznetzov, Emma de Caunes. Prod: Caravan Production/ADR.

WHO'S NEXT?

Script and Dir: Felix Tissi. Phot: Daniel Leippert. Players: Rossanna Mortara, Yves Progin. Prod: Insert Film/arte/ZDF.

ADRIAN FRUTIGER –
TYPOGRAPHER

Documentary. Script: Anne Cuneo, Thomas Kubiak. Dir: Cuneo. Phot: Kubiak. Prod: Fama Film/Eva-Film and TVs.

EIN ZUFALL IM PARADIES
(Coincidence in Paradise)

Documentary. Script and Dir: Matthias von Gunten. Phot: Pio Corradi. Prod: T & C Edition AG.

CHRONIQUE VIGNERONNE

Documentary. Script and Dir: Jacqueline Veuve. Phot: Hugues Ryffel. Prod: Les Productions Crittin & Thiébaud/Aquarius Films Production/TVs.

LE DEFI DU KHAN-TENGRI (The Challenge of Khan-Tengri)

Documentary. Script, Dir and Phot: K-soul Chrix. Prod: Triangle Vert.

ELF FREUNDE (Eleven Friends)

Documentary. Script and Dir: Miklos Gimes, Michele Andreoli. Phot: Pio Corradi. Prod: Offside Film/TVs.

GENET A CHATILA (Genet in Chatila)

Documentary. Script and Dir: Richard Dindo. Phot: Ned Burgess. Players: Mounia Raoui. Prod: Lea Produktion/Les Films d'Ici.

Still from Wolfgang Panzer's BILL DIAMOND
photo: Camera Obscura Distribution

EVITAS GEHEIMNIS (Evita's Secret)

Documentary. Script and Dir: Frank Garbely. Phot: Adrian Zschokke. Prod: Triluna Film/TVs.

HUG ' LES HÔPITAUX UNIVERSITAIRES DE GENEVÉ (HUG – University Hospitals of Geneva)

Documentary. Script and Dir: Richard Dindo.Phot: Patrice Cologne. Prod: Ciné Manufacture.

JEAN NOUVEL – L'ESTHETIQUE DU MIRACLE (The Aesthetic of the Miracle)

Documentary. Script and Dir: Beat Kuert. Phot: Reinhard Schatzmann, Kuert. Prod: Al Castello/TVs.

DIE REISEN DES SANTIAGO CALATRAVA (The Journies of Santiago Calatrava)

Documentary. Script and Dir: Christoph Schaub. Phot: Matthias Kälin. Prod: T & C Film/SF DRS.

SCHLAGEN UND ABTUN (Hit and Stop)

Script and Dir: Norbert Wiedmer. Phot: Peter Guyer. Prod: Biograph Film/SF DRS.

CLOSED COUNTRY

Documentary. Script: Kaspar Kasics, Stefan Mächler. Dir: Kasics. Phot: Matthias Kälin. Prod: eXtra Film/SF DRS.

STEPS OF MINDFULNESS – A JOURNEY WITH THICH NHAT HANH

Documentary. Script, Dir and Phot: Thomas Lüchinger. Prod: roses for you.

PASTRY, PAIN AND POLITICS

Short. Script and Dir: Stina Werenfels. Phot: Patrick Cady. Players: Viola Harris, Neza Selbuz, Jack Carter. Prod: Dschoint Ventschr.

FUGUE (Run Away)

Animation. Script, Dir and Phot: Georges Schwizgebel. Prod: Studio GDS.

Producers

Alhena Films SA

(production and distribution)
8, rue des Moraines
CH-1227 Carouge
Tel: (41 22) 823 0303
Fax: (41 22) 823 0304

Ascot/Elite

(production and distribution)
see address under Distributors

Balzli & Cie Filmproduktion

Altenbergstrasse 16
CH-3013 Bern
Tel/Fax: (41 31) 332 9438

CAB Productions SA

17, rue du Port-Franc
CH-1003 Lausanne
Tel: (41 21) 321 1500
Fax: (41 21) 321 1509

Carac Film AG

Zinggstrasse 16
CH-3007 Berne
Tel: (41 31) 372 0040
Fax: (41 31) 372 0481

Catpics Coproductions AG

Steinstrasse 21
CH-8003 Zürich
Tel: (41 1) 451 2358
Fax: (41 1) 462 0112

Ciné Manufacture SA

21, rue du Bugnon
CH-1003 Lausanne
Tel/Fax: (41 21) 311 5858

Arthur Cohn

Gellertstrasse 18
CH-4052 Basel
Tel: (41 61) 312 1242
Fax: (41 61) 312 0717

C-Films AG
Hallenstrasse 10, P.O.Box
CH-8032 Zürich
Tel. (41 1) 253 6555
Fax (41 1) 251 5253
e-mail: c-films@c-films.ch

Condor Films AG
Restelbergstrasse 107
CH-8044 Zürich
Tel: (41 1) 361 9612
Fax: (41 1) 361 9575

**Dschoint Ventschr
Filmproduktion AG**
Zentralstrasse 156
CH-8003 Zürich
Tel: (41 1) 456 3020
Fax: (41 1) 456 3025
e-mail: dvfilm@dschointventschr.ch

Fama Film AG
(production and distribution)
Balthasarstrasse 11
CH-3014 Bern
Tel: (41 31) 992 9280
Fax: (41 31) 992 6404
e-mail: famafilmag@access.ch

J.M.H. Productions SA
PO Box 58
CH-2005 Neuchâtel 5
Tel: (41 32) 729 0020
Fax: (41 32) 729 0029

Bernard Lang AG
(production and distribution)
Dorfstrasse 14d
CH-8427 Rorbas-Freienstein
Tel: (41 1) 865 6627
Fax: (41 1) 865 6629
e-mail: langfilm@kino.ch

**Les Productions
Crittin & Thiébaud SA**
3, rue des Sources
CH-1205 Geneva
Tel: (41 22) 329 5983
Fax (41 22) 321 2512
e-mail:pat@cortex.ch

T & C Film AG
Seestrasse 41a
CH-8002 Zürich
Tel: (41 1) 202 3622
Fax: (41 1) 202 3005
e-mail: tcemail@tcfilm.ch

Thelma Film AG
Josefstrasse 106
CH-8031 Zürich
Tel: (41 1) 271 8124
Fax: (41 1) 271 3350

Triluna Film AG
Neugasse 6
CH-8005 Zürich
Tel: (41 1) 273 0053
Fax: (41 1) 273 0106
e-mail: trilunafilm@access.ch

Vega Film AG
Kraftstrasse 33
CH-8044 Zürich
Tel: (41 1) 252 6000
Fax: (41 1) 252 6635
e-mail: vegafilm@access.ch

Distributors

Alexander Film
Lägernstrasse 6, PO Box 590
CH-8037 Zürich
Tel: (41 1) 362 8443
Fax: (41 1) 361 1603

Alhena Films SA
(production and distribution)
see Producers

Alpha Films SA
PO Box 176
CH-1211 Geneva 12
Tel: (41 22) 789 4545
Fax: (41 22) 789 3555

Buena Vista Int. Ltd
Am Schanzengraben 27
CH-8002 Zürich
Tel: (41 1) 289 2200
Fax: (41 1) 289 2222

Columbus Film AG
Steinstrasse 21
CH-8036 Zürich
Tel: (41 1) 462 7366
Fax: (41 1) 462 0112
e-mail: info@columbusfilm.ch

Elite Film AG
Molkenstrasse 21
CH-8026 Zürich
Tel: (41 1) 298 8181
Fax: (41 1) 298 8189

Fama Film AG
(production and distribution)
see Producers

Filmcooperative
Heinrichstrasse 114, PO Box 1366
CH-8031 Zürich
Tel: (41 1) 448 4422
Fax: (41 1) 448 4428
e-mail: filmcoopi@swissonline.ch

Focus Film AG
Mittelstrasse 14, PO Box
CH-8034 Zürich
Tel: (41 1) 382 3388
Fax: (41 1) 382 3389

Frenetic Film AG
Bachstrasse 9, PO Box
CH-8038 Zürich
Tel: (41 1) 483 0660
Fax: (41 1) 483 0661

Bernard Lang AG
(production and distribution)
see under Producers

Look Now!
Staffelstrasse 10
CH-8045 Zürich
Tel: (41 1) 201 2440
Fax: (41 1) 201 2442

Monopole Pathé Films SA
Neugasse 6, PO Box 1827
CH-8031 Zürich
Tel: (41 1) 271 1003
Fax: (41 1) 271 5643

Praesens Film AG
Münchhaldenstr. 10, PO Box 322
CH-8034 Zürich
Tel: (41 1) 422 3832
Fax: (41 1) 422 3793

Rialto Film AG
Neugasse 6
CH-8005 Zürich
Tel: (41 1) 444 2277
Fax: (41 1) 444 2280

Sadfi SA
8, rue de Hesse, PO Box
CH-1211 Geneva 11
Tel: (41 22) 311 7767
Fax: (41 22) 781 3119

Stamm Film AG
Löwenstrasse 20, PO Box
CH-8023 Zürich
Tel: (41 1) 211 6615
Fax: (41 1) 212 0369

Trigon-Film, Filmverleih Dritte Welt
Bahnhofstrasse 11
CH-4118 Rodersdorf
Tel: (41 61) 731 1515
Fax: (41 61) 731 3288
e-mail: trigon-film@bluewin.ch

Twentieth Century Fox
PO Box 1049
CH-1211 Geneva 26
Tel: (41 22) 827 1717
Fax: (41 22) 343 9255
e-mail: danielbe@foxinc.com

UIP (Schweiz) GmbH
Signaustrasse 6, PO Box 295
CH-8032 Zürich
Tel: (41 1) 383 8550
Fax: (41 1) 383 6112

Warner Bros. Inc.
Studerweg 3, PO Box
CH-8802 Kilchberg
Tel: (41 1) 715 5911
Fax: (41 1) 715 3451
e-mail: wbt@x8.net.ch

Useful Addresses

Swiss Film Center
Neugasse 6, PO Box
CH-8031 Zürich
Tel: (41 1) 272 5330
Fax: (41 1) 272 5350
e-mail: swissfilms@filmnet.ch

Swiss Short Film Agency
2, rue du Maupas
CH-1004 Lausanne
Tel: (41 21) 311 0906
Fax: (41 21) 311 0325
e-mail: agency@filmnet.ch

Federal Office of Culture
Film Department
Hallwylstrasse 15
CH-3003 Berne
Tel: (41 31) 322 9271
Fax: (41 31) 322 9273
e-mail: cinema.film@bak.admin.ch

Pro Helvetia
Arts Council of Switzerland
Film Department
Hirschengraben 22, PO Box
CH-8024 Zürich
Tel: (41 1) 267 7171
Fax: (41 1) 267 7108
e-mail: phmail@pro-helvetia.ch

Swiss Film Producers' Association SFP
Zinggstrasse 16
CH-3007 Berne
Tel: (41 31) 372 4001
Fax: (41 31) 372 4053

Swiss Film and Video Producers
Weinbergstrasse 31
CH-8006 Zürich
Tel: (41 1) 266 6446
Fax: (41 1) 262 2996
e-mail: ams@access.ch

Procinéma
Swiss Association of Exhibitors and Motion Pictures Distributors
PO Box 8175
CH-3001 Berne
Tel: (41 31) 387 3700
Fax: (41 31) 387 3707

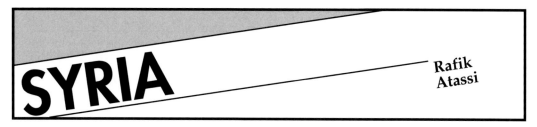

SYRIA
Rafik Atassi

On the threshold of the twenty-first century, Syrian film-makers' prospects look more doubtful than ever. Granted, the last year has witnessed the completion of six new films, but all of them had initially been given green lights in previous years. Two came from the National Film Organisation (NFO), the sole producer of long features in Syria for the past two decades. They are **Breeze of the Soul**, by Abdullatif Abdulhamid (*Verbal Messages*), and **A Land for Strangers**, by Samir Zekra (*Half-Metre Incident*).

Abdulhamid's tragi-comedy, with sadness at its core, proved a failure in the cinemas and lasted only one week in Damascus, despite huge publicity and positive reviews. *A Land of Strangers* took the prize for best Arabic film at the Cairo Film Festival, but when it is released at home it may well face the same fate as *Breeze of the Soul* at the box-office, given its heavy subject matter: the life of the Syrian thinker Abdul Rahman Al-Kawakbi (1852–1902), author of *The Characteristics of Despotism and The Struggle Against Slavery*, which presented a picture of enlightened Islam in the face of fundamentalism.

The other four films were produced through independent companies – a relatively new phenomenon in Syria. **Nasser**, the biopic directed by the Syrian-born British film-maker Anwar Kawadri (*Nutcracker*) and shot in Egypt with

Egyptian actors and technicians, may be the most expensive film in the history of Syrian cinema, with a budget that rose above $2m. The film deals with the late Egyptian president Jamal Abdul Nasser's relationship with Israel, the revolution against the monarchy, the Suez Crisis of 1956, and other incidents, up to his death in 1970.

Another independent production was **Al-Twaibi**, by Bassel Khatib, who transformed the TV series written by Nabeel Suleiman into a two-hour film about one of the rebels against Turkish oppression in Syria early this century. **A1**, the third independent production, is an experimental film directed by newcomer Mohammad Ali Adeep and covering numerous aspects of life, death and other human issues in an abstract yet simple style.

The surprise of the year was Syria's first full-length animated feature. **The Jug: A Tale from the Orient**, produced and directed by the brothers Ammar and Tahseen Shurbaji, cost more than $1m and took four years to be completed. Its story, taken from the *Tales of A Thousand and One Nights*, and computerised animation attracted large numbers of children and adults and it became one of the top-grossing films of the year.

Thus the picture looks brilliant on the surface: six films in one year, something which has not happened for the past 25 years. But it is the future which is making

Still from NASSER AND ARAFAT

Syrian film-makers anxious. Only one film, *Box of the Globe (Sandouk Al-Dunia)*, is said to be under preparation at NFO. To be directed by Osama Mohammad, it has been waiting to go into production for two years. Similarly, the other Syrian features mentioned in *IFG 1999*, Ghassan Shmeit's *Zahr Al-Rumman* and Waha Al-Raheb's *Dreams (Aghlam)* are no nearer to shooting. Unless there is some kind of miracle in the provision of film funding, Syria's film-makers will find themselves almost unemployed at the start of the third millennium.

RAFIK ATASSI has been a film critic for more than 25 years and has written many articles and books on Arabic cinema. A member of the high organising committee of the Damascus Film Festival, he has served as a jury member at many regional and international film festivals. He is currently director of programmes for the Syrian Satellite Channel.

Recent and Forthcoming Films

BREEZE OF THE SOUL

Script and Dir: Addullatif Abdullhamid. Phot: Abdo Hamza. Players: Bassam Kusa, Salim Sabri, Lina Hawarneh.

A LAND FOR STRANGERS

Scrip and Dir: Samir Zekra. Phot: Hanna Ward. Players: Bassam Kusa, Iman Al-Ghuri, Osama Ashour. Prod: NFO.

JAMAL ABDUL NASSER

Dir: Anwar Kawadri. Players: Khaled El-Sawi, Hisham Saleem, Abla Kamel, Jameel Rateb. Prod: Haya Films.

THE JUG: A TALE FROM THE ORIENT

Dir: Ammar and Tahseen Shurbaji. Prod: Al-Nejm for Artistic Productions.

A1, A FIRST OF A KIND

Script and Dir: Mohammad Ali Adeeb. Prod: Mak TV and Cinema Productions.

AL-TWAIBI

Script: Nabeel Suleiman. Dir: Bassel Khateeb. Photo: Hisham Maleh. Players: Ayman Zeidan, Khaled Taja, Norman Asaad/ Prod: Cham Al-Dawlia.

Producers

National Film Organisation
Rawda
Damascus
Tel: (963 11) 333 4200

Haya for Artistic Production
Bashir Ghaiah
Salheia
Damascus
Tel: (963 11) 221 8144

Nader Atassi
Fardous St
Damascus
Tel: (963 11) 221 6009

Tahseen Kawadri
Tigheez St
Damascus
Tel: (963 11) 223 6767

Ghanem Films
Malki
Damascus
Tel: (963 11) 333 6279

Al-Nejm
Baramkeh
Damascus
Tel: (963 11) 222 3730

Igraa Films
Khateeb St
Damascus
Tel: (963 11) 444 1446

Cham Al-Dawkia
Mezz
Damascus
Tel: (963 11) 613 3382

Al-Tawam
Kafr Sousa
Damascus
Tel: (963 11) 212 4040

Ara Films
Fine Arts Square
Damascus
Tel: (963 11) 442 0083

Mak for TV and Cinema
Abou Rummaneh
Damascus
Tel: (963 11) 332 1000

Al-Surriah
Mezza
Damascus
Tel: (963 11) 613 4020

Aleppo Al-Dawlia
Sabeel
Aleppo
Tel: (963 21) 331 2752

Syrian TV
Omayad Square
Damascus
Tel: (963 11) 221 2000
Fax: (963 11) 222 5374

Momen Mulla
Rokn El-deen
Damascus
Tel: (963 11) 512 284

Ara for Artistic Prod
Fine Arts Square
Damascus
Tel: (963 11) 442 008

Distributors

Tiba and Abboud
Fardous St
Damascus
Tel: (963 11) 222 1096

Mamoun Serri
Fardous St
Damascus
Tel: (963 11) 221 1188

Shamra
Mezza
Damascus
Tel: (963 11) 666 5601

Ibrahim Nejma
Aleppo St.
Damascus
Tel: (963 11) 331 2193
Venus
Mezza
Damascus
Tel: (963 11) 611 5433

Useful Addresses

Cham Cinemas
Maysaloun St
Damascus
Tel: (963 11) 223 2300

Boruq
Mazraa
Damascus
Tel: (963 11) 444 9306

Saad
Baghdad St
Damascus
Tel: (963 11) 442 7153

Daoud Sheikhani
Rawda
Damascus
Tel: (963 11) 333 3491

Haysam Hatahet
Salheia
Damascus
Tel: (963 11) 222 2212

Abdul Masih Attia
Tijara
Damascus
Tel: (963 11) 232 0021

Dureid Laham
Abou Rummaneh
Damascus
Tel: (963 11) 333 1601

Syndicate of Artists
Baghdad St
Damascus
Tel: (963 11) 444 5809

TAIWAN

Derek
Elley

The past year will go down as one of the more fractious in Taiwan's recent film history, though with hindsight the bickering may turn out to have been just a storm in a teacup. The rows centred on the 1998 Golden Horse Awards, whose judges gave seven prizes to US-based actress Joan Chen's directorial debut *Xiu Xiu: The Sent-Down Girl*, with nothing going to critical favourites Tsai Ming-liang (*The Hole*) or Wang Shau-di (the animated *Grandma and Her Ghosts*), prompting Tsai to withdraw from the event. Controversy has rarely been absent from these awards, and of more interest was the hoo-ha over the government's annual film-making subsidies (the so-called *fudao jin*), a dispute which had been simmering for some time.

Set up in the late 1980s, the *fudao jin* system was originally meant to encourage local production by making monetary awards for scripts. Several film-makers have benefited, including Ang Lee at the start of his career. However, many scripts were never filmed, and the process acquired an unwelcome reputation for simply being a cash-cow for writers. The whole 'art vs. commerce' debate blew up again in 1998 with the news that two commercial movies – *Ninja Army* (*Renzhe bing*) and *Na Cha vs. the Monkey King* (*Na Zha danao Meihouwang*) – were being awarded $310,000 (NT$10m) each. Worse, the scripts had already been made into films and been released in cinemas.

The row brought to the surface again the parlous commercial state of Taiwanese cinema and how, in many people's eyes, the industry had long been hijacked by film-makers who garnered awards at festivals but cared naught for the industry or audiences. A prime example is FIPRESCI favourite Tsai, whose *The Hole*, lauded by critics, ran for three days in Taipei before being yanked.

There are signs that things may slowly be changing, though it will be a while – and require another generation of film-makers – before Taiwan discovers whether it still has an industry left. Production is running at around 20 features a year (60% of which were government-aided during the past year), with a huge gap between the artier movies selected by international festival programmers, and films with purely local appeal. Even Chu Yen-ping, the island's one-man commercial film industry, complained that 1998 had been one of his worst years ever, with the loss of many traditional East Asian export markets.

Desperately seeking husband

One film gave major cause for hope – the comedy-drama **The Personals** (*Zhenghun qishi*), by former critic Chen Kuo-fu, whose previous movies have often been an uneasy mix of fanciful ambition and soft-centred whimsy. An almost Hal Hartley-like exercise, centred on a thirtysomething doctor (Rene Liu) who advertises for a potential husband, the film is immaculately scripted and luminously acted by Liu, in a role that confirms her as the island's finest young actress, following sterling work in films like Sylvia Chang's *Siao Yu*. Almost entirely composed of a series of meetings with potential spouses, but with a surprising final twist, it also signals Chen as a director of new maturity and observation.

Though it is slickly made, and never takes its audience for granted, *The Personals* is still specialised fare; but it points the way for a new kind of quality entertainment, free of the introverted vanity which has plagued Taiwanese cinema during the 1990s. In Taipei it drew an encouraging 40,000 admissions in March 1999, and was admired by audiences who bothered to see it at Cannes, where it was tucked away in Un Certain Regard, rather than being given the Competition berth it deserved. It is, quite simply, one of the finest Taiwanese movies of the decade.

Co-produced with the government-funded Central Motion Picture Corp. (CPMC), on a budget of $500,000, *The Personals* was the latest production by Zoom Hunt Intl., a company set up in 1997 by former CMPC producer Hsu Li-kong. Hsu, who was previously responsible for launching the international careers of directors as diverse as Tsai and Lee, plans to direct Liu in the contemporary melodrama *Night Flight*, as well as expanding Zoom Hunt into distribution and finally getting Lee's long-planned swordplay drama, the $6m **Crouching Tiger Hidden Dragon**, off the ground. Starring Chow Yun-fat, the movie finally started shooting in China in late summer 1999.

The secret history

More specialised than *The Personals*, but possessed of a powerful spirituality, was Wan Jen's **Connected to Fate** (*Chaoji*

guomin), a continuation of his examination of Taiwan's hidden political history, first pursued in his previous film, *Super Citizen Ko* (1995). Where the earlier movie looked in retrospect at the anti-communist terror of the 1940 and 1950s, *Connected to Fate* centres on the islanders' relationship with the aboriginal population, here symbolised through a lonely Taiwanese taxi driver's strange friendship with the ghost of an executed killer. Rather too esoteric for foreign tastes, and requiring some knowledge of local history and society, it is still a movie of considerable sweep and power, venturing into areas hardly touched by other film-makers, and directed with Wan's customary finesse.

Other films of the past year have ranged across the usual small bandwidth of accessibility. The best was Chen Yu-hsun's **Love Go Go** (*Aiqing laile*), a quirky comedy of manners focused on a small group of oddball characters looking for love in the big city. The worst was Lin Cheng-sheng's **March of Happiness** (*Tianma chafang*; later changed to *Xingfu jinxingqu* for its Cannes showing), a relentlessly small-scale, introverted drama about two young lovers

Hsiao Shu-shen and Lim Giong in MARCH OF HAPPINESS

during the late 1940s, roughly the same period shown in Hou Hsiao-hsien's *City of Sadness*. Dryly directed and listlessly acted, it was a major disappointment from the director of *A Drifting Life* and *Murmur of Youth*, though Lin's previous film, *Sweet Degeneration*, had already started to show signs of this overly-mannered style.

Of interest were **Darkness and Light** (*Heianzhi guang*), a family drama set in a fishing village, the third feature of Chang Tso-chi (*Ah Chung*), and Chen Yi-wen's first feature, **Jam** (*Guojiang*), a film in four overlapping segments that shows the influence of Edward Yang, for whom Chen had previously worked as an assistant.

Yang himself has been preparing for the past year his part of a trio of films funded by Japan's Pony Canyon going under the series title **Y2K** ('Y' referring to Yang, 'K' to Hong Kong's Stanley Kwan, and '2 to one of the ideograms in Japanese Shunji Iwai's name). Yang finally started shooting in summer 1999.

Taiwan's other internationally-known name, Hou Hsiao-hsien, was scheduled to start in autumn 1999 on his next feature, a contemporary drama set in Taipei's rave scene. His contract with Japan's Shochiku at an end, Hou has found French finance for the new movie, which he planned to shoot on 16mm. On a sadder note, May 1999 saw the death, from a heart attack, of Tang Pao-yun, one of the major female stars of Taiwanese cinema of the 1960s and 1970s. She was 54.

Golden Horse Awards 1998

The following awards were presented in Taipei on December 12, 1998:

Best Film: *Xiu Xiu: The Sent-Down Girl*.**
Best Director: Joan Chen (*Xiu Xiu: The Sent-Down Girl*).
Best Actor: Lopsang Chunpei (*Xiu Xiu: The Sent-Down Girl*).
Best Actress: Lu Lu (*Xiu Xiu: The Sent-Down Girl*).
Best Supporting Actor: Eric Tsang (*Hold You Tight*).*
Best Supporting Actress: Shu Qi (*Portland Street Blues*).*
Best Original Script: Mabel Cheung, Alex Law (*City of Glass*).*
Best Adapted Script: Yan Geling, Joan Chen (*Xiu Xiu: The Sent-Down Girl*).
Best Photography: Jungle Ma (*City of Glass*).
Best Visual Effects: Centro Digital (*The Storm Riders*).*

Best Art Direction: Huang Wen-ying, Tsao Chih-wei (*Flowers of Shanghai*).
Best Sound Effects: Tsang King-cheung (*City of Glass*).
Best Costume Design: Lee Pik-kwan (*The Storm Riders*).
Best Action Direction: Jackie Chan's Stunt Team (*Who Am I?*).*
Best Original Music: Johnny Chen (*Xiu Xiu: The Sent-Down Girl*).
Best Original Songs: Johnny Chen (*Xiu Xiu: The Sent Down Girl*).
Best Editing: Maurice Li (*City of Glass*).
Golden Horse Film Festival Audience Award: *City of Glass*.
Special Jury Prize: Rene Liu (*The Personals*).
Main Jury Prize: *Flowers of Shanghai*.
Best Documentary: *Amah's Secret*.
Best Animated Film: no award.
Best Short: no award.
Lifetime Achievement Award: Chou Tien-su.
* Hong Kong production
** technically a US production

Forthcoming Films

WO HU CANG LONG (Crouching Tiger Hidden Dragon)

Dir: Ang Lee. Players: Chow Yun-fat, Michelle Yeoh, Cheng Pei-pei, Chang Chen, Zhang Ziyi. Prod: Zoom Hunt. Shot in China.

A ONE AND A TWO

Dir: Edward Yang. Players: Wu Nien-jen, Ise Ogata. Co-production with Japan.

DIANYIN WU SHI

Dir: Hou Hsiao-hsien. Players: Maggie Cheung, Jack Kao, Pauline Chen. Co-production with France.

YE BEN (Night Flight)

Dir: Hsu Li-kong. Players: Rene Liu. Prod: Zoom Hunt.

THE CANDIDATE

Dir: Peter Lee: Prod: Zoom Hunt.

Useful Addresses

Central Motion Picture Corp. (CMPC)
8/F 116 Hanchung St
Taipei
Tel: (886 2) 371 5191
Fax: (886 2) 331 0681

Chang-Hong Channel Film & Video Co.
3/F, No. 9, Alley 6, Lane 166
Section 3, Hsinyi Rd
Taipei
Tel: (886 2) 705 2603
Fax: (886 2) 709 0334

Long Shong Pictures
2/F, 113 Hankou St
Section 2
Taipei
Tel: (886 2) 311 0249
Fax: (886 2) 314 5157

Scholar Films Co.
10/F, 88 Omei St
Taipei
Tel: (886 2) 361 5850
Fax: (886 2) 311 9692

3-H Films
3/F, No. 19, Lane 2
Wanli St
Taipei
Tel: (886 2) 230 0136

Taiwan Film Centre
4/F, No. 19, Lane 2
Wanli St
Taipei
Tel: (886 2) 239 6026
Fax: (886 2) 239 6501

Zoom Hunt Intl. Prods. Co.
Tel: (886 2) 2761 7879
Fax: (886 2) 2761 6876

THAILAND — Anchalee Chaiworaporn

The economic turmoil that swept South East Asia from the middle of 1997 finally started threatening the box-office returns of Hollywood movies in Thailand in the fourth quarter of 1998. Up until then, Hollywood films had been relatively unaffected, since they were still considered the best-value entertainment among audiences. Fewer Hollywood films were distributed in 1998 than in 1997: 196 (out of a total of 260 movies), down from 219. For the first time in the past several years, all of the top ten highest grossers were American blockbusters and *Titanic* broke all of Thailand's box-office records, taking in $5.9 million, to surpass *The Lost World: Jurassic Park*.

Large-scale multiplex construction continued, but the new domestic Arthouse project, designed to screen "sidebar" independent movies bought from the block-sales system, was closed down after just nine months. Most distributors saw grosses slip by 30–40% in the fourth quarter, bringing into question their release strategies. Most movies have been given the widest possible release on their

opening weekend, and then immediately pushed aside into second-run theatres.

Unsurprisingly, local production continued to decline. Only 13 local films were released in 1998 (down from 30 in 1997). Major studios have drastically cut their production slates and B-movie producers have gone bust. Worst of all, none of the 13 films made a profit, or even grossed $1m. However, in stark contrast to the prevailing mood, a new Thai production company, BEC Film, has emerged. Despite the box-office failure of its first offerings, BEC Film is one of the most encouraging arrivals on the Thai film scene since the economic downturn began.

New directors who started out in television have continued to move across to features. Of these, Phinyo Roo-tham was the most successful, with **O-Negative**. Though it was not a commercial success, the film collected several major Thai critics' and national awards, including Best Movie and Best Director. Thakonkiat Veerawan retained the romantic plot familiar from many of his successful television series for his feature debut, **Kamphaeng**, but the repetitious formula did not fare well with critics or audiences.

The most exciting film has come from Penek Ratanaruang, who brought Thai film-making to the attention of international critics and audiences with his directorial debut, *Fun Bar Karaoke*. His new work, **Simple Men**, again focuses on the everyday lives of Thai people after the economic bubble has burst. Inspired by front-page stories, *Simple Men* is set in one day in Bangkok and looks at how the devaluation of the local currency has affected Thai people's moral and human value.

Alternative film-making continues to flourish. With his directorial debut **Mysterious Object at Noon**, Apichat-phong Weerasethakul has created a cons-iderable stir. This mock-documentary about Thai people's lives in four different regions became the first Thai film to be supported by the Rotterdam Film Festival's Hubert Bals Fund and is expected to be released in 2000.

Still from SIMPLE MEN

ANCHALEE CHAIWORAPORN is a film writer and critic for Thai and international periodicals, including *Variety*.

Recent and Forthcoming Films

KAMPHAENG

Dir: Thakolkiat Weerawan. Players: Kirkphol Massaya-wanich, Ketmanee Phichairon-narongsongkhram. Prod: Grammy Film.

MYSTERIOUS OBJECTS AT NOON

Script, Dir and Phot: Aphichat-phong Weerasetthakul. Prod: Cinema Factory.

SIMPLE MEN

Script and Dir: Pen-ek Ratanaruang. Players: Lalita Punyopas. Prod: Five Star Productions Co. Ltd./Film Factory Ltd.

Producers

Cinema Factory
44/17 Ladprao 15
Jatujak
Bangkok 10500
Fax: (66 2) 938 5648

Film Factory Ltd.
95 Soi Sukhumvit 99
Bangchak

Phrakanong
Bangkok 10250.
Fax: (66 2) 332 2817

Five Star Productions Co. Ltd.
157/9 Soi Areesamphan 2
Bangkok 10310
Fax: (66 2) 246 2105/245 7931

Grammy Film
209/1 CMIC Tower B

Sukhumvit 21
Bangkok 10110
Fax: (66 2) 664 0246

Kantana Production
333 Soi Ratchadanivej 19
Pracha-u-tit Rd
Huay Kwang
Bangkok 10310
Fax: (66 2) 275 4530

New Breed Pictures
301/61 Soi Panich-a-nun
Sukhumvit 71
Bangkok 10110
Fax: (66 2) 392 3447

RS Film
419/1 Ladphrao 15
Jatujark
Bangkok 10900
Fax: (66 2) 511 2324

Saha Mongkol Film Co., Ltd
1081/5 Phaholyothin Rd
Phyathai
Bangkok 10400
Fax: (66 2) 271 0620

Tai Entertainment
79/23 Srinakarin Rd
Nongbon
Pravej
Bangkok 10260
Fax: (66 2) 366 0377

Useful Address

Thai Film Foundation
21/1 Sukhumvit 61
Klong Toey
Bangkok 10110
Fax: (66 2) 437 9818

TUNISIA — Roy Armes

The past year saw the release of just two, characteristically interesting Tunisian features, one co-produced with the CCM, the national cinema centre in Morocco, the other with a French company. The director responsible for one of them, Taïeb Louhichi, had already established an international reputation with his first two features.

The first, *The Shadow of the Earth*, was a slow and moving story of an isolated rural community torn apart by natural forces and the pressures of modern life; the second, *Layla My Reason*, in a very different mode, was an adaptation of the traditional tale *Le fou de Layla*, and told of the poet Qays and his frustrated love for the beautiful Layla.

Louhichi's third feature, **Moon Wedding** (*Noces de Lune*), is a fresh departure: a tale of disaffected youth in contemporary Tunis, told with the director's customary flair and elegance. The film focuses on a group of five young people (a girl and four boys, two of whom are from rich families)

who zoom carelessly through the outskirts of the city on their motorbikes.

The group reaches a highpoint of unity when they lightheartedly bring together in marriage two illiterate drop-outs, Pierrot and Madonna. But a late-night drinking session then leads to the accidental death of one of their number, a crisis which causes the group to disintegrate. The death ends their idyll, but Louhichi resolutely refuses to condemn his young protagonists.

Mohamed Ben Smaïl had made a reputation as an actor in both French and Tunisian features and directed two documentaries before he embarked on his first feature, **Tomorrow I Burn** (*Demain Je Brule*), in which he plays the lead. The protagonist, Lotfi, is already a broken and defeated man before he leaves his wife and two children in Paris, to return to his native Tunis. There he meets a succession of old friends and visits old haunts but nowhere is he able to make meaningful connections. The whole film follows a trajectory towards inevitable death.

Recent Films

NOCES DE LUNE
(Moon Wedding)

Script and Dir: Taïeb Louchichi. Phot: Dominique Le Rigoleur. Players: Mess Hattou, Mohamed Hédi Moumen, Rym Riahi. Prod: Tanit Productions (Tunis)/CCM (Morocco).

DEMAIN JE BRULE
(Tomorrow I Burn)

Script and Dir: Mohamed Ben Smaïl. Phot: Youssef Ben Youssef. Players: Mohamed Ben Smaïl, Amel Hedhili, Slah Msaddak, Nejib Belkadhi, Jalila Bourhane, Sémia Rhalem, Mohamed Ben Becher. Prod: Nomadis Images (Tunisia)/Les Ateliers de l'Arche (France).

Useful Addresses

Carthage Image (Formerly SATPEC: Film Laboratory)
017 20 avenue Taeib Mehri
Gammarth 2003
Tel: (216 1) 740 944

Canal Horizons Tunisie
(Television Company)
rue de la Monnaie
Tunis 1000
Tel: (216 1) 333 100
Fax: (216 1) 333 104

Journées Cinématographiques de Carthage (Biennial Film Festival)
5 rue Ali Belhouane
2070 La Marsa
Tel: (216 1) 745 355
Fax: (216 1) 745 564

SeptièmArt
(Film journal)
B.P. 992
1045 Tunis
Tel: (216 1) 256 904

Festival International du Film Amateur de Kelibia (FIFAK)
(Film Festival)
B.P. 116
1015 Tunis
Tel: (216 1) 280 298

TURKEY

Atilla Dorsay

Miraculously, cinema at the end of the century is playing the same part in the daily life of the Turks as it did some 20 years ago. The nationwide increase in the number of cinemas, the incredible box-office success of some local films and the pitiful standard of most TV broadcasting have resulted in the total cinema audience almost doubling in the past three years.

Of the 160 films released in Turkey in 1998, 110 were American, 20 were European, and a dozen were locally produced – a small share but made up of interesting and successful features. The veteran Tunç Basaran was responsible for two of the 12. **Please Don't Go** (*Sen de Gitme*) was an adaptation of a novel by the woman writer Ayla Kutlu about the sad love story of a Turkish girl and a French soldier during the short period when Hatay, at the Syrian border, was under

Still from PLEASE DON'T GO

French control. **Kaçiklik Diplomasi** (literally, *Graduate of Insanity*) was a lucid observation of a woman's tragic decline into a world of madness. Both films were of reasonable quality, but had poor box-office results.

Films which questioned Turkey's politics and history were in fashion. The TRT-State

TV Company financed **Republic** (*Cumhuriyet*), about the foundation of the Turkish state by Kemal Atatürk in the 1920s. Released during the celebration of the seventy-fifth anniversary of the Republic, it was a big crowd-pleaser.

Two young directors made films which were in direct opposition to this official reading of history. Reis Çelik, in his second film **Goodbye Tomorrow** (*Hoşçakal Yarin*), told the true story of Deniz Gezmis and his two friends, young political rebels who were hanged in the early 1970s. His documentary-like style and his courage in dealing with a tormented period of recent history in a non-official and personal way gained the approval of the public. Turgut Yasalar, in his first film **The Leopard's Trail** (*Leoparin Kuyrugu*), dealt with the same period and enjoyed more modest success.

The almost-veteran Sinan Çetin had another huge box-office hit with **Propaganda**, an Italian-like rural comedy about the catastrophic installation of a Turkish-Syrian border in a small eastern village. His film was crude and grotesque, but it nevertheless pleased the audiences, selling more than a million tickets. Ömer Vargi drew on the experience of the successful producer of big hits such as *The American* and *The Bandit* to turn his first-time directing effort **Everything's Gonna be Great** (*Hersey Çok Güzel Olacak*) into a pleasant comedy and a big box-office hit With two irresistible leads, one a TV personality the other a well known musician, it sold almost 1.3 million tickets.

New wave, classic release

A group who call themselves The New Moviemakers has emerged. They are all cinema school graduates and work as a team. Their first efforts were two films shot simultaneously with a shared crew and employing similar, complementary stories and themes. **On Board** (*Gemide*), by Serdar Akar, was stronger than **Azize**, by Kudret Sabanci. Both dealt with the small-time crooks and conmen who operate at night in Istanbul, and had a very fresh feel and enormous sincerity. The films pleased the

critics, but were a flop at the box-office. However, *On Board* enjoyed the prestige of being selected for the Critics Fortnight in Cannes.

A major event was the first domestic commercial release – after 17 years – of the most famous Turkish film ever made: **Yol**, written by Yilmaz Güney and directed by Serif Gören. Many people, including some young critics discovered it for the first time, and the public response was good.

The Turks also worked hard abroad, especially directors based in Germany. Films such as **The Wound** (*Yara*), by Yilmaz Arslan, were big successes in festivals. Turkish director Kutlug Ataman made a controversial second film, **Lola and Bilidikid**, a co-production about the Turkish gay and transvestite community in Germany. The film premiered in the Panorama section at Berlin and was heading for a summer 1999 release in Turkey. Ferzan Özpetek, who lives in Italy, followed *Hammam* with **Harem Suare**, another typically Turkish story, set in the last days of the Ottoman harem. It was chosen as the closing film in Un Certain Regard at Cannes.

Probably the most important film to emerge from the past year was **Journey to the Sun** (*Güneşe Yolculuk*). The second film by the young woman director, Yesim Ustaoglu, it tackled a sensitive subject, the present-day friendship between a Turkish boy and a Kurdish boy in Turkey. This was a political film without being polemical, dealing sensitively with an important subject and showing the documentary origins of its director. Shown for the first time at Berlin, where it won two sidebar prizes, it then collected all the major awards in the national section at the Istanbul festival, although, sadly, at press time there was no date set for a domestic theatrical release.

ATILLA DORSAY was born in 1939 in Izmir and has been a film critic since 1966. He is the author of 15 books on the cinema, is president of SIYAD, the Turkish film critics' association, and a member of the organising committee of the Istanbul Film Festival.

Recent and Forthcoming Films

AZIZE
(Azize – A Madonna in Laleli)

Script: Kudret Sabanci, Önder Çakar, Serdar Akar. Dir: Sabanci. Players: Güven Kirac, Istar Gökseven, Ella Manea. Prod: Yeni Sinemacilik.

GEMIDE (On Board)

Script: Serdar Akar, Önder Çakar. Dir: Akar. Players: Erkan Can, Naci Tasdögen, Ella Manea. Prod: Yeni Sinemacilar.

GÜNESE YOLCULUK
(Journey to the Sun)

Script and Dir: Yesim Ustaoglu. Players: Nevruz Sahin, Nazmi Kirik, Mizgin Kapazan. Prod: IFR.

HERSEY COK GÜZEL OLACAK
(Everything's Gonna Be Great)

Script: Ömer Vargi, Cem Yilmaz, Hakan Haksun. Dir: Vargi. Players: Cem Yilmaz, Mazhar Alanson, Selim Nasit. Prod: Filma Cass.

HOSCAKAL YARIN
(Goodbye Tomorrow)

Script and Dir: Reis Çelik. Players: Berhan Simsek, Tuncer Necmioglu, Tuncel Kurtiz. Prod: RH Politic Productions International.

Still from PROPAGANDA

KACIKLIK DIPLOMASI

Script and Dir: Tunç Basaran. Players: Ayda Aksel, Selcuk Yöntem, Güler Ökten. Prod: Mine Film.

KAYIKCI (The Boatman)

Script: Metin Belgin, Ülkü Karaosmanoglu. Dir: Biket Ilhan. Players: Memet Ali Alabora, Katerina Mousatsos. Prod: Sinevizyon Film-Turkey/Maraton Films-Greece.

LEOPARIN KUYRUGU
(Leopard's Trail)

Script and Dir: Turgut Yasalar. Players: Yetkin Dikinciler, Devrim Nas, Hakan Piskin, Tardu Flordun. Prod: Planet Film.

LOLA VE BILIDIKI
(Lola and Bilidikid)

Script and Dir : Kutlug Ataman. Players: Gandi Mukli, Erdal Yildiz, Baki Davrak, Inge Keller. Prod: C-O Productions-Turkey/ Zero Film-Germany.

PROPAGANDA

Script: Sinan Çetin, Gülin Tokat. Dir : Sinan Çetin. Players: Metin Akpinar, Kemal Sunal, Meltem Cumbul, Rafet el Roman. Prod: Plato Film.

YARA (The Wound)

Script and Dir: Yilmaz Arslan. Players: Yelda Kaymakci Reynaud, Nur Sürer, Halil Ergün, Füsun Demirel. Prod: Y.A. Filmproduktion- Germany.

Producers/ Distributors

Özen Film
Sakızağaci Caddesi, 21
Beyoğlu
Istanbul
Tel: (90 212) 7070/71
Fax: (90 212) 244 5851

Umut Sanat
Halaskargazi Caddesi
Gezi Ethem Paşa Sitesi, 214/7
80220 Şişli
Istanbul
Tel: (90 212) 230 4041
Fax: (90 212) 232 3583

Warner Bros
Topcu Cad. Uygun Is Merkezi. No 2/6
80090 Taksim
Istanbul
Tel: (90 212) 237 2000
Fax: (90 212) 237 2600

Useful Addresses

CASOD
(The Association of Actors)
Istiklal Caddesi
Atlas Sinemasi Pasaji–C Blok 53/3
Beyoğlu
Istanbul
Tel: (90 212) 251 9775
Fax: (90 212) 251 9779

FILM-YÖN
(The Association of Directors)
Ayhan Işik Sokak, 28/1
Beyoğlu
Istanbul
Tel: (90 212) 244 0138
Fax: (90 212) 245 7194

Istanbul Kültür ve Sanat Vakfi
(The Istanbul Culture and Arts
Foundation)
Istiklal Caddesi, Louvre Apt. 146
800070 Beyoğlu
Istanbul
Tel: (90 212) 293 3133
Fax: (90 212) 249 7771

**SIYAD–Sinema Yazarları
Derneği**
(The Association of Film Critics)
Atilla Dorsay–Akçam Sokak 17/6
4. Levent
Istanbul
Tel: (90 212) 264 0683
Fax: (90 212) 269 8284

TÜRSAK
(The Turkish Cinema and
Audiovisual Culture Foundation)
Gazeteci Erol Dernek Sokak
11/2 Hanif Han
Beyoğlu
Istanbul
Tel: (90 212) 244 5251
Fax: (90 212) 251 6770

UNITED KINGDOM
Philip Kemp

The British film industry, independent producer-director Bill Cartlidge remarked not long ago, is "permanently ill, but goes into remission now and then". If so, for the past three or four years the patient has at least been sitting up and taking solid food. In recent months, though, the consultants may have felt some cause for concern. Nothing yet so serious as a relapse, for sure: but the rate of recovery has unmistakably slowed almost to a standstill. A temporary plateau, a breathing-space before further improvement – or is this as good as it gets, with a downturn in prospect?

Pessimists can point to some ominous statistics. Production figures are down: in 1998 the number of films shot in Britain (by British or overseas companies) dropped to 94, as against the record level of 124 in 1997; wholly British productions fell off proportionately more, down to 42 from 72 the previous year. Co-productions, whether UK-US or UK-European, were similarly down.

Overall investment fell sharply, down by 24% from $1.1bn (£676m) to $844m. And despite the continuing increase in the number of screens – and the mass appeal of *Titanic* – admissions were down for only the second time in 15 years. Exhibitors blamed the football World Cup for spoiling the summer blockbuster season; though others pointed out that the big-budget popcorn fare was no great shakes, either critically or at the box-office.

Even so, one can justifiably put a more favourable spin on these statistics. A drop in production may be no bad thing: the previous glut saw too many mediocre films being produced, often without a hope of cinematic release. The average budget for a wholly-UK production (not necessarily an index of quality, of course) rose from $3.3m in 1997 to $4.3m in 1998. And despite decreased output, Britain was able to field 55 films at the 1999 Cannes Festival, more than any other country except the US and France. Many of them were very well received and it bodes well for the future that several of the most impressive were by first-time directors, including Damien O'Donnell's **East is East**, Jasmin Dizdar's **Beautiful People** and Lynne Ramsay's **Ratcatcher**.

Though overall funding is down, it has been heartening to see City institutions starting to dabble in film. Traditionally the City has steered clear of the movie industry, seeing it as too erratic and unpredictable. Well-publicised debacles like the collapse of Goldcrest in the 1980s did not help. But recently, encouraged by government initiatives on 100% tax breaks, the attitude has softened – most notably at leading accountants Ernst & Young, who have announced a $30m debut slate of projects. According to the Ottawa Consulting Group, private-sector financing of the UK film industry is forecast to rise from its present $120m to an annual $600m by 2004.

Whose money is it, anyway?

Despite the sacking of Britain's first Films Minister, Tom Clarke, and his replacement by the all-but-invisible Janet Anderson, the government's low-key but useful support of the industry continues. The much-derided idea of a "voluntary levy" has been scrapped; in its place a "skills fund" for training up new talent is proposed. The 100% tax breaks on films costing $24m or less are guaranteed for a further two years,

and government funding over the same period is expected to total $233.5m.

Up to now, much of this public funding has been channelled through the Arts Council. This is set to change under plans to set up a new umbrella body, the Films Council, which will not only handle all government subsidy for the industry, but oversee the present British Film Institute, British Screen and British Film Commission. Is this thrifty pooling of resources or another layer of superfluous bureaucracy? The jury is still out on the proposals, but many feel that, rather than tinkering with the production side, the government should focus on distribution, the perennial problem of the British film industry.

Fears that the strong pound would hurt British studio facilities, driving overseas productions elsewhere, seemed to be realised when George Lucas' next two *Star Wars* episodes transferred on cost grounds from Leavesden Studios to the new Fox Australia complex in Sydney. But Leavesden soon recouped the business and, along with other British studios, remains busy. Doubts hover over the future of Ealing Studios: the National Film and Television School, which

Vinnie Jones in the most successful British film of 1998, Guy Ritchie's LOCK, STOCK AND TWO SMOKING BARRELS
photo: S. Pearson/PolyGram

Let's just say, we've had a few heavyweights in our time.

BBC Films has been fortunate over the last few years to feast on a diet of some of the world's most prodigious directors. But this fact isn't down to luck, moreover, it's down to our incisive instinct for choosing the right script and our ability of unearthing new and refreshing talent.

So, it's no coincidence that BBC Films has attracted such big names as Roger Michell, John Madden, Bernardo Bertolucci and Stephen Frears. And also tempted many actors of a similar size. Judi Dench, Kate Winslet, Helena Bonham Carter and Hugh Grant to name but a few.

Yet our real talent has to be the new talent we are discovering today. As they will be the big stars of tomorrow. Incidentally, BBC Films was responsible for three of the four nominations in the 'Best Newcomer Category' at the last BAFTA awards.

BBC Films

THE BIG NAME'S ON THE BIG SCREEN

BBC FILMS, CENTRE HOUSE, 56 WOOD LANE, LONDON W12 7SB UNITED KINGDOM. TEL: +44 20 8743 8000 FAX: +44 20 8740 9609

was to move there, now has other plans. Another historic venue, though, has been preserved: London's oldest production centre, the former Gainsborough Studios in Islington (where Hitchcock started out) will continue to house film shoots.

In Scotland, plans are afoot for the first-ever Scottish film studios. The currently favoured site is near Edinburgh, in a venture whose backers include Sony and Sean Connery's Fountainbridge Films. The Isle of Man, too, may soon acquire its first purpose-built studios, following the success of *Waking Ned* – set in Ireland, but shot in the unspoiled Manx countryside.

Celtic tales

Altogether, there's a strong Celtic element within the present revitalisation of British cinema. The sense of reborn national pride that led to the setting up of the Scottish Parliament and the Welsh National Assembly has also inspired, in both countries, films with no trace of the conventional tourist image. In Wales, the label of 'the Welsh *Trainspotting*', formerly attached to Keith Allen's 1997 *Twin Town*, fitted this year's **Human Traffic**, the debut of writer-director Justin Kerrigan, far better. Kerrigan's study of drugged-up clubbers in downtown Cardiff shares much of *Trainspotting*'s headlong energy, if little of its sophistication. No less roundly Welsh, but utterly remote in mood and mode, is **Solomon and Gaenor**, Paul Morrison's poignant tale of cross-racial romance in the mining valleys, shortly before the First World War.

In Scotland itself, the momentum launched by *Shallow Grave* and *Trainspotting* shows no sign of slowing down. Ken Loach moved north of the border to make **My Name is Joe**, whose characteristically Loachian mix of dour humour and class-conscious anger slotted perfectly into its Glasgow setting. The Cannes-acclaimed *Ratcatcher*, Anthony Nielson's hard-bitten thriller **The Debt Collector** and Genevieve Jolliffe's edgy, unsettling **Urban Ghost Story** all make powerful use of their urban Scottish settings.

Peter Mullan in MY NAME IS JOE
photo: Joss Barratt/Film Four

So does one of the most impressive directorial debuts of the year, Peter Mullan's **Orphans**. Mullan, who played the title role in *My Name is Joe*, directed a couple of well-regarded shorts before making his feature debut as writer-director. *Orphans* starts out grounded in Loachian realism, but soon takes off into realms of deliriously surreal imagery that Mullan's mentor would scarcely countenance.

The film follows four bereaved adult siblings through the long night preceding their mother's funeral. Each reacts differently but self-destructively, plunging into his or her personal purgatory in a Glasgow mired in a stew of boozy, casual violence, tears and Catholic obscurantism. Socially and emotionally dysfunctional, snared by the traps of class and culture, these characters are orphaned in every sense of the word.

At once distressing, scary and savagely funny, Mullan's film – shot in neon-garish colours and acted to the hilt by a committed cast – swings abruptly from tragedy to farce, depicting a society torn by maudlin, self-romanticising despair. Just occasionally – as in the funeral sequence – the tone is misjudged, but for most of its length the film deftly sustains its balancing act.

Sticking on home turf

It is perhaps an index of growing national self-confidence that the present generation of British film-makers generally feel less need to court the American market with the 'big international pictures' that have so often in the past come crashing down in flames. The unexpected runaway success of *The Full Monty* seems to have convinced people that national, and even provincial, stories can exert worldwide appeal, and that our own history and culture give us ample material to work with.

In very different ways, four of the year's films tried to tap into the national heritage without getting pompous or reverential: John Madden's witty, Bard-spoofing **Shakespeare in Love** (whose US-financed triumph at the Oscars reawakened the debate on what exactly constitutes a British film); **Hilary and Jackie**, Anand Tucker's account of the troubled relationship

Joseph Fiennes in SHAKESPEARE IN LOVE
photo: Laurie Sparham/Miramax Universal

between doomed-genius cellist Jacqueline Du Pré and her sister; John Maybury's mordant study of Francis Bacon, **Love Is the Devil**; and Brian Gibson's disarming **Still Crazy**, in which a fifth-rate 1970s rock group, now paunchy and past-it, go back on the road.

Even when current British film-makers do range further afield for setting and subject matter, they seem able to keep things incisive and light-footed, avoiding the lumbering portentousness of such

Peter Mullan's ORPHANS was one of the year's most striking feature debuts   *photo: The Kobal Collection*

Kate Winslet seeking adventure in Morocco in Gillies MacKinnon's HIDEOUS KINKY   *photo: Sophie Baker*

1980s predecessors as *Revolution* or *The Mission*. In **Gods and Monsters**, Bill Condon wittily and movingly dramatised the last days of *Frankenstein* director James Whale; with **Love and Death on Long Island**, Richard Kwietniowski offered a *Lolita*-lite tale of a London man of letters infatuated with a dim young American bit-part actor. Both, in dealing with elderly, gay Englishmen adrift in alien America, gave due weight to the darker intimations of their material without letting them swamp the social comedy.

The same goes for **Hideous Kinky**, the latest from the versatile MacKinnon brothers, director Gillies and screenwriter Billy. Taking a break after the sombreness of their stark First World War drama, *Regeneration*, the MacKinnons plunged with gusto into the colour and turmoil of Morocco in the early 1970s. The uprooted Brit in this case is a young Englishwoman, Julia, living hand to mouth in Marrakech with her two small daughters, following the hippie dream and planning – without much concept of what it entails – to become a Sufi. Her wayward, well-meaning fantasies are seen through the eyes of her

daughters – especially the younger, whose laconic voice-over reveals a far surer grip on reality than her mother's.

The film resists the temptation to poke easy fun: Julia (a warm, very physical performance from Kate Winslet) may be misguided but is never ludicrous. Her affair with street acrobat Bilal (Saïd Taghmaoui from *La Haine*) conveys genuine affection on both sides, beyond the easy lure of the exotic stranger. At the same time it is hinted – without the message ever being rammed home – how as Westerners we buy into the surface attraction of alien cultures, using them as an escape route from whatever inadequacies or disappointments we have left behind. Vividly photographed by John de Borman, *Hideous Kinky* is a visual delight, but leaves behind a quiet sense of poignant regret.

There was nothing in the least quiet about **Lock, Stock and Two Smoking Barrels**, perhaps the most ultra-hyped British film of the year. A gleefully violent farce about murderous London gangs of varying degrees of ineptitude, Guy Ritchie's film had energy and attitude to spare, but overdosed

Hugh Grant and Julia Roberts repeating the Four Weddings *formula in NOTTING HILL*

photo: *Clive Coote*

on flashy visual gimmicks and Tarantinish bravura. It struck a chord in cinemas, however, with an $18m take that made it the most successful domestic release of 1998. As a result, a dozen or more laddish gangland clones have gone into production.

Love still in the air

The staple commodities of British cinema have long been romantic comedies and costume dramas (*Shakespeare in Love*, of course, neatly managed to be both). Romantic comedy is currently marking time, as typified by the carefully calculated, just-like-*Four Weddings and a Funeral* mixture of **Notting Hill**, and **Among Giants**, written by Simon Beaufoy, author of *The Full Monty*, which replayed his smash-hit comedy in a minor key – and sank at the box-office. Originality can, however, pay dividends in this genre. Under the guise of a carefree comedy of sexual permutations, David Kane's debut feature, **This Year's Love**, slipped in some pessimistic determinism borrowed from *La Ronde* and took a very respectable $5m.

British costume drama, though, does seem to be undergoing a sea-change – into something fiercer and altogether less reverential than the Austen and Forster adaptations of recent years. Even the light-hearted *Shakespeare in Love* kicked off with a torture scene, as did the far darker **Elizabeth**. Calling in Shekhar Kapur, the director of *Bandit Queen*, to handle this account of Gloriana's younger years proved a shrewd stroke. Untrammelled by any residual veneration for the glories of the Elizabethan Age, Kapur turned an incredulous gaze on a cruel, barbaric world.

An equally disenchanted view of England's other supposed golden age, the Victorian era, came in David Yates's **The Tichborne Claimant**. This was an account of the most notorious real-life cause célèbre of the period, when a man claiming to be the long-lost heir to one of the richest estates in Britain suddenly turned up in Australia. Money, class, family squabbles, convoluted legal shenanigans: this is a story with all the ripe ingredients of a great Victorian novel, and Yates tells it with suitable gusto, abetted by a modern sense of political irony.

Christopher Eccleston plotting in ELIZABETH
photo: Alex Bailey/Gramercy Pictures

Here, as in *Elizabeth*, the tale is all the more pointed for being seen through non-English eyes. In this case, the detached outsider is the narrator, a black African family servant (played with grave dignity by John Kani). Through him, Yates shows us Victorian society as a parade of dangerous Gilbertian grotesques, high on their own pomposity, but lethal when their interests are threatened. Graced with a gallery of incisive performances, most notably a masterly portrayal of twinkling malice from the seemingly immortal John Gielgud, *The Tichborne Claimant* often recalls an earlier classic of period satire, *Kind Hearts and Coronets*.

The battle continues

Eighteen months after its completion, Yates's film was still awaiting a UK release – another casualty of Britain's hopelessly skewed distribution set-up. Many films fail to secure a release – not always deservedly – and those that do come out often suffer from inadequate publicity and exposure.

Many, such as *Hideous Kinky* and *Orphans*, find themselves pushed into the cramped arthouse ghetto, from which they can only escape with the aid of exceptional luck, strong Hollywood backing – or Oscar-related buzz, as with *Gods and Monsters*.

Distribution, as ever, remains the bottleneck that constricts the industry. Five distributors, all closely linked to Hollywood majors, still control some 80% of the UK market, severely limiting the outlets for all but mainstream Hollywood product. Only one independent UK company, Entertainment, is a significant player, with a 7% share, while the future of London-based PolyGram Filmed Entertainment (PFE) has hung in the balance since its sale to Seagram in early 1998. After various bids and rumours, the current scenario is that Seagram will preserve PFE as an autonomous entity, albeit trading as Universal Pictures International.

Several newcomers, such as Mel Gibson's Icon, Winchester, Alliance, and the City-backed Redbus have recently entered the fray, and the UK now has its first gay distribution company in Millivres Multimedia. But the independent sector remains tiny and beleaguered, and more radical measures are badly needed to redress the balance. The government, which in the first flush of electoral success promised action on this front, has gone strangely silent on the whole question – having evidently registered the magnitude of the task. But it has to be tackled, if the always-talented British film industry is not to succumb to another of the near-fatal relapses that have dogged its history.

Pete Postlethwaite and Rachel Griffiths in AMONG GIANTS

Recent and Forthcoming Films

ALL THE LITTLE ANIMALS

Script: Eski Thomas. Dir: Jeremy Thomas. Phot: Mike Molloy. Players: John Hurt, Christian Bale, Daniel Benzali. Prod: Recorded Picture Co.

THE AMERICAN

Script: Michael Hastings. Dir: Paul Unwin. Phot: Tony Miller. Players: Matthew Modine, Diana Rigg, Brenda Fricker. Prod: BBC Films/Irish Screen.

AMONG GIANTS

Script: Simon Beaufoy. Dir: Sam Miller. Phot: Witold Stok. Players: Pete Postlethwaite, Rachel Griffiths, James Thornton, Lennie James. Prod: Capitol/British Screen/BBC Films.

BEAUTIFUL PEOPLE

Script and Dir: Jasmin Dizdar. Phot: Barry Ackroyd. Players: Charlotte Coleman, Charles Kay, Rosalind Ayres, Roger Sloman. Prod: Tall Stories.

BIRTHDAY GIRL

Script: Tom and Jez Butterworth. Dir: Jez Butterworth. Phot: Oliver Stapleton. Players: Nicole Kidman, Ben Chaplin, Vincent Cassel, Matthieu Kassovitz. Prod: Portobello/HAL/Miramax/Film Four.

THE CLANDESTINE MARRIAGE

Script: Sam Donovan. Dir: Christopher Miles. Phot: Mark Tanner. Players: Nigel Hawthorne, Joan Collins, Timothy Spall. Prod: RGO.

COMPLICITY

Script: Brian Elsley, based on the novel by Iain Banks. Dir: Gavin Millar. Phot: David Odd. Players: Jonny Lee Miller, Brian Cox, Keeley Hawes, Paul Higgins. Prod: J&M.

CROUPIER

Script: Paul Mayersberg. Dir: Mike Hodges. Players: Clive Owen, Kate Hardie, Alex Kingston, Gina McKee. Prod: Film Four/Little Bird/TATfilm/Sept Film/Compagnie des Phares et Balises.

THE DEBT COLLECTOR

Script and Dir: Anthony Nielson. Phot: Dick Pope. Players: Billy

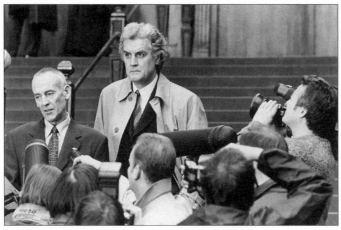

Billy Connolly in Anthony Nielson's THE DEBT COLLECTOR
photo: The Kobal Collection

Connolly, Ken Stott, Francesca Annis, Iain Robertson. Prod: Film Four.

DIVORCING JACK

Script: Colin Bateman. Dir: David Caffrey. Phot: James Welland. Players: David Thewlis, Rachel Griffiths, Richard Grant, Laura Fraser. Prod: BBC Films/Winchester/Scala.

EAST IS EAST

Script: Ayub Khan-Din. Dir: Damien O'Donnnell. Phot: Brian Tufano. Players: Om Puri, Linda Bassett, Jordan Routledge, Archie Panjabi. Prod: Film Four/BBC Films.

8½ WOMEN

Script and Dir: Peter Greenaway. Phot: Sacha Vierny, Reinier van Brummelen. Players: John Standing, Matthew Delamere, Vivian Wu, Amanda Plummer. Prod: Movie Masters/Woodline/Continent/Delux.

GODS AND MONSTERS

Script and Dir: Bill Condon. Phot: Stephen M Katz. Players: Ian McKellen, Brendan Fraser, Lynn Redgrave. Prod: Flashpoint/BBC Films.

GREY OWL

Script: William Nicholson. Dir: Richard Attenborough. Phot: Roger Pratt. Players: Pierce Brosnan, Annie Galipeau, Nathaniel Arcand, Renee Asherson. Prod: Beaver/Ajwaan.

HIDEOUS KINKY

Script: Billy MacKinnon, based on the novel by Esther Freud. Dir: Gillies MacKinnon. Phot: John de Borman. Players: Kate Winslet, Saïd Taghmaoui, Bella Riza, Carrie Mullan. Prod: Film Consortium/BBC Films.

HILARY AND JACKIE

Script: Frank Cottrell Boyce. Dir: Anand Tucker. Phot: David Johnson. Players: Emily Watson, Rachel Griffiths, David Morrissey, James Frain. Prod: Film Four/ Intermedia.

HUMAN TRAFFIC

Script and Dir: Justin Kerrigan. Phot: David Bennett. Players: John Simm, Lorraine Pilkington, Shaun Parkes, Danny Dyer, Nicola Reynolds. Prod: Metrodome/Irish Screen.

THE LOST SON

Script: Margaret Leclere, Eric Leclere, Mark Mills. Dir: Chris Menges. Phot: Barry Ackroyd. Players: Daniel Auteuil, Natassja Kinski, Katrin Cartlidge, Ciaran Hinds. Prod: Film Consortium/ Scala/Ima/Canal Plus.

LOVE, HONOUR AND OBEY

Script and Dir: Dominic Anciano, Ray Bardis. Phot: John Ward. Players: Jude Law, Rhys Ifans, Sadie Frost, Jonny Lee Miller, Ray Winstone. Prod: Fugitive.

LOVE'S LABOURS LOST

Script and Dir: Kenneth Branagh. Phot: Alex Thompson. Players: Branagh, Alicia Silverstone, Natascha McElhone, Carmen Ejogo. Prod: Shakespeare Film Co/Intermedia/Pathe.

MAD COWS

Script: Sara Sugarman, Sasha Hails. Dir: Sugarman. Phot: Pierre Aim. Players: Anna Friel, Joanna Lumley, Greg Wise, Anna Massey. Prod: Flashlight.

MANSFIELD PARK

Script and Dir: Patricia Rozema. Phot: Mick Coulter. Players: Embeth Davidtz, Jonny Lee Miller, Alessandro Nivola, Frances O'Connor. Prod: HAL/ Miramax/BBC Films.

MICKEY BLUE EYES

Script: Mark Lawrence, Adam Scheinman, Robert Kuhn. Dir: Kelly Makin. Phot: Donald Thorin. Players: Hugh Grant, Jeanne Tripplehorn, James Caan, Burt Young. Prod: Simian/Castle Rock.

NOTTING HILL

Script: Richard Curtis. Dir: Roger Michell. Phot: Michael Coulter. Players: Hugh Grant, Julia Roberts, Rhys Ifans, Emma Chambers. Prod: Working Title/PolyGram.

OLD NEW BORROWED BLUE

Script: John Forte.Dir: Michael Winterbottom. Phot: Benoit Delhomme. Players: Yvan Attal, Dervla Kirwan, Christopher Eccleston, Alun Armstrong. Prod: Miramax/Channel Four)

PLUNKETT & MACLEANE

Script: Robert Wade, Neil Purvis, Charles McKeown, Selwyn Roberts. Dir: Jake Scott. Phot: John Mathieson. Players: Robert Carlyle, Liv Tyler, Jonny Lee Miller, Michael Gambon. Prod: Working Title/PolyGram.

A La Ronde-style set of London love affairs made THIS YEAR'S LOVE a box-office success

photo: Paul Chedlow

RATCATCHER

Script and Dir: Lynne Ramsay. Phot: Alwin Kchler. Players: Tommy Flanagan, Mandy Matthews, William Eadie, Lynne Ramsay Jr. Prod: Holy Cow/Pathé /BBC Scotland.

SOLOMON AND GAENOR

Script and Dir: Paul Morrison. Phot: Nina Kellgren. Players: Ioan Gruffudd, Nia Roberts, Sue Jones Davis, William Thomas. Prod: S4C/Film Four/September.

THIS YEAR'S LOVE

Script and Dir: David Kane. Phot: Robert Alazraki. Players: Kathy Burke, Jennifer Ehle, Ian Hart, Douglas Henshall, Catherine McCormack, Dougray Scott. Prod: Kismet/Entertainment.

THE TICHBORNE CLAIMANT

Script: Joe Fisher. Dir: David Yates. Phot: Peter Thwaites. Players: John Kani, Robert Pugh, Robert Hardy, Barry Humphries. Prod: Bigger Picture Co.

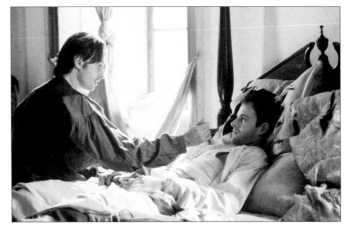

Jonny Lee Miller (in bed) and Robert Carlyle in PLUNKETT AND MACLEANE   *photo: Jaap Buitendijk/PolyGram*

THE TRENCH

Script and Dir: William Boyd. Phot: Tony Pierce-Roberts. Players: Paul Nicholls, Daniel Craig, Julian Rhind-Tutt, Danny Dyer. Prod: Portman/Skyline/Blue PM/Galat.

THE WAR ZONE

Script: Alexander Stuart. Dir: Tim Roth. Phot: Seamus McGarvey.

Players: Ray Winstone, Tilda Swinton, Lara Belmont, Freddie Cunliffe. Prod: Portobello/Film Four/Fandango/Mikado/JVC.

WONDERLAND

Script: Laurence Coriat. Dir: Michael Winterbottom. Phot: Sean Bobbitt. Players: Ian Hart, Gina McKee, Molly Parker, Jack Shepherd. Prod: Revolution/ Kismet.

David Thewlis in trouble in DIVORCING JACK   *photo: Marcus Robinson*

Producers

Alibi Films
12 Maiden Lane,
London WC2E 7NA
Tel: (44 171) 845 0410
Fax: (44 171) 836 6776

Arcane Pictures
46 Wetherby Mansions,
Earl's Court Square,
London SW5 9DJ
Tel: (44 171) 244 6590
Fax: (44 171) 565 4495

BBC Films
56 Wood Lane,
London W12 7SB
Tel: (181) 743 8000
Fax: (181) 749 7520

Celador Productions
39 Long Acre,
London WC2E 9JT
Tel: (44 171) 240 8101
Fax: (44 171) 497 9541

Company Pictures
184-192 Drummond Street,
London NW1 3HP
Tel: (44 171) 388 9277
Fax: (44 171) 388 8107

DNA Films Ltd
72–73 Margaret Street
1st Floor
London W1N 7HA
Tel: (44 171) 485 4411
Fax: (44 171) 485 4422

Dogstar Films
5 Sherwood Street,
London W1V 7RA
Tel: (44 171) 287 5944
Fax: (44 171) 287 1786

Ecosse Films
12 Quayside Lodge,
Watermeadow Lane,
London SW6 2UZ
Tel: (44 171) 371 0290
Fax: (44 171) 736 3436

Figment Films
2-4 Noel Street,
London W1V 3RB
Tel: (44 171) 287 3209
Fax: (44 171) 287 3503
e-mail: figment@globalnet.co.uk

Filmfour Ltd
76-78 Charlotte Street,
London W1P 1LX
Tel: (44 171) 868 7700
Fax: (44 171) 868 7769

Flashlight Films Ltd
10 Golden Square,
London W1R 3AF
Tel: (44 171) 287 4252
Fax: (44 171) 287 4232
e-mail: flashlightfilms@compuserve.
com

Granada Film
London Television Centre, 16th Floor,
Upper Ground,
London SE1 9LT
Tel: (44 171) 737 8681
Fax: (44 171) 737 8682

Gruber Films
74 Margaret Street,
London W1N 7HA
Tel: (44 171) 436 3413
Fax: (44 171) 436 3402
e-mail: office@gruberfilms.com

Heyday Films
5 Denmark Street,
London WC2H 8LP
Tel: (44 171) 836 6333
Fax: (44 171) 836 6444

Little Bird Co.
7 Lower James Street,
London W1R 3PL
Tel: (44 171) 434 1131
Fax: (44 171) 434 1803
e-mail: karen@littleb.demon.co.uk

Merchant Ivory Productions
46 Lexington Street,
London W1R 3LH
Tel: (44 171) 437 1200
Fax: (44 171) 734 1579

Miramax & HAL Films
Elsley House,
24-30 Great Titchfield Street,
London W1P 7AD
Tel: (44 171) 535 8300
Fax: (44 171) 535 8301

Pagoda Film & TV Corp.
20th Century House,
31-32 Soho Square,
London W1V 6AP
Tel: (44 171) 534 3500
Fax: (44 171) 534 3501

Parallax Pictures
7 Denmark Street,
London WC2H 8LS
Tel: (44 171) 836 1478
Fax: (44 171) 497 8062

Pathé Productions Ltd
4th Fl., Kent House,
14-17 Market Place,
Great Titchfield Street,
London W1N 8AR
Tel: (44 171) 323 5151
Fax: (44 171) 631 3568

Rafford Films
26-27 Oxendon Street,
London SW1Y 4LT
Tel: (44 171) 839 1800
Fax: (44 171) 839 3600
e-mail: algscott@aol.com

Rocket Pictures
7 King Street Cloisters,
Clifton Walk,
London W6 0GY
Tel: (181) 741 9090
Fax: (181) 741 9097

Samuelson Productions
9 Hanover Street, 4th floor,
London W1P 7LJ
Tel: (44 171) 495 3414
Fax: (44 171) 495 3415

Sarah Radclyffe Productions
83-84 Berwick Street, 5th floor,
London W1V 3PJ
Tel: (44 171) 437 3128
Fax: (44 171) 437 3129

Scala Productions
15 Frith Street,
London W1V 5TS
Tel: (44 171) 734 7060
Fax: (44 171) 437 3248
e-mail: scalaprods@aol.com

Scott Free
42-44 Beak Street,
London W1R 3DA
Tel: (44 171) 437 3163
Fax: (44 171) 439 2478

The Bigger Picture Company
Ealing Studios,
Ealing Green,
London W5 5EP
Tel: (181) 758 8566
Fax: (181) 567 5475

The Film Consortium
6 Flitcroft Street,
London WC2H 8DJ
Tel: (44 171) 691 4440
Fax: (44 171) 691 4445

Toledo Pictures Ltd
30 Oval Road,
London NW1 7DE
Tel: (44 171) 485 4411
Fax: (44 171) 485 4422
e-mail: toledopix@aol.com

Tony Kaye Productions
33 Tottenham Street,
London W1P 9PE
Tel: (44 171) 323 1511
Fax: (44 171) 323 1711

Working Title Films
Oxford House, 76 Oxford Street,
London W1N 9FD
Tel: (44 171) 307 3000
Fax: (44 171) 307 3001

Distributors

Alliance Releasing
2nd Fl.,184-192 Drummond Street,
London NW1 3HP
Tel: (44 171) 391 6900
Fax: (44 171) 383 0404

Artificial Eye Film Ltd.
14 King Street,
London WC2E 8HM
Tel: (44 171) 240 5353
Fax: (44 171) 240 5242

Blue Dolphin Film & Video Ltd.
40 Langham Street,
London W1N 5RG
Tel: (44 171) 255 2494
Fax: (44 171) 580 7670

British Film Institute
21 Stephen Street,
London W1P 1PL
Tel: (44 171) 255 1444
Fax: (44 171) 436 7950

Buena Vista International
Beaumont House,
Kensington Village,
Avonmore Road,
London W14 8TS
Tel: (181) 222 2890
Fax: (181) 222 2795

Columbia TriStar Film Distributors
Sony Pictures Europe House
25 Golden Square
London W1R 6LU
Tel: (44 171) 533 1111
Fax: (44 171) 533 1015

Entertainment Film Distributors
27 Soho Square,
London W1V 6HU
Tel: (44 171) 439 1606
Fax: (44 171) 734 2483

Feature Film Co.
68-70 Wardour Street,
London W1V 3HP
Tel: (44 171) 734 2266
Fax: (44 171) 494 0309

Film Four Distributors
Castle House,
75-76 Wells Street,
London W1P 3ER
Tel: (44 171) 436 9944
Fax: (44 171) 436 9955

Gala Film Distributors
26 Danbury Street,
London N1 8JU
Tel: (44 171) 226 5085
Fax: (44 171) 226 5897

ICA Projects
12 Carlton House Terrace,
London SW1Y 5AH
Tel: (44 171) 930 0493
Fax: (44 171) 873 0051
e-mail: info@ica.org.uk

Metrodome Films
3rd Fl., 25 Maddox Street,
London W1R 9LE
Tel: (44 171) 408 2121
Fax: (44 171) 409 1935

Metro Tartan
79 Wardour Street,
London W1V 3TH
Tel: (44 171) 734 8508
Fax: (44 171) 287 2112

Pathé Distributions
4th Fl., Kent House,
14-17 Market Place,
Great Titchfield Street,
London W1N 8AR
Tel: (44 171) 323 5151
Fax: (44 171) 631 3568

Twentieth Century Fox
20th Century House,
31 Soho Square,
London W1V 6AP
Tel: (44 171) 437 7766
Fax: (44 171) 434 2170

U.I.P.
UIP House,
45 Beadon Road,
London W6 0EG
Tel: (44 171) 636 1655
Fax: (44 171) 636 4118

Universal Pictures International
4th Floor, Oxford House,
76 Oxford Street,
London W1N 0HQ
Tel: (44 171) 307 1300
Fax: (44 171) 307 1301

Warner Bros.
20/24 Broadwick Street,
London W1V 1FG
Tel: (44 171) 465 4808
Fax: (44 171) 465 4290

Sales Companies

Alibi Films
12 Maiden Lane,
London WC2E 7NA
Tel: (44 171) 845 0410
Fax: (44 171) 836 6776

Jane Balfour Films
Burghley House,
35 Fortess Road,
London NW5 1AQ
Tel: (44 171) 267 5392
Fax: (44 171) 267 4241
e-mail: jbf@janebalfourfilms.co.uk

Capitol Films
23 Queensdale Place,
London W11 4SQ
Tel: (44 171) 471 6000
Fax: (44 171) 471 6012

Film Four International
76-78 Charlotte Street,
London W1P 1LX
Tel: (44 171) 868 7700
Fax: (44 171) 868 7769
www.filmfour.uk

Goldcrest Film International
65-66 Dean Street,
London W1V 6PL
Tel: (44 171) 437 8696
Fax: (44 171) 437 4448

IAC Films
19-21 Tavistock Street
London WC2E 7PA
Tel: (44 171) 836 6545
Fax: (44 171) 836 6564

Icon Films
56 Kingsdown Parade,
Bristol BS6 5UQ
Tel: (117) 924 8535
Fax: (117) 942 0386

Intermedia
9-13 Grosvenor Street,
London W1X 9FB
Tel: (44 171) 495 3322
Fax: (44 171) 495 3993

J&M Entertainment
2 Dorset Square,
London NW1 6PU
Tel: (44 171) 723 6544
Fax: (44 171) 724 7541

Portman Entertainment Group Ltd.
167 Wardour Street
London W1V 3TA
Tel: (44 171) 468 3434
Fax: (44 171) 468 3455

The Sales Company
62 Shaftesbury Avenue,
London W1V 7DE
Tel: (44 171) 434 9061
Fax: (44 171) 494 3293
e-mail: salesco@btinternet.com

Summit Entertainment
118-120 Wardour Street,
London W1V 3LA
Tel: (44 171) 494 1724
Fax: (44 171) 494 1725

United Artists Int'l
10 Stephen Mews, Office 718,
London W1P 1PP
Tel: (44 171) 333 8877
Fax: (44 171) 333 8878

Victor Film Co.
2B Chandos Street,
London W1M 9DG
Tel: (44 171) 636 6620
Fax: (44 171) 636 6511
e-mail: post@victor-film-co.demon.co.uk

Vine International Pictures
Astoria House,
62 Shaftesbury Avenue,
London W1N 7DE
Tel: (44 171) 437 1181
Fax: (44 171) 494 0634
e-mail: vine@easynet.co.uk

Winchester Film & TV Sales
29-30 Kingly Street,
London W1R 9LB
Tel: (44 171) 434 4374
Fax: (44 171) 287 4334

Useful Addresses

British Academy of Film and Television Arts (BAFTA)
195 Piccadilly,
London W1V 0LN
Tel: (44 171) 734 0022
Fax: (44 171) 734 1792

British Board of Film Classification (BBFC)
3 Soho Square,
London W1V 6HD
Tel: (44 171) 439 7961
Fax: (44 171) 287 0141
e-mail: webmaster@bbfc.co.uk

British Actors Equity Association
Guild House,
Upper St. Martins Lane,
London WC2H 9EG
Tel: (44 171) 379 6000
Fax: (44 171) 379 7001

The British Council
Films, Television, & Video Dept.
11 Portland Place,
London W1N 4EJ
Tel: (44 171) 389 3065
Fax: (44 171) 389 3041

British Film Commission
70 Baker Street,
London W1M 1DJ
Tel: (44 171) 224 5000
Fax: (44 171) 224 1013

British Film Institute
21 Stephen Street,
London W1P 1PL
Tel: (44 171) 255 1444
Fax: (44 171) 436 7950

British Screen Finance
14-17 Wells Mews,
London W1P 3FL
Tel: (44 171) 323 9080
Fax: (44 171) 323 0092

Cinema Exhibitors' Association (CEA)
22 Golden Square,
London W1R 3PA
Tel: (44 171) 734 9551
Fax: (44 171) 734 6147
e-mail: cea@cinemauk.ftech.co.uk

Directors' Guild of Great Britain
15-19 Great Titchfield Street,
London W1P 7FB
Tel: (44 171) 436 8626
Fax: (44 171) 438 8646

Independent Television Association
ITV Network Centre,
200 Grays Inn Road,
London WC1X 8HF
Tel: (44 171) 843 8000
Fax: (44 171) 843 8158
e-mail: publicaffairs@itc.org.uk

Independent Television Commission
33 Foley Street,
London W1P 7LB
Tel: (44 171) 255 3000
Fax: (44 171) 306 7800

London Film Commission
20 Euston Centre
Regent's Place
London NW1 3JH
Tel: (44 171) 387 8787
Fax: (44 171) 387 8788
e-mail: lfc@london-film.co.uk

PACT
45 Mortimer Street,
London W1N 7TD
Tel: (44 171) 331 6000
Fax: (44 171) 331 6700
e-mail: inquires@pact.co.uk

Scottish Screen
74 Victoria Crescent Road,
Glasgow G12 9JN
Tel: (141) 302 1700
Fax: (141) 302 1711

UNITED STATES — Harlan Jacobson

I n the US in 1998-99, Life once again outperformed Filmed Entertainment, even though film had a great year at the box-office. US filmgoers turned in $6.95 billion according to the Motion Picture Association of America, up some 9.2% over 1997 (*Variety* put the total at $6.88 billion, up 9.9%). *Titanic* propelled the first two quarters into 19.1% and 15.9% gains over the previous year, the summer third quarter was up 8.9% and the Christmas quarter down 6.9%. Total admissions hit 1.48 billion, up 6.7% to a 40-year high, according to the MPAA (*Variety* reported admissions of 1.30 billion, up 5.5%).

Despite this bottom-line success, it was impossible for Hollywood's fantasy factories to come up with an assault on the public's dream life more sustained than that provided by Washington, as Americans were riveted to their TV screens by the Biggest Scandal of all, the attempt to take down a president. The industry was thrilled by the summer performance of the malevolent comet twins, **Deep Impact** ($140m domestic gross) and **Armageddon** ($200m), which both saw fit to obliterate large chunks of the East Coast, and both showed strong, noble presidents who accepted the inevitable: that their terms in office could be shortened by natural forces.

On TV news bulletins, however, was a real president caught up in the tragi-comedy – bordering on farce – of a failed coup masterminded by out-party plotters and sanctimonious hypocrites, using the very stuff of Hollywood folklore: the sexual/emotional Achilles heel of a self-made man, up from nowhere, the product of America's lasting contribution to mankind, the meritocracy. Bill Clinton somehow outlasted and outmanoeuvred the plotters.

Irony of ironies, it slowly dawned on the Republic that in Clinton it finally had a movie star, an outsized personality who could carry the big picture – which is more than the Republican saint, Ronald Reagan, ever did in 1940s Hollywood. Bill Clinton was so charismatic that John Travolta's rendition of him in Mike Nichols' failed **Primary Colors** ($39m) was limp in comparison. If DreamWorks – suggested by some, before the impeachment business, as the President's post-term destination of choice – had any sense they would offer Clinton a role in front of the camera.

Politically incorrect?

In America, everybody's a critic, and media criticism in the wrong hands can be a dangerous thing: the very Reverend Cotton Mather reincarnated himself as a televangelist and denounced the purple Teletubby with a triangle-shaped aerial as a gay agent subliminally intended to corrupt Christian youth. No sooner was **Tarzan** ($130m), Disney's rather complex, computer-assisted disquisition on adoption and discrimination, released to rave reviews (one week after the rather dismal **Instinct** had uncannily followed the exact same plotline of 'man prefers apes to humans') than various New Sensitive Male academics took to the airwaves to denounce both the film and the tie-in doll for an exaggerated chest-to-waist ratio that surely will lead to a generation of deep male neuroses and a revived trend toward bulking up, initiated by Arnold Schwarzenegger back in the stone age of *Pumping Iron*.

In short, the relationship between fantasy – the lifeblood of Hollywood, after all – and the development of the psyche is not greatly appreciated or understood here. And so, after the Colorado high school massacre, the President hauled the National Association of Theatre Owners into what the Right Wing Crazies on Disney's ABC-owned talk radio line-up now call the Oral Office, and made them vow to start checking ID cards for R-rated movies (no one under 17 admitted without parent or guardian).

Of course, Hollywood has for 30-plus years lived and died by the tacit understanding that the rating system was never intended to be enforced. It was created to placate Congress during the nervous 1960s, and subsequently to remain purely a public relations palliative meant to assure gullible parents that the pot-smoking, gun-toting, carnal sophisticate that the 1990s American teenager has become would never see a movie featuring sex and violence – even if in the end the good guy nails the good girl and shoots the bad guy.

Of the 509 films released in the US in 1998, of which 490 were new features, 432 were rated R. When I worked them out,

those numbers gave 84% R-rated. When the MPAA did the math, however, they computed R-rated films at 65%, in a nifty, nonsensical little pie-chart. And since 1968, the MPAA says, 55% of the 14,926 films it has rated have been R. No matter whether it is 84%, or 65%, or 55%, the same theatre that cards kids has an absolutely vital interest, therefore, in not monitoring which auditorium the adolescent miscreants subsequently enter. Stay tuned, however, to see whether the holy-rollers scare the production departments into making sanitised, sugar-coated movies by this time in 2000, an election year.

Money talks

Hollywood seems to have worked itself into an economic corner, where the average negative cost per picture is $52m and the ratio of production to marketing has started moving towards one to one. This situation is addressed with band-aid solutions: eliminating a few pork-barrel housekeeping deals here, negotiating a little tougher on rentals there, or even

THE AVENGERS typified Hollywood's lack of imagination in 1998   *photo: David Appleby/Warners*

Faber and Faber Film Books

'Faber's catalogue of film books is one of the deepest and widest around.'
Esquire

As the century draws to a close, the passion for film has generated a desire in audiences to cease being mere spectators and to become active practitioners of the craft of film-making. The ease and availability of new equipment has made this dream a reality.

This is the context in which Faber and Faber has committed itself to reflect the best in contemporary movie-making concentrating on both Film-maker and the Script.

Faber publishes the best contemporary writing for the screen by the most talented and adventurous writers working in the medium.

Collected Screenplays
Andrei Tarkovsky £17.99

The Loss of Sexual Innocence
Mike Figgis £6.99

Topsy-Turvy
Mike Leigh £8.99

Girl, Interrupted
James Mangold £6.99

Ride With the Devil
James Schamus £6.99

Rushmore
Wes Anderson & Owen Wilson £9.99

Shakespeare in Love
Tom Stoppard & Marc Norman £6.99

Lulu on the Bridge
Paul Auster £9.99

Seven and 8mm
Andrew Kevin Walker £7.99

The Winslow Boy and The Spanish Prisoner
David Mamet £11.99

Ratcatcher
Lynne Ramsey £6.99

Sleepy Hollow
Tim Burton £12.99

ff

CLASSIC SCREENPLAYS

Faber's Classic Screenplay Series presents the finest writing from those masters who have helped make the cinema the great art form of the twentieth century.

The Apartment
Billy Wilder and I. A. L Diamond £8.99
introduced by Mark Cousins

Billy Wilder won two Academy Awards ® – as co-screenwriter and director – for this mordant comedy about getting ahead in the corporate world. **The Apartment** is a beautifully judged piece of writing saved from cynicism by Wilder's tenderness towards his central characters.

Sweet Smell of Success
Clifford Odets and Ernest Lehman £8.99

Sweet Smell of Success is the smartest and most cynical film of the 1950s; a vicious dissection of the world of public relations and journalism. This edition includes a specially commissioned introduction by Ernest Lehman, and an appreciation of the film's director, Alexander Mackendrick, by the writer/director of **Copland**, James Mangold.

The Exorcist and Legion
William Peter Blatty £9.99

One of the most terrifying films ever made, **The Exorcist** now returns in published form to haunt another generation. Included are the full texts of **The Exorcist's** legendary 'lost scenes' and excised dialogue, as well as the original text of Blatty's extraordinary sequel.

Brief Encounter
Noel Coward £8.99

One of the best-loved of British films, Coward's tour de force of repressed middle-class sexuality, as brought to the screen by David Lean in 1946.

North by Northwest
Ernest Lehman £8.99

North by Northwest, Hitchcock's best-loved romantic thriller, is now published to celebrate the centenary of Hitchcock's birth. Includes an introduction from the author.

Performance
Donald Cammell £8.99

A peerless study of crime, class, sex, drugs and rock 'n' roll from one of the most exciting and enigmatic figures in British cinema. Professor Colin MacCabe introduces this archetypal sixties film.

FILM BIOGRAPHIES

The biography series is intended to illuminate the current state of cinema by examining the lives and work of those who have created the cinema language we use today.

Stanley Kubrick
Vincent LoBrutto £14.99

Stanley Kubrick was described by Orson Welles as a genius. Despite worldwide controversy and acclaim, the public knows little about this reclusive and intensely private man. Vincent LoBrutto's comprehensive biography of Kubrick contains interviews with those who knew him during his formative years and meticulously recounts the making of Kubrick's masterworks.

Coppola
Peter Cowie £12.99

This is the definitive portrait of Francis Ford Coppola – the director of the **Godfather** trilogy**, Apocalypse Now, The Conversation, Rumble Fish** and **One from the Heart.** More than any of his contemporaries, Coppola's career brilliantly expresses the drive and invention of the American cinema.

James Whale
James Curtis £14.99

James Whale directed some of the most stylish and unusual movies of the 1930s and influenced a generation of film-makers, but he was most successful in a genre he virtually invented: horror. This book covers Whale's extraordinary life, from the poverty of England's Black Country to his career as a director in Hollywood.

Sam Peckinpah: . . . If They Move, Kill 'Em!
David Weddle £12.99

'A great introduction to Peckinpah for a younger generation of film students.' *Martin Scorsese*. David Weddle has written the first major biography of Peckinpah's dramatic life. Peckinpah was both a grim nihilist and a hopeless romantic, a film-maker who defined his era with films such as **The Wild Bunch** and **Straw Dogs.**

David Lean
Kevin Brownlow £16.99

Kevin Brownlow spent many hours with Lean, who talked openly about a career that lasted over fifty years. This is the definitive biography of Britain's greatest film-maker, the creator of some of the most memorable and poignant scenes in cinema history.

Sergio Leone
Christopher Frayling £20.00

Groundbreaking films such as his Spaghetti Westerns with Clint Eastwood, and the magisterial **Once Upon a Time in the West**, made Sergio Leone one of the most popular directors in world cinema. This first ever biography of Leone lovingly explores his work, and casts light upon the little-known details of his life.

About Lindsay Anderson
Gavin Lambert £14.99

A rich, personal assessment fo the tempestuous life and work of the **If . . .** director, by his close friend.

ff

Monkey Business: The Lives and Legends of The Marx Brothers

Simon Louvish £12.00

The much-praised biographer of W.C. Fields has written a definitive, in-depth, entertaining and analytical work, based on archival research about the Marx brothers' life, their era and the roots of their humour.

The Quiet Man: Searching for John Ford

Joseph McBride £20.00

No one captured the landscape and faces of the American people the way Ford did. This book attempts to penetrate Ford's habitual reticence about his inner life and also provides insight into Ford's prodigious –140 movies – film career.

Fassbinder: The Life and Work of a Provocative Genius

Christian Braad Thomsen £16.99

This book tells the story of German enfant terrible Rainer Werner Fassbinder. It details the essential characteristics of his short but brilliant life, and discusses in depth each of Fassbinder's 44 films.

Man on the Flying Trapeze: The Life and Works of W. C. Fields

Simon Louvish £14.99 pbk £20.00 hbk

The acclaimed life of America's most beloved, if cantankerous, comic genius, it tells the curious tale of an actor who became his image, of a man who could not separate his private from his working life, and who became hopelessly intertwined with the character he himself had invented.

Special Offer for Variety Readers

Spend over £20

on the selected Faber film titles

and receive a

free copy of *Shakespeare in Love* worth £6.99

For regular film title information and a free Faber film catalogue, please include your address on the order form.

DIRECTORS ON DIRECTORS

As enduring as the films themselves are the words of the film-makers as they struggle to translate their dreams onto the screen. Our Directors series brings readers into intimate contact with some of the essential film-making of this century.

Lynch on Lynch
edited by Chris Rodley £11.99
No one sees the world quite like David Lynch and, having seen one of his films, the world will never seem the same again. In this volume, Lynch speaks about his movies from **Eraserhead** through to **Lost Highway**.

Scorsese on Scorsese (new edition)
edited by David Thompson and Ian Christie £11.99
foreword by Michael Powell
Scorsese's controversial films are a record of the most personal achievement in American cinema. This new, revised edition includes chapters on **Goodfellas, Cape Fear, The Age of Innocence, Casino** and **Kundun**.

Kazan on Kazan
edited by Jeff Young £12.99
Elia Kazan re-defined American film acting and was responsible for **On the Waterfront, A Streetcar Named Desire** and **East of Eden**. His demand for an authentic intensity of performance from his actors brought a powerful emotionalism to American movies and created moments of cinema that live for ever in the memory.

Gilliam on Gilliam
edited by Ian Christie £9.99 pbk £17.99 hbk
The wildly imaginative Monty Python animator who became a cinematic visionary (**Brazil, Twelve Monkeys**) explains his unique vision, and unravels the myths and controversies that have surrounded his career. Quite apart from his bracingly irreverent humour, Gilliam is a lucid, thoughtful commentator on his own work, as well as on the contemporary cinema. There is ample use of his drawings and storyboards.

Burton on Burton
edited by Mark Salisbury £11.99
The offbeat visionary behind **Beetlejuice, Batman** and **Edward Scissorhands**.

Hitchcock on Hitchcock
edited by Stanley Gottlieb £12.99
Most other biographies have focused on Hitchcock's American period. This one redressesthe balance between that work and the films that were done in Britain, and is meticulously researched and illuminating.

The Godfather Book
Peter Cowie £14.99

Peter Cowie has had access to Coppola's archives and, in addition to recounting the dramas encountered in the making of this masterpiece, offers an analysis of the themes and historical inspiration that underpin the **Godfather** trilogy.

A Personal Journey Through American Movies
Martin Scorsese £14.99

Martin Scorsese's masterly account of American movies is balanced between subjective enthusiasm and objective analysis. Lavishly illustrated and strikingly designed, this book is essential reading for anyone interested in movies.

Me and Hitch
Evan Hunter £3.99

Hunter is as frank as he is illuminating, describing his experiences working with Hitchcock on the screenplay of **The Birds** and **Marnie** in a manner that is vivid and entertaining.

Projections 10: Hollywood Film-makers on Film-making
edited by Mike Figgis £12.99

For this specially edited **Projections** Mike Figgis, director of **Internal Affairs** and **Leaving Las Vegas**, accepted an invitation to return to Los Angeles in late 1998 and document the Hollywood dream factory.

Conversations with Billy Wilder
Cameron Crowe £20.00

Billy Wilder is one of the acknowledged masters of modern cinema. Here, for the first time ever in published form, he explores his own life and work and takes us behind the scenes of such classic movies as **Double Indemnity, The Lost Weekend, The Apartment** and **Some Like It Hot**.

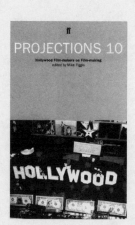

Getting Away With It
Steven Soderbergh £12.99

An account of an unusual year from the director of **Out of Sight**. Plus, Soderbergh interviews a directorial hero of his – Richard Lester.

Watching
Tom Sutcliffe £14.99

In this book Thomas Sutcliffe, the respected television critic, takes some of the fundamental elements of film – screen size, freeze-frame, opening shots, even punches – and opens our eyes to the effect they have on our senses.

My Time with Antonioni
Wim Wenders £12.99

Wenders reflects on his cherishable collaboration with the maestro on **Beyond the Clouds**.

Seventy Light Years
Freddie Young £17.99

The late cinematographer, thrice Oscar-winner for his work with David Lean, looks back on his 'lucky' life, from youthful apprenticeship to desert adventures with **Lawrence of Arabia**.

ff

ORDER FORM

Qty	SCREENPLAYS			
_ _	Collected Screenplays	Andrei Tarkovsky	0 571 14266 4	£17.99
_ _	The Loss of Sexual Innocence	Mike Figgis	0 571 20153 9	£ 6.99
_ _	Topsy-Turvy	Mike Leigh	0 571 20206 3	£ 8.99
_ _	Girl, Interrupted	James Mangold	0 571 20211 X	£ 6.99
_ _	Ride With the Devil	James Schamus	0 571 20163 6	£ 6.99
_ _	Rushmore	Wes Anderson & Owen Wilson	0 571 20012 5	£ 9.99
_ _	Shakespeare in Love	Tom Stoppard & Marc Norman	0 571 20108 3	£ 6.99
_ _	Lulu on the Bridge	Paul Auster	0 571 19586 5	£ 9.99
_ _	Seven and 8mm	Andrew Kevin Walker	0 571 20098 2	£ 7.99
_ _	The Winslow Boy and The Spanish Prisoner	David Mamet	0 571 20074 5	£11.99
_ _	Ratcatcher	Lynne Ramsey	0 571 20349 3	£ 6.99
_ _	Sleepy Hollow	Tim Burton	0 571 20223 3	£12.99
	CLASSIC SCREENPLAYS			
_ _	The Apartment	Billy Wilder and I.A.L Diamond	0 571 19409 5	£ 8.99
_ _	Sweet Smell of Success	Clifford Odets and Ernest Lehman	0 571 19410 9	£ 8.99
_ _	The Exorcist and Legion	William Peter Blatty	0 571 20015 X	£ 9.99
_ _	Brief Encounter	Noel Coward	0 571 19680 2	£ 8.99
_ _	North by Northwest	Ernest Lehman	0 571 20184 9	£ 8.99
_ _	Performance	Donald Cammell	0 571 20189 X	£ 8.99
	FILM BIOGRAPHIES			
_ _	Stanley Kubrick	Vincent LoBrutto	0 571 19393 5	£14.99
_ _	Coppola	Peter Cowie	0 571 19677 2	£12.99
_ _	James Whale	James Curtis	0 571 19285 8	£14.99
_ _	Sam Peckinpah	David Weddle	0 571 17884 7	£12.99
_ _	David Lean	Kevin Brownlow	0 571 19168 1	£16.99
_ _	Sergio Leone	Christopher Frayling	0 571 16438 2	£20.00
_ _	About Lindsay Anderson	Gavin Lambert	0 571 17775 1	£14.99
_ _	Monkey Business: The Lives and Legends of the Marx Brothers	Simon Louvish	0 571 19350 1	£12.99
_ _	The Quiet Man: Searching forJohn Ford	Joseph McBride	0 571 20075 3	£20.00
_ _	Fassbinder: The Life and Work of a Provocative Genius	Christian Braad Thomsen	0 571 17842 1	£16.99
_ _	Man on the Flying Trapeze:		0 571 19772 8	£14.99 pbk
	The Life and Times of W. C. Fields	Simon Louvish	0 571 17610 0	£20.00 hbk
	DIRECTORS ON DIRECTORS			
_ _	Lynch on Lynch	ed. by Chris Rodley	0 571 19548 2	£11.99
_ _	Scorsese on Scorsese	ed. David Thompson & Ian Christie	0 571 17827 8	£11.99
_ _	Kazan on Kazan	ed. by Jeff Young	0 571 19217 3	£12.99
_ _	Gilliam on Gilliam	ed. by Ian Christie	0 571 20280 2	£ 9.99 pbk
			0 571 19190 8	£17.99 hbk
_ _	Burton on Burton	ed. by Mark Salisbury	0 571 17393 4	£11.99
_ _	Hitchcock on Hitchcock	ed. by Stanley Gottlieb	0 571 19136 3	£ 9.99
	GENERAL			
_ _	The Godfather Book	Peter Cowie	0 571 19011 1	£14.99
_ _	A Personal Journey Through American Movies	Martin Scorsese	0 571 19455 9	£14.99
_ _	Me and Hitch	Evan Hunter	0 571 19306 4	£ 3.99
_ _	Projections 10: Hollywood Film-makers on Film-making	ed. by Mike Figgis	0 571 19357 9	£12.99
_ _	Conversations with Billy Wilder	Cameron Crowe	0 571 20162 8	£20.00
_ _	Getting Away With It	Steven Soderbergh	0 571 19025 1	£12.99
_ _	Watching	Tom Sutcliffe	0 571 19036 7	£14.99
_ _	My Time With Antonioni	Wim Wenders	0 571 20076 1	£12.99
_ _	Seventy Light Years	Freddie Young	0 571 19793 0	£17.99

_ _ Please send me a free Film Catalogue

_ _ Please send me a free copy of *Shakespeare in Love* screenplay for orders over £20 (Offer closes end of March 2000)

I enclose a cheque for [£ _____] made payable to Faber Book Services or please charge my:

Access ☐   Visa ☐   Amex ☐   Delta ☐   Diners Club ☐   Switch ☐   Switch Issue No. _____

Account No. ☐☐☐☐☐☐☐   Expiry Date _____

Name _____

Address _____

_____

Signed _____   Date _____

Send to:
Sharon Horton,
Faber and Faber,
3 Queen Square,
London,
WC1N 3AU

ff

Postage and packing free for UK delivery. For Overseas orders please allow 20% of order value.
Please allow 28 days for delivery. Offer ends March 2000 and is subject to availability.

sending productions out to shoot in Vancouver, Minneapolis and Adelaide. With so much "runaway production" around, it was telling that Steven Spielberg and partners gave up on their plans to build a new DreamWorks production facility in LA, while over on the potentially less pricey East Coast, Robert DeNiro and Miramax seem close to building a studio in New York's old Brooklyn Navy Yard.

Better solutions are needed for the basic problem: Hollywood is so hamstrung about what constitutes an acceptable fantasy that fantasy itself has escaped its borders and is being acted out everywhere from schoolyards to halls of governance. The economics are out of whack and the nightly news is hotter than what's on screen. It makes no sense to pay Travolta $20m per picture, when Clinton does the star turn better, and yet Hollywood is shackled to the 'Travoltacracy' and cannot compete with reality.

Disney's Michael Eisner settled with DreamWorks' Jeffrey Katzenberg for a rumoured $260m, for the latter's share of revenue from projects initiated while he was at Disney. Katzenberg wanted more, perhaps triple that figure; Eisner wanted to give the man he called a midget less. It was titillating, but overshadowed the more interesting story: Disney, which under Walt, was not known as a company that had Jews on its board or in senior management positions, became a colossus with their help, post-Walt.

One look at major production style and you can smell the fear. The suits are no longer sure what works, and the result has been a spate of pictures that look like they have been put through a genre blender. Old TV shows continue to serve as source material for Hollywood's lack of imagination, either by retooling old series for the big screen, or as a thematic jumping off point in hopes of attracting the 18-25s and their Baby Boomer parents. **Wild Wild West** ($110m at press time), **The X-Files Movie** ($84m), **The Avengers** ($24m), and **Star Trek: Insurrection** – talk about the bankruptcy of ideas.

The wars at home

Finally released from the grip of Leonardo DiCaprio and *Titanic*, the US went off to the Second World War again. America's cumulative box-office champ, Steven Spielberg, led the way with **Saving Private Ryan**, which racked up $200m and earned him another Best Director Oscar. Spielberg competed on the aesthetic axis against a ghost, Terrence Malick, who returned after 20 years with **The Thin Red Line**, which whiffed ($34m) in the money department. The critical verdict was split between noble failure and aesthetic fraudulence.

Pundits deemed these sagas as healthy, fin-de-siècle pulse-taking. Since network TV anchors had themselves written books about the war, this was hardly a surprise. The networks' own morning talk shows continued their transformation into publicity machines, relentlessly flipping from any excuse to re-bury Nicole Brown Simpson and Princess Di to welcoming films stars onto the mock living room set to promote that week's film, every single one of which was invariably "a joy to make".

The decline in the American educational system is gleaned from TV "producers", meaning kids, apparently being trained only to respond to celebrity availability, as opposed to making critical judgement about who or what is actually worth seeing and hearing. The rise of the celebrity agents and publicists who created and serve the $20m stars in the last decade has dovetailed with the expiration of the class of boiler-room war veterans who used to run the Hollywood sales departments – places in which how the picture actually did at the end of the day mattered.

The absence of accountability might very well account for the public's perception that Hollywood now only makes a load of expensive crap. Hanging above the desk of the late *Variety* legit editor Hobe Morrison was a needlepoint motto that read "It Ain't Creative Unless It Sells", a point of some contention and confusion that keeps changing shape: 20 years ago the counter argument (swatted away by Hobe) was "It Ain't Creative If It Sells".

Tom Hanks in SAVING PRIVATE RYAN

Terrence Malick directing THE THIN RED LINE

Both are true; but given the transformation of publicists from sandwich board artists into cop-like figures who restrict access to people and information, the new interpretation of Hobe's handiwork seems to be "If It Sells, Or It Doesn't Sell – Who Cares?" The corollary has become "It Must Be Creative Because the Publicist Tells The Talk-Show Host It Is."

Studio shifts, Bard worship

The public and the craftspeople, however, know this is all the Emperor's New Clothes. Even the industry's own estimate of things – condensed into Oscar nominations – again favoured the indies and the little guys, the most prominent of which have continued their consolidation into major studios – not without acute pain over the compromise of their original mission. From the studios' perspective, there is a long-term, strategic admission that they can't make 'A' pictures any more and so have gone out and essentially vertically reintegrated the industry, theatres with distributors, schlock with 'A' pictures.

Yet the indie scene was going through its own changes. Universal unloaded PolyGram, the very profitable Gramercy, which made some $500m in its brief career as a distributor, and the edgy but less profitable October ($100m over five years) to Barry Diller in a bit of backstage dealing that ended up as USA Films, owned in no small percentage by Universal. Presumably the move, which resulted in the consolidation of two very good companies into one, also let MCA chairman Edgar Bronfman appease his Seagrams folks over Universal's less profitable film entities. Companies moving up over the past year included Lions Gate, Artisan, The Shooting Gallery, Strand and Goldwyn.

There was precious little aggregate box-office for arthouse fare such as **Pi**, **Three Seasons**, **Affliction**, **Happiness**, **A Walk on the Moon**, **A Simple Plan** (and its analog, the misunderstood **Very Bad Things**) or the grey area studio films: **Pleasantville**, **Election**, or even Spike Lee's **Summer of Sam**, which along with **Analyze This** all but declared the end of the Romantic Mafia movement. But one thing a fat economy eventually permits is something other than escapist fantasy; in fact, it encourages the demand for adult investigation. All of the above titles deal with various senses of dislocation – temporal, sexual, familial, mental, or ethical – and differ only in the personal vision of the director on how to end a film: up or down.

The completely elegant and winning **Shakespeare in Love**, financed by Miramax, shot in London, simply blew all the big Second World War guns out of the honours water, capturing 14 Oscar nominations, seven statuettes, and $100m at the box-office. The media quickly misinterpreted *Elizabeth* and *Shakespeare in Love* as proof of a Shakespeare boom (such is the need for end of millennium mush about stock-taking).

Yet *Elizabeth* had as much to do with *The Godfather* as Elizabethan England, and *Shakespeare in Love* was not by Shakespeare but a fantasy about him. Go tell "Shakespeare Boom" to Fox Searchlight, which arrived on the heels of *Shakespeare*'s Oscar conquest with the release of a star-studded **A Midsummer Night's Dream**, and the subsequent hordes of Americans who didn't go see it; maybe they could tell from the hype that the film was marzipan. Miramax, however, continued its boom with high-profile, successful Oscar campaigns for *Shakespeare* and Roberto Benigni's *Life is Beautiful*, the two films to emerge most successfully from its strategy of 'buy everything and see what works'.

Force majeure

Of course, the story of the year was the wait for **Star Wars Episode One: The Phantom Menace**. And what a difference

Nick Nolte in Paul Schrader's AFFLICTION

two decades make. In 1977, it is little remembered, Fox got hauled into court for illegally conditioning the sale of what was supposed to be its big summer hit, Sidney Sheldon's *The Other Side of Midnight*, on an exhibitor's agreement to play this little sci-fi thing by the kid who did *American Graffiti*. This time, Lucas' deal with Fox basically let him keep all the money, plus *Phantom Menace* scared all the summer films other than Mike Meyers' **Austin Powers: The Spy Who Shagged Me** out of May and June release dates.

That *Phantom Menace* opened during Cannes did not seem to matter: Fox made sure the critics all saw it before they left, and 98% of the critics proceeded to pronounce it a bust. True, *Phantom Menace* suffers from arriving at the tail end of the genre it created. In 1977, it offered a wonderfully inventive mise-en-scène and, in embracing military techno-solutions, might as well have been a political crystal ball, presaging the coming Reagan era. *Phantom Menace*, by contrast is merely a well-detailed fable at the comic book level.

The culture of the Jedi Knights has turned into a training manual for Canadian Mounties. Gone is the *Star Wars* irreverence: royalty relying on the inventiveness of the working-class; Han Solo was the personification of the can-do Yanks who won the real (Second World) war. By contrast, Liam Neeson's Jedi Knight is limned with Christ-like implications to no particular end, and Ewan McGregor failed to penetrate the essential strength of the young Obi Wan Kenobi any further than the haircut.

At the end of the day, did it matter that *Phantom Menace* did not attract the repeat business of adults, à la *Titanic* last year or *Star Wars* in 1977? The film still made more than $400m, as the trade had predicted, and served as a rising tide that lifted all boats, including *The Spy Who Shagged Me* ($200m-plus).

Within one six-month period, Lucas and Malick both released new films for the first time in 20 years – and demonstrated that they had not really grown up in that period. Both films seemed frozen in amber, while films by their contemporaries, Spielberg and Scorsese, reflect maturation and life experience. Malick seems to have led a pair of producers around by the nose, and Lucas' immense wealth has deprived him of the force when it comes to film-making. A good career also includes canny judgement of risk-taking. Accuse Spielberg of careerism by all means, but he takes chances; and beg Scorsese and Jim Jarmusch to think about their careers instead of only taking chances. What's needed in Hollywood is the will to adulthood.

HARLAN JACOBSON covered the entertainment industries from New York for seven years for *Variety*, edited *Film Comment* for eight, and for nearly 25 years has written worldwide on film and pop culture. In 1992, with his wife, Susan Jacobson, he formed Talk Cinema, a preview screenings-and-discussion series, which has sites in eight US cities.

Joan Allen and Jeff Daniels in PLEASANTVILLE   *photo: Ralph Nelson/New Line*

George Clooney in OUT OF SIGHT, one of the year's most impressive thrillers, and arguably the best Elmore Leonard adaptation to date *photo: Merrick Morton/Universal*

Bill Pullman (right) as the unconventional, eponymous detective in ZERO EFFECT, Jake Kasdan's brilliant directorial debut *photo: Gemma La Mana/Castle Rock*

Christina Ricci and Ivan Serciei in Don Roos' spiky comedy, THE OPPOSITE OF SEX
photo: Bob Akester/Sony Pictures Classics

Recent and Forthcoming Films

AMERICAN BEAUTY

Script: Alan Ball. Dir: Sam Mendes. Phot: Conrad Hall. Players: Kevin Spacey, Annette Benning, Thora Birch, Wes Bentley, Mena Suvari. Prod: The Jinks/Cohen Company.

ANY GIVEN SUNDAY

Script: Josh Logan. Dir: Oliver Stone. Players: Al Pacino, Cameron Diaz, Dennis Quaid, Lauren Holly, Sean "Puffy" Combs, Tom Arnold. Prod: Illusion Ent. Group/Shuler Donner-Donner Prods.

THE ASTRONAUT'S WIFE

Script and Dir: Rand Ravich. Phot: Allen Daviau. Players: Blair Brown, Nick Cassavetes, Johnny Depp, Clea DuVall, Joe Morton, Donna Murphy, Tom Noonan, Charlize Theron. Prod: New Line Cinema.

BONE COLLECTOR

Script: Jeremy Iacone. Dir: Philip Noyce. Phot: Dean Semler. Players: Denzel Washington, Angelina Jolie, Queen Latifah, Ed O'Neill, Michael Rooker. Prod: Collector of Bones Prods.

BOWFINGER

Script: Steve Martin. Dir: Frank Oz. Phot: Ueli Steiger. Players: Steve Martin, Eddie Murphy, Robert Downey Jr., Heather Graham, Christine Baranski, Jamie Kennedy, Terence Stamp. Prod: Imagine Ent.

BRINGING OUT THE DEAD

Script: Paul Schrader. Dir: Martin Scorsese. Phot: Robert Richardson. Players: Nicolas Cage, Patricia Arquette, John Goodman, Ving Rhames, Tom Sizemore, Marc Anthony, Mary Beth Hurt, Aida Turturro. Prod: Paramount/Touchstone.

DOUBLE JEOPARDY

Script: Douglas Cook. Dir: Bruce Beresford. Phot: Peter James. Players: Tommy Lee Jones, Ashley Judd, Bruce Greenwood, Annabeth Gish, Roma Maffia. Prod: Paramount.

DUDLEY DO-RIGHT

Script and Dir: Hugh Wilson. Phot: Donald Thorin. Players: Brendan Fraser, Sarah Jessica Parker, Alfred Molina, Eric Idle, Robert Prosky, Alex Rocco. Prod: Davis Ent./Joseph Singer Ent./ Universal.

END OF DAYS

Script: Andrew Marlow. Dir and Phot: Peter Hyams. Players: Arnold Schwarzenegger, Robin Tunney, Gabriel Byrne, Kevin Pollak. Prod: Lucifilms/Beacon Communications.

EYES WIDE SHUT

Script and Dir: Stanley Kubrick. Phot: Larry Smith. Players: Tom Cruise, Nicole Kidman, Sydney Pollack, Todd Field, Marie Richardson, Alan Cumming, Rade Serbedzija, Leslee Sobieski. Prod: Warner Bros.

50 VIOLINS

Script: Pamela Gray. Dir: David Fincher. Phot: Jeff Cronenweth. Players: Meryl Streep, Angela Bassett, Aidan Quinn, Gloria Estefan, Jane Leeves, Cloris Leachman, Kieran Culkin, Isaac Stern, Itzhak Perlman, Arnold Steinhardt, Mark O'Connor, Michael Tree, Diane Monroe, Karen Briggs. Prod: Craven-Maddalena Films/Fifty Fiddles.

FIGHT CLUB

Script: Jim Uhls. Dir: David Fincher. Phot: Jeff Cronenweth. Players: Brad Pitt, Edward Norton, Helena Bonham Carter, Meat Loaf, Jared Leto. Prod: Fox 2000.

FLAWLESS

Script and Dir: Joel Schumacher. Phot: Declan Quinn. Players: Robert De Niro, Philip Seymour Hoffman, Barry Miller, Rory Cochrane, Daphne Rubin-Vega. Prod: Tribeca Prods/MGM.

FOR LOVE OF THE GAME

Script: Dana Stevens. Dir: Sam Raimi. Phot: John Bailey. Players: Kevin Costner, Kelly Preston, Jena Malone. Prod: Universal.

GIRL INTERRUPTED

Script and Dir: James Mangold. Players: Winona Ryder, Angelina Jolie, Brittany Murphy, Clea DuVall, Whoopi Goldberg, Vanessa Redgrave. Prod: Red Wagon Prods/3 Arts Ent./Columbia.

THE GREEN MILE

Script and Dir: Frank Darabont. Phot: David Tattersall. Players: Tom Hanks, Michael Clarke Duncan, David Morse, Bonnie Hunt, James Cromwell, Michael Jeter, Graham Greene, Sam Rockwell, Patricia Clarkson, Harry Dean Stanton. Prod: Castle Rock Ent.

HANGING UP

Script: Delia Ephron, Nora Ephron. Dir: Diane Keaton. Players: Meg Ryan, Lisa Kudrow, Diane Keaton. Prod: Laurence Mark Prods/Columbia.

ISN'T SHE GREAT

Script: Paul Rudnick. Dir: Andrew Bergman. Phot: Karl Walter Lindenblaub. Players: Bette Midler, Nathan Lane, Stockard Channing, David Hyde Pierce, John Cleese. Prod: Lobell/Bergman Prods.

LAKE PLACID

Script: David E. Kelly. Dir: Steve Miner. Phot: Daryn Okada. Players: Bill Pullman, Bridget Fonda, Oliver Platt, Brendan Gleason. Prod: BEI Lake Placid Prods.

MAGNOLIA

Script and Dir: Paul Thomas Anderson. Phot: Robert Elswit. Players: Julianne Moore, William H. Macy, Tom Cruise, Luis Guzman, Philip Baker Hall, Philip Seymour Hoffman, Ricky Jay, John C. Reilly, Melora Walters, Henry Gibson, April Grace, Felicity Huffman. Prod: Ghoulardi Films/New Line Cinema.

MAN ON THE MOON

Script: Scott Alexander. Dir: Milos Forman. Phot: Anastas Michos. Players: Jim Carrey, Danny DeVito, Courtney Love, Paul Giamatti, Vince Schiavelli. Prod: Jersey Films/Universal.

MISSION: IMPOSSIBLE SEQUEL

Script: Michael Tolkin. Dir: John Woo. Players: Tom Cruise, Ving Rhames, Dougray Scott, Steve Zahn, Thandie Newton, Luther Stickell. Prod: Paramount.

MYSTERY MEN

Script: Neil Cuthburt. Dir: Kinka Usher. Phot: Stephen Burum. Players: Gordon Forlani, Janeane Garofalo, Greg Kinnear, Jennifer Lewis, William H. Macy, Kel Mitchell, Lena Olin, Paul Reubens, Geoffrey Rush, Ben Stiller, Wes Studi, Tom Waits, Eddie Izzard, Pras. Prod: Universal Pictures/Lawrence Gordon Prods.

THE NINTH GATE

Script and Dir: Roman Polanski. Players: Johnny Depp, Lena Olin, Frank Langella, James Russo. Prod: Artisan Ent.

RUNAWAY BRIDE

Script: Sara Parriott. Dir: Garry Marshall. Players: Julia Roberts, Richard Gere, Joan Cusack, Rita Wilson, Hector Elizondo, Paul Dooley. Prod: Paramount/Walt Disney/Interscope/Lakeshore.

SIXTH SENSE

Script and Dir: M. Night Shyamalan. Phot: Tak Fujimoto. Players: Bruce Willis, Toni Collette, Olivia Williams, Haley Joel Osment, Donnie Wahlberg.

SUPERNOVA

Script: David Campbell Wilson. Dir: Walter Hill. Phot: John Seale. Players: James Spader, Angela Bassett, Robert Forster, Lou Diamond Philips, Robert Tunney. Prod: United Artists/Imperial Ent.

THE TALENTED MR. RIPLEY

Script and Dir: Anthony Minghella. Phot: John Seale. Players: Matt Damon, Gwyneth Paltrow, Jude Law, Cate Blanchett, Philip Seymour Hoffman, Philip Baker Hall, Sergio Rubini. Prod: Mirage Enterprises/Timnick Films.

THE WORLD IS NOT ENOUGH

Script: Neal Purvis. Dir: Michael Apted. Players: Pierce Brosnan, Denise Richards, Sophie Marceau, Robert Carlyle. Prod: United Artists/Danjaq Prods.

Producers

Alliance Atlantis
808 Wilshire Blvd., 3rd Floor,
Santa Monica, CA 90401
Tel: (1 310) 899 8000
Fax: (1 310) 899 8100

American Zoetrope
916 Kearny Street,
San Francisco, CA 94133
Tel: (1 415) 788 7500
Fax: (1 415) 989 7910

Beacon Communications Inc.
1041 N. Formosa Ave.
Santa Monica Bldg., #207
Los Angeles, CA 90046
Tel: (1 323) 850 2651
Fax: (1 323) 850 2613

Brillstein-Grey Entertainment
9150 Wilshire Blvd., #350
Beverly Hills, CA 90212
Tel: (1 310) 275 6135
Fax: (1 310) 275 6180

Cappa Production
(Martin Scorsese)
445 Park Ave., 7th Floor
New York, NY 10022
Tel: (1 212) 906 8800
Fax: (1 212) 906 8891

Castle Rock Entertainment
335 N. Maple Drive, #135
Beverly Hills, CA 90210
Tel: (1 310) 285 2300
Fax: (1 310) 285 2345

Cinergi Pictures Entertainment
2308 Broadway
Santa Monica, CA 90404
Tel: (1 310) 315 6000
Fax: (1 310) 828 0443

Donner Productions Richard
4000 Warner Blvd., Bldg. 102,
Burbank, CA 91522
Tel: (1 818) 954 4437
Fax: (1 818) 954 4908

DreamWorks SKG
100 Universal City Plaza,
Building 10,
Universal City, CA 91608
Tel: (1 818) 695 5000
Fax: (1 818) 733 6153

The Robert Evans Company
The Lubitsch Bldg., #117
5555 Melrose Ave.
Hollywood, CA 90038
Tel: (1 323) 956 8800
Fax: (1 323) 862 0070

Finerman Productions, Wendy
10100 Santa Monica Blvd., Ste 420,
Los Angeles, CA 90067
Tel: (1 310) 369 8800
Fax: (1 310) 369 8808

40 Acres & a Mule Filmworks
(Spike Lee)
8899 Beverly Blvd., Ste 401,
Los Angeles, CA 90048
Tel: (1 310) 276 2116
Fax: (1 310) 276 2164

Fox Filmed Entertainment
10201 W. Pico Blvd.,
Los Angeles, CA 90035
Tel: (1 310) 369 1000
Fax: (1 310) 369 3155

Hanna Barbera Productions
15303 Ventura Blvd.
Sherman Oaks, CA 91403
Tel: (1 818) 977 7500
Fax: (1 818) 977 7510

Hollywood Pictures
(Distributed through Buena Vista)
500 South Buena Vista St.
Burbank, CA 91521
Tel: (1 818) 560 1000/4383
Fax: (1 818) 842 9046

Imagine Entertainment
9465 Wilshire Blvd, 7th Floor
Beverly Hills, CA 90212
Tel: (1 310) 858 2000
Fax: (1 310) 858 2020

King World Productions
12400 Wilshire Blvd. #1200
Los Angeles, CA 90025
Tel: (1 310) 826 1108
Fax: (1 310) 207 2179

Kopelson Entertainment
2121 Avenue of the Stars, Ste. 1400
Los Angeles, CA 90067
Tel: (1 310) 369 7500
Fax: (1 310) 369 7501

Kushner-Locke Intl.
11601 Wilshire Blvd., 21st Floor
Los Angeles, CA 90025
Tel: (1 310) 445 1111
Fax: (1 310) 445 1191

The Ladd Company
Chevalier 117
5555 Melrose Ave.
Hollywood, CA 90038
Tel: (1 323) 956 8203
Fax: (1 323) 862 1115

MGM/UA
2500 Broadway St., Ste. E-2029
Santa Monica, CA 90404
Tel: (1 310) 449 3000
Fax: (1 310) 449 3069

Miramax Films
7966 Beverly Blvd
Los Angeles, CA 90048
Tel: (1 323) 951 4200
Fax: (1 323) 951 4215

Morgan Creek Productions
4000 Warner Blvd., Bldg. 76
Burbank, CA 91522
Tel: (1 818) 954 4800
Fax: (1 818) 954 4811

New Line Cinema Corp.
(Distributor/Producer)
116 North Robertson Blvd. #200
Los Angeles, CA 90048
Tel: (1 310) 854 5811
Fax: (1 310) 854 1824

New Regency Productions Inc.
10201 W. Pico Blvd., Bldg. 12
Los Angeles, CA90035
Tel: (1 310) 369 8300

Peters Entertainment
4000 Warner Blvd., Bldg 15,
Burbank, CA 91522
Tel: (1 818) 954 4960
Fax: (1 818) 954 4976

Red Wagon Productions
10202 W. Washington Blvd.,
Astaire Bldg., Ste. 1200,
Culver City, CA 90232
Tel: (1 310) 244 4466
Fax: (1 310) 244 1480

Ruddy-Morgan Organization
9300 Wilshire Blvd., Ste. 508
Beverly Hills, CA 90212.
Tel: (1 310) 271 7698
Fax: (1 310) 278 9978

Saban Entertainment
4000 West Alameda Avenue,
Ste. 500
Burbank, CA 91505
Tel: (1 310) 235 5100
Fax: (1 310) 235 5102

The stag day from hell featured in VERY BAD THINGS   photo: Robert Zuckerman/PolyGram

Silver Pictures
4000 Warner Blvd., Bldg. 90
Burbank, CA 91522
Tel: (1 818) 954 4490
Fax: (1 818) 954 3237

Spelling Entertainment Group Inc.
5700 Wilshire Blvd., #575
Los Angeles, CA 90036
Tel: (1 213) 965 5700
Fax: (1 213) 965 5895

Tisch Company, Steve
3815 Hughes Ave., Culver City
CA 90232
Tel: (1 310) 838 2500
Fax: (1 310) 204 2713

Trimark Pictures
(Distributor/Producer)
2644 30th St., 2nd Floor,
Santa Monica
CA 90405
Tel: (1 310) 399 8877
Fax: (1 310) 392 0252

Universal Television Group
100 Universal City Plaza
Universal City, CA 91608
Tel: (1 310) 360 2300

Warner Bros. Studio
4000 Warner Blvd.,
Burbank, CA 91522
Tel: (1 818) 954 6000
Fax: (1 818) 954 2089

Wildwood Enterprises Inc.
(Robert Redford)
1101 Montana Ave., #E
Santa Monica, CA 90403
Tel: (1 310) 395 5155
Fax: (1 310) 395 3975

Wind Dancer Films
1040 North Las Palmas, Bldg 2,
Hollywood, CA 90038
Burbank, CA 91521
Tel: (1 323) 645 1200
Fax: (1 323) 645 1255

Winkler Films Inc.
211 S. Beverly Drive, #200
Beverly Hills, CA 90212
Tel: (1 310) 858 5780
Fax: (1 310) 858 5799

Distributors

Alliance Releasing Corp.
121 Bloor Street, Ste 800
Toronto
Ontario M4W 3M5, Canada
Tel: (1 416) 967 1141
Fax: (1 416) 960 0971

Buena Vista Pictures (Disney)
500 South Buena Vista St.
Burbank, CA 91521
Tel: (1 818) 560 4020
Fax: (1 818) 841 2679

King World Entertainment
12400 Wilshire Blvd., Ste. 1200,
Los Angeles, CA 90025
Tel: (1 310) 826 1108
Fax: (1 310) 207 2179

Miramax Films
Tribeca Film Center
375 Greenwich Street
New York, NY 10013
Tel: (1 212) 941 3800
Fax: (1 212) 941 3949

Paramount Pictures
5555 Melrose Ave.
Hollywood, CA 90038
Tel: (1 323) 956 5000
Fax: (1 323) 862 1703

Sony Pictures Entertainment Inc.
10202 West Washington Blvd.
Culver City, CA 90232
Tel: (1 310) 244 4000
Fax: (1 310) 244 2626

TriStar
10202 West Washington Blvd.
Culver City, CA 90232
Tel: (1 310) 244 7700
Fax: (1 310) 244 1468

Twentieth Century Fox
10201 West Pico Blvd.
Los Angeles, CA 90035
Tel: (1 310) 369 1000
Fax: (1 310) 369 2735

Warner Bros. Pictures
(Distributor)
4000 Warner Blvd.
Burbank, CA 91522
Tel: (1 818) 954 6000
Fax: (1 818) 954 2222

Universal Pictures Inc.
100 Universal Plaza
Universal City, CA 91608
Tel: (1 818) 777 1000

USA Films
65 Bleecker Street
New York, NY 10012
Tel: (1 212) 539 4000
Fax: (1 212) 539 4099

Useful Addresses

Academy of Motion Picture Arts and Sciences
8949 Wilshire Blvd.
Beverly Hills, CA 90211
Tel: (1 310) 247 3000
Fax: (1 310) 859 9619

American Film Institute
John F. Kennedy Center for the
Performing Arts

Washington D.C. 20566
Tel: (1 202) 416 7815
Fax: (1 202) 659 1970

The Directors Guild of America
7920 Sunset Blvd.,
Los Angeles, CA 90046
Tel: (1 310) 289 2000
Fax: (1 310) 289 2029

Independent Feature Project
104 W. 29th Street, 12th Floor
New York, NY 10001
Tel: (1 212) 465 8200
Fax: (1 212) 465 8525

Motion Picture Association of America (MPPA)
15503 Ventura Blvd.
Encino, CA 91436
Tel: (1 818) 995 6600
Fax: (1 818) 382 1784

ShoWest
116 North Robertson Blvd., Ste. 708
Los Angeles, CA 90048
Tel: (1 310) 657 7724
Fax: (1 310) 657 4758

VENEZUELA

Irene
Herrera

Though the 1990s have been a largely optimistic decade for Venezuelan film, the tough political and economic situation in 1998 resulted in a significant reduction in production activity, as the budget of the Autonomous National Center for Cinematography (CNAC) was cut by 60%, from $2m to $800,000.

More than 90% of Venezuelan film production depends on subsidy from CNAC, the government-financed organisation which almost disappeared after new president Hugo Chavez took office in February 1999. Despite protests from film-makers and guilds, CNAC's future remains uncertain; it can now scarcely

afford to finance one feature and three shorts for 1999. The various film-making guilds are lobbying hard for new legislation which would take greater account of distribution and exhibition and, perhaps, give CNAC a completely autonomous budget, rather than leaving it at the mercy of sudden government cuts.

Directors and producers, obliged increasingly to look for alternative funding in the private sector, have been establishing co-production agreements with other Spanish-speaking countries. Argentina and Venezuela have signed a co-production agreement; urban drama **Glue Sniffer** (*Huelepega*) and revenge thriller

Devil Gold (*Oro Diablo*) will be co-produced with Spain; psychological drama **Death Drives the Birds Away** (*Los Pájaros se van con la Muerte*), thriller **Carnival Monday** (*Lunes de Carnaval*) and the first children's movie produced in Venezuela since 1985, **Oscar's Magic Adventure** (*La Mágica Aventura de Oscar*), are Mexican-Colombian-Venezuelan co-productions.

Only four Venezuelan features were released in 1998: **Rude Awakening** (*Amaneció de Golpe*), directed by Carlos Azpurua, Oscar Lucien's **Skin** (*Piel*), Alejandro Saderman's **100 Years of Forgiveness** (*Cien Años de Perdón*) and the privately-financed musical-comedy *Lonely Guy* (*Muchacho Solitario*). Early in 1999, Gustavo Balza's debut **The Valley** (*El Valle*) became the first release from the new generation of film-makers.

Between them these productions participated in more than 50 film festivals and won nine awards, including Best Film at the XXIV edition of the Huelva Iberoamerican Film Festival in Spain, for Azpurua's *Rude Awakening*, a drama about four families, set during the 1992 coup led by Chavez. Of the 130 titles released in 1998, Azpurua's was one of just two national productions to break into the box-office top 20, with 168,333 admissions – a minute figure compared to *Titanic's* record-breaking two million spectators.

Pop idols, national hero

Despite the problems, there were still events to cheer. For the first time in recent years, a Venezuelan production is being distributed in Spain, North and South America by a US major, Buena Vista International. Already premiered in Latin and Caribbean cities, the $2m **Lonely Guy** will be seen in US cities with large Latin populations. Directed by César Bolívar and starring Servando & Florentino, one of Venezuela's most popular teenage salsa acts (responsible for the 1996 box-office success *The First Time*), it reached 210,000 admissions in Venezuela.

Beatríz Valdés as MANUELA SAENZ, Simón Bolivar's lover in Diego Rísquez's new feature film

Perhaps the biggest and most ambitious motion picture project ever developed in Venezuela was in pre-production when this article went to press. **Bolívar – The Liberator** will tell the life story of Simon Bolívar (1783–1830) liberator of Venezuela, Colombia, Ecuador, Peru, Bolivia and Panama.

The film may cost as much as $100m, with investment coming from several countries and principal roles to be played by Hollywood and British names. Venezuelan Edgard Meinhardt Iturbe, originator and producer of the project,

plans to films scenes from Bolívar's life at the actual European and Venezuelan locations. Interest in Latin America's war of independence was also fuelled by Diego Risquez, who recently shot **Manuela Sáenz**, about Bolívar's lover. The film is expected to be released in 2000.

IRENE CAROLINA HERRERA has worked as an art director for several short films and has just written and directed her first short, *The Confession*. She has contributed to numerous publications in Venezuela and currently edits the film magazine, *Producción & Distribución*.

Recent and Forthcoming Films

MANUELA SÁENZ

Script: Leonardo Padrón. Dir: Diego Rísquez. Players: Beatríz Valdés, Mariano Alvarez. Prod: Producciones Guakamaya.

Young sailor Herman Melville arrives at a lonely Peruvian port in 1856 and meets Manuela Sáenz, lover of Simón Bolívar, hero of the South American revolution, and tries to save her from dying of diptheria. She sees her entire life pass before her eyes.

LA MAGICA AVENTURA DE OSCAR
(Oscar's Magic Adventure)

Script: Yutzil Martínez, Diana Sánchez, Joelle Lecoin. Dir: Sánchez. Players: Carlos Montilla, Linsabel Noguera, Alberto Rudiño, Bárbara Garofalo, Samantha Dagnino. Prod: Tango Bravo Producciones/Philippe Toledano.

Eight-year-old Oscar sets out to rescue his mother, who has been kidnapped by the evil Mr Black. Together with his little sister Miranda and his dog Mac he encounters friends and enemies.

Marcelo Cesán in Henrique Lazo's LET'S START ALL OVER

LUNES DE CARNAVAL
(Carnival Monday)

Script: Claudio Nazoa and Malena Roncayolo. Dir: Roncayolo. Players: Mimi Lazo, Armando Gutiérrez, Luis Felipe Tovar, Juan Carlos Alarcón. Prod: T y M Films.

Mariantonia, an innocent nine-year old girl who lives in a quiet little town called San Jorge, is suddenly forced to take part in adult life when the new town sheriff begins a reign of terror.

LOS PÁJAROS SE VAN CON LA MUERTE
(Death Drives the Birds Away)

Script: Edilio Peña and Thaelman Urgelles. Dir: Urgelles. Prod: T y M Films.

Psychological drama. A mother and daughter live tormented by the memory of the husband who abandoned them. Their obsessive hatred and attachment to this man lead to destruction.

HUELEPEGA (Glue Sniffer)

Script: Nestor Caballero and Elia Schneider. Dir: Schneider. Prod: Joel Films.

Grim drama exploring the lives of homeless children in Latin American cities, and their merciless, inexorable relationship with drugs.

ORO DIABLO (Devil Gold)

Script: Sonia Chocrón. Dir: José Ramón Novoa. Players: Laureano Olivarez, Roberto Hernández, Jenny Noguera, Pedro Lander, Yanis Chimaras. Prod: Joel Films.

Revenge drama set in Papayal, a gold mining town where life has lost all value. Isabel, a beautiful, innocent girl is wrongfully accused of attempting to steal the town's gold stocks. Driven by hatred, she destroys her enemies.

BORRÓN Y CUENTA NUEVA
(Let's Start Over)

Script: Ana María Uslar. Dir: Henrique Lazo. Players: Gustavo Peraza. Mimi Lazo, Elba Escobar, Marcelo Cezán, Carolina Perpetuo.

A series of romantic adventures in an unstable city lead to tragedy, satire and deceit.

EL IRRIGADOR (The Irrigator)

Script: Roberto Rodríguez and Milton Crespo. Dir: Crespo. Players: Laura Altieri, Gabriel Blanco, Toco Gómez, Dalila Colombo, Carlos Cruz. Prod: Producciones Tizaral.

In Pueblo Rico, an oil-mining town where the stocks appear to have run out, exposure to toxic waste gives a young man the power to locate petroleum beneath the ground. The townsfolk begin to worship him.

MUCHACHO SOLITARIO
(Lonely Guy)

Script and Dir: César Bolívar. Players: Servando & Florentino, Ivonne Reyes, Miguel Ferrari. Prod: Montaner Entertainment Group.

Hard-working Juan and David are united through their music after inheriting a truck which they use to distribute soda throughout the country. An adventurous, entertaining film propelled by magical dreams and an innovative soundtrack.

KURÚ-KURÚ

Script and Dir: Rafael Marziano Tinoco. Prod: Makatoa Media Producciones.

Tragi-comedy following a day in the lives of four very different characters, anti-heroes who come together in an unexpected climax in the back alleys of Caracas.

100 AÑOS DE PERDON
(100 Years of Forgiveness)

Script and Dir: Alejandro Saderman. Players: Orlando Urdaneta, Daniel Lugo, Mariano Alvarez, Aroldo Betancourt. Prod: Antonio Llerandi and Liz Mago.

One Christmas, four childhood friends are reunited and because of their desperate financial states, decide to rob a bank.

Laura Altieri submerged in a cave in Milton Crespo's debut, THE IRRIGATOR

TRAMPA PARA UN GATO
(Trap for a Cat)

Script and Dir: Manuel De Pedro. Players: Amado Zambrano, Alejandro Faillace, Gregorio Milano, Yasmín Hernández. Prod: Marco Antonio Pérez, Jota y Joropo.

Action-drama set during the civil war in El Salvador and based around Radio Venceremos, the secret radio station that became the voice of the guerrilla forces, heard worldwide. The Army mounts a helicopter attack on the station but the guerillas set a trap.

LA NAVE DE LOS SUEÑOS
(The Ship of Dreams)

Script: Ciro Durán, Dunav Kuzmanich. Dir: Durán. Players: Oscar Borda, Lourdes Elizarraras, Gledys Ibarra, Ramiro Meneses. Prod: G3/Joyce Ventura.

Six Venezuelan stowaways on a ship bound for New York face a terrible dilemma when one of them has a life-threatening accident: should they search for help from the ship's crew, or let their friend die and pursue their "American dream".

ALFREDO SADEL

Script and Dir: Alfredo Sánchez. Documentary about the Venezuelan singer Alfredo Sadel, featuring the recollections of friends and colleagues, including Placido Domingo.

Producers

Alter Producciones
Ave. Diego de Losada
Qta. Alter
San Bernardino
Caracas
Tel: (58 2) 527 197/511 923
Fax: (58 2) 552 7297

Bolivar Films
Av. Luis Guillermo Villegas Blanco
Edif. Bolívar Films. Sta
Eduvigis
Caracas
Tel: (58 2) 283 8455
Fax: (58 2) 284 1011
www.bolivarfilms.com

Caral Cine
2da transversal
Qta. El Laurel
Sta. Eduvigis
Caracas
Tel: (58 2) 283 9944
Fax: (58 2) 285 9056

Centro de cinematografía de La Universidad de los Andes
Altos Comedor
Universitario
Entrada Vía Chorros de Milla
Mérida
Tel: (58 74) 401 725/401 720/441 514

Cine Marte
Calle Santa Ana con Calle Lecuna
Boleíta Sur
Caracas
Tel: (58 2) 239 5376
Fax: (58 2) 239 2073

Cine Sur C. A.
Av. Principal de San Marino
Qta. Siboney

Chacao
Caracas
Tel: (58 2) 261 8685/266 7667
Fax: (58 2) 266 7667

Pablo de la Barra Producciones
3era transversal con 4ta avenida
Edificio Elite
Apto. 105, Los Palos Grandes
Caracas
Tel: (58 2) 283 4990/284 3484
Fax: (58 2) 149 355 057
e-mail: amaru@truevision.net

Premiere Producciones
Primera Av. De los Palos Grandes
Edif. Roxul
piso 3. Ofc. 31
Caracas
Tel: (58 2) 286 1291/6967
Fax: (58 2) 284 338
e-mail: alopezsojo@cantv.net

Producciones 800
Edifcio Torre Financiera
Oficina Mezanina M-0
Ave. Beethonven (al lado de Maxy's)
Urbanización Bello Monte
Caracas 1060
Tel: (58 2) 751 7076/752 1821/166243862

Producciones Doble Ele
Avenida Principal de Prados
del Este
Residencias
los Copigües
piso 7, apto. 7-4
Lomas de Prados del Este
Caracas
Tel: (58 2) 976 8273/261 8685
Fax: (58 2) 266 7667
Cel. (58 2) 16 6302854

Producciones Tango Bravo
4ta Avenida entre 9na
Y 10ma. Transversal
Qta. Turandot
Los Palos Grandes
Caracas
Tel: (58 2) 283 4829/285 9237
Fax: (58 2) 285 9213
e-mail: tango.bravo@cantv.net

T&M Films
Ave. Luis Guillermo Villegas Blanco
Edif. Rivera, Piso 1
oficina 11, Santa Eduvigis
Caracas
Tel: (58 2) 283 4653/285 4747
Fax: (58 2) 283 4653
e-mail: tymfilms@facilnet.com

TVA
Av. El Retiro
Qta. 34, El Rosal
Caracas 1060
Tel: (58 2) 952 5727
Fax: (58 2) 953 0778

Distributors

Blancica
3era Av. Las Delicias
Sabana Grande
Edif. Las Delicias PB
Caracas
Tel: (58 2) 762 9781
Fax: (58 2) 762 4264

Cineven 2.000
Alberto Benaim
4ta Avenida entre 9na
Y 10ma.
Transversal
Qta. Turandot
Los Palos Grandes

Caracas
Tel: (58 2) 283 4829/283 7156
Fax: (58 2) 285 9237

Di Fox
Av. Las Palmas
Edif. Las Palmas
Piso 3
Caracas
Tel: (58 2) 781 7511
Fax: (58 2) 782 5087

Korda Films
Ed. Teatro Altamira PH
Altamira Sur
Caracas
Tel: (58 2) 762 6030

Movie Movie Asesoramientos
Av. Libertador, cruce con
Av. Las Palmas
Edif. Teatro Las Palmas
Sótano 1. Of. 7
Caracas
Tel: (58 2) 793 7158

Roraimex
Av. Las Palmas
Ed. Las Palmas
Mezzanina
Caracas
Tel: (58 2) 793 7377

Tepuy Films
Av. Libertador
Torre EXA, PH 1
El Rosal
Caracas 1060
Tel: (58 2) 953 3363/0942
Fax: (58 2) 953 6880
e-mail: tepuy@hdq.true.net

Venefilms
Av. Rómulo Gallegos
Esq. El Carmen
Ed. Torre Samán, piso 1
of. 11, Los Dos Caminos
Caracas
Tel: (58 2) 762 9781/239 6417

Useful Addresses

Asociación Nacional de Autores Cinematográficos (ANAC)
Urb. Avila, Av
San Gabriel
Qta. Primavera
Alta Florida
Tel: (58 2) 740 366/741 954

Asociación Nacional de Exhibidores
Av. Rómulo Gallegos
Esq. El Carmen
Ed. Torre Samán
psio 1, of. 11
Los Dos Caminos
Caracas
Tel: (58 2) 237 0397/1262
Fax: (58 2) 239 6417

Cámara de la Industria del Cine y del Video
Tel: (58 2) 283 4829/7156
Fax: (58 2) 285 9237

Cámara Venezolana de Productores de Largometrajes (CAVEPROL)
4ta Avenida entre 9na

Y 10ma
Transversal
Qta. Turandot
Los Palos Grandes
Caracas.
Tel: (58 2) 283 4829/7156
Fax: (58 2) 285 9237

Centro Nacional Autónomo de Cinematografía (CNAC)
Av. Ppal de Los Ruices
Edificio Centro Monaca
Ala Sur, Piso 2
Los Ruices
Caracas
Tel: (58 2) 238 6494/1050
Fax: (58 2) 237 4942
e-mail: presidencnac@true.net

Venezuela Film Commission
Av. Ppal de Los Ruices, Edificio
Centro Monaca
Ala Sur
Piso 2. Los Ruices
Caracas
Tel: (58 2) 238 6494/1050
Fax: (58 2) 237 4942
e-mail: venefilmcomis@true.net

Sindicato Profesional de Trabajadores de Radio, Cine, TV y Afines del
Distrito Federal y Estado Miranda
Av. Nivaldo
Qta. San Joseph
no. 175, La Florida
Caracas
Tel: (58 2) 744 444
Fax: (58 2) 731 0976

ZIMBABWE
Judy Kendall

The news for cinema has not been good in Zimbabwe this year. Two of the main production houses, Central Film Laboratories and Framework, have gone bust, and the giants of 1996–97, *Flame* and *Kini and Adams* (co-produced by Framework International with France and Burkina Faso), both of which held great promise after scooping many awards, fared poorly when released in, respectively, Johannesburg and Paris.

The new genre of "African Cinema", which had looked so promising in recent years is floundering, failing to gain for itself that essential popular audience needed to secure future investment. On a more positive note however, African TV broadcasters are increasingly interested in showing "African Cinema" on their channels. TV films may well be the way forward for Zimbabwe.

The annual Southern African Film Festival (SAFF) was held in October 1998. Established as an attempt to balance West Africa and Burkina Faso's FESPACO with a Southern African festival, it disappointingly failed to attract much media coverage, a point bemoaned by Stephen Chifunyise, Zimbabwe's Minister of Education, Sport and Culture. Among issues aired during the festival was the question of co-production and how it might curtail a director's freedom.

Michael Games' new feature film, *Escape from Angola*, to be shot in Zimbabwe before the end of 1999, shows that foreign directors are still attracted to Zimbabwe's attractive filmic conditions: stunning scenery, low labour costs and technical provision. Harare boasts one of Africa's few training schools, the UNESCO Zimbabwe Film and Video

Training Project, as well as the African Script Development Fund.

As for local films, there is little to show, apart from Nobert Fero's debut feature, **Matters of The Spirit**. Filmed in both Shona and English, it draws on Fero's experience of working as a hospital drama therapist, and explores the story of a mentally disabled woman and her struggle to get accepted by the community. Fearing rejection, she feels obliged to hide the truth and complications soon result.

In the short film category, Manu Kurewa's *Tomorrow* (*Mangwana*), having featured in the Cinefoundation category at Cannes in 1998, received a special mention at SAFF 1998. The story is of an ageing Scottish farmer who, after a car crash in the Zimbabwean bush, is obliged to accept the hospitality of an elder of the local village – a man he would normally never meet on equal terms. It also won an award as Best Short at the 1998 Southern Africa Film and TV Market in South Africa.

As regards local films in production, Zimmedia is producing M-NET's series of short films by woman directors in Africa, **Mama Africa**. The directors include Ingrid Sinclair, the winner of the best documentary award for *Tides of Gold* at the 1998 SAFF. At press time, Sinclair was still seeking finance for her new film, **The Captain**, about genocide in Rwanda.

Producers

Chameleon Film Productions
11 Smit Crescent
Eastlea
PO Box Cy2918

Media for Development Trust
135 Union Avenue
PO Box 6755
Harare
Tel/Fax: (263 4) 729 066
e-mail: mfd@mango.zw

Mighty Movies
Production House
7 Cambridge Ave

Newlands
PO Box HG 993
Highlands
Harare
Tel: (263 4)746 530/776 214
Fax: (263 4) 746 550
e-mail: mighty@id.co.zw

The Southern African Film Festival
Isaac Meli Mabhikwa
Box CY 724
Causeway
Harare
Tel/Fax: (263 4) 704 227
e-mail: SAFF@zin.surf.co.zw

Z Promotions (Pvt) Ltd
PO Box 6109
Harare
Tel: (263 4) 726 795
Fax: (263 4) 726 796
e-mail: film@internet.co.zw

FESTIVALS

The Thessaloniki International Film Festival's First 40 Years

by Alexis Grivas

"Michel Demopoulos has been able to give a new vitality to the Festival and open it to a young audience. During the Festival, in this town, you breathe not oxygen but cinema."

Bernardo Bertolucci

Born in 1960, as a modest "Week of Greek Cinema", the Thessaloniki International Film Festival has, 40 years later, become an annual event focused on the discovery and promotion of new directors from all over the world – a true celebration of film. For ten days in mid-November, approximately 70,000 viewers, as well as hundreds of Greek and foreign guests of the festival, attend screenings of more than 150 films in the city's seven cinemas.

Newcomers in the competitive section meet veterans showcased in retrospectives and special screenings. Films are shown in front of the young, vital, cinema-loving Thessaloniki audiences; and, in the parallel events such as concerts and art exhibitions, cinema is united with the other arts.

The festival took on its present dynamic and international character in 1992, under the direction of Michel Demopoulos, with the financial support of the Greek Ministry of Culture, in collaboration with the Municipality of Thessaloniki and other

Theo Angelopoulos, director and President of the Thessaloniki Int'l Film Festival photo: Rassias

local institutions – and with the unanimous support of the city's population.

The international recognition for the new face of the festival is illustrated by the participation in its jury of such notables as István Szabó, Nelson Pereira dos Santos, Chantal Akerman, Ivan Passer, Goran Paskaljević, Yoichiro Takahashi, Nikos Papatakis, Paul Leduc, Jerry Schatzberg, Georgi Chenguelaiia, Dariush Mehrjui, Elliot Stein, Pascal Bonitzer, Lino Micciché, David Thewlis, Aurore Clément, Maia Morgenstern, Dean Tavoularis, Adrienne Mancia, Beki Probst, Giuglielmo Biraghi, Eric Heumann and many others.

Location, location...

"Both city and festival love to combine tradition with innovation ... this most hospitable of festivals and most elegant of Greek cities." – *Sight and Sound*

Thessaloniki, the second largest city in Greece and the country's largest export port, is a lively metropolis of one million inhabitants. At the crossroads of East and West, the site of an harmonious blending of

The headquarters of the Thessaloniki Int't Film Festival   *photo: Rassias*

people and civilisations, the city is one of the major financial and commercial centres of South-eastern Europe. Thessaloniki's rich cultural tradition is enhanced by its modern museums, art galleries, libraries and other institutions.

Blending tradition with modernity, Thessaloniki's inhabitants have a reputation for friendly hospitality. The guests of the festival are given the opportunity to join in the everyday life of this most joyful city and also visit prominent historical sites such as Vergina.

To cut a long story short...

"Since 1960, the Thessaloniki Film Festival has been the most important showcase of Greek cinema and, for the last few years, one of the most significant festivals for first and second films from all over the world."
– *La Repubblica*

The first Week of Greek Cinema was organised in 1960 by the International Thessaloniki Fair (known today as Helexpo) and realised the dream of a group of local intellectuals and the desire of the city's inhabitants. Two years later, the festival was taken on by the Ministry of Industry, which was then supervising Greek film production.

In 1966, the event was officially named the Greek Film Festival, and a first attempt was made to hold an international film festival at a different date. The imposition of a dictatorship the following year caused this plan to fall through. Foreign participants were limited to a small, non-competing section, complementary to the Greek festival (a set-up which had already existed since 1961).

The state's attitude towards cinema, and especially the enforcement of severe censorship, caused intense displeasure among film unions, a displeasure that did not dissipate even with the fall of the dictatorship in 1974. The rift between the state and the film industry widened during the first years of democratic rule, and reached its peak in 1977, with the holding of two separate festivals: one organised by the government and one by the film unions.

The decisive step for the settling of the dispute was made in 1981, when the festival became the responsibility of the Ministry of Culture. The next, crucial move was made in 1986, when a permanent institution for organising the festival was legally established, under the supervision of the Ministry. There followed several short-lived efforts to expand the goals of the festival, while its directorship changed three times. Finally, in 1991, Michel Demopoulos was named as director, and the following year he gave the event the form it has today.

Based on the new law, in force since 1998, the Thessaloniki Film Festival is an autonomous organisation, with Theo Angelopoulos as its President, Michel Demopoulos as its Vice-President and Artistic Director, a small Executive Council (comprising representatives from Helexpo, the Municipality of Thessaloniki and the Advisor for Film to the Ministry of Culture), and the larger General Assembly (representing film unions and other institutions). Financially, 59% of the festival's expenses are covered by state sponsorship through the Ministry of Culture, 16% by its own income and 25% by other institutions (co-organisers, sponsors, advertisers etc.).

And the winners were...

"It's a wonderful festival. To meet new directors is a necessity. They represent the future of the cinema."   – István Szabó

The International Competition section is open to first and second films by directors from all over the world. To date, this section has featured films from 39 countries: Australia, Azerbaijan, Belgium, Canada, China, Colombia, Czech Republic, Czechoslovakia, Finland, France, Georgia, Germany, Greece, Guinea-Bissau, Hungary, Iran, Ireland, Italy, Japan, Kazakhstan, Korea, Lithuania, Mexico, Netherlands, New Zealand, Norway, Poland, Portugal, Russia, Spain, Switzerland, Taiwan, Tajikistan, Tunisia, Turkey, Ukraine, United Kingdom, United States and Yugoslavia.

The competition has seen numerous world premieres: Antoine Desrosières' *A la belle étoile*, Lucas Belvaux's *Pour rire*, Peter Wooditsch's *Hey Stranger*, Jeremy

Abbas Kiarostami with a poster announcing his photographic exhibition in Thessaloniki in 1997
photo: Rassias

Claude Chabrol, guest of honour during a retrospective of his work in 1997   *photo: Rassias*

Podeswa's *Eclipse*; and European premieres: Sergei Livnev's *Serp I molot*, We Nien-jen's *Do-san*, Alexander Payne's *Citizen Ruth*, Robert Jaan Westdijk's *Zusje*, Makoto Shinozaki's *Okaeri* and Shinji Aoyama's *Chinpira*.

The prizes awarded each year by the seven-member international jury include the Golden Alexander for Best Film (accompanied by a $50,000 cash prize), the Special Jury Award – Silver Alexander (plus $35,000), as well as awards for Best Direction, Best Screenplay, Best Actor, Best Actress and Artistic Achievement.

To date, the Golden Alexander has been awarded to the following films: Sally Potter's *Orlando* (UK) and Aleko Tsabadze's *Night Dance* (Georgia) in 1992, Sotiris Goritsas' *From the Snow* (Greece) in 1993, Wang Xiaoshuai's *The Days* (Hong Kong/China) in 1994, He Jianjun's *The Postman* (China) in 1995, Udayan Prasad's *Brothers in Trouble* (UK) in 1996, Sue Brooks' *Road to Nhill* (Australia) in 1997, and Yoichiro Takahashi's *Fishes in August* (Japan) in 1998.

FIPRESCI also votes for the best film at Thessaloniki each year. The winners of the FIPRESCI award have been: *Orlando* (UK, 1992), *18* (Taiwan, 1993), *Do-san* (Taiwan, 1994), *Okaeri* (Japan, 1995), Jacques Deschamps' *Méfie-toi de l'eau qui dort* (France, 1996), Tom Tykwer's *Winterschlafer* (Germany, 1997) and *Fishes in August* (Japan, 1998). Finally, the public's award, established in 1996, has gone to Srdjan Dragojević's *Lepa sela lepo gore*

Jules Dassin and Sotiris Goritsas (winner of the Golden Alexander in 1993)

Irene Papas and Manoel de Oliveira attending the Thessaloniki Int'l Film Festival in 1997   photo: Rassias

(Yugoslavia), Tykwer's *Winterschlafer*, and Bruno Podalydes' *Dieu seul me voit* (France).

A Greek showcase

"The Festival gives Greek film-makers the opportunity to meet their fellows from abroad and promote Greek cinema which, for a while, had become stagnant."
– Le Monde

Of course, the Thessaloniki Festival remains – even now, when what used to be the National Competition section is simply the Greek Film Festival – the most prestigious showcase for Greece's annual film production – a slate of films that always provides surprises and challenging topics.

In the early years, the festival featured such internationally acclaimed film-makers as Nikos Koundouros and Michael Cacoyannis (with their international successes *Young Aphrodites* and *Electra*, respectively), but also other significant directors such as Takis Canellopoulos, Grigoris Grigoriou and Vassilis Georgiadis.

In the late 1960s and early 1970s, a younger generation of film-makers appeared: Theo Angelopoulos, Pandelis Voulgaris, Alexis Damianos, Costas Ferris, Nikos Panayiotopoulos, Nikos Nikolaidis, Nikos Perrakis, Tonia Marketaki, Frida Liappa and others, who were first noticed at Thessaloniki, and went on to become known internationally. More recently, it is thanks to the festival that we have come to know promising young directors such as

Sotiris Goritsas, Pericles Hoursoglou, Constantinos Giannaris and Antonis Kokkinos.

A universal panorama

"I just want to say how thrilled and flattered I am to be part of the New Horizons section of the Thessaloniki International Film Festival."
– David Cronenberg

Dimitri Eipides and Atom Egoyan at a press conference at the 34th festival

The festival's New Horizons section presents each year a panorama of contemporary film production, giving special emphasis to all that is new, dynamic and radical in world cinema. Bruno Dumont, Lodge Kerrigan, Takeshi Kitano, Jacques Doillon, Mohsen Makhmalbaf, Erick Zonca, Aki Kaurismäki, Jim Jarmusch, Cedric Kahn, Gregg Araki, Laetitia Masson, Aleksandr Rogoschkin and Olivier Assayas are among the film-makers whose work has been featured in the New Horizons section – and many of them came to Thessaloniki to mark the occasion.

New Horizons director Dimitri Eipides has chosen many films that go on to meet with great critical acclaim internationally. Thus, films such as Nikita Mikhalkov's *Burnt by the Sun*, Scott Hicks' *Shine*, Jan Sverak's *Kolya* and André Téchiné's *Les roseaux sauvages* were screened in Thessaloniki before being nominated for Academy Awards. Also, tributes to Atom Egoyan and Abbas Kiarostami were held by New Horizons as early as 1992, before these film-makers had been celebrated at Cannes.

New Horizons also organised special tributes to Hal Hartley in 1993, Michael Haneke and Charles Burnett in 1994, Sergei Bodrov and Jan Sverak in 1996, Friðrik Thór Friðriksson, Errol Morris, Tony Gatlif, Tsai Ming-liang and Aleksandr Sokurov in 1997, and Ventura Pons, Marcel Gisler and François Ozon in 1998. In 1993, the main event of the Festival was the David Cronenberg retrospective, along with the European premiere of an exhibition, "The Strange Objects of David Cronenberg's Desire".

New Horizons also presents selections of films which are representative of new trends in film-making in various countries, for example "New Russian Cinema", "Treasures of Iranian Cinema" and "American Independents". Finally, New Horizons has established a series of especially popular midnight screenings of controversial films: classic cult movies such as Andy Warhol's *Lonesome Cowboys*, David Lynch's *Eraserhead*, or Jim Sherman's *The Rocky Horror Picture Show*, as well as more recent productions, Paul Thomas Anderson's *Boogie Nights* and Anna Kokkinos' *Only the Brave*.

A Balkan meeting point

"In Thessaloniki, I had the feeling that the situation for cinema in the Balkans is getting better and better."
– Lucian Pintilie

Its geographical position at the centre of Northern Greece and at the base of the Balkan peninsula, makes Thessaloniki the ideal location for Balkan countries to meet and present their new films. That is why the Balkan Survey section, which began in 1994, immediately met with an enthusiastic response among all Balkan countries, while at the same time being especially appreciated by the Festival's western guests, who were given a rare opportunity to experience another side of the Balkans, beyond that which is presented by the western press.

As early as 1995, the festival administration won an honorable mention by the

Bernardo Bertolucci's press conference during the retrospective of his work in 1996   *photo: Rassias*

FIPRESCI committee for the selection and presentation of this program. Each year, the Balkan Survey presents a selection of new films from all over the Balkans (Albania, Bosnia, Bulgaria, Yugoslavia, Croatia, Romania, Slovenia, Turkey and Macedonia), from directors such as Goran Marković, Milco Manchevski, Erden Kiral, Peter Popzlatev, Vinko Bresan, Metod Pevec, Krassimir Kroumov, Mircea Daneliuc, Vladimir Prifti and Kutlug Ataman.

There have also been tributes to the work of Omer Kavur, Zivojin Pavlović and Eduard Zahariev, as well as a complete retrospective of the films of Lucian Pintilie. In 1997, a memorable section of the Balkan Survey, entitled "Times of Turmoil", presented films dealing with the dramatic events that had recently shaken the Balkans.

Easterly wind

"I think this festival will become increasingly important as a film centre between East and West."
– Nagisa Oshima

Foreseeing very early on that Asian cinema was becoming a dynamic new force, Michel Demopoulos scoured the depths of this huge market for films to participate in the festival's international competition. The response of the international jury members to these films encouraged him to continue this search, thus enriching the festival's program with a new section, Asian Vision, which began in 1998.

All-time classics

"Thessaloniki promises friends of the cinema a real celebration. The festival, directed exceptionally by Michel Demopoulos, offers, beyond the selection of new films from all over the world, a wide choice of retrospectives and special tributes."   – *Cahiers du Cinéma*

Thessaloniki has successfully organised comprehensive retrospectives of the work of many eminent film-makers. John Cassavetes, Jules Dassin, David Cronenberg, Nagisa Oshima, Kryzsztof Kieślowski, Nanni Moretti, Bernardo Bertolucci, Lucian Pintilie, Claude Chabrol, Arturo Ripstein, Ken Loach, Jean-Daniel Pollet, and Greek directors Yorgos Tzavellas, Tonia Marketaki, Michael Cacoyannis, Frida Liappa, Grigoris Grigiriou, Takis Canellopoulos and Nikos Koundouros have all been honoured with retrospectives.

Dassin, Oshima, Moretti, Bertolucci, Pintilie, Chabrol, Loach, Cacoyannis and

Samira Makhmalbaf at a press conference at the 1998 event   *photo: Rassias*

Nagisa Oshima and Theo Angelopoulos at a dinner during the 38th Thessaloniki Int'l Film Festival

Dean Tavoularis holding the honorary Alexander that was awarded to him and Aurore Clément, both members of the international jury at the 38th Thessaloniki Int'l Film Festival   *photo: Rassias*

Otar Iosseliani introducing his film to the Thessaloniki audience in 1996

Wang Xiaoshuai, winner of the Golden Alexander in 1994

Koundouros came to the festival, introducing their films and talking with audiences and the media. Smaller tributes, with the screening of selected films, have been held for Manoel de Oliveira, Akira Kurosawa, Peter Greenaway and Greek actress Irene Papas. Many restored versions of classic films have also been screened at Thessaloniki, including Orson Welles' *Don Quixote* and *Touch of Evil*, Jean Renoir's *Le carrosse d'or* and, to the accompaniment of live music, silent films such as Giovanni Pastrone's *Cabiria*, Fritz Lang's *Metropolis* and Georg Wilhelm Pabst's *Mademoiselle Docteur*.

Not just films

"The Thessaloniki International Film Festival has developed into an exceptionally enriching event."   – *Allgemeine Zeitung*

Apart from film screenings, the festival each year organises events that connect cinema to other art forms: painting, music, theatre and photography. Recent years have seen concerts by Michael Nyman,

István Szabó, president of the international jury, presents We Nien-jen with the Silver Alexander in 1994

Manoel de Oliveira, Irene Papas and festival director Michel Demopoulos at the 38th Thessaloniki Int'l Film Festival
photo: Rassias

Audiences awaiting the start of a show at the 35th Thessaloniki Int'l Film Festival in 1994

Ingrid Caven, Gato Barbieri and Zbigniew Preisner, as well as exhibitions featuring works by famous directors: paintings and collages by Sergei Paradjanov, drawings and objects by Sergei Eisenstein, paintings by Peter Greenaway, and the photography of Abbas Kiarostami.

Especially memorable were the 1993 exhibition, "David Cronenberg's Strange Objects of Desire" (featuring objects made for his films *The Fly, Naked Lunch, Shivers, Dead Ringers, Scanners* and *Videodrome*); 1994's video installation by Nam Jun Paik; the 1995 exhibition of photographs by Josef Koudelka, taken during the filming of Angelopoulos' *Ulysses' Gaze*; and, in 1998, the presentation of Peter Greenaway's prop-opera, *100 Objects That Represent the World*.

Looking ahead

The aim of the festival, according to Michel Demopoulos, is to constitute a pole of resistance to the conformity that dominates the cultural scene; to promote a brave, and forward-looking concept of cinema as a multifarious art; and to cut inroads of free,

alternative expression into the monopoly of thought which has spread through powerful channels into the area of cinema.

Indeed, the Thessaloniki Festival believes that it has achieved this aim, and is determined to continue on a course that leads to new forms of expression and innovative approaches; for these are the only means of providing answers to the questions posed by the cultural and social changes taking place in the world.

Ken Loach during a retrospective of his work in 1998
photo: Rassias

Guide to Leading Festivals

Adriaticocinema

June 2000

Third edition of the first festival which involves three seaside resorts of the Adriatic coast: Bellaria Igea Marina, Cattolica and Rimini, known for their formerly individual film festivals (Mystfest, Riminicinema and Anteprima). Adriaticocinema combines research, experimental and independent cinema with entertainment. It includes films, conferences, awards, meetings and debates with film-makers and actors in the native region of Federico Fellini. There are special competitions for Italian independents and international film schools, a prize for the best international first feature film of the season, as well as an international preview section and retrospectives. Organising director: Gianfranco Miro Gori. *Inquiries to:* Adriaticocinema, Via Gambalunga 27, 47900 Rimini, Italy. Tel: (39 05) 412 6399/2627. Fax: (39 05) 412 4227. e-mail: adriaticocinema@comune.rimini.it

Amiens

November 10–17, 2000

A competitive festival in northern France for both shorts and features. There are also retrospectives, as well as a "Cinémas du Monde" series, which includes works from Africa, Latin America and Asia. *Inquiries to:* Amiens International Film Festival, MCA, Place Léon Gontier, 80000 Amiens, France. Tel: (33 3) 2271 3570. Fax: (33 3) 2292 5304. e-mail: amiensfilmfestival@burotec.fr

Austin Film Festival

October 2000

The original film festival dedicated to recognising the screenwriter's contribution to the motion picture and television

Comuni di
Bellaria Igea Marina,
Cattolica, Rimini

Regione Emilia Romagna
assessorato alla cultura
assessorato al turismo

Ministero per i Beni e le Attività Culturali
Dipartimento dello Spettacolo

Provincia di Rimini

Commissione europea
Programma MEDIA II

adriaticocinema
festival di Bellaria Igea Marina, Cattolica, Rimini

COLPO D'OCCHIO 7/99

June 2000

Italian independent film competition
Film school competition
International previews
Retrospectives
Federico Fellini Award
'Gran Giallo città di Cattolica' Award
Meetings, seminars, debates

Adriaticocinema
via Gambalunga, 27
47900 Rimini (Italia)
tel. 0541-22627-52038-26399
fax 0541-24227
E-mail:
adriaticocinema@comune.rimini.it

tel: +47 55 32 25 90 , fax: +47 55 32 37 40 , e-mail: biff@bgnett.no
bergen international film festival, georgernes verft 3, n-5011 bergen, norway

industry. As such, Austin holds the Heart of Film Screenplay Competition, the four-day Heart of Film Screenwriter's Conference, which features more than 40 panels on the art, craft, and business of screen writing conducted by over 80 industry professionals. The festival lasts one week and includes a competition for Best Narrative Film, Best Feature, Best Short, Best Student Short Film. *Inquiries to:* Austin Film Festival, 1604 Nueces, Austin, TX 78701, USA. Tel: (1 512) 478 4795. Fax: (1 512) 478 6205.

Bergen

October 20–27, 2000

Norway's beautiful capital of the fjords is launching an annual film festival to coincide with Bergen's EU appointment as one of the "European Culture Cities". There will be a main programme, and sidebars, focusing on arthouse films and new media. There will be a Jury Prize and an Audience Award. *Inquiries to*: Bergen Int'l Film Festival, Georgernes verft 3, N-5011 Bergen, Norway. Tel: (47 55) 32 25 90. Fax: (47 55) 32 37 40. e-mail tiff@bgnett.no.

**20ᵗʰ Amiens
International Film
Festival**

*November, 10ᵗʰ-17ᵗʰ
2000*

*Information/
accreditation form:*
Tel: +33 3 22 71 35 70
Fax: +33 3 22 92 53 04
e-mail: amiensfilmfestival @ burotec.fr

Berlin

February 10–21, 2000

Approaching its Golden Jubilee, and moving to the spectacularly modernistic Potsdamerplatz, Berlin is generally accepted to be the most efficiently-organised of the world's festivals, although arrangements should be made as far in advance as possible. In addition to the competitive programme (with its Golden Bears and Silver Bears dispensed by an international jury) and information section, there is a retrospective as well as screenings of all new German films, and the Forum of Young Cinema, directed by Ulrich Gregor, where many of the most imaginative films are screened. Festival Director: Moritz de Hadeln. *Inquiries to:* Berlin International Film Festival, Potsdamer straße 5, D-10785 Berlin, Germany. Tel: (49 30) 2592 0202. Fax: (49 30) 2592 0299. Telex: 185255. e-mail: info@ berlinale.de. Website: www.berlinale.de.

AWARDS 1999
Golden Bear: **The Thin Red Line** (USA), Malick.
Jury Grand Prix: **Mifunes sidste sang - Dogme 3** (Denmark), Kragh-Jacobsen.
Best Director: Stephen Frears for **The Hi-Lo Country** (USA).
Best Actor: Michael Gwisdek for **Nachtgestalten.**
Best Actress: Juliane Köhler and Maria Schrader for **Aimée & Jaguar** (Germany).
Best Short: **Faraon (Pharaoh)** by Sergej Ovtscharov & **Masks** by Piotr Karwas.

Brisbane

July–August, 2000

Now in its ninth year, Brisbane screens shorts, fiction features and documentaries on film and video. There is also the Chauvel Award for a distinguished contribution to Australian feature film-making, retrospectives, and an Asia Pacific Focus. *Inquiries to:* Brisbane International Film Festival, P.O. Box 94, Brisbane Albert St., Queensland 4002, Australia. Tel: (61 7) 3224 4114. Fax: (61 7) 3224 6717. e-mail: pftc@pftc.com.au. Website: www.pftc.com.au.

Cannes

May 10–21, 2000

Cannes remains the world's top festival, attracting key American independents and personalities, as well as entries from other countries. Cannes includes two official sections: the Competition and "Un Certain Regard." There are also the Directors' Fortnight screenings, as well as the much-improved Marché (MIF) with its extended new facilities in 2000, the Critics' Week, and innumerable other useful screenings (e.g. the Australian, New Zealand, and Scandinavian films). The great advantage of Cannes is that everyone of importance attends the event. *Inquiries to:* Festival International du Film, 99 boulevard Malesherbes, 75008 Paris, France. Tel: (33 1) 4561 6600. Fax: (33 1) 4561 9760. Website: www.cannes-fest.com.

AWARDS 1999
Palme d'Or: **Rosetta** (Belgium), Dardenne.
Grand Prix: **L'Humanité** (France), Dumont.
Best Actor: Emmanuel Schotté for **L'Humanité**.
Best Actress: Séverine Caneele for **L'Humanité** and Emilie Dequenne for **Rosetta**.
Best Direction: Pedro Almodóvar for **Todo sobre mi madre** (Spain).
Best Screenplay: Youri Arabov for **Moloch** (Russia).
Jury Prize: Manoel de Oliveira.
Technical Prize: Tu Juhua for **The Emperor and the Assassin** (China).
Caméra d'Or: **Marana Simhasanam** by Murali Nair.

Cartagena

March 3–10, 2000

Ibero-Latin American films with features, shorts, docus and a TV and video market. Inquires to: Cartagena Film Festival, Baluarte de San Francisco, Calle San Juan de Dios, A.A. 1834, Cartagena, Colombia. Tel: (57 5) 660 0966. Fax: (57 5) 660 0970, 660 1037.

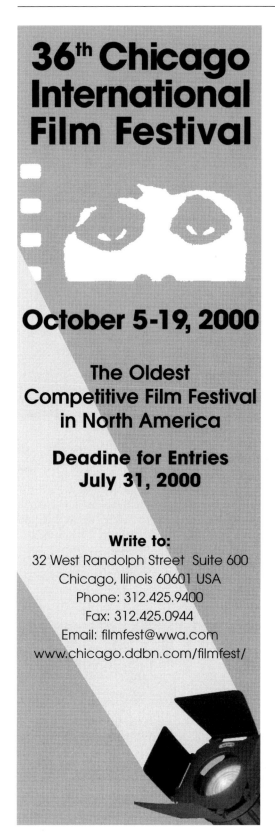

36ᵗʰ Chicago International Film Festival

October 5-19, 2000

The Oldest Competitive Film Festival in North America

Deadine for Entries July 31, 2000

Write to:
32 West Randolph Street Suite 600
Chicago, Ilinois 60601 USA
Phone: 312.425.9400
Fax: 312.425.0944
Email: filmfest@wwa.com
www.chicago.ddbn.com/filmfest/

Ada Choi attending the 1999 Centro Espressioni Cinematografiche

Centro Espressioni Cinematografiche

April 8–15, 2000

The second edition of "Far East Film" (Udineincontri XIII), held in the Teatro Nuovo cultural centre of Udine, north-eastern Italy, will continue to dwell on the best of popular cinema from across the Orient. This coming year's programme will also embrace Japan and other countries from Southeast Asia. Personal tributes, archive restorations, and genre surveys are included. *Inquiries to:* Centro Espressioni Cinematografiche, Via Villalta 24, 33100 Udine, Italy. Tel: (39 04) 3229 9545. Fax: (39 04) 3222 9825. E-mail: cecudine@tin.it. Website: www.udineincontri.it.

Chicago

October 5–19, 2000

Now in its fourth decade, the Chicago International Film Festival is the oldest competitive event in North America. It spotlights the latest work by established international directors as well as seeking out works by new directors. The festival bestows its highest honour, the Gold Hugo, on the best feature film in its International Competition, with separate prizes for documentaries, student films, and shorts. Chicago is the only US site to award the FIPRESCI prize for first and second time directors, judged by a jury of top international film critics. *Inquiries to:* Michael Kutza (founder & artistic director) Chicago International Film Festival, 32 W. Randolph St., Suite 600, Chicago, IL 60601,

Michael Douglas receives the Chicago Festival's Lifetime Achievement Award from founder and artistic director Michael Kutza

USA. Tel: (1 312) 425 9400. Fax: (1 312) 425 0944. e-mail: filmfest@wwa.com. Website: www.chicago.ddbn.com/filmfest/

AWARDS 1998

Gold Hugo: **The Hole** (Taiwan) Tsai Ming-Liang.
Special Jury Prize: **Wind with the Gone** (Argentina), Agresti.
FIPRESCI prize: **The Outskirts** (Russia), Lutzik.
Best Actress: Alessandra Martines for **Chances or Coincidences** (France).
Best Actor: The ensemble in **Friendly Fire** (Brazil).
Best Documentary: **Angel on My Shoulder** by Donna Deitch (US).
Best Short Narratives: **Little Sisters** (Scotland), Goddard and **Lovely** (Scotland), Drysdale.

Cinéma Tout Ecran

September 18–24, 2000

The first and, until recently, the only festival to devote its programme to films of artistic quality produced by television. The main criteria for selection are the film-maker's distinct view of the world and his story-telling style. Highlights of the festival include the International Competition (three major prizes), New TV Series, Retrospective, Thematic Night, an international selection of shorts, and professional seminars. *Inquiries to:* Cinéma Tout Ecran, Maison des Arts du Grütli, 16 rue du Général-Dufour, CP 5305, CH-1211 Geneva 11, Switzerland. Tel: (41 22) 328 8554. Fax: (41 22) 329 6802. e-mail: info@cinema-tout-ecran.ch Website: www. cinema-tout-ecran.ch

Clermont-Ferrand

February 4–12, 2000

Every year the Clermont-Ferrand Short Film Festival offers an international competition (with 44 countries represented in 1999), a national competition alongside additional programmes. Altogether over 350, mainly fiction but also animation, documentary and experimental short films are offered to large and enthusiastic public, who totalled over 122,000 in 1999. *Inquiries to:* Clermont-Ferrand Short Film Festival, 26 rue des Jacobins, 63000 Clermont-Ferrand, France. Tel: (33 4) 7391 6573. Fax: (33 4) 7392 1193. e-mail: festival@gdebussac.fr Website: www.shortfilm.gdebussac.fr

MAIN AWARDS 1999

International Festival:
Grand Prix: **Motifs (Patterns)** (Ireland), Sheridan.
Prix spécial du jury: **La vie dans le brouillard (Life in Fog)** (Iran), Ghobadi.
Prix Recherche: **Phil Touches Flo** (US), Birdsell.
Prix du Public: **En el espejo del cielo** (Mexico), Salces.
National Festival:
Grand Prix (ex aequo): **Un beau jour sans conséquence**, Bouhnik (best director award) and **Aïd el kebir**, Albou (best screenplay award).
Prix spécial du jury: **Des heures sans sommeil**, Meier.

5th International Film and Television Festival

cinéma tout écran

Geneva, 20 - 26 September•'99

Cinéma tout écran is the first International Film Festival to dedicate its program to «films d'auteur» produced by/for television

Cinéma tout écran Case postale 5305
CH-1211 Geneva 11 Switzerland
Phone +4122 328 85 54
Fax +4122 329 68 02
info@cinema-tout-ecran.ch

23rd Denver International Film Festival

OCTOBER 12-19, 2000

Inquiries to:

Denver International Film Festival   Phone   303.595.3456
1430 Larimer Square, Suite 201   Fax   303.595.0956
Denver, Colorado 80202 U.S.A.   e-mail   dfs@denverfilm.org

www.denverfilm.org

DENVER FILM SOCIETY

Jane Horrocks at the 1998 Denver Int'l Film Festival
photo: Larry Laszlo

Denver

October 2000

The Denver International Film Festival, an invitational exposition of film, presents approximately 150 films over eight days and plays host to more than 60 film artists. New international feature releases, cutting-edge independently-produced fiction films and documentaries, animation, experimental works, children's programmes and short subjects are included in the festival. In addition, a number of acclaimed international film artists are honoured with tributes. The festival presents a Lifetime Achievement Award, the John Cassavetes Award, the Krzysztof Kieślowski Award for Best European Film, the Starz! Cinema Award to the best independent film without US distribution and the Encore People's Choice Award for the most popular feature-length fiction film and feature-length documentary. Entry fee: $30 ($20 for students). The Denver Film Society also produces the Aurora Asian Film Festival in June and the Denver Jewish

Film Festival in August. *Inquiries to:* Denver Film Society, 1430 Larimer Square, Ste. 201, Denver, Colorado 80202 USA. Tel: (1 303) 595 2345. Fax: (1 303) 595 0956. e-mail: dfs@denverfilm.org. Website: www. denverfilm.org

Edinburgh

August 13–27, 2000

The oldest continually-running film festival in the world, Edinburgh is also one of the most accessible. Emphasis on new films, innovation and excellence in film-making world-wide, UK films and young directors, with retrospectives and seminars particularly well-chosen by Lizzie Francke. There's an offbeat sparkle to the Edinburgh mix of local audiences. The event also features the New British Expo, a unique showcase of British film production. Now aided by Film Four as a major sponsor. Inquiries: Edinburgh International Film Festival, 88 Lothian Road, Eduinburgh EH3 9BZ, Scotland. Tel: (44 131) 228 4051. Fax: (44 131) 229 5501. e-mail: info@edfilmfest.aug.uk. Website: www.edfilmfest.aug.uk.

Espoo Ciné

August 22–27, 2000

Espoo Ciné has established itself as *the* annual showcase of contemporary European – primarily long feature – cinema in Finland. Whereas the traditional section will appeal to every movie buff in Finland, the ever-growing fantasy film selection will attract everyone hungry for stimulation of the imagination. Espoo Ciné is a member of the European Fantasy Film Festivals' Federation and organises every year a Méliès d'Argent fantasy film competition. And the listing of other treats goes on and on: US indies as well as new highlights from other continents, the best of the contemporary Finnish cinema, outdoor screenings, retrospectives, sneak previews, seminars, film-maker guests of honour. *Inquiries to:* Espoo Ciné. P.O. Box 95, FIN-02101 Espoo, Finland. Tel: (358 9) 466 599. Fax: (358 9) 466 458. e-mail: espoocine@cultnet.fi. Website: www. espoo.fi/cine.

Fajr International Film Festival

February 1–11, 2000

The Festival has flourished as a competitive event and aims to provide a bridge between Eastern and Western cinemas. Fajr focuses mainly on Iranian films but, since 1998, has incorporated an international competition section. *Inquiries to:* Fajr International Film Festival, Farhang Cinema, Dr. Shariati Ave., Gholhak, Tehran 19139, Iran. Tel: (98 21) 200 2088-90. Fax: (98 21) 267 082.

AWARDS 1999
Best Film: **The Color of God** (Iran), Majidi.
Best Director: Ebrahim Hatamikia for **The Red Ribbon** (Iran).
Best Actress: Azita Hajian for **The Red Ribbon** (Iran).
Best Screenplay: Feng Xiaoning for **The Red River Valley** (China).
Special Jury Prize: **The Perfect Circle** (Bosnia/France), Kenović.

21th FESTIVAL DES 3 CONTINENTS

NANTES - November 23 - 30 th, 1999

70 feature-length fiction films from Africa, Latin & Black America and Asia in competitive and non competitive sections

Tel: (33) 2 40 69 74 14 - Fax: (33) 2 40 73 55 22
e-mail: f3c@franceplus.com

Fantasporto

February 25–March 4, 2000

The Oporto International Film Festival, now going into its 20th edition, specialises in fantasy and science-fiction films in its Official Competitive section. This festival also includes the 10th New Directors Week with an official competition, a Fantasia section dedicated to Eastern films and a Retrospective section. The Festival director, Mario Dorminsky, is preparing, with the help of the Portuguese Film Institute, a programme on Portuguese cinema for the benefit of the foreign guests. The Festival runs now in 8 theatres (2,700 seats altogether) and screens nearly 300 feature films each year. The leading Portuguese newspapers, radio stations and television networks all cover the Festival. Attendance hovers around the 100,000 mark. *Inquiries to:* Fantasporto/Oporto International Film Festival, Multimédia Center Vinema Novo, Rua da Constituição, 311 4200 Porto, Portugal. Tel: (351 2) 507 3880. Fax: (351 2) 550 8210. e-mail: fantas@caleida.pt.Website: www.caleida.pt/fantasporto.

Melvin van Peebles and Jia Zhang-ke attending the Festival des 3 Continents

AWARDS 1999
Best Film: **Cube** (Canada), Vincenzo Natali.
Best Director: Lars Von Trier for **The Kingdom 2** (Denmark).
Best Actor: Kevin McKidd & Gary McCormack for the **Acid House** (UK).
Best Actress: Sofie Gråbøl for **Credo** (Denmark).
Best Screenplay: Lars Von Trier & Niels Vorsel for **The Kingdom 2** (Denmark).
Best Special Effects: Bob Munroe & John Mariella for **Cube** (Canada).
Best Short: **Trigon** (Germany), Niklas Roy.

Festival Des 3 Continents

November 22–29, 2000

The only annual competitive festival in the world for films originating solely from Africa, Asia and Latin and Black America. The aim of the 22-year-old festival is to present the cultural values of these groups in a non-paternalistic and objective way. One of the few festivals where genuine discoveries may still be made. *Inquiries to:* Alain and Philippe Jalladeau, Directors, Festival des 3 Continents, B.P. 43302, 44033 Nantes Cedex 1, France. Tel: (33 2) 4069 7414. Fax: (33 2) 4073 5522.

Filmski Festival Ljubljana

November 6–9, 1999

A Slovenian event that concentrates on retrospectives (Kiarostami in 1998, for example), offering world premieres of Slovenian films, and presenting independent productions by highly creative and promising directors. The winner in this latter section receives the Kingfisher Award (10,000 DEM), and there are also documentaries and a round-up of the cream of other festivals. *Inquiries to:* Cankarjev Dom, Prešernova 10, 1000 Ljubljana, Slovenia. Tel: (386 61) 176 7150. Fax: (386 61) 22 42 79. E-mail:jelka.stergel@cd-cc.si

Peter Weir receiving the Douglas Sirk Award at FilmFest Hamburg, flanked by the Mayor of Hamburg, Ortwin Runde, and the festival director, Josef Wutz   *photo: Baernd Fraatz*

Filmfest Hamburg

September 25–October 1, 2000

This competitive event is held every year around the last weekend of September, and attracts more than 30,000 spectators. The varied programme of some 80 to 100 titles previews some Hollywood productions but focuses primarily on indie pictures from all over the world. The Douglas Sirk Prize is awarded by the Filmfest and the City of Hamburg to a major personality each year (Peter Weir in 1998). Especially good as a launch-pad for offbeat films. *Inquiries to*: Filmfest Hamburg, Postfach 500 480, 22704 Hamburg, Germany. Tel: (49 40) 399 19 00 0. Fax: (49 40) 399 19 00 10. E-mail: filmfest-hamburg@t-online.de. Website: www.filmfesthamburg.de

Flanders International Film Festival (Ghent)

October 10–21, 2000

Belgium's most prominent yearly film event, which celebrated its Silver Jubilee in 1998 and attracts an annual attendance of over 70,000, with the prime focus on "The Impact of Music on Films". The competitive Ghent Festival awards grants up to $130,000 and screens around 150 features and 80 shorts, most without a Belgium distributor. Outside the competitive section, screenings include Country Focus, a Film Spectrum of international titles receiving their world, European or Benelux premieres as well as a tribute to an important film-maker. Deadline for entry forms: August 10. *Inquiries to:* Flanders International Film Festival-Ghent, 1104 Kortrijksesteenweg, B-9051 Ghent, Belgium. Tel: (32 9) 221 8946, 242 8060. Fax: (32 9) 221 9074. e-mail: info@filmfestival.be Website: www.filmfestival.be.

AWARDS 1998

Best film: **Die Siebtelbauern** (Austria), Ruzowitzky.
Best director: **Rosie** (Belgium), Toye.
Best composer of music: **Claire Dolan** (France/UK), music by Simon Fisher Turner and Ahnin Mishan.

Fort Lauderdale

October 20–November 14, 2000

Screens more than 100 films from around the world, including features, documentaries, shorts and student films. The festival will present Lifetime Achievement Awards to outstanding industry leaders in the fields of acting, directing, producing, writing and composing. The popular event (65,000 admissions in 1998) also offers a film competition with cash prizes and a host of gala events on the beaches and waterways of South Florida. *Inquiries to:* The Fort Lauderdale International Film Festival, 1402 East Las Olas Blvd., Fort Lauderdale, FL 33301, USA. Tel: (1 954) 760 9898. Fax: (1 954) 760 9099. e-mail: brofilm@aol.com. Website: www.ftlaudfilmfest.com.

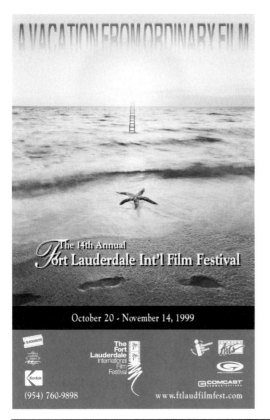

Large audience at the Ljubljana Film Art Festival

Andrzej Wajda at the Polish Cultural Institute in Berlin after receiving the American Cinema Foundation's Freedom Award

AWARDS 1998
Best Film: **The General** (Ireland).
Best Foreign Film: **The Inheritors** (Germany).
Best Director: John Boorman for **The General** (Ireland).
Best Actor: Roberto Benigni for **La Vita e bella** (Italy).
Best Actress: Birgit Doll for **Suzie Washington.** (Austria) and Fernanda Montenegro for **Central Station** (Brazil).

Freedom Film Festival
February 24–March 2, 2000

Founded in 1997 by the American Cinema Foundation, this showcase of films from Eastern and Central Europe is dedicated to bringing light to Eastern Europe's history and creating opportunities for its film-makers. Films screened represent the cutting edge of the struggle for many kinds of freedom: personal, political, economic and artistic. The festival is held at the time of the AFM in L.A., and reprised overseas, participating at Karlovy Vary, Moscow, and Baku. *Inquiries to:* American Cinema Foundation, 9911 W. Pico Blvd., Suite 510, Los Angeles, CA 90035, USA. Tel: (1 310) 286 9420. Fax: (1 310) 286 7914. E-mail: acinema@cinemafoundation.com. Website: www.cinemafoundation.com

FREEDOM FILM FESTIVAL 2000
BERLIN LOS ANGELES KARLOVY VARY MOSCOW BAKU

FILMS FROM EASTERN EUROPE AND CIS COUNTRIES
THEMES: FREEDOM AND LIVING HISTORY
PRESENTED AND CURATED BY THE AMERICAN CINEMA FOUNDATION

A showcase of new and classic films from Eastern Europe and the CIS countries which contribute to our understanding of political freedom, memorialize the victims of tyranny, and celebrate the priceless gift of a free and pluralistic culture. This initiative supports and promotes a film culture of enduring, humanistic values.

In Berlin in February: gala presentation of the Andrzej Wajda/Philip Morris Freedom Prize to a filmmaker at the height of their powers. Screenings of new films and retrospectives from the Stalinist era to the present.

In Los Angeles in February/March: the third Freedom Film Festival is Hollywood's annual remembrance of the human rights abuses caused by decades of Communist rule in Europe, reminding our own filmmakers that from time to time history will make profound and unexpected demands on their courage.

At the Karlovy Vary International Film Festival in July: the jury convenes to select the winner of the 2001 Andrzej Wajda/Philip Morris Freedom Prize, and the ACF celebrates the "East Of The West" section of the festival, which presents films from Eastern Europe and beyond.

At the Moscow International Film Festival in July: the ACF supports the Cinema Forum Of The CIS and Baltic Countries.

At the Baku Film Festival in October: the Freedom Film Festival presents new films from Eastern Europe at one of the leading festivals in Central Asia.

Fribourg

March 12–19, 2000

Features, shorts, and documentaries from Asia, Africa, and Latin America unspool at this Swiss springtime event. There is a competitive section. *Inquiries to*: Fribourg International Film Festival, Rue de Locarno 8, 1700 Fribourg, Switzerland. Tel: (41 26) 322 2232. Fax: (41 26) 322 7950. E-mail: info@fiff.ch.

Geneva Film Festival

October 2000

Annual event that aims to introduce "Stars of Tomorrow" – actors known in their own country but not yet on a global scale. There is a lively competitive section and numerous guest appearances, tributes and seminars. In the past decade, at least four films starring winners of the main Geneva prize have gone on to triumph at the Academy Awards. *Inquiries to:* Festival du film de Genève, 35 rue des Bains, C.P. 5615, CH-1211 Genève, Switzerland. Tel: (41 22) 809 9450. Fax: (41 22) 809 9444. e-mail: info@festival-ffg.ch Website: www.festival-ffg.ch.

Gijón International Film Festival

November 2000

With a calling card of "the best young cinema worldwide," the 38-year-old Gijón Festival has become a springboard for edgy, independent, and first-time directors. Set in lovely northern Spain, Gijón features an official competition section and is probably one of Spain's top five festivals. Festival Director: José Luis Cienfuegos. *Inquiries to:* Gijón International Film Festival, Paseo de Begona, 24-entlo., P.O. Box 76, 33205 Gijón, Spain. Tel: (34 98) 534 3739. Fax: (34 98) 535 4152. e-mail: festcine@las.es Website: www.las.es/gijonfilmfestival/

Göteborg

January 28–February 6, 2000

Now in its 23rd year, Göteborg has established itself as among the best film festivals in Norden and as one of the key events in Europe, with an attendance of almost 105,000 enthusiastic spectators always ready to give spontaneous applause. Hotels and cinemas are conveniently close to one another. Swedish TV broadcasts live from the festival and selects a couple of films to screen each year. *Inquiries to:* Göteborg Film Festival, PO Box

Barry Adamson, Matthew Harrison and Fele Martinez, three of the jury members at Gijón in 1998

7079, S-402 32 Göteborg, Sweden. Tel: (46 31) 410 546. Fax: (46 31) 410 063. e-mail: goteborg@filmfestival.org. Website: www. goteborg.filmfestival.org.

Haugesund-Norwegian International Film Festival

August 27–September 3, 2000

Held in the west coast region of Haugesund every summer, the Norwegian International Film Festival has become one of the country's major film events, attended by many international visitors and over 1,000 representatives from the Norwegian and Scandinavian film world. Award-winning films receive "Amanda Statuettes," and the "New Nordic Film" market runs parallel to the Festival. Festival Director: Gunnar Johan Løvvik. Programme Director: Christin Berg. Honorary President: Liv Ullmann. *Inquiries to:* P.O. Box 145, N-5501 Haugesund, Norway. Tel: (47 52) 734 430. Fax: (47 52) 734 420. e-mail: imfpo@filmfestivalen.no. Website: www.filmfestivalen.no.

Helsinki Film Festival – Love & Anarchy

September 2000

An important film festival in Finland, now in its 12th year. Helsinki promotes international and daring quality film-making to Finnish audiences and distributors. True to its subtitle, "Love and Anarchy," the event uncompromisingly challenges limits of cinematic expression and experience alike. Non-competitive. *Inquiries to:* Helsinki Film Festival, PO Box 889, FIN-00101 Helsinki,

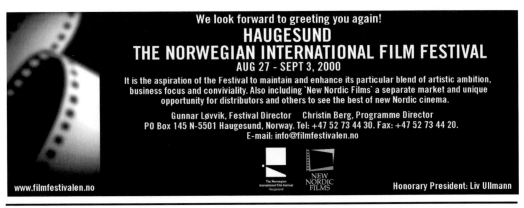

Opening reception at the 23rd Hong Kong Int'l Film Festival

Finland. Tel: (358 9) 684 35230. Fax: (358 9) 684 35232. e-mail: lanerva@hiff.fi. Website: http://love-and-anarchy.cultnet.fi.

Hong Kong

April 12–17, 2000

Regularly includes a selection of Asian product and a Hong Kong Cinema Retrospective among 200 films and videos shown at various venues. The festival has been recognised as a valuable showcase of Asian works that allows the West to discover the riches of Chinese cinema. *Inquiries to:* Senior Manager, Festivals Office, Urban Services Department, Level 7, Administration Building, Hong Kong Cultural Centre, 10 Salisbury Road, Tsimshatsui, Kowloon, Hong Kong. Tel: (852) 2734 2903. Fax: (852) 2366 5206.

Huelva

November 2000

The main objective of Huelva's Iberoamerican Film Festival (Spain) is to show and promote films of artistic quality which contribute to the best knowledge of the cinematography produced in the Iberoamerican area, including the USA, as far as Latin film-maker's productions are concerned. It has become one of the world's key rendezvous for anyone connected with Latin American movies. It enables European buyers and film buffs to catch the latest developments from across the Atlantic. e-mail: festihuelva@ayuntamientohuelva.es Website: www.festihuelva.otd.es

The 24th Hong Kong International Film Festival
12~27. 4. 2000

A FIPRESCI Award for Young Asian Cinema has been installed for the event

For information, please contact:
Senior Manager,
Hong Kong International Film Festival,
Level 7, Hong Kong Cultural Centre Administration Bldg.,
Hong Kong SAR, China.
Tel: (852) 2734 2903   Fax: (852) 2366 5206
E-mail: hkiff@hkiff.com.hk   Web site: www.hkiff.org.hk

Presented by
the Provisional Urban Council
of Hong Kong

AWARDS 1998
Jury's Colón de Oro: **Traiçao** (Brasil), Fontes, Torres, Fonseca.
Public's Colón de Oro: **Coraje** (Peru), Durant.

Independent Feature Film Market

September, 2000

The Independent Feature Film Market (IFFM) is the original and longest-running market devoted to new, emerging American independent film talent. Since 1979, the IFFM has presented the industry with its first look at such landmark films as: *American Dream, Blood Simple, The Brothers McMullen, Clerks, Dancemaker, Daughters of the Dust, Poison, Roger & Me, Stranger Than Paradise, Welcome to the Dollhouse,* and many others. The IFFM screens nearly 300 film projects, including Works-in-Progress, and presents over 100 copyrighted feature-length scripts. Deadline: mid-May. *Inquiries to:* Independent Feature Project, 104 West 29th Street, 12th Floor, New York, NY, 10001, USA. Tel: (1 212) 465 8200. Fax: (1 212) 465 8525. Website: www.ifp.org.

India

January 10–20, 2000

Annual, non-competitive event recognised by IFFPA. There is a substantial information section, a new competition for features made by Asian women, a comprehensive "Cinema of the World" section, foreign and Indian retrospectives, and a film market, as well as a valuable panorama of the best Indian films of the year, subtitled in English. Circulates between the major city venues of India, north and south. *Inquiries to:* International Film Festival of India, 4th Floor, Lok Nayak Bhavan, Khan Market, New Delhi 110 003, India. Tel: (91 11) 461 5953, 469 7167. Fax: (91 11) 462 3430.

International Film Festival Mannheim-Heidelberg

October 13–21, 2000

A festival for young independent film-makers from all over the world. The event

Please contact:
Heinz Badewitz, Director
Lothstraße 28
D-80335 München
Tel: +49-89/129 74 22
Fax: +49-89/123 68 68

INTERNATIONAL HOF FILMDAYS

Every Last Week in October

THE HOF SOCCER DREAM TEAM:
① ATOM EGOYAN
② JOHN SAYLES
③ VOLKER SCHLOENDORFF
④ HERBERT ACHTERNBUSCH
⑤ GEORGE A. ROMERO
⑥ TERENCE DAVIES
⑦ ROBERTO BENIGNI
⑧ VINCENT WARD
⑨ DAVID CRONENBERG
⑩ JIM JARMUSCH
⑪ JOHN CARPENTER
⑫ ROGER CORMAN
⑬ NEIL JORDAN
Ⓐ WERNER HERZOG
Ⓑ WIM WENDERS
Ⓒ PAUL COX
COACH: SAM FULLER

SUBSTITUTES:
MONTE HELLMAN | PAUL BARTEL
MEHDI CHAREF | DETLEV BUCK
DORIS DÖRRIE | ALEX COX
BRIAN DE PALMA | SÖNKE WORTMANN
JOHN WATERS | PERCY ADLON

which gave early recognition to Truffaut, Fassbinder, Kieślowski, Jarmusch, and more recently, Bryan Singer and Thomas Vinterberg, presents features, shorts, and documentaries in competition, with cash prizes of 10,000 DM for the best feature films, 10,000 DM for the best documentary and and 5,000 DM for the best short film. (Deadline for entry: July 25). Films in the Official Programme are also shown in the "New Film Market", reserved for international buyers and distributors. Parallel to the annual event, the "Mannheim Meetings", a market for film projects, takes place. *Inquiries to:* Dr. Michael Koetz, International Filmfestival Mannheim-Heidelberg, Collini-Center, Galerie, D-68161 Mannheim, Germany. Tel: (49 621) 102 943. Fax: (49 621) 291 564. e-mail: ifmh@ mannheim-filmfestival.com. Website: www. mannheim-filmfestival.com.

AWARDS 1998
Best Fiction Film: **Max et Bobo** (Belgium), Fonteyne.
Best Documentary: **Titinaki-Jidai** (Japan), Shigeno.
Best Short: **Troie** (Russia), Berschadeski.
Rainer Werner Fassbinder Prize: **Confessions of a Sexist Pig** (US), Sandy Tung.

Internationale Hofer Filmtage

October 24–29, 2000

Dubbed the "Home of Films" by Wim Wenders, Hof is famous for its thoughtful selection of some 50 features. Founded by the directors of the New German Cinema, Hof enjoys a high reputation among German film-makers and American cult figures like Roger Corman, Monte Hellman, John Sayles, and Henry Jaglom, all of whom have

Hülya Uçansu, festival director, with Jerry Schatzberg at an exhibition of his photographs, held during the Istanbul Festival

attended retrospectives in their honour. Directed by one of the most respected German film enthusiasts, Heinz Badewitz, Hof has enjoyed a rising reputation these past 33 years. A screening in Hof can often result in a distribution deal. *Inquiries to:* Postfach 1146, D-95010 Hof, Germany: or Heinz Badewitz, Lothstr. 30, D-80335 Munich, Germany. Tel: (49 89) 129 7422. Fax: (49 89) 123 6868. e-mail: info@hofer-filmtage.de. Website: www.hofer-filmtage.de

Istanbul

April 15–30, 2000

The only film festival which takes place in a city where two continents meet, the Istanbul International Film Festival, recognised as a specialised competitive event by IFFPA, acts as a valuable showcase for distributors internationally. Attendance reaches 100,000 every year. Now in its 19th edition, this dynamic event focuses on features dealing with the arts (literature, music, cinema, dance, etc.) with other thematic sections such as tributes, selections from World Festivals, "A Country – A Cinema", and a panorama of Turkish cinema. *Inquiries to:* Ms. Hülya Uçansu, Istanbul Kültür ve Sanat Vakfı, Istiklal Cad. Luvr Apt. No. 146, Beyoglu 80070, Istanbul, Turkey. Tel: (90 212) 293 3133/34/35. Fax: (90 212) 249 7771. e-mail: film.fest@istfest-tr.org. Website: www.istfest.org.

Jerusalem International Film Festival

July 6–15, 2000

One of Israel's most prestigious cinematic events, which brings to Jerusalem over 150 films in a wide spectrum of themes and categories: Best of International Cinema, Documentaries, Israeli Cinema, Mediterranean Cinema, Animation, Short Films, American Independents, Avant Garde, New Directors, Jewish Themes, Classics and Restorations and Special Tributes. Prize categories include the Wolgin Awards for Israeli Cinema, Lipper Award for Best Israeli Screenplay, international awards, like the Wim van Leer "In the Spirit of Freedom" for films focusing on human rights, the

Encounters in İstanbul

İSTANBUL FOUNDATION FOR CULTURE AND ARTS

19th INTERNATIONAL İSTANBUL FILM FESTIVAL

FILM

15 - 30 APRIL 2000

Contact: Mrs. Hülya Uçansu, Director
Address: İstiklal Caddesi, 146 Beyoğlu 80070, İstanbul -Turkey
Phone: (90-212) 293 31 33 ext. 20, 21
website: http://www.istfest.org
e-mail: film.fest@istfest-tr.org

Light Project for Maiden's Tower by Maria Wirkkala - 5th International İstanbul Biennial (1997)

Corporate Sponsors

KOÇBANK   BAYTUR İNŞAAT TAAHHÜT A.Ş.   MARMARA İSTANBUL   RENAULT   DHL WORLDWIDE EXPRESS

Mediterranean Cinema Award and the Films on Jewish Themes Award. *Inquiries to:* Jerusalem Film Festival, P.O. Box 8561, Jerusalem 91083. Tel: (972 2) 671 5117. Fax: (972 2) 673 3076. e-mail: festival@jer-cin.org.il. Website: www.jer-cin.org.il.

Karlovy Vary

July 5–15, 2000

The festival in Karlovy Vary is one of the oldest international festivals. The annual programme includes an international

JERUSALEM FILM FESTIVAL

Director: Lia van Leer

July 6-15, 2000

35th Karlovy Vary International Film Festival

The most prestigeous cinema event in the Czech Republic

5th – 15th July 2000

- **Feature Films Competition**
- **Hors Concours Sections**
  Horizons – The Best of Last Seasons
  Another View
  Forum of Independents
  East of the West
- **Czech Cinema**
- **Retrospectives**
- **Special Events**

Contact address: Film Servis Festival Karlovy Vary, Panská 1, 110 00 Praha 1, Czech Republic
Tel: +420 2 24 23 54 12, Fax: +420 2 24 23 34 08, E-mail: foundation@iffkv.cz, Internet: http:www.iffkv.cz

selection of feature films in competition, judged by an international jury which awards the Crystal Globe for best film, best direction, best actor and actress in a leading role and a special jury prize. Particular attention is paid to Czech cinema and films from the countries of the former Communist bloc. The 1999 festival featured US independents, the retrospective Belgian Surrealism and Film, a thematic retrospective of French region films, a representative selection of Canadian animated films, an extensive retrospective of Kazakhstan films, new German films and a tribute to the late Yugoslav director Dušan Vukotić. *Inquiries to:* Karlovy Vary International Film Festival, Panská 1, CZ 11000 Prague 1, Czech Republic. Tel: (420 2) 2423 5412. Fax: (420 2) 2423 3408. e-mail: foundation@iffkv.cz. Website: www.iffkv.cz.

AWARDS 1998
Grand Prix: **Le cœur au poing (Streetheart)** (Canada), Binamé.
Special Prize: **Full Moon** (Russia), Shakhnazarov.
Best Director: Charles Binamé for **Le cœur au poing (Streetheart).**
Best Actress: Julia Stiles for **Wicked** (USA).
Best Actor: Olaf Lubaszenko for **Sekal Has To Die** (Czech Republic/Poland/France/Slovakia).

La Rochelle

June 24–July 4, 2000

Fighting against the inroads of television, that cinematic polymath Jean-Loup Passek builds a bridge between past and future cinema with his popular and distinguished festival held in this French resort (71,000 attendance this summer). The event includes a profusion of new features and thematic programmes, sometimes with magnificent discoveries (the Arne Skouen and Anna Sten retrospectives in 1999, for example). *Inquiries to:* Festival International du Film de La Rochelle, 16 rue Saint Sabin, Paris 75011, France. Tel: (33 1) 4806 1666. Fax: (33 1) 4806 1540.

Leeds International Film Festival

October 2000

An emerging major on the British film festival scene, Leeds IFF is the largest arts event organised by the city of Leeds, the centre of the North of England. Featuring the UK's only competitive section, Leeds IFF

Jean Loup Passek, Norwegian director Arne Skouen, and Godfried Talboom, at the 1999 La Rochelle festival
photo: Régis d'Audeville

XXVIIIe FESTIVAL INTERNATIONAL DU FILM DE LA ROCHELLE

directed by jean-loup passek   **23 JUNE - 3 JULY, 2000**

100 LONG FEATURE FILMS   300 SCREENINGS   NON COMPETITIVE

3 MAIN SECTIONS

● Retrospectives devoted to the work of past filmmakers

● Tributes to contemporary directors, in their presence

● Le Monde Tel Qu'il Est (The World As It Is), a selection of unreleased films from all over the world.

Festival International du Film de la Rochelle
16, rue Saint Sabin, 75011 Paris
Phone: (1) 48 06 16 66 Fax: (1) 48 06 15 40

LEEDS CITY COUNCIL PRESENTS

leeds international
FILM FESTIVAL 2000
T: +44 (0)113 247 8398
E: filmfestival@leeds.gov.uk
W: www.leedsfilm.com

also has unique sidebars including Fenomenon for cult film, Evolution for interactive entertainment, Voices of Cinema for special guest interviews, and the Fringe Film Festival, where cutting-edge work is screened in the city's cafes and bars. Inquiries to: Leeds International Film Festival, The Town Hall, The Headrow, Leeds, LS1 3AD, UK. Tel: (44 113) 247 8398/ Fax: (44 113) 247 8397. e-mail: filmfestival@leeds.gov.uk. Website: www.leedsfilm.com

Le Giornate del Cinema Muto (Sacile; formerly Pordenone)

October 14–21, 2000

This unique event last year moved from Pordenone following the demolition of Cinema Verdi, the festival's venue for 17 years. Its new home is the enchanting town of Sacile, 15km from Pordenone. An inland island formed by a loop in the river Livenza, Sacile was traditionally "the garden of Venice" – as witnessed by the wealth of old palaces and historical monuments. Now, for one week each autumn, this little Italian town is overrun by a devoted band of scholars, collectors, archivists, and enthusiasts who travel from around the world for the "Giornate del Cinema Muto," established in 1982 and dedicated to silent films. 1997 saw the start of the Griffith

19th Pordenone Silent Film Festival

LE GIORNATE DEL CINEMA MUTO

October 14-21, 2000

Louis Feuillade

For further information:
Le Giornate del Cinema Muto   Tel: +39-0432-980458
c/o La Cineteca del Friuli   Fax: +39-0432-970542
Via Bini, Palazzo Gurisatti   E-mail: gcm@proxima.conecta.it
33013 Gemona (UD) Italia   www.cinetecadelfriuli.org/gcm/

Project, a long-term commitment to show every extant film by D.W. Griffith. They show alongside a wealth of other rarities and rediscoveries all presented with live musical accompaniment. There's also a Film Fair devoted to scripts and books on the cinema. Director: David Robinson. *Inquiries to:* Le Giornate del Cinema Muto c/o La Cineteca del Friuli, Palazzo Gurisatti, Via Bini 33013 Gemona (UD), Italy. Tel: (39) 0432 980 458. Fax: (39) 0432 970 542. e-mail: gcm@proxima.conecta.it. Website: www. cinetacadelfriuli.org/gcm/

Locarno

August 2–12, 2000

Under director Marco Müller, Locarno has become a place where world and European premieres are regular occasions, and where serious buyers go to discover creative film-makers. More than 1,000 accredited journalists from over 30 countries are surrounded by an international attendance of 170,000. Every night 7,000 people sit in front of the giant screen in Piazza Grande to discover the lively and varied programmes. Müller can justifiably claim that Locarno is now one of the world's top half-dozen festivals. *Inquiries to:* Festival Internazionale del Film, Via della Posta 6, CH-6600 Locarno, Switzerland. Tel: +41-91-756 2121. Fax: +41-91-756 2149. E-mail: info@pardo.ch. Website: www.pardo.ch.

London

November 2000

Presented at the National Film Theatre and at cinemas throughout the capital. The programme comprises around 180 features and documentaries, as well as a showcase for shorts. Aside from the British section there is a very strong international selection including the *Evening Standard* Film on the Square, Asia, Africa, and Latin America as well as Europe's largest and most influential selection of US independents. The festival attracts over 400 UK and international press and provides a buyers/sellers liaison office. *Inquiries to:* London Film Festival, South Bank, London SE1 8XT, UK. Tel: (44 171) 815 1322. Fax (44 171) 633 0786. e-mail: sarah.lutton@bfi.org.uk.

festival de
cine espanol
de málaga

Contact address:
Ramos Marin, 2
29012 Malaga
SPAIN
Tel.: 34 95 222 82 42
Fax: 34 95 222 77 60

Malaga Spanish Film Festival

May/June 2000

A Sunny Southern Festival

Competitive sections for full-length features and shorts, retrospectives, documentaries, tributes

Málaga Spanish Film Festival

May / June 2000

After its second edition in 1999, which saw massively increased attendance from Spanish film professionals, the Malaga Spanish Film Festival has established itself as a key event for the local industry, offering world premieres of recent productions, plus retrospectives, tributes and prize money to films in competition, worth some $150,000. Set in the sunny southern resort, the Festival also includes a documentary section and round tables whcih attract notable Spanish producers and actors. Inquiries to: Salomon Castiel, Director, Málaga Spanish Film Festival, Ramos Marin 2-2c, 29012 Málaga, Spain. Tel: (34 95) 222 8242. Fax: (34 95) 222 7760.

AWARDS 1999
Best Film: **Las Huellas borradas** (Spain/Argentina), Gabriel.
Best Actress: Asunción Balaguer for **Las Huellas borradas** (Spain/Argentina).
Best Actor: Sergi López for **Lisboa** (Argentina).
Audience Prize: **Se buscan Full Monties** (Spain).

MIFED (Milan)

Late October 2000

Long-established film market held in the expansive Milan Fair, particularly well-attended by buyers and sellers from all over the world. Third on the annual calendar after the American Film Market and the Cannes Film Festival, Mifed's atmosphere is more sober and business-like. Rivalry with the London Screenings has provoked MIFED to start its own "special screenings" slightly ahead of the main gathering. *Inquiries to:* E.A. Fiera Internationale di Milano, Largo Domodossola 1, 20145 Milano, Italy. Tel: (39 02) 4801 2912/4801 2920. Fax: (39 02) 4997 7020. e-mail: mifed@fmd.it. Website: www.fmd.it/mifed.

Mill Valley

October 5–15, 2000

The Mill Valley Film Festival presents a wide variety of international programming that is shaped by a commitment to cultural and artistic excellence. This intimate and

welcoming event of unusually high calibre and dedication is set in a beautiful small town just north of San Francisco. The eleven-day, non-competitive festival includes the prestigious New Media/ Videofest, as well as the Children's Film Fest, tributes, seminars and special events. *Inquiries to:* Mill Valley Film Festival, 38 Miller Avenue, Suite 6, Mill Valley, CA 94941, USA. Tel: (1 415) 383 5256. Fax: (1 415) 383 8606. e-mail: info@finc.org Website: www.finc.org

Montréal World Film Festival

Late August – early September 2000

Established as a major competitive festival in Montreal in late summer, this is the only such event recognised by the IFFPA in North America. Behind its success lies the remarkable personality of Serge Losique. There are several categories (Official Competition, Hors Concours Section, Cinema of Today: Reflections of Our Time, Cinema of Tomorrow: New Trends, Latin American Cinema, Focus on One Country's Cinema, Panorama Canada, TV films, tributes). Public attendance is extremely high, and the number of foreign personalities swells each year. With its bilingual facilities and its proximity to several major North American outlets, Montreal is the ideal location for such an event. *Inquiries to:* World Film Festival (International Film Festival of Montreal), 1432 de Bleury St., Montreal, Quebec, Canada H3A 2J1. Tel: (1 514) 848-3883. Fax: (1 514) 848 3886. e-mail: ffm@interlink.net. Website: www.ffm.montreal.org.

AWARDS 1998

Grand Prix of the Americas (best film): **The Quarry** (Belgium/France), Hänsel and **Vollmond** (**Full Moon**) (Switzerland/Germany), Murer.
Special Grand Prix of the Jury: **Sunbird** (China), Xueqi, Liping.
Best Director: **2 Seconds** by Manon Briand (Canada).
Best Actress: Ingrid Rubio for **El Faro** by Eduardo Mignogna (Argentina/Spain).
Best Actor: Hugo Weaving for **The Interview** by Craig Monahan (Australia).
Best Screenplay: **The Man with Rain in His Shoes** by Maria Ripoll, screenplay by Rafa Russo (Spain/UK).

Netherlands Film Festival

September 20–29, 2000

Since 1981, Holland's only event presenting an overview of the entire output of Dutch film-making for the year. A selection of Dutch features, shorts, documentaries, and television dramas are screened and judged. The Grand Prix of the Dutch Film, Golden Calf Award, is presented in 14 categories. The competition programme comprises about 150 features, documentaries, short films and television drama productions, all completed in the 12 months previous to the festival. Including more than 50 premieres. Retrospectives on the history of Dutch cinema and special programmes address various aspects of Dutch film. The Holland Film Meeting is the international sidebar of the festival and includes a Market Programme and a co-production platform, for Dutch and European producers with a project-in-progress, which is an initiative to encourage Dutch film talent. *Inquiries to:* Nederlands Film Festival. P.O. Box 1581, 3500 BN Utrecht, The Netherlands. Tel: (31 30) 232 2684. Fax: (31 30) 231 3200. e-mail: ned.filmfest@inter.nl.net. Website: www. filmfestival.nl.

WORLD FILM FESTIVAL
MONTRÉAL 2000

Keep your agenda open
at the end of August

Montreal World Film Festival
1432 de Bleury St.
Montréal (Québec) H3A 2J1
Tel. : (514) 848-3883 / **Fax :** (514) 848-3886
E-mail : ffm@Interlink.net / **Web site :** http://www.ffm-montreal.org

VISA

THE NOOSA INTERNATIONAL FILM FESTIVAL

OCTOBER 2000

NOOSA, QUEENSLAND, AUSTRALIA

Australia's only international competitive film festival, held annually in Australia's premier resort town.

Address: Suite 1, 218 Crown Street, EAST SYDNEY NSW 2010 AUSTRALIA
Postal: PO Box 828, BONDI JUNCTION NSW 1355 AUSTRALIA
Tel: 61-2-9360 5384 - **Fax:** 61-2-9360 7893
Email: noosafilmfest@ozemail.com.au - **Internet:** www.noosafilmfestival.com

AWARDS 1998

Golden Calf for Best Full-Length Feature: **Felice...felice**, Pieter van Huyates and Suzanne van Voorst.
Golden Calf for Best Director: **The Polish Bride**, Karim Traïdia.
Golden Calf for Best Actor: Johan Leysen for **Felice...felice.**
Golden Calf for Best Actress: Monic Hendrickx for **The Polish Bride.**
Golden Calf for Best Short Film: **Nussin**, Clara van Gool.

New York

September 22–October 9, 2000

Now in its 38th year, the New York Film Festival has resisted the temptation to grow into a major market offering hundreds of films, instead limiting the programme to 25–30 international features and shorter works selected from nearly 1,000 entries annually. Attendance has been well over 95% for the past decade, and each selection receives extensive coverage in local, national and even international media. *Inquiries to:* Film Society of Lincoln Center, 70 Lincoln Center Plaza, New York, NY 10023–6595, USA. Tel: (1 212) 875 5638. Fax: (1 212) 875 5610. Website: www.film.linc.com.

Noosa

September 2000

The Noosa Film Festival, Australia's first competitive international film event, launched in Queensland in September 1999. Among the guests attending were Tom Skerritt, Jason Biggs, Ron Judkins, and Linus Roache, alongside Australian personalities such as Bryan Brown, Gillian Armstrong, Jack Thompson and Rachel Ward. There are competitive sections for features, shorts, and documentaries, as well as symposia. Inquiries to: Noosa Film Festival, P.O. Box 1557, Noosa Heads, Queensland 4567, Australia. Tel: (61 7) 5447 2410. Fax: (61 7) 5447 2860. E-mail: noosaboxoffice@noosafilmfestival.com. Website: www.noosafilmfestival.com

Nordische Filmtage Lübeck

November 2–5, 2000

Annual event held in the charming medieval town of Lübeck (north of Hamburg). The Festival throws a spotlight on Scandinavian and Baltic cinema, enabling members of the trade, critics and other film-goers to see the best of the new productions. It also features a large documentary section. Celebrates its 42nd anniversary in the year 2000. *Inquiries to:* Nordische Filmtage Lübeck, D-23539 Lübeck, Germany. Tel: (49 451) 122 4102. Fax: (49 451) 122 4106. e-mail: filmtage-@luebeck.de. Website: www.filmtage. luebeck.de

Nyon

May 1–7, 2000

Specialises in creative documentaries. This recently rejuvenated event, entitled "Visions du Réel", includes two competitions, market screenings, film-makers, spectators, buyers, forums, and is a stimulating source of ideas for new projects. *Inquiries to:* Visions du Réel, case postale 593, CH-1260 Nyon, Switzerland. Tel: (41 22) 361 6060. Fax: (41 22) 361 7071. e-mail: docnyon@iprolink.ch.

Oberhausen

April 27–May 2, 2000

Now in its 46th year, the International Short Film Festival, Oberhausen remains one of the world's premiere short film festivals. It includes a wide selection of international and German issues in the media field. *Inquiries to:* Oberhausen International Short

Film Festival, Grillostrasse 34, D-46045 Oberhausen, Germany. Tel: (49 208) 825 2652/2318. Fax: (49 208) 825 5413. e-mail: kurzfilmtage_oberhausen@uni-duisburg.de. Website: www.uni-duisburg.de/HRZ/IKF/home.html.

Odense

August 2000

Denmark's only international short film festival invites unusual films that displays an original and delightful sense of imagination – along the lines of the fairytales of Hans Christian Andersen. All 16mm and 35mm films can participate. Maximum length is 45 minutes. *Inquiries to:* Odense Film Festival, Vindegrade 18, DK-5000 Odense C, Denmark. Tel: (45) 6613 1372, ext. 4044. Fax: (45) 6591 4318. e-mail: filmfestival@post.odkomm.dk. Website: www.filmfestival.dk.

AWARDS 1998
Grand Prix: **The Oath** (Holland), Penning
Most Imaginative Film: **Possum** (New Zealand), McGann
Most Surprising Film: **Kal** (Bulgaria), Simidchiev

XIX INTERNATIONAL CHILDREN'S FILM FESTIVAL OULU

20-26 NOV 2000
15 new feature films in competition

Torikatu 8,
SF-90100 Oulu, Finland
Tel: +358 8 8811293, 1294
Fax: + 358 8 8811290
E-mail:oek@oufilmcenter.inet.fi

Oulu International Children's Film Festival

November 20–26, 2000

The only annual festival of full-length feature films for children in Scandinavia. The event is competitive and screens both recent films and retrospective seasons. Oulu is located in northern Finland and contains some excellent modern architecture. *Inquiries to:* Oulu International Children's Film Festival, Torikatu 8, SF-90100 Oulu, Finland. Tel: (358 8) 881 1293. Fax: (358 8) 881 1290. e-mail:raimo.kinisjarvi@oufilmcenter.inet.fi Website: www.ouka.fi./oek

Palm Springs

January 13–24, 2000

Celebrating its 11th anniversary this year, the Nortel Palm Springs International Film Festival is a glittering event, screening over 150 films from 25 countries, including US and international premieres. Founded by the late Sonny Bono, the festival offers seminars, panels and workshops on various aspects of film-making and hosts a black-tie Awards Gala. The event has grown rapidly from a three-day event in 1990, to its current length of 12 days. *Inquiries to:* Nortel Palm Springs International Film Festival, 1700 E. Tahquitz Canyon Way #3, Palm Springs, CA 92262, USA. Tel: (1 760) 322 2930. Fax: (1 760) 322 4087. Website: www.psfilmfest.org.

Pesaro

June 2000

Focuses on the work of new directors and emergent, innovative cinemas, including non-fiction, animation, shorts and videos. For the past 34 years, this Mediterranean resort has been the centre for lively screenings and debates. In recent seasons, the Festival programme has been devoted in part to a specific country or culture. The main festival is coupled each year with a special retrospective of Italian cinema. In addition, each October the Festival organises a five-day themed retrospective. *Inquiries to:* Mostra Internazionale del Nuovo Cinema (Pesaro Film Festival), Via Villafranca 20, 00185 Rome, Italy. Tel: (39 06) 445 6643 491 156. Fax: (39 06) 491 163. e-mail: pesarofilmfes@mclink.it. Website: www.comune.pesaro.ps.it

Portland

February 11–28, 2000

The 23rd Portland International Film Festival is an invitational event presenting over 100 films from two dozen countries. New international features, documentaries and shorts enjoy an audience of over 35,000 people from throughout the Northwest. Special programmes include classic silents with live orchestra performances, visiting artists, children's programming, an annual Pacific Rim Showcase and "Cine-Lit," a special selection of new Hispanic-language films and symposiums on literature. *Inquiries to:* Portland International Film Festival, Northwest Film Center, 1219 S.W. Park Avenue, Portland, OR 97205, USA. Tel: (1 503) 221 1156. Fax: (1 503) 294 0874. e-mail: info@nwfilm.org. Website: www. nwfilm.org.

Raindance

February 24-March 2, 2000

Founded in 1997 by the American Cinema Foundation, this showcase of films from Eastern and Central Europe is dedicated to bringing light to Eastern Europe's history and creating opportunities for its film-makers. Films screened represent the cutting edge of the struggle for many kinds of freedom: personal, political, economic and artistic. The festival is held at the time of the AFM in L.A., and reprised overseas, participating at Karlovy Vary, Moscow, and Baku. Inquiries to: American Cinema Foundation, 9911 W. Pico Blvd., Suite 510, Los Angeles, CA 90035, USA. Tel: (1 310) 286 9420. Fax: (1 310) 286 7914. E-mail: acinema@cinemafoundation.com. Website: www.cinemafoundation.com

Rotterdam

January 26–Feburary 6, 2000

The largest film festival in Benelux, the 29th Rotterdam International Film Festival has a reputation for programming innovative, independent new work alongside more commercial productions. New film talents from all over the world compete for three Tiger Awards (10,000 Euro plus guaranteed theatrical and television release in the Netherlands). More than 200 features –

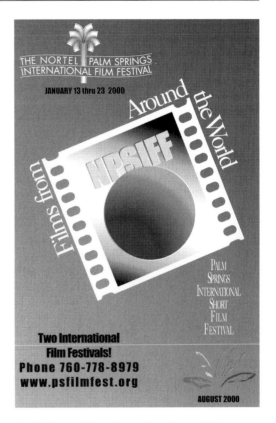

including 60 international or European premieres – offer an overview of contemporary world cinema. The festival also hosts CineMart, the leading co-production market for independent film-makers, producers, sales agents, distributors and financiers. Rotterdam's Hubert Bals Fund supports film-makers from developing countries. *Inquiries to:* Rotterdam Film Festival, P.O. Box 21696, 3001 AR Rotterdam, Netherlands. Tel: (31 10) 890 9090. Fax: (31 10) 890 9091. e-mail: tiger@iffrotterdam.nl. Website: www.iffrotterdam.nl.

San Francisco

April 20–May 4, 2000

The oldest film festival in the Americas, in its 43rd year, the San Francisco International Film Festival continues to rise in importance and popularity. Last year's event broke box-office records for the sixteenth year in a row, with over 77,000 film-goers. The festival presents over 100 features and 70 shorts from around the world. Special awards include the recently-established SKYY Prize, a $10,000 cash award designed to launch an emerging film-maker into the US marketplace. Attendees at last year's event included festival honoree Sean Penn, Robin Wright Penn, The Talking Heads and Jeremy Northam, and directors Jonathan Demme, David Mamet and Arturo Ripstein. *Inquiries to:* San Francisco International Film Festival, 1521 Eddy Street, San Francisco, CA 94115-4102, USA. Tel: (1 415) 929 5000. Fax: (1 415) 921 5032. e-mail: sfiff@sfiff.org.

San Sebastian

September 2000

Held in an elegant Basque seaside city, the Donostia-San Sebastian Festival remains one of the most important film festivals in Spain in terms of glamour, competition, attendance, facilities, partying and number of films. Events include the Official Competitive section, Zabaltegi and a variety of meticulous retrospectives. The city is known for its superb gastronomy, beautiful beaches and quaint streets. The festival usually attracts a large number of international celebrities, national and

international press, talent, and film buffs. A special jury awards the New Director's Prize to a first or second-time producer and director, worth 25 million pesetas (approx. $160,000). Director: Diego Galan. *Inquiries to:* San Sebastian International Film Festival, Apartado de Correos 397, 20080 Donostia, San Sebastian 20080, Spain. Tel: (34 943) 481 212. Fax: (34 943) 481 218. e-mail: ssiff@sansebastianfestival.com. Website: www.sansebastianfestival.com

AWARDS 1998
Golden Shell: **El Viento se llevo lo que (**Argentina), Agresti.
Special Jury Award: **Gods and Monsters** (UK), Condon and **A la place du cœur** (France), Robert Guédiguian.
Best Director: Fernando León de Aranoa for **Barrio** (Spain).
Best Actress: Jeanne Balibar for **Fin août, debut septembre** (France).
Best Actor: Ian McKellen for **Gods and Monsters** (UK).
Best Photography: Rodrigo Prieto for **Un embrujo** (Mexico).
Jury Award: **Don** (Iran), Jalili.

Santa Barbara International Film Festival
May 2–12, 2000

An eleven-day event held in the glamorous seaside resort of Santa Barbara, California, just 90 minutes north of Los Angeles. Under the artistic direction of seasoned producer, Renée Missel, the SBIFF has received worldwide recognition for its diverse programming and has grown to be a major cultural event since its inception in 1986. A jury of industry professionals select winners in several categories, including Best US Feature Film, Best Foreign Feature Film, Best Director, Best Documentary Feature, Best Short, and Best of the Fest Audience Award. This year's theme will be American Comedy. *Inquiries to:* SBIFF 1216 State Street, Ste 710, Santa Barbara, CA 93101-2623, USA. Tel: (1 805) 963 0023. Fax: (1 805) 962 2524. e-mail: sbiff@west.net. Web: www.sbfilmfestival

SPONSORED BY CENTRAL

1 - 11 June 2000

Nottingham's 10th International CRIME, MYSTERY AND THRILLER FILM FESTIVAL

Shots
I N   T H E   D A R K

Previews and Premieres
Guests / Retrospectives
Shorts / Summer School

"The chambers are loaded.
All that remains is to pull the trigger".
The Big Issue

To join the free mailing list, phone
(+44 0) 115 952 6600 / fax **(+44 0) 115 952 6622**
email: **Enquiries@ broadway.org.uk**

Broadway 14-18 Broad St, Nottingham NG1 3AL, UK

Shots in the Dark
June 1–11, 2000

Britain's unique festival celebrating the crime, mystery and thriller genres, featuring the best line-up of previews of thrillers and special guests. The festival also includes major themed retrospectives, a "Mystery" film and short film programme, as well as a summer school and "In the Frame" young people's video-making competition. Tenth anniversary of the festival will be in June 2000. *Inquiries to:* Shots in the Dark, Broadway, 14-18 Broad Street, Nottingham, NG1 3 AL. UK Tel: (44 115) 952 6600. Fax: (44 115) 952 6622.

Sitges: Festival Internacional de Cinema de Catalunya
October 2000

The 32nd edition of Sitges: Festival Internacional de Cinema de Catalunya presents films from all over the world in its usual sections: Fantàstic, the Festival's core competitive section devoted to fantasy, Gran Angular, for non-fantasy films, a selection of the most recent international productions, Seven Chances, seven films with little chance of being commercially distributed, chosen by seven critics, Anima't, a selection of the latest animation trends, Retrospectiva, a selection of classics from the history of cinema, and Brigadoon, an alternative space with projections in new formats. *Inquiries to:* Sitges '99: Festival Internacional de Cinema de Catalunya, Av. Josep Tarradellas 135, Esc. A 3 2, 08029 Barcelona, Spain. Tel: (34 93) 419 3635. Fax: (34 93) 439 7380. e-mail: cinsit@sitgestur.com Website: www.sitges.com/cinema

Solothurn Film Festival

January 18–23, 2000

Held every year since 1966, the Festival is a source of up-to-date information and gives a representative survey of all forms of creative film and video in Switzerland of the preceding year. It presents a selection of films and videos by Swiss directors and foreign directors resident in Switzerland, as well as co-productions between Switzerland and foreign countries. The event is covered by the Swiss and foreign media (press, radio, television). This year there will be a special programme with international short fiction films. *Inquiries to:* Solothurn Film Festival, Postfach 140, CH 4504, Solothurn, Switzerland. Tel: (41 32) 625 8080. Fax: (41 32) 623 6410, e-mail: filmtage@cuenet.ch. Website: www.filmtage-solothurn.ch.

South Africa Film & TV

November 1999

Sithengi (the Southern African International Film and Television Market) will mark its fifth year in 2000. Held in the exquisite city of Cape Town, Sithengi has become Africa's leading media and entertainment event, featuring a TV programme Market, the Co-Production Forum, and Africa's only Locations Expo. Sithengi also hosts the Cape Town Film Week. Business conducted at Sithengi exceeds $75 million, and is well patrionised by broadcasters from throughout Africa. Inquiries to: Sithengi, P.O. Box 52120, Waterfront 8002, Cape Town, South Africa. Tel: (27 21) 430 8160. Fax: (27 21) 430 8249. E-mail: info@sithengi.co.za. Website: www.sithengi.co.za

OgilvyOne

STOCKHOLM INTERNATIONAL FILM FESTIVAL

10 - 19 november 2000

Tel: +46 8 677 50 00
www.filmfestivalen.se
program@cinema.se

Stockholm

November 10–19, 2000

The Stockholm International Film Festival is in its 11th year as the leading competitive film festival in Northern Europe and the fastest growing one. It is the only Scandinavian festival recognised by FIAPF, it hosts a FIPRESCI jury and is also a member of European Coordination of Film Festivals. Quentin Tarantino, Steve Buscemi, Joel and Ethan Coen, Lars von Trier, Dennis Hopper, Gena Rowlands, Neil Jordan and Elia Kazan are among the many personalities who have enjoyed the only festival in the world that operates 24 hours per day. When leaving Stockholm, Hopper stated, "I just wish my whole life was like this festival." Some 80 films have gained distribution in connection with the Stockholm International Film Festival over the years. *Inquiries to:* The Stockholm International Film Festival, P.O. Box 3136 S-103 62 Stockholm, Sweden. Tel: (46 8) 677 5000. Fax: (46 8) 200 590. e-mail: program@cinema.se Website: www.filmfestivalen.se

AWARDS 1998
Best Film: **The Wounds** (Yugoslavia), Dragojević.
Best First Feature Film: **Seul contre tous** (France), Noé.
Best Actress: Yuri Kinugawa for **Memory and Desire** (New Zealand).
Best Actor: Milan Marić and Dušan Pekić for **The Wounds** (Yugoslavia).
Best Screenplay: Todd Solondz for **Happiness** (USA).
Life Time Achievement Award: Gena Rowlands.
FIPRESCI Awards:
  Best Film: **Acid House** (UK), McGuigan.
  Best Nordic Film: **Georgica**.
Audience Award: **Happiness** (USA), Todd Solondz.

Sundance Film Festival

January 20–30, 2000

Sponsored by Robert Redford's Sundance Institute, this winter festival ranks among America's most respected displays of American independent cinema. Between 120 and140 dramatic and documentary films are presented in the Independent Feature Film Competition each year , serving as indicators of the current trends. 58-70 short films are screened each year. *Inquiries to:* Sundance Film Festival, P.O. Box 16450, Salt Lake City, UT 84116, USA. Tel: (1 801) 328 3456. Fax: (1 801) 575 5175.

AWARDS 1999
Grand Jury Prize (Dramatic): **Three Seasons**, Bui.
Grand Jury Prize (Documentary): **American Movie**, Smith.
Film-Makers Trophy (Dramatic): **Tumbleweeds** , O'Connor.
Film-Makers Trophy (Documentary): **Sing Faster: The Stagehand's Ring Cycle**, Else.

Taipei

November 2000

Held annually, the Taipei Golden Horse Film Festival aims to appreciate the art of film, to promote both domestic and international film, and to encourage understanding among different cultures through film art. Founded in 1964, the Festival is sponsored by the Government of the Republic of China (ROC) and the Motion Picture Development Foundation of ROC. The two main divisions of the film festival include Golden Horse Awards, a competition for Chinese-language films, and the International Film Exhibition, a non-competitive showcase of wide range of outstanding films from all over the world. Entry deadline: August 31. *Inquiries to:* Taipei Golden Horse Film Festival, 7F, No. 45 Chilin Road, Taipei, Taiwan, 104. Tel: (886 2) 2567 5861. Fax: (886 2) 2531 8966. e-mail: tghff@ms14.hinet.net. Website: www. goldenhorse.org.tw.

Tampere

March 8–12, 2000

The 30th year of one of the leading short film festivals in the world. This event - famous for its international sauna party - attracts every year entries from over 60 countries; the 700 professionals and over 25,000 spectators can see over 400 short films in some 100 screenings during five daus and nights. The International competition has awards for the best documentary, fiction and animation. The programme offers an interesting collection of top quality retrospectives and tributes from all over the world. There is also an extensive series of open debates and training seminars for professionals. The market include shorts and documentaries from northern and eastern Europe. *Inquiries to:* Tampere Film Festival, P.O. Box 305, 33101 Tampere, Finland. Tel: (358 3) 213 0034. Fax: (358 3) 223 0121. e-mail: film.festival@ tt.tampere.fi. Website: www.tampere.fi/ festival/film.

AWARDS 1999

Grand Prix International: **Youfek** (Iran), Shaykh-Aleslami.
Special Prize of the Jury: **A Viagem** (Portugal/France), Boustani.
Audience Award: **Pavel and Lyalya** (Russia/Israel), Kossakovsky.

TORINO FILM FESTIVAL
CINEMA GIOVANI

via Monte di Pietà, 1
10121 Torino, Italy
tel. (+39) 011 5623309
fax (+39) 011 5629796
e-mail: info@torinofilmfest.org
website: http://www.torinofilmfest.org

Director: Stefano Della Casa

18° Torino Film Festival
November 17/25, 2000

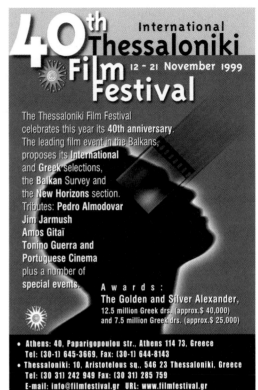

Telluride

September 1–4, 2000

A truly unique, friendly gathering in the historic mining town of Telluride, a spectacular location in the mountains of Colorado. The Festival continues to be one of the world's most influential, as famous directors, players and critics descend on the Sheridan Opera House and other theatres. The dedication of both organisers and participants to the art of cinema gives Telluride a sincere, authentic feel – not forgetting the "surprise" element, with the programme only announced on the first day! *Inquiries to:* The National Film Preserve Ltd., P.O. Box B1156, Hanover, New Hampshire 03755, USA. Tel: (1 603) 643 1255. Fax: (1 603) 643 5938. e-mail: Tellufilm@aol.com. Website: www.telluridefilmfestival.com

Thessaloniki International Film Festival

November 2000

In its 40th year, the oldest and one of the most important film events in Greece. Thessaloniki targets a new generation of film-makers as well as high-quality independent films made by established directors. The International competition (for first or second features) awards the Golden Alexander (approx. $38,000) and the Silver Alexander (approx. $23,000). Other sections include the Greek film panorama, retrospectives, Balkan survey, New Horizons and a number of special galas and exhibitions. *Inquiries to:* International Thessaloniki Film Festival, 40 Paparigopoulou street, 114 73 Athens, Greece. Tel: (30 1) 645 3669. Fax: (30 1) 644 8143. e-mail: info@filmfestival.gr. Website: www.filmfestival.gr

AWARDS 1998

Best full length film award – Dolgen Alexander: **Fishes in August** (Japan), Takahashi.
Special jury award - Silver Alexander: **The Flight of the**

Bee (Korea, Tajikistan),Usmanov and Hun Min and **Knoflikari (The Buttoners)** (Czech Republic), Zelenka.
Best director award: Constantine Giannaris for **Apo tin akri tis polis (From the Edge of the City)** (Greece).
Best screenplay award: Petr Zelenka for **Knoflikari (The Buttoners)** (Czech Republic).
Best actress award: Jeanne Balibar for **Dieu seul me voit (God's Got My Number)** (France)
Best actor award: Mehmet Kurtulus for **Kurz and schmerzlos (Short Sharp Shock)** (Germany)
Artistic ahievement award: **A rrum da woon shee chul (Spring in My Hometown)**
Special mention: **Sib (The Apple)** (Iran), Makhmalbaf

Torino Film Festival

November 17–25, 2000

Well-organised event (formerly known as the Festival Internazionale Cinema Giovani) which takes place each autumn and focuses exclusively on films made by new directors. There is a competitive section for shorts, features, and Italian independents, as well as a section for retrospectives and spotlights. The Festival has been recognised as a top showcase for hot new international talent and dubbed second only to Venice on the crowded Italian festival circuit. *Inquiries to:* Torino Film Festival, Via Monte di Pietà 1, 10121 Torino, Italy. Tel: (39 011) 562 3309. Fax: (39 011) 562 9796. e-mail: info@torinofilmfest. org. Website: www.torinofilmfest.org

Toronto International Film Festival

September 7–16, 2000

A rich diversity of world cinema featured yearly with over 250 films in 10 days. The event offers hundreds of films and film-makers, in a wide range of international programmes: Galas, Special Presentations, Contemporary World Cinema, Planet Africa, Dialogues, Talking with Pictures, Reel to Reel, Directors Spotlight, Midnight Madness, Perspective Canada Discovery, and Masters. There is also a Rogers Industry Centre that includes a Sales Office and Symposium. *Inquiries to:* Toronto International Film Festival, 2 Carlton St., 16th Floor, Toronto, Ontario, Canada M5B 1J3. Tel: (1 416) 967 7371. Fax: (1 416) 967 9477. Public Box Office: (416) 968-FILM. e-mail: tiffg@torfilmfest.ca. Website: www. bell.ca/filmfest.

Tromsø International Film Festival

January 18–23, 2000

Possibly the world's northernmost film event, far beyond the Arctic Circle, this "Winter Wonderland" festival focuses on contemporary art films and documentaries, 35mm feature-length films from all continents. *Inquiries to:* The Arctic Film Festival, Tromsø, Postbox 285, N - 9253 Tromsø, Norway. Tel: (47) 7760 5150. Fax: (47) 7760 5151. e-mail: filmfestival@tromsokino.no Website: www.tromsokino.no/filmfestival.

Umeå

September 15–20, 2000

Now in its 15th year. An annual, non-competitive event screening around 100 features and 50 shorts, including a number of Swedish premieres, from around the world. The Festival has gained considerable standing as a gateway for film distribution in Sweden and the Nordic countries and is the

largest film festival in Northern Scandinavia. Director Thom Palmen's lively programme includes an international panorama, innovative, funny shorts, Swedish and Nordic documentaries, and special guests. The popular "Camera Obscura" section features obscure films and restored or neglected classics. Also seminars and workshops. *Inquiries to:* Umeå International Film Festival, Box 43, S-901 02 Umeå, Sweden. Tel: (46 90) 133 388/356. Fax: (46 90) 777 961. e-mail: film.festival@ff.umea.com. Website: www.ff.umea.com

Valladolid

October 20–28, 2000

Now in its 45th year, an annual, well-organised, popular Spanish festival offering competition for features, shorts and documentaries. It also features a non-competitive section for retrospectives, film schools, and Spanish cinema and exhibits. The 1998 sidebars featured Liv Ullmann, Takeshi Kitano, Bert Haanstra, José Luis Dibildos, the Academia de Teatru Si Film, Bucharest and films based on the works of Mario Benedetti. *Inquiries to:* Teatro Calderón, C/Leopoldo Cano, s/n, 4a planta, 47003 Valladolid, Spain. Tel: (34 983) 305 700,77,88. Fax: (34 983) 309 835. e-mail: festvalladolid@seminci.com. Website: www.seminci.com.

AWARDS 1998
Golden Spike: **My Name Is Joe** (UK/Germany/Spain), Loach.
Silver Spike: **Die Siebtelbauern** (Austria), Ruzowitzky.
"Pilar Miro" Prize to the Best New Director (shared): Christophe Ruggia for **Le gone du Chaâba** (France), Shane Meadows for **Twentyfourseven** (UK).
Best Actor: Peter Mullan for **My Name Is Joe** (UK/Germany/Spain).
Best Actress: Ariadna Gil for **Lágrimans negras** (Spain).
Best Cinematography: Ashley Rowe for **Twentyfourseven** (UK).

Vancouver

September–October, 2000

Now in its 18th year, this festival has grown into an event of considerable stature. About 130,000 people attend more than 250 films from all parts of the world,

Richard Farnsworth, Anne Wheeler and Robert Wisden at the Victoria Independent Film & Video Festival
photo: Barbara Pedrick

and the Canadian city's natural beauty adds to the hospitality offered to guests. Areas of special focus are East Asia, Canada, Documentaries and the Annual Trade Forum. *Inquiries to:* Alan Franey, 410-1008 Homer Street, Vancouver, B.C., Canada V6B 2X1. Tel: (1 604) 685 0260. Fax: (1 604) 688 8221. e-mail: viff@viff.org. Website: www.viff.org.

Venice

September 2000

In the hands of Alberto Barbera, fresh from the Turin Festival, the oldest world film festival is trying to speed itself up for the new century. Its Lido facilities need major expansion in order to accommodate a rising flood of features, shorts and experimental works, which are increasingly sunchronised with other multimedia branches within the Biennale of Art – Venice's unparalleled international gold-mine. *Inquiries to:* La Biennale di Venezia, San Marco, Cà Giustinian, 30124 Venice, Italy. Tel: (39 041) 521 8711. Fax: (39 041) 523 6374. e-mail: das@labiennale.it Website: www.labiennale.org

AWARDS 1998
Golden Lion for best film: **Cosí ridevano** (Italy), Amelio.
Special Jury Gran Prix: **Terminus Paradis** (Romania/France),Lucian Pintilie.
Silver Lion for best direction: Emir Kusturica for **Black Cat, White Cat** (Yugoslavia).
Coppa Volpi for best actress: Catherine Deneuve for **Place Vendôme** (France).
Coppa Volpi for best actor: Sean Penn for **Hurlyburly** (USA).
Osella d'Oro for best original screeplay: Eric Rohmer for **Conte d'automne** (France).
Fiprseci Award: **Bure Baruta** (Yugoslavia), Paskaljević.

Victoria Independent Film and Video Festival

February 4–10, 2000

Set in beautiful Victoria, the 6th annual festival includes seven days of feature films, documentaries, shorts and a chance to come face to face with the who's who of the film world in a laid-back setting. The festival also features a two-day film forum, film discussions, a fun filled opportunity for the public to try film-making first hand (in one evening), an art exhibition (with a film theme, of course), and video installation. Inquires to: Victoria Independent

Film and Video Festival, 101-610 Johnson Street, Victoria British Columbia, Canada V8W 1M4. Tel: (1-250) 389 0444. Fax: (1 250) 380 1547. Website: www.coastnet.com/~cinevic

Wellington

July 14–30, 2000

29-year-old festival screening an invited programme of around 100 features and 50 shorts. Along with its Auckland sibling, the event provides a non-competitive New Zealand premiere showcase for a striking diversity of film and video styles. An archival component also enjoys considerable prominence. Now in their second decade under the direction of the apparently tireless Bill Gosden. *Inquiries to:* Wellington Film Festival, Box 9544, Morion Square, Wellington, New Zealand. Tel: (64 4) 385 0162. Fax: (64 4) 801 7304. e-mail: enzedff@actrix.gen.nz. Website: www.enzedff.co.nz.

Wine Country Film Festival

July–August, 2000

Set in the heart of Northern California's premium wine country, the event accepts feature film, shorts, documentaries, animation, student films and videos. The five categories are: independent features, international films, films that have a social comment, films about the arts and films about the environment. Generally non-competitive, but with a short film, documentary, and a new directors' prize. Many of the films are shown outdoors in spectacular wine country settings. *Inquiries*

to: P.O. Box 303, Glen Ellen, CA 95442, USA. Tel: (1 707) 996 2536. Fax: (1 707) 996 6964.

WorldFest-Flagstaff

November 3–12, 2000

Previously held in Charleston, South Carolina, this annual independent film festival, now held in Flagstaff, Arizona, offers premieres of independent and international features, shorts, documentaries, and video. The 10-day event also offers in-depth film and video production seminars, from screen-writing to directing and producing independent feature films. Screenings are held in a three-screen theatre, and a select programme of 40-50 new features and 60 shorts are premiered with directors in attendance. Worldfest screens only independent films, and no major studio films are accepted. It is the sister festival to the spring WorldFest-Houston. *Inquiries to:* WorldFest-Flagstaff, P.O. Box 56566, Houston, TX 77356, USA. Tel: (1 713) 965

9955. Fax: (1 713) 965 9960. e-mail: worldfest@aol.com. Website: www.vannevar.com/worldfest

WorldFest-Houston

April 2000

Celebrating its 33rd year, the Festival offers competition for independent features, shorts, student films, TV Productions and commercials, music videos and screenplays. WorldFest is the largest film and video competition in the world in terms of the number of entries received. It is the only truly Independent Film Festival in North America as it no longer accepts major studio films. Festival Founding Director J. Hunter Todd operates a new Discovery Festival programme which automatically notifies the major 200 international film festivals of the WorldFest winners. The programme co-ordinators also submit all student, short and screenplay winners to the top US agents and agencies. *Inquiries to:* WorldFest-Houston, P.O. Box 56566, Houston, TX 77256, USA. Tel: (1 713) 965 9955. Fax: (1 713) 965 9960. e-mail: worldfest@aol.com. Website: www.vannevar.com/worldfest

World Festival of Animated Films

June 2000

The organisers in Zagreb aim to make the Festival a gathering place for creators and fans of animated films from all over the world, where recent world production is judged and the past is recalled with relevant national, personal or thematic retrospectives. The event features a competitive section but still reserves a segment, entitled "Below the Line," for those works that just missed selection for the prize category. *Inquiries to:* Koncertna direkcija Zagreb Animafest, Kneza Mislava 18, 10000 Zagreb, Croatia. Tel: (385 1) 461 1709. Fax: (385 1) 461 1808/7. e-mail: kdz@zg.tel.hr. Website: www.animafest.hr.

Other Festivals and Markets of Note

Alcalá de Henares Film Festival, Plaza del Empecinado 1, 28801 Alcalá de Henares, Madrid, Spain. Tel: (34 91) 881 3934. Fax: (34 91) 881 3906. (*Competition for Spanish shorts and new directors, plus a panorama of international shorts and cartoons Nov. 10–18.*)

Alexandria International Film Festival, 9 Orabi Str. 111, Cairo, Egypt. Tel: (20 2) 574 1112. Fax: (20 2) 576 8727. (*Competitive, mainly for Mediterranean countries and for first films internationally – Sept.*)

American Film Market, 10850 Wilshire Blvd., 9th floor, Los Angeles, CA, 90024. USA. Tel: (1 310) 446 1000. Fax: (1 310) 446 1600. (*Efficiently-run market primarily for English-language theatrical films. Buyers must be accredited – Feb. 24-March 3.*)

Ann Arbor Film Festival, P.O. Box 8232, Ann Arbor, MI 48107, USA. Tel: (1 734) 995 5356. Fax: (1 734) 995 5396. Website: aafilmfest.org (*Presenting experimental films from all over the world – March 14–19.*)

Annecy/MIFA, Centre International du Cinéma d'Animation, B.P. 399, 74013 Annecy Cedex, France. Tel: (33 4) 5010 0900. Fax: (33 4) 5010 0970. Website: www.annecy.org. (*Long-established international and competitive animated film festival with a useful market (MIFA) to further the sale and distribution of animated films – June 5–10.*)

Antarctic Film Festival, 2543 2nd Street, Santa Monica, CA 90405, USA. Tel: (1 310) 396 2759. e-mail: info@antarctic-filmfest.com. Website: www.antarctic-filmfest.com. (*Competitive event for films and videos – August 24–31, 2000.*)

Arab Film Festival, 2 Plaza Avenue, San Francisco, CA 94116, USA. Tel: (1 415) 564 1100. Fax: (1 415) 642 4780. Website: www.aff.org (*Arab films featured in a Bay Area location.*)

Art Film Festival (Trencianske Teplice) Konventna 8, Bratislava, Slovak Republic, 81103. Tel: (421 7) 5441 9479/81. Fax: (42 17) 5441 1679. e-mail: festival@artfilm.sk (*The Festival encourages interest in and promotion of art films – June.*)

Asian American International Film Festival, Asian Cinevision, 37 East Broadway, New York, NY. 10002, USA. Tel: (1 212) 925 8685. Fax: (1 212) 925 8157. (*Showcases works by established and emerging Asian and Asian American film-makers – July.*)

Aspen Shortfest & Filmfest, 110 E. Hallam, Ste. 102, Aspen, CO. 81611, USA. Tel: (1 970) 925 6882. Fax: (1 970) 925 1967. e-mail: aspenfilm.org. Website: www.aspenfilm.org. (*Features documentaries – Sept. Short subject competition – April 5–9.*)

Atlantic Film Festival, P.O. Box 36139, Halifax, NS B3J 3S9 Canada. Tel: (1 902) 422 3456. Fax: (1 902) 422 4006. e-mail: festival@atlanticfilm. com. Website: www. atlanticfilm.com. (*Features documentaries, shorts and workshops. Incorporates Screen-scene children's festival – Sept. 15–23.*)

Auckland International Film Festival, P.O. Box 9544, Wellington 6001, New Zealand. Tel: (64 4) 385 0162. Fax: (64 4) 801 7304. e-mail: enzedff@actrix.gen.nz. (*A leading showcase of over 100 features and 50 shorts. Twinned annually with the Wellington Film Festival – July 7–23.*)

Augsburg Children's Film Festival, Filmbüro Augsburg, Schroeckstrasse 8, 86152 Augsburg, Germany. Tel: (49 821) 349 1060. Fax: (49 821) 349 5218. (*New international feature films for children Nov. 3–12.*)

Banff Festival of Mountain Films, The Banff Centre for Mountain Culture, Box 1020, Stn. 38, Banff, AB, Canada TOL OCO. Tel: (1 403) 762 6125. Fax: (1 403) 762 6277. e-mail: cmc@banffcentre.ab.ca. Website: www.banffcentre.ab.ca/cmc/ (*International competition for all films and videos related to mountains and the spirit of adventure – Nov.*)

The Bilbao International Documentary and Short Film Festival, Colon de Larreategui, 37, 4 dcha., 48009 Bilbao. Tel: (34 94) 424 8698. Fax: (34 94) 424 5624. (*Long-running festival in the northern Spanish industrial town of Bilbao - Nov.*)

Birmingham International Film & Television Festival, 9 Margaret St., Birmingham B3 3BS, UK. Tel: (44 121) 212 0777. Fax: (44 121) 212 0666 (*Growing provincial festival which features both film and television – Nov. 15–26.*)

Bite the Mango Film Festival, National Museum of Photography, Film & TV, Pictureville, Bradford, BD1 NQ West Yorkshire, UK. Tel: (44 1274) 773 399. Fax: (44 1274) 770 217. (*Annual film festival for South Asian and Black Film and TV – Sept. 22–30.*)

Bogota Film Festival, Calle 26 No. 4–92, Santa Fe de Bogota, Colombia. Tel: (57 1) 282 5196, 243 1901. Fax: (57 1) 342 2872. e-mail: cidc@coll.telecom.com.co. *(International competition for new directors. France is the Guest of Honour this year – Sept.)*

Boston Film Festival, P.O. Box 516, Hull, MA. 02045, USA. Tel: (1 781) 925 1373. Fax: (1 781) 925 3132. *(Approximately 50 films including studio releases, American independents, documentaries and short subjects – Sept. 8–17.)*

Bradford Film Festival, National Museum of Photography Film & TV, Pictureville, Bradford, BD1 1NQ West Yorkshire, UK. Tel: (44 1274) 773 399. Fax: (44 1274) 770 217. *(Features a competitive section for new European film-makers, previews of new releases, sections of unreleased film, retrospectives and Widescreen Weekend – March.)*

British Short Film Festival, Room A214-BBC TV Centre, Wood Lane, London W12, UK. Tel: (44 181) 743 8000. Fax: (44 181) 740 8540. *(Only competitive short film festival in UK – Sept. (tbc))*

Brussels Festival of Cartoons and Animated Films, Folioscope, rue de la Rhetorique 19, B–1060 Brussels, Belgium. Tel: (32 2) 534 4125. Fax: (32 2) 534 2279. e-mail: Folioscope@skynet.be *(Showcase for the newest, most interesting works in animation – Feb. 28-March 10.)*

Brussels International Festival of Fantasy, Thriller and Science Fiction Films, 144 Avenue de la Reine, 1030 Brussels, Belgium. Tel: (32 2) 201 1713.Fax: 210 1469. *(Competitive international selection. Special side-events include the Unusual Fashion Show and Painting and Sculpture competitions – March 17–Apr. 1.)*

Brussels International Film Festival, 30 chaussée de Louvain, 1210 Brussels, Belgium. Tel: (32 2) 227 3980. Fax: (32 2) 218 1860. *(Competitive festival featuring films from all countries – Jan. 19–30.)*

Cairo International Film Festival, 17 Kasr El Nil St., Cairo, Egypt. Tel: (20 2) 392 3562. Fax: (20 2) 393 8979. *(Competitive, aimed at showing major international films, usually not available – Nov.–Dec.)*

Cairo International Children's Film Festival, 17 Kasr El Nil Str., Cairo, Egypt. Tel: (20 2) 392 3562. Fax: (20 2) 393 8979. *(Organised by the General Union of Arab Artists. Competitive – March.)*

Camerimage, Foundation Tumalt, Rynek Nowomiejski 28, 87 100 Torun, Poland. Tel: (48 56) 652 2179. Fax: (48 56) 621 0019.Website: www.man.torun.pl/camerimage. html. *(International event celebrating the art of cinematography. Includes a competition, film workshops and equipment presentations – tbc May or Sept.)*

Canyonlands Film Festival, 1102 East 5th Avenue, Durango Colorado, 81301 USA. Tel: (1 970) 382 9528. e-mail: canyonfilm@hotmail.com Website: http://moab-utah.com/film *(Competitive, with awards including Best of Festival, Best Documentary, Best Dramatic Feature, etc. – April 6–9.)*

Cape Town International Film Festival, University of Cape Town, Private Bag, Rondebosch 7700, South Africa.Tel: (27 21) 423 8257.Fax: (27 21) 424 2355 e-mail: filmfest@hiddingh.uct.ac.za. *(Longest established film festival in South Africa. Non-competitive, transgressive in tone – Nov.)*

Cartoons on the Bay, Rai Trade, Via Umberto Novaro 18, 00195 Rome, Italy. Tel: (39 06) 3749 8315. Fax: (39 06) 3735 3521. E-mail: cartoonsbay@raitrade.it Website: www.raitrade.rai.it/cartoonsbay. *(International Festival of Television Animation, Competition, Conference and Workshop, promoted by RAI Radiotelevisione Italian, organised by RAI Trade – Apr. 14–18.)*

Chicago International Children's Film Festival, Facets Mulimedia, 1517 W. Fullerton, Chicago, IL 60614, USA. Tel: (1 773) 281 9075. Fax: (1 773) 929 5437. *(Largest competitive festival for children's films in North America, screening films and videos from 25 countries – Oct. 12–22 (tbc))*

Chicago Latino Cinema, 600 S. Michigan Ave., Chicago, IL 60605, USA. Tel: (1 312) 431 1330. Fax: (1 312) 360 0629. Website: www.chicagolatinocinema.org *(Aims to promote awareness of Latino culture through film and video – April 7–19.)*

Cinefest: The Sudbury Film Festival, 21840 Elm Street, Sudbury, Ontario P3C 1S8, Canada. Tel: (1 705) 688 1234. Fax: (1 705) 688 1351. Website: www.cinefest.com *(Aims to programme the best of contemporary Canadian cinema –Sept. 18–24.)*

Cinekid, 249, 1017 XJ Amsterdam, The Netherlands. Tel: (31 20) 624 7110. Fax: (31 20) 620 9965. e-mail: engelzx@xsyall.nl. *(International film and TV festival for children and young adults – Oct. 21–20.)*

Cinéma Méditerranéen Montpellier, 78 Avenue du Pirée, 34000 Montpellier, France. Tel: +33–4–99 13 73 73. Fax: +33–4–99 13 73 74. e-mail: cinemed@mnet.fr. Website: www.cinemed.tm.fr *(A major meeting-place of Mediterranean cinema – Oct. 27-Nov. 5.)*

Cinéma Italien Rencontres D'Annecy, Bonlieu Scène Nationale, 1 rue Jean Jaurès, BP 294, 74007 Annecy Cedex, France. Tel: (33 450) 334 400. Fax: (33 450) 518 209. *(Feature films from Italy, with tributes and retrospectives. Competitive – early Oct.)*

Cinemagic Festival for Young People, Fourth Floor, 38 Dublin Road, Belfast BT2 7HN, Ireland. Tel: (44 1232) 311 900. Fax: (44 1232) 319 709. *(Children's films in competition Dec.)*

Cinemayaat (Arab Film Festival) 2 Plaza Avenue, San Francisco, California, 94116. Tel: (1 415) 564 1100. Fax: (1 415) 704 3139. *(Features innovative curatorial perspective and presents exciting selection of films/videos from the Mashreq and the Maghreb. Non-competitive – Sept.)*

Cinequest San Jose Film Festival, P.O. Box 720040, San Jose, CA, USA. Tel: (1 408) 995 5033. Fax: (1 408) 995 5713. e-mail: sjfilmfest@aol.com. Website: www. cinequest.org. *(Competition of features, documentaries and shorts, with accompanying tributes, seminars, entertainment – Feb. 24–March 4.)*

Cleveland International Film Festival, 1621 Euclid Ave. #428, Cleveland, OH 44115–2017, USA. Tel: (1 216) 623 0400. Fax: (1 216) 623 0103. *(International "World Tour" progamme with specials like family films, American independents and lesbian and gay films – March 16–26.)*

Cork Film Festival, Hatfield House, Tobin Street, Cork, Ireland. Tel: (353 21) 271 711. Fax: (353 21) 275 945. e-mail: ciff@indigo.ie Website: www.corkfilmfest.org/ciff/. *(Features documentaries, animation, art films, fiction and sponsored shorts. Competitive for shorts – 2nd week in Oct.)*

Deauville Festival of American Film, 36 rue Pierret, 92200 Neuilly-sur-Seine, France. Tel: (33–1) 41 34 20 00.Fax: (33–1) 47 58 77 77. *(Deauville celebrated its 25th anniversary in 1999. Showcase for US features and independent films – early Sept.)*

Diagonale, Mariahilfer str. 113, A–1060 Vienna, Austria. Tel: (43 1) 216 1303. Fax: (43 1) 216 1303200. e-mail: wien@diagonale.at

Website: www.diagonale.at *(Festival of Austrian Film -March 27- April 2.)*

Dublin Film Festival, 1 Suffolk Street, Dublin 2, Ireland. Tel: (353 1) 679 2937. Fax: (353 1) 679 2939. e-mail: dff@iol.ie. Website: www.iol.ie/dff/. *(Amicable Irish festival focusing on world cinema with special emphasis on Irish film – March/April.)*

Dublin Lesbian & Gay Film Festival, OutHouse, 6 South William Street, Dublin 2, Ireland. Tel: (353 1) 672 7211. Fax: (353 1) 679 1306. e-mail: dublinlesbiangayfilm@ ireland.com Website: www.iftn.ie/ dublingayfilm. *(Now in its eight year the Dublin Lesbian & Gay Film festival is Europe's second largest, with a world-wide perspective and a special emphasis on Irish films north and south – Aug. 3–7.)*

Duisburg Film Week, Am König-Heinrich-Platz, D–47049 Duisburg, Germany. Tel: (49 203) 283 4171. Fax: (49 203) 283 4130. e-mail: filmwoche.vhs@duisburg.de. *(Dedicated to German-language documentaries – Nov. 6–12.)*

Emden International Film Festival, An der Berufsschule 3, 26721 Emden, Germany. Tel: (49 4921) 915 533/535. Fax: (49 4921) 915 591/599. *(Focusing on North-Western European films, particularly from Germany and the UK – May 31—June 7.)*

European First Film Festival (Premiers Plans), Festival d'Angers, 54 Rue Beaubourg, F–75003 Paris, France. Tel: (33 1) 4271 5370. Fax: (33 1) 4271 0111. *(Competitive festival for European first films, including features, shorts, and film schools – Jan. 21–30.)*

femme totale International Women's Film Festival Dortmund, c/o Kulturbüro Stadt Dortmund, Kleppingstr. 21–23, D–44122 Dortmund, Germany. Tel: (49 231) 502 5162. Fax: (49 231) 502 2497. e-mail: femmetotale@compuserve.com Website: www.inter-net-work.de *(Biennial festival with changing themes highlighting films made as a result of women's efforts. Non-competitive – March.)*

Festival of French Cinema, Tel Aviv Cinematheque, 2 Sprintzak Street, Tel Aviv, Israel. Tel: (972 3) 691 7181. Fax: (972 3) 696 2841. *(Screens new French fare, many Israeli premieres, with tributes and retrospectives – April.)*

Festival International du Film Francophone de Namur, 175 rue des Brasseurs, 5000

Namur, Belgium. Tel: (32 81) 241 236. Fax: (32 81) 224 384. *(Feature films, shorts and documentaries from French- speaking countries, with retrospectives and first-time directors. Competitive –Sept. 22-Oct. 3.)*

Festival Dei Popoli, Borgo Pinti 82r, 50121 Firenze, Italy. Tel: (39 055) 244 778. Fax: (39 055) 241 364. e-mail: fespopol@dada.it. Website: www.festivalpopoli.org. *(Includes documentaries on social issues and films on history. Partly competitive – second week in Nov.)*

Festival du Cinema International en Abitibi-Temscamingue, 215 Avenue Mercier, Rouyn-Noranda, Quebec J9X 5WB, Canada. Tel: (1 819) 762 6212. Fax: (1 819) 762 6762. e-mail: fciat@sympatico.ca Website: www.telebec.qc.ca/fciat. *(Short and medium length features from animation to documentary – Oct. 28–Nov. 2.)*

Figueira da Foz, Post Box 50 407, 1709 Lisbon Codex, Portugal. Tel: (351 1) 812 6231. Fax: (351 1) 812 6228. *(One of Portugal's most established film events Sept.)*

Filmfest München, Kaiserstrasse 39, D–80801, Munich, Germany. Tel: (49 89) 381 9040. Fax: (49 89) 381 90426. *(International screenings, TV movies and retrospectives – June. 24-Jul. 1.)*

Filmfestival Max Ophüls Prize, Mainzerstrasse 8 66111 Saarbrucken, Germany. Tel: (49 681) 39452. Fax: (49 681) 905 1943. *(Competitve event for young directors from German-speaking countries – Jan. 25–30.)*

Florida Film Festival, Enzian Theatre,1300 South Orlando Ave., Maitland, Florida 32751, USA. Tel: (1 407) 629 1088. Fax: (1 407) 629 6870. Website: www.enzian.org. *(Specialises in independent American films with special sections for features, shorts, documentaries and non-competitive spotlight films – June 10–19.(tbc))*

Focus on Asia Fukuoka International Film Festival, c/o Fukuoka City Hall, 1–8–1, Tenjin, Chuo-ku, Fukuoka 810 8620, Japan. Tel: (81 92) 733 5170. Fax: (81 92) 733 5595. *(Dedicated to the promotion of Asian Film. Non-competitive – Sept.)*

Future Film Festival, Via Pietralata 55/a- 40122 Bologna, Italy. Tel: (39 051) 520 629. Fax: (39 051) 523 816. e-mail: fff@clarence. com *(The first Italian festival about new technologies in animation cinema - Jan 21–25.)*

Galway Film Fleadh, Cluain Mhuire, Monivea Road, Galway, Ireland. Tel: (353 91) 751 655. Fax: (353 91) 770 746. e-mail: gafleadh@iol. Ie Website: ireland.iol.ie/ ~galfilm/fleadh *(Screens Irish, European, and international features and premieres. Last year's theme was "Family." Accompanied by the Galway Film Fair, Ireland's only film market -July 4–9.(tbc)*

Haifa International Film Festival, 142 Hanassi Avenue, Haifa 34 633, Israel. Tel: +972 4 8353 521/522. Fax: +972 4 8384 327. e-mail: haifaff@netvision.net.il Website: www.haifaff.col.il. *(Includes a broad spectrum of new films from around the world, special tributes, retrospectives and other events – Oct. 12–18.)*

Hawaii International Film Festival, 1001 Bishop Street, Honolulu, Hawaii 96813, USA. Tel: (1 808) 528 3456. Fax: (1 808) 528 1410. *(Seeks to promote cross-cultural under- standing – Nov. 3–12.)*

Heartland Film Festival, 613 N. East Street, Indianapolis, Indiana 46202, USA. Tel: (1 317) 635 9405. Fax: (1 317) 635 4201. e-mail: hff@pop.iquest.net. Website: www. heartlandfilmfest.org. *(Established in 1991 in Indianapolis, Indiana, to honour and reward film-makers whose work explores the human journey, artistically expressing hope and respect for positive values of life – Oct 19–29. tbc.)*

Hébraïca Montpellier, 500 Boulevard d'Antigone, 34000 Montpellier, France. Tel: (33 4) 6715 0876. Fax: (33 4) 6715 0872. *(Theatre Festival, Conferences, Showcases Jewish and Israeli films. Competitive – March.)*

Holland Animation Film Festival, Hoogt 4, 3512 GW Utrect, Holland. Tel: (31 30) 233 1733. Fax: (31 30) 233 1079. *(Animation from all over the world, competition for applied animation – Nov 15–19.)*

Hometown Video Festival, The Alliance for Community Media, 666 11th Street, NW #806, Washington, DC 20001, USA. Tel: (1 202) 393 2650. Fax: (1 202) 393 2653. *(Independent community producers from the US and abroad – July.)*

Huesca Film Festival, Calle del Parque, 1,2, Circulo Oscense, 22002 Huesca, Spain. Tel: (34 974) 212 582. Fax: (34 974) 210 065 *(Well- established festial in Northern Spain with long- features, hommages and a strong short film competition - June.)*

Hungarian Film Week, Magyar Filmunió, Vérosligeti, Fasor 38, 1068 Budapest, Hungary. Tel: (36 1) 351 7760. Fax: (36 1) 351 7766. *(Competitive national festival showcasing Hungarian production from the past year – Feb.)*

Independent Film Days, Filmbüro Augsburg, Schroeckstrasse 8, 86152 Augsburg, Germany. Tel: (49 821) 349 1060. Fax: (49 821) 349 5218. *(International event for documentary and independent features, with retrospectives, national focus and symposium of film students – Nov.)*

International Documentary Film Festival-Amascultura, Rua Angola, Olival Basto, 2675 Odivelas, Portugal. Tel: (351 1) 938 8407. Fax: (351 1) 938 9347. e-mail: amascultura@mail.telepac.pt. *(International documentaries – Nov. 11–17.(tbc)*

International Documentary Filmfestival – Amsterdam (IDFA), Kleine-Gartman-plantsoen 10, 1017 RR Amsterdam, The Netherlands. Tel: (31 20) 627 3329. Fax: (31 20) 638 5388. e-mail: info@idfa.nl. Website: www.idfa.nl. *(Creative documentary films of all lengths, including numerous awards and a special "Kids & Docs" section. Includes the Forum, a market for international co-financing of documentaries – Nov 22–30.)*

International Film Camera Festival "Manaki Brothers", 8. Mart #4, 91100 Skopje, Republic of Macedonia. Tel/fax: (389 91) 211 811. e-mail: ffmanaki@unet.com.mk. *(Held in Bitola, Republic of Macedonia, in remembrance of the brothers Yanaki and Milton Manaki, the first cameramen on the Balkans – Sept. 27-Oct.1.)*

International Festival of New Latin American Cinema, Calle 23 No. 1155, Vedado, Havana, Cuba. Tel: (53 7) 34169. Fax: (53 7) 334 273. *(Competitive event and market for Latin American and International Films – Dec.)*

International Film Festival, Museum-strasse 31, A–6020 Innsbruck. Austria. Tel: (43 664) 120 7458. Fax: (43 512) 581762. e-mail: ffi.cinematograph@tirolkultur.at. Website: www.tirolkultur.at/cinema. *(Films about Africa, America and Asia, Austrian premieres – early May 31-June 4.)*

International Film Festival of Uruguay, Lorenzo Carnelli 1311, Casilla de Correo 1170, 11200 Montevideo, Uruguay. Tel: (5982) 408 2460. Fax: (5982) 409 4572. e-mail: cinemuy@chasque.apc.org. Website: www.cinemateca.org.uy. *(Uruguayan event running April 15–30, 2000, with a Children's Festival from July 13–14, 2000.)*

International Film Forum "Arsenals," Marstalu 14, P.O. Box 626, Riga, LV 1047, Latvia. Tel: (371 7) 221 620. Fax: (371 7) 820 445. e-mail: programm@arsenals.lv. *(Latvia's biggest film event, dedicated to innovative film-making – Sept. 16–24.)*

International Short Film Festival Oberhausen, Grillostrasse 34, D–46045 Oberhausen, Germany. Tel: (49 208) 825 2652. Fax: (49 208) 825 5413. e-mail: info@kurzfilmtage.de. *(A competitive short film and video festival and market – May 4–9.)*

International Student Film Festival, Tel Aviv Cinémathèque, 2 Sprintzak Street. Tel Aviv, Israel. Tel: (972 3) 691 7181. Fax: (972 3) 696 2840. *(Workshops, retrospectives, tributes, premieres – June.)*

The World Animation Celebration, 30101 Agoura Court, Suite 110, Agoura, CA 91301, USA. Tel: (1 818) 991 2884. Fax: (1 818) 991 3773. E-mail: animag@aol.com. Website: www.animag.com.

International Women's Film Festival, Maison des Arts, Palace Salvador Allende, 94000 Creteil, France. Tel: (33 1) 4980 3898. Fax: (33 1) 4399 0410. e-mail: filmsfemmes@wanadoo.fr. Website: www.g.debussac.fr/filmfem. *(Features, shorts and animated films all made by women – March 24–April 2.)*

Israel Film Festival, Israfest Foundation, 6404 Wilshire Blvd., Suite 1240, Los Angeles, CA. 90048, USA. Tel: (1 213) 966 4166. Fax: (1 213) 658 6346. *(US showcase for Israeli features, shorts, documentaries and TV dramas – Feb. in LA, March in NY.)*

Junior Dublin Film Festival, Irish Film Centre, 6 Eustace Street, Dublin 2, Ireland. Tel: (353 1) 671 4094. Fax: (353 1) 677 8755. *(Showcases the best in world cinema for young people and includes workshops and seminars – Nov. 21-Dec 1)*

Kidfilm Festival, USA. Film Festival, 2917 Swiss Ave., Dallas, Texas 75204, USA. Tel: (1 214) 821 6300. Fax: (1 214) 821 6364. *(Showcases new and classic children's films from around the world – Jan. 10–23.)*

Kraków International Short Film Festival, c/o Apollo Film, ul. Pychowicka 7, 30–364 Kraków, Poland. Tel: (48 122) 676 340. Fax: (48 122) 671 552. *(Poland's oldest international film festival and respected short film showcase – May.)*

Kudzu Film Festival, P.O. Box 1461, Athens, GA 30603, USA. Tel: (1 706) 227 6090. Fax: (1 706) 227 6090. *(Celebrates emerging talent and cultural diversity through features, shorts and documentaries – Oct. 18–21.)*

Kiev International Film Festival "Molodist", 6 Saksagansky Street, 252033 Kiev, Ukraine. Tel: (380 44) 246 6798. Fax: (380 44) 227 4557. e-mail: molodist@gu. kiev.ua. *(Ukraine's largest international film event and annual competition – Oct. 21–29.)*

Latin American Film Festival, Metro Pictures, 79 Wardour Street, London W1V 3TH, UK. Tel: (44 171) 434 3357. Fax: (44 171) 287 2112. *(Films from Latin American countries, including features, documentaries and shorts Sept. 1–14)*

Leeds International Film Festival, Town Hall, Headrow, Leeds LS1 3AD, UK. Tel: (44 113) 247 8389. Fax: (44 113) 247 8397. *(Premieres, previews, retrospectives, director tributes, workshops and special events – Oct.)*

Los Angeles International Film Festival, AFI Festivals, 2021 N. Western Avenue, Los Angelos, CA 90027, USA. Tel: (1 323) 856 7707. Fax: (1 323) 462 4049. e-mail: afifest@afionline.org. Website: www. afifest.com. *(L.A.'s most prominent film festival – Oct.)*

Ljubljana International Film Festival, Cankarjev Dom, Presernova 10, 1000 Ljubljana, Slovenia. Tel: (386 61) 212 600. Fax: (386 61) 224 279. *(Independents and previews of films coming to Slovenian cinemas. Nov. 6–19.)*

Local Heroes International Screen Festival, National Screen Institute, 3rd floor, 10022–103 St., Edmonton, Canada T5J 0X2. Tel: (1 403) 421 4084. Fax: (1 403) 425 8098. E-mail: filmhero@nsi-canada.ca. Website: www.nsi-canada.ca. *(Independent, non-competitive, seminars etc. – Feb. 18–26.)*

London Lesbian & Gay Film Festival, National Film Theatre, South Bank, London SE1 8XT. UK. Tel: (44 171) 815 1323. Fax: (44 171) 633 0786. *(Films made by or about gays and lesbians –April.)*

Lucas International Children's and Young People's Film Festival, Deutsches Filmmuseum, Schaumainkai 41, 60596 Frankfurt/Main, Germany. Tel: (49 69) **2123 3369**. Fax: (49 69) **2123 7881**. *(New films for children and young people – Sept.)*

Margaret Mead Film & Video Festival, American Museum of Natural History, 79th St. at Central Park West, New York, N.Y. 10024, USA. Tel: (1 212) 769 5305. Fax: (1 212) 769 5329. *(International documentary and ethnographic festival includes shorts and features –Nov.)*

Marseille 2000 Documentary Film Festival, 3 Square Stalingrad, 13001 Marseilles, France. Tel: (33 4) 9504 4490. Fax: (33 4) 9504 4491. *(Specialising in documentaries, the Festival is a rich showcase for talent – June.)*

Melbourne International Film Festival, P.O.Box 2206, Fitzroy 3065, Melbourne, Victoria, Australia. Tel: (61 3) 9417 2011. Fax: (61 3) 9417 3804. *(The oldest festival in the Southern hemisphere incorporating international features, animation, documentary and experimental works – July 22–Aug 8.)*

"Message to Man" Film Festival, Karavannaya 12, 191011, St. Petersburg, Russia. Tel: (7 812) 235 2660. Fax: (7 812) 235 3995. *(Programme includes international competition and special programmes, such as Russian documentaries, French films, a children's programme, Nordisk Panorama and retrospectives – Jun.)*

Miami Film Festival, Film Society of Miami, 444 Brickell Ave. no.229, Miami, Florida 33131. USA. Tel: (1 305) 377 3456. Fax: (1 305) 577 9768. e-mail: mff@gate.net. Website: www.miamifilmfestival.com. *(Festival emphasis is on Hispanic cinema, featuring an Audience Award – Feb. 18–27.)*

Midnight Sun Film Festival, Malminkatu 36 B 102, 00100 Helsinki, Finland. Tel: (358 9) 685 2242. Fax: (358 9) 694 5560. *(International and silent films, as well as award-winners from Cannes, Berlin, Locarno, and Stockholm film festivals – June 14–18.)*

Minneapolis/St.Paul International Film Festival, University Film Society, Minnesota Film Center, 425 Ontario Street SE, Minneapolis, MN 55414. Tel: (1 612) 627 4431. *(Event built up over 16 years by the reliable Al Milgrom. Screens scores of foreign films, especially Scandinavian – Apr. 14–29.)*

Montréal International Festival of New Cinema and New Media, 3668 Boulevard Saint-Laurent, Montreal, Quebec H2X 2V4,

Canada. Tel: (1 514) 847 9272. Fax: (1 514) 847 0732. e-mail: montrealfest@fcmm.com Website: www.fcmm.com (*Focuses on independent cinema and seeks to explore quality experimental films as an alternative to conventional commercial cinema – Oct. 12–22.*)

Moscow International Film Festival, 10/1 Khokhlovsky per., Moscow, 109028, Russia. Tel: (7 095) 917 2486. Fax: (7 095) 916 0107. E-mail: miff@cityline.ru Website: www.miff.ru (*Competitive only for full-length features – July.*)

NAT-Annual Film Festival of Denmark, NatFilm Festivalen, Festivalsekretariat, Store Kannikestræde 6, 1169 Copenhagen, Denmark. Tel: (45) 3312 0005. Fax: (45) 3312 7505. e-mail: natfilm@centrum.dk. Website: www.filmfest.dk. (*Offers offbeat retros and tributes from various countries March 3–19.*)

New Directors/New Films, The Film Society of Lincoln Center, 70 Lincoln Center Plaza, New York, N.Y. 10023, USA. Tel: (1 212) 875 5610. Fax: (1 212) 875 5636. (*A forum for works by new directors co-sponsored by the Museum of Modern Art and The Film Society of Lincoln Center – March 24-April 9.*)

New England Film and Video Festival, Boston Film/Video Foundation, 1126 Boylston Street, room 201, Boston, MA 02215, USA. Tel: (1 617) 536 1540. Fax: (1 617) 536 3576. e-mail: Devon@bfvf.org Website: www.bfvf.org (*Since 1976, competitive regional festival devoted to new works by professionals and students in New England. Residency required for eligibility – April.*)

New Orleans Film and Video Festival, P.O. Box 50819, New Orleans, LA. 70150, USA. Tel: (1 504) 523 3818. Fax: (1 504) 529 2430. (*Eleventh annual festival includes international features, workshops and indie film competition – Oct.*)

New York Exposition of Short Film and Video, New York Expo, 532 LaGuardia Place, Suite 330, New York, NY 10012, USA. Tel: (1 212) 505 7742. e-mail: nyexpo@aol.com Website: www.yrd.com/nyexpo (*Showcases both traditional, well-crafted work and challenging, experimental productions – Dec.*)

Northwest Film and Video Festival, Northwest Film Center, 1219 S.W. Park Ave., Portland, Oregon 97205, USA. Tel: (1

503) 221 1156. Fax: (1 503) 226 4842. Website: www.nwfilm.org (*Annual survey of new moving-image art produced in the US Northwest. Features, shorts and documentaries – Nov. 3–10.*)

Ökomedia, Ökomedia Institute, Habsburgerstr. 9a, D–79104 Freiburg, Germany. Tel: (49 761) 52 024. Fax: (49 761) 555 724. e-mail: oekomedia@t-online.de (*Screenings of international film and television productions which offer an up-to-date review of ecological and environmental issues - early Oct.*)

Open Air Filmfest Weiterstadt, Film fest Weiterstadt, c/o Pollitt, Bahnhofstrasse 70, D-64331 Weiterstadt, Germany. Tel: (49 6150) 12185. Fax: (49 6150) 14073. e-mail: sfk@hrzpub.tu-darmstadt.de Website: www.home.pages.de/~sfk/weiterstadt/filmfest (*Germany's oldest and largest open air film festival - Aug. 10-14.*)

Oslo Animation Festival, Skippergt. 17, Box 867, 0104 Oslo, Norway. Tel: (47 23) 119 300. Fax: (47 23) 119 310. (*Nordic and international animation, with retros and student fims. Competitive – April 26–30.*)

Palm Beach International Film Festival, 1555 Palm Beach Lakes Blvd., Suite 403, West Palm Beach, Florida 33401 USA. Tel: (1 561) 233 1044. Fax: (1 561) 683 6655. (*Approximately 50 films, which include studio releases, American independents, documentaries and short subjects – April.*)

Palm Springs International Short Film Festival, 1700 E. Tahquitz Way, #3, Palm Springs, CA 92262, USA. Tel: (1 760) 322 2930. Fax: (1 760) 322 4087. (*Largest competitive short film festival in North America. Student, animation, documentary and international competition. Seminars and workshops – July/Aug.*)

Panorama of European Cinema, Minoos 10–16, 11 743 Athens, Greece. Tel: (30–1) 929 96 001. Fax: (30–1) 902 8311. (*In its 12th year in 1999, the event includes European Competition Section-Sept. 23-Oct.8.*)

Peniscola International Comedy Festival, Patronato Municipal de Turismo, Festival de Cine, Plaza Constitucion, s/n, 12598 Peniscola (Castellon). Tel: (34 964) 474 901. Fax: (34 964) 481 521. (*Hugely enjoyable local comedy festival set in a spectacular Mediterranean seaside resort - June.*)

Pia Film Festival, 5–19 Sanban-cho, Chiyoda-ku, Tokyo, Japan. Tel: (81 3) 3265

1425. Fax: (81 3) 3265 5659. (*Aims to nurture new, unique voices and emergent talent. Competitive for amateurs, with an invitational showcase – Jul.*)

Philadelphia Festival of World Cinema, International House, 3701 Chestnut Street, Philidelphia, PA 19104, USA. Tel: (1 215) 895 6593. Fax: (1 215) 895 6562. (*Festival screens a world-wide range of features, documentaries and shorts – April 27-May 6.*)

Pusan International Film Festival, Room 208, # 1393 Woo 1 Dong, Hacuudac-Ku, Pusan, Korea. Tel: (82 51) 747 3010. Fax: (82 51) 747 3012. e-mail: program@piff.org Website: www.piff.org (*Launched in 1996 PIFF is celebrating the best in world cinema with the emphasis on Asian films – Oct.*)

RAI Trade Screenings, Rai Trade, Via Umberto Novaro 18, 00195 Rome, Italy. Tel: (39 06) 3749 8257/8473/8330. Fax: (39 06) 3701 343. Website: www.raitrade.rai.it (*Opportunity for international programming buyers to view audio-visual material from Rai for broadcast, home video, music, merchandising and publishing rights – Sept./Oct.*)

Rio De Janeiro Film Festival, Cima – Centro de Cultura, Informacão e Meio-ambiente, Rua Fernandes Guimarães, 39–4th floor, Botafogo, Rio de Janeiro, Brasil. Tel/Fax: (55 21) 295 1060/ 3792/0756. e-mail: cima@visualnet.com.br (*Rio Festival has brought together two events which co-existed for the last decade: RioCine Festival and MostraRio – Sept.*)

Rouen, Festival du Cinéma Nordique, 22 rue de la Champmesle, 76000 Rouen, France. Tel: (33 2) 35 98 28 46. Fax: (33 2) 35 70 92 08. (*Competitive festival of Nordic cinema, including retrospective and information sections – March 15–26.*)

Saint Louis Film Festival, 55 Maryland Plaza, Suite A, St. Louis, MO 63108–1501, USA. Tel: (1 314) 454 0042. Fax: (1 314) 454 0540. e-mail: info@sliff.org Website: www.sliff.org (*Showcases approximately 100 US and international independent and studio "art" films – Oct./Nov.*)

St. Petersburg Festival of Festivals, 190 Kamennostrovsky Ave., St. Petersburg 197101, Russia. Tel: (7 812) 237 0304, 237 0072. Fax: (7 812) 394 5870. (*Features international productions as well as local fare. Non-competitive – June 23–29.*)

San Francisco International Asian American Film Festival, c/o NAATA, 346

9th Street, San Francisco, CA., 94103, USA. Tel: (1 415) 863 0814. Fax: (1 415) 863 7428. e-mail: festival @naatanet. (*Film and video works by Asian-American and Asian artists – March 13–20.*)

San Francisco International Lesbian and Gay Film Festival, Frameline, 346 Ninth Street, San Francisco, CA. 94103, USA. Tel: (1 415) 703 8652. Fax: (1 415) 861 1404. (*Focus on gay and lesbian themes – June 15–25.*)

São Paulo International Film Festival, Alameda Lorena, 937 no. 303, 01424-001 São Paulo, Brazil. Tel: (55 11) 883 5137. Fax: (55 11) 853 7936. (*Competitive event with features and shorts from around 60 countries. Emphasis on independents – Oct.*)

Seattle International Film Festival, 801 East Pine Street, Seattle, Washington 98122, USA. Tel: (1 206) 464 5830. Fax: (1 206) 264 7919. e-mail: mail@seattlefilm.com Website: www.seattlefilm.com. (*Unusual Northwest Pacific coast event that has done a great deal to establish Dutch cinema in the US – May/June.*)

Singapore International Film Festival, 29A Keong Salk Road, 089136 Singapore. Tel: (65) 738 7567. Fax: (65) 738 7578. (*Showcases the best of Asian and world cinema. Competitive Asian section – April.*)

Sydney Film Festival, P.O. Box 950, Glebe, NSW 2037, Australia. Tel: (61 2) 9660 3844. Fax: (61 2) 9692 8793. e-mail: sydfilm@ ozonline.com.au. (*Broad-based, non-competitive event screening new international films and Australian features and shorts – June 9–23*)

Taormina International Film Festival, Corso Umberto 19, 98039 Taormina, Italy. Tel: (39 094) 221 142. Fax: (39 094) 223 348. (*Competitive and non-competitive event in Sicily, stressing films by new English-language directors – July*)

Tokyo International Film Festival, 3rd floor, Landic Ginza, Bldg. II 1–6–5 Ginza, Chuo-ku, Tokyo 104-0061, Japan. Tel: (81 3) 3563 6305. Fax: (81 3) 3563 6310. Website: www.tokyo-filmfest.or.jp. *(Major international event with competition and sidebars – late Oct.-early Nov.)*

Troia International Film Festival, Avenida Luisa Dodee 65, 2900 Setubal Codex, Portugal. Tel: (351 65) 525 908. Fax: (351 65) 525 681. *(Held in a summer recreational area on the tip of a peninsula. Features a wide variety of categories. Competitive – Early June.)*

Udine Incontri Cinema, Centro Espressioni Cinematografiche, Via Gregorutti 25, 33100 Udine, Italy. Tel: (39 432) 522 717. Fax: (39 432) 601 421. e-mail: cecudine@tin.it. *(Annual themed event which, since 1998, has focused on East Asian cinema, with special emphasis on Hong Kong and Chinese cinema – April.)*

Uppsala Short Film Festival, P.O. Box 1746, S–751 47 Uppsala, Sweden. Tel: (46 18) 120 025. Fax: (46 18) 121 350. e-mail: uppsala@shortfilmfestival.com Website: www.shortfilmfestival.com. *(The only international short film festival in Sweden. Competitive – Oct.)*

USA Film Festival, 2917 Swiss Ave., Dallas, Texas 75204, USA. Tel: (1 214) 821 6300. Fax: (1 214) 821 6364. *(Eight-day festival featuring new US and foreign independents. Competition for US shorts with cash prizes – April 27-May 4.)*

Valencia Film Festival, Plaza Arzobispo, 2 acc. B, Valencia 46003, Spain. Tel: (34 96) 392 1506. Fax: (34 96) 391 5156. *(Competitive section for films made in and around the Mediterranean – Oct.)*

Viennale, Stiftgasse 6, A – 1070 Vienna, Austria. Tel: (43 1) 526 5947. Fax: (43 1) 523 4172. e-mail: office@viennale.or.at Website: www.viennale.or.at. *(Presents a line-up of new international films, independent and new cinema, creative documentaries, shorts, tributes programmes dedicated to directors, actors or producers – Oct.13–25.)*

Vila do Conde Festival Internacional de Curtas Metragens, Auditório Municipal, Praça de República, 4480 Vila do Conde, Portugal. Tel: (351 52) 641 644. Fax: (351 52) 646 516. *(Competitive for both Portuguese and international short films. Adjoining market for shorts – July.)*

Virginia Film Festival, Dept. of Drama, Culbreth Road, Charlottesville, VA 22903, USA. Tel: (1 804) 982 5277. Fax: (1 804) 924 1447. Website: www.virginia .edu / ~vafilm. *(Annual event dedicated to the study of American cinema in relation to international films, with classics, premieres and discussions – late Oct.)*

Warsaw, P.O. Box 816, 00–950 Warsaw 1, Poland. Tel: (48 22) 853 3636. Fax: (48 22) 853 1184. e-mail: festiv@wff.org.pl Website: www.wff.org.pl *(Audience-oriented, 12-day event which has been screening current, invitation-only productions since 1985 – Oct. 5–16.)*

Washington, DC International Film Festival (Filmfest DC), P.O. Box 21396, Washington, DC 20009, USA. Tel: (1 202) 724 5613. Fax: (1 202) 724 6578. *(Celebrates the best in world cinema – April 19–30.)*

XV Muestra de Cine Mexicano en Guadalajara, Alemania #1370, col Moderna, CP 44190 Guadalajara, Jalisco, México. Tel: (523) 615 4953/ 615 4922. Fax: (523) 615 5002. e-mail: Muestra@cencar. udg.mx *(Competition festival both national and international, short films only national – March.)*

Antonio Banderas, Anthony Hopkins and Catherine Zeta-Jones, at the premiere of THE MASK OF ZORRO in San Sebastian

FILM SCHOOLS

AUSTRALIA

Australian Film, Television and Radio School, P.O. Box 126, North Ryde, NSW 1670.

AUSTRIA

Universität für Musik und darstellende Kunst, Abteilung für Film und Fernsehen, Metternichgasse 12, A-1030 Vienna. Tel (43-1) 713 5212-113. Fax: (43-1) 713 5212-114. Director: Mr. Wolfgang Gluck, member of AMPAS, Director's Branch.

BELGIUM

Archimedia, European Training Network for the Promotion of Cinema Heritage, Cinémathèque Royale, 23 rue Ravenstein, 1000 Brussels. Tel: (32 2) 507 8403. Fax: (32 2) 513 1272. e-mail: archimedia@ledoux.be.

Institut des Arts de Diffusion (I.A.D.), Rue des Wallons No. 77, B 1348 Louvain-la Neuve.

Institut National des Arts du Spectacle et Techniques de diffusion (I.N.S.A.S), Rue Thérésienne, 8, 1000 Brussels. Tel (32 2) 511 92 86. Fax: (32 2) 511 0279. e-mail: sec@insas.be Website: www.insas.be

Koninklijke Academie voor Schone Kunsten-Gent, Academiestraat 2, B-9000 Gent.

CANADA

Queen's University, 160 Stuart St., Kingston, Ontario K7L 3N6. Tel: (1 613) 533 2178. Fax: (1 613) 533 2063. e-mail: film@post.queensu.ca Website: www.film.queensu.ca. In its four-year B.A. (Honours) degree programme and three-year B.A. degree programme, the Department of Film Studies provides an integrated approach to film criticism, history and production.

Sheridan College, Faculty of Visual Arts, 1430 Trafalgar Road, Oakville, Ontario, L6H 2L1. Tel: (1 905) 845 9430 ext. 2958. Fax: (1 905) 815 4041. Dean: Scot Turner. Intensive and award-winning diploma programmes in: Classical Animation, International Summer School of Animation, Computer Animation, Computer Graphics and Media Arts. Summer workshops available from May to August.

Simon Fraser University, School for the Contemporary Arts, 8888 Univeristy Drive, Burnaby, B.C. V5A 1S6. Tel: (1 604) 291 3363. Fax: (1 604) 291 5907.

Vancouver Film School, 400-1168 Hamilton Street, Vancouver B.C. V6B 2S2. Tel: (1 604) 685 5808. Fax: (1 604) 685 5830. President: James Griffin. A unique training centre that offers five programmes in communication production: Film Production, Multimedia Production, Classical Animation, Computer Animation, and Acting for Film and Television. All programmes have been designed with industry consultation and are taught by industry professionals. Specialising in shorter (one year) and intensive formats, students create their own graduate productions.

University of Manitoba, Film Studies Program, 367 University College, Winnipeg, Manitoba R3T 2M8. Tel: (1 204) 474 9581. Fax: (1 204) 474 7684. e-mail: film@umanitoba.ca Basic film-making and screenwriting, the Film Studies Program at the University of Manitoba will be offering advanced filmmaking beginning in January 2000.

University of Windsor, Ontario N9B 3P4. Film, radio, TV.

York University, Faculty of Fine Arts, Film & Video Dept., 4700 Keele Street, Toronto, Ontario M3J 1P3.

CZECH REPUBLIC

FAMU, Film and Television Faculty, Academy of Performing Arts, Smetanovo nábr. 2, CZ 116 65 Prague 1. Tel: (420 2) 2422 9176. Fax: (420 2) 2423 0285. Dean: Karel Kochman.

DENMARK

European Film College, DK-8400 Ebeltoft. Tel: (45) 8634 0055. Fax: (45) 8634 0535. Principal: Kjeld Veirup. Summer season: international, intensive training courses for professionals of the industry. Sept.-April: eight-month undergraduate courses for students from all over the world. No special qualifications required except English language.

The National Film School of Denmark, Theodor Christensen's Plads 1, 1437 Copenhagen K. Tel: (45) 3268 6400. Fax: (45) 3268 6410. e-mail: info@filmskolen.dk

FINLAND

Taideteollinen korkeakoulu, elokuvataiteen osasto, University of Art and Design Helsinki UIAH, Department of Film and TV, Pursimiehenkatu, 29-31 B, SF-00150 Helsinki.

FRANCE

La Femis (École Nationale Supérieure de de Formation et Métiers de L'Image et du Son, 6 rue Francoeur, 75018 Paris. Tel: (33 1) 5341 2101. Fax: 33 1) 5341 2109. President: Alain Auclaire. Director: Gérard Alaux.

Conservatoire Libre du Cinéma Français (C.I.C.F.), 9 quai de l'Oise, 75019 Paris. Tel: (33 1) 4036 1919. Fax: (33 1) 4036 0102.

ESEC (Ecole superieure études cinematographique), 21 rue de Citeaux, 75012 Paris. Tel: (33 1) 4342 4322. Fax: (33 1) 4341 9521. L'ESEC gives a national diploma.

GERMANY

Deutsche Film and Fernsehakademie Berlin GmbH, DFFB, Heerstrasse 18-20, 14052 Berlin.Tel: (49 30) 300 9040. Fax: (49 30) 300 90461. Director: Prof. Reinhard Hauff. Four-year course deals with theories of film-making, film-history, and all aspects of practical film and TV production, script-writing, direction, camerawork, editing and special effects.

Filmakademie Baden-Würtenberg, Mathildenstraße 20, 71638 Ludwigsburg, Germany. Tel: (49 7141) 969 235. Fax: (49 7141) 969 297.

Hochschule für Fernsehen und Film, Frankenthaler Strasse 23, D-81539 München. Tel: (49 89) 689 570. Fax: (49 89) 689 57189. Website: www.hff-muenchen. mhn.de. President: Prof. Dr. Albert Scharg. Approx. 340 students, 80 staff. Four-year course provides instruction in the theory and practice of film and TV. Facilities provide for work in 16 and 35mm as well as video equipment. Studies are free and begin each Fall. Ask for details about the two-step admission process in Jan. each year.

HONG KONG

Hong Kong Academy for Performing Arts, School of Film and Television, 1 Gloucester Road, GPO Box 12288, Wanchai, Hong Kong. Dean: Mr. Richard Woolley. Tel: (852) 2584 8626/8679. Fax: (852) 2802 4372.

HUNGARY

Szinbáz-es Filmmiivészeti Föiskola, Vas u. 2/c, 1088 Budapest. Rector: Péter Huszti. General Secretary: László Vadäsz.

The London International Film School

- Training film makers for 40 years •
- Graduates now working worldwide •
- Located in Covent Garden in the heart of London •
- 16mm documentary & 35mm studio filming •
- Two year Diploma course in film making •
- Commences three times a year: January, May, September •

London International Film School,
Department IG14. 24 Shelton Street, London WC2H 9HP
Tel: 0171 836 9642/0171 240 0168 Fax: 0171 497 3718
Email: info@lifs.org.uk Web Page: http://www.lifs.org.uk

One of the many international events held by MAGICA in Italy

INDIA

Film and Television Institute of India, Law College Road, Pune 411 004. Tel: (91 20) 331 817. Fax: (91 20) 330 416. e-mail: filminst@pne. vsnl. net.in Director: Dr. Mohan Agashe. Chairman: Girish Karnad.

IRELAND

European School of Animation, Senior College, Ballyfermot Road, Dublin 10. Tel: (353 1) 626 9421. Fax: (353 1) 626 6754. e-mail: infoscb.cdcec.ie

ISRAEL

Department of Cinema and Television, Tel Aviv University, Ramat Aviv, Tel Aviv. Tel: (972 3) 640 8403. Fax: (972 3) 640 9935.

ITALY

MAGICA, Master Europeo in Gestione di Impresa Cinematografica e Audiovisiva, Via Lucullo 7 int. 8, 00187 Rome, Italy. Tel: (39 06) 420 0651. Fax: (39 06) 420 10898. e-mail: courses@ audiovisual.org Website: www. audiovisual.org. An international organisation offering on-line (via Internet) and in-class audiovisual and multimedia management and creative training for professionals and graduates. Specialisations include: screenwriting, audio-visual law and economics, multi-media studies, co-production, audiovisual management in all areas of production and distri-bution. All the programmes are designed and taught by European and US industry professionals.

Scuola Nazionale di Cinema, Via Tuscolana 1524, 00173 Rome. Tel: (39 06) 722 941. Fax: (39 06) 721 1619. e-mail: snccn@tin.it. President: Lino Miccichè. General Director: Angelo Libertini. Director-coordinator: Caterina D'Amico.

JAPAN

Nihon University College of Art, Asahiganoka 2-42, Nerimaku, Tokyo, 176. Head of Film Depart-ment: Professor Toru Otake.

NETHERLANDS

Maurits Binger Film Institut, Nieuwezijds Voorburgwal 4-10, 1012 RZ Amsterdam NL. Tel: (31 20) 421 2048. Fax: (31 20) 638 3002. e-mail: binger@mbi.ahk.nl. Core programme of around 15 film-makers per half-year working together to develop numerous feature film projects. Also serves as a centre for the film community at large to exchange ideas, gain inspiration, and use the facilities.

Nederlandse Film en Televisie Academie, Ite Boeremastraat 1, 1054 PP Amsterdam.

POLAND

Panstwowa Wyzsza Szkola Filmowa, Telewizyina i Teatralna, 61/63 Targowa str., 90 323 Lódz. Tel: (48 42) 674 8088. Fax: (48 42) 674 8139. e-mail: swzfilm@ mazurek.man Website: www. filmowka.lodz.pl

ROMANIA

Universitatea de Arta Teatrala si Cinematografica "I.L. Caragiale", str. Matei Voievod nr. 75-77, sector 2, 73224, Bucharest. Tel: (40 1) 252 8112. Fax: (40 1) 252 5881. Dean: Elisabeta Bostan.

SPAIN

University of Valladolid, Cátedra de Historia y Estética de la Cinematografica, 47002, Valladolid. Tel: (34 983) 423 611. Fax: (34 983) 423 611. Director: Sr. Dr. Francisco Javier de la Plaza Santiago.

ECAM (Escuela de Cinematografia de la Comunidad de Madrid), Juan de Orduña 3, Ciudad de la imagen, 28223 Pozuelo de Alarcón, Madrid. Tel: (34 91) 512 1060. Fax: (34 91) 512 1070. e-mail: escuelacine@ecam.es Created in 1995 a popular three-year course especially strong on film direction.

Centre d'Estudis Cinematograficos de Catalunya, Caspe 33, principal, 08010 Barcelona, Spain. Tel: (34 93) 412 0484. Fax: (34 93) 318 8866. Three-year course run by Hector Faver in the theory and practice of film, including direction, scriptwriting and acting.

ESCAC (Escola Superior de Cinema Audiovisuals de Catalunya), Immaculada 35, 08017 Barcelona, Spain. Tel: (34 93) 212 1562. Fax: (34 93) 417 2601. Four-year course approved by the University of Barcelona split between general theory and specialist courses in screenwriting, production, direction, cinematography, sound, post-production and art-direction.

SWEDEN

Department of Cinema Studies University of Stockholm, Borgvägen 1-5, Box 27062, S-102 51 Stockholm. Tel: (46 8) 647 7627. Fax: (46 8) 665 0723.

Dramatiska Institutet (College of Theatre, Film, Radio, and Television), Borgvägen, Box 27090, S-102 51 Stockholm. Head of School: Kjell Grede.

UNITED KINGDOM

University of Bristol, Department of Drama, Film and Television Studies, Cantocks Close, Woodland Road, Bristol BS8 1UP. Tel: (44 117) 928 7838. Fax: (44 117) 928 8251.

University of Derby, School of Arts and Design, Britannia Mail, Mackworth Road, Derby DE22 3BL. Tel: (44 13) 3262 2281. Fax: (44 13) 3262 2760. e-mail: s.greenhough@derby.ac.uk. MA/FT/PT in Film with TV studies. B.A. (Honours) – subject to validation.

University of Westminster, Harrow School of Design and Media, Watford Road, Northwick Park, Harrow, HA1 3TP. Tel: (44 171) 911 5903. Fax: (44 171) 911 5955

London International Film School, 24 Shelton Street, London WC2H 9HP. Tel: (44 171) 836 9642. Fax: (44 171) 497 3718. e-mail: info@lifs.org.uk. Website: www.lifs.org.uk. Principal: Martin M. Amstell. Offers a practical, two-year Diploma course to professional levels. About half of each term is devoted to film production and the other half to practical and theoretical tuition. All students work on one or more films each term and are encouraged to experience different skill areas. Facilities include two cinemas, shooting stages, rehearsal stages, and 15 cutting rooms. Equipment includes 16 and 35mm Panavision, Arriflex and rostrum cameras, Nagra recorders, Steenbeck editing machines and U-matic video. Faculty is permanent and visiting professionals. Entrance requirements: a degree or art or technical diploma, with exceptions for special ability or experience. Applicants must submit samples of their work and be proficient in English. New courses commence each Jan., April and Sept.

Middlesex University, Faculty of Art and Design, Cat Hill, Barnet, Herts EN4 8HT. Tel: (44 181) 362 5021. Fax: (44 181) 362 6339.

National Film and Television School, Station Road, Beaconsfield, Bucks, HP9 1LG. Tel: (44 1494) 671 234. Fax: (44 1494) 674 042. Director: Stephen Bayly. Head of Production: Anne Skinner. Training in all areas of film and television programme making.

Newport School of Art and Design, University of Wales College, Newport, College Crescent, Caerleon, PO BOX 179, Gwent NP18 3YG. Tel: (44 1633) 430 088. B.A. (Hon.) Film and Video, Animation, and Media and Visual Culture.

University of Westminster, School of Communication, Watford Road, Nortwick Park, Harrow, Middlesex, HA1 3 TP. Tel: (44 171) 911 5000. Fax: (44 171) 911 5943.

Royal College of Art, Department of Film and Television, Kensington Gore, London SW7 2EU. Tel: (44 171) 590 4444. Fax: (44 171) 590 45 00. 35 Students.

The Surrey Institute of Art and Design, Farnham Campus, Falkner Road, Farnham, Surrey GU9 7DS. Tel: (44 1252) 722 441. Fax: (44 1252) 892 616. Website: www.surrart.ac.uk

University of Stirling, Film and Media Studies, Stirling FK9 4LA. Tel: 01786 46 75 20. Fax: 01786 46 68 55. Head of Department: Dr. Raymond Boyle.

UNITED STATES

Information on the thousands of US film schools and courses can be obtained in the *American Film Institute's Guide to College Courses in Film and Television*, which can be ordered at Publications, The American Film Institute, 2021 North Western Avenue, Los Angeles, CA 90027.

URUGUAY

Escuela de Cinematografia, Chucarro 1036, CP 11300 Montevideo. Tel: (598 2) 709 7637. Fax: (598 2) 707 6389. e-mail: cinevid@chasque.apc.org

FILM ARCHIVES

ARGENTINA

Cinemateca Argentina, Salta 1915, CP 1137 Buenos Aires. Tel: (54 11) 4306 0548/0561. Fax: (54 11) 4306 0592. Executive Director: Mrs. Paulina Fernandez Jurado. Established in 1949. Stock: 12,000 film titles, 6,250 books, collection of film periodicals, 352,000 film stills, 6,600 film posters. The collection of micro-filmed clippings holds files on individual films and on foreign and Argentine film personalities. The library is open to researchers and students. The Cinemateca operates one film theatre with daily screenings.

AUSTRALIA

Archives office of Tasmania, 77 Murray Street, Hobart, Tasmania, Australia 7000. Tel: (61 3) 6249 9013. Fax: (61 3) 6249 9015. State Archivist: Ian Pearce.

State Film Archives, Library and Information Service of Western Australia, Alexander Library Building, Perth Cultural Centre, Perth, WA 6,000. Tel: (61 8) 9427 3310. Fax: (61 8) 9427 3276. e-mail: gfoley@tom.liswa.wa.gov.au Film Archivist: Gerard Foley. Stock: 3,800 Western Australian titles.

AUSTRIA

Österreichisches Filmarchiv, Obere Augartenstr. 1, 1020 Vienna. Tel: (43 1) 216 1300. Fax: (43 1) 216 1300100

Österreichisches Filmmuseum, A-1010 Vienna, Augustinerstr. 1. Tel: (43 1) 5337 0540. Fax: (43 1) 5337 05625. Directors: Peter Konlechner and Prof. Peter Kubelka. Stock: app. 14,000 film titles, and an extensive library and collection of stills and photographs.

BELGIUM

Royal Film Archive, 23 rue Ravenstein, 1000 Brussels. Tel: (32 2) 507 8370. Fax: (32 2) 513 1272.

BRAZIL

Cinemateca Brasileira, Caixa Postal 12900, 04092 São Paulo. Tel: (55) 577 4666. Fax: (55) 577 7433. Director: Thomaz Farkaz.

Cinemateca do Museu de Arte Moderna, Caixa Postal 44, CEP 20021-140, Rio de Janeiro, RJ. Tel: (55 21) 210 2188. Tel/fax: (55 21) 220 3113. e-mail: mam@mamrio.com.br Director: Lucia Lobo

BULGARIA

Bulgarska Nacionalna Filmoteka, ul. Gourko 36,1000 Sofia. Tel: (359 2) 987 3740, 871 392. Fax: (359 2) 876 004.

CANADA

La Cinémathèque Québécoise, 335 boul de Maisonneuve est. Montréal, Québec H2X 1K1.Tel: (1 514) 842 9763. Fax: (1 514) 842 1816. Curator: Robert Daudelin.

Conservatoire d'Art Cinématographique de Montréal, 1455 de Maisonneuve West, Montréal, Québec. Director: Serge Losique.

National Archives of Canada, Visual and Sound Archives, 344 Wellington Street, Room 1036, Ottawa, Ontario, K1A 0N3. Tel: (1 613) 995 7504. Fax: (1 613) 995 6575. Director: Betty Kidd.

CHINA

China Film Archive, No3, Wen Hui Yuan Road, Xiao Xi Tian, Haidian District, Beijing, 100088. Tel: (86 10) 6225 0916. Fax: (86 10) 225 9315.

CZECH REPUBLIC

Národní filmovy archiv, Malesicka 12-14, 130 00 Praha 3. Tel: (4202) 894 686 Fax: (420) 897 3057. Director/Curator: Vladimir Opéla.

DENMARK

Danish Film Institute/Archive & Cinematheque, Vognmagergade 10, DK-1120 Copenhagen K. Tel: (45 33) 74 34 00. Fax: (45 33) 74 35 99. Director: Dan Nissen. Stock: 27,500 film titles, 54,000 books, 350 periodicals subscribed to, 2,300,000 film stills, 18,500 posters, three cinemas (178, 140, and 42 seats) used for daily screenings and for researchers and students. DFI/Archive & Cinematheque also publishes a magazine, "Kosmorama."

EGYPT

National Archive of Egyptian Film, c/o National Film Centre, City of Arts, Al Ahram Road, Giza. Tel: (20 2) 585 4801/0897. Fax: (20 2) 585 4701. President: Prof. Dr. Madkour Thabet.

FINLAND

Suomen elokuva-arkisto, Pursimiehenkatu 29-31 A, P.O. Box 177, FIN-00151 Helsinki. Tel: (358 9) 615 400. Fax: (358 9) 6154 0242. E-mail: sea@sea.fi. Website: www.sea.fi. Director: Matti Lukkarila. Stock: 7,200 feature film titles, 26,000 shorts and advertising film (spots), 20,000 video cassettes, 20,000 books, 160 magazines (currently subscribed), 10,500 dialogue lists and scripts, 326,000 different stills, 110,000 posters and 41,000 documentation files. The archive arranges regular screenings in Helsinki and eight other cities.

FRANCE

Cinémathèque française, 4 rue de Longchamp, 75116 Paris. Tel: (33 1) 53 65 74 75. Fax: (33 1) 53 65 74 96. President: Jean Saint Geours.

Cinémathèque de Toulouse, rue du Taur, BP 80024, 31080 Toulouse Cedex 6. Tel: (33 5) 6230 3010. Fax: (33 5) 6230 3012. Director: Pierre Cadars.

Cinémathèque Universitaire, 3 rue Michelet, 75006 Paris. Tel: (33 1) 4586 4853. Fax: (33 1) 4586 5643

Institut Lumière, 25 rue du Premier-Film, 69008 Lyon. Tel: (33 4) 7878 1895. Fax: (33 1) 7801 3662. President: Bertrand Tavernier.

Musée du Cinéma de Lyon, 69 rue Jean Jaurès. 69100 Villeurbanne. Tel: (33 4) 7853 2769. Fax: (33 4) 7233 7925. President: Paul Génard. Stock: 1,600 film titles, 1,000 film stills, 50 posters.

Service des Archives du Film du Centre National de la Cinématographie, 7 bis rue Alexandre Turpault, 78392 Bois d'Arcy Cedex. Tel: (33 1) 3014 8000. Fax: (33 1) 3460 5225.

GERMANY

Arsenal/Kino der Freunde der Deutschen Kinemathek, Welserstrasse 25, 10777 Berlin. Tel: (49 30) 219 0010. Fax: (49 30) 218 4281. The nearest equivalent of Britain's NFT. Programming: Ulrich and Erika Gregor, Milena Gregor. The Freunde also runs a non-commercial distribution of about 800 films, most of them from the International Forum, the independent second main programme of the Berlin Film Festival, organised by the Freunde.

Bundesarchiv-Filmarchiv, Fehrbelliner Platz 3, 10707 Berlin. Tel: (49 30) 86811. Fax: (49 30) 868 1310. E-mail: barch@barch-fa. uunet.de

Deutsches Filmmuseum Frankfurt am Main, Schaumainkai 41, D-60596 Frankfurt am Main. Tel: (49 69) 2123 8830. Fax: (49 69) 2123 7881. e-mail: filmmuseum@stadt-frankfurt.de Director: Prof Walter Schobert. Deputy Director and Head of Archives: Hans-Peter Reichmann. Cinema: Kitty Vincke.

Deutsches Institut für Filmkunde, Schaumainkai 41, 60596 Frankfurt am Main. Tel: (49 69) 961 2200. Telefax: (49 69) 620 060. e-mail: mieles@em.uni-frankfurt.de. Website: www.filminstitut.de Director: Claudia Dillmann. Financial Director: Helmut Possmann. Deputy director: Ursula Von Keitz. Stock: 10,000 film titles, 70,000 books, 260 periodicals, 140,000 programmes, 16,000 dialogue lists, 5,000 scripts. Also newspaper clippings, advertising material.

Filmmuseum Berlin Deutsche Kinemathek Potsdamer Strasse 2, 10785 Berlin, Germany. Uta Orluc Chief Librarian. (new address from summer 2000)

Münchner Stadtmuseum/Filmmuseum, St. Jakobsplatz 1, D-80331 München. Tel: (49 89) 2332 2348. Fax: (49 89) 2332 3931. e-mail: 101657.3365@ compuserve.com. Director: Dr. Stefan Drössler. Founded in 1963, this municipal film archive runs a daily cinema programme. Film archive holds approx. 5,000 titles, including many restored silent German film classics, New German cinema, and the Orson Welles Collection. Estate holdings from G. W. Pabst, Dr. Arnold Fanck etc. Library holds over 6,000 film books, 10,000 film periodicals.

Stiftung Deutsche Kinemathek, Heerstrasse 18-20, 14052 Berlin. Tel: (49 30) 300 9030. Fax: (49 30) 300 90313. Director: Hans Helmut Prinzler. Stock: 8,000 film titles, 1,500,000 film stills, 15,000 posters, 60,000 film programmes, 10,000 scripts etc. The Kinemathek's library of books and periodicals is amalgamated with that of the Deutsche Film-und-Fernsehakademie-Berlin, in the same building.

HUNGARY

Magyar Filmintézet, Budakeszi ut 51b, 1021 Budapest. Tel:and fax: (36 1) 200 8739. Director: Vera Gyürey. Stock: 7,022 feature titles, 8,713 short films, 3,756 newsreels, 13,224 books, 3,710 periodicals, 2,708 scripts, 5,381 manuscripts, 143,159 stills, 15,365 posters. In addition to housing the archive, the institute does research into the history of cinema, particularly Hungarian cinema, and encourages the development of film culture in Hungary.

Szinház-és Filmmüvészeti Foiskola, Vas utca 2/c, Budapest 1088. Tel/Fax: (36 1) 329 4790. Rector: Péter Huszti. General Secretary: Lajos Tiszeker.

ICELAND

Kvikmyndasafn Islands (National Film Archive of Iceland), Vesturgötu 11-13, 220 Hafnarfjolgur. Tel: (354) 565 5993. Fax: (354) 565 5994. Nearly 400 titles in the collection, documentaries being the larger part of it. Numerous sources of information regarding Icelandic films and the national film history.

INDIA

National Film Archive of India, Ministry of Information and Broadcasting, Government of India, Law College Road, Pune 411 004, India. Tel: (91 212) 565 2259. Fax: (91 212) 567 0027. Director: L.K. Upadhyaya.

IRAN

National Iranian Film Archive, Baharestan Square, Tehran. Tel: (98 21) 324 1601. Director: Mohammad Hassan Khoshnevis.

ISRAEL

Israel Film Archive/Jerusalem Cinémathèque, P.O. Box 8561, Jerusalem 91083, Israel. Tel: (972 2) 672 4131. Fax: (972 2) 673 3076. Director: Lia van Leer. Stock: 20,000 prints: international, Israeli, Jewish film collections. Books, periodicals, stills, posters and scripts. Film documentation and educational programme for school children and adults. Permanent exhibition of early cinema apparatus and cinema memorabilia. 6000 members. Screening five films every day in two auditoriums. Organisers of the Jerusalem Film Festival.

Tel Aviv Cinémathèque (The Doron Cinema Centre), 2 Sprintzak Street, Tel Aviv. Postal address: P.O. Box 20370, Tel Aviv 61203. Tel: (972 3) 6917 1818. Fax: (972 3) 696 2841. Director: Alon Garbuz. Stock: 20,000 video cassettes, 7,000 books, periodicals, stills, posters, scripts. 1,500 screenings yearly, various activities, lectures and seminars for the general public, and special morning educational programmes for schools. Publishes Israel's only film magazine, "Cinematheque."

ITALY

Cineteca del Comune di Bologna Via Galliera 8, 40121 Bologna. Tel: (39 051) 228 975. Fax: (39 051) 261 680. e-mail: cineteca@ comune.bologna.it. Website: www2.comune.bologna.it/bologn a/cineteca.

Cineteca del Friuli, Via Bini, Palazzo Gurisatti, 33013 Gemona del Friuli (Udine). Tel: (39 0432) 980 458. Fax: (39 0432) 970 542. e-mail: cdf@proxima.conecta.it. Website: http://.cinetecadelfriuli.org/gcm/ Established in 1977, this excellent Italian archive conceived the idea for the Pordenone Silent Film Festival, and organises regular screenings. Stock: 2,000 film titles, 3,000 newsreels, 18,000 books. Director: Livio Jacob.

Cineteca Nazionale, Via Tuscolana n. 1524, 00173 Rome. Tel: (39 06) 722 941. Fax: (39 6) 721 1619. Director: Angelo Libertini. The Director of Scuola Nazionale di Cinema - Cineteca Nazionale: Lino Micciché. Director-coordinator: Adriano Aprá.

Fondazione Cineteca Italiana, Via Palestro 16, 20121 Milano. Tel: (39 2) 799 224. Fax: (39 2) 798 289. President: Gianni Comencini.

Fondazione Federico Fellini Via Angherà 22, 47900 Rimini. Tel (39 0541) 50085. Fax: (39 0541) 24885. e-mail: fellini@comune.rimini.it Director: Gainfranco Angelucci.

Museo Nazionale del Cinema - Fondazione Maria Adriano Prolo, Via Montebello, 15,1, 10124 Turin. Tel: (39 011) 815 4230. Fax: (39 011) 812 2503. e-mail: museo-cinema@to2000.net President: Mario Ricciardi.

Museo Internazionale del Cinema e dello Spettacolo (M.I.C.S.), Casella Postale 6104-00195 Rome. Tel: (39 6) 370 0266. Fax: (39 6) 3973 3297. Director: Jose Pantieri. The M.I.C.S. has organised in Italy and abroad a remarkable amount of fair, exhibitions, conferences, re-searches, publications, experi-mental coursees etc. Film archives and bank (about 5,000 rare and antique films, mostly silent. Photo library (some two million photos from 1850 to present, daguerrotypes, etc). Film/TV library (books and publications on film/show, original scripts) Newpaper library (specialised periodcals/ magazines). Image restoration laboratory (to preserve and study images). Museum (optical devices, relics, movie-cameras, lenses, projectors, costumes, props, original posters, rarities, historical documents, letters, memorabilia, etc.)

JAPAN

Kawakita Memorial Film Institute, 18 Ichibancho, Chiyodaku, Tokyo 102-0082. Tel: (81-3) 3265 3281. Fax: (81-3) 3265 3276. e-mail: kmfi@kawakita-film.or.jp. President: Mrs. Masayo Okada.

National Film Center, 3-7-6 Kyobashi, Chuoku, Tokyo. Chief Curator: Masatoshi Ohba.

LATVIA

Riga Film Museum, Smerla str. 3. Postal address: P.O. Box 391, Riga LV 1047. Tel: (371 2) 520 655, 529 845. Tel/Fax: (371 2) 754 5099. e-mail: kinomuz @com.latnet.lv.

LUXEMBOURG

Cinémathèque Municipale de la Ville de Luxembourg, 10 rue Eugene Ruppert, L-2453 Luxem-bourg. Tel: (352) 4796 2644. Fax: (352) 407 519.

MEXICO

Cinemateca Luis Buert, Calle 5, Oriente 5, Apdo. Postal 255, Puebla, Pue.

Cinemateca Mexicana, Museo Nacional de Antropologia, Calzada M. Gandhi, México 6, D.F.

Cineteca Nacional, Av. Mexico-Coyoacán 389, Col. Xoco, C.P. 03330 Mexico, DF. Tel: (52 5) 688 8814. Fax: (52 5) 688 4211. e-mail: srm@spin.com.mx.

Direccion General de Activi-dades Cinematograficas Filmo-teca UNAM, Circuito Exterior Dr. Mario de la Cueva s/n, Ciudad Universitaria, 04510 México, D.F. Tel: (52 5) 622 9594. Fax: (52 5) 622 9585. e-mail: trujillo@servidor. unam.mex General Director: Biol. Iván Trujillo.

NETHERLANDS

Netherlands Audiovisual Archive – Department film archive. P.O. Box 1799, 2280 DT Rijswijk. Tel: (31 70) 356 4109, 390 7200. Fax: (31 70) 364 7756, 307 0428. Head: Mr. Paul Kusters, MA.

Nederlands Filmmuseum (Stich-ting), Vondelpark 3, 1071 AA Amsterdam. Postal Address: Postbus 747 82, 1070 BT Amsterdam. Tel: (31 20) 589 1400. Fax: (31 20) 683 3401. E-mail: filmmuseum@nfm.nl Website: www.nfm.nl Director: Mrs. V. F. Blotkamp-de Roos. Head of distribution department: Mr. R. Hadders.

NEW ZEALAND

The New Zealand Film Archive, P.O. Box 11-449, Wellington. Tel: (64 4) 384 7647. Fax: (64 4) 382 9595. e-mail: nzfa@actrix.gen.nz.

The New Zealand Film Archive Auckland PO Box 68 747, Newton, Auckland. Tel/fax: (64 9) 379 0688. e-mail: nzfaauck@iprolink.co.nz

NORWAY

Henie-Onstad Art Centre, 1311 Hovikodden, Oslo. Director: Gavin

Jantjens. Tel: (47 67) 80 48 80. Fax: (47 67) 54 32 70.

Norske Film Institut, P.B. 482 Sentrum, 0105 Oslo. Tel: (47 22) 474 500. Fax: (47 22) 474 599. e-mail: nfi@nfi.no Managing Director: Erling Dale. Director/curator: Vigdis Lian. Head of Cinémathèque: Kjell Billing.

PANAMA

Cinemateca del GECU, Universidad de Panama, Apartado 6-1775, El Dorado, Panama. Tel: (507) 223 9324, 264 2737. Fax: (507) 264 2737. e-mail: gecu@ancon.up.ac.pa Stock includes films, books, periodicals, film stills and posters. It has a small theatre with three daily screenings. Director: Roberto Enrique King.

POLAND

Filmoteka Narodowa, ul. Pulawska 61, 00-975 Warszaw. Tel: (48 22) 845 5074.

Muzeum Kinematografi, Pl Zwyciestwa 1, 90312 Lódz. Tel: (48 42) 674 0957. Fax: (48 42) 674 9006.

PORTUGAL

Cinemateca Portuguesa, Rua Barata Salgueiro 39-1250 Lisboa. Tel: (351 1) 354 6279. Fax: (351 1) 352 3180. Director: João Bénard da Costa.

ROMANIA

Arhiva Nationala de Filma, Str. Dem I Dobrescu nr. 4-6, Bucharest. Tel/Fax: (40 1) 313 4904. General Manager: Bujor T. Ripeanu.

RUSSIA

Gosfilmofond of Russia, Belye Stolby, Moskovskaia oblast 142050. Tel: (7 095) 546 0535. Fax: (7 095) 546 0512.

SERBIA & MONTENEGRO

Jugoslovenska Kinoteka, Knez Mihailova 19, 11000 Belgrade. Tel: (381 11) 622 555, 550 471 (Archive). Fax: (381 11) 622 587, 555 015 (Archive). Director: Radoslav Zelenovic Head of Archive: Stevan Jovicic. Programme Director: Dinko Tucakovic.

SPAIN

Filmoteca Espaa 19, Carretera Dehesa de la Villa, s/n. 28040 Madrid. Tel: (34 91) 549 0011. Fax: (34 91) 549 7348. Director: José María Prado.

Filmoteca de la Generalitat de Catalunya, Portal de Santa Madrona, 6-8 Barcelona 08001. Tel: (34 93) 412 5640. Director: Antoni Kirchner.

SWEDEN

Cinemateket, Svenska Film Institutet. Filmhuset, Box 27126, S-102 52 Stockholm. Tel: (46 8) 665 1100. Fax: (46 8) 661 1820. Head of Programme & Information: Jan-Erik Billinger. Director: Joen Wenjstrom. Head of archives: Rolf Lindfors. Head of Documentation: Margareta Nordström. Stock: 17,800 film titles, 41,000 books, 250 subscriptions to periodicals, 1,500,000 film stills, 31,000 posters, and unpublished script material on 7,600 foreign films and 1,900 Swedish films. The collection of microfilmed clippings holds 52,000 jackets on individual films, 16,500 jackets on film personalities and jackets on general subjects classified by the FIAF scheme. Cinemateket has four daily screenings at two theatres in Stockholm. A selection of the yearly programme is also shown in Göteborg and Malmö.

SWITZERLAND

Cinémathèque Suisse, 3 Allée Ernest Ansermet, 1003 Lausanne (Postal address: P.O. Box 2512, 1002 Lausanne). Tel: (41 21) 331 0101. Fax: (41 21) 320 4888. Curator: Hervé Dumont. Stock: 53,000 titles (1,500,000 reels), 600 apparati, 40,000 posters, 5,000,000 film references, 19,000 books, and 1,500,000 stills. Three projections each day.

TAIWAN

Chinese Taipei Film Archive, 4F, No. 7 Ching-Tao East Road, Taipei, Taiwan, R.O.C. Tel: (886 2) 392 4243, 2396 0760. Fax: (886 2) 2392 6359. Director: Edmond K. Y. Wong.

TURKEY

Turkish Film and Television Institute, 80700 Kislaönü-Besiktas, Istanbul. Tel: (90 212) 266 1096. Faxx: (90 212) 211 6599. e-mail: sinematv@msu.edu.tr Prof. Sami Sekeroglu. The Institute is a science and art centre which is engaged in education, research and archiving on cinema and television. Stock: 6,000 film titles, 3,500 video titles. Library of books, periodicals, newspaper clippings and photos available to researchers.

UNITED KINGDOM

Imperial War Museum, Lambeth Road, London SE1 6HZ. Tel: (44 171) 416 5291/2. Fax: (44 171) 416 5299. Keeper of the Film and Video Archive: Roger Smither. Deputy: Paul Sargent. Stock: over 120 million feet of actuality film relating to conflict in the 20th Century, from Britain and other countries. Viewing facilities for students and researchers *by appointment only*; public film screenings.

National Film and Television Archive, British Film Institute, 21 Stephen Street, London W1P 1LN. Tel: (44 171) 255 1444. Fax: (44 171) 580 7503. Head of Collections, BFI: Caroline Ellis. Curator: Anne Fleming. Stock: 275,000 film and television titles, over 5,000,000 black-and-white stills, 700,000 colour transparencies, 18,000 posters, 2,500 set-designs. Viewing service for students and researchers.

The Scottish Film and Television Archive, 74 Victoria Crescent Road, Glasgow G12 9JN. Tel: (44 141) 302 1742. Fax: (44 141) 302 1713.

UNITED STATES

Academy of Motion Picture Arts and Sciences, Centre for Motion Picture Study, Academy Film Archive, 333 South La Cienega Blvd., Beverly Hills, California 90211. Tel: (1 310) 247 3027. Fax: (1 310) 657 5431. e-mail: mfriend@oscars.org Director: Michael Friend.

American Cinematheque, 1800 N. Highland Ave., #717, Hollywood 90028. Executive Director: Barbara Zicka Smith. A viewer-supported arts organisation dedicated exclusively to the public exhibition of film and video. Permanent home at the Egyptian Theatre (6712 Hollywood Blvd.) will open in Dec. 1998.

American Film Institute/National Center for Film and Video Preservation, 2021 North Western, Los Angeles, CA 90027. Tel: (1 323) 856 7600.

Archive Films/Archive Photos, 530 West 25th Street, New York, NY 10001-5516 USA. Tel: (1 212) 822 7800. Fax: (1 212) 645 2137. e-mail: sales@archivefilms.com Website: www.archivefilms.com Contact: John McQuaid. Archive Films is a leading historical footage library with more than 40,000 hours of stock footage including Hollywood feature films, newsreels, TV news, silent films, documentaries, and vintage industrial and educational films, and many specialty collections. Archive Photos has over 20,000,000 photographs, en-gravings and drawings spanning 3,000 years of world history.

George Eastman House/International Museum of Photography and Film, 900 East Avenue, Rochester, N.Y. 14607. Tel: (1 716) 271 3361 Fax: (1 716) 271 3970. e-mail: film@geh.org Website: www.eastman.org Senior Curator of Film: Dr. Paolo Cherchi Usai.

Harvard Film Archive, Carpenter Center for the Visual Arts, Harvard Univ, 24 Quincy Street, Cambridge, MA 02138. Tel: (1 617) 496 6046. Fax: 91 617 495 6197) Curator: tbc. Films (16mm, 35mm, video); 4,000 titles.

The Library of Congress, Motion Picture, Broadcasting and Recorded Sound Division, Washington, DC 20540-4690. Tel: (1 202) 707 5840. Fax: (1 202) 707 2371. Telex: 64198. Chief of division: David Francis. Head of Moving Image Section: Patrick

Loughney. Head of Recorded Sound Section: Samuel Brylawski. The nation's largest public research collection and preservation archive for motion pricutres, videos, TV & radio broadcast and sound recordings available to qualified researchers, 8:30 to 5:30 pm, M-F, through the facilities of the Film and Television Reading Room and the REcorded Sound Reference Center in the James Madison building.

Museum of Modern Art, Department of Film and Video,11 West 53rd Street, New York, NY 10019. Tel: (1 212) 708 9600. Fax: (1 212) 333 1145. Chief Curator: Mary Lea Bandy. Curators: Steve Higgins, Larry Kardish. Stock: 17,500 film titles, 2,500 books, 250 periodicals, 4,000,000 film stills. The excellent research and screening facilities of the department are available to serious students only by appointment with the supervisor, Charles Silver; 1,000 of its films are available for rental, sale, and lease. Stills Archive open by appointment with Mary Corliss.

National Museum of Natural History/Human Studies Film Archives, Rm E307, 123 Smithsonian Institution, Washington DC 20560. Tel: (1 202) 357 3349. Fax: (202) 357 2208. Director: John P. Homiak.

Pacific Film Archive, University Art Museum, 2625 Durant Avenue, Berkeley, California 94720.

UCLA Film and Television Archive, 302 East Melnitz Hall, University of California, 405 Hilgard Avenue, Los Angeles, CA 90024. Tel: (1 310) 206 8013. Fax: (1 310) 206 3129.

UCLA Film and Television Archive Commercial Services. 1015 North Cahuenga Blvd, Hollywood, CA 90038. Tel: (1-323) 466 8559. Fax: (1-323) 461 6317.

The Wisconsin Center for Film and Theater Research, 816 State Street, Madison, Wisconsin 53706. Tel: (1 608) 264 6466. Fax: (1 608) 264 6472.

URUGUAY

Cinemateca Uruguaya, Lorenzo Carnelli 1311, Casilla de Correo 1170, Montevideo. Tel: (598 2) 408 2460, 409 5795. Fax: (598 2) 409 4572. e-mail: cinemuy@chasque. apc.org

Mary Pickford, whose screen presence is so lovingly recreated by Kevin Brownlow and Robert Cushman in Mary Pickford Rediscovered *(Abrams)*

BOOK REVIEWS

A new volume by Kevin Brownlow illuminates any year, and **Mary Pickford Rediscovered** (Harry N. Abrams, New York and London) should beguile anyone with a sympathetic eye for the silent film era. Enriched by more than 230 black-and-white photographs from the files of the Academy of Motion Pictures Arts & Sciences, this book resurrects the legendary, winsome appeal of "America's Sweetheart". There are images from all her major films, carefully introduced and annotated by Brownlow, in the style of a catalogue raisonné, and a characteristically relaxed account of how the author tracked down the actress in her seventies – and induced her to talk at length about her work. Robert Cushman's archival labours help to make this luscious tribute a valuable addition to any library.

Biography

The season's best biography analyses in passionate detail the extraordinary life of Europe's greatest director since Bergman. **Fassbinder**, by Christian Braad Thomsen, translated from the Danish by Martin Chalmers (Faber, London), describes the German whirlwind as "a provocative genius", and there is no doubting the turbulence and abundance of his output: 44 films in 14 years, not forgetting countless stage productions. His magnum opus, *Berlin Alexanderplatz*, ran to more than 16 hours, and alone would justify any career in television. The book makes one wonder how Fassbinder's name has been so swiftly forgotten by a new generation. Thomsen's shrewd, sympathetic portrait brings the man to life, warts and all.

Veteran journalist Tom Hutchinson interviewed Rod Steiger when both men were young, and has now written a sympathetic, anecdotal account of the star's troubled life and career. **Rod Steiger**

(Gollancz, London) evokes a vanished world, with Steiger learning his craft alongside Brando, Monroe and Bogart, then winning an Oscar for *In the Heat of the Night*, before lapsing into depression and all-too rare screen appearances. It is unusual to read a book that suggests so powerfully the friendship between author and subject. Truly, an "intimate biography."

Ian Christie has edited **Gilliam on Gilliam** (Faber, London), the eighteenth such interview book in the Faber stable. Terry Gilliam may not be in the same league as Orson Welles, as Christie would wish, but his brand of antic humour and 1960s anarchism has produced underrated films such as *Time Bandits* and *The Fisher King*, while anyone who has seen the restored version of *Brazil* on LD or DVD will recognise the eye of a master. Gilliam talks cogently and wittily, and accounts of his travails with the Hollywood and British studio systems make an engrossing read.

Chris Salewicz has written a useful handbook to the work of one of the most perplexing men in Hollywood North: **George Lucas** (Orion Books, London), and the paperback includes the full *Variety* reviews of each of Lucas's features. Starting out as assistant to Francis Coppola, and writing the screenplay for *THX 1138* between 4 a.m. and 6 a.m. each morning while on the road as assistant on *The Rain People*, Lucas has become the reticent (yet not timid) commander of the richest empire in the movie world.

Screenplays

A sumptuous benchmark for script publishing is set by **Titanic, James Cameron's Illustrated Screenplay** (Harper Collins, New York; Boxtree, London). Stuffed with colour photographs, it is set out like an original typed manuscript, with deletions and other amendments marked in red. On every left-hand page there are pictures from and comments about certain sequences. This is a volume truly worthy of its subject, prefaced with an interview with Cameron by the diligent Randall Frakes.

The screenplays pioneered by Faber, like the best DVDs, usually have "extras" attached that bring the script into sharper focus. **Jerry Maguire and A Jerry Maguire Journal**, by Cameron Crowe (Faber, London), includes the deft and witty screenplay, of course, but also an engrossing description of Crowe's race to finish the film, Tom Cruise's commitment to it, plus some bonus materials about the production.

Lulu on the Bridge (Henry Holt, New York; Faber, London) marks Paul Auster's debut as a director. The book contains the entire shooting script, which sheds considerable light on a film that seems part myth, part dream, and part thriller. **Dancing at Lughnasa** (Faber, London) also has literary merit, for the film owes much to Brian Friel's original Irish play.

Reference and History

Einaudi Editore of Torino have made an imposing start to their massive **Storia del cinema mondiale** project with a 1,253 page tome devoted to European trends and stars, with a second volume to follow on national cinemas. Written by several historians, this scholarly survey is immaculately edited by Gian Piero Brunetta, and will – pending translation into other languages – surely belong on the shelves of any film buff conversant with Italian. The illustrations have been chosen with obvious pleasure and fastidiousness. The indexes have been compiled with similar care, and the whole enterprise commands admiration.

Martin Schaub's **The Swiss Cinema** (Pro Helvetia, Zurich) may be neither the first nor the most exhaustive study of the subject, but it is published usefully in English. Schaub, perhaps his country's best movie critic, tells a poignant and well-illustrated tale of a national cinema that flickered into flame during the 1960s (Tanner, Goretta, Gloor,

Soutter) and has since survived thanks to government support.

Glam!, by Barney Hoskyns, also has a melancholy undertow, tracing the glitter rock revolution in British pop culture during the early 1970s. The book will appeal to fans of Todd Haynes's *Velvet Goldmine*, and maybe even Kubrick's *A Clockwork Orange*. Although Jay Leyda's classic history of Soviet film, *Kino*, is 40 years old, it remains the standard work on its subject. Now Denise J. Youngblood has written **The Magic Mirror, Moviemaking in Russia 1908-1918** (University of Wisconsin Press / Eurospan, London). In deft strokes, she evokes a fertile pre-Revolutionary era in which costume dramas rubbed shoulders with experiments in narrative.

Projections 9 (Faber, London) turns its attention to modern French cinema, in association with that nation's finest film magazine, *Positif*. There are interviews with 21 directors, from the most august (Bresson, Resnais) to the newest kids on the block (Kassovitz, Audiard). Together they form an almost mesmerising image of film-making in a country where the auteur remains undisputed king.

Fifteen years ago we reviewed the first edition of **Quinlan's Film Directors** (Batsford, London). Now it has appeared in a revised and expanded edition. Many of the 700 film-makers represented had not made an impact in 1983; others have retreated in importance. More orthodox than David Thomson's biographical dictionary, less comprehensive than Ephraim Katz's encyclopaedia, Quinlan's tome is unpretentious, quite good on arcane facts (viz the entry on Paul Wendkos), and well illustrated.

Slim in format yet most rewarding for fans of Maghreb cinema is Roy Armes' **Omar Gatlato** (Flicks Books, Trowbridge, UK). Merzak Allouache directed this comic and poignant film in 1976, and Professor Armes subjects it to a close reading that keeps a weather-eye cocked for wider cultural references. **Sin in Soft Focus, Pre-Code Hollywood**, by Mark A. Vieira (Harry

N. Abrams, New York), unveils the often subtle consequences of the Production Code of 1930, whereby Hollywood was meant to outlaw all things lewd, violent and vulgar. Directors like Lubitsch, Mamoulian and Sternberg used lighting, ambivalent dialogue and humour to slither past the Code's rigid stance. The lush illustrations are alone worth the price of admission.

Some of the most striking posters of our time have come from the brilliant pen and brush of Renato Casaro. The best of his work is included in a spectacular coffee-table volume, **In the Limelight: Renato Casaro, Movie Art** (PGM Art World, Siegfried Hafner, Munich). With parallel texts in English and German, and colour reproductions of exceptional quality, this book pays tribute to an art form only now being recognised as both valuable and culturally important. Casaro deserves to be ranked alongside Mucha, Lautrec and Bonnard as a poster artist who will surely be collected in the new millennium.

Finally, a delight in store for foodies and film buffs alike: Ismail Merchant's **Paris: Filming and Feasting in Paris** (Harry N. Abrams, New York). Spiced with 40 recipes, this colourful volume flits from one experience to another in Merchant's beguiling career. He and James Ivory have shot *Jefferson in Paris*, *Surviving Picasso* and other films on location in Paris, and his joy in all things French is irresistibly contagious.

Peter Cowie

JEFFERSON IN PARIS, one of the films mentioned by Ismail Merchant in his lavish FILMING AND FEASTING IN PARIS (Abrams)

photo: Touchstone Pictures

Variety Books

In addition to the *International Film Guide*, *Variety* edits a number of books on films and film-making. The past year has seen a revived version of the **Variety Movie Guide** (Perigee, New York; Boxtree, London), with more than 8,500 reviews from the paper's pages, abridged and edited by Derek Elley to make a perfect companion for the home cinema enthusiast. **The Variety Almanac** (Boxtree, London), released in the US as the **Variety Insider** (Perigee, New York), is a goldmine of information concerning film, TV, theatre, music, video and even books. As a reference source, it draws on *Variety*'s unique knowledge of box-office records, and its lists cover everything from Oscars to Grammys.

Also still available is **Variety's Guide to Film Festivals**, **The Emmys** and **The Grammys** (all three released by Perigee, New York). Should you have difficulty obtaining any of these titles, contact *Variety* bureaux in Los Angeles (+1 323 965 4476), New York (+1 212 337 7002) or London (+44 171 520 5222)

FILM BOOKSHOPS POSTERS & RECORDS

AUSTRALIA

Electric Shadows Bookshop, City Walk, Akuna Street, Canberra, ACT 2601. Tel: (61 262) 488 352. Fax: (61 262) 471 230. e-mail: esb@electricshadowsbookshop. com.au. Website: www. electricshadowsbookshop.com.a u. Free quarterly catalogue available. Listing new film books & video. Australian material highlighted.

Movie Buffs, P.O. Box 508, Hawthorn, Victoria 3122. Free catalogue available listing movie books, magazines, posters and memorabilia.

CANADA

Theatrebooks, 11 St. Thomas Street, Toronto, M5S 2B7. Tel: (1 416) 922 7175. Fax: (1 416) 922 0739. e-mail: action@ theatrebooks.com. Website: www.theatrebooks.com. Founded first as a source of theatre, opera, and dance books. Theatrebooks has also been developing a first-class film book collection since 1982. Worldwide mail-order is handled.

FRANCE

Atmosphère, Libraire du Cinema, 10 rue Broca, 75005 Paris. Tel: (33 1) 4331 0271. Fax: (33 1) 4331 0369. Atmosphere offers a wide range of film publications, with a large stock of stills, postcards, posters of new and old movies of all origins and sizes. Also stocks back issues of magazines. Open every day except Sunday from 11 a.m. to 7 p.m. Atmosphere sets up shop during the Cannes festival, too.

Cinedoc, 45-53 Passage Jouffroy, 75009, Paris. Tel: (33 1) 4824 7116. Fax: (33 1) 4483 0634. e-mail:

cinedocuments@thema.net. Website: www.cinedoc.com. Posters, books, stills, pressbooks, magazines, etc.

Cine-Folie, La Boutique du Cinéma, 14 rue des Frères Pradignac, 06400 Cannes. Tel: (33 4) 9339 2299. Stills, books, posters, postcards.

Cinemagence, 12 rue Saulnier, 75009 Paris. Tel: (33 1) 4246 2121. Fax: (33 1) 4246 2020. Stills, posters, magazines, books. Mail-order service. Free catalogue.

Contacts Champs-Elysées, 24 rue du Colisée, 75008 Paris. Tel: (33 1) 4359 1771. Fax: (33 1) 4289 2765. Cinema bookshop was established 41 years ago in the Champs-Elysées area, close to the film production companies. Amply stocked with French and foreign-language books on technique, theory, history and director monographs. Also magazines. Reliable mail-order service. Free "new aquisitions" list. Open year round.

Gilda, 36 rue de Boudonnais, 75001, Paris. Tel: (33 1) 42 33 60 00. K7 videos, books, film magazines, compact disc videos, CDs, CD Roms.

GERMANY

Buchhandlung Walther König, Ehrenstr. 4, 56072 Koln. Tel: (49 221) 205 9625 Fax: (49 221) 205 9640. Offers a comprehensive catalogue of international titles in the film department, also useful antiquarian department.

Buchhandlung Langenkamp, Beckergrube 19, D-2400 Lübeck. Tel: (49 451) 7647.. Fax: (49 451) 72645

H. Lindemann's Bookshop, Nadlerstrasse 4+10, D-70173

Stuttgart 1. Tel: (49 711) 2489 9977. Fax: (49 711) 236 9672. Photography and film literature. Catalogue available.

Kiepert Taschenbuchladen, Hardenbergstr. 4-5, D-10623 Berlin. Tel: (49 30) 311 880. Fax: (49 30) 311 88 120. Good selection of film paperbacks.

Sautter + Lackmann, Filmbuchhandlung, Admiralitädstr. 71/72 D-20459 Hamburg or Postfach 11 04 31, 20404 Hamburg. Tel: (49 40) 373 196. Fax: (49 40) 365 479. Mainly books, but also videos etc.

Marga Schoeller Bucherstube, Knesebeckstr. 33, D-10623 Berlin. Tel: (49 30) 881 1122. Fax: (49 30) 881 8479. One of the fabled literary haunts of western Europe, Marga Schoeller's shop is justly proud of its film book selection.

Verlag fur Filmschriften Christian Unucka, Am Kramerburg 7A, D-85241 Hebertshausen. Tel: (49 8131) 13922. Fax: (49 8131) 10075. Books, posters, programmes, stills, postcards, videos, rare items, etc.

ITALY

Libreria dello Spettacolo, via terraggio 11, 20123 Milan. Tel: (39 2) 864 51730. Fax: (39 2) 864 51730

Il Leuto, via Monte Brianzo 86, 00186 Rome. Tel: (39 06) 868 687. Fax: (39 06) 869 269.

THE NETHERLANDS

Ciné-qua-non, Staalstraat 14, 1011 Amsterdam. Tel: (31 20) 625 5588. Books, new & second-hand, posters & stills.

SPAIN

Alphaville, Martin de los Heros 14, 28008 Madrid. Tel: (34 91) 559 3836.

Filmoteca Española, Cine Dore, Santa Isabel 3, Madrid. Tel: (34 91) 369 4673. Well-stocked bookstore dealing with movie topics.

El Espectador, Consell de Cent, 475 bis, 08013 Barcelona. Tel: (34 93) 231 6516. Specialising in cinema and video books, magazines, etc.

Ocho y Medio, Martin de los Heros 23, 28008 Madrid. Tel: (34 91) 559 0628. Fax: (34 91) 541 2831. e-mail: alphalib@isid. es/ochoymedio@arrakis.es. Website: www.ochoymedio. arrakis.es. Friendly bookstore just up the road from the Alphaville. A wide range of Spanish and foreign-language books.

Ramon Serina, Aribau 114, 08026 Barcelona. Tel: (34 93) 454 9633. A specialist collection of books, photos, magazines, press books, posters and programmers ons ale to the public in Spain and abroad.

SWEDEN

Movie Art of Sweden, Sodra Hamngatan 2, 411 06 Goteborg. Tel: (46 31) 151 412. Fax: (46 31) 115 1445. e-mail: info@ essemposters.se. Website: www. movieartofsweden.com. New and vintage film posters, stills, postcards, props, t-shirts. Postal service available.

SWITZERLAND

Filmbuchhandlung Hans Rohr, Oberdorfstr. 3 CH-8024 Zurich. Tel: (41 1) 251 3636. Fax: (41 1) 251 3344. In its long-established existence,

Hans Rohr has offered an efficient and reliable service when it comes to dealing with mail-order inquiries for literally any film, book or magazine in print.

Librairie du Cinema, 9 rue de la Terrassiere, CH-1207, Geneva. Tel: (41 22) 736 8888. Fax: (41 22) 736 6616. E-mail: cinema@ worldcom.ch. Immaculate display of posters, books, stills, postcards, photos, soundtrack CD's and videos. A veritable treasure trove for the movie buff.

UNITED KINGDOM

The Cinema Bookshop, 13-14 Great Russell Street, London WC1B 3NH. Tel: (44 171) 637 0206. Fax: (44 171) 436 9979. Fred Zentner's film bookshop close to the British Museum has succeeded by virtue of prompt and friendly service and an eye for rare items.

The Cinema Store, Unit 4B/C, Orion House, Upper Saint Martin's Lane, London WC2H 9EJ. Tel: (44 171) 379 7838. Fax: (44 171) 240 7689. e-mail: cinemastor@ aol.com. Website: www. atlasdigital.com/cinemastore. Fine selection of magazines, toys and models, laser discs, posters

etc. in Paul McEvoy and Neil Palmer's friendly and recently expanded store now stocking rare/new VHS, soundtracks and trading cards. Mail-order catalogue £1.

Anne FitzSimons, 62 Scotby Road, Scotby, Carlisle, Cumbria CA4 8BD. Tel: (44 1228) 513 815. Small stock of ephemera and second-hand and out-of-print books on the cinema, and other entertainment. Catalogue twice a year. Private premises. Postal only.

Flashbacks, 6 Silver Place, (Beak Street) London W1R 3LJ. Tel/Fax: (44 171) 437 8562. e-mail: flashbacks@compuserve.com. Most impressively stocked establishment which, in London's West End caters for those interested in movie ephemera – posters, stills, pressbooks – from many countries and every period of cinema history. Also extensive mail-order service. (No catalogues issued, but individual requests responded to. Monday to Saturday, 10:30-7).

Greenroom Books, 11 Bark Lane, Addingham, Ilkey, West Yorkshire LS29 ORA. Tel/Fax: (44 1943) 830 497. Mail-order service for books on the preforming arts.

David Henry, 36 Meon Road, London W3 8AN, England. Tel: (44 181) 932 5152. e-mail: filmbook@netcomuk.co.uk. Mail-order business catalogues upon request.

Hollywood Superstore, 16-18 St. Giles High Street, London WC2H 8LN. Tel: (44 171) 836 3736. Movie photos, posters, books, magazines, and vintage memorabilia. Open Mon-Sat. 10-6)

Ed Mason, c/o Rare Discs, 18 Bloomsbury Street, London WC1B 32A. Tel: (44 171) 580 3516. Recently re-located, large and carefully assembled stock of memorabilia. Contact Ed Mason on (171) 736 8511 for further info.

Movie Boulevard, 3 Cherry Tree Walk, Leeds LS2 7EB. Tel: (44 113) 242 2888. Fax: (44 113) 243 8840. Welcome north of England addition to the ranks of shops specialising in soundtracks, videos, laserdiscs and memorabilia. Headed by the enthusiastic Robert Wood.

Filmbooks, Pullman Everyman Cinema, Holly Bush Vale, London NW3 6TX. Tel: (44 171) 431 4828. Fax: (44 171) 435 2292. Full selection of books, directories, magazines, trade papers, videos, gifts and postcards.

Offstage Film & Theatre Bookshop Offstage Film & Theatre Bookshop, 37 Chalk Farm Rd, London, NW1. Tel: (44 171) 485 4996. (44 171) 916 8046. Bright square space crammed with play and film scripts and books on all aspects of theatrical, broadcast and cinematic media, including criticism, stagecraft, comedy, writing and education.

The Reel Poster Gallery, 72 Westborn Grove, London W2 5SH. Tel: (44 171) 727 44 88. Fax: (44 171) 727 4499. London's first gallery dedicated to original vintage film posters. An extensive yet selective stock includes posters of all genres, from Westerns to science fiction, and Hollywood

classics to cult titles, seen through the eyes of artists from various countries.

Zwemmer Media, 80 Charing Cross Road, London WC2. Tel: (44 171)240 4157. Fax: (44 171) 240 4186. Large selection of new and out-of-print film books, from early film-making to digital video. Mail-order inquires.

UNITED STATES

Applause, 211 West 71st Street, New York, NY 10021. Tel: (1 212) 496 7511. Fax: (1 212) 721 2856. Now one of the few – and certainly the only uptown – film and showbiz bookstores in Manhattan.

Cinema Books, *4753 Roosevelt Way NE, Seattle, WA 98105. Tel: (1 206) 547 7667.* Fine selection of film books and magazines, with space also devoted to TV and theatre. Mail-orders welcome.

Cinemonde, 138 Second Ave North, Suite 104, Nashville, TN 37201. Tel: (1 615) 742 3048. Fax: (1 615) 742 1268. Installed in a capacious gallery in Old Nashville, Cinemonde is a poster store for movie buffs. Items are meticulously stored and displayed, and the colorful catalogue is a collector's item. In addition, Cinemonde has a search service in San Francisco for hard-to-find vintage posters, headed by the movie poster consultant for Sotheby's, New York (1932 Polk St., San Francisco, CA 94109. Tel: (1 415) 776 9988. Fax: (1 415) 776 1424).

Dwight Cleveland, P.O. Box 10922, Chicago, IL 60610-0922. Tel: (1 773) 525 9152. Fax: (1 773) 525 2969. Buys and sells movie posters.

Collectors Book Store, 6225 Hollywood Blvd., Hollywood, CA. 90028. Tel: (1 323) 467 3296. Fax: (1 323) 467 4536. Offers a superlative range of posters, stills, lobby cards, TV and film scripts.

Cinema Paradiso, 162 Bleecker Street, New York, NY 10012. Tel: (1 212) 677-8215. Fax (1 212) 505 0582. Specializing in international

movie posters, stills, vintage, originals. Open 365 days a year.

Samuel French's Theatre & Film Bookshop, (2 Locations) 7623 Sunset Boulevard, Hollywood, CA 90046. Tel: (1 213) 876 0570. Fax: (1 213) 876 6822. Extended evening hours at 11963 Ventura Boulevard, Studio City, CA 91604. Tel: (1 818) 762 0535. e-mail: samuelfrench@ earthlink.net. Website: www. samuelfrench.com. The world's oldest and largest play publisher (est.1830) operates a separate film and preforming arts bookshop. Complete range of new movie and preforming arts books available: directories, reference, writing, acting biography, screenplays, etc. World-wide mail-order service. The staff prepares meticulous catalogues that include more data than similar publications, and they strive to have any book in the English language from publishers throughout the world.

Gotham Book Mart, 41 West 47th Street, New York, NY 10036. Tel: (1 212) 719 4448. This famous literary bookshop in mid-Manhattan, est. in 1920, is the only New York City bookstore offering new, used and out-of-print film and theatre books. Also, an extensive stock of "quality" film magazines dating from the 1950's to present.

Larry Edmund's Bookshop, 6644 Hollywood Blvd., Hollywood, CA 90028. Tel: (1 213) 463 3273. Fax: (1 213) 463 4245. The stills collection alone is a goldmine for any film buff. Back numbers of movie annuals, posters, lobby cards and largest collection of new and used books in the world.

Limelight Film and Theatre Bookstore, 1803 Market Street, San Francisco, CA 94103. Tel: (1 415) 864 2265. Fax: (1 414) 864 7753. Derek G. Mutch runs this lively store for film and theatre books. Collection includes plays, screenplays, biographies, history and criticism of films and film and television technique.

Movie Madness, 1083 Thomas Jefferson Street, Washington, DC 20007. Current, classic and campy movie posters available at this unique store in Georgetown.

Jerry Ohlinger's Movie Material Store Inc., 242 West 14th Street, New York, NY 10011. Tel: (1 212) 989 0869. Fax: (1 212) 989 1660. Jerry Ohlinger's emporium stocks a wealth of stills from the 1930's through the 1990's, specializing in colour material. Posters are also plentiful, and there are some magazines as well.

MAGAZINES

The following list amounts to a selection only of the world's hundreds of film publications. Editors wishing to receive a free listing must send sample copies (preferably opening a sample subscription for us). Address: IFG, Variety, 6 Bell Yard, London WC2A 1EJ, UK.

ARGENTINA

ENTERTAINMENT HERALD

Corrieres 2817 3-A 1015, Buenos Aires, Argentina.

AUSTRALIA

CINEMA PAPERS

116 Argyle Street, Fitzroy, Victoria, Australia. Tel: 613 9416 2644. Fax: 613 9416 4088. e-mail: cp-edit@eis.net.au. Excellent large-format Australian bi-monthly, packed with information and pictures, useful for anyone monitoring the industry in Oz.

FILM HISTORY

John Libbey and Co. Pty Ltd., Level 10, 15-17 Young Stret, Sydney NSW 2000. Tel: (61 2) 9251 4099. Fax: (61 2) 9251 4428. Articles on the historical development of the motion picture, in a social, technological and economic context. Quarterly.

THE MACGUFFIN

177 Simpson Street, East Melbourne 3002, Australia. e-mail: <muffin@labyrinth. net.au>. Scholarly newsletter focusing on the films of Alfred Hitchcock. Intelligent and jargon-free.

BELGIUM

CINE-FICHESDEGRANDANGLE

Rue d'Arschot 29, B-5660 Mariembourg, Belgium. Tel: (32 60) 31 21 68. Fax: (32 60) 31 29 37. e-mail: grand.angle@mail.micro-center.be. Monthly review of new films and videos.

CINE & MEDIA

Rue du Saphir 15, 1040 Brussels, Belgium. Tel (32 2) 734 4294. Fax: (32 2) 734 3207. e-mail: sg@ocic.org. Multilingual (French, English and Spanish) bi-monthly published by the International Catholic Organisation for Cinema and the Audiovisual, with reports from all continents.

FILM & TELEVISIE + VIDEO

Cellebroerstraat 16, B-1010 Brussels, Belgium. Extensive reviews of major new film and video releases, profiles and interviews, festival news.

MEDIAFILM

Cellebroerstraat 16, B-1010 Brussels, Belgium. Serious Belgian quarterly, with extensive reviews, analysis and focus on directors. Quareterly.

SOUNDTRACK!

Astridlaan 171, 2800 Mechelen, Belgium. Tel: (32 15) 41 41 07. Fax: (32 15) 43 36 10. e-mail: pophost.eunet.be. Excellent quarterly for film music collectors.

STARS

Rue d'Arschot 29, B-5660 Mariembourg, Belgium. Tel: (32 60) 31 21 68. Fax: (32 60) 31 29 37. e-mail: grand.angle@mail.micro-center.be. Quarterly publication giving actors' biographies and filmographies.

BOLIVIA

IMAGEN

Casilla 1733, La Paz, Bolivia. Magazine of the Bolivian New Cinema Movement.

CANADA

CINÉ-BULLES

4545 avenue Pierre-de-Coubertin, CP 1000, Succursale M. Montréal, Canada H1V 3R2. Remarkable and informative Québécois quarterly that may just be the best in Canada.

KINEMA

Fine Arts (Film Studies), University of Waterloo, Waterloo, Ont. N2L 3G1, Canada. A journal of history, theory and aesthetics of world film and audiovisual media. Twice yearly.

THE NIGHTINGALE REPORT

45 Barclay Road, Toronto, Ontario M3H 3EZ, Canada. Fortnightly newsletter aimed at Canadian film and television industry. News and comprehensive listings.

24 IMAGES

3962, rue Laval, Montréal, QC H2W 2J2, Canada. Exceptionally attractive French/Canadian quarterly, witty and well-informed.

CHILE

ENFOQUE

Publicaciones y Audiovisuales, Linterna Mágica Ltda., Casilla 15, Correo 34, Santiago, Chile. Occasional quarterly taking an in-depth look at the Chilean/Latin American markets and new-releases.

CHINA, REPUBLIC OF

CITY ENTERTAINMENT

Flat B2, 17/F, Fortune Factory Building, 40 Lee Chung Road, Cahiwan,Hong Kong. Tel: (852) 2892 0155. Fax: (852) 2838 49320. e-mail: cityent@wlink.net Website: www.webhk. com/cityent Indispensable Hongkong biweekly for anyone interested in Chinese cinema. In Chinese.

FILM APPRECIATION

The National Film Archive of the R.O.C., 4th Floor, 7 Ching-tao East Road, Taipei, Taiwan R.O.C. Taiwan's premier serious film journal, published as a bi-monthly. Focus on the cinematic output of Taiwan, Hong Kong and mainland China, as well as from Chinese communities overseas.

POPULAR CINEMA

(Dazhong dianying), 22 Beisanhuan donglu 22, Peking, China. Leading mainland Chinese monthly, also carrying pieces on Hongkong, Taiwan and foreign cinema.

WORLD SCREEN

China Film Press, 22 Beisanhuandonglu, Beijng 100013, China. Monthly, primarily devoted to new/classic features from around the world, with artist profiles and events.

COLOMBIA

KINETOSCOPIO

Carrera 45, no. 53-24, Apartado 8734, Medellin, Colombia. Tel: (574) 513 4444, ext. 151. Fax: (574) 513 2666. e-mail: aramos@colomboworld.com Quarterly covering international and Latin American cinema, Colombian directors and festival news.

CUBA

CINE CUBANO

Calle 23, no. 1115 Apdo. 55, Havana, Cuba. Vital information on all Latin American cinema, unfortunately only in Spanish.

CZECH REPUBLIC

CINEMA

Václavské nám. 15, 11000 Prague, Czech Republic. A glossy Czech monthly.

DENMARK

KOSMORAMA

The Danish Film Museum, Vognmagergade 10, 1120-Copenhagen K, Denmark. A changed, chunkier, more academic format for Kosmorama, which appears twice yearly (in Danish).

FINLAND

FILMJOURNALEN

Finlandssvenskt filmcentrum, Nylandsgatan 1, 20700 Åbo, Finland. Tel: (358 2) 250 0410. Fax: (358 2) 250 04321. e-mail: filmcent@ netti.fi Passionate Swedish-language quarterly focusing on Nordic and Finnish cinema.

FILMIHULLU

Malminkatu 36, FI-00100 Helsinki, Finland. Finnish film and TV magazine with perverse if passionate critical approach, appearing eight times a year.

FRANCE

CAHIERS DU CINEMA

Editions de l'Etoile, 9 passage de la Boule Blanche, 75012 Paris, France. Celebrated French journal now enjoying a second lease of life after a long spell in the wilderness.

POSITIF

19 Villa Croix Nivert, 75015 Paris, France. In-depth interviews, articles, all immaculately researched and highly intelligent. By a clear margin, this is Europe's best film magazine. New large format.

PREMIERE

151 rue Anatole France, 92300 Levallois-Perret, France. Tel: (33 1) 4134 9111. Fax: (33 1) 4134 9119. France's familiar movie monthly, packed with information, reviews and filmographies.

STUDIO MAGAZINE

41/43 rue de Colonel Pierre-Avia, 75015, Paris, France. Tel: (33 1) 56 88 88 88. Fax: (33 1) 45 66 48 52. Glossy, beautifully designed monthly with reviews, articles and interviews.

GERMANY

EPD MEDIEN

Postfach 50 05 50, 60 394 Frankfurt am Main, Germany. Tel: (49 69) 580 98141. Fax: (49 69) 580 98 261. e-mail: medien@epd.de. Highbrow German publication covering , radio, T.V., and the press. Bi-weekly.

KINO: GERMAN FILM + INTL. REPORTS

c/o Holloway, Helgoländer Ufer 6, 10557, Berlin, Germany. Tel: (49 30) 391 6167. Excellent magazine published twice a year also includes special issues devoted to both German cinema and international festival reports. Features reviews, interviews and credits.

THE LIMITED EDITION ONLINE

K.S.Z.-Verlag, Linzer Str. 5, 53604 Bad Honnef, Germany. Tel/fax: (49 2224) 104 68. Website: www.leonline.de Available only

via internet. Featuring extensive reviews this website is devoted to movies, DVDs and soundtracks; it's updated on a weekly basis..

WELTWUNDER DER KINEMATOGRAPHIE

Postfach 100 274, D-10562 Berlin, Germany. Tel: (49 30) 6908 8185. e-mail: DGFK@SNAFU.de. Fascinating, well-researched title, with detailed articles on the past, present and future of cinematography and the technical art of film-making. Yearly.

HUNGARY

FILMKULTURA

Solymár u. 8, 1032 Budapest, Hungary. Essays and reviews on Hungarian and international cinema. Six times a year.

FILMVILAG

Pozsonyi út 20, H-1137 Budapest, Hungary. Monthly with reviews and interviews.

INDIA

CINEMAYA

B 90 Defence Colony, New Delhi 110 024, India. Tel: (91 11) 461 7127/ 464 7482. Fax: (91 11) 462 7211. e-mail: cinemaya@nde.vsni. net.in Informative, elegant magazine, published quarterly in English since 1988, on all aspects of the Asian film industry. Is the official journal of NETPAC (Network for promotion of Asian Cinema).

SPECIAL EFFECT

B/4, Balgachia Villa, Calcutta 700 037, India. Formerly *Magic Lantern*, this Indian film quarterly mixes interviews and reviews with insightful comment, and surveys different trends in Indian cinema.

IRAN

CINEMA

No. 123 Jami, Hafez Avenue, Tehran. Reports and reviews on local and international cinema.

CINEMA AND THEATRE

No. 1/1 Omrani Alley, North Bahar Street, Tehran. Articles on theoretical aspects of cinema and theatre.

CINEMA AND VIDEO

No. 1073, Rudaki Street, Jomhuri Square. Reports and features on cinema and video.

CULTURE AND CINEMA

P.O. Box 15175-338 Tehran, Iran. Monthly magazine featuring Iranian cinema.

FILM AND CINEMA

No. 18 Safa Alley, Kushk Street, Saadi Avenue, Tehran. Features focusing on theoretical aspects of cinema.

FILM AND VIDEO

No. 5 Laal Alley, Etesami Street, Fatemi Avenue, Tehran. Reports and features on cinema and video.

FILM INTERNATIONAL

No. 12 Sam Alley, Hafez Avenue, Tehran. English-language quarterly journal that offers a cross-cultural review of

international cinema, focusing on the film art in Asia.

FILM MONTHLY

P.O. Box 11265-5872 Tehran. Reviews and features on the latest releases.

FILM REPORT

3rd Floor, 123 Jami St., Hafez Ave., Tehran, Tehran, Iran. Reviews and features on the latest releases.

THE IMAGE

No. 15 Golriz Street, Motahhari Avenue. Reports and features on cinema and photography.

WORLD OF IMAGE

No. 46 Khorshid Alley, Tus Street, Talequani Avenue Theoretical aspects of cinema and photography.

ISRAEL

CINEMATHEQUE

P.O. Box 20370, Tel Aviv 61203, Israel. Fine monthly Israeli magazine (with summary in English) dwelling on seasons at the Tel-Aviv Cinémathèque but also reporting on world festivals etc.

ITALY

BIANCO E NERO

1524 via Tuscolana, 00173 Rome, Italy. Tel: (39 06) 722 9369/249. Fax: (39 06) 722 9369. e-mail: biancoen@tin.it Italian bimonthly that boasts a reputation for scholarship second to none in its country.

CINECRITICA

Via Yser, n.8-00198 Rome, Italy. Dense Italian quarterly focussing on world cinema.

CINEMA & CINEMA

1 via Battibecco, 40123 Bologna, Italy. Respected quarterly.

CINEMA & VIDEO INTERNATIONAL

Via Tevere 46B, 00198 Rome, Italy. Monthly for audiovisual professionals in English and Italian.

CINEMAZERO

Piazza Maestri del Lavoro 3, 33170 Pordenone, Italy. Serious Italian bi-monthly covering international cinema, with festival news and book reviews.

GRIFFITHIANA

Cineteca del Friuli, Via Bini, Palazzo Gurisatti, 33013 Gemona (Udine), Italy. Tel: (39 0432) 970 542. Fax: (39 0432) 970 542. e-mail:cdf@proxima.conecta.it. Website: www.cinetecadelfriuli.org/gcm/. Distribution agent in North America: Bilingual Review/Press, Hispanic Research Center, Arizona State University, PO BOX 872702, Tempe, AZ 85287-2702, USA. e-mail: gary.keller@asu.edu. Italian quarterly devoted exclusively to the study of silent cinema and animation. Each issue is a miracle of schoplarship and devotion. In English and Italian.

IMMAGINI & SUONI

FIAIS, Casella postale 6306, 00195 Rome, Italy. Tel: (39 06) 370 0266. Fax: (39 06) 39 733 297. Published by the International Federation of Film Archives. In French and Italian.

LA MAGNIFICA OSSESSIONE

Piazza Palermo, 10B, 16129 Genova, Italy. Published by the Cinema department of Genova University, this academic quarterly has numerous articles on cinema history.

NUOVO CINEMA EUROPEO

Via delle Cinque Giornate 15, 50129, Florence, Italy. Chunky bi-monthly report on Italian film industry, in English with Italian summary. Includes industry news, such as box-office, markets and foreign sales.

QUADERNI DI CINEMA

Via Benedetto Varchi 57, 50132 Florence, Italy. Wide-ranging Italian bi-monthly, striving to match cultural politics with an enthusiastic appreciation of film.

RIVISTA DEL CINEMATOGRAFO

Via Giuseppe Palombini, 6-165 Rome, Italy. Tel: (39 06) 663 7514. Fax: (39 06) 663 7321. e-mail: infoeds@tin.it. Website: www. cinematografo.it. Important Italian monthly.

SEGNOCINEMA

Via G Prati 34, Vicenza. Glossy Italian bi-monthly packed with profiles, reviews and photographs. September issue lists complete guide to all titles released the previous season.

KOREA

KOREA CINEMA

(Yeonghwa), Korean Film Commission, 206-46 Chongnyangni-dong, Tongdaemun-gu, Seoul. Tel: (82-2) 958 7584. Fax: (82-2) 958 7550. e-mail: dustinyu@hanmail.net Published once a year, a promotion guide for Korean cinema.

KOREAN FILM NEWS

Yeonghwa), Korean Film Commission, 206-46 Chongnyangni-dong, Tongdaemun-gu, Seoul. Tel: (82-2) 958 7584. Fax: (82-2) 958 7550. e-mail: dustinyu@hanmail.net Published twice a year.

NETHERLANDS

HOLLAND ANIMATION NEWSBRIEF

Hoogt 4, 3512 GW Utrecht, The Netherlands. Quarterly newsletter from the Holland Animation Foundation.

SKRIEN

Vondelpark 3, 1071 AA Amsterdam, The Netherlands. Tel: (31 20) 589 1447. Fax: (31 20) 689 0438. e-mail: skrien@xsiall.nl Excellent Dutch magazine that appears with regularity and enthusiasm. Monthly.

NEW ZEALAND

ONFILM

P.O. Box 6374, Wellington, New Zealand. A film, television and video magazine for New Zealand, with location reports and a production survey.

NORWAY

Z FILMTIDSSKRIFT

Dronningensgate 16, 0152 Oslo, Norway. Enthusiastic quarterly with a focus on film theory and history, both Norwegian and international. Now with useful summaries in English.

PERU

EL REFUGIO

José Granda 460, Lima 27, Peru. South American monthly with reviews and features on world cinema.

LA GRAN ILUSIÓN

Universidad de Lima, Oficina de Distribución y Venta de Publicaciones, Av. Javier Prado Este s/n Monterrico, Apartado 852, Lima, Peru. Weighty journal with essays on international contemporary and classic cinema.

POLAND

FILM

Pulawska 61, 02595 Warsaw, Poland. Popular Polish monthly with international slant.

KINO

Chelmska 19/21, 00-724 Warsaw, Poland. Tel: (48 22) 841 6843. Fax: (48 22) 841 9057. e-mail: kino@free.ngo.pl. Culturally inclined Polish monthly designed to promote European cinema, with interviews, reviews and essays.

PORTUGAL

CINEMA NOVO

Apartado, 78, 4002 Porto Codex, Portugal. Bi-monthly Portuguese magazine dealing with international and Portuguese topics.

ROMANIA

PRO CINEMA

Str. Luterana nr. 11, et. 2, sector 1, Bucharest, Romania. Tel: (40 1) 303 3967. Fax: (40 1) 303 3855. Monthly with reviews, profiles and interviews.

RUSSIA

ISKUSSTVO KINO

9 ul. Usievicha, 125319 Moscow, Russia. Chunky, theoretical, most authoritative Russian film monthly.

SPAIN

CINEMANIA

Gran Via 32, 2°, 28013 Madrid, Spain. Founded in 1995. Tel: (34 91) 538 6104. Fax: (34 91) 522 2291. e-mail: cinemania@ progresa.es. Upmarket monthly with news, interviews, reports, feature articles and TV and video coverage.

DIRIGIDO POR

Conseil de Cent 304, 2°, 1°, Barcelona 08007, Spain. Tel: (34 93) 487 6202. Fax: (34 93) 488 0896. This handsomely-produced Spanish monthly throws the spotlight each issue on a particular genre, studio or director of international renown.

FANTASTIC

Gran Via de las Corts Catalanes 133,3, 08014 Barcelona, Spain. Tel (34 93) 223 3760. Fax: (34 93) 421 8048. Breezy consumer monthly focusing on young stars. 46,000 readers.

FOTOGRAMAS

Gran Via de les Corts Catalanes 133, 3°, 08014 Barcelona, Spain. Tel: (34 93) 223 0353. Fax: (34 93) 432 2907. e-mail: fotograms@iberonline.esAn institution, fifty years old in 1996. A glossy monthly with authoritative film reviews, news, on-location reports and features.

IMAGENES DE ACTUALIDAD

Consell de Cent, 304, 2.0, 1.ª, 08007 Barcelona, Spain. Tel: (34 93) 487 6202. Fax: (34 93) 488 0896. e-mail: dirigidopor@ idgrup.ibernet.com Glossy, well-presented international magazine with strong Hollywood bias. Monthly.

NICKELODEON

Bárbara de Braganza 12, 28004 Madrid, Spain. Tel: (34 91) 308 5238. Fax: (34 91) 308 5885. Website: www.nickel-odeon.com. Important new quarterly from Spain, very well illustrated and researched. First issue offers an in-depth look at Spanish cinema.

SRI LANKA

CINESITH

142 Abeyratne Mawatha, Boralesgamuwa, Sri Lanka. Tel: (94 77) 318 610. Fax: (94 1) 509 553. e-mail: ashley@sri.lanka.net Sri Lanka's only serious film magazine focuses on national and international cinema with special reference to Asia. Recognised as a reference journal in the Sri Lankan Universities. Now in its 15th year.

SWEDEN

FILMHÄFTET

Box 101 56, 100 55 Stockholm, Sweden. Egghead periodical with features on international directors, retrospectives, and Scandinavian television.

FILMRUTAN

Box 82, 851 02 Sundsvall, Sweden. Organ of the Swedish Federation of Film Societies, this unpretentious monthly has, with the demise of *Chaplin*, become Sweden's most important film magazine. Features, film, book and record reviews.

SWITZERLAND

AVANT PREMIERE

Case Postale 5615, 1211 Geneva 11, Switzerland. Colourful monthly with lengthy reviews of new releases, as well as a pullout brochure on Swiss production and distribution.

CINE-BULLETIN

Bederstr. 76, Postfach, CH-8027 Zürich, Switzerland. Tel: (41 1) 204 1780. Fax: (41 1) 280 2850. E-mail: sennhause@email.ch Serious Swiss monthly in French and German with box office and films in production.

FILM BULLETIN

Postfach 137, CH-8408 Winterthur, Switzerland. Tel: (41 52) 226 0555. Fax: (41 52)

222 0051. e-mail: info@filmbulletin.ch. Website: www.filmbulletin.ch. Informative, straightforward look at international cinema, with useful Swiss material also. Bi-monthly. Strong in film history, many essays on the work of famous directors and interviews with camera men and other people of the profession.

RECTANGLE
CAC Voltaire, Rue Général-Dufour 16, 1204 Geneva, Switzerland. Tel: (41 22) 320 7878. Fax: (41 22) 320 8893. e-mail: cacvolt@iprolink.ch Only film magazine in the Suisse romande, and admirably poised between the theoretical and researchist approach to the cinema, with a fresh and lively layout.

ZOOM
Bederstrasse 76, Postfach, 8027 Zürich, Switzerland. Swiss monthly highlighting new releases, with interviews and good festival coverage. In German.

UNITED KINGDOM
BLACK FILMMAKER
Church Road, Hendon, London, NW4 4EB, UK. e-mail: bfm@ivc.leevalley.co.uk

EMPIRE
1st Floor, Mappin House, 4 Winsley Street, London W1N 7AR, UK. Supercharged fanzine monthly with profiles, reviews and behind-the-scenes reports.   Often far ahead of its rivals in breaking news and interviews.

MUSIC FROM THE MOVIES
1 Folly Square, Bridport, Dorset DT6 3PU, UK. Tel/fax: (44 1308) 427 057. e-mail: ftmy@halto.co.uk Informative quarterly devoted to all aspects of film music and its composers, with articles, interviews and soundtrack reviews.

PICTURE HOUSE
5 Coopers Close, Burgess Hill, W. Sussex RH15 8AN. Admirable quarterly devoted to the cinema buildings of the past.

SIGHT AND SOUND
British Film Institute, 21 Stephen Street, London W1 1PL, UK. Apart from its reference guide to most films released in the UK., this once-celebrated magazine is still a pale shadow of its former authority. Slight improvement in the past year.

TALKING PICTURES
3b Glengarry Road, East Dulwich, London SE22, UK. Quarterly booklet with interviews, reviews and articles on film culture in the UK., now expanding in size and coverage.

TOTAL FILM
Future Publishing, 99 Baker Street, London W1M 1FE, UK. Tel: (44 171) 317 2600. Fax: (44 171) 317 2644. e-mail: totalfilm@futurenet. co.uk. The UK's fastest growing monthly mainstream movie magazine covering everything from Hollywood blockbusters to European arthouse cinema. Editor: Ema Cochrane. Current ABC: 66,474.

VERTIGO
20 Goodge Place, London W1P 1FN. e-mail: vertigo.lusia@lineone.net

UNITED STATES
AMERICAN PREMIERE
8421 Wilshire Blvd., Penthouse; Beverly Hills, CA 90211, USA. Bi-monthly industry magazine, free to members of the Academy of Motion Picture Arts and Sciences.

ANIMATION MAGAZINE
Bill Buck, 30101 Agoura Court, Suite 110, Agoura, California 91301, USA. Tel: 1 818) 991 2884. Fax: (1 818) 991 3773. Website: www.animag. com The only international publication focusing on the global animation industry. Monthly.

AUDIENCE
P.O. Box 215, Simi Valley, CA 93062-0215, USA. Tel: (1 805) 584 6651. AUDIENCE. www.audiencemag.com. Billed as an "informal commentary on film", this witty, well-informed online version of the magazine founded in 1968 features articles and reviews, both recent and retrospective.

CINEASTE
PO Box 2242, New York, NY 10009, USA. Tel/fax: (1 212) 982 1241. e-mail: cineaste@cineaste.com Perhaps the finest anti-establishment movie magazine, never afraid to tackle controversial issues and never prone to Hollywood worship. Interviews are especially good in *Cineaste*.

CINEFANTASTIQUE
P.O. Box 270, Oak Park, III. 60303, USA. Tel: (1 708) 366 5566. Fax: (1 708) 366 1441. e-mail: cmail@cfg.com. An enthusiastic, well-written, beautifully produced bi-monthly with a special emphasis on horror, fantasy and s-f films now in its 30th year of publication.

CINEMA JOURNAL
Dept. of Communications, University Plaza, Georgia State University, Atlanta, GA 30303, USA. Scholarly essays concerned with the study of the moving image from diverse methodological perspectives, with information on upcoming events and research opportunities.

CLASSIC IMAGES
P.O. Box 809, Muscataine, IA52761, USA. Formerly "Classic Film Collector," a good source for film buffs eager to enlarge their library of movies. Monthly.

FEMME FATALES
5023 Frankford Ave., Baltimore, MD 21206. Tel (1 410) 488 8147. Published every three weeks.

FILMMAKER MAGAZINE
110 West 57th Street, New York, Ny 10019-3319, USA. Tel: 212-581-8080. Fax: 212-581-1857. Aimed at independent film-makers, this quarterly offers interviews, news and sound advice.

FILM COMMENT
Film Society of Lincoln Center, 70 Lincoln Center Plaza, New York, NY 10023, USA. Tel: (1 212) 875 5614. Fax: (1 212) 875 5636. e-mail: rtvfc@aol.com Informative, feisty, and usually uncompromising articles as well as interviews on wide-ranging international topics. Still the best US bi-monthly on the cinema.

FILM CRITICISM
Allegheny College, Box D, Meadville, PA 16335, USA. Tel: (1 814) 332 4333/ 4343. Fax: (1 814) 332 2981. e-mail: lmichael@alleg.edu Scholarly essays on film history, theory and culture. Tri-Quarterly.

FILM JOURNAL INTERNATIONAL
Sunshine Group Worldwide, 244 West 49th Street, Suite 200, New York, NY 10019, USA.

Tel: (1 212) 246 6460. Fax: (1 212) 265 6428. e-mail: sunshine@maestro.com Monthly magazine covering international exhibition.

FILM LITERATURE INDEX
Film and Television Documentation Centre, State University of New York, 1400 Washington Avenue, Albany, NY 12222, USA. Fax: (1 518) 442 5367. e-mail: fatcod@cnsvax@albany.edu The most comprehensive international index to the journal literature of film and television.

FILM QUARTERLY
University of California Press, 2120 Berkeley Way, Berkeley, California 94720, USA. Tel: (1 510) 601 9070. Fax: (1 510) 601 9036. e-mail: ann.martin@ucpress.ucop.edu Publishes readable discussions of issues in contemporary film, TV and video, substantive film reviews and interviews, and analyses of independent, documentary, avant-garde and foreign films. Comprehensive book reviews.

HONG KONG FILM MAGAZINE
601 Van Ness Avenue, Suite E3728, San Francisco, California 94102, USA. Quarterly focusing on the Hong Kong cinema scene, featuring news, reviews and interviews. In English.

INTERNATIONAL DOCUMENTARY ASSOCI-ATION (IDA)
1551 South Robertson Boulevard, Suite 201, Los Angeles, CA 90035-4257, USA. Fax: (1 310) 785 9334. e-mail: ida@artnet.net Website: www. documentary.org The only publication to focus exclusively on non-fiction film and video. Presents new work and ideas in the documentary field with informative articles, reviews and interviews. Published ten times a year.

JUMP CUT
P.O. Box 865, Berkeley, California 94701, USA. Tel: (1 510) 658 2221. Fax: (1510) 658 2269. e-mail: jhess@igc.apc.org Published only once or twice a year, this magazine contains an extraordinary amount of closely-woven text.

LITERATURE/FILM QUARTERLY
Salisbury State University, Salisbury, Maryland 21801, USA. Tel: 1-410 334 3495/ 543 6446. Fax: 1-410 543 6068. e-mail: "jxwelsh@ssu.edu Scholarly quarterly with film and book reviews, interviews and articles. Manuscripts invited for submission. Circulates coast to coast in the US and Canada and abroad. Now in its 27th year.

MOVIELINE
1141 South Beverly Drive, Los Angeles, CA 90035, USA. Intelligent, irreverent and refreshingly candid Hollywood monthly. Great interviews.

WIDE ANGLE
The Johns Hopkins University Press, Baltimore, Maryland 212180, USA. Scholarly, thematically arranged journal. Wide range.

URUGUAY
CINEMATECA REVISTA
Lorenzo Carnelli 1311, Casilla de Correo 1170, Montevideo, Uruguay. Bright magazine with international slant published by Cinemateca Uruguaya. Ten times a year.

Trade and Technical

BELGIUM

MONITEUR DU FILM
36 rue des Frambosiers, 1180 Brussels, Belgium. Monthly.

FRANCE

LE FILM FRANÇAIS
90 rue de Flandre, 75947 Paris Cedex 19, France. Lightweight weekly with news, reviews, box-office and production schedules.

GERMANY

BLICKPUNKT-FILM
Stahlgruberring 11a, 81829 Munich, Germany. Tel: (49 89) 451 140. Fax: (49 89) 451 14444. e-mail: emv@e-media.de. Strong on box-office returns and marketing, this German weekly also covers the video and TV market.

ENTERTAINMENT MARKT
Stahlgruberring 11a, 81829 Munich, Germany. Tel: (49 89) 451 140. Fax: (49 89) 451 14444. e-mail: emv@e-media.de. Bi-weekly business magazine that covers the German video, CD-ROM, computer games, from multimedia to business news. The trade magazine for innovative dealers, distributors, decisionmakeres and market leaders.

FILM-ECHO/FILMWOCHE
Marktplatz 13, 65183 Wiesbaden, Germany. Tel: (49 611) 36 09 80. Fax: (49 611) 37 28 78. e-mail: filmeco@aol.com. Doyen of the German trade. Weekly.

MÜNCHEN FILM NEWS
Schwanthalerstr. 69, 80336 Munich, Germany. Tel: (49 89) 544 60250. Fax: (49 89) 544 60 260. A monthly put out by Munich's Informationbüro Film containing festival reports, films in production, personalities and other news concerning the Munich film scene. Specials in English.

VIDEO VOCHE
Trade magazine for software dealers. Tel: (49 89) 451 140. Fax: (49 89) 451 14444. e-mail: emv@e-media.de. As the market leader, it provides the latest facts and trends on a weekly basis.

ITALY

ACTINGNEWS
Via Belluno 1, 00161 Rome, Italy. Comprehensive weekly reports on Italian film starts. Four market issues have English translations.

CINEMA D'OGGI
Viale Regina Margherita 286, 00198 Rome, Italy. Fornightly. Interviews with producers.

GIORNALE DELLO SPETTACOLO
Via di Villa Patrizi 10, 00161 Rome, Italy. Box-office data, legal requirements, technical information etc.

JAPAN

MOVIE/TV MARKETING
Box 30, Central Post Office, Tokyo, 100-8691 Japan. Tel: (81 3) 3587 2855. Fax: (81 3) 3587 2820. e-mail: movie@sepia.ocn.ne.jp Monthly from Japan — in English.

NORWAY

FILM OG KINO
Dronningensgate 16, 0152 Oslo, Norway. Tel: (47 22) 47 46 28. Fax: (47 22) 47 46 98. e-mail: kalle@kino.no. Wide-ranging and with a more expressive layout. Covering new releases in cinema as well as national and international trade matters and festival reports. Now the best film magazine in Scandinavia.

SPAIN

CINEINFORME & TELE
Gran Via 64, 28013, Madrid, Spain. Tel: (34 91) 541 2129. Fax: (34 91) 559 8110. e-mail: exportfilm@cineytele.com 38-year-old monthly that covers Spanish and international film, video and TV development.

CINEVIDEO 20
Apartado 2016, 28080 Madrid. Tel: (34 91) 519 6586. Fax: (34 91) 519 5119. e-mail: cinevideo@cinevideo20.es Features technologies of film, video, computer, studio facilities, satellite and cable for a Spanish readership.

EURO-MOVIES INTERNATIONAL
News-Movies, SCP, San Gaudencio 7, Sitges, 08870, Barcelona, Spain. Tel: (34 91) 527 6189. Fax: (34 91) 468 7820. Spanish and Latin American panorama, with reviews, festival news and television section.

LA GRAN ILUSION
Cines Renoir Plaza España, Marin de los Heros 12, 28008 Madrid, Spain. Tel: (34 91) 542 2702/3. Enterprising monthly published by distributor/exhibitor Alta Films with news and views on Alta releases and the Spanish cinema in general.

UNITED KINGDOM

IMAGE TECHNOLOGY — JOURNAL OF THE BKSTS
67-71 Victoria House, Vernon Place, London WC1B 4DA, UK. Tel: (44 171) 242 8400. Fax: (44 171) 405 3560. e-mail: movimage@bksts.demon.co.uk Website: www.bksts.demon. co. uk Covers technologies of motion picture film, television and sound at professional level. Ten times yearly.

MOVING PICTURES INTERNATIONAL
34-35 Newman Street, London W1P 3PD, UK. European-orientated trade paper published in London, with daily editions at numerous festivals.

SCREEN INTERNATIONAL
33-39 Bowling Green Lane, London, EC1R 0DA, UK. Weekly, UK.-oriented trade organ.

UNITED STATES

AMERICAN CINEMATOGRAPHER
ASC Holding Corp., 1782 N. Orange Dr., Hollywood, CA 90028, USA. Glossy monthly on film and electronic production techniques.

BOXOFFICE
155 S. El Molino Ave, Suite 100, Pasadena, California, 91101, USA. Tel: (1 626) 396 0250. Fax: (1 626) 396 0248. e-mail: editorial@boxoffice.com; advertising@boxoffice.com Website: www.boxoffice.com Business monthly for the Hollywood and movie theatre industries.

THE HOLLYWOOD REPORTER
5055 Wilshire Boulevard, Los Angeles, CA 90036-4396, USA. Daily.

VARIETY
5700 Wilshire Boulevard, Suite 120, Los Angeles, CA 90036. The world's foremost newspaper (daily and weekly) of the entertainment business.

National Organs

AUSTRALIA

AFC NEWS
GPO Box 3984, Sydney NSW 2001, Australia. Tel: (61 2) 9321 6444. Fax: (61 2) 9357 3631. e-mail: info@afc.gov.au Website: www.afc. gov.au Monthly, with regular production and multimedia reports, industry statistics, funding approvals and Australian films at international markets and festivals and awards won.

BELGIUM

CINEMA, CINEMA
Ministère de la Culture Française, avenue de Cortenbur 158, 1040 Brussels, Belgium.

CANADA

FILM CANADA YEARBOOK
Cine-communications, Box 152, Station R, Toronto, Ontario M4G 3Z3, Canada. Tel (1 416) 696 2382. Fax: (1 416) 696 6496. e-mail: patfilm@globalserve.net. Comprehensive directory of the Canadian film industry for over a decade.

BURKINA FASO

FEPACI NEWS
01 BP. 2524 Ouagadougou 01, Burkina Faso. Monthly newsletter of the Pan-African Federation of film-makers.

GERMANY

KINO
Export-Union des Deutschen Films, Türkenstr. 93, D-80799 München. Tel: (49 89) 390 095. Fax: (49 89) 395 223. E-mail: export-union@german-cinema.de Information on new German features (in production and already released), and selected personalities of the German film industry. Published four times a year in English, with a yearbook also available.

ISRAEL

ISRAEL FILM CENTRE INFORMATION BULLETIN
Ministry of Industry and Trade, 30 Agron Street, Jerusalem, Israel. Yearly review of Israeli film industry and catalogue of Israel films.

NEW ZEALAND

NZ FILM

P.O. Box 11546, Wellington, New Zealand. Tel: (64 4) 382 7680. Fax: (64 4) 384 9719. e-mail: marketing@nzfilm.co.nz. News from the New Zealand Film Commission, a twice yearly round-up of the country's film industry.

SPAIN

ACADEMIA

Sagasta 20, 3° drcha., 28004 Madrid, Spain. Tel: (34 91) 593 4648. Fax: (34 91) 593 1492. Excellent quarterly with articles, news and opinions of members of Spain's Academy of the Arts and Cinematographic Sciences.

BOLETIN

Sagasta 20, 3 dcha., 28004 Madrid. Tel: (34 91) 593 4648. Fax: (34 91) 593 1492. Highly useful monthly published by Spain's Academy with the latest industry news and film production updates.

Index to Advertisers